PARTNERS IN REVOLUTION

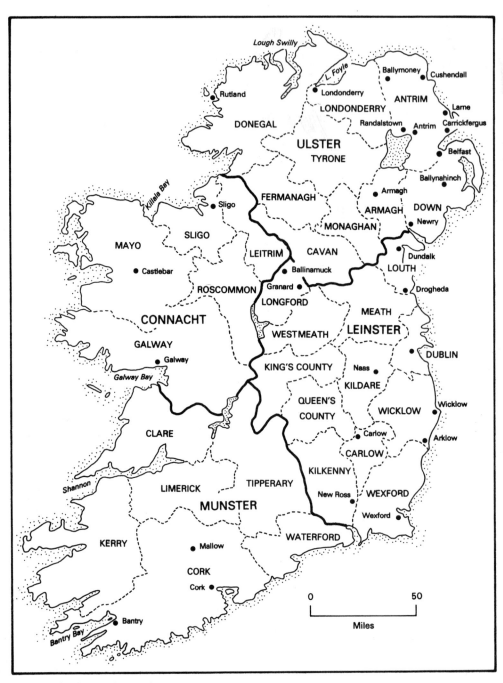

Map 1. Ireland in the eighteenth century

PARTNERS IN REVOLUTION
The United Irishmen and France

MARIANNE ELLIOTT

Yale University Press · New Haven & London

1982

For Trevor and my parents, Sheila and Terry Burns

Designed by Caroline Williamson.
Filmset in Monophoto Baskerville by Thomson Press (India) Ltd, New Delhi.
Printed in Great Britain by Butler & Tanner Ltd, Frome, Somerset.

Library of Congress Cataloging in Publication Data
Elliott, Marianne, 1948–
    Partners in revolution.

    Bibliography: p.
    Includes index.
    1. Ireland—Politics and government—1760–1820.
2. United Irishmen.   3. Ireland—Relations—France.
4. France—Relations—Ireland.   I. Title.
DA948.5.E38   1982   941.507   82–8523
ISBN 0–300–02770–2   AACR2

CONTENTS

LIST OF PLATES

MAPS

ACKNOWLEDGEMENTS

No writer is an island, and for a work involving research in three countries the present writer is more indebted than most to the help of family, friends, archivists and various research foundations. My first debt is to my parents, for the original interest in this topic arose from their early tutelage in Irish history and from the vivid repertory of United Irish plays staged by my father's amateur dramatic company, the Rosemary Theatre Group in Belfast. If I have succeeded in infusing my characters with the same life as such dramatic representations, I will be well satisfied. Later, as a student at Queen's University of Belfast, my interest in the period was further encouraged by the teaching of Professor J. C. Beckett, Dr. P. J. Jupp and Dr. A. T. Q. Stewart, and by the advice of Professor Michael Roberts. To them I owe a particular debt for helping to launch the research programme which has produced the present book. At Oxford University I was fortunate to have the guidance of Professor R. C. Cobb, to whose knowledge of France and continuing friendship I owe more than I can say.

I wish also to thank Professor L. M. Cullen, Dr. M. R. Beames, Dr. J. A. Hone, Dr. K. M. Berryman, Dr. D. G. Boyce, Dr. W. H. Crawford, Dr. A. P. W. Malcomson, Dr. P. D. H. Smyth, Clive Emsley, Dan Davin, Dr. C. J. Woods, Dr. J. Stevenson and Mlle A. Joly for their readiness to answer my queries through the years; and my particular thanks go to Dr. E. A. O. Whiteman, Dr. Gwynne Lewis, Dr. Colin Lucas, Professor Olwen Hufton, Dr. J. R. Dinwiddy, Dr. R. F. Foster, Professor Glanmor Williams, Mike Collinge and Maurice Hutt, whose friendship and support through various crises was indispensable to the completion of the book. Mme S. Grassot, Mr. Frank MacDermot and Professor Alun Davies did not, alas, live to see the publication of this work; but I hope that they might have enjoyed a work which they did so much to encourage in its earlier stages. The hospitality of many friends has been invaluable in the different cities in which I have worked, and I would like to thank in particular Susan Paton, Brendan Keith, Phil Powell, Wendy Newell, Ron and Joy Carmichael, Roy and Aisling Foster and Margot and Ciaran Fee.

To the help of the staff of the libraries and archives used in the course of its research, this book is of course particularly indebted; and I wish to thank in Ireland the staff of the Public Record Office of Northern Ireland, the Linenhall Library and the Belfast Central Library, the State Paper Office, the National Library of Ireland, the Royal Irish Academy, Trinity College Manuscript Room, and the Department of Irish Folklore in University College, Dublin; in England, the staff of the Bodleian Library, Oxford, the Public Record Office, the British Library, the Institute of Historical Research and the County Record Offices of Kent and Hampshire; in Wales, the library staff of University College, Swansea, particularly Miss K. M. Dale and Dr. F. G. Cowley; and in France, the staff of the Archives Nationales, particularly Mme D. Devos, the Bibliothèque Nationale, the Archives des Affaires Étrangères, the Archives de la Guerre, and the Archives département-ales de la Seine et Maritime.

I am grateful for research awards from the Twenty-Seven Foundation, the British Academy, the Sir Ernest Cassel Educational Trust, and most of all from the University of Wales, who awarded me a two-year research fellowship at University College of Swansea, during which period most of this book was written. My colleagues in the History Department at Swansea always listened cheerfully to my ideas; this book owes much to the companionship and intellectual stimulus which they supplied and I am particularly grateful to Peter Stead for help with the title.

I am indebted to Mrs. Mary Morris-Davis for permission to use the Bland-Burges papers in Oxford, to the Marquise des Roys for permission to use the Hoche Papers in Rouen, and to the Comte Patrice de la Tour de Pin, not only for his permission to use the O'Connor papers at his château in Bignon, but for the hospitality and entertaining account of family history which I received there. Dr. J. R. Dinwiddy and Dr. Sean Connelly were kind enough to read an earlier version of the book; I hope that the final version has done justice to their expert and helpful criticisms. I have made every effort to contact holders of copyright material, and hope that this general acknowledge-ment will be accepted if any oversight has occurred.

Mrs. Pat Rees typed the book with remarkable skill and patience, and I owe a particular debt to Caroline Williamson and John Nicoll of Yale University Press, the former for her meticulous and perceptive copy-editing of the typescript and her design for the lay-out of the book, the latter for wanting to publish it in the first place, and both for making the process of its publication such an enjoyable experience.

Since the book is based primarily on original sources, I have adhered to original spelling—mistakes and all—in the quotations. I have translated all the quotations from French sources, except in one or two instances where the flavour would have been lost by doing so. Some of the illustrations have been supplied by the National Library of Ireland, the British Museum, the Mansell Collection, the Bibliothèque Nationale, and I am grateful to all these for reproduction permission. Most of the illustrations were prepared by Roger Davies, and the maps were drawn by Mrs. Glenys Bridges. I would like to thank them for their patience and for their expert corrective to my amateurishness in both fields and the British Library for permission to reproduce the maps on pp. 80, 148 and 349.

But my greatest debt is to my husband, Trevor, who has endured my whims and obsessions since the book was first mooted, and who has been my most constant and helpful critic. For this, and more, I owe the publication of this book to him.

Swansea, January 1982. Marianne Elliott.

ABBREVIATIONS

A.A.E.	Archives des Affaires Etrangères, Quai d'Orsay, Paris
A.A.G.	Archives Administratives de la Guerre, Château de Vincennes, Paris
A.H.G.	Archives Historiques de la Guerre, Château de Vincennes, Paris
A.D.S.M.	Archives Départementales de la Seine-Maritime, Rouen
A.h.R.f.	*Annales historiques de la Révolution française*
A.N.	Archives Nationales, Paris
B.N.	Bibliothèque Nationale, Paris
B.L.	British Library, London
Bodl.	Bodleian Library, Oxford
E.H.R.	*English Historical Review*
F.H.S.	*French Historical Studies*
G.P.O.	Post Office Archives, London
Hants. C.R.O.	Hampshire County Record Office, Winchester
H.M.C.	Historical Manuscripts Commission
I.H.S.	*Irish Historical Studies*
I.S.P.O.	Irish State Paper Office, Dublin Castle
Kent C.R.O.	Kent County Record Office, Maidstone
N.L.I.	National Library of Ireland
Parl. Deb.	*Parliamentary Debates*
Parl. Hist.	*Parliamentary History*
Parl. Reg.	*Parliamentary Register*
P.R.O.	Public Record Office, London
P.R.O.N.I.	Public Record Office of Northern Ireland, Belfast
R.I.A.	Royal Irish Academy, Dublin
T.C.D.	Trinity College Dublin
U.J.A.	*Ulster Journal of Archaeology*

INTRODUCTION

The most important legacy of the 1790s to Irish history is that of militant republicanism. It was born in 1795 when the United Irish Society decided to seek French assistance in a rebellion against English rule in Ireland. Thereafter the French alliance became the driving force behind the Irish republican movement, and well into the next century it sustained the romantic myth of early Irish republicanism by offering the United Irish survivors an honourable asylum in France. It is that republican alliance which forms the principal theme of this book.

The United Irishmen started life in 1791 as one of the many advanced reform associations that arose in the wake of the American and French Revolutions. Although Ireland then as now was predominantly catholic, the early leadership of the United Irishmen was drawn largely from the protestant mercantile and professional classes of Belfast and Dublin.[1] At the outset they were republican in the manner of the classical republicanism of the English 'country' or 'real Whigs', the eighteenth-century 'Commonwealthmen' or the writers of the Enlightenment, accepting monarchy but seeking to curb the powers of central government, to preserve fundamental liberties and to secure religious toleration. Their transformation into a militantly anti-English, anti-monarchical republican movement was produced by the reaction of a general European crisis upon the peculiar historical situation in Ireland. The extent to which thinking men at the end of the eighteenth century considered themselves cosmopolites is too often ignored. It was this sense of belonging to a wider reform movement, which had spurred the French, the Dutch, the Belgians, the Savoyards and the Poles to revolt against oppression, which made an alliance with France such a natural alternative for the United Irishmen when faced with total suppression at home.[2] Forced

1. R. B. McDowell, 'The Personnel of the Dublin Society of United Irishmen 1791-4,' *I.H.S.* II (1940-1), 12-53 lists 130 protestants and 140 catholics as members of the Dublin society, with the protestants as the most active leaders.
2. For the use of the term republican in the eighteenth century see C. Robbins, *The Eighteenth-Century Commonwealthman* (Cambridge, Mass., 1959), also *Two English Republican Tracts*, ed. C. Robbins (Cambridge, Mass. 1969), 41-9; Y. Durand, *Les Républiques aux Temps des Monarchies* (Paris, 1973), 7-11. For an account of eighteenth-century cosmopolitanism, see T. J. Schlereth, *The Cosmopolitan Ideal in Enlightenment Thought* (Notre Dame, 1977).

underground in 1795, they spilled over their island boundaries to enlist the help of fellow democrats in England and to seek the military support already proffered by France and her allies. Over the next three years, the reorganization of the scattered recesses of English disaffection along United lines, and the despatch of five French invasion forces and incalculable quantities of arms to Ireland, testified to the effectiveness of the United Irishmen's external activities.

The most enduring strength of the United Irishmen lay in such external activities, in their ability to move with ease among England's plebeian democrats and at another level to negotiate as equals with French, Spanish or Dutch officials. Indeed, after 1798 the Society's leadership operated almost entirely in exile, in England, Hamburg or in France. But although there have been a considerable number of able studies of various European countries in the context of the struggle between revolutionary France and the old monarchies, the British Isles have never been given similar treatment, except as a small part of R. R. Palmer's general study on the concept of an 'Atlantic Revolution'.[3] It is true that whilst the revolutionary minorities of Belgium, Holland or the Rhineland were nurtured by France, assisted militarily and ultimately subsumed into an extended French empire, no successful invasion of the British Isles occurred and no republican government on the French model was erected. In other respects, however, the crisis in Ireland in the 1790s followed a similar pattern to that of many other countries with sizeable revolutionary groups looking to France for support and inspiration. Ireland too had an internal French party which played upon popular grievances; she too sent her patriot exiles to France and experienced similar, albeit unsuccessful, attempts at French invasion; she too suffered the reactionary backlash incurred by this juncture of internal disaffection with French-inspired republicanism. Of course the peculiar character of each country determined its internal response to the end-of-century crisis, and the reaction of Ireland provides a notable, if disturbing, reminder that the pattern of an 'Atlantic Revolution' cannot be applied unmodified to every country caught up in that crisis. Nevertheless, it was the interplay of French and continental politics with United Irish plans for the home movement and with Irish popular expectations which determined that reaction, and the United Irish Society can only be fully understood in the wider context of the European crisis in general and French policies in particular.

I

The decision to accept French help against England was not lightly taken by the United Irish leaders. Many felt uncomfortable as militant republicans,

3. R. R. Palmer, *The Age of Democratic Revolution*, 2 vols. (London, 1959 and 1964), II, especially ch. 14.

and the relationship between a future Irish republic and England was left unclear in their political plans. Their convinced francophilia, which they shared with most advanced reformers of the day, and their ideological commitment to the freedom of peoples to decide their own destinies caused them to view the suppression of the reform movement at home and the war against France as part of a monarchical conspiracy against the rights of national self-determination. Early overtures from France permitted them to regard themselves as legitimate combatants when they eventually opened official negotiations with France in 1795–96. This alliance with France, and their sense of involvement in an ideological war which knew no national boundaries, helped legitimize their revolt in their own minds, temporarily papering over their own doubts and inconsistencies, and allowing them to view themselves as allies in arms rather than as suppliants of France. Moreover, the widespread discontent in Ireland and the population's sense of alienation from their rulers was such a universally-known fact that the United Irishmen could plausibly claim to represent the interests of an entire nation in the struggle against a foreign conqueror, rather than those of a revolutionary elite. The confident tone which they therefore adopted in their negotiations did not entirely remove the scepticism and caution with which France had come to regard the claims and demands of foreign patriot groups, but the diplomatic achievements of a Society which in the first year of such negotiations could boast no real strength at home were impressive.

Under the first Directory (1795–97), the United Irishmen held a unique position among the many patriot groups negotiating for French assistance. The Belgians, the Dutch and the Swiss had already exhausted French patience with their squabbling and bad faith; the Irish had arrived late on the scene, and had yet to encounter the internal divisions and disputes which the experience of frustrated exile had produced among other foreign revolutionaries. The conclusion of peace with Prussia in 1795 and Austria in 1797 did not permit France to assist many such groups. But England was France's most enduring enemy, at war constantly from 1792 to 1815, apart from the short respite of Amiens; and her early involvement in the civil war in the Vendée, one of the most emotive episodes of the war, had raised France's desire for revenge against England to the proportions of a crusade. After 1798 Ireland became less and less significant in French military plans, which were by then being dictated by Bonaparte, with his grandiose schemes for knocking England out of the war. Until 1798, however, most French officials recognized that a direct attack on England would be foolhardy and that the easiest way to weaken her was rather to invade her neighbouring dependency, which had shown itself more than willing to welcome and assist the French forces. The United Irishmen accordingly received considerable support from the French Directory; and a detailed analysis of their role in Directorial war strategy occupies an important place in this book.

II

The eighteenth century in Ireland was ostensibly a period of remarkable tranquillity by comparison with the turbulent times before and afterwards; and the enigma of the development of modern Irish republicanism from such a background has not been fully explained. Below such apparent tranquillity, however, lay deeply-seated hopes, fears and historical grievances upon which the end-of-century crisis reacted. Loyalist fears have been looked at in a number of recent works.[4] But there has been little analysis of the effects of the United Irish dissemination of revolutionary ideals on popular opinion; and whilst I recognize that the people cared little for politics and normally supported organizations like the United Irish Society from economic or religious motives, nevertheless all the evidence shows that they were well informed of events in the continental war and of the benefits which might result from a French invasion of Ireland. A better understanding of the catholic secret society, the Defenders, is essential to any estimate of the primitive political ideas of the Irish lower classes, for it was the Defenders rather than the United Irishmen that they joined, and it was the alliance between the two which gave the impression of an expanding United movement after 1795. Originating in Ulster in the 1780s, in response to protestant sectarian attacks, the Defenders are frequently dismissed as a secret agrarian society in the same tradition as the Whiteboys of the 1760s. Unlike the peasant protesters in the Whiteboys, however, the main strength of the Defenders lay in the towns and centres of rural industry. All the signs are that they were republicans before the United Irishmen and that it was their peculiarly catholic interpretation of French promises and United Irish ideals which was espoused by the ordinary people.[5] Despite loyalist fears, however, the Irish catholics were not natural rebels, and there was nothing approximating to a nationalist movement before the 1790s, let alone any attack on the existing government or the English connection. But the confiscations of native land in the seventeenth century, and its redistribution to a protestant ruling class, had created a historical situation in which the latter lived in fear of a catholic rising to regain their ancestral possessions.

---

4. See P. Gibbon, *The Origins of Ulster Unionism* (Manchester, 1975); idem, 'The Origins of the Orange Order and the United Irishmen', *Economy and Society*, 1 (1972), 135–63; A. T. Q. Stewart, *The Narrow Ground: aspects of Ulster 1609–1969* (London, 1977).

5. Some excellent work on the Defenders can be found in J. G. O. Kerrane, 'The Background to the 1798 Rebellion in County Meath' (Nat. Univ. of Ireland M.A. thesis 1971), and M. R. Beames, 'Peasant Disturbances, Popular Conspiracies and their Control; Ireland 1798–1852' (Univ. of Manchester Ph.D. thesis 1975). T. MacNevin's *The Lives and Trials of A. H. Rowan ... the Defenders ... and other Eminent Irishmen* (Dublin, 1846) simply paraphrases pamphlet accounts of Defender trials; for fuller accounts see *A Complete Collection of State Trials*, ed. T. B. and T. J. Howell, 33 vols. (London, 1809–28); see M. Elliott, 'The Origins and Transformation of Early Irish Republicanism', *International Review of Social History*, XXIII (1978), 405–28, for an account of the Defenders and their historiography.

Modern historians tend to overcompensate for the religious prejudices of their predecessors by playing down religious divisions as a cause of Irish strife, concentrating instead on the socio-economic factors and ignoring the relationship between the two. Every traveller in eighteenth-century Ireland remarked on the intensity of popular pride in the past, and on the way in which the resentment of the upper levels of catholic society at the dispossessions of the seventeenth century had been absorbed by the catholic populace as a whole. The consciousness of the protestants that their power rested on the historical phenomena of confiscation and plantation dictated their attitudes to the catholics. They resisted catholic emancipation tooth and nail, arguing that numbers alone would turn catholic equality into catholic superiority, and that a reversal of the land settlement would follow as a matter of course. Whitehall was shocked and embarrassed at such antiquated bigotry, but made little effort to understand the reasoning behind it.

The United Irishmen would never consciously have encouraged catholic hopes of a reversal of the land settlement, or risked the possibility of a catholic revenge campaign against the protestant dispossessors. They were political rather than social reformers, seeking the support of all religious denominations in their pursuit of national self-determination; and their insistence on the need for French military assistance stemmed as much from their fears of how the catholic lower classes would conduct themselves in a rebellion as from their desire for independence from English rule. But in pursuit of their ideal of incorporating all religious persuasions into a genuinely national movement, they joined forces with the primitive catholic nationalism of the Defenders. The alliance of a secret catholic movement, which did envisage a reversal of the land settlement, with an advanced republican leadership and a hostile French government poised to assist their joint attack on the established order terrified the protestant nation and was responsible for the brutal repression which helped to provoke the 1798 rebellion. The imminence of French invasion gave a new sense of urgency to the latent hopes and fears of both sides and was a crucial ingredient in the holocaust of that year.

After the disasters of 1798 no further action was possible without French aid. The people were cowed and unwilling to rise again unless assured beforehand of success by a French victory on Irish soil. The rump of the United Irish leadership still at liberty was in exile on the Continent, barred from Ireland by a stringent Banishment Act, their standing and confidence as negotiators rapidly deteriorating as Irish rebel fugitives flocked to the Continent, swelling the numbers of foreign refugees already clamouring for French assistance. The United Irishmen had been forced into dependence on outside stimuli, and like so many other exiled revolutionaries before them their fate had become irretrievably tied to that of France. It is at this stage that the history of the United Irishmen falls into line with that of the many other foreign patriots who had already experienced defeat, exile, total dependence on France, and the frustration, bitterness, internal bickering and ultimate disenchantment with French promises which followed in due course. The last two chapters of this book examine this period in the history of the United Irish movement and the efforts made by successive French governments to cope with a larger refugee problem, of which the plight of the United Irishmen formed but a part. It was difficult for the United men to retain any of their old confidence in negotiations when they were simultaneously petitioning for relief, and their inability to agree on future policies, their nagging of French officials and tiresome reiteration of old promises, made a poor showing with a new and less sympathetic French regime. From 1804 there was a steady trickle of disillusioned United Irishmen to America. But their experience in France after 1798 was not identical to that of the the the Dutch, the Belgians, or the Italians. Irish disillusionment with the French alliance was never sufficient to outweigh its obvious advantages, and in Ireland and France alike the French government could have aroused the support of an Irish party of rebellion at any time up to 1815.

III

An account of United Irish activities in England is fundamental to a proper understanding of their aims and development, particularly after 1797; and since E. P. Thomson's seminal work *The Making of the English Working Class* (1963) English historians have come to recognize the importance of United Irish involvement in underground political movements of the period, particularly in their shadowy offshoot, the United Englishmen.[6] This book does not pretend to give a full account of the United Englishmen or attempt to slot them into the pattern of industrial or subsistence troubles of the period, the growth of early workers' combinations or the patchwork survival of a democratic reform movement (all of which form the backdrop to the activities of the United movement on the mainland). Rather it examines the United Englishmen as an appendage to the United Irish Society and tries to

---

6. Much of this is still locked up in theses, see e.g. J. Walvin, 'English Democratic Societies and Popular Radicalism 1791–1800' (York Univ. D.Phil. thesis 1969); J. A. Hone, 'The Ways and Means of London Radicalism 1796–1821' (Oxford Univ. D.Phil. thesis 1975); A. Booth, 'Reform, repression and revolution: radicalism and loyalism in the North-West of England, 1789–1803' (Lancaster Univ. Ph.D. thesis 1979); and J. L. Baxter, 'Origins of the Social War: a history of the economic, political and cultural struggles of working people in South Yorkshire 1750–1850' (Sheffield Univ. Ph.D. thesis 1976). See also M. I. Thomis and P. Holt, *Threats of Revolution in Britain 1789–1848* (London, 1977), ch. 1; A. Goodwin, *The Friends of Liberty* (London, 1979); and C. Emsley, *British Society and the French Wars 1793–1815* (London, 1979), particularly ch. 4. Although I have sometimes disagreed with E. P. Thompson's assumptions and use of evidence, my own research has invariably supported conclusions which he has reached on the basis of English archival material alone.

show that they were directly modelled on the Irish parent society and can only be understood in the context of the latter's extended programme to enlist support for an Irish revolution. But to look for an English movement tightly organized in graduated divisions like the United Irishmen would be incorrect. The United Englishmen were as amorphous as the myths which have developed around them seem to suggest. They were a loose federation of surviving London Corresponding Society members, of isolated pockets of disaffection, of the extreme fringes of the workers' combinations, and of the Irish workforce on the mainland. Alone, the movement was a paltry body, a handful of agitators playing upon disturbances caused by non-political grievances. Its strength lay in its participation in a wider United Irish programme, firmly based on expectations of French military assistance.

The efforts made by the London government to counter such subversion have also been examined. In the early 1790s the policy of the English government towards Ireland differed little from that pursued by its predecessors throughout the eighteenth century. It had little sympathy for the fears and difficulties of the Irish ruling classes. In most matters Ireland was expected to govern and defend itself in much the same way as the English counties did through the unpaid local magistracy, and policies which London forced on Dublin Castle frequently failed to recognize the plight of the Anglo-Irish gentry, who felt themselves encircled by an alienated, and frequently hostile, catholic majority. But when events in Ireland directly affected England's interests, as they did in dramatic fashion when the United Irishmen joined with the conspirators on her very doorstep and upset her war policy by their activities on the Continent, England showed that she could act swiftly and effectively to prevent infection from Ireland, even if she ignored the reasons for its indigenous growth. The British government's mobilization of the domestic and foreign intelligence service to deal with such conspirators is impressive, and in time it became so well informed of United activities that it was able to manipulate them for propaganda purposes: at home to frighten the loyal majority into supporting wartime security measures, and abroad, particularly after the revelations concerning the international set of revolutionaries in Hamburg, to play on the widespread European fear of French-inspired subversion.

* * *

The United Irish Society cannot be treated in a purely Irish context. It was its association with France which decided its development after 1795 and which, with its incursion onto the British mainland, made it such a threat to England at a time of involvement in a major European war. By 1803 that association had become essential to the Society's continued existence. As an organized movement it had collapsed in Ireland in 1798, though the continuing expectations of French help and knowledge of a United party still operating in France kept the remnants of a republican movement alive in Ireland long after its formal organization had disappeared. Deepening reaction at home had already placed more emphasis on the Society's external operations before 1798, but àfter that year its leadership operated almost entirely in exile. In England it did not long survive the double failure of 'Despard's Conspiracy' and 'Emmet's Rebellion'; but in France and Hamburg it remained active as an organization until 1806, and individual United men were still consulted by the French government right up to 1815. After 1798 it was a mere tool in the French armoury, despite its struggle to maintain the pretence of independence, and it was the United Irishmen's bitterness and disillusionment at this altered situation which led to the eventual dispersal of the continental movement. Without the support and asylum provided by France, however, they could not have survived the mounting repression at home from 1797 onwards. The French alliance was as essential to the Society's continued existence as it had been to its ability to attract widespread support in Ireland and England in the first place. This is why that alliance is the dominant theme of this book and why I consider the pursuit of that theme important to the understanding of a movement which occasioned such disruption in both islands, which has remained the inspiration behind militant Irish republicanism, and which the London government considered 'the most powerful engine, in the hands of conspirators, against the Government of their country, which has ever yet been devised'.[7] I have tried to rescue the United Irishmen and the '98 rebels from the sterility of hero-worship; the English and Irish governments, the Irish loyalists and the French Directory from the damnation of their detractors; and the exiles and refugees on the Continent from obscurity. Above all the book examines the human frailties and the accidents which determined the French muddle and the Irish catastrophe, destroying the reform euphoria which had swept through late eighteenth-century Ireland, and transforming the United Irish Society into a pitiful rump of exiles by 1799.

---

7. *Report from the Committee of Secrecy of the House of Commons relative to the proceedings of different persons and societies in Great Britain and Ireland engaged in a treasonable conspiracy* (1799) in *Reports from the Committees of the House of Commons, printed by order of the House 1715–1801*, 15 vols. (London, 1803), x, 789.

PART ONE

1791–1795 : The United Irishmen Formation and Transformation

When exultant we tell how our fathers of yore,
   Their wrongs and oppressions were wont to redress,
How firmly they waded through rivers of gore,
   And forced from proud despots those rights we possess;
When we boast of our own revolution and laws,
   Yet reprobate men who have spurn'd base controul,
We may shew an acquaintance with Liberty's cause,
   But we strongly evince a contraction of soul.

We deem ourselves lodg'd under Liberty's tree,
   Where the whole human race might with comfort recline;
We boast of the blessing—and, Britons, shall we
   At the joyous approach of our neighbours repine?
Forbid it—ye ofspring of men who were tried,
   Of men, who unshackled both body and mind;
Forbid it—and learn, ere you dare to deride,
   That the cause of the French is the cause of mankind!

O! spurn the mean prejudice, Britons, and say,
   If your Fathers were right, how can Frenchmen be wrong?
The will of oppressors both scorn'd to obey,
   And asserted those rights which to mortals belong
Yet the struggles of these are to infamy hurl'd
   While the actions of those we with triumph rehearse:
But the bright orb of reason now peeps on the world,
   And the thick clouds of prejudice soon shall disperse.

Ye! soon shall these truths far and wide be convey'd.
   'Spite of Pindars quaint prattle and Burke's raving din,
That the thrones of *true* Kings by the PEOPLE are made
   And when kings become tyrant's—submission is sin!
That the power of oppressors can ne'er be of Heav'n,
   A being all-just—cannot justice despise:
A Being all-just—EQUAL RIGHTS must have giv'n;
   And who robs man of these must offend the All-wise.

('A new SONG addressed to ENGLISHMEN', taken from the United Irish chapbook *Songs on the French Revolution* (Belfast, 1792)—I.S.P.O. 620/19/88ª)

CHAPTER ONE

Reform to Republicanism:
the eighteenth-century Background

The idea of a general European crisis at the end of the eighteenth century, upon which the American and French Revolutions reacted, is now generally accepted by historians. But if Ireland reflects this general response to the French Revolution, the results were unique. In most countries the revolutionaries formed a tiny part of the population; many had already tried and failed to effect their ideals by revolutionary means and thereafter required outside military aid to replace non-existent national support. For the Dutch, the Belgians, the Poles or the Swiss, the French Revolution offered little hope unless France agreed to back them with military assistance. In Ireland, however, the majority catholic population was traditionally pro-French and had been estranged from its established rulers by exclusion from the economic and political life of the country. The seventeenth century had witnessed the confiscation of native, catholic-owned land on a massive scale and its transfer to imported English or protestant settlers. A brutal penal code was then devised by the latter to prevent any reversal of the land settlement or the restoration of the powers accruing to land ownership. With most of the catholic leaders already in exile by the close of the seventeenth century, the penal laws were designed to ensure that catholic society remained leaderless and politically powerless; and the handful of upper-class catholics who survived the penal laws were so afraid of losing the property remaining to them that they became almost servile in their loyalty. In consequence there was no movement among the catholics to win back lost rights for most of the eighteenth century. Instead, demoralized and leaderless, the catholic populace expended its aggressiveness in verse, messianic prophecies and endemic, though localized, agrarian warfare.

It was within the protestant community, rather than among the discontented catholic majority, that revolutionary nationalism developed spasmodically and took off in the last two decades of the century. A movement for greater independence from English control was already far advanced before 1789, but participation of the catholics in the extended powers of the political nation was not envisaged and those protestant reformers who argued otherwise were ostracized. As long as the protestant minority recognized that the basis

3

of its power lay in the conquest and subsequent repression of the catholic majority and ultimately on the support of English arms, it was unlikely that any movement for greater autonomy within the context of continuing British rule would be extended to a demand for outright independence. It was the situation created by the French Revolution which eventually brought about an alliance between the extreme protestant reformers and the catholics, giving the latter the leadership which alone could have turned their passive discontent to revolutionary ends. By the mid-1790s Ireland possessed the means of liberating itself without foreign aid; that its leaders eventually joined the wave of patriot exiles in France seeking such aid owed more to their continuing fears of popular catholic passions than to any real military necessity.

I

There was a strange dichotomy between popular catholic thinking and popular action in eighteenth-century Ireland. In bardic poetry and street ballads the catholics expressed their resentment at the confiscations of preceding centuries and pined for a golden age when their ancestors had owned the land and the gaelic Brehon Law had been in force. But few spoke of patriotism or revulsion at English rule, or if they did they expressed the traditional bardic lament at the disappearance of their patrons and their loss of status, rather than any popular nationalism.[1] Indeed, gaelic Ireland had proved singularly indifferent to English rule since it was first introduced in the twelfth century. Any opposition had consistently come from within the Anglo-Irish protestant community rather than from the old Irish, and the struggle of the 1790s which launched modern Irish republicanism had started out as an internecine conflict within the ruling protestant elite. The only two major outbreaks of popular catholic violence before the 1780s, the Houghers of 1709–13 and the Whiteboys of the 1760s and 1770s, were directed at specific local grievances like land enclosures, methods of tithe payment, or rent increases, and had no political content.[2] Even Jacobitism remained weak in Ireland; the Irish did not forget that the Stuarts had been responsible for further land confiscations and had proved as hostile to the Irish as the other English monarchs. Jacobite songs were popular because

1. G. D. Zimmermann, *Songs of Irish Rebellion. Political Street Ballads and Rebel Songs* (Dublin, 1967), particularly 9, 25–7, 29–31; T. C. Croker, *Researches in the South of Ireland* (London, 1824), 182; J. C. Beckett, *The Anglo-Irish Tradition* (London, 1976), 18, 46; L. M. Cullen, 'The Hidden Ireland: Re-assessment of a Concept', *Studia Hibernica*, 9 (1969), 7–47.
2. M. Elliott, 'The Origins and Transformation', 408–9; M. Wall, 'The Whiteboys', in *Secret Societies in Ireland*, ed. T. D. Williams (Dublin, 1973), 13–25; J. S. Donnelly Jr., 'The Whiteboy Movement, 1761–5', *I.H.S.* xxi (1978), 20–54; M. R. Beames, 'Peasant Disturbances', 1–16; idem, 'Peasant Movements: Ireland, 1785–1795', *Journal of Peasant Studies*, 2 (1975), 502–6.

they were written in gaelic and voiced some vague sense of grievance felt by all.[3]

The truth is that much of eighteenth-century vernacular literature reflects the grievances of the surviving noble stock rather than those of the Irish people. Under the old gaelic land-holding system, the principle of hereditary ownership was virtually unknown. Rather, land was held in common by clans, septs or extended families. An elected chief who controlled clan land would possess only a small portion by hereditary right. Below him society was organized in a rigidly hierarchical structure with his own relatives at its apex; it then descended through various collateral septs (cousin branches) and sometimes a few non-related septs, each division possessing in turn its own elected chieftain and at the very bottom of the social scale its 'churls', or landless labourers. Few therefore actually 'owned' land by hereditary right, and the status of inferior septs was progressively eroded by more powerful chiefs who manipulated the Brehon Law. The desire for a more permanent hold on land and power was a constant source of dispute within the upper echelons of gaelic society, and many took advantage of the Tudor policy of 'surrender and re-grant' to convert their elective chieftainships into hereditary lordships on the English model, depressing the status of sub-chiefs to that of mere tenants, and reducing the number of Irish land-owners.[4] The old Brehon system was therefore less rosy than its eighteenth-century eulogists cared to admit, and only a handful would have been justified in claiming dispossessed ancestry as a result of land confiscation in the seventeenth century. But the crucial difference between the old gaelic structure and that of post-plantation times was that everybody, even the unfree 'churl', was given a common stake in the well-being of the clan. The system was designed to cater for the needs of all on clan lands, and although its pastoral and nomadic nature made it uneconomic, it did ensure a right of share in the produce and a fixed social status for each one of its members. It provided a security which the development of capitalistic farming in the

---

3. J. O'Daly, *Reliques of Irish Jacobite Poetry*, 2nd edn. (Dublin, 1949), iii–iv; also J. Hardiman, *Irish Ministrelsy or Bardic Remains of Ireland*, 2 vols. (London, 1831), i, xxiv–xxviii and ii, xliii, 27, 31, 61; G. Cornewall Lewis, *On Local Disturbances in Ireland* (London, 1836), 3; D. Hyde, *A Literary History of Ireland*, 7th edn. (London, 1920), 594, and 517–30 for his attempt to read nationalism into such Jacobite poetry.

4. See K. Nicholls, *Gaelic and Gaelicised Ireland in the Middle Ages* (Dublin, 1972), especially 8–12, for the best short account of the gaelic land-holding system; also G. Sigerson, *History of the Land Tenure and Land Classes of Ireland* (London, 1871), ch. 1; W. F. Butler, 'Irish Land Tenures: Celtic and Foreign', *Studies*, xiii (1924), 291–305, 524–40. See N. Canny, 'Hugh O'Neill and the changing face of Gaelic Ulster', *Studia Hibernica*, x (1970), 7–35, for an account of the changes taking place in Irish landholding even before the confiscations and plantations, also his 'Early Modern Ireland: An Appraisal Appraised', in *Irish Economic and Social History*, iv (1977), 62. M. Perceval–Maxwell, 'The Ulster Rising of 1641, and the depositions', *I.H.S.*, xxi (1978), 144–67, provides many examples of the deep gulf between the Irish gentry and people.

eighteenth century shattered, and almost every incident of agrarian turmoil thereafter was a collective attempt to enforce these long-standing customs, and was sparked off by an attack on accepted rights.[5]

The operation of this collective gaelic system would have been in living memory in the early eighteenth century. Although there had been several attempts to destroy it—the Elizabethan conquest, the Ulster plantation, the Cromwellian settlement and the Williamite confiscations—the process of plantation and re-settlement was uneven, and in many areas the hereditary and the gaelic systems co-existed well into the seventeenth century. Large tracts of land were given to individuals who simply imposed their ownership on the existing structure, and many remained absentees. Even in Ulster, where the original plan had been to replace the Irish completely with imported settlers, the new owners found it more convenient to retain them to work the land. Hence, although the ownership was changed, the infrastructure was not, for the Irish remained in 'occupancy'.[6] Many of the Irish chieftains were already dead or in exile, but the status of the collateral septs was debased to that of mere tenancy, and it seems to have been their sense of grievance at lost ancestral rights which was gradually assimilated into popular catholic thinking. Every traveller and social commentator remarked upon the prevalence of peasant resentment at ancestral dispossession, at their long memory of the exact boundaries of the lands belonging to their families, and their firm belief that they would one day be restored.[7] The early training of at least one catholic who later became a United Irishman had included tours of such estates and vows of vengeance against the 'invaders' who had taken them.[8] Historically, the ancestors of most eighteenth-century catholics would have been the landless members of the septs; but it is important to remember that the concept of individual landholding or ownership was still a novel one. When they spoke of their ancestors, they spoke rather of the clan or extended family, and Arthur Young remarked on this in his *Tour in Ireland* of 1776.[9] A sense of historical right to the land therefore did exist,

5. R. D. Crotty, *Irish agricultural production: its volume and structure* (Cork, 1966), 1–3, and Sigerson, *History of the Land Tenure*, 3–5.

6. See the contributions of A. Clarke and R. D. Edwards in *A New History of Ireland*, III: *Early Modern Ireland*, ed T. W. Moody, F. X. Martin and F. J. Byrne (Oxford, 1976), 168–232; also T. W. Moody, 'The Treatment of the Native population under the scheme for the Plantation of Ulster', *I.H.S.*, 1 (1938–9), 51–63.

7. L. M. Cullen, *An Economic History of Ireland since 1660* (London, 1972), 77; J. G. Simms, *Jacobite Ireland* (London, 1969), 5–6 and idem, *The Williamite Confiscation in Ireland, 1690–1703* (London, 1956), 58, 80. See Rev. J. Hall, *Tour Through Ireland*, 2 vols. (London, 1813), II, 144–5, for examples of peasant memories of confiscations etc.; also Croker, *Researches in the South of Ireland*, 182, 225, and P.R.O. H.O. 100/44/5–10. Dervla Murphy, *A Place Apart* (Harmondsworth, 1978), 203–4, cites the remarkable survival of catholic resentment at ancestral confiscation into the 1970s.

8. *Memoirs of Miles Byrne*, ed. by his widow, 2nd. edn., 2 vols. (Dublin, 1906), I, 3.

9. A. Young, *A Tour in Ireland*, ed. C. Maxwell (Cambridge, 1925), 193–4.

though the logical extension of resentment from the local object, the landlord or agent, to the government and the English monarchy, was not actually made. Despite the recurring references to hopes of a reversal of the land settlement in Defender oaths, or popular interpretations of United Irish or French intentions, there is no sign that such vague laments produced any ideas of political revolution in the catholic populace. The process of plantation, of self-exile by the Irish nobles and the workings of the eighteenth-century penal laws, left catholic Ireland degraded and leaderless, and some outside element would have been required to focus such nebulous discontent on any specific object.[10]

But if catholic resentment was passive for most of the eighteenth century, its existence explains the depth of protestant paranoia. The protestants were never in any doubt about the potential dangers of liberalism on the part of the 'conquerors'. They recognized that their power rested on confiscations and on the suppression of the majority and they were convinced that the catholics sought every opportunity to reverse the land settlement and massacre the protestants. Little wonder that the prospect of former chiefs actually returning in 1729, when England permitted France to recruit openly for her Irish regiments in Ireland, should have raised an anguished protest from the protestants; and fears that the catholics kept a register of the forfeited lands were fuelled by the appearance in 1769 of a perfectly innocent antiquarian map, outlining the areas formerly occupied by the gaelic septs. The catholics had to be kept in an inferior position at all costs; sheer numbers (twice that of the episcopalians and all the dissenting sects together, and increasing steadily while the others remained static or registered only a marginal increase) would mean catholic domination if they were ever admitted to equal rights with the protestants.[11]

The aim of the penal statutes passed against the catholics in the first half of the eighteenth century was accordingly to ensure that they would never be able to acquire the property or the position which would entitle them to a say in the country's government. They were disfranchised and debarred from all political or legal office, and they could not acquire or bequeath land or property. Added to the confiscations of the preceding century, the net result was to further reduce the land remaining in catholic hands to

10. M. Beresford, 'Ireland in French Strategy, 1691–1789', (Univ. of Dublin M. Litt. thesis 1975), 4, estimates that 18,000 went to serve in the Irish regiments in France between 1690 and 1691, and recruiting continued thereafter. Simms, *Jacobite Ireland*, 259–60.
11. M. Beresford, 'Ireland in French Strategy', 44–5, 52, 146–55, 163, 167; *Northern Star*, I, nos. 9, 12–14, 67. Such protestant fears were made more explicit at the time of the catholic relief campaign in the early 1790s, see the letters of Dublin Castle to London in P.R.O. P.R.O. 30/8/331/1, W.O. 30/63/55, and H.O. 100/42/246–9; also *The Life of William Wilberforce*, ed. by his sons R. I. and S. Wilberforce, 5 vols. (London, 1838), II, 163; and *H.M.C. Dropmore MSS.*, II, 318.

only 5 per cent by 1778, and to deprive them of their natural leaders.[12] Catholic talent was instead channelled into trade, as the only career left open. But this scarcely posed a threat to the protestant ascendancy, when political power was so firmly rooted in the land, and a predominantly urbanized mercantile community was too divorced from the mass of the catholic people to provide any local leadership.[13] The catholic religion itself was heavily penalized, and had the religious clauses of the penal code been fully implemented, it would have been virtually eradicated by the middle of the century. It was however the economic and political power of the religion which the state sought to crush; bereft of both, catholicism was no longer a threat and the more barbaric penalties against its practice were allowed to fall into disuse. They remained nevertheless on the statute book, highlighting one of the major weaknesses of English and protestant rule in Ireland. The Irish were only half-conquered, half-repressed; the remaining freedom only emphasized the injustice of persecution, and a country which was neither fervently religious nor nationalistic before the seventeenth century was both by the nineteenth. The gradual repeal of the penal statutes in the last decades of the eighteenth century only aggravated the insult of those remaining, and since each improvement was forced from a grudging ascendancy, resentment rather than gratitude was the result.

The penal code fulfilled its desired purpose, and as a political force the catholics were mute for most of the century. But it never entirely removed protestant fears of a catholic resurgence. The seventeenth-century conflict supplied enough horror stories to sustain such fears, and the 1641 'massacre' during the catholic rising in Ulster, the siege of Derry in 1690 and the sectarian legislation of James II's last Irish parliament became the stock-in-trade of protestant scaremongering. The numbers killed in 1641 do not merit the epithet 'massacre', but from a recent analysis of the depositions of witnesses, M. Perceval–Maxwell has shown that enough murders were committed to justify some of the protestant scare stories. Certainly A. T. Q. Stewart has found that in areas which had seen such atrocities in 1641, the United Irish Society, with its emphasis on religious union, remained weak a hundred and fifty years later. The evidence collected by specially appointed commissioners

<hr>

12. R. D. Edwards, *An Atlas of Irish History* (London, 1973), 166, estimates that the percentage of land in catholic hands declined from 90% in 1603 to 5% in 1778. J. G. Simms, 'The Restoration 1660–85', in *A New History of Ireland*, III, ed. Moody *et al.*, 420–53; and idem, *The Williamite Confiscation*, 196; Simms estimates that the percentage of land in catholic hands declined from 59% in 1641 to 22% in 1688 and 14% in 1703.
13. S. J. Connolly, 'Catholicism and Social Discipline in Pre-Famine Ireland', 2 vols. (New Univ. of Ulster D.Phil. thesis 1977), I, 147–9; M. Wall, 'The rise of a catholic middle class in eighteenth-century Ireland,' *I.H.S.*, XI (1958–9), 91–115. It is important to remember, however, that there were also many catholics in such rural middle-class groups as the middlemen and graziers.

in the aftermath of 1641 was carefully selected for use as propaganda against the Irish. It is not surprising, therefore, that the intensely protestant Sir John Temple, writing in 1646, the first to use the depositions for presentation to the public, should have provided an account which aggravated protestant insecurity well into the following century. Temple's book went through eight editions by 1812, helping to make the vision of another catholic massacre a constant spur to eighteenth-century protestant fanaticism, and providing one of the main arguments in favour of the penal laws.[14] John Wesley was chilled by the blood-curdling accounts of 1641 still circulating in the middle of the eighteenth century. Every minor riot, every sign of catholic re-organization or of foreign invasion, would automatically trigger rumours of another protestant massacre and provoke the immediate revocation of catholic gun licences.[15] It was such fears which reconciled the Anglo-Irish ascendancy to total domination by England.

England never understood such fears, especially after the Jacobite threat had receded. The sectarian spoutings of the Irish protestants, which had found a ready audience in the Dublin parliament, sounded archaic at Westminster after the Union of 1801, and deeply embarrassed government supporters in England. Protestant submission to control from London had been the price of their supremacy; but their fear of a catholic backlash was such that it produced what had never existed in the first place, and as the catholic regeneration proceeded, the protestants were forced to sign away any power independent of England in return for continued protection. The isolation of the Anglo-Irish ascendancy became increasingly apparent in the eighteenth century. The narrowness of its base came under mounting attack both from a vocal reform group within the protestant nation itself, and from the rising catholic middle class and an English government which demonstrated its control of Irish politics by forcing unwelcome reforms upon the Dublin government. The challenge had started as a revolt within the ascendancy's own ranks against excessive English influence in Ireland's affairs. For much of the latter half of the eighteenth century, protestant paranoia and catholic resentment were latent, ignited only by crises. The long quiescence of the catholics and the growing prosperity of the country created a novel sense of confidence, independence and in many ways a

14. Perceval–Maxwell, 'The Ulster Rising'; Stewart, *The Narrow Ground*, 108; Sir J. Temple, *The Irish Rebellion; or, an history of the beginning and first progresses of the general rebellion raised within the kingdom of Ireland upon the ... 23 Oct. 1641 ...* (London, 1646). For examples of attempted refutations of Temple's claims see J. Curry, *An Historical and Critical Review of the Civil Wars in Ireland* (Dublin, 1750); and idem, *Historical Memoirs of the Irish Rebellion in the year 1641* (London, 1758); see also D. Berman, 'David Hume on the 1641 Rebellion in Ireland', *Studies*, LXV (1976), 101–12.

15. Beresford, 'Ireland in French Strategy', 44–5; *The Journals of the Rev. John Wesley*, 4 vols. (London, 1827) II, 68.

sense of their own Irishness among some protestants, and their struggle to lessen England's clutch on national resources was to provide the first outside influence which would pull the catholic populace back into the mainstream of national politics.

Despite their insulation from the catholic population and their dependence on England, the Anglo-Irish ascendancy felt themselves to be thoroughly Irish. Once their supremacy was firmly established, they began to question England's stranglehold over the country's political and economic life. England's mercantilist regulation of Ireland's commerce, her control of patronage and the chief plums of Irish office and, most of all, her power to legislate for Ireland and to quash Irish bills at will, made a mockery of such dearly-won supremacy. The ascendancy politicians were not original thinkers. Habit and cultural ties dictated a flow of ideas from English rather than native origins; they had absorbed completely the ideas of the English country Whigs and in particular their earliest prophet, John Locke. But the concept of a contract between ruler and ruled, of parliamentary sovereignty and the balanced constitution as safeguards to liberty and property, had profound implications for the Anglo-Irish constitutional connection, and had been adapted to the Irish situation by two writers in particular, Locke's contemporary and friend, the Dublin M.P. William Molyneux, and writing some fifty years later, the Dublin apothecary and political journalist Dr. Charles Lucas.

Molyneux's argument was to be reiterated by successive generations of protestant patriots: he claimed that Ireland and England were two separate kingdoms, the King acting in a dual capacity as King of Ireland and of England alike, not as King of England ruling over Ireland; and he called upon antiquity to show that this had been generally accepted since the days of Henry II. The compact had been made between the Irish people and the King, not between them and the English parliament. It was the King who granted their laws and liberties; they owed no allegiance to any intermediary authority, and the English parliament had no powers to supersede the parliament of Ireland or bind it by English statutes. Since the Irish in giving homage to the King had been granted the same rights as Englishmen, their representative institutions could not be controlled by any superior authority—in this case the English parliament. Molyneux also rehearsed the argument later adopted by the Americans that no man could submit to laws to which he had not consented.[16] These arguments formed the basis of the mid-century

16. W. Molyneux, *The Case of Ireland's being bound by Acts of the Parliament in England, stated* (Dublin, 1698); on Molyneux see R. R. Madden, *The History of Irish Periodical Literature*, 2 vols. (London, 1867), I, 42–62; and Robbins, *The Eighteenth-Century Commonwealthman*, 137–55. Charles Lucas was the principal figure of the mid-eighteenth century to rehearse Molyneux's arguments in a continuous flow of addresses and pamphlets, but particularly in his paper the *Citizens Journal*; see also the pamphlet, *The Ursurpations of England. The Chief Sources of the Miseries of Ireland* (Dublin, 1780).

campaign of the so-called 'patriots' in the Irish parliament to restore rights thought to have been usurped by the parliament in London. It culminated in 1779–80, in the grant of free trade, and the measures of 1782–83, granting legislative independence to the Irish parliament. The American and French Revolutions therefore had less impact on Irish thinking than is commonly supposed. They simply highlighted existing grievances and theories and, most important, provided the occasions to do something about them.

Nationalist polemic of the nineteenth and twentieth centuries was virtually to ignore the role of late eighteenth-century protestantism in the development of Irish nationalism. It is true that the conflicts of the 1790s reduced the number of protestant nationalists to a mere handful and introduced the novelty of sectarianism into the national struggle. But it had not always been so, and there had been a gaelic revival too in the eighteenth century, sponsored not by the catholics, as in the next century, but by the protestant ascendancy in its period of confident liberalism. Starting in the 1760s, it formed part of the romantic folk and Ossianic revival sweeping Europe at the time; the fashionable world of the Dublin intelligentsia was caught up in a wave of patriotism which had clear political undertones, and reformers of all hues, including future United Irishmen like the Ulster presbyterian physician and poet Dr. William Drennan, participated in the revival.[17] In particular this new surge of romantic nationalism added weight to the campaign of the 'patriot' party in the Irish parliament, the representatives of the 'real Whig' tradition of constitutional resistance to excessive ministerial influence, who were to achieve their most notable successes in the 1770s and 1780s under the leadership of Henry Flood and his successor Henry Grattan.

It was, however, the activities of the Volunteer companies rather than those of the gaelic revivalists or the 'patriots' which carried reform into every corner of the country. The Irish Volunteers were the embodiment of one of the most cherished principles of the Glorious Revolution, the right of every citizen to arm in defence of his property. They originated in Ulster in 1778 when the American war had denuded Ireland of troops and exposed her coasts to the threat of invasion by the French. Although they rapidly spread to other parts of the country, they were widely regarded as an Ulster phenomenon and survived in the province long after they had disappeared elsewhere.[18] Composed of the most respectable members of Irish society,

17. P. Rafroidi, *L'Irlande et le romantisme* (Paris, 1972), 211–72; N. Vance, 'Celts, Carthaginians and Constitutions: Anglo-Irish Literary Relations 1780–1820', forthcoming *I.H.S.* I am grateful to Dr. Vance for permission to consult a typescript of this paper.
18. D. H. (Peter) Smyth, 'The Volunteer Movement in Ulster: Background and Development 1745–85' (Queen's Univ. of Belfast Ph.D. thesis 1974), 21; *The Irish Sword*, XIII, no. 52 (1978–9), commemorative issue on the Volunteers, especially the contributions of P. Smyth and K. P. Ferguson, 185–216. See also T. G. F. Patterson, 'The County Armagh Volunteers of 1778–1793', U.J.A., 3rd ser. IV (1941), 101–27; V (1942), 36–61; VI (1943), 69–105.

protestants of some property, who could at least afford to supply their own uniform and equipment, the Volunteers were initially home-guard units in the militia tradition. But unlike the militia, they were, and remained, entirely independent of government control. They were proud of this independence and used it to promote the reform spirit which was sweeping the Irish political nation at the end of the 1770s. The 'patriot' party's stance against the interference of British ministers in Irish affairs was shaping itself into a call for free trade and legislative independence for the Irish parliament, and had been taken up by the English Whig opposition as part of their own campaign against excessive ministerial interference in the English parliamentary process. Under colonels who were also prominent in the political reform campaign, the Volunteers quickly assumed the position of the reformers' battering-ram. They possessed the ability to extend political agitation farther afield than at any other time since the Williamite wars, and the threat implicit in such support from armed battalions gave the reformers' campaign a particular advantage at the time of Britain's struggle with the American colonies. The outcome of the campaign was the grant of free trade for Ireland in 1779–80 and more importantly the so-called 'constitution' of 1782, which, whilst reserving the connection between the two countries, removed all restrictions on the Irish parliament's ability to legislate for Ireland, apart from the royal veto. The issues raised by the campaign for free trade and legislative independence perpetuated Volunteer participation in the reform debate; and during the 1780s parliamentary reform, the privileges of the established Church, the extention of 'real Whig' demands for religious toleration to include catholic emancipation, and even the connection with England were aired in a manner which would be penalized as treasonable in the next decade.

With the Volunteer convention which met at Dungannon on 15 February 1782, the debate of constitutional issues by extra-parliamentary bodies was given temporary respectability. The convention became the symbol of Ireland's independence from excessive English influence and the immense pride in her ability to win reform through such extra-parliamentary means was matched by the indignation when the tradition came under the hammer in the 1790s. It is crucial to understand this euphoria of the 1780s, and protestant pride in the institutions and practices associated with it, in order to appreciate the violent reaction produced by their suppression in the following decade. The native experience was always uppermost in propelling the reformers of the 1780s towards republicanism in the 1790s. The protestant political nation, however loyal it might be to the English connection, had long resented the stranglehold of England over the country's economic and political life; the supineness of the Irish parliament, unable to initiate its own legislation, corrupted by government pensions in the gift of an Irish executive appointed from London, particularly offended protestant national

Plate 1. The Lisburn and Lambeg Volunteers, 1782 (National Library of Ireland)

pride, and had already created a climate of opinion in favour of making parliament more responsive to the needs of the nation. The debate took off after the victory of 1782, and for the next two years the Volunteers were in the forefront of the campaign for parliamentary reform. In their demands they were clearly influenced by the example of the reform campaign in England, they consulted with its leading figures, and in September the Ulster Volunteers put forward a plan of reform which called for a redistribution of seats, shorter parliaments, an extension of the franchise to leaseholders, the ballot, registration of voters and a total exclusion of placemen and pensioners. The recommendations were discussed in detail at another national convention meeting in Dublin two months later, and were incorporated into a reform bill which Flood presented to parliament. The membership of the convention reflected the same wide spectrum of support that had mustered for the legislative independence campaign. But a group of more radical protestant thinkers, which included future United Irishmen like Dr. William Drennan, the popular Dublin merchant and member of the Dublin corporation James Napper Tandy, and Archibald Hamilton Rowan, a member of the Ulster land-owning class, chafed at the timidity of some of the delegates. The proposal to consider granting the franchise to the catholics, even on the exclusive basis of £50 property owners (which Drennan estimated would admit no more than 500–1000) proved particularly divisive. Although most sincerely wanted some measure of parliamentary reform, the threat of any popular commotion to attain it was enough to sink the whole issue with its more aristocratic supporters, and the convention fizzled out without protest after Flood's bill had been defeated in parliament.

The debate brought out a considerable body of support for reform. Issues were aired which were to become central to the United Irishmen's programme and, most importantly, it had brought together a body of men which included several who were to be founder United Irishmen and who were committed to the idea that the constitution could not continue in its present form. Ridicule was thrown on the opinion that the 1688 constitution was immutable. Drennan criticized the habit of always identifying with English Whig heroes and suggested that it was time for the Irish to seek their own identity in their gaelic past. The question of separation from England altogether was openly debated, and six years later, as part of the reform debate which had continued throughout the decade, a young protestant barrister, Theobald Wolfe Tone, published a pamphlet in which he 'advanced the question of separation with scarcely any reserve, much less disguise; but . . . made not the smallest impression!' Well might Tone have marvelled at the chain of events which by the time he wrote these words in 1796 had made him a republican exile for expressing ideas which he and others had talked of openly only a few years before.[19]

The contradiction between the fight for Irish rights and the exclusion of the majority of the Irish people from any participation in those rights was not immediately apparent to the protestant reformers. The Volunteers as a whole still thought in terms of a protestant state, and Grattan alone of the reforming politicians argued for the full introduction of the catholics to political rights. Catholic quiescence had not only bred a sense of false security within the political nation, but had also produced a contempt for, or at best, a misunderstanding of the intellect of the catholic majority. Even the United Irish leaders had been conditioned to think of the catholic populace as brutalized and illiterate.[20] The language and imagery which the parliamentary opposition used, with little thought of the consequences, accordingly played upon popular aspirations for a reversal of the land settlement which

19. *The Drennan Letters, 1776–1815*, ed. D. A. Chart (Belfast, 1931), 17–34; F. J. Bigger, 'The National Volunteers of Ireland, 1782', *U.J.A.*, 3rd ser. xv (1909), 141–8; *H.M.C. Charlemont MSS.*, I, 391–428; J. Lawless, *The Belfast Politics Enlarged* (Belfast, 1818), 111–224; R. B. McDowell, *Irish Public Opinion 1750–1800* (London, 1944), 97–118. For Tone's pamphlet, *Spanish War! An Inquiry How Far Ireland is Bound, of Right, to Embark in the impending Contest on the Side of Great Britain* . . . (Dublin, 1790) see *Life of T. W. Tone*, ed. by his son W. T. W. Tone, 2 vols. (Washington, 1826), I, 33, 325–40.

20. See e.g. *Drennan Letters*, 223 (the full letter is in P.R.O.N.I. T.765/546); also W. J. MacNeven, *Pieces of Irish History* (New York, 1807), 230; *H.M.C. Charlemont MSS.* II, 179–80.

the reformers scarcely imagined to exist. In words which shocked most protestant politicians, opposition members emulated their English counterparts by appealing to the unenfranchised to support their campaign in parliament, calling on them to avenge their wrongs against England, and proclaiming the right to revolt if their demands went unanswered.[21]

The effect of such political vaporizing on the mass of the catholics is difficult to assess. But it almost certainly contributed to their growing sense of confidence in the last decades of the century. Nothing can be more false than the picture of the ordinary Irish people as degraded and priest-ridden. Theirs was a religion composed of saints, miracles, superstitions, prophecies and deeply entrenched local traditions. The dictates of the catholic church commanded conformity only insofar as they accorded with such traditions, and repeated church edicts against traditional forms of popular lawlessness were ignored. Moreover, despite their exclusion from any formal education, a flourishing oral culture and a tradition of hedge-school teaching produced a relatively high level of literacy among the Irish people.[22] The image of Irish rural society in which the impoverished and degraded cottier class is the dominant element comes later, from the era of the Great Famine. At the end of the eighteenth century the pressure of an increasing population upon the land had not yet eroded the 'social mix', as Louis Cullen calls it, of rural Ireland, which included solvent tenant farmers, dairymen, artisans, domestic workers and a large migrant labour force, as well as cottiers. Land-holdings were normally too small to support a family and some form of supplementary income was necessary, either from seasonal employment or from domestic industry such as brewing, distilling or weaving; and the Royal and Grand Canals, under construction at this time, provided considerable opportunity for casual employment. A highly mobile rural workforce accordingly bridged the gap between urban and rural society, and both Defenderism and the United Irish system frequently reached more remote areas through returning tradesmen or labourers, rather than by means of official missionaries.[23]

21. *The Parliamentary Register: or, History of the Proceedings and Debates of the House of Commons of Ireland*, 15 vols. (Dublin, 1784–95), x, 240–6; *The Correspondence of the Rt. Hon. John Beresford*, ed. the Rt. Hon. W. Beresford, 2 vols. (London, 1854), I, 55, 70.

22. P. J. Dowling, *The Hedge Schools of Ireland* (Dublin, 1935), especially 47–72; A. Atkinson, *Ireland Exhibited to England, in a political and moral Survey of her Population*, 2 vols. (London, 1823), I, 167; Hall, *Tour Through Ireland*, I, 241; Connolly, 'Catholicism ... in Pre-Famine Ireland', I, 165–8, 217–22 and II, 350–418; see also, J. O'Driscoll Esq., *Views of Ireland, Moral, Political and Religious*, 2 vols. (London, 1823), I, 138–55; and P.R.O.N.I. D.607/C/56, for limited clerical control over the people.

23. J. H. Johnson, 'The Two Irelands', in *Irish Geographical Studies in honour of E. Estyn Evans*, ed. N. Stephens and E. Glasscock (Belfast, 1970), 224–41; L. M. Cullen, 'The Cultural Basis of Modern Irish Nationalism', in *The roots of nationalism: studies in northern Europe*, ed. R. Mitchison (Edinburgh, 1980); A. J. Fitzpatrick, 'The Economic Effects of the French Revolutionary and the Napoleonic Wars in Ireland', (Manchester Univ. Ph.D. thesis 1973), 98–9.

Ireland witnessed the same efflorescence of local reform groups and reading clubs as England during these years, and it was from groups within her primitive industrial society that more remote parts of Ireland learnt of Paine and the French Revolution long before the United Irishmen reached them. Francis Higgins, one of the government's longest serving and most reliable agents, described them as 'clubs of Journeymen, artificers, and tradesmen ... something ... above the common rabble' who had learnt their revolutionary principles from 'reading newspapers', or from 'Paine's politics of *Liberty and Equality*'. They went under various titles, the 'Sons of Freedom', the 'Philanthropic Society', the 'Liberty Boys' or the 'Friends of Parliamentary Reform', and many were eventually subsumed into Defenderism and less completely into the United Irishmen.[24]

An inability to read was not necessarily a barrier to knowledge of contemporary events, and information received over the next few years showed that the language of the more radical reformers, and the claim to natural human rights—which the American and French revolutionaries had put forward against the threat of despotism—had been absorbed into the threats and oaths of popular Irish protest. This is not to say that the people who took the oaths fully understood the import of such theories or the significance of the events in France which they celebrated. It is important to recognize the uneven response to the political events of the 1790s, and the present account will concern itself primarily with those more prosperous areas in the north, the east and the midlands, the heartlands of Defenderism and the United Irishmen. But no area could remain unaffected by the crisis of those years; the very fact of intensified repression and an increasing military presence brought the poorer areas into direct contact with it. Everywhere there are signs that the idea of a French invasion had taken a firm hold on popular imagination; it had given a new twist to old hopes of a restoration of catholic power, and although this sectarian interpretation of the current political crisis was no foundation for a national revolutionary movement, the enthusiastic response of the people of Connacht to the French invasion of 1798 was to be a token of the kind of support the French might have received even from those areas where political consciousness was weak.

The catholic church leaders and the rising catholic middle class would have been the last to have consciously promoted current reform trends with

24. For the local clubs, see Kent C.R.O. U840/O143/3 and O144/8, P.R.O. H.O. 100/34/75–6; *Drennan Letters*, 92; *State Trials*, xxvi, 395; R. R. Madden, *The United Irishmen, their Lives and Times*, 1st. ser., 2 vols. (London, 1842), I, 116. For examples of local tradesmen and workmen bringing new ideas back to their home counties, see P.R.O. H.O. 100/44/115–8; Croker, *Researches in the South of Ireland*, 16, 182; Kerrane, 'The Background to ... 1798', 31; and J. Hewitt, 'Ulster Poets 1800–1870', (Queen's Univ. of Belfast, M. A. thesis 1951), 105–9. For the dissemination of United Irish literature, see I.S.P.O. 620/19/29, 33, 73, 101; 620/34/54; and P.R.O. H.O. 100/43/145–51.

the catholic populace, let alone ideas about a restoration of catholic rights and catholic lands. Both worked on the principle that submission to the system would eventually improve their lot, and the thriving mercantile class had no desire to draw attention to the loop-holes in the penal code which had allowed them to prosper. Moreover the Catholic Relief Act of 1782 had repealed the clauses against catholic ownership of land, enabling many catholics to become landlords and middlemen in their own right. By the 1790s, therefore, they freely admitted that they had no desire to reverse the land settlement, since they, as well as the protestants, would be the victims.[25] Consequently, although a catholic committee of sorts had existed since 1759, its unobtrusive attempts to secure the removal of the worst aspects of the penal code scarcely commanded catholic attention. Indeed, time was to show that the catholic hierarchy and middle class were only marginally less afraid of popular passions than was the protestant ascendancy, and it is not surprising that the political interest of the catholic populace should have been revived rather by protestant radicalism. There was no trace of dis-affection towards England either in the secret agrarian societies of the eighteenth century or in popular oral culture. Indeed, if anything catholicism had been depoliticized; support for the Stuarts had faded rapidly after 1745, and Edward Bancroft, the French agent sent in 1779 to sound Irish opinion, found the catholics pacified by government concessions and totally uninterested in independence.[26] From the 1790s onwards, however, even before the rising of 1798 had involved the ordinary people in direct conflict with the British forces, the desire for independence becomes a common facet of popular protest. Although the older agrarian tradition of the Whiteboys persisted into the nineteenth century, from the Defenders there stretches a long tradition of the popular subversive society. There is nothing inherent in eighteenth-century catholic society to explain such a sudden alteration in popular thinking, besides the exposure to radical propaganda.

II

It was from Ulster that the extremes of both radicalism and reaction radiated through the rest of the country at the end of the century. The apparent conversion of Ulster from extreme radicalism to extreme loyalism in the course of the 1790s has baffled many commentators. But the transformation was not as dramatic as it appears, and Ulster was never the republican stronghold of contemporary propaganda. There was no rapid takeover of

25. Tone, *Life*, I, 354; D. Corkery, *The Hidden Ireland*, 2nd edn. (Dublin, 1925), 31–6.
26. A. Temple Patterson, *The Other Armada* (Manchester, 1960), 75; see also Beresford, 'Ireland in French Strategy', 209, 254–61; Cornewall Lewis, *On Local Disturbances*, 3; Zimmermann, *Songs of Irish Rebellion*, 36.

the province by the United Irishmen, and apart from Antrim and Down the other Ulster counties registered insignificant numbers. That Ulster should have produced such opposing movements as Orangeism and the United Irishmen or Defenderism was a product of its peculiar historical development. The land settlement of Ulster in the seventeenth century had proceeded along quite different lines from that of the rest of the country, and the manner in which the province was 'planted' was to produce the conflicting forces of advanced liberalism and bitter sectarianism in the following century.

Most of the native catholic chiefs had fled from Ulster by 1607, and Armagh, Derry, Cavan, Tyrone, Fermanagh and Donegal had been granted by King James I to so-called 'undertakers', including several companies of the City of London, to plant with English and Scottish settlers. But the 'undertakers' had not entirely fulfilled the terms of the agreement. Enough settlers were not forthcoming, and it was found economically essential to retain the Irish to work the land. In many areas, therefore, the Irish were not removed, but their status was depressed, and they were exploited, confined to less productive land, and forced to pay higher rents and accept shorter leases than the imported settlers. Cultural and economic divisions were compounded, and as late as the 1780s the terms 'Scotch' and 'Irish' were used in Armagh, Orangeism's homeland, to denote the opposing groups of presbyterians and catholics.[27]

In the eighteenth century Ulster was the most densely populated province in the country, and with lower-class protestants and catholics living in such proximity any demographic change or economic slump made it the centre of sectarian rivalry. Competition for tenants had forced many seventeenth-century landlords to grant long and favourable leases, and security of tenure contributed to the growing sense of confidence and stability as the eighteenth century progressed. But from the middle of the century the remarkable rise of the linen industry and a rapidly expanding population produced immense pressure on the land at a time when the long leases were falling due, and the landlords, anxious to participate in the new prosperity, were raising rents, attracting outsiders who might inject capital into neglected land, or removing substantial farmers and establishing new contracts directly with the old sub-tenants. A new and bitter competition for land was the result, and although Armagh's independent cottier-weavers derived their livelihood principally from a thriving linen industry, they considered a plot of land which was adjacent to a favourable market centre, and on which they could fall back in hard times, a prerequisite for their trade. The catholics had come to the weaving trade late in the century; but by the 1780s linen-induced

27. P.R.O.N.I. T.1722/42; Clarke and Edwards, in *A New History of Ireland*, III, ed. Moody *et al.*, 187–232; P. Robinson, 'British Settlement in County Tyrone 1610–1666', *Irish Economic and Social History*, v, (1978), 5–26; T. W. Moody, *The Londonderry Plantation, 1609–41* (Belfast, 1949).

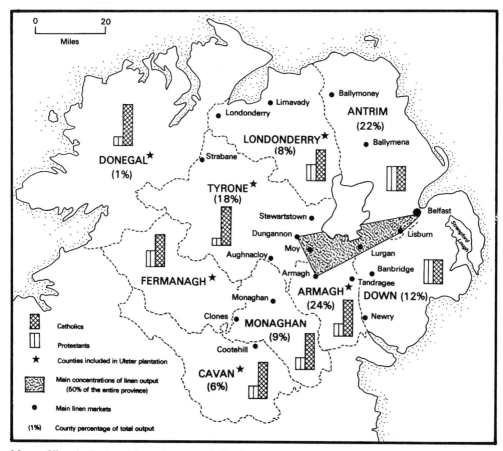

Map 2. Ulster in the late eighteenth century, indicating main linen markets, religious breakdown of population and plantation counties. (Linen statistics based on Crawford and Trainor, *Aspects of Irish Social History*, 72–4; religious statistics on Beaufort's 1792 figures in Wakefield, *An Account of Ireland*, II, 630–1. But see Elliott, *Origins and Transformation*, 415, for certain reservations about eighteenth-century statistics.)

prosperity and the relaxation of the penal legislation against land-holding had made them a real threat in the market for land in which to re-invest their weaving profits, and had given rise to protestant revenge gangs such as Nappach Fleet and the Peep O'Day Boys, to which the catholics responded with Defenderism. In 1785 the Nappach Fleet captain had prepared his men for their nocturnal foray against the catholics with warnings about the 'many Papists ... who have taken the oath of allegiance, having got long leases, and of course ... arms to shoot the sparrows from their grain ... '.[28] It was in such areas, where the protestant weavers were struggling to maintain their plebeian ascendancy against competition from the catholic weavers, that Orangeism was to thrive; and because these protestants were not entirely dependent on the land for their livelihood they could identify more easily with—and be mobilized by—reactionary landlords, creating a protestant

28. P.R.O.N.I. T.1722/8.

sense of identity in contradistinction to the catholics. The 'linen triangle' of Lisburn, Dungannon and Armagh town became the focus of the Orange–Defender conflict, and the slump of the mid-1790s produced sectarian warfare of such intensity that the course of Irish history was radically altered thereafter.

In contrast, Antrim and Down had been settled peacefully and progressively by waves of Scottish families before the official plantation of the province began in 1609. The area remained predominantly presbyterian in religion and experienced little of the lingering resentment at dispossession felt in other areas. Its economy was based primarily on middle-range farming and a more independent and largely presbyterian middle-class, with a group identity developed in contradistinction to an episcopalian ascendancy rather than to the catholics. It is scarcely surprising, therefore, that north-east Ulster, with only a sprinkling of catholics and a more homogeneous population than elsewhere, should for the moment have become the vanguard of political liberalism.[29]

Although the reform euphoria of the early 1780s had largely evaporated by the end of the decade, the debate had been sustained by a core of advanced radicals, particularly in the North, where the Volunteers had continued their political activities when companies had fizzled out elsewhere in the country. The Ulster presbyterians had a long history of conflict with the established authorities in Ireland, and if the catholics had been won over by the gradual relaxation of the penal laws, the presbyterians were only further alienated when there had been no corresponding relaxation in those laws which excluded them from public office and penalized their church. It was the 'New Light' or non-subscribing presbyterians who led the way in the radicalization of Ulster reformism at the end of the century. They were latitudinarians, who were deeply influenced by the liberal thought of the Scottish universities in the early eighteenth century, and had formally seceded from the presbyterian synod in 1726 in protest at its efforts to secure orthodoxy by requiring subscription to the Westminster confession of faith.

The 'New Light' presbyterians were therefore the most radical thinkers of eighteenth-century dissent; they were fiercely independent and felt a strong sense of provincial pride in their reputation for advanced thinking. At first

---

29. See Gibbon, *The Origins of Ulster Unionism*, 22–34; and idem, 'The Origins of the Orange Order', 135–63, for details of the economic background to the tensions in Ulster at this time. See also C. Gill, *The Rise of the Irish Linen Industry* (Oxford, 1925), 1–2, 129–32, 144–5; W. H. Crawford, *Domestic Industry in Ireland. The Experience of the linen industry* (Dublin, 1972), 24–37; idem, 'Landlord-Tenant Relations in Ulster 1609–1820', *Irish Economic and Social History*, II, (1975), 5–21; Johnson, 'The Two Irelands,' 230–1; and for the north-east coast in particular see G. Benn, *A History of the Town of Belfast From the Earliest Times to the Close of the Eighteenth Century*, 2 vols (London, 1877–80), 317–18, 416; M. Perceval-Maxwell, *The Scottish Migration to Ulster in the Reign of James I* (London, 1973).

they had supported the Northern Whig Club, established in 1789 by the veteran reformer and Volunteer colonel, the Earl of Charlemont.[30] But by 1791 they had become disillusioned by its tameness and a group began meeting separately in Belfast to discuss filling the void in the reform campaign left by the Club's inadequacy and by the apparent abdication of the parliamentary opposition from reform agitation. They had exchanged letters about an alternative reform organization with Drennan and Tone, as the recognized scribes of the advanced reformers, and Drennan had replied suggesting some kind of 'benevolent conspiracy' or 'plot for the people' to achieve 'the Rights of Man and the Greatest happiness of the Greatest Number'.[31] The forthcoming Volunteer celebration for the anniversary of the fall of the Bastille was recognized as the most suitable occasion on which to revive the reform campaign. But although Tone and Drennan were asked to prepare addresses for the occasion, the continuing reluctance in reform circles to discuss the catholic issue diluted their impact. Charlemont, most of the Northern Whig Club, and many Volunteers themselves were hostile to the idea of including the catholic franchise in their reform programme. But Charlemont's nervous caution about the catholics, and that of his main ally in Belfast, Dr. Alexander Haliday, was representative even of reforming opinion in the province. Gradual admission of the catholics to political rights, preceded by a national programme of education to prepare them, was acceptable enough. But few were enthusiastic about granting such rights immediately, and most, even the leading catholics, thought the association of catholic rights with advanced reform would bring the two down together.

This area of deepening uncertainty at the heart of the reform campaign was welcomed by government: '. . . the Popery question will not produce ferment,' wrote Edward Cooke, one of the Under-Secretaries at the Castle. 'None of the Protestant gentry are sincere in it. They all wish it to be defeated, and where they seem to countenance it, it is merely for electioneering purposes. The North in general is indisposed to the question, and in no part inclined to it but as leading to reform in parliament; and the coupling of the questions makes against the Catholics.'[32] Few therefore were totally committed to catholic emancipation, even the United Irishmen viewing it as an inferior, though essential, element of parliamentary reform. But catholic emancipation

---

30. W. T. Latimer, *A History of the Irish Presbyterians* (Belfast, 1893), 146–53, 171–6; see also I.S.P.O. 620/19/11–12, 25.

31. *Drennan Letters*, 54–60; also F. MacDermot, *Theobald Wolfe Tone*, 3rd edn. (Tralee, 1969), 59–62, and R.I.A. MS. 25. K. 53 for their correspondence. See Rogers, *The Irish Volunteers*, 201–6, and P.R.O. H.O. 100/34/35 for the Northern Whig Club and its loss of public support.

32. P.R.O.N.I. T.3229/2/7, Cooke to Auckland, 6 Apr. 1795. See Rogers, *The Irish Volunteers*, 194–6, M. Wall, 'The United Irish Movement', *Historical Studies*, v (1965), 122–40; P.R.O.N.I. T.1722/50–6; and *H.M.C. Charlemont MSS.*, ii, 160, 179–86 on the Volunteer reaction in particular.

eventually became the issue dividing reformers, for the heated opposition which greeted it in parliament forced them to make it their central concern, and the publicity it attracted reactivated all the old protestant fears.

In Belfast all references to the catholic issue were dropped in July 1791 in the interests of unanimity; and although those who had contacted Tone and Drennan firmly believed in the need to involve all Irishmen in a reformed parliament, they recognized the strength of opposition to such beliefs, and seem to have deferred the inauguration of their new society in consequence. In September, Tone's pamphlet *An Argument on behalf of the Catholics of Ireland* temporarily broke the stalemate of the summer and autumn. The events of July had convinced Tone that, enlightened as the Belfast reformers might appear, they had nevertheless failed to shed their prejudices against the catholics. 'I sat down accordingly and wrote a pamphlet, addressed to the dissenters ... the object of which was to convince them that they and the Catholics had but one common interest and one common enemy [i.e. excessive English influence in their country]; that the depression and slavery of Ireland was produced by the divisions existing between them, and that, consequently, to assert the independence of their country and their own individual liberties, it was necessary to forget all former feuds, to consolidate the entire strength of the whole nation, and to form for the future but one people.' The pamphlet was a masterpiece of journalistic propaganda, considered by Tone's biographer, the late Frank MacDermot, to be the finest of all his publications. Its impact was immense, and so far achieved Tone's aim of shattering dissenter timidity on the catholic issue that even Haliday, the arch-gradualist, found its arguments difficult to refute. The pamphlet was reprinted and distributed by both the Belfast reformers and the Dublin catholics, and secured for Tone a hallowed reputation with both.[33]

As a result, Tone was invited to Belfast the following month to help found the Society of United Irishmen. Besides Tone's friend, Thomas Russell, then an army ensign stationed in Belfast, the other ten founder members were prominent presbyterian merchants in Belfast, those same Volunteers who had mooted such a club earlier in the year, but had been deterred by the anti-popery which Tone for the moment had dispersed. They were Samuel Neilson (a prominent woollen draper), Samuel McTier (Drennan's brother-in-law), William Sinclair (owner of a linen mill), William McCleery, William and Robert Simms (all tanners), Henry Haslett (a shipbroker), William Tennent (a merchant), Thomas McCabe (a watchmaker), Gilbert McIlveen (a linen draper), and John Campbell (an apothecary). The declared object

---

33. Tone, *Life*, I, 52–3, and 341–66 for the pamphlet; see also *H.M.C. Charlemont MSS.*, II, 160, 179; W. E. H. Lecky, *A History of Ireland in the Eighteenth Century*, 5 vols. (London, 1892), III, 13; and I.S.P.O. 620/19/29, Tone to Chambers, 13 Oct. 1791, for its impact. MacNeven, *Pieces of Irish History*, 16, claims that 10,000 copies were printed in Belfast alone.

of the new society was parliamentary reform, its means the union of the Irish people. Its foundation principles, drawn up by Tone and reiterating many of the points in his pamphlet, declared: '... That the weight of English influence in the Government of this country is so great, as to require a cordial union among ALL THE PEOPLE OF IRELAND, to maintain that balance which is essential to the preservation of our liberties ... That the sole constitutional mode by which this influence can be opposed, is by a complete and radical reform of the people in Parliament ... That no reform is practicable, efficacious, or just, which does not include *Irishmen* of every religious persuasion ... With a Parliament thus reformed, everything is easy; ... and we do call on and most earnestly exhort our countrymen in general to follow our example, and to form similar societies ... for the promotion of constitutional knowledge, the abolition of bigotry in religion and politics, and the equal distribution of the rights of man through all sects and denominations of Irishmen.'[34]

Tone and Russell then travelled to Dublin and communicated details of the Belfast club to Tandy and several other notable reformers. The Dublin Society of United Irishmen was accordingly set up in November, with Tandy as secretary and Simon Butler, a prominent barrister, as chairman. The Dublin Society soon came to be regarded as the movement's principal branch, and it was from Dublin that the main United Irish policy document issued on 5 December 1791.

> The object of this institution is to make an United Society of the Irish nation; to make all Irishmen Citizens—all Citizens Irishmen; ...
>
> In thus associating, we have thought little about our ancestors, much of our posterity. Are we forever to walk like beasts of prey, over the fields which these ancestors stained with blood? In looking back, we see nothing ... but savage force, ... savage policy ... an unfortunate nation, 'scattered and peeled, meted out, and trodden down!' ... But we gladly look forward to brighter prospects; to a people united in the fellowship of freedom; to a parliament the express image of the people; to a prosperity established on civil, political, and religious liberty; to a peace—not the gloomy and precarious stillness of men brooding over their wrongs; but that stable tranquillity which rests on the rights of human nature, ...
>
> We agree in thinking that there is not an individual ... whose happiness can be established on any foundation so rational and so solid, as on the happiness of the whole community. We agree, therefore, in the necessity of giving political value and station to the great majority of the people ...

34. Tone, *Life*, I, 367–8. See F. J. Bigger, 'The Northern Star', *U.J.A.* 2nd ser., I (1895), 33–5, for the professions of the paper's proprietors.

Plate 2. Theobald Wolfe Tone in Volunteer Uniform (Madden, *United Irishmen*)

Plate 3. Lord Edward Fitzgerald (Madden, *United Irishmen*)

... Without, therefore, an impartial and adequate representation of the community ... our late revolution [1782] we declare to be fallacious and ideal—a thing much talked of, but neither felt nor seen ... and nothing remains to the people, who, of right are everything, but a servile majesty and a ragged independence.[35]

Both addresses were reprinted in the newly established United Irish paper, the *Northern Star*. Published in Belfast, it became the Society's principal mouthpiece and quickly outdistanced all other provincial newspapers in popularity, though it would be some time before the Society's rapid progress along the eastern seaboard was mirrored elsewhere.[36]

The United Irish Society was the most radical and most influential of all the British political clubs generated by the reform euphoria of the early 1790s, and it could boast a membership impressive in wealth, intellectual ability and social standing. In a detailed analysis of the 400 nominal and about 200 active members of the Dublin Society alone, Professor R. B. McDowell has found 30 attorneys, 26 barristers, 24 physicians and apothecaries (of which Drennan, James Reynolds from Tyrone and William James MacNeven, one

35. *Northern Star*, I, no. 3; also reproduced in Madden, *United Irishmen*, 1st ser., II, 315–17.
36. See *Northern Star*, I, nos. 4, 9 and 27; and *H. M. C. Charlemont MSS.*, I, 160, for the early spread of the Society.

of the catholic committee, were the most prominent), over 100 merchants, including the successful woollen merchant Oliver Bond, the poplin manufacturer Richard McCormick and the wealthy iron-founder Henry Jackson, a fellow of Trinity College, and a number of prominent booksellers and printers, including John Chambers and John Stockdale. In addition the English and Scottish radicals Tom Paine and Thomas Muir had been made honorary members.[37] The landed influence in the Society was rather smaller, though Archibald Hamilton Rowan was heir to substantial estates in Ulster and his rakish youth at Eton and Cambridge would have matched that of any of the Irish aristocracy. Simon Butler was brother to Lord Mountgarret, whilst Mathew Dowling, agent to Lord Cloncurry, would later recruit Cloncurry's son and heir, Valentine Lawless, into the Society.

But the aristocratic connection which justifiably attracts most attention now, as it did at the time, is that between the Society and Lord Edward Fitzgerald. Descended from one of the oldest, most esteemed and largest landowners among Ireland's aristocratic families, he was the son of the twentieth Earl of Kildare (first Duke of Leinster) and Lady Emily Mary Lennox, daughter of the Duke of Richmond, sister of Lady Holland. He did not formally join the United Irish Society until 1796, because of pressure from his elder brother, the second Duke of Leinster; but he openly consorted with its leaders and publicly proclaimed his support. Edward was a natural soldier, courageous to a fault. He had already distinguished himself as a young officer in North America, the West Indies and Canada, but was cashiered from the army in 1792 after participating in a republican banquet in Paris, at which all hereditary titles and distinctions were renounced.[38] He was elected M.P. for Kildare in 1790 and had a brief and reluctant parliamentary career, distinguished solely by his dramatic intervention against the suppression of the Volunteers in January 1793, when he accused the Irish parliament and the Lord Lieutenant of being the King's worst subjects. The incident alienated him from the Irish establishment and endeared him to the Irish radicals in equal measure, and Tandy and Rowan in particular became completely enamoured of this open-hearted young nobleman, whose enthusiasm for the French Revolution had become a way of life. Indeed he had only just returned with his new French wife Pamela, popularly believed to be the illegitimate daughter of Philippe (Egalité) Duc d'Orleans, one of the French revolutionary leaders. In fact Pamela was Anne or Nancy Syms, taken from an English foundling hospital by Egalité in 1780, and reared since the age of six with his own children. But the myth played such a part in creating the reputation of Lord Edward as an advanced democrat that it has

37. McDowell, 'The Personnel of the Dublin Society of United Irishmen 1791–4'; idem, *Ireland in the Age of Imperialism and Revolution* (Oxford, 1979), 386–7.
38. See below p. 55.

survived nearly two centuries of scholarly research, and with Edward's style of dressing and of cropping his hair in the French republican style, long before it became common United Irish practice, Drennan was correct in thinking that 'he and his elegant wife will lead the fashion of politics in a short time'.

But in these early years it was the legal profession which set the tone of Society proceedings; and people like Simon Butler, Leonard McNally, William Todd Jones, Edward Lewins, Henry Sheares, Mat Dowling, Tone and Thomas Addis Emmet were constantly in the public eye as authors of its rules and addresses. Emmet, only lately returned from his training at the Temple in London, was particularly influential. Like all the Emmets, particularly his father, the eminent physician Dr. Robert Emmet, Thomas was renowned for his eloquence; but the way in which he could turn opinion at Society meetings in favour of his cautious and moderate policies caused even his friend Drennan to criticize him for possessing 'more eloquence than energy, more caution than action'.[39]

The traditional and simplistic picture of the United Irish Society is that of a body of advanced reformers, in which a few militant republicans, notably Tone, were totally enamoured of France and the writings of Tom Paine, and came to dominate the Society, as the war, the excesses of the French, and government repression frightened away the moderate majority. In fact, the aims and beliefs of the United Irish Society before 1794 were confused, and apart from the central aims of catholic emancipation and a radical reform of parliament, there appear to have been as many opinions on detail as there were individuals. No full programme of reform was worked out until February 1794, and even then there were many differences of opinion.[40] One is left with the impression that the Society started out with a fluid philosophy and developed its ideas to meet situations or obstacles as they arose. Subsequent claims that the movement might have been rescued from its drift towards republicanism by a radical measure of parliamentary reform, even after it had opted for a republican solution in 1795–96, are indisputable.[41] In 1794 its plan of parliamentary reform simply reiterated the central points of the Westminster Association's programme of 1780, which had become the essence of British radical demands by the early 1790s. It called for universal manhood suffrage, annual parliaments, equal electoral districts, payment for M.P.s, and the abolition of property qualifications for parliamentary candidates; open voting, valued by Irish landlords as a means of influencing their catholic tenants, was retained. The secret ballot was rejected, as a potential means of

---

39. P.R.O.N.I. T.765/380; also *Drennan Letters*, 51, 75, 81, 88–9, 119, 122, 125 for Emmet, and 126, 131, 134 and P.R.O.N.I. T.765/382, 386A, 387–8 for Fitzgerald. T. Moore, *The Memoirs of Lord Edward Fitzgerald* (London, 1897), chs. i–xvi.
40. T. W. Moody, 'The Political Ideas of the United Irishmen', *Ireland Today*, iii (1936), 15–25.
41. See e.g. MacNeven, *Pieces of Irish History*, 196, 206, 227.

extending central government control, and it is symptomatic of the United Irishmen's Whiggish principles that they should have considered landlord power the lesser evil.[42]

United Irish readings in political philosophy were impressively wide, encompassing Irish products such as Molyneux and Swift, the Whig philosophers Locke, Hume, Ferguson and Adam Smith, the French *philosophes*, of which Mirabeau was the undoubted favourite, and contemporaries such as Burke, Paine, Godwin, Thelwall and Price. But although they were attracted by Paine's claims for popular participation in government on the basis of natural rights, and although his theory of cheap government accorded well with their own desire to reduce corruption and taxation, their arguments were taken almost exclusively from Locke. They were 'real Whigs' before they were militant republicans, and the history of the Society's republican phase showed that many might have preferred to remain so. Like Locke, they argued that the people had certain inalienable rights which they had entrusted to a government for protection, and in true country-Whig style they churned out the well-worn theory of the 'ancient constitution' to show how the original principles of such a trust had been abandoned. Both the Glorious Revolution of 1688 and their own of 1782 had only partially restored such principles; 1688 was appropriate for its time, 1782 was 'a mere flower of the day', and renovation was long overdue. None of the Whig philosophers would have advocated the continuing participation of the common weal in the political process, but even here the United Irishmen denied innovation, and in an elaborate reconstruction of the governing process in Saxon times, they argued for the existence of such popular participation before the Norman conquest.[43] Indeed, despite their interest in gaelic culture, they were very much outer Britons in their political thinking.

Their demand for universal suffrage did not signify any egalitarian thinking. Social reform was scarcely discussed. They lamented the burden of the tithe and hearth-tax on the poor and the sufferings of the small manufacturers during the war with France, but only in the context of their attack on church privileges, or their anti-war campaign. There was no trace of any social programme beyond the abolition of tithes and hearth-tax, the establishment of a national system of education by a reformed parliament, and a reduction of taxation indirectly through cheaper government and the abolition of sinecures. The House of Lords, interrogating the United Irish state prisoners in 1798, could not believe that they expected to satisfy the people by such means, without also fulfilling popular expectations of a redistribution of the land, and after the bloodshed of the 1798 rebellion their claim that the people

42. I.S.P.O. 620/53/1, *A Plan of an Equal Representation of the People of Ireland in the House of Commons. Prepared for public Consideration by The Society of United Irishmen in Dublin.*
43. See e.g. *Northern Star*, i, nos. 10, 52, 54, 96–9; ii, 315–18; *Drennan Letters*, 93–4.

were 'very much attached to parliamentary reform' seemed naïve in the extreme.[44] But if their understanding of rural Irish needs was limited, they were outspoken critics of popular urban protest, they denounced it as the work of 'a handful of idle and wicked men' and were found instead among those who turned out to repulse the Belfast and Antrim weavers in 1792 when they demonstrated for better wages.[45] They abhorred social disorder and their preferred means of securing reform was by peaceful union, by the united efforts of all religious denominations working within the constitutional system, rather than by the popular will arrayed in arms. Parliamentary reform was their ultimate goal until 1795, with the re-admission of the catholics to political rights as the necessary pre-requisite; even after the republicanization of their political aims there was no corresponding extension of their social programme.[46] By all accounts, therefore, the Irish people might have considered the changes involved in a United Irish republic as little more than a palace revolution, and the course which popular agitation was to take after the United Irishmen had faded away was unlikely to have been dramatically altered.

There are vague references to the other side of Locke's contract theory in United Irish writings, to the people's right to resort to arms if government betrayed its trust. But until 1794–95, when a decision in favour of force was taken, such references were few and ill-defined. For the early United men to arm in defence of one's rights was to become a Volunteer, and the United leaders remained very attached to the principle of volunteering long after the Volunteers were officially suppressed.[47] Indeed the first United Irishmen were particularly sensitive about the topic of armed resistance or accusations that they were French-style republicans and levellers. 'By Liberty we never understood unlimited freedom, nor by Equality the levelling of property, or the destruction of subordination,' they insisted in their address to the Volunteers of December 1792.[48] Nor are there any signs that some United leaders had been working to sever the connection with England from the outset, even if such an accusation was frequently levied against Tone after his famous letter of 1791, in which he transmitted the resolutions for the new Society to Russell.

> My unalterable opinion is that the Bane of Irish prosperity is the
> influence of England. I believe that influence will ever be exerted while
> the connection between the Countries continues. Nevertheless, as I know

44. MacNeven, *Pieces of Irish History*, 194–234. See also *Northern Star*, I, nos. 50, 66, 68; and Jemmy Hope's comments in T.C.D. MS. 7253/4.
45. *Northern Star*, I, nos. 50, 52; II, no. 21.
46. Madden, *United Irishmen*, 1st ser., II, 296–319.
47. *Northern Star*, I, nos. 99, 100, 101; II, nos. 60, 318.
48. *Northern Star*, I, no. 101, also 95; II, nos. 15, 21; Madden, *United Irishmen*, 1st ser., II, 322–6; and Russell's notebook for 1793 in I.S.P.O. 620/15/6/1–3.

that opinion is, *for the present*, too hardy, tho a very little time may
establish it universally, I have not made it a part of the resolutions.
. . . I have not said one Word that looks like a wish for *separation*, tho I
give it to you and to your friends as my most decided opinion that such
an event would be a *regeneration* for this Country.

As a private note attached for his friend's attention only, Tone had worded
his opinions loosely. The context in which they appeared, and his words and
actions until then, uphold his later claim that by the word 'separation' he
had intended some alteration in the existing connection rather than its
repudiation altogether. In the context of the time Tone's language was
moderate and the following year he prepared an address for the Bastille Day
celebrations supporting the constitution and denouncing republicanism. In
his diary for 1796 he explicitly rejected the idea that he had been a militant
republican in 1791. He did accept the possibility of using force in the last
instance, but without enthusiasm, and when confronted with the prospect of
armed French help in 1794, he shied away from it as a 'most severe and
grievous remedy' to be used only as a last resort.[49]

The United Irishmen admired other republics, but as a form of government they considered republicanism unsuited to Ireland. They were
totally committed to the concept of a limited monarchy and felt that only
government refusal to carry out reform could drive the people towards republicanism. The only alteration they would have liked in the existing monarchy was one to which every party, even the Jacobites, had subscribed at some
time or other: the idea of a dual monarchy, rather than the King of England
ruling over Ireland.[50] Particularly noticeable was their faith in the justice of the
King, despite the manifest evil of his ministers, and they displayed a defiant
loyalism to his person when taunted by his officials. When the militia, with
apparent official support, ran amok in Belfast in 1793, smashing the windows
of United Irishmen's houses, Thomas McCabe ostentatiously illuminated his
one surviving pane during the ensuing celebrations for the King's birthday.[51]
Drennan privately accepted the epithet 'Republican', but defined it in the
same terms as did the 'real Whigs', as a reformer rath . than an anarchist;
'you are not, I believe a republican,' Drennan wrcte to Sam McTier, his
brother-in-law in Belfast, 'but not many years will elapse till this persuasion
will prevail, for nothing else but the public happiness as an end, and the public
will as the power and means of obtaining it, is good in politics and all else is
job.' What did the term republic mean anyway, argued the *Northern Star*, but

49. Tone, *Life*, I, 116, 495–510; Tone's letter to Russell, 9 Jul. 1791, is in R.I.A. 23. K. 53; *Drennan
Letters*, 89, 168; MacDermot, *Theobald Wolfe Tone*, 60–2.
50. *Northern Star*, I, nos. 87, 97, 100; Tone, *Life*, I, 329, 348–9; and see Beresford, 'Ireland in
French Strategy', 170, for Jacobite ideas on this.
51. Benn, *A History of . . . Belfast*, I, 651–3; see also *Drennan Letters*, 166.

public good, upon which principle every good government should act?[52]

As for the connection with England, the matter was discussed less by the United Irishmen than by their predecessors in the 1780s. When it was discussed, they admitted that there would be little regret if a separation occurred, though it was never spoken of as anything more than a hypothesis. They clearly considered England to have abused the relationship and felt that some new 'association' on a more equitable basis should be established. Even after the 1798 rebellion the leading United men were prepared to accept a common monarch and some kind of federal connection between the two countries. It was British control of the Irish parliament of which they complained, and if that could have been redressed by parliamentary reform they would have happily accepted the connection on a revised basis. 'I have only proposed to set up a reformed Parliament as a barrier against that mischief which every honest man that will open his eyes, must see in every instance overbears the interest of Ireland,' Tone's 1791 letter had continued; and in another letter he explained United attitudes towards the connection with England. It was written to the editor of *Faulkner's Journal* in July 1793, in reply to accusations by Fitzgibbon, the Lord Chancellor, in the same paper. Whilst admitting that he found the character of the connection objectionable and accepting a remote possibility of separation if England proved impervious to demands for reform, Tone blamed 'the misconduct of ministers' for the abuses, and insisted that the union could be preserved and fortified by a reform based on the 'equal rights' of the two countries.

> My theory of politics, since I had one, was this: What is the evil of this country? British influence. What is the remedy? A reform in Parliament. How is that attainable? By a union of all the people ... But of this creed, separation makes no part. If it were *res integra*, God forbid but I should prefer independence; but Ireland being connected as she is, I for one do not wish to break that connection, provided it can be, as I am sure it can, preserved consistently with the honor, the interests, and the happiness of Ireland.[53]

In general, therefore, the United Irishmen agreed that the connection should be preserved in a modified form.

After the outbreak of hostilities between England and France in 1793, the continuing support of the United Irishmen for the French became the main basis for attacks on their constitutionalism. United Irish response to events in France, however, was inconsistent, and never as uncritical as generally

---

52. *Drennan Letters*, 54; *Northern Star*, 1, no. 84; and see B. L. Add. MS. 35143 fo. 90 for Place's definition of republicanism.

53. See Tone, *Life*, 1, 495–510, for the letter to the editor of *Faulkner's Journal*; also 545–9, 556–9. See also *Northern Star*, ii, no. 397 for the U.I. attempt to outline an alternative type of connection with England.

assumed. They argued that the French were simply fighting for the liberty which already existed in the British Isles: they rejoiced at their successes, not because they wanted to introduce French practices into Ireland 'but because that people were thus enabled to choose their own government . . . the natural and unalienable right of every people'.[54] But the defence of that natural right involved them in a whole series of polemical contortions to explain the blood-letting, the coups, and the political jockeying of the first years of the French Republic. Attempts were made to explain away the events of 10 August 1792, when the Parisian people rose with the loss of some 1500 lives, and the September massacres of the same year as 'accidential irregularities', products of the temporary inability of the Assembly to control 'the mob'. The murder of the Princesse de Lamballe and the execution of the King and Queen were condoned as a necessary excision of enemies to permit the continued growth of liberty. Similar arguments were invoked to justify the fall of former heroes like Danton or Robespierre, notwithstanding the eulogies lavished upon them when they had been in power. Louis's execution was reluctantly accepted as necessary, though the United Irishmen were more reticent on this than on any of the other controversial events in France, and their popularity declined sharply because of the intense revulsion with which the royal executions were generally greeted in Ireland. The bloodletting of the Terror contributed to the Society's unusual reticence in the years 1793–94, and it was only after Robespierre's fall that the old confidence in France returned. The innate conservatism and religiosity of the United Irish conscience was clearly upset by the extremes and the growing irreligion of the new Republic, and many felt uncomfortable at being thus obliged to condone morally reprehensible acts in the interests of liberty. Attention was diverted instead to the French attempt to maintain the rule of law, the rights of private property, and, by renouncing any intention of conquest in the war, the rights of other peoples to self-deter-mination. But on the whole they were neither very clear nor very consistent about what was happening in France before 1795, and were genuinely shocked at suggestions that their francophilia extended to calling in French assistance. 'We abhor the idea, of any foreign interference with the people or government of our own country . . . abuses exist in the administration of Ireland—but we wish to see these abuses corrected by the good sense of the Irish Nation, not by interference from abroad.'[55] That they did eventually accept French assistance in 1795 was due not to its inherent attraction but to the timing of

54. *Northern Star*, ii, no. 21; see also I.S.P.O. 620/19/88ᵃ, chapbook 'Songs on the French Re-volution' (Belfast, 1792).
55. *Northern Star*, ii, no. 21, also i, nos. 42, 71, 73, 74, 82 and ii, nos. 10 and 21; MacNeven, *Pieces of Irish History*, 32, 66, 70; *Drennan Letters*, 109, 112, 171, 175; P.R.O.N.I.T.765/261, 440; Tone, *Life*, i, 246; I.S.P.O. 620/21/23, Russell's diary, 1793. For Ireland's shocked reaction to the royal executions, see J. Hall Stewart, 'The French Revolution and the Dublin Stage, 1790–94', *Royal Society of Antiquaries of Ireland: Journal*, xci (1959), 188–92; R. B. McDowell, *Irish Public Opinion 1750–1800* (London, 1944), 151–4.

the offer. It came at the end of a year in which all the gains of the last two decades had been lost and the constitutional channels through which the popular will could influence parliament closed.

But it was not entirely the force of circumstances which turned the United Irishmen into republicans, as commonly claimed by their apologists. Despite their conservatism in matters of political and social reform, the United Irishmen epitomized certain attitudes already marked in the earlier Irish reform movement, but which were crystallized in response to the unusual events of the 1790s. The first was a fundamental contempt for the Irish parliament as an institution, and a recurrent tendency to resort instead to extra-parliamentary conventions. In Whig theory parliament was the essential check on the monarch, and Locke's idea of a 'trust' and a 'contract' between the ruler and the ruled had been transposed from a relationship between monarch and people to one between monarch and parliament. There are no signs of a similar contempt for their own parliament among the English radicals of the 1790s, possibly because it was endowed with a vocal opposition which consistently opposed the war and the emergency measures which accompanied it.[56] In Ireland the United Irishmen saw their own opposition, on whom they had relied to carry through the desired reforms, instead throwing their support behind the war and tamely submitting to the suppressive measures introduced in consequence. The shock at such a betrayal was immense and contributed to their growing conviction that the entire Irish body was corrupt.[57].

The United Irishmen claimed that the 1782 'constitution' had not ensured Irish legislative independence, and they denounced England's continuing ability to dictate to their parliament through influence and corruption. Their programme for parliamentary reform accordingly devoted as much attention to removing this inlet of British influence as to the extension of the franchise. This explains the retention of the *viva voce* vote—in opposition to current reform trends—as being less open to corrupt influence. They soon realized, however, that the Irish parliament was incapable of reforming itself. Their dispute had not initially been with England but with the 'wretched set of politicians' in Dublin. The events of 1793–95, however, were to reveal the Irish government and parliament as mere cyphers of England, and the odium was accordingly transposed to the connection itself.[58]

56. See, however, T. M. Parssinen, 'Association, Convention, Anti-Parliament in British Radical Politics, 1771–1848', *E.H.R.* 88 (1973), 504–33.

57. *Drennan Letters*, 141–2, 188–9; *Northern Star*, II, nos. 47, 209, 323; Tone, *Life*, I, 285–6, 304; T.C.D. MS. 2041/1, 32, 80; T. Russell, *Letter to the People of Ireland on the Present Situation of the Country* (Belfast, 1796).

58. *Drennan Letters*, 91, also 166–7; see also *Northern Star*, I, no. 99; II, no. 397; and C. H. Teeling, *Sequel to the History of the Irish Rebellion*, I.U.P. reprint of 1876 edn. (Shannon, 1972), 162–3. For their complaint at excessive English influence in and their general contempt of the Irish parliament see *Northern Star*, I, *no.* 97 and II, nos. 60 and 342; P.R.O.N.I. T.765/383; also Drennan's *Letters of Orellana*, in Lawless, *Belfast Politics*, 154–224.

The resort to arms was also a logical step in terms of the United Irishmen's concept of Irish nationhood. When Locke's concept of a government ultimately answerable to the people was applied to Ireland, and England became totally identified with the stubborn refusal to admit the catholics to political rights, the struggle for reform inevitably became one for national liberation. 'It is not upon external circumstances, upon the pledge of man or minister, we depend, but upon the internal energy of the Irish Nation,' the United Irishmen had claimed in 1792, and, as they followed through their arguments on popular will and the theory of contract, gradually the idea of the nation in arms took shape. Irish historians have pointed to vague glimmerings of Irish nationalism before the end of the eighteenth century.[59] But the all-embracing quality of United Irish reformism and its elevation to a programme of national rights was relatively novel in Irish history. Like so much of United Irish ideology, however, it was developed situationally. It had originated as a mode of campaigning for political reform: the union of the Irish people would remove any dependence on the Irish and English politicians alike; that union must first be brought about by the admission of the catholics to political rights; and 'the internal energy of the Irish Nation' would do the rest. For generations the catholics had been looked upon as degenerate and debased, unfit to participate in the political process. By the 1790s the United Irishmen felt that they had been regenerated by the efforts of the enlightened elements among their protestant countrymen. Since they were now considered as part of one nation, the continued rejection of their rights by English-backed officials came to be regarded as a national insult. 'The connexion with England is preached up as if Ireland must perish without . . .', wrote the *Northern Star* on 20 October 1795. 'This may be good policy for English settlers; but it is time for them to . . . boast as good a title in being Irishmen as they can find in conquest.'[60]

Nevertheless, although their own sense of injustice and the direction of their political ideology pointed to a national rising as the only real means of attaining reform, their political tutelage within the anglicized eastern sea-board did not prepare them for an easy transition to direct action. The *Northern Star* for 1795 reflects their soul-searching about the full implications of the contract theory. Writing in 1828, the Ulster United leader Charles Teeling still felt obliged to explain in detail their reasons for seeking foreign assistance, outlining the repressive legislation of the period and showing how the offer of French help came just at the moment when the worst effects were being felt.[61] The introduction of a mercenary army would not be the first occasion on which the United Irishmen would be obliged to jettison their Whig principles. Even in its republican phase, United Irish discomfiture at being forced into

---

59. *Nationality and the Pursuit of National Independence, Historical Studies*, xi ed. T. W. Moody (Belfast, 1978), especially the contributions of Donnchadh O Corráin, 1–35, and Aidan Clarke, 57–71. *Northern Star*, i, no. 97.
60. *Northern Star*, ii, no. 397, also i, nos. 55, 97, 98, and ii, nos. 19, 338, 340, 397.
61. Teeling, *Sequel to the History of the Irish Rebellion*, 188–9; *Northern Star*, ii, nos. 317, 397.

such a role caused persistent bickering and indecision. Accordingly, many tried to explain this transition from theoretical to active republicanism by pointing to official persecution and government refusal to grant reasonable reform. But the United Irishmen themselves gave scant consideration to the complexities of the Irish situation and to the genuine fears of the protestants. The result was the impasse which produced militant republicanism and the accompanying sectarian warfare.

CHAPTER TWO

Defenderism and the Protestant Backlash

Although the membership of the United Irishmen remained small and select in the years 1791–95, and their operations were confined almost entirely to north-east Ulster and the Dublin area, the Irish authorities looked upon them as dangerous subversives from the outset. In the circumstances this was not an unreasonable reaction. The United Irishmen were the offspring of the Volunteers, and their continuing association with the older body meant that they were in effect an armed organization even before they officially armed in 1796. It was in partnership that the two spread rapidly through the eastern seaboard in 1792, and though the Volunteer revival was more muted in Dublin than in Ulster, in both areas it was associated with the rise of the United Irishmen. This revival of the Volunteers alarmed the government, for they had been discredited in the late 1780s and were now fast becoming the military wing of an outspoken radical organization. They were suppressed altogether in 1793, when the United Irishmen attempted to remodel them as a national guard, with a uniform so similar to that of the French body as to give the government serious cause for alarm on the eve of the declaration of war.[1] It was neither the association with France, however, nor the fact that the 'levellers' were arming which caused most concern; it was rather their connection with the subject of catholic emancipation at a time when the rapid spread of the militantly catholic Defenders presented the image of the catholics arming against the protestants. It would be difficult to over-emphasize the role of the catholic emancipation crisis of 1792–95 in pushing the United Irishmen towards full-blown republicanism, destroying the heady optimism of the previous decade and the nascent force of protestant nationalism, and proclaiming a future of sectarian conflict. Sectarian consciousness had always been a part of protestant group identity; but because of the low density of the protestant population else-

---

1. See government correspondence of Jan–Feb. 1793 in P.R.O. H.O. 100/42/214–15, 287–90 and 100/43/15–16, 89 and 91–4; also P.R.O. 30/8/331/98–104, and I.S.P.O. 620/19/28; see *Northern Star*, I, nos. 34, 50, 52, 56–8, 78, 87, 90, 99, 101; and II, nos. 15–19 for the rapid spread of the Volunteers in association with the United Irishmen.

where it was virtually unknown as a bond of union among catholics outside Ulster, and only became so in the 1790s.

The repeal of the main clauses of the penal code started in the mid-1770s, and those outlawing the catholic religion were repealed in 1782. But there was still considerable protestant reluctance to extend political rights to the catholics, and though they could no longer deny the loyalty of the catholic population, they were determined that political power should remain firmly in protestant hands. Although the Catholic Relief Acts of 1778 and 1782 granted the catholics the same rights of purchase and possession of land as the protestants, they were still forbidden to purchase land situated in a parliamentary borough. The Volunteers and the parliamentary opposition had split on the issue of catholic emancipation in the 1780s. But catholic expectations and protestant fears had been aroused by the campaign, and with the more militant rump of the Volunteers proclaiming their continuing support for catholic reform, there was little chance that either would be permitted to subside. When the campaign was renewed in 1790–91, therefore, opposition by the majority of protestants was immediate and implacable. They genuinely believed that the catholics sought parliamentary representation not as an end in itself, but as the means of reviving James II's court of claims to confiscate protestant property. In Dublin the catholics had been organized in a national committee to push for repeal of the penal laws since the 1750s. But latterly the body had been dominated by the conservatism of the catholic prelates and had been dormant since 1783. After 1790 it witnessed a spectacular revival, with the radicals among the catholic middle classes assuming control. Protestant fears were exacerbated when they joined forces with the United Irishmen, thereby creating the impression that the catholics and democrats were massing against the ruling elite. Even noted protestant reformers cautioned the campaigners against such agitation on the catholic issue and reminded them that their own positions rested on past confiscations.[2]

Protestant fears were further intensified by the knowledge that the most outspoken leaders in the catholic committee—the Dublin merchant John Keogh, the poplin manufacturer Richard McCormick, and the attorney Edward Lewins—were also prominent in the Dublin Society of United Irishmen. Tone was appointed agent for the catholic committee in July 1792; another United man, Simon Butler, was their legal adviser; and such was the nature of the catholic campaign mounted by the United Irishmen themselves, that government thought the catholics and the northern 'levellers' were in league to bring down the existing social structure. Moreover, each sign

---

2. *Northern Star*, I, nos. 9, 13–14; Tone, *Life*, I, 149–50; and for protestant fears in general, see P.R.O. 30/8/331/64–72, 80–3, *H.M.C. Dropmore MSS.*, II, 318 and Powell, 'The Background to the Wexford Rebellion', 48–9.

of opposition by the protestant authorities was forcing the catholic committee to take an increasingly radical stance. Mitford's Act of 1791 had repealed much of the penal legistation against the catholics on the British mainland, and their Irish co-religionists could reasonably expect an extension of similar privileges to Ireland. But the attempts of the catholic committee to petition the Irish parliament for a further relaxation in the penal code were haughtily brushed aside, and in 1791 not one M.P. could be found to present their petition. The catholic leadership would have been content to drop the matter altogether, but such submissiveness rankled with their more radical co-religionists, and when the catholic lords and prelates formally seceded from the committee in December 1791 the radical catholics dropped all pretense at restraint and came out with an unequivocal demand for the total repeal of all remaining penal legislation. The following year the committee responded to a parliamentary taunt about its unrepresentative character by sending delegates throughout the country to arrange for elections to a catholic convention. The decision had already been taken to appeal over the heads of the Dublin politicians directly to the administration in London, and the elected catholic convention met in Dublin in December 1792 to prepare the petition.[3]

This appeal to England was a particular affront to the Dublin parliament, since the protestants felt that England needed them to rule a country which they still considered potentially disloyal, and that she would always support them against the majority population. At the close of the century, however, England tended to view the Irish catholics in the light of their less numerous and more docile English co-religionists and was particularly insensitive to protestant fears of encirclement. Throughout the difficult period of the 1790s the English ministers usually sought swift and short-term remedies for Irish troubles, with little thought for the subtleties of the problem or the long-term consequences of their actions. It is easy to condemn the bigoted intransigence of the Irish politicians, but in the circumstances it is difficult not to agree with their bitter accusations that English neglect, punctuated by ham-fisted interference, only exacerbated their problems.[4]

Westmorland, the Lord Lieutenant, was anxious to prevent an alliance between the radicals and the catholics and did not anticipate any difficulty in extending the benefits of Mitford's Act to Ireland. But when he became aware of the strength of protestant opposition to even a mild measure of catholic reform, he tried to convince the Prime Minister of the need for caution if anything at all were to be achieved. 'In a country where Every man holds his estate and political consequence by dispossession of Catholics

3. I.S.P.O. 620/19/37 and 45–7; Lecky, *Ireland in the Eighteenth Century*, III, 22–64; *Drennan Letters*, 56–79; MacNeven, *Pieces of Irish History*, 18–34.
4. *Beresford Correspondence*, II, 16.

allowance must be made for even unreasonable apprehension; it is a common conversation that if the Protestant Interest must have a struggle for their property, it is wiser to resist in the first instance ... '. The protestants had argued that any concession would simply encourage more radical demands, and that the catholics would never be satisfied until they had full political control; and when everything short of the franchise and the right to sit in parliament was indeed granted to them in Langrishe's Act of 1792, and catholic agitation for further concessions intensified, Westmorland had to endure the bitter protestant taunt that they had predicted as much.[5]

The protestants felt betrayed; their fears had been intensified by England's handling of the situation, and catholic discontent had not been proportionally allayed. But worse was still to come. Westmorland warned that England should recognize her dependence on the protestant loyalists to rule Ireland, and although he felt that the catholics should be won by concessions, these should not be granted in such a way as to undermine protestant authority. Pitt had been quite happy to grant the catholic franchise in 1792, independently of any outside pressure. But his handling of the situation had indeed created the impression that he was giving way to intimidation and riding roughshod over the Irish parliament and government in the process. When the catholic petition was eventually taken to London in January 1793, it was intimated to the delegates that the required act would be forced upon the Dublin parliament, and so in fact it was in the session which opened in February.

But the Catholic Relief Act of 1793, giving catholics the vote but not the right to sit in parliament, had already been robbed of any conciliatory effect. England's actions had destroyed the protestant ascendancy's veneer of confident security, forcing it to express its fears in increasingly shrill warnings and publicly exposing its ill-will towards the catholics. Whitehall's stance had made a mockery of the boasted legislative independence of 1782. It had undermined the protestants' authority by showing that they could not ultimately rely on British support, and had introduced a note of grim determination into their reaction to internal discontent. Yet things could have been very different. Westmorland had noted that many protestants were not opposed to a 'gradual' removal of catholic disabilities; but such hesitant reformism needed patient cultivation, not the shock tactics meted out by the English government and the Irish radicals. The year 1793 accordingly became the Irish protestants' *ne plus ultra* at a time when, as they had predicted, catholic demands had escalated to include full emancipation.[6]

---

5. See P.R.O. H.O. 100/34 and P.R.O. 30/8/331/64–70, 96–8; I.S.P.O. Westmorland Corr., I, 3–16 and II, 1–2, 80–3, for Westmorland's correspondence with Pitt and Dundas, Dec. 1791–May 1792.
6. See P.R.O. H.O. 100/42/65–6, 246–9, for an account of the debates in the Irish parliament; *Drennan Letters*, 72, 75–7, 96; *Northern Star*; II, no. 4; and Tone, *Life*, I, 240–67.

This shattering of loyalist confidence had been achieved without any visible gain of catholic goodwill. Tone was baffled by the reasoning behind the 1793 Act. Government had admitted the catholic people to the constitution but excluded their leaders. 'By their exclusion from the two houses of Parliament, the whole body of the Catholic gentry . . . are insulted and disgraced . . . branded with a mark of subjugation, the last relic of interested bigotry . . . If the Catholics deserved what has been granted, they deserved what has been withheld; . . . They receive a benefit with one hand, and a blow with the other, and their rising gratitude is checked by their just resentment . . . the radical and fundamental defect of the bill is, that it still tends to perpetuate distinctions, and, by consequence, disunion amongst the people. While a single fibre of the old penal code, that cancer in the bosom of the country, is permitted to exist, the mischief is but suspended, not removed, the principle of contamination remains behind and propagates itself.'[7] At the end of the year relations between the catholic leaders and the Irish government had never been worse; the bitterness of one side at such grudging reforms was interpreted as ungratefulness by the other, and respective attitudes became entrenched. Looking back from 1802, Lord Redesdale attributed the disasters which had occurred in Ireland in the preceding decade to 'the measures of the government in 1792 and the succeeding years, by which they lost the attachments of the Protestants, without gaining that of the Roman Catholics'.[8] The events of 1792–93 had terminated Ireland's liberal era at one fell swoop. The gulf between the protestant establishment and the rest of the population was shown for what it was, and before long the catholic leaders would throw in their lot with the militant republicans to win those rights which the Irish politicians were manifestly determined to withhold.

In 1792–93, however, protestant fears were not as unreasonable as they appeared. For the first time since the organized banditry of the Tories and Rapparees at the turn of the century, latent catholic hopes of a reversal of the land settlement were being played upon by agitators of a higher social status. The campaign of the United Irishmen and the catholic committee gave rise to a whole spectrum of expectations among the catholic populace, partially justifying loyalist fears that their ultimate object was far more sinister than parliamentary reform. It was the activities of the militantly catholic Defender movement in particular which confounded the constitutional agitation in protestant thinking with the vision of a catholic uprising. The secret society has become such a part of modern Irish history that one tends to assume its ancient vintage. In the late eighteenth century, however, it was still something of a novelty, having made its appearance only in 1760,

7. Tone, *Life*, I, 100–3.
8. *The Life and Correspondence of the Rt. Hon. Henry Addington, First Visc. Sidmouth*, ed. the Hon. G. Pellew, 3 vols. (London, 1847), I, 206.

possibly, as M. R. Beames suggests, as a consequence of masonic influences from the Continent.[9] The oath-bound society was considered sinister and subversive in the 1790s, and Defenderism was to confirm the protestants' worst fears concerning such secret organizations.

The Defenders inaugurated a new era in the history of the Irish secret society. With them the traditional attacks on tithes, rents, hearth-tax, county-cess or church dues became identified with vague ideas of revolution, and it was the Defenders and their offspring, the Ribbonmen, who sustained the notion of foreign-assisted revolution during the long interval between the collapse of the United Irishmen and the reappearance of organized republicanism with Fenianism. The Defenders had originated in Armagh in the mid-1780s, a non-denominational movement to defend the catholics from attacks by militant protestant groups like Nappach Fleet and the Peep O' Day Boys. The intense competition among the weavers of Armagh was exacerbated by trade slumps such as that which revived protestant attacks in 1792, and helped to spread Defenderism. In these areas where lower-class protestants and catholics lived and worked in such proximity, the catholics posed a threat unknown to isolated upper-class protestants elsewhere, and it was in similar areas outside Ulster, where the two religious groupings were in direct economic competition, that Defenderism and later, Orangeism, spread rapidly.[10] It was as a sectarian catholic body that Defenderism spread outside Armagh after 1790 into the rest of Ulster, along the eastern seaboard and into the midlands during 1792-93, and over the next two years it was reported also to have reached the more rural provinces of Connacht and Munster.

It is important to recognize, however, that Defenderism was never a peasant movement, although in the vocabulary of the authorities it became for a time the generic term for every kind of disturbance. Its strength lay in the more urban and industrialized areas, and when it did extend into the rural hinterland, it remained confined to the same social elements which dominated its membership in its more prosperous strongholds. The older Whiteboy tradition prevailed in rural Ireland, and although the agrarian bands sometimes adopted Defender oaths, their methods and aims remained wholly traditional. The Defenders proper did not generally attack property and we can be sure that the widespread 'houghing', the slaughter of livestock, which was reported from the west in these years, had no connection whatsoever with Defenderism. Although the Defenders' social demands were sometimes indistinguishable from those of the secret agrarian societies, in general they were to be found conducting well-organized arms' raids, drilling, or swearing-in new areas.

9. Beames, 'Peasant Disturbances', 22; Donnelly, 'The Whiteboy Movement', 27.
10. P.R.O.N.I. T.1722; see also Donnelly, 'The Whiteboy Movement,' 22, 38-9 and Fitzpatrick, 'The Economic Effects of the . . . Wars on Ireland', 120-3, 236-7, for the decline in prosperity in the 1790s among skilled tradesmen and labourers.

One nineteenth-century commentator saw them as Irish '*sans culottes*',[11] a description which is not quite as far-fetched as it may appear. Their member-ship seems to have been taken largely from among the weavers, the labourers, and the tenant farmers who were also involved in some kind of domestic industry, and above all from among a growing artisan class in the towns. Evidence taken in 1795 about two Defender societies in Dublin shows their membership to have included a skinner, a weaver, an apprentice to a cutler, a member of the Fermanagh militia, a publican, a dairyman, several porters, a journeyman tanner and a journeyman tobacconist.[12] As such, the Defenders were only one step nearer the peasantry than the United Irishmen them-selves, and in their attempt to incorporate the Defenders, the United Irishmen were merely recruiting the more politically conscious catholics in areas already converted to the United system. They remained as remote from the mass of the catholics after 1795 as they had done before and their attempt to create a truly national movement never entirely got off the ground.

The Irish authorities were baffled by the Defenders, who seemed to be lacking in any central purpose and appeared rather to adapt their programme to the grievances of the different areas in which they operated. 'In all other risings of the populace there was some avowed object, or some general grievance to complain of,' wrote the pro-government *Freeman's Journal*. 'The Defenders . . . on the contrary can or do allege none. One talks of paying no hearth money, another of paying no tithes, a third of paying no rent for potato ground and some others shout out Liberty and Equality.'[13] The paper summarized accurately enough the general social aims of the Defenders, which by 1795 the government was able to define as the desire to regulate payment of tithes, church-cess, rents, particularly for potato ground, and to lower dues paid to the priests. These were fairly traditional demands, voiced by other protest groups before the Defenders, and the ambition of many adherents undoubtedly extended no further.[14]

But there was a sense of system in Defenderism, a co-ordination between different areas, which set it apart from the more traditional, localized agrarian societies. 'Their plans have the appearance of method . . . ,' wrote one army officer from Tyrone; and Friar Phillips, a government agent who had in-sinuated himself into the Defenders in 1795 and whose efforts brought him

11. *Irish Rebellions: No. 11. The United Irishmen* (London, 1866), 42.
12. The information on the Defenders is taken from I.S.P.O. 620/22/19–51 and S.O.C. 1015–16; Kent C.R.O. U840/O144–6, O150; P.R.O. H.O. 100/42–4 and H.O. 100/58/201–7; *State Trials*, xxv, 749–84 and xxvi, 225–462; MacNevin, *The Lives and Trials of . . . Eminent Irishmen*, 291–4; *Report on the Proceedings in Cases of High Treason . . . Dublin, Dec. 1795* (Dublin, 1796); Kerrane, 'The Background to . . . 1798', Beames, 'Peasant Disturbances', and Hogan, 'Civil Unrest in . . . Connacht', 30–1, 45–52, 61–5.
13. *Freeman's Journal*, 8 Jan. 1793.
14. I.S.P.O. 620/22/19/12–21.

a rough reward some months later when he was fished out of the River Lagan, found that the Defender hand-signs were recognized in every town on the road from Kildare to Dublin.[15] Standardized oaths too were found in every county penetrated by the movement. But what distinguished Defenderism most from previous secret societies was its distinct revolutionary tone, and its rapid progress after 1792 is a classic example of how catholic consciousness had been aroused by the campaign of upper-class reformers. Their oaths were a hotchpotch of biblical imagery and other religious references, but they had also absorbed much of the language of the advanced reformers. One handbill spoke of restoring their laws to their 'primitive purity'; another claimed that 'All men were born equal; we will have no king but the Almighty.' Most Defenders were encouraged to expect some startling improvement in their material situation and this was closely associated with the old idea that the protestants must be ousted before the catholics could prosper. 'I expected that I would get what livings you, and the like of you have, for myself,' one former Defender told Counsellor Curran in the Louth trials of 1794, and he agreed that they had planned 'to knock the Protestants on the head, and . . . take their places'.[16]

This anticipation of revenge against the protestants was one of the main elements in Defender thinking; but they also spoke of 'overturning the King's Government in this kingdom' and of seeking French help, long before the United Irishmen had contemplated either, and their documents are full of French revolutionary imagery. 'Are you consecrated?' asks their common form of oath, 'I am—to what?—To the National Convention—to quell all nations—to dethrone all Kings, and plant the Tree of Liberty in our Irish land—whilst the French Defenders will protect our cause, and the Irish Defenders pull down the British laws . . . ' From the end of 1792 followers were being told to expect French help and the result was a novel sense of confidence in the advent of the millennium. Although there was a general sense of some change in France which might benefit Ireland, it is unlikely that many fully understood the exact nature of events there, and one former Defender testifying at the 1794 trials was clearly confused when asked why he thought an anti-catholic country like revolutionary France should wish to help the Irish catholics. It is difficult to understand this conviction in French willingness to help, even before war had been declared. But some kind of approach does appear to have been made to France, and there is evidence of extensive, even sophisticated plans for insurrection in the winter of 1792–93. It is unlikely that such preparations could have been co-ordinated by the social classes composing the main body of Defenderism, and the existence of leaders from a higher social class seems indisputable. But there is little information on their identity. Government suspected the local catholic

---

15. Kent C.R.O. U840/O144/4, W. C. Lindsay to R. Lindsay, 6 Apr. 1795; and for Friar Philips, see U840/O150/3; I.S.P.O. 620/22/19/11 and 14; and P.R.O.N.I. D.272/73/149.
16. *State Trials*, xxv, 757 and 767.

leaders, and though the attempts to incriminate several Drogheda merchants in 1794 came to nothing, there does appear to have been some connection between the Defenders and those involved in the local promotion of the catholic petition.

In the winter of 1792–93 a Defender war raged in counties Down, Cavan, Meath, Monaghan, Kildare and Dublin. Although the aims of the 'insurgents' included the traditional demands for rent and tithe regulation, their chief purpose was apparently to denude the protestants of their arms. Many protestants fled to the towns for protection and Louth was so badly disturbed that an infantry and cavalry regiment were quartered there. The reckless confidence of the attackers unnerved the protestants and the suppression was predictably brutal. In a small ambush at Ballyboro in Meath, a group of Defenders attempted to rescue a captured leader. They were attacked by the military and the local gentry; forty-seven were killed and with few exceptions the remainder were arrested. They admitted that they had fought that winter in expectation of 'an equal distribution of property', 'assistance from France', 'the conditions of Limerick', and 'to destroy the Protestant religion'. Predictably, the whole issue of the plantation settlement, the confiscations and catholic aspirations was revived in the press in these months. Arms were known to have reached the Defenders from England and the Continent, and the knowledge that the lower order of catholics were generally armed contributed to the protestant panic of that winter.[17]

A stringent Arms Act to prevent the sale and purchase of arms and to facilitate selective disarming was carried through parliament without opposition in December. That it was used primarily against the Volunteers and the United Irishmen was not accidental. The government and the loyalists alike could not believe that the lower-class catholics possessed the ability to organize themselves so effectively without assistance from men 'of Superior Rank'. It was certainly true that the militant language of the parliamentary opposition, the United Irishmen and the catholic committee helped generate a new confidence among the lower-class catholics. But efforts to implicate noted United and catholic leaders came to nothing.[18] At

17. For the disturbances see P.R.O. H.O. 100/42/13–14 (Louth); 27–8 (Meath and Monaghan); 194–8 (Meath and Cavan); also 100/43/71–3 (the numbers tried at the Meath Assizes) and 145–51; also the *Report Presented to the House of Lords*, 7 Mar. 1793, in *Journals of the House of Lords, Ireland, 1634–1800*, 8 vols. (Dublin, 1779–1800), VII, 128–30. For the supplies of arms reaching Ireland clandestinely, see P.R.O. H.O. 42/22–3; H.O. 32/3; and P.R.O. 30/8/331/90–5. For Defender expectations see H.O. 100/44/115–8, 147–50; and *State Trials*, xxv, 754, 757, 761.
18. For the belief that the disturbances were promoted by outside leaders see P.R.O. H.O. 100/42/65–6, 196–8; 100/43/321–2; 100/44/115–8; *State Trials*, xxv, 749–84; and *Report . . . to the House of Lords*, 1793. For the attempt to implicate the United and catholic leaders, see Tone, *Life*, I, 476–86; *Northern Star*, II, no. 19; and John Sweetman, *A Refutation of the Charges Attempted to be made against the Secretary of the Sub-Committee of the Catholics of Ireland, Particularly that of Abetting Defenders* (Dublin, 1793).

this stage, the United Irishmen were desperately anxious to avert violence, however violent they may have appeared in speech, and in August 1792 Wolfe Tone, Samuel Neilson and John Keogh were sent to those parts of Ulster worst affected by the Defender disturbances, in an effort to calm the sectarian warfare deemed to be jeopardizing the progress of the catholic reform campaign.[19] There may have been contacts between some of the United leaders and the Defenders, for such was the freedom of individual action in these years that the Society never succeeded in imposing central control, even after secrecy compelled more efficient organization. Napper Tandy's associations with the Louth Defenders are undeniable. Personal curiosity rather than official United policy had motivated his mission, and the more level-headed United men denounced such flirtations with subversive movements as provocative. Tandy epitomized the independence, demagoguery and sheer vanity of many in the United Irish Society and catholic committee alike. They taunted the authorities in a manner which invited the repressive measures ultimately invoked against them, and what appeared as sedition was frequently little more than bravado.[20]

In the spring assizes of 1793, the Irish authorities tried to set an 'awful example' to 'the deluded' by passing capital sentences on twenty-one Defenders and transporting thirty-seven more. But the recurrent crises of the 1790s ensured Defender survival, and the riots against the 1793 Militia Act further extended the movement outside its original home in the more industrialized areas. With the declaration of war between Britain and France in February 1793 and the removal of many regular soldiers from Ireland in consequence, Westmorland secured the passage of an Irish Militia Act to supply 16,000 men for home defence. But militia raised for home duties during the American War had been sent overseas, and the new Act met with universal resistance. The catholic rural areas had always suffered most in past levies, since county sheriffs frequently shifted the whole burden onto the catholics. By the summer of 1793, therefore, anti-militia riots raged in almost every country. The regular troops seemed powerless against such turmoil, and priests and gentry who tried to restore order were attacked with equal vehemence by the angry crowds. The loyalists were convinced that a popish rebellion was in progress and the riots intensified their reaction.

The riots were a spontaneous response to a measure which threatened to remove many families' breadwinners, and in the worst-affected areas like Leitrim, Sligo and Roscommon, Defenderism was in fact weak. But

19. Tone, *Life*, I, 169–77; MacNeven, *Pieces of Irish History*, 48, 52; I.S.P.O. 620/19/89, 'Address by "An Irish Man" to the Peep of Day Boys and Defenders, to put aside their differences'.
20. *Drennan Letters*, 115, 122–3 and 141; MacNeven, *Pieces of Irish History*, 48–9; *Northern Star*, I, no. 24. See also Drennan's remarks in P.R.O.N.I. T.765/372 and 380; also I.S.P.O. 620/19/73 and 620/53/198.

Plate 4. Archibald Hamilton Rowan (National Library of Ireland)

Plate 5. Henry Grattan (by C. G. Stuart in Lord Ashbourne, *Pitt: some Chapters of his Life and Times* (London, 1898))

the riots did show how the ordinary people had identified current political events with their own plight and how political agitators could easily turn popular turmoil to their own ends. Many of the rioters saw the act as the manifestation of some wider evil and were overheard to claim that the French would arrive shortly, that 'they should all soon get Estates' and 'that not one Protestant should be alive in a month'. One land agent writing from Sligo felt that 'the 1st motive stated for these outrages is the Militia, but he believes the real one to be the late Popery Act, from the violent Opposition given to it by the Protestants, and the great exertions made by the Papists, and the infinite benefits the people of that persuasion were taught to think would arise from that law to everyone, and that not only Religious Equality, but one of Property would be produced, but now they find this to be a dream and that they are determined to effect by force that equality of property, they vainly hoped for'.[21] The Defenders took an active role in the riots in counties where they were already organized, and by May their movement had spread also into riot-torn areas like Sligo and Leitrim. The authorities were not entirely wrong therefore in seeing 'something more sinister' behind the riots.[22]

21. P.R.O. H.O. 100/44/7–10, information from Mr. Wynne's agent, 26 May 1793; see also H.O. 100/44/115–18 for similar reports from Sligo. For the riots see H.O. 100/43/319–22, 331; H.O. 100/44/5–10 and 195; and *Northern Star*, II, nos. 43–4.
22. P.R.O. H.O. 100/43/321–2, Westmorland to Dundas, 25 May 1793.

But they still held the United Irishmen rather than the Defenders responsible and the militia riots confirmed their determination to tame the Society.

The English officials in Dublin had never reacted as violently towards the United Irishmen as did career Irish politicians like Toler, the Solicitor General and Fitzgibbon, the Chancellor, with whom several future United Irish leaders had been in dispute for many years prior to the Society's inception. Their conflict with such leading officials was therefore simply a continuation of their earlier reform tactics into less suitable times; but the younger leaders condemned them for provoking the authorities unnecessarily and causing them to single out the Society in a personal vendetta.[23] The Society's promotion of the new 'National' Volunteers at the end of 1792 had genuinely alarmed many in government circles; and it was seized upon by certain politicians as a God-given opportunity to crush both.[24] But although the proclamation of 8 December against the Dublin Volunteers was a total success, in the North they continued to meet, their United Irish members becoming more aggressive in response to the threat from government. On 14 December the United Irish Society issued an address to the Volunteers of Ireland which Dublin Castle regarded as verging on treason. They called upon the Volunteers to take up arms again in defence of Ireland and their rights, to push ahead with parliamentary reform and full catholic emancipation and to go again in convention to Dungannon as they had done in the 1780s. The first Belfast Volunteer Company, led by the town's United men, issued a similar address four days later. 'We say that it is the Right of the People to be represented in Parliament—*taxation without representation is* O P P R E S S I O N.' Six months before such language would have been unexceptionable. But by this stage the country was on course for war with France. Westmorland's determination to tame the North was temporarily interrupted by the Defender 'insurrection' of that month. But in January, Archibald Hamilton Rowan and the proprietors of the *Northern Star* were prosecuted for printing and distributing the Dublin pamphlet, and such was government's conviction that the whole town of Belfast was infected that they were forced to come to Dublin instead to answer the charges.[25]

Rowan was charged with seditious libel, and had he been tried immediately he might have escaped lightly. But he was not tried until January 1794, after a year which had seen the growing clash between the United Irishmen and the authorities, and he was sentenced to two years' imprisonment, fined

23. *Drennan Letters*, 83 5, 88 90; *Northern Star*, I, nos. 16, 32, 47, 52, 97, and II, no. 209; also I.S.P.O. 620/42/18 and P.R.O.N.I. T.765/358.

24. See P.R.O. H.O. 100/42/13–14; P.R.O. 30/8/331/98–104; and P.R.O.N.I. D.607/B/380; for this hardening of government attitudes.

25. For the addresses and arrests see P.R.O.N.I. T.765/364–6 and *Northern Star*, I, no. 101, and II, nos. 9 and 11. For the spread of the Volunteers, especially in Ulster, see P.R.O. H.O. 100/42/287–90; 100/43/15–16 and 145–51.

Plate 6. Volunteers parading up High Street, Belfast, at the commemoration of the storming of the Bastille, 14 July 1792 (National Library of Ireland)

£500 and asked to provide three securities for his future good behaviour. Rowan was the most respected and popular of the United leaders, and this draconian sentence was one of the many factors which contributed to the United Irishmen's conversion to active republicanism the following year.[26] For much of 1793 they were still confused about their identity, operating simultaneously as a nostalgic remnant of the 1780s reform movement and as a vehicle of Painite ideas and French sympathies. The Ulster leaders participated in the Ulster reform convention meeting at the Volunteer shrine in Dungannon in February 1793. It consisted of as many old Volunteers and Northern Whigs as United Irishmen and though it reiterated United Irish demands for full catholic emancipation and parliamentary reform based on universal suffrage, it re-affirmed its loyalty to the concept of a mixed monarchy and expressed its abhorrence of republicanism. The document which issued from Dungannon was mild enough, but it called for a national reform convention, and government intervened immediately with a Convention Act to prevent any future representative assemblies meeting outside parliament.[27]

26. *State Trials*, XXII, 1034–1190. For the shocked reaction of the United Irishmen see *Northern Star*, II, nos. 219–26, 230–3, 241; and P.R.O.N.I. T.765/457, 461, 464–6, 471.
27. *Northern Star*, II, nos. 14–15; *Drennan Letters*, 135–7.

The time had come to crush the menace in Ulster, and in the report of a secret parliamentary committee which appeared in March, the turmoil of recent years was attributed entirely to Belfast and the United Irishmen. The proclamation against volunteering and unlawful assemblies was extended to Ulster in the same month and the recent Arms (Gunpowder) Act had at last given government power to act against Belfast, the fountain-head of Irish sedition.[28]

On Monday and Tuesday 4–5 March, arms raids were made by the authorities in Lisburn and Belfast. On Saturday troop reinforcements were sent into Belfast from outlying areas and the soldiers made no secret of their intention to teach the town a lesson for its wayward behaviour. As a detachment of cavalry passed through the town, a group of Belfast people forced a fiddler to play the French revolutionary song, 'Ça Ira'. The soldiers insisted on changing the tune to 'God Save the King'. They were clearly in a belligerent mood, and, as a confrontation seemed likely, some armed Volunteers hastily assembled. The opposing groups were dispersed by the intervention of the district commander, Major General Whyte; but the dragoons took their revenge that afternoon, spilling out of the inns in which they were quartered, tearing down inn and shop signs dedicated to democratic figures and symbols, and attacking the houses of known radicals. The attacks had no government authorization, despite United claims to the contrary, but many officers had also taken part in their men's misbehaviour, and the failure of the authorities to reprimand the offenders was taken as a tacit admission of collusion.

Accounts of the incident differ in important details: Whyte claimed that the troops were provoked by a stone-throwing crowd; the Belfast Town Committee, which met on 10 March to investigate the incident, unanimously condemned the troops as having planned the attack before their arrival, the crowd around the fiddler, a mere 'rabble consisting of ten or twelve boys and ragamuffins', simply providing the occasion. Certainly Westmorland had planned to subdue the town; Whyte had been sent there with special powers to order in extra troops, and in retrospect government was glad of the excuse provided by the incident to apply the proclamation against the assembling of armed men. The Volunteers protested at the implications of disloyalty in the proclamation, but to no avail. United Irish support had plummeted in the Belfast area; they were held responsible for drawing the wrath of the military on the town, and it is not as surprising as it may appear to find that Ulster, alone of the Irish provinces, passively accepted the application of the Militia Act.[29]

28. *Report . . . to the House of Lords*, 1793; P.R.O. H.O. 100/34/243–4 and 100/43/89, Cooke and Hobart's letters to Nepean, 8 Feb. and 12 Mar. 1793; *Northern Star*, II, nos. 18–19.
29. For the United Irish version see *Northern Star*, II, nos. 19–21; *Drennan Letters*, 143, 147–8, 152–6; Tone, *Life*, I, 270–2; MacNeven, *Pieces of Irish History*, 54–8; see also H. Joy and W. Bruce, *Belfast Politics* (Belfast, 1794), 122–30 and R. Jacob, *The Rise of the United Irishmen, 1791– 1794* (London, 1937), 163–4. For Westmorland's reaction see P.R.O. H.O. 100/43/145–51.

The period 1791 to 1792 had been one of overwhelming optimism among the Irish reformers, and the annual festivities on Bastille Day were more an expression of hope in the dawning everywhere of a new enlightened era than a celebration for a revolution in one country only. But the increasing militancy of the Defenders and the declaration of war with France raised the spectre of a Jacobin-inspired revenge campaign by the catholics. By the middle of 1793 the protestant nationalism of the previous decades was virtually dead and even Westmorland was surprised at the overwhelming support which his repressive legislation received in the Irish parliament. United Irish addresses altered radically in 1793. There was none of the confidence of their early attacks on government; they had become pessimistic and defensive in tone, already showing signs of their growing despair at ever securing reform by constitutional means. Their despair reached new heights when they saw the Irish parliamentary opposition slavishly supporting the war and the attendant repressive legislation. Until 1793 the United Irishmen had been professed supporters of the parliamentary system. Tone had never quite trusted the opposition, but he had personal motives for not doing so, and was unrepresentative of United opinion, which had always considered them the essential channel for reform. This 'desertion' of 1793 consequently had a profound effect on the United Irishmen. It had removed one of their last hopes of change by constitutional methods and this new sense of despair and shock at the sudden crash from such optimistic heights is expressed in their address to 'the People of Ireland.'

> At the opening of this session, every man thought ... that the Catholics must be completely emancipated, and a radical reform in Parliament effectuated, but the delusion was soon removed. It was suddenly discovered that it was necessary to have a *strong* government in Ireland; ... The War had been approved by Parliament, 36,000 men have been voted ... the gunpowder bill is passed; the volunteers of Dublin have been insulted, their artillery has been seized; soldiers hourly are seen with a Police Magistrate at their head parading the streets, entering and searching the houses of citizens for arms; and finally the officers of the only society which had spirit to observe on those proceedings, are seized and thrown into prison.[30]

With Butler, Bond and Reynolds also in prison for querying the authority of the House of Lords to examine witnesses under oath, the Society felt that the country was being 'rushed to arbitrary government'. But worse was yet to come.

The government seemed determined to prove the Society a treasonable organization. A Defender prisoner was bribed to testify that Tandy had

---

30. Madden, *United Irishmen*, 1st. edn., ii, 335. See *Northern Star*, ii, nos. 19–24, and MacNeven, *Pieces of Irish History*, 65–6, for this growing sense of alarm and despair.

sworn him into the Defenders, an accusation that had an element of truth sufficient to convince Tandy that he had little choice between the gallows and self-exile. Fitzgibbon, the Lord Chancellor, publicly accused Henry Sheares and his younger brother John of being in the pay of France, and similar accusations were made against other prominent leaders.[31] The cumulative effect of such harassment was to increase United Irish conviction that constitutional agitation could achieve nothing, and from the end of that year some were already meeting in semi-secret groups. Repentant United men later rebuked the Irish government for failing to see that reform would have satisfied most United Irishmen and for forcing them into republicanism by failing to grant it. The Irish officials, however, were not the calculating tyrants of radical propaganda, using the excuse of the war to crush opposition. They were convinced that the United Irishmen were already militant republicans, and their correspondence of early 1793 reveals a genuine crisis of confidence in their own ability to control domestic discontent in time of war.[32]

Nevertheless, the suddenness of the official clamp-down, and the impasse reached in 1793 after a decade of heightened expectation, left the Society 'stunned'. Even sympathizers now spoke of it in hushed tones; meetings were scantily attended and confidence was fading. The United Irishmen were being forced to consider their future development. Initially they spoke in even stronger terms of their essential constitutionalism and at last published their reform programme in February 1794. But they realized that there was little hope of any early success, and a period of aimlessness succeeded their virtual suppression in 1793. Thomas Addis Emmet later described their sense of despair, the absence of any direction in their thinking, and the passive waiting on events. 'The press had been overawed and subdued: numberless prosecutions had been commenced against almost every popular publication; but particularly against the *Northern Star*. The expectations of the reformers had been blasted, their plans had been defeated, and decisive measures had been taken by government to prevent their being resumed. It became therefore necessary to await for new events, from which might be formed new plans.'[33] It was the events of the next two years, reacting upon the Society's sense of frustrated helplessness, which pushed it towards militant republicanism. Of these events, the most important was the French offer of military assistance.

31. I.S.P.O. 620/42/18; see also *Trial of Francis Graham for Attempting to suborn Joseph Corbally, Taylor to swear that A. H. Rowan and J. Napper Tandy Esqs. were at the Head of the Defenders* (Dublin, 1794).

32. For signs of government alarm, see I.S.P.O. Westmorland Corr. IV, 56 and 104; P.R.O. H.O. 100/34/163, 100/42/13–14 and 31–2.

33. MacNeven, *Pieces of Irish History*, 70; *Drennan Letters*, 153, 166–71; P.R.O.N.I. T.765/430–2; I.S.P.O. 620/21/23, Russell's diary tracing the progress of their disillusionment. See also Higgins's information, early 1794, I.S.P.O. 620/21/27–38, and Madden, *United Irishmen*, 1st ser. 1, 222, for the declining attendance at United Irish meetings.

CHAPTER THREE

The Cause of the French

Ireland responded to the French Revolution with a spontaneity lacking elsewhere in the British Isles.[1] Old Jacobite sympathies have sometimes been invoked to explain such enthusiasm, but there is little evidence to support this. It is true that after the defeat of the Jacobite army in Ireland in 1690 a steady stream of Irish catholics, the so-called 'wild geese', had gone to fight in the armies of the catholic powers on the Continent. But Ireland did not move in support of the 1745 Jacobite rebellion on the British mainland; if the catholics had not been excluded from joining the British army in the penal era there can be little doubt that fewer would have joined the Irish brigades on the Continent; and in the 1790s, when the descendants of the 'wild geese' came to Ireland as fugitive French émigrés, they were simply repulsed by the Irish people as enemies of the French Revolution.[2] Irish trading, educational and smuggling connections with France had created a sense of catholic identity independently of the Stuarts, and there is enough information to show that even in areas unaffected by Defenderism, the people recognized that the turn of events in France had created a situation in which they might again expect outside assistance to secure their historical rights.[3]

Protestant reformers too had traditionally looked outside Ireland, to America, to the Continent and to England for their inspiration. They were cosmopolites long before the French Revolution took place, and in the early 1790s the struggles of the Poles, the Dutch and the Savoyards received almost as much attention as those of the French. 'If the Irish are in some respects a century behind us in point of civilization,' warned one English officer serving in Ireland, 'they are at least two centuries before us in their

1. *Northern Star*, i, nos. 2, 8, 46, 51, 56, 65, 84; and ii, no. 15; McDowell, *Irish Public Opinion*, 141–78. For the Irish addresses to France, see Teeling, *Sequel*, 186; *Dublin Evening Post*, 15 Nov. 1792; *Réimpression de l'Ancien Moniteur*, 31 vols. (Paris, 1858–63), 12, p. 533; A. Aulard, *La Société des Jacobins*, 6 vols. (Paris, 1889–1897), iv, 221–2.
2. P.R.O. H.O. 100/44/351–6, Hobart to Nepean, 6 Aug. 1793; W.O. 1/612/29–33, Camden to Dundas [1795]; and *Northern Star*, i, no. 82.
3. For traditional contacts with France see Hardiman, *Irish Ministrelsy*, ii, 55–67; Beresford, 'Ireland in French Strategy', ch. iii; R. Hayes, *The Last Invasion of Ireland* (Dublin, 1937), 187.

Revolutionary principles; and if we are to be agitated hereafter by those doctrines which now shake Europe to her centre, we are as likely to have them imported from Ireland as from France; . . . Thelwall and Hardy [leaders of the London Corresponding Society] would be very secondary firebrands among the United Irishmen.'[4] It was a warning which England ignored to her cost. But it was in the nature of Ireland's recent history for such reformers to see their own efforts as part of a wider British campaign on the one hand, and the French Revolution as a reflection of their own reform struggle on the other. In 1789 they considered the French to have won the combined gains of 1688 and 1782, but to have extended them to include a truly representative system of government for which countries like Ireland still struggled. They viewed the events in France as both an example to peoples everywhere and a warning to governments who refused reform, and even the future Lord Castlereagh felt that no government could afford to ignore the peoples they claimed to govern after the example of the Revolution in France. Political patronage soon altered his early reformist sympathies, but his belief in the irreversibility of the reform trend after 1789 was shared by all like-minded Britons, and the glowing accounts of events in France were designed as much to further native campaigns for reform as to express support for the French. Perhaps the most important effect of the French Revolution and of Paine's writings on Irish society was to push the protestant reformers into what previously would have been considered an unnatural alliance with the catholics. The spectacle of a catholic country like France revolutionizing itself, the dogma of natural rights, the enthusiasm of the Irish catholics for the French Revolution and the United Irish platform of national union convinced many protestants that the catholics were not as 'unfit for liberty' as they had generally assumed.[5] Nevertheless the decision to take the Defenders into alliance was not lightly taken, and was only finally brought about by direct French intervention.

France had been dragged into war by a small but vociferous Brissotin war party, and until the downfall of the Committee of Public Safety successive governments remained bitterly divided on the nature of the war in general and their policy towards foreign revolutionaries in particular. In the first months of the war, however, it was the bombastic statements of the Brissotins which moulded the hopes of the foreign patriots, and the famous November decree of 19 November 1792, offering fraternity and assistance to all peoples wishing to recover their liberty, is a case in point. It was the product of a

---

4. N.L.I. MS 54[A]/111, [George Dallas] to Dundas, 20 Sept. 1797. *Northern Star*, 1, no. 97, 'Address of the Society of United Irishmen in Dublin to the Delegates for promoting a reform in Scotland', epitomizes the United Irishmen's conception of themselves as part of a wider British movement.
5. MacNeven, *Pieces of Irish History*, 12–15. *H.M.C. Charlemont MSS.*, II, 153; *Northern Star*, I, nos. 28, 38.

particularly heady session in the Convention in which the French Revolution had been hailed as the harbinger of universal liberty by several delegations of foreign patriots. But it was a deep embarrassment for Lebrun, the Foreign Minister, who desperately sought to convince those countries still at peace with France that she had no desire to interfere with the independence of other nations or to intervene in support of 'every riot or seditious movement' abroad. The decree had been passed in 'a burst of enthusiasm', he insisted, and had little chance of practical application.[6]

Time was to prove the truth of Lebrun's assertions. The decree was diluted by several amendments and finally laid to rest by Danton in April 1793. It had terminated rather than initiated an era of international brotherhood, and the fall of the more internationally-minded Girondins, early defeats in the war, and mounting internal difficulties heralded an intensely introspective regime the following year. Robespierre had always been suspicious of foreigners. His fears were played upon by Saint-Just and prompted increasingly bitter clashes with Brissot before the latter's downfall in June 1793. Such xenophobia was not a new departure; the foreign patriot groups in Paris in the first days of the Revolution were treated with less respect than they cared to admit in their home propaganda, and this inherent hostility to foreigners continued long after Robespierre's downfall. France would never have actively assisted rebellion where it could have been promoted more cheaply by moral encouragement alone, and Robespierre spoke for most Frenchmen in January 1794 when he publicly renounced any idea of French support for international revolution. Interference in neutral countries was entirely ruled out. If the subjects of an enemy rebelled, France would support them; but she could not be expected to foot the bill for the preliminary revolutionization. In this attitude successive French governments of the 1790s were to remain entirely consistent, and foreign patriots had to prove themselves capable of winning their own liberty to qualify for French support.[7]

Despite such attempts to undo the damage caused by the euphoric statements of the early months of the war, the belief in French internationalism had

---

6. See Lebrun's correspondence in A.A.E. Corr. Pol. Ang. 582 fos. 41–52; 583 fos. 210–12, 348–60; 584 fos. 19–22, 67–79, 92–5, 177–8; and 586 fos. 71–4.

7. *Réimpression de l'Ancien Moniteur*, 11, pp. 177–8, P.J.B. Buchez and P. C. Roux–Lavergne, *Histoire parlementaire de la Révolution française*, 40 vols. (Paris, 1834–8), XIII, 122–69; M. Bouloiseau, *La République jacobine* (Paris, 1972), 74–7; *Discours de Danton* ed. A. Fribourg (Paris, 1910), 398–400; and Aulard, *La Société des Jacobins*, III, 614–20, v, 633–5 for Robespierre's remarks. For the foreign patriots in Paris see A. Méautis, *Le Club helvétique de Paris, 1790–91, et la diffusion des idées révolutionnaires en Suisse* (Neuchâtel, 1969), expecially 93–115; P. Sagnac, *Le Rhin Français pendant la Révolution et l'Empire* (Paris, 1917), 58–9; S. Schama, *Patriots and Liberators* (London, 1977), especially 149–57; A. Gieysztor *et al.*, *Histoire de Pologne* (Warsaw, 1972), 410–11. For the changing attitude of France to such foreign revolutionaries see J. P. McLaughlin, 'The Annexation Policy of the French Revolution 1789–1793' (London Univ. Ph.D. thesis 1951), and S. S. Biro, *The German Policy of Revolutionary France*, 2 vols. (Cambridge, Mass., 1957), I, 63–5, 103–18.

been firmly implanted alike in the minds of the foreign revolutionaries and their home governments. England was alarmed by the rapid success of French arms, and the November decree was a primary factor in pushing her into a war, for which the opening of the Scheldt provided the occasion.[8] As events on the Continent gradually convinced Britain of the necessity of war, the same events were eliciting an increasingly inflammatory response from the United Irishmen. The Belfast Volunteers, with Sam McTier at their head, had met on 28 October to celebrate the French victory at Valmy. In Dublin the authorities just managed to prevent a similar demonstration. But parts of the capital were illuminated, along with Belfast and several other towns in Antrim and Down, to celebrate the expulsion of the allied armies from France. A country which had gloried in its Volunteering tradition rejoiced at the vision of French republicanism in arms and a citizen army in conflict with foreign oppressors, and the passage of the November decree was hailed as 'the day on which the National Convention of France decreed assistance to all peoples struggling for liberty'.[9] That the United Irishmen had no intention of seeking French support or of armed resistance at this stage was no consolation to a government which was given every reason to think otherwise.

The United Irishmen had no group of representatives in France to witness the vicissitudes of the early years of the war, and did not experience the disillusionment of other patriot groups at their treatment by the French. There was a handful of Irish radicals in Paris in the heady days of 1792 who were shortly to join the United Irish Society. They left Paris before the declaration of war and the inevitable French reaction against British subjects which ensued, and brought back to the United movement an excessive sense of optimism in French goodwill. Arthur O'Connor had visited Paris that year and had met General Lafayette. As a member of the Irish parliament since 1790, he had always voted with the government, but his attitude changed after his return from France, and he was to become one of the most outspoken of the United leaders in the Society's republican phase.[10] Lord Edward Fitzgerald had become so enamoured of French principles that when he returned from Paris at the end of 1792 even the United Irishmen thought him a secret French agent and feared the ill-repute he might bring to a Society still seeking to establish its constitutionalism. John and Henry Sheares had, like Lord Edward, joined the Jacobin Club in Paris and later, as members of the French National Guard, had actually formed part of the contingent attending the King's trial. Henry's outspoken support for France, after

8. *Parl. Hist.* xxx, 344–97; xxxii, 582; xxxiv, 1442; E. D. Adams, *The influence of Grenville on Pitt's Foreign Policy, 1787–1798* (Washington, 1904), 20–1; and A.A.E. Corr. Pol. Ang. 584 fos. 67–9 for Chauvelin's analysis of the causes of the war.

9. *Northern Star*, i, no. 98, also no. 90; I.S.P.O. 620/21/23, Russell's comments on the French victories, 21 Feb. 1793. For government reaction see I.S.P.O. Priv. Offic. Corresp. viii^A /1/3/242.

10. Frank MacDermot, 'Arthur O'Connor', *I.H.S.*, xv (1966), 48–69.

his return to Ireland, convinced many that he was a violent republican, and even Drennan feared the possible effects of his election to the Society's presidency in April 1793.[11]

But the Irish in Paris had formed no separate grouping. Rather they had adhered to the short-lived English Club, or Friends of the Rights of Man Associated at Paris, in which delegates from the London-based Society for Constitutional Information predominated.[12] It was as part of an English group that on Sunday 18 November they participated in the festivities at White's Hotel in the rue Croix-des-Petits-Champs in Paris. Representatives from many foreign patriot groups in Paris, deputies from the Convention, soldiers from the French army and the various foreign legions in French service gathered there to celebrate French victories and the advent of 'the Great Republic of Man'. The presence of the Dublin-born General Dillon who had fought for France since 1762, was of particular significance for Ireland; he spoke of his own part in the expulsion of the foreign invader from France and of 'his willingness ... to perform ... similar services to his own country'. Shortly afterwards a deputation of English and Irish presented the address of congratulation voted at this gathering to the Convention. 'The British and Irish citizens, now in Paris ... have considered it their duty to offer the representatives of such a great nation, their congratulations on these events which are of such importance to all peoples aspiring to be free ... It is for the French nation to free all Europe ... let us hope that the victorious soldiers of liberty will not relinquish their arms until no tyrants or slaves remain ... We are not alone in holding such beliefs; we are certain that they are shared by the vast majority of our compatriots ... ' In the wake of the November decree, the address produced another display of euphoric internationalism. The deputation was cheered continuously and Grégoire, the president of the Convention, assured them that 'the wishes you have expressed for the liberation of the oppressed will be realized ... the celebration you have held in honour of the French Revolution, is the prelude to that of nations everywhere'. The occasion was fully reported in the Irish press and added to the list of United Irish toasts, another of the accumulating signs of apparent French sympathy for their cause.[13]

11. See P.R.O.N.I. T.765/386, 421 and 426; P.R.O. H.O. 100/34/134; and 100/43/161 for suspicions of Lord Edward and Sheares; and T.C.D. MS. 4833 (Sheares MSS.) for Henry's activities in Paris.

12. For the English in Paris see W. A. L. Seaman, 'British Democratic Societies in the Period of the French Revolution, 1789-1799', (Univ. of London Ph.D. thesis 1954), 223-61; J. G. Alger *Englishmen in the French Revolution* (London, 1889) and idem, 'The British Colony in Paris 1792-1793', *E.H.R.* xiii (1898), 672-94; and *The Despatches of Earl Gower, 1790-1792*, ed. O. Browning (Cambridge, 1885), 260-9.

13. *Archives parlementaires. Receuil complet des débats législatifs et politiques des Chambres françaises, 1ʳᵉ série: 1787-1799*, 91 vols. (Paris, 1879-1976), liii, 635-6; Sheares's account in T.C.D. MS. 4833; *Northern Star*, i, nos. 97-8 and *Dublin Evening Post*, 6 Dec. 1792.

Despite English fears, France had no intention of promoting disturbances in Britain, even after war had broken out between the two countries in February 1793. Any diversion of English attention from events on the Continent was welcome, but early experiences with the Belgian patriots had hardened French attitudes towards foreign revolutionaries, and in any case they had little desire to antagonize England unnecessarily. The 1792 November decree was not a true reflection of French policy, which until the dissolution of the first Committee of Public Safety in July 1793 was still predominantly moderate and pacifist in character. Prussia and England were looked to as potential friends, and peaceful overtures were even made to Austria. There was little support for enemy dissidents, and the decision to invade the Rhineland, in response to an invitation from the Rhenish patriots, raised a howl of opposition to this despatch of 'armed ambassadors' abroad.[14] Indeed, neither England nor France had any clear idea of their aims in the conflict or the form it would take, and in the first months of 1793 the plans of both were marked by confusion and lack of direction. Only at the end of the year did the two countries recognize the impossibility of an early peace and the need for a determined struggle and a coherent war policy. Until then they had been dragged along by interested parties, England by the supporters of the French royalists, France by the foreign revolutionaries and the Brissotin war party. The result was that England found herself irretrievably linked to the royalist struggle within France, and France to a policy of intervention and annexation abroad. But it was England's early promotion of civil war in France, long before France herself had given any serious thought to supporting the disaffected in the British Isles, which altered French opinion and determined the nature of the ensuing struggle.

Neither relished the promotion of internecine warfare. The English ministers acted with a reserve towards the royalists bordering at times on downright hostility. It was only the missionary zeal of the War Minister, William Windham, with the powerful backing of Grenville at the Foreign Office, which made support for the royalists in France a focal and, in the long absence of any other direction, a dominant part of English war policy.[15] By the end of 1793 the French belief that the English people were natural friends had entirely evaporated, and with England supporting a bloody

14. Biro, *The German Policy of Revolutionary France*, I, 146; and see A.A.E. Corr. Pol. Ang. 587 fos. 96–113, and P.R.O. F.O. 27/41–2, for Lebrun's overtures to England Feb.–May 1793.
15. See J. Holland Rose, in *Cambridge History of British Foreign Policy*, 3 vols. (Cambridge, 1922–3), I, 236–52 on the confusion of British policy at this period; and F. Masson, *Le Département des Affaires Étrangères pendant la Révolution, 1787–1804* (Paris, 1877), ch. VIII, for similar aimlessness in France. See also J. R. Taylor, 'William Windham and the Counter-Revolution in the North and West of France 1793–1801', (Manchester Univ. M.A. thesis 1967), 31–42; *The Journal and Correspondence of William, Lord Auckland*, ed. the Bishop of Bath and Wells, 4 vols. (London, 1861–2), II, 513–16; III, 44–6, 62–8, 85–99, 137–210. I am also grateful to Kim Berryman for her advice on English attitudes towards the royalists.

civil war in the Vendée, the desire for revenge became an important factor in French war policy. At the same time the woolly attitude towards Ireland gave way to a firm policy of armed intervention. Despite French reluctance to help foreign revolutionaries until they had proved themselves, the desire for revenge made Ireland a special case, and the logistical difficulties of supplying and maintaining military support at a distance made a swift victory more necessary and a full-scale French invasion more likely in Ireland than in any other country with a strong internal revolutionary movement. Reports reaching France at the end of 1792 suggested that Ireland was ripe for revolution, and as the crisis in the Vendée worsened, Ireland's potential utility in the conflict with England was gradually recognized.[16]

Britain's fears of such sponsorship of internal dissidents were real enough, for although she too had secret agents in France before the declaration of war, notably the talented Irishman Charles Somers, it required time to establish the reliability of secret sources, and Somers's assurances that France was in no position to send help to anyone carried little weight.[17] The English government was concerned at the proliferation of French agents operating in Britain, secretly or otherwise, on the eve of the war, and even official French representatives warned Lebrun that this confusion of agents only provoked England unnecessarily. Whitehall was not to know that such activities derived from the chaos in the Paris ministries and from a good deal of freelancing on the part of agents and ministers alike, rather than from overall policy. Many of these agents openly flirted with the British democrats and undoubtedly gave rise to greater expectations among the few subversives than France would have cared to satisfy.[18]

Since the reins of control were so loose over the French agents it is probable that Jean Benoist's encounter in November 1792 with representatives of a so-called Irish 'Revolutionary Committee' in London was accidental. They claimed that the committee had been formed within the wider campaign for catholic emancipation to ensure that the catholic petition made such demands as to guarantee almost certain rejection. The catholics might then be converted to the idea of separation from England and the establishment of an Irish republic. They hoped that the Volunteers would also join, and efforts had already been made to win over the Irish fighting in the royalist regiments in Prussia and in the Low Countries. They had purchased large supplies of arms in England and hoped to secure assistance in money and munitions from France. France's response was cautious, though Lebrun

---

16. See A.A.E. Corr. Pol. Ang. 587 fos. 9 and 43. For reports to the French government on the state of Ireland, see A.A.E. Corr. Pol. Ang. 582 fos. 197–202, 219–28; 583 fos. 47–50, 153–5; 584 fos. 67–9, 215–17, 408–11; 587 fos. 349–50; Mem. et Doc. Ang. 53 fos. 133–6; and *H.M.C. Dropmore MSS.*, II, 480–1.

17. P.R.O. F.O. 27/40–41, Somers's reports.

18. For the squabbling of the various agents, see A.N.AF III 63 and A.A.E. Corr. Pol. Ang. 582 fos. 123–4. For signs of contact with British democrats, see Corr. Pol. Ang. 582 fos. 135–6, 174–7.

agreed that the project offered an excellent opportunity for weakening England, and the committee's agent was invited to Paris for further consultation.

The ensuing negotiations showed that had the Catholic Relief Act of 1793 been rejected, the post-1795 coalition of catholic leaders, Defenders and United Irishmen might have been achieved several years earlier. We know nothing of the identity of the London group. But Lord Edward Fitzgerald later claimed that he and some of the delegates who were sent with the catholic petition to London had spoken with French officials.[19] The official catholic delegates cannot have been among those who approached Benoist initially, since they would not have been in London. But Benoist's informants seem to have been involved with both the official catholic campaign and with the Defenders, and leading Defenders were known to have been in London at the time buying arms. Certainly these secret discussions would have shown that the Irish government's attempt to implicate some leading catholics with the Defenders was less misdirected than commonly supposed. They were not, however, a formal delegation from any established group in Ireland, and their claims for a 'Revolutionary Committee' were greatly exaggerated. The incident indicates that a few men had already begun to think in terms of a French-assisted revolt; but the Catholic Relief Act, the purge of the Defenders, the reserve of the United Irishmen, and the confusion in French politics prevented any further progress in the negotiations. The absence of any references to the discussions when more serious relations were established with France some years later reveals the whole incident for what it was, a casual approach to one of the many French agents who almost invited such encounters by their activities in London.

Nor was there any immediate sequel in France. Instead the mission of the Irish agent Richard Ferris, a priest who had resided in France for many years, highlights the confusion of French politics at the beginning of 1793, the uncertainty about policies to be adopted in the war and towards the foreign patriots in particular. As a former student of the Irish College in Paris, Lebrun was excited by the prospect of an Irish republic, but he was anxious to conceal his enthusiasm and not to commit France to any policy which might embarrass her attempts to regain England's friendship. In reply to Ferris's requests, the French temporized, promised an invasion of Ireland when the campaign in the Low Countries had been completed, and seemed anxious to retain him in Paris for some future use, but were devoid of any immediate suggestions. It was only later in the year that interest in Ferris revived, when the Committee of Public Safety started to formulate a constructive war policy against England.[20]

19. A.A.E. Corr. Pol. Ang. 589 fos. 249–53, Lord Edward's claims to Reinhard in 1796, and P.R.O.N.I. T.765/386.
20. For a full account of the mission see A.A.E. Corr. Pol. Ang. 584 fos. 9–11, 98–9; and 587 fos. 296–300, 306–7, 312–13, 319 and 325.

Ferris was critical of France's feeble response to suggestions of an under-cover campaign in Britain. Sending forty or fifty agents to spread the truth about their revolution was no way to conquer nations, he had remarked disdainfully, and he cited the inadequate planning of the mission of four young seminary students to Ireland, which would have destined it to certain failure had Britain's own intelligence service been more effective. The mission in question was another example of the inefficiency, lack of positive direction and essential rawness of French intelligence in the first year of the war. It was designed to disseminate propaganda about the French Revolution in Ireland. Its leader was William Duckett, a young Kerryman, and like his three companions, Edward Ferris, Nicholas Madgett and Sidderson, he was a student from the Irish College in Paris. The choice of such novices for a semi-permanent mission was a token of the rupture of any continuous intelligence tradition from the days before the Revolution, and Somers dismissed them as 'not at all qualified for such a mission . . . a parcel of young fellows just escaped from an Irish Seminary here', and posing no threat to British security.[21] Lack of adequate preparation threatened to destroy the mission at the outset. The four were arrested in London and left to sink by the carelessness of French agents already operating there. They were eventually released, possibly screened by those novice qualities which Somers had mocked, and Whitehall's failure to discover any incriminating information in consequence. They soon became experts in the business of espionage, however, providing one of the most consistent pieces of under-cover activity of the period, and in Duckett one of France's most dedicated agents. Duckett divided his time between England and Ireland, mingling with local radicals and mounting an attack on the British government in the *Morning Chronicle* and the *Northern Star*. The others had a roving mission in Ireland, having been instructed to lead 'a wandering life, in order to increase their contacts, and enable them to exert the greatest influence on popular thinking'. They were left entirely free to work out their own campaign on the spot, though Sidderson and Madgett did eventually become leading militants in the United Irish movement, and all continued to supply Duckett with information on Ireland many years after the official mission had terminated.[22]

By 1793 Thomas Paine had set himself up in Paris as the political philosopher of Ireland's coming revolution, the most prominent member of the

---

21. P.R.O. F.O. 27/42, Somers to [Bland Burges], 4 Mar. 1793.
22. N.L.I. pos. 210, MS. Life of William Duckett, by R. Duckett (Bordeaux, 1946), 75; A.A.E. Corr. Pol. Ang. 582 fos. 353, 359–60; and R. Hayes, *Biographical Dictionary of Irishmen in France* (Dublin, 1949), 86. For Sidderson and Madgett, see *Dublin Evening Post*, 18 July 1795, A.H.G. B[11]1, Duckett's memoir, 1 Nov. 1796; P.R.O. H.O. 100/86/224 and F.O. 33/17/26. For the mission see A.A.E. Mem. et Doc. Ang. 19 fos. 382–8, Personnel 1re sér. 25 fo. 297; A.N. AF III 370 doss. 1814 fos. 9–15 and BB[4]122 fo. 284. Duckett's articles are in the *Morning Chronicle*, 17 Nov. and 3 Dec. 1794 and *Northern Star*, II, no. 304.

group of Anglo-Irish exiles who had attended the White's Hotel celebrations and who were promoting the idea of a British revolution with the declining Girondin regime. They included William Duckett, several well-known English radicals—John Hurford Stone, Robert Merry and Sir Robert Smith—all members of the Society for Constitutional Information—William Jackson, an Irish clergyman, who had spent most of his working life in England, Lieutenant Colonel Eleazer Oswald, an American, and Nicholas Madgett, a Kerryman, cousin to one of the four seminarists sent on mission, an exile of long standing who had been in and out of government employment under the monarchy and who would soon become chief of the *Bureau de Traduction* attached to the Committee of Public Safety.[23] Unlike most patriot exiles, the Madgett–Paine circle spoke for no home movement, had little knowledge of current developments in Ireland, and while they did sustain French interest, they were also responsible for promoting many false ideas and assumptions which were to prove impossible to remove when an official United Irish embassy to Paris was established in 1796–97.

Shortly before he left for London and Ireland in November 1792, Lord Edward Fitzgerald had talked with Paine about the possibility of French support for an Irish revolution. They had agreed that the Irish Volunteers were an ideal engine of revolution, and with Henry Sheares had worked out a mode of correspondence with Ireland. Paine communicated to Lebrun Lord Edward's suggestion that if 40,000 Volunteers could be financed and kept in the field for three months, Ireland would be liberated. Eleazer Oswald was accordingly commissioned to travel to Ireland 'to sound out the dispositions of the Irish people'. Passport difficulties necessitated a circuitous journey via Norway and Oswald only arrived in Dublin on 8 May 1793. He could not have arrived at a more inopportune moment. The Defenders had been silenced, the Volunteers disarmed, many United leaders were in prison and the Society seemed totally demoralized. Oswald was taken by Lord Edward to consult with Butler, Bond, Rowan, Reynolds and several other United leaders, including possibly Thomas Addis Emmet and Lewins. Their conversation showed that the leading United men had never entirely dismissed the idea of a French-supported revolution in Ireland as a legitimate means of attaining their ends. They found any proposal for liberating their country attractive, but felt nothing could be done in the present situation.

It is instructive to compare the Irish accounts of the mission with that of Oswald. Lewins later wrote: 'Thomas Paine ... sent the American Oswald

23. For Madgett see A.A.E. Personnel 1er sér. 47 fos. 83–9; P.R.O.N.I. D.3030/302; Masson, *Le Département des Affaires Étrangères*, 354, 366; and Hayes, *Biographical Dictionary*, 105. For Jackson see F. MacDermot, 'The Jackson Episode in 1794', *Studies*, 27 (1938), 77–92; A.A.E. Personnel 1er sér. 39 fos. 148–53; and J. Taylor, *Records of My Life*, 2 vols. (London, 1832), II, 319–32.

to Lord Edward Fitzgerald with an offer of 20,000 men, arms, munitions and money from the Brissotin party, then in power, to help the Irish shake off the English yoke and to establish their independence. Ireland was not then sufficiently prepared for such a revolution and the proposal was rejected.' Rowan, who had actually spoken with Oswald, claimed that he had offered French help for the independence movement and a French loan to maintain 40,000 Volunteers for four months. The French documents, however, tell of no firm instruction to offer either money or men. Indeed all the evidence suggests that this mission, which was so important in inflating Irish expectations of French assistance, was entirely in the tradition of all the other secret missions to the British Isles in these months, and was to have been purely fact-finding in character. Oswald had not directly communicated with Lebrun and it is possible that Paine may have added the offer of financial support which was made in Dublin. Thereafter the offer seems to have been embellished in the process of transmission to the other United leaders. Lewins was not given to exaggeration; if he believed that an offer of large-scale French assistance had been made, we can be sure that the belief was commonly held by all the other leaders.[24] Oswald's mission accordingly contributed to the growing belief that French help was there for the asking.

Oswald returned to France in June to a political crisis which was to culminate in the annihilation of the Girondins and the re-structuring of the Committee of Public Safety. Lebrun had been removed in May; Paine had shared the decline of his friend Danton, and the Dantonist Foreign Minister, Deforgues, was ill-acquainted with the background to Oswald's mission. He was nevertheless blamed for its apparent failure and the excessive expenditure involved in the route via Norway. It was ammunition for Danton's detractors and the question of the Foreign Minister's secret expenditure was blown into a full-scale attack by the supporters of Robespierre. The upshot was the severe curtailment of any future expenditure without the prior consent of one of the executive committees. The measure could have done little to arrest the chaos of ministerial finances, but it did check ministerial freedom of action, destroyed the secrecy with which preparations for such missions had hitherto been surrounded, and confined future missions to a shoe-string budget. Intelligence files were consequently opened to British scrutiny.[25]

After Paine's fall from favour, the mantle of responsibility for Irish affairs fell to Madgett, now in the *Bureau de Traduction* attached to the Marine Ministry. The date of the appointment is uncertain, but by mid-1793 Madgett

24. For the Irish account of the mission, see MacNeven, *Pieces of Irish History*, 71; and A.N. AF IV 1671 plaq. 1 fos. 99–105 (Lewins's account). For Oswald's reports and correspondence after his return, see Corr. Pol. Ang. 587 fos. 167, 176.
25. *H.M.C. Dropmore MSS.*, ii, 456–7 and 551; M. Marion, *Histoire financière de la France depuis 1715*, 6 vols. (Paris, 1914–31), iii, 171–3.

was already looked upon as a spokesman on England and Ireland, and his office inevitably became the semi-official medium of communication between the French government and the disaffected British subjects. A government employee, who also considered himself an exiled patriot, was a rare asset to any group of exiles. But there were no United Irishmen in Paris to benefit from Madgett's position and Ireland continued to be viewed as part of a wider British campaign. Shortly before his appointment, Madgett had already secured official sanction for the re-organization of the British exiles in Paris. He had pointed to the *émigrés* in London and the British spies known to be operating in Paris and suggested a co-ordinated effort between the Foreign, War and Marine Ministries to purge Paris of spies and to disseminate French propaganda in the British Isles. At first Lebrun was hesitant about fostering any venture which might provoke English retaliation. Some kind of group or committee, however, does appear to have been formed which included Jackson, Oswald and Robert Smith. For the next two years all intelligence operations in the British Isles were organized through Madgett and his circle, and although officially the fact-finding element remained dominant in such missions, there is evidence of empire-building on the part of Madgett.[26] This was certainly true in the case of William Jackson, who conducted the most important Irish mission of these years.

France had emerged from the internal turmoil of 1793 convinced that it had been perpetrated by England and determined on revenge. The western and southern parts of the country were torn by royalist and federalist revolts; the coasts were harassed by enemy fleets; Toulon had been betrayed to the English, and Dunkirk had almost followed suit after a prolonged bombardment; the early gains of the war had been reversed, and Dumouriez, France's best general, had defected to the enemy. Until the end of 1793 France had never seriously contemplated a direct offensive against England and early naval plans had been entirely defensive in character.[27] By September, however, plans for a direct attack on England were launched in an atmosphere of rising anglophobia. These measures, claimed the Committee of Public Safety, were 'the fruit of the mistrust which England has inspired in us; for they have barbarously violated our national rights in a manner hitherto unknown. They seemed to think that the best way of waging war against a new Republic, was by corruption rather than combat . . . ', and Saint-Just, who delivered the address to the Convention, decisively laid to rest

26. See A.A.E. Corr. Pol. Ang. 587 fos. 20–1, 45–6; and A.N. BB³ 36 fo. 116, for Madgett's and Lebrun's correspondence on the organization of such a 'Comité révolutionnaire'. A.N. GG¹ 36, Madgett's letter of 17 Aug. 1799; A.A.E. Personnel, 1ᵉʳ sér. 47 fo. 83, and 65 fos. 57–64.

27. A.N. GG¹ 67 fos. 3–14; L. Lévy-Schneider, *Le Conventionnel Jeanbon Saint-André, 1749–1813*, 2 vols. (Paris, 1901), I, 415–16; N. Hampson, *La Marine de l'An II. Mobilisation de la flotte de l'océan* (Paris, 1959), 56.

the myth of international brotherhood.[28] The impossibility of sending the proposed 100,000 men to England was quickly realized and the scheme whittled down to an attack on the Channel Isles. At first the pretense of the full-scale attack was maintained, partly to distract French attention from internal troubles; but the scheme was abandoned altogether when the arrests of the Hébertists and Dantonists had cleared the political air.[29] The new chauvinism of French politics banished all ideas of active help for foreign patriots. But the upsurge of feeling against England had created a more widespread interest in the Irish situation. Deforgues, Bruix, one of the naval commanders and a future Minister of Marine, and General Hoche, fresh from combatting the effects of England's perfidy in the Vendée, had all urged the Committee to concentrate its naval efforts against Ireland. 'It is there that you must fight the English,' wrote Hoche, '. . . a landing in England itself can never be considered as anything but a chimera.' At the end of 1793 Ferris was persuaded to return to England to report on English support for the royalists and to attempt to revive discontent in Ireland.[30]

It was Jackson, however, who, at Madgett's suggestion, was chosen to travel to Ireland. The mission was sponsored by the Marine Ministry, which was not experiencing the same rigorous scrutiny as Foreign Affairs, and there was a marked element of free-lancing by Madgett and his British colleagues. Jackson had spoken with Jeanbon Saint-André and learnt of his support for an Irish invasion, but the instructions were delivered by Madgett, and although they represented a new trend in favour of the Irish, there seems to have been little official backing for the promise of armed help which Jackson eventually made to the United Irishmen. John Stone provided Jackson with introductions to Benjamin Beresford (his brother-in-law in Hamburg), and in England to his brother William Stone and the veteran radical Horne Tooke. Jackson was to sound out the Irish and English opposition politicians on their opinion of a French invasion of England and of Ireland in particular.

Jackson arrived at Hull on 26 January 1794, travelled to London and immediately contacted Stone's brother. William, unlike his brother, was no great admirer of France and had already given information from John's letters to the English government.[31] He assured Jackson that the English people were in general anti-French and secured the opinions of several opposition politicians in support of his claim. The member for Calne, Ben-

28. A.A.E. Corr. Pol. Ang. 588 fos. 47–50 (Saint-Just's report, 16 Oct.), also fos. 37–8.

29. Lévy-Schneider, *Jeanbon Saint-André*, II, 674–746; Aulard, *Recueil des actes*, x, 568–70; A.N. AF III 186ᵇ doss. 857.

30. E. Guillon, *La France et l'Irlande sous le Directoire* (Paris, 1888), 73. For Ferris's mission see A.A.E. Corr. Pol. Ang. 588 fos. 19–20; Bodl. Burges Dep., correspondence of Oct. 1793; and P.R.O. F.O. 27/43.

31. P.R.O. F.O. 27/40/363, Earl Stanhope to Grenville, 18 Dec. 1792.

jamin Vaughan, agreed to compose a memorandum on the state of English opinion, which Stone subsequently delivered to Jackson. None of those consulted by Jackson had suspected his real purpose, and William Stone boasted among his associates that his action had saved the country from invasion.[32]

Before he left for Ireland, Jackson called on his old friend John Cockayne, a London solicitor. Cockayne immediately contacted Pitt and was urged to accompany his friend to Ireland. From that moment the English and Irish governments were fully apprised of Jackson's movements. The two men arrived in Dublin on 3 April 1794 and Jackson hoped to have completed his mission there in time to catch the same vessel returning to Hamburg from Hull. They took lodgings in Dame Street, close to the United Irishmen's meeting place, and soon secured introductions to the leading United men through the barrister Leonard McNally, who had been a law student with Cockayne in London. However, in the aftermath of the arrest and trial of Rowan, there was an acute fear of informers among the United Irishmen, and Jackson experienced considerable difficulty in securing their trust. Lord Edward refused to meet him; Tone was convinced that he was an English *agent provocateur*, and others thought him a trouble-maker sent from the Society for Constitutional Information.[33] At a dinner given by McNally, Jackson made informal overtures to the United leaders and succeeded in turning the conversation to the possibility of a French invasion of Ireland. McNally dismissed the possibility out of hand; Samuel Butler treated it as a joke and Jackson's mission might have become a second version of Oswald's had not Lewins taken his comments seriously and arranged a meeting between Jackson and Rowan in Newgate prison.

Events moved rapidly after the first meeting. Rowan dismissed Butler's remarks as unrepresentative of the United Irishmen and exaggerated the republican element in the Society. His enthusiasm seems to have been returned with correspondingly exaggerated promises of French support by Jackson. Jackson was excited by this reception and wrote telling William Stone that he had postponed his return to England because he had met with greater support in Ireland than he had anticipated. He agreed that a statement on Ireland should be sent to France, and Rowan asked Tone to write it. Fortunately for Tone his involvement went no further than the composition of this address, for he suspected that Jackson was a government spy, and through the influence of friends in government circles he was to be spared prosecution on his undertaking to leave the country. Rowan had in fact

32. *State Trials*, xxv, 1248–59; P.R.O. T.S. 11/555/1793; T.S. 11/1067/4935; I.S.P.O. 620/21/ 19; and A.A.E. Corr. Pol. Ang. 588 fos. 171–6, information given by Vaughan on his arrival in France, 28 May 1794.
33. See I.S.P.O. 620/21/28 for the fear of informers; MacDermot, *Theobald Wolfe Tone*, 120; Tone, *Life*, I, 111–12, 114–20, and *Dublin Evening Post*, 1 May 1794 for reactions to Jackson.

Plate 7. The late Rev. William Jackson (National Library of Ireland, from *Walker's Hibernian Magazine*, 1795)

Plate 8. Leonard McNally (National Library of Ireland)

asked Tone to travel to France and act as United Irish agent to the Committee of Public Safety. After some initial flirtation with the proposition, Tone had declined, and Dr. Reynolds was chosen instead. Tone distrusted Jackson and was glad of the excuse of legal duties to remove himself to Drogheda. On his return he discovered to his horror that Rowan had given copies of his memorandum to Jackson, who had promptly sent them through the open post to France, using the intermediaries of the merchant house of Chapeaurouge in Hamburg and the French minister to Holland, D'Audibert Caille. The packages were intercepted and Jackson was arrested on 26 April.

Initially the mission had little impact on Ireland. The *Northern Star* and *Dublin Evening Post* devoted only a few lines to the arrest, and the occasional references to Jackson over the next twelve months were submerged in the coverage given to the escape and flight of Rowan after he heard of Jackson's arrest, to the trial of the *Northern Star* proprietors, and to the English treason trials at the end of 1794. The *Northern Star* considered Jackson a British spy sent to entrap Rowan, and consciously played down the affair.[34] Public interest was only aroused at the time of his trial in April 1795, and the publicity was inspired by the government in the naïve belief that by revealing the plot, it could frighten supporters and terminate its development. France

34. *Northern Star*, II, nos. 243–4, 330, 346, 348; *Dublin Evening Post*, 28 Apr.–3 May, 3 Jun., 1 Jul., 8 Nov. 1795; *Faulkner's Journal*, 29 Apr., 3 May, 8 Nov. 1794 and 25 Apr.–9 May 1795; *State Trials*, xxv, 838.

could not have publicized her interest in Ireland to better effect. In contrast to the indifference of the United Irishmen, the government treated Jackson's arrest as a major coup. He was placed in close confinement and under heavy guard. Every effort was made to secure witnesses to his handwriting, and the papers taken when William Stone was arrested on 3 May were sent over from England. The Irish government clearly expected the conspiracy to fade after such publicity; it made no attempt to protect its channel of information by shielding Cockayne, and much against his will he was forced to give evidence at the trial.

Whitehall went even further afield to expose the full extent of the conspiracy, and many felt that the safety of the kingdom depended on the conviction of those involved. Lord St. Helens, British minister at the Hague, was instructed to intercept the correspondence of D'Audibert Caille, and extra staff were recruited to the 'Secret Office' in London—which dealt with the interception of foreign mail—to cope with the new volume of mail from the Low Countries. Chapeaurouge had already been placed under arrest by the Hamburg authorities for trading with France, and the Hamburg Senate was pressurized by Britain to reveal the contents of his captured papers in the hope of discovering Jackson's letters to France. Such efforts produced no new information, for Jackson had sent only two letters to France, and they had already reached their destination before the mission was discovered.[35] Neither the English nor the Irish government seemed particularly concerned about the conviction of Jackson himself; rather they hoped to use him as a witness against those with whom he had negotiated in both countries. Nevertheless, Dublin Castle was shocked at London's lack of concern about the effects in Ireland of its determination to incriminate Jackson's associates in England. The Irish Chancellor and Attorney General had been aghast at England's suggestion that Jackson should be encouraged to turn evidence, and they warned that 'it would ruin government in the opinion of the public, and it would be thought, as is now insinuated that Jackson was sent merely to entrap the others'. They entertained little difficulty of securing a conviction, since unlike the English law of treason that in Ireland required the evidence of only one witness for a conviction. The evidence against Tone was insufficient and they thought him 'hardly worth punishing' anyway. But Whitehall sought to salvage even this scrap and insisted, too late as it turned out, that he should not be allowed to emigrate. Even Cockayne threatened to let them down. He had objected to Jackson's arrest in the first place, pleaded with Pitt that he had agreed to the mission on

35. Bodl. Burges Dep., correspondence with Lord St. Helens and Lord Malmesbury, June 1794; P.R.O. F.O. 33/9, correspondence of Grenville and Fraser, June–July 1794; G.P.O. Archives, Post 42/70 (Postmaster General's Reports), II, 142G. fo. 195; A.N. GG¹ 67 no. 2 fos. 30–9, letters of Madgett and Jackson, 1794–5.

the understanding that he would never have to undergo 'the Disgrace of a common Informer', and proved a reluctant accuser in court.[36]

This sudden interest of England in Ireland's disaffected subjects was a by-product of her campaign against her own. The involvement of Jackson and Stone with some of the leading members of the English parliamentary opposition might also have been used to stem the bitter attack which they were making on the government's counter-subversive measures. In future years Ireland was to supply government with a rich fund for counter-attack, but in 1794–95 it proved a disappointment. John Stone's letters were sifted for any references to the radicals and opposition Whigs, but nothing was found; and since Vaughan, Rowan and Reynolds had fled, Jackson's trial was poor compensation. Despite the thin prosecution case against Jackson, the Castle had fulfilled its main aim of publicly revealing the conspiracy in open court and many felt that Jackson himself might have been spared the death penalty. The prosecution had tried to show that the initiative for the mission had come from a group of internal traitors rather than from the French.[37] The United Irishmen were not named in the indictment, but the association was unmistakeable and official repression of the Society was thus retrospectively justified.

But Dublin had seriously miscalculated on the timing and the publicity given to the trial. In 1794 both Defenderism and the United Irishmen were in decline, the country was calmer than it had been for years, and Jackson's arrest had excited little interest outside the group intimately acquainted with his designs. The account given by Rowan when he arrived in France indicated that some of these had already decided to accept the French offer and to abandon their constitutional stance. But the early stages of the Society's republicanization were confused, and appear to have owed as much to pressure from lower social groups in Ulster as to the hesitant conversion of the original leaders. The Belfast United Irishmen had long ceased to meet formally, but one branch had happened to escape official vigilance because of 'the obscurity of its members'. It was this branch and another political club quite separate from the United Irishmen, and said to have been composed of 'mechanics, petty shop-keepers and farmers', who were the first to join together as an oath-bound republican organization. They retained the name of the United Irishmen, but it was not simply a continuation of the original Society, and for some time the main United leaders

---

36. P.R.O. P.R.O. 30/8/327/94–100, P.R.O. 30/8/331/222–8, 238–41 and H.O. 122/3/136 for government correspondence, Apr.–May 1794 and Apr. 1795, particularly on Cockayne's testimony. See also P.R.O. T.S.11/555/1793, T.S.11/1067/4935 and *State Trials*, xxv, 798, for London's efforts to secure firm evidence.

37. *State Trials*, xxv, 786–94, and P.R.O. T.S. 11/1067/4935, brief on behalf of the crown. Cockayne had told Rowan that the Privy Council had been more interested in incriminating Rowan himself than Jackson, see Rowan's account in A.A.E. Corr. Pol. Ang. 588 fos. 262–4.

remained unaware of its development. It spread rapidly in the North and its surviving documents illustrate Thomas Addis Emmet's claim that it was 'from the base of society' that the idea of a secret organization seeking a French-assisted revolution gradually worked its way up through the middling and upper ranks of the original Society, just at the time when events in Ireland and the Jackson episode were generating similar ideas at the top.

There is no evidence that former United leaders were associated with this body until after Jackson's trial, but by the end of July 1795 the original Belfast United leaders had assumed control. Such developments were a token of the blurring of former distinctions between the various elements opposed to the government; 'all parties were speculating upon some change' wrote Emmet, and many were coming to recognize that ultimately it was English influence which sustained Irish oppression. Another reform bill had just been defeated in the Irish parliament; it had been of derisory tameness and yet was rejected overwhelmingly. The debates had also been marked by the opposition's rejection of the United Irishmen's plan of reform.[38] Jackson's mission had jolted many into recognizing another way of attaining reform, and Rowan was encouraged by the catholic and United leaders alike to represent their changed opinions to the French government.

In France, Rowan had audiences with Madgett and leading French political figures like Jeanbon Saint-André, Robespierre and Couthon, and made demands which were to remain the core of United Irish representations in France thereafter. He delivered a copy of Tone's memoir, which outlined the state of opinion in Ireland, and assured France that an invasion would meet with overwhelming Irish support. He added that many feared conquest rather than liberation at the hands of France and the French should issue assurances to the contrary when the invasion took place. News of Jackson's arrest and the representations of Vaughan and Rowan had revived French interest in Ireland. Jeanbon was fully committed to an Irish invasion attempt and it seems likely that it might have become official policy had the *coup d'état* of Thermidor not removed the Committee of Public Safety and inaugurated another interval of political turmoil. But although the confusion of the Thermidorean period forced Rowan to America, the documentation of this first United Irish approach to France was to play an important role in the revival of interest under the Directory and in the establishment of a permanent Irish mission in Paris after the false start of 1794.[39]

38. Lecky, *Ireland in the Eighteenth Century*, III, 229–31; and see MacNeven, *Pieces of Irish History*, 67–8, 76–7, and I.S.P.O. 620/22/7ᵇ, 28 and 41 for this new republican United movement. Clearly the Ulster United leaders felt that it required some kind of formal control, see Tone, *Life*, I. 284 and T.C.D. MS. 868/1/1 for Russell's account.
39. For Rowan's and Jeanbon Saint-André's communications with the Committee of Public Safety see *The Autobiography of Archibald Hamilton Rowan*, ed. W. H. Drummond, I.U.P. reprint of 1840 edn. (Shannon, 1972), 213–18; A.A.E. Corr. Pol. Ang. 588 fos. 184–8, 196, 262–4, 267–9, 274–80, 313–18; also Personnel 1ᵉʳ sér. 65 fos. 57–64; and A.N. AF II 294 doss. 2464 fos. 42–4.

For the moment the prospect of a republican alliance in Ireland was held in suspension by the revival of reform hopes in 1795. For much of 1794 speculation had been rife on the outcome of Pitt's coalition negotiations with the Portland Whigs. The Whigs were known to want the Irish Viceroyalty, and towards the end of the year the pro-catholic and liberal-minded Earl Fitzwilliam was appointed. The catholic leaders were encouraged to believe that the reforms withheld in 1793 would now be granted. The moribund catholic committee became active again and mounted an intensive petitioning campaign for catholic emancipation. When Fitzwilliam eventually arrived in Ireland he found catholic expectations at such a height that the refusal of reform might have caused outright rebellion. His public announcements thereafter, and the removal of the Castle politicians most opposed to emancipation, convinced everybody in England and Ireland alike that he was preparing to defy Pitt's instructions against the measure. Fitzwilliam had indeed drawn up the terms of a catholic bill when he was abruptly recalled on 23 February after a sharp reprimand from Whitehall.[40] Rumours of such a recall had already created a crisis in Ireland; it was just one more example, commented the *Northern Star*, of how English rule worked to Ireland's disadvantage. The catholic leaders warned that if their just demands were again rejected, they would cease meeting as a separate body and 'merge their cause with that of the Nation', i.e. with the United Irishmen. To give substance to the threat they travelled through Belfast en route for London with another catholic petition, openly associating with the United Irish leaders, and flaunting the presence of Tone in their delegation at a time when he was under suspicion of treason.

The day of Fitzwilliam's departure, 25 March 1795, was seen by moderates and radicals alike as a disastrous turning point in the country's history. Dublin city went into mourning; its shops were closed and its inhabitants appeared dressed as for a funeral. 'Yesterday will be remembered as the most ominous and fatal to the interests of Ireland that has occurred within the present century,' wrote the *Northern Star*, '. . . It is not easy to afford an idea of the awfulness of the scene. The populace carefully abstained from riot, but they were loud in their curses and execrations against the British Cabinet, and the plunderers and peculators whose dark agency procured the recall of so independent and honest a man . . . unhappy Ireland! . . . the curtain falls upon the great drama of your prosperity . . . You are to be surrendered to the old and unhallowed dominion of jobs, insults, plunder, schisms, persecutions revilings and oppressions! . . . the members of the

---

40. For a general account of the viceroyalty, see R. B. McDowell, 'The Fitzwilliam Episode', *I.H.S.* XVI (1966), 115–30; Lecky, *Ireland in the Eighteenth Century*, III, 238–341; E. A. Smith, *Whig Principles and Party Politics* (Manchester, 1975), ch. 7. For the build-up of catholic expectation, see *Northern Star*, II, nos. 279–95; MacNeven, *Pieces of Irish History*, 80; and P.R.O. H.O. 100/46/152–7. For Fitzwilliam's correspondence with London, see H.O. 100/46/259–76 and P.R.O. 30/8/325/1/31–3. Fitzgibbon had stirred up a hornet's nest by references to the King's coronation oath etc., P.R.O.N.I. T.3229/1/7.

Plate 9. Earl Fitz-
william (by Grozier in
Ashbourne, *Pitt*)

Good Old System of Terror, dined yesterday . . . to celebrate the event of the
departure of Earl Fitzwilliam, and with him—IRISH INDEPENDENCE!'[41]
Fitzwilliam's departure did indeed mark the end of an era in which Ireland
had enjoyed remarkable prosperity and an accompanying sense of optimism
that the old divisions and fears were fading. Even the most committed republicans admitted that they had expected great things from his viceroyalty,
and a sudden calm had descended as the country awaited the expected
reforms. The catholic leaders had held back from more extreme methods
until their bitterness at the deception of 1795 placed them in the vanguard of
the United Irish militants. Prominent catholics like Mathew Dowling,
Richard McCormick, Butler, Lewins and Henry Jackson were reported to be
'inciting the working people to riot' in the disturbances which erupted in
Dublin shortly after Fitzwilliam's departure. They had started on 31 March
when Fitzwilliam's successor, Lord Camden, had arrived. That day saw
intense rioting in the city, and the unpopular politicians held responsible

41. *Northern Star*, II, nos. 326, 333, 338, 342.

for Fitzwilliam's recall barely escaped with their lives.[42] In England the catholic delegates were snubbed and they returned bitterly resentful of the English and Irish governments alike. A huge catholic meeting, at which over 4,000 were said to have attended, listened to the delegates tell of their insulting neglect in London and pledged 'that the Catholics of Ireland, refused this time, would never again seek the favour of a British Cabinet . . . The present . . . was the last time the Catholics would ever assemble in a distinct body—their cause being no longer a distinct cause, but adopted by their Protestant brethren as the common cause of Ireland.' Lewins, MacNeven and others also spoke in terms which showed that they had finally laid to rest the old idea that England was sympathetic to their claims; the evil genius was no longer the Castle clique, but the English connection itself.[43]

Jackson had finally been brought up for trial on 23 April and was convicted on the 30th; but he cheated the court's justice by taking poison, and died before sentence was passed. At the same time the debate on the much publicized Catholic Bill was taking place in the Irish House of Commons, culminating in its defeat on 5 May. The contrast between liberty at the hands of France as offered by Jackson and the refusal of all reform by the Irish ascendancy was drawn by many at the time, among them Arthur O'Connor, shortly to become one of the most militant of the United leaders. In his speech on the Catholic Bill, he warned that the Irish people had already imbibed many of the new ideas sweeping Europe, and after the late revelations at Jackson's trial would no longer tamely accept the 'costly venality, injury, insult, degradation and poverty which the English connection forced on them'. The *Northern Star* was more menacing, citing Locke's claim 'that the people retain the supreme power to remove or alter the legislative body when they find it acting contrary to the trust reposed in them', and presenting the solution held out by Jackson as the alternative to official tyranny.[44]

The summer and autumn of that year witnessed the worst disturbances in the country since 1793. Economic distress had sparked off the disturbances in the west, but in Ulster and Leinster they were accompanied by a more uniform and bitterly militant Defenderism.[45] It was the so-called 'Armagh

---

42. On the riots see Kent C.R.O. U840/O143/5; P.R.O.N.I. T. 3229/2/7; and *Northern Star*, II, no. 340. On the sense of bitterness at the recall, and signs that many who had been holding back in expectation of reform now became militant republicans, see MacNeven, *Pieces of Irish History*, 177, 206; and S. McSkimmin, *Annals of Ulster* (Belfast, 1849), 3.

43. P.R.O. P.R.O. 30/8/327/319, McNally's information, 30 Mar. 1795; *Northern Star*, II, nos. 342–4; and Kent C.R.O. U840/O143/6, Higgins's information, 9 Apr. 1795. T. Wyse, *Historical Sketch of the Late Catholic Association of Ireland*, 2 vols. (London, 1829), I, 137, shows that the catholics did not meet again as a body until 1805.

44. *Parl. Reg.*, xv, 208–361; *Northern Star*, II, no. 345–6, 351.

45. Kent C.R.O. U840/O144 and C212/1; I.S.P.O. 620/22/8, 19, 30–51; and P.R.O. P.R.O. 30/8/326/16–21, 42–4. See also Kerrane, 'The Background to . . . 1798', 56–60, and Hogan, 'Civil Unrest in . . . Connacht', 42–67.

Outrages' which were directly responsible for disseminating the more active and sectarian brand of Defenderism outside Ulster. The conflict between the Defenders and the protestant Peep O'Day Boys had continued intermittently throughout the 1790s. But a particularly intensive outbreak in Armagh in 1795 had pushed the upper-class protestants into alliance with the latter, and when they were upgraded to the Orange Order later that year, their intensified campaign against the catholics had the tacit sanction of the local authorities. In the purge which followed, thousands of catholics were forced to flee to other parts of the country, taking their Defenderism and their antagonism to such biased authority with them. Camden regarded intimidation on such a massive scale with dismay and for a long time was completely opposed to Orangeism. But his inability to stop local attacks without the help of the factious local gentry created the impression that the campaign against the catholics had government sanction.[46]

It was to the 'Armagh Outrages' that the United Irishmen attributed their rapid expansion after 1795. Despite the occasional twinge at Defender aspirations for a reversal of the land settlement, they found that the aims of those Defenders who now attached themselves to the United movement in great numbers accorded well with their own, and a determined campaign was mounted from 1795 onwards to unite the two movements. Plans for a new oath-bound United Irish Society had been completed by May 1795. Divisions would be limited to thirty-six to preserve secrecy, and delegates would be elected every three months to higher committees on an ascending scale from district, to baronial, to county and finally to provincial level. Every new member would be proposed by two existing members and would take the oath before all the other members. The prinicipal goal would be 'a republican government, with separation from England', and a national committee of five would provide the nucleus for this future government. The new society had not spread beyond Antrim and Down when a resolution was taken to send a delegate to France. Although many of the original United leaders were not yet involved in the new system, its members felt that an established figure would be better received in France, and they approached the former Belfast leaders, who unanimously suggested Tone. Tone arrived in Belfast on 2 May to take ship for America and accepted the 'appointment'; it was one which had already been made independently by his United colleagues in Dublin.[47]

The Dublin Society had been officially suppressed in 1794, but the Jackson

46. Elliott, 'Origins and Transformation', 424–5; P. Tohall, 'The Diamond Fight of 1795 and the Resultant Expulsions', *Seanchas Ardmhacha*, 3 (1958), 17–50; *H.M.C. Charlemont MSS.*, II, 265; and Kent C.R.O. U840/O173/1. For Camden's attitude see P.R.O. H.O. 100/64/168–72, letter to Portland, 6 Aug. 1796. There were similar attacks in Antrim and S. Down, see Hogan, 'Civil Unrest in ... Connacht', 84–7 and P.R.O.N.I. D.607/C/104^A, 143.
47. MacNeven, *Pieces of Irish History*, 100–8, 117–18, 178–9.

and Fitzwilliam episodes had injected its remnants with a new militancy. Lewins flaunted his association with Jackson and became something of a hero in the eyes of Dublin's working population. He was one of the small group of United men who recommenced meetings secretly at the Sheares's house. The others seem to have been Thomas Addis Emmet, Thomas Russell, John Keogh and Richard McCormick, and they fully endorsed Tone's plan of using his American exile as a stepping-stone to France. On arrival in Philadelphia, he was 'to wait on the French Minister, to detail to him, fully, the situation of affairs in Ireland ... to obtain a recommendation to the French Government, and ... to set off instantly for Paris, and apply, in the name of my country, for the assistance of France, to enable us to assert our independence'.[48] In Belfast Tone had seen his old United friends Samuel Neilson, William Sampson, the Simmses, the McCrackens, Dr. McDonnell and Charles Teeling. He was told of the approach by the new United societies, of the expected merger with the Defenders and the hopes of French assistance.

Thus were the different strands of discontent coming together behind the common aim of securing a French invasion. France had not directly created this republican spirit which swept through Ireland in 1795; rather the long exposure to French ideas as interpreted by Paine and the United Irishmen, the increasing signs of official immobility and the emotional atmosphere of the Fitzwilliam episode had created a climate in which Jackson's offer of French assistance seemed the only way out of the impasse. In view of the events of the past three years, the United Irishmen had been given every reason to think that France was eager to supply military assistance. This conviction that she had already committed herself to helping Ireland was to dominate Irish republican thinking for the next decade. From the outset, therefore, the Irish mission was based on a fundamental misunderstanding, for successive French ministers had taken care to avoid giving such a commitment. But the Jackson episode had also supplied the Irish government with the means of finally crushing the movement by furnishing it with the talented services of Leonard McNally. McNally was so terrified of the consequences of his association with Jackson that he sold his services to the Castle and henceforth became its most reliable and consistent source of information on United Irish developments. Indeed until 1797, when another top leader, Samuel Turner, also joined government service, Dublin's domestic intelligence system revolved largely around McNally.[49]

Jackson's mission closed the constitutional period of the United Irish

---

48. Tone, *Life*, I, 125–8; and Lewins's account in A.N. AF IV 1671 plaq. 1 fos. 99–105; for the revival in Dublin see Higgins's information of 6 and 24 June 1795 in Kent C.R.O. U840/O143/5, 10, and O147/11, and O147/4 for Tone's stay in Belfast.

49. W. J. Fitzpatrick, *Secret Service under Pitt* (Dublin, 1892), 174–210; for his first reports, see Kent C.R.O. U840/O143 and O144; I.S.P.O. 620/10/121; and P.R.O.N.I. D.607/C.

Society. The removal of Fitzwilliam and the rejection of the Catholic Relief Bill of 1795 terminated the brief honeymoon between the catholics and the government, and the two discontented elements of Irish society were left to join together. Their republicanization was not at first inevitable. But the declaration of war in 1793 had initiated a series of events which transformed the United Irishmen from a small group of radical reformers into an even smaller group of ardent republicans, and eventually into a huge insurrectionary force active throughout Ireland. The war, by effectively terminating the movement for reform and branding criticism of the authorities as semi-treasonable, erased the moderate element in the United Irish Society. Left to themselves, the radicals, conditioned by one and a half decades of opposition to English influence and several years of exaggerated support for the French, were ready to resort to more militant means. The mission of Jackson determined the character which those means were to assume and the alliance with the Defenders followed as a matter of course. The potential for rebellion was there; it only required organization. The significance of the events of 1793–95 was not that they created widespread republicanism, but that they temporarily provided existing discontent with a republican and pro-French leadership.

PART TWO

1796–1798: United Irish Embassy to France

'I am here a kind of Ambassador incognito'.

[A.N. AF IV 1671 plaq. 1 fo. 82, Tone to Clarke, 18 Jul. 1796.]

CHAPTER FOUR

1796: Tone, the Directory and Bantry Bay

The inauguration of a more stable political regime in France and the temporary agreement of Irish aspirations with French war strategy secured a favourable reception for United Irish proposals in 1796. The Directory's reputation has been blackened by a long series of able detractors; but a progressive exoneration has continued since Albert Goodwin's pioneering article of 1937.[1] In 1796 the five-man Directory was a hard-working team whose determination to re-establish order through strictly constitutional means was hampered by an apathetic population, an intractable political nation and a constitution which rendered it financially powerless. Ultimately these difficulties were to make constitutional procedure impossible; personal quarrels, political coups, nullified elections and a mercenary foreign policy characterized its final years. But in 1796, at a time when expansionism was not yet a part of French war policy, when Directors like La Revellière brought to the regime surviving traces of republican internationalism, and Carnot an intense hatred of England, the Irish republicans could still expect a fair hearing.

Tone was sensible enough to recognize that appeals to the principles of fraternity were outmoded. Instead the material and diplomatic gains which the French and Irish might win in co-operation against a common enemy were carefully rehearsed. As an exercise in secret diplomacy, United Irish tactics in the years 1796–97 were impressive. The early United Irish negotiat-

---

1. A. Goodwin, 'The French Executive Directory—a re-evaluation', *History*, XXII (1937), 201–18. The first works to study the Directory at length were invariably hostile; see e.g. L. Sciout, *Le Directoire*, 4 vols. (Paris, 1895); A. Sorel, *L'Europe et la Révolution Française*, V; and A. C. Thibaudeau, *Mémoires sur la Convention et le Directoire*, 2 vols. (Paris, 1824), II. Mildly revisionist were R. Guyot, *Le Directoire et la Paix de l'Europe* (Paris, 1911), the work of J. Godechot and G. Lefebvre, and most recently D. Woronoff, *La République bourgeoise* (Paris, 1972). Recent historians tend to adopt a more favourable approach, see e.g. I. Woloch, *Jacobin Legacy: the democratic movement under the Directory* (Princeton, 1970); S. T. Ross, 'The Military Strategy of the Directory: the Campaigns of 1799', *F.H.S.*, V (1967), 170–87; C. H. Church, 'In Search of the Directory', in *French Government and Society 1500–1850. Essays in Memory of Alfred Cobban*, ed. J. F. Bosher (London, 1973), 261–94; M. Lyons, *France Under the Directory* (Cambridge, 1975); and C. Lucas, 'The Directory and the Rule of Law', *F.H.S.* X (1978), 231–60.

Plate 10. Theobald
Wolfe Tone in French
Uniform (after a portrait
by Charlotte Sampson
Tone in Tone, *Life*)

ors in Paris considered themselves the courted party and there was little of
that humble pleading for assistance, or that nagging urgency which the
French found so tiresome in their successors. United Irish negotiations with
France were to achieve their greatest success in 1796. The recent memory of
those unsolicited promises of help from Oswald and Jackson and the social
stature and political expertise of the Irish agents endowed the negotiations
with an air of confident professionalism which commanded respect. Much
of the appeal of Tone's autobiographical *Life* comes from his exaggerated
sense of modesty, his disarming naïvety and ability to laugh at his own
weaknesses. But this personal account of the Irish negotiations with France
can mislead. Such doubts are absent from his official correspondence
with the French authorities; rather there is a fixity of purpose, a firm grasp
of detail and an air of confidence in the attractiveness of the Irish proposals.

As an example of wishful thinking and misinformation, however, the early
Irish negotiators in Paris fell into the same category as the minority patriot

groups who sought French help throughout the revolutionary wars and progressively reduced their own plausibility by exaggerating the revolutionary potential of their compatriots. No full restructuring of the United Irish Society had taken place before Tone's departure from Ireland, and fewer than a dozen leaders were responsible for inaugurating negotiations with France. For the next three years United Irish high politics took precedence over internal organization and remained in the hands of a professional elite from the eastern seaboard counties. They were secret diplomats rather than national leaders, with little first-hand experience of popular Irish aspirations, and their accounts of the Irish situation were too often dictated by an ideal of enlightened revolution rather than by any reference to Irish realities.

I

Tone had arrived in Philadelphia in August 1795, justifiably amazed at the Irish government's short-sightedness in thus permitting him access to a French minister on neutral territory. Encouraged by Rowan and Reynolds, who had taken refuge in America, he called upon Adet, the French ambassador there, on 9 August. But he was surprised at his lukewarm reception. Adet promised to forward to France a short memoir on the situation in Ireland, but rejected any suggestion that Tone should himself travel to the Continent. The truth was that Adet suspected Tone of being a British spy, and only transmitted his memoir in October, after having satisfied himself to the contrary. In November, when Tone received a letter from Russell, Keogh and the Simmses, urging him to fulfil his engagement of travelling to France, he returned to find Adet more responsive. Tone's claims had been upheld by the other Irish exiles in Philadelphia, and Adet was now convinced that an independence movement was organizing in Ireland. Tone arrived in France on 1 February 1796, secured a coach passage to Paris on the 10th, and finally arrived there two days later. Rowan's correspondence with Madgett, detailing the information brought by Tone from Ireland, had already predisposed the Directory in his favour, and within two days of his arrival he had a profitable audience with the French Foreign Minister, Charles Delacroix.[2]

The Directory had continued its predecessors' policies towards foreign dissidents, and they were normally encouraged to show their hand by rising before France would lend support. At a working breakfast with Tone on 18 February, Madgett, to whom Delacroix had delegated the Irish nego-

2. See Tone, *Life*, I, 131–5, and 283–4, 289–93 for the text of the letters sent from Belfast in Sept. 1795; and A.A.E. Corr. Pol. Ang. 589 fos. 23–4, 111–15 for French correspondence concerning Tone and Rowan.

Map 3. Paris in the 1790s (1792 map, British Library)

1. Place Vendôme—Lewins's address 1799
2. Jacobins
3. Rue Vivienne—Hôtel des Étrangers, Tone's address 1796
4. Palais Royal
5. Rue Croix-des-Petits-Champs—White's Hotel 1792
6. Rue Saint Honoré—O'Connor's address 1804
7. Hôtel de Ville
8. Quai Malaquet (or Malaquais)—Ministry of Police
9. Rue du Colombier—United Irish Committee 1798
10. Rue des Cordeliers—Duckett's address June 1796—renamed rue de l'École-de-Médecine, United Irish Committee-room 1799
11. Palais du Luxembourg—seat of the Directory
12. Rue de Vaugirard—General Clarke's bureau
13. Rue de Cherche-Midi—Thomas Addis Emmet's address 1803
14. Rue du Bac—Ministry of Foreign Affairs
15. Rue de Varenne—War Ministry
16. Rue de Grenelle—Interior Ministry
17. Rue Notre-Dame-des-Champs—Tone's address 1798
18. Irish College

tiations, raised the possibility of the Irish rising before the French invaded the country. Tone was indignant: 'I told him most certainly not; that if a landing were once effected, everything would follow instantly ... that if 20,000 French were in Ireland, we should in a month have an army of 100,000, 200,000, or, ... 300,000 men, but that the *point d'appui* was indispensable ... and if that was not effected, the people would not move, unless in local riots and insurrections, which would end in the destruction of the ringleaders.' Tone demanded the appointment of a famous French general to the Irish expedition. Upon arrival, he was to issue proclamations guaranteeing property and renouncing all idea of conquest, and he was to conclude an offensive and defensive alliance with the native leaders.[3] These were hefty demands from a stripling diplomat. What advantages could he offer in return?

Tone claimed that the overwhelming majority of the Irish people and many of the gentry were anti-English; they were deterred from rebelling only by insufficient military expertise, but would rise to join a French invasion force; and since the majority of the militia were sworn Defenders the rising would be certain to succeed. Ireland liberated would deprive England of her main source of recruits and force her out of the war. French officials were sceptical about the revolutionary commitment of the Irish catholics; Tone never quite managed to remove their reservations, and the United Irishmen were later accused of exaggeration. Tone was certainly misleading in his denial of religious conflict in Ireland; but it was a genuine delusion of most United leaders, nurtured on the reformism of the 1780s and early 1790s, and the bitter sectarianism exported from south Ulster by the Defenders and the Orangemen had post-dated Tone's departure. His belief in the widespread disaffection of the catholic population was common among the protestant establishment, of which Tone, after all, was a member. The persistent refusal of French officials to credit this republican transformation of a nation which they had always believed to be staunchly Jacobite and royalist led Tone to over-emphasize his claims.[5] But the Directory should by now have been sufficiently practised in negotiating with other patriot groups to have divested his account of its inevitable polemic. A recurring weakness in the Directory's war policy was its tendency to snatch at the

3. For Tone's claims and early negotiations see Tone, *Life*, II, 14–77, 181–204; A.N. AF III 64 doss. 264, AF III 186[b] doss. 857 and BB[4] 103 fos. 135–44.
4. For the accusations that Tone misled the French see *Report from the Committee of Secrecy of the House of Commons* [*Ireland*] (Dublin, 1798), 15; Teeling, *Observations on the '... Battle of the Diamond'* 8–13; R. Kee, *The Green Flag* (London, 1972), 80, 132; W. B. Kennedy, 'French Projects for the Invasion of Ireland 1796–8', (Univ. of Georgia Ph.D. thesis 1966), 55–7.
5. Tone, *Life*, II, 49–53, 57–8, 92–3, and A.H.G. B[11]1, Tone's observations on instructions for a secret agent to Ireland. Tone clearly failed to remove French scepticism on this point, see A.N. AF III 186[b] doss. 858, Hoche's letter of 16 Jul. 1796, and A. Debidour, *Recueil des actes du Directoire exécutif*, 4 vols. (Paris, 1910–17), II, 489–91.

most attractive of alternative means of weakening an enemy, with little thought of the effects it might have on overall strategy. In the case of Ireland a peak of self-delusion was attained, as France sought to deal a mortal blow to England's war plans with the minimum of effort on her own part. Tone was shocked at the lack of care taken to forewarn the Irish of French plans. He was conscious of his increasing removal from home developments and repeatedly urged the Directory to establish some means of communication with Ireland.

The process by which Ireland was incorporated into the Directory's campaign against England sheds much light on its general war policy. Early commentators like Sorel claimed that the Directory had consciously perpetuated the war to provision and occupy its armies and ambitious generals and to fill its coffers with requisitions and indemnities extorted from enemy territories. Whilst the policies of the second Directory might have occasionally conformed to such a pattern, it is not equally applicable to the first Directory which fell in September 1797. In 1796 the Directors could not have perpetuated war for war's sake against the prevailing atmosphere of public pacifism to which they themselves subscribed. Peace had become a panacea to terminate France's crises of subsistence and finance and to destroy its domestic enemies, royalist and Jacobin alike.[6] But the Directory could see too many conflicting schemes for attaining this double package of external peace and internal stability, and frequently diluted their efficacy by pursuing several simultaneously. In addition, insufficient control over civil and military personnel permitted underlings to propagate their own pet schemes, and the vacuum left by indecisiveness or disagreement at the centre was quickly filled by ambitious generals like Bonaparte. At the beginning of 1796 the Directory could have destroyed the coalition against France by a concentrated attack on either Austria or England. Reubell, the Director charged with the conduct of foreign policy, would have preferred the former. His Alsatian background and his commitment to a natural frontier policy dictated a preference for concentrating French forces on the Rhine, rather than squandering them in unpredictable naval ventures. England was wrong in her belief that Reubell was her most dangerous protagonist within the French executive; his belligerency stopped at the Rhine.[7] It was rather Carnot who sought an all-out war against England.

6. See e.g. Sorel, *L'Europe et la Révolution Française*, v, 12–13; Sciout, *Le Directoire*, ii, 228–48. But see P. Sagnac, *Le Rhin Français pendant la Révolution et l'Empire* (Paris, 1917), 110–14, on efforts to restrain troop requisitions and Goodwin, 'The French Executive Directory', 211–12. See also A. Aulard, *Paris pendant la réaction thermidorienne et sous le Directoire*, 5 vols. (Paris, 1898–1902), iii, 169, 191, 256–8, 328, 339, 341, 361, 367, 497–9, on popular pre-occupation with peace in 1796.

7. Biro, *The German Policy of Revolutionary France*, i, 378, ii, 491–2, 508; B. Nabonne, *La Diplomatie du Directoire et Bonaparte d'après les papiers inédits de Reubell* (Paris, 1951), 42–58. On England's fears of Reubell see P.R.O. F.O. 27/47, memoir of Apr. 1796 and F.O. 27/50, Malmesbury's despatches of Jul.–Aug. 1797.

Plate 11. Public Audience by the Directors in the Luxembourg (Mansell Collection)

Carnot's anglophobia, like that of Hoche, had been fashioned by involvement with the counter-revolution in the west of France. England's promotion of civil war in France had made her the one exception to French popular pacifism, and in the first months of Tone's mission there was a real, if uneasy, consensus on plans for an offensive against England. Prior to his arrival, the Directory had already agreed to attack England as soon as the rebels in the west had been crushed. Funds had been earmarked to send secret missions to Britain and Hoche was commander designate of an expedition to be sent against some undecided part of British territory.[8] Tone's timely arrival decided its destination as Ireland, and on 19 June preparations for an Irish expedition were officially inaugurated.[9] But Tone's negotiations had not run smoothly; a lack of clarity on the terms to be granted to the Irish republicans, and a sense that Ireland was being used in a tug-of-war between competing officials, detracted from his sense of triumph.

At an early stage in the negotiations Tone had sensed some kind of competition between the officials involved. Frustrated by the slowness of negotiations conducted through the medium of Madgett, he had by-passed the Foreign Ministry, and with a forwardness which astonished even himself had taken matters directly to Carnot. On 24 February, Tone walked from his lodgings

8. M. Reinhard, *Le Grand Carnot*, 2 vols. (Paris, 1950), II, 216–20; see A. Sorel, 'Les Vues de Hoche', *Revue de Paris*, IV (Jul.–Aug. 1895), 232. A.N. AF III 337 doss. 1470 fos. 1–3, arrêté of 26 Dec. 1795. See also E. Desbrière, *Projets et tentatives de débarquement aux îles britanniques*, 4 vols. (Paris, 1900–2) I, 57–69.

9. Debidour, *Recueil des actes*, II, 660–2; A.H.G. B¹¹1, the Directory to Hoche, 19 Jun. 1796 and the arrêté of 21 Jul. 1796.

in the rue Vivienne to the Luxembourg, rehearsing en route the argument
he intended putting to the Director. It was Carnot's day for public audience,
but a word from one of the clerks on Tone's behalf secured a private hearing.
Half a dozen others had been accorded the same privilege 'personnages . . .
like myself, of great distinction', mused Tone as he let the others go first to
ensure maximum privacy for his own audience. Inside Carnot's chamber,
after some initial embarrassment at having to explain himself in French, Tone
outlined the situation in Ireland and the purpose of his mission. Then with
unreserved frankness he told of his negotiations with the Foreign Affairs
Ministry and of his disappointment that matters of such importance should
have been entrusted to 'a mere commis' like Madgett.[10]

Tone considered such backbiting justified by the urgency of his mission;
but it was symptomatic of his inexperience in the early stages of his negotiations, it betrayed his ignorance of the state of French high politics and only
served to exacerbate relations between the different groupings. Carnot's
control of the conduct of war under the Committee of Public Safety had been
a poor training for the moderate regime of the Directory. At first he readily
conformed to the practice of presenting despatches for the approval of his
colleagues and of securing a general consensus on policy before acting. But he
was caught in a conflict between efficient habit and democratic propriety.
He was as eager as his colleagues for peace, but his former training dictated
total war against an enemy to secure that peace and entailed frequent incursions into the preserve of Foreign Affairs. His mounting impatience at the
way in which foreign policy was handled by Reubell and Delacroix quickly
dissolved his initial constitutionalism. Within the Directory his only real
supporter was the ineffectual and visionary Letourneur, and his isolation was
intensified by his own irascibility, aloofness and increasing conservatism.[11]
It was to Carnot's declining fortunes that Tone had nailed the Irish cause when
he succeeded in transferring Irish affairs almost entirely to the War Ministry.
Tone's account of his negotiations with Delacroix and Madgett fuelled
Carnot's anger at the inefficiency of Foreign Affairs. Madgett had been
puffing up his own importance by revealing too much information to Tone,
and Delacroix smarted at Carnot's reprimand for such laxity. Foreign
Affairs had long been notorious for inefficiency, disloyalty and financial
wastefulness; but it is difficult not to detect an element of party conflict
behind Carnot's attack on these breaches of security, for which Delacroix
was not entirely responsible. Madgett's tongue-wagging and bouts of drunken-
ness posed a real threat to the Directory's policy against England, and he

10. Tone, *Life*, ii, 28 and 25–31.
11. T. Aubin, 'Le rôle politique de Carnot, depuis les élections de germinal an V jusqu'au coup
d'État du 18 fructidor', *A.h.R.f.*, no. 49 (1932), 37–51 and M. Martin, 'Les journaux militaires
de Carnot', *A.h.R.f.*, no. 229 (1977), 404–28.

had already leaked information on the Irish expedition to Richard Cadman Etches, then British agent in charge of the prisoner-of-war exchange programme.[12]

When Tone next called on Carnot on 14 March, he was introduced to General Clarke, a second-generation Irishman at the head of the *Cabinet Topographique et Géographique* in the War Ministry, and Carnot's chief disciple there. Tone chafed at having thus been handed over once again to a 'subaltern'. But as Clarke directed him through various corridors lined with bulging boxes labelled, '*Armée du Nord*', '*Armée du Rhin*' and so on, Tone's opinion changed. He quickly came to recognize Clarke as Carnot's mouthpiece, and although he maintained contact with Foreign Affairs, his relationship with Madgett lacked its former seriousness of purpose.

But Clarke held some very unusual opinions on Ireland which shocked Tone out of his naïve belief that France recognized the intrinsic merits of an independent Irish republic. Opinions formed during French negotiations with the Irish Jacobites persisted. Clarke for instance was convinced that the Irish catholics would prefer a Stuart monarch to a republican government, and that members of the Irish ascendancy, even Fitzgibbon, would support such a restoration. 'Flat nonsense', thought Tone. The Duke of Leinster 'being a good Irishman' might conceivably 'join the people' after the outbreak of revolution; but as for Fitzgibbon, who had cried out for Tone's blood after the Jackson episode, Fitzgibbon with his principles, property and situation, Tone thought such a suggestion so preposterous that it scarcely merited a reply. He managed to represent the foolishness of both ideas to Clarke, but failed to remove another of which Carnot, Clarke and a good many others remained firmly convinced.[13]

After the civil war in the west of France was subdued in the course of 1795, there was a widespread desire among Frenchmen to inflict on Britain the same devastation which she had helped promote in France. The ferocious and endemic banditry of the groups of peasants, brigands and deserters in the royalist-promoted *chouannerie* was particularly resented, and in 1793 Hoche had suggested promoting a *chouannerie* in Britain. The idea gathered strength after June 1795, when English ships landed a force of French royalists at Quiberon Bay in Brittany; and when Tone first learnt of the project in April 1796, Carnot and Hoche had already initiated preparations for a secret expedition to England under General Humbert. Convicts, prisoners of war, and a multitude of other unsavoury elements of which France wished to be rid, were pouring into the western ports to form 'special corps, composed of ex-chouans ... disruptive elements from the French army ... the scum

12. See P.R.O. F.O. 27/47, Etches's report of 25 Apr. 1796; see also Masson, *Le Départment des Affaires Étrangères*, 3.
13. Tone, *Life*, II, 49–53.

Plate 12. General Clarke
(Bibliothèque Nationale)

of the Republic ... [and] a corps of 12 to 1500 convicts taken from the
Brittany prisons'.[14] In the Paris cafés, reported the Minister of Police in
June, ' ... they have but one desire as far as England is concerned, her
total destruction, ... if the French government seeks revenge, it should
cast all our conspirators, our Jacobins, our supporters of the 1793 Constitution
... onto the English coasts and urge them to exercise all their anarchical
and revolutionary talent in that island'.[15] The establishment of a *chouannerie*
in Britain was to become an obsession with Carnot; and when the bad press
given to these social dregs assembling for Humbert's expedition alienated
his colleagues and tarnished the idea of a French-sponsored *chouannerie*,
Carnot secretly continued to promote his pet scheme. During his term as
president of the Directory in the summer of 1796, he acted with a remarkable
degree of independence, and his projects invariably suffered on discovery.[16]

14. A.H.G. MR 501, Armée de l'Ouest ... Expédition d'Irlande, undated order.
15. Aulard, *Paris ... sous le Directoire*, III, 258. For further details of plans to establish a *chouannerie*
see Desbrière, *Projets et Tentatives*, I, 61–9; Debidour, *Recueil des actes*, II, 176–8; A.N. AF IV
1671 plaq. 1 fo. 65; and P.R.O. F.O. 27/44 and F.O. 74/18/67.
16. For Carnot's personal involvement see Debidour, *Recueil des actes*, II, 688 and A.N. AF III
57 doss. 227. For similar activities in other countries see Biro, *The German Policy of Revolutionary
France*, II, 610–15 and I.S.P.O. 620/29/60.

The increased flow of information on the Irish Defenders encouraged Carnot to think that Ireland might become England's Vendée. Clarke raised the matter with Tone on 2 April. He explained how the Directory planned to distract and embarrass the Irish government by landing a band of 'blackguards' in the country prior to the main invasion force. Tone objected that such a scheme would merely produce localized insurrections, which would be easily suppressed before the main invasion attempt. Every man of property, fearful of indiscriminate plunder, would scurry to the protection of government and an excuse would be provided to reduce Ireland to such a state of military and political subjection that any future revolutionary attempt would be impossible. 'I cannot blame France', he wrote in his diary that evening, 'for wishing to retaliate on England, the abomination of La Vendée and the Chouans, but it is hard that it should be at the expense of poor Ireland. It will be she and not England that will suffer, and the English will be glad of it, for they hate us next to the French ... Poor Pat! I fear he is just now in a bad neighbourhood.' Tone did not relish this 'horrible mode of war' in England either. It proved a constant irritant in his relations with Clarke; by the end of April he had decided that he did not much like the fellow after all, and had once more gravitated towards Delacroix and Madgett.

By then the novelty of Paris had worn off and Tone was becoming increasingly frustrated at the apparent lack of progress in his negotiations. Carnot and Clarke seemed determined to tell him as little as possible, though he had heard rumours that preparations for an Irish expedition had actually commenced. The bungling inefficiency of the Foreign Affairs Ministry, where his memoranda were periodically lost by Madgett or his fellow translators, intensified his exasperation. Inactivity, conscious isolation from other English-speaking exiles, and disgust at Parisian frivolity made him pine for his wife and family. He was forced to move into cheaper lodgings, and by mid-June had only sufficient finance for another month. He had not heard from Ireland since the previous November, although he had consistently represented the urgency of despatching an agent from France to the United Irish leaders. Delacroix and Clarke were searching for a suitable candidate, but Tone considered their recommendations an insult. Duckett he unjustly dismissed as a scoundrel because of an insignificant incident at their first encounter, which Tone interpreted as a ruse by Duckett to encourage disclosures. His patience snapped when an Irish Capuchin friar called Fitzsimons was proposed. Tone's inherent anti-clericalism bristled at the thought of introducing a priest into the business, especially when Fitzsimons saw an Irish revolution as a means of restoring the forfeited catholic lands. Recognizing that he would have little say in the matter, Tone seized upon a trifling incident in which Fitzsimons was supposed to have revealed his stupidity by asking if letters lately intercepted to the Portuguese minister in Rio de Janeiro were in English, to work himself into something of a frenzy about the idiocy of sending such a 'blockhead' to Ireland.

How can I explain myself to such a damned dunce, or intrust the
safety of my friends, not to speak of the measure itself, to a blockhead
that has not sense enough to keep his mouth shut, or count five on his
fingers? ... Is not this most terribly provoking, for it seems to be a thing
settled, that he shall go ... I objected, all along, to priests, as the worst
of all possible agents, and here is one who is the worst of all possible
priests ... If he goes to Ireland, the people there will suppose that we
are laughing at them ... I suppose he will talk Portuguese to the Irish,
by way of keeping the secret .. At all events, I will not communicate
with him, 'that's flat'.[17]

Tone need not have been so upset; Carnot and Clarke had no intention of
appointing one of Delacroix's discoveries, nor for that matter of confiding
the final identity of the agent to Tone. Initially Eugene Aherne, a physician
and a seasoned agent from Madgett's circle, was chosen in April to fulfil
the mission, apparently with the agreement of all concerned. Aherne had
only recently returned from a successful mission to Scotland, and Tone was
to see a good deal of him in the next few months, having taken lodgings in
the same house. Tone acted as chief adviser for his planned mission. In
particular he gave Aherne a list of people to contact which included John
Keogh, Richard McCormick, Thomas Russell, Charles Teeling, Robert
Simms, Samuel Neilson, Oliver Bond, William J. MacNeven, and possibly
Thomas Addis Emmet. But April, May and June passed by with no sign of
Aherne's imminent departure.[18]

Towards the end of May another agent, Richard O'Shee, Clarke's cousin,
had been substituted. Although Delacroix was told of the substitution, the
excuse used was that Tone and Aherne were by now too closely associated.
The agent must produce information entirely independently of Tone, and
Delacroix was again reprimanded for releasing details about the Directory's
intentions to Tone. Delacroix complied with orders to conceal information
on O'Shee's mission and neither Tone, Aherne nor Madgett ever discovered
the substitution.[19] O'Shee was instructed to study the organization of the
Defenders, to discover if they consisted of catholics only or if they were in
alliance with the northern presbyterians; to see what kind of government
they sought; if a monarchy (which from the general tenor of the instructions
the Directory still believed), to suggest that France would find a Stuart
claimant; if they preferred an Irish Lord he was to become acquainted with
their candidate and urge on him the advantages of a French alliance. He

17. Tone, *Life*, II, 80–5, 98–9.
18. Tone, *Life*, II, 90–141; also A.N. AF III 186[b] doss. 859, Madgett to Clarke, 30 Aug. 1796;
and A.A.E. Presonnel 1re sér. I. fos. 264–8; and A.N. BB[3] 107 fos. 180–90 for Aherne's career.
19. A.A.E. Corr. Pol. Ang. 589 fos. 259–62 and A.N. AF III 57 doss. 224 fos. 7–9 for Delacroix's
and Carnot's correspondence, May–Jun. 1796.

JEAN REWBEL

*Député des Districts de Colmar
et Schelestat à l'Assemblée Nationale en 1789.*

A Paris, chez L'AUTEUR, Quay des Angulins, Nº 71. au 5º

CARNOT.

B.R

Revellière Lépeaux.

Revellière Lépeaux

M. Paul . BARRAS.

*Membre du Directoire Exécutif.
Né à Foxempheux, près Barjols, dépt. du Var. le 26 j. 1765.*

Place Rue du Théatre Français Nº 4

Plates 13–16. The Directors Reubell, Carnot, La Revellière-Lépeaux and Barras (Bibliothèque Nationale)

was to contact the Defender chiefs, promise at least 10,000 French soldiers and arms for 20,000 more; these would arrive in the north or north-west of Ireland, and the Irish would be expected to rise simultaneously. Finally he was to establish communication routes with France through Cadiz, Copenhagen, Hamburg, Stockholm and Amsterdam. Despite appearances, these instructions were not a sign that the Directory mistrusted Tone's claims. Tone had represented the Defenders as the largest revolutionary group in Ireland, but claimed that an alliance had taken place between them and the presbyterians (the United Irishmen) and that he represented both in consequence. Moreover, his comments on Aherne's instructions were incorporated into those issued to O'Shee.[20]

Carnot wanted O'Shee to discover the names of the chief Defenders from Tone, but in the presence of Delacroix, to prevent O'Shee communicating the details of his mission to Tone. There is no sign that any such audience ever took place. Was there an element of sabotage in Delacroix's non-compliance? Delacroix was certainly bitter at the way in which he had been by-passed by Carnot and Clarke in current negotiations with Austria, and they now threatened to do the same over Ireland. He knew little of foreign affairs on taking office, though he was a passionate supporter of Reubell's Rhineland policies and has consequently been dismissed as the Director's lap-dog. But Delacroix liked the trappings and power of office and resented decisions on foreign affairs being taken over his head, especially by other departments. His action in this case typified the excessive individualism which so weakened the Directory. There was little sense of corporate spirit among ministers, and a destructive unilateralism percolated down through the lower levels of their departments. 'Every man here must do everything himself,' Tone had complained, and the secretiveness, competition and lack of co-operation, even between officials in the same department, had shocked him.[21] Delacroix had begun to take quite a personal interest in the Irish business, and the substitution of O'Shee for Aherne had savoured too much of party rivalry to be accepted lightly, especially when his own position had so recently been threatened by Carnot's attempt to replace him.[22] There was little Delacroix could do openly to challenge Carnot's actions; but in matters of secret service he could act with a certain degree of independence, and it is here that the destructive conflict between the component parts of the central machine can best be analyzed.

In the context of the search for a suitable agent for Ireland, there was

20. A.N. AF III 186ᵇ doss. 859, instructions to O'Shee, undated. A.H.G. B¹¹1, 'Observations sur les Instructions delivrées', by Tone; A.N. AF III 57 doss. 224 fo. 7, Delacroix to Clarke, 30 May 1796.

21. Tone, *Life*, II, 38, 90–91.

22. See Biro, *The German Policy of Revolutionary France*, II, 496–7, 610–12; and A.A.E. Corr. Pol. Ang. 589 fos. 241–5 and 264–5 for Delacroix's intense interest in Irish affairs.

already something decidedly suspicious about the instructions issued by Delacroix to Jean Mengaud in April 1796. His mission to England and Scotland to report on public opinion and on the state of the economy had received official Directory backing. His instructions, however, concentrate on Ireland, with similar queries on the Defenders to those later issued to O'Shee.[23] But the main culprit in this practice of sending double and frequently conflicting missions was Carnot. Not satisfied with the despatch of Mengaud to England in April, Carnot sent his own private emissary there in June. The appointment of Jean Berthonneau was a product of Carnot's determination to proceed with plans for an English *chouannerie*. In choosing Berthonneau, a young Bordeaux merchant recommended by a friend, Carnot stepped outside normal intelligence procedure. The Foreign Ministry tended to appoint agents to English missions from a pool of professionals who had performed similar missions in the past, and Delacroix had already rejected Berthonneau's services in January.[24] Ostensibly Berthonneau was to report on *émigré* activities in Hamburg, and as such his mission was financed from the Foreign Ministry's secret service funds. But Delacroix never actually saw the secret instructions drawn up by Clarke and Carnot.

These instructions are quite astonishing and survive as a monument to the intense bitterness caused in France by England's involvement in the Vendée. Berthonneau was to create as much havoc in England through the medium of internal dissidents as England had done in France. He was to establish a network of agents throughout the country, using the militants in the popular societies to organize sporadic revolts. Prisoners were to be liberated and used to fire arsenals and ships in port. Popular antipathy towards the *émigrés* was to be fanned; popular discontent at bread shortages, food prices, low wages and various other grievances was to be used to turn workers against their employers, servants against their masters and students against their tutors. The Irish immigrants would supply the principal agents for this promotion of internal havoc, in much the same way as the royalists had done in France, and Humbert would land an advanced guard to help establish the nucleus of Carnot's cherished *chouannerie*. Berthonneau's work in England, Humbert's landing, Hoche's invasion of Ireland, a joint invasion of England by Hoche and the liberated Irish—a Quiberon in reverse—were the components of Carnot's scheme to destroy the English enemy.

From the outset the fate of the mission became entangled with the political divisions in France. Normally arrangements for the onward travel of a secret agent from Hamburg would have been made through the resident French minister, on instructions from the Minister of Foreign Affairs. When Berthon-

23. For Mengaud see A.A.E. Corr. Pol. Ang. 589 fo. 215; 591 fos. 174–88; Corr. Pol. Ham. 109 fo. 262; and Personnel, Arrêtés et Décrets 8 fo. 83.

24. A.A.E. Personnel 1^{re}sér. 8 fos. 104–40.

neau arrived in Hamburg, however, he found no funds, no passport, and the French minister in official retirement at Altona because of a dispute between France and the Hamburg Senate. Bewildered at finding no further instructions, Berthonneau lingered in Hamburg beyond the eighteen days prescribed by his instructions and quickly became the dupe of the city's professional spies. Hamburg, as Europe's main neutral seaport, had attracted a sizeable body of freelance agents. Many were French *émigrés*, feeding off England's ready munificence in matters of foreign intelligence, or seeking to ingratiate themselves with France as a preliminary to eventual repatriation. In Berthonneau's case their task was facilitated by the action of Delacroix, who had discovered the duplicity of Clarke and Carnot, and retaliated by sending a package through the open post to Berthonneau, clearly labelled 'Government Agents'. In view of Delacroix's subsequent efforts to disrupt the mission, this failure to use a special messenger can scarcely be dismissed as an oversight. In addition he ordered Jean Colleville, one of his own agents in Hamburg, to accompany Berthonneau to England, and to report back on his activities. In London Colleville informed the royalist agent Dutheil of Berthonneau's mission. But he secured a promise that no arrests would be made, and thereby dispelled Berthonneau's suspicions that he was a British spy. Berthonneau used Colleville as a courier to carry despatches to Clarke; but many found their way instead to Delacroix. Only the first two ever reached Clarke, and Berthonneau's sense of isolation intensified as his appeals for instructions and funds went unheard. He made an attempt to contact the English democrats, but lack of funds forced him to reveal his mission to some London creditors. His fears of betrayal grew apace, and he was in hiding with his English brother-in-law in London when he was eventually recalled at the end of that year. His return was an embarrassment to Carnot, and he was snubbed.[25]

The incident further cooled relations between Foreign Affairs and Carnot's supporters, but it was only at a later date that Carnot's freelancing in the campaign against England began to tarnish the Irish project in the eyes of his colleagues. In the summer of 1796, when an uneasy peace still reigned on the Continent, when there was an excess of restless generals and soldiers in the French interior, and the opportunity was presented of putting England out of the war, government support for the Irish expedition was unanimous. On 19 June the Directory had outlined its strategy for forcing England to make peace. A fleet would sail to the West Indies in August, landing 5,000 troops in Ireland en route; a further 6,000 French and 5,000 Dutch soldiers would

25. For Berthonneau's and Colleville's mission see A.H.G. B¹¹1, instructions of [Feb. 1796]; A.N. AF III 51ᵃ doss. 188 pᶜᵉˢ 76, 83–4; AF III 59 doss. 230–1; AF III 186ᵇ doss. 859; and A.A.E. Corr. Pol. Ham. 110–12.; Corr. Pol. Ang. 589 fos. 288–9, 398, and 590 fo. 287; also Mem. et Doc. Fonds Bourbon 590 fos. 254–5; P.R.O. F.O. 27/51–2 and F.O. 33/12/51.

arrive in Ireland in September and smaller forces under Generals Humbert and Quantin would land simultaneously in Wales and south-west England. The following day Hoche was made commander of the Irish expedition. Carnot was triumphant: 'Citizen General, the executive Directory has made known to you its views on Ireland which we wish to separate from England. As for myself, I see in the success of this operation the downfall of our most irreconcilable and most dangerous enemy. I see in it a guarantee of French repose for centuries to come.'[26] Carnot was still mesmerized by the idea of Ireland as England's Vendée; he could never quite see the conflict between his vision of Ireland as a dumping ground for French trouble-makers and his genuine desire to help the Irish republicans, and the June plans were consequently full of incongruities. The Dutch contingent was to be composed of foreign deserters and clothed in uniforms captured from the English at Quiberon. Hoche's force would include a thousand convicts, and by the end of the summer Humbert's *chouan* force, originally destined for England, was also attached.[27]

However, French plans for the future government of a liberated Ireland also show that the havoc envisaged by Carnot was to be limited in its application. France also wanted Ireland as an ally in the final conflict against England. The problems of reconciling a *chouannerie* with the promotion of an ally's prosperity were not yet apparent and many of Tone's recommendations were incorporated into the instructions issued to Hoche on 19 July. Hoche was to establish a republican form of government with an elective convention and an executive composed of the members of the catholic committee and 'l' assemblée de l'union' (an indication of France's continuing lack of clarity about the United Irishmen). Although no sympathy would be shown to the protestant aristocracy and clergy, disruption would be minimized, and civil officials would not be removed where possible. But the religious issue still worried the French. It had been the main point of discussion when Hoche and Tone finally met in Paris on 12 July, and the instructions of the 19th re-stated French fears. France would have preferred the establishment of some form of natural religion; but Ireland seemed ill-prepared for such a departure, and toleration and equal status for all existing religions were prescribed instead. If the Irish insisted on a monarchical form of government, the candidate should be Irish, catholic and firmly opposed to England. In return the Irish would be expected to form a powerful navy, to help in an invasion of England, and to grant favourable terms to French commerce. On the whole Tone

---

26. Debidour, *Recueil des actes*, II, 688–9, and see note 9.
27. For the continuing preparations for a *chouan*-like project see A.D.S.M. Papiers Hoche, 1 Mi 54/97/1096, 1 Mi 57/123/1544, 1 Mi 59/135/1760 and 1 Mi 60/139/1842; A.N. AF III 186ᵇ doss. 859, AF III 377 doss. 1900 fos. 1–2, AF III 437 doss. 2527; and A.H.G. B¹¹1 and MR 501.

would have found little to query in such modest proposals, though he remained
as ignorant of French plans for Ireland after his meeting with Hoche as he
had done before. Even the caution clause, granting ultimate control of
government to France while her soldiers remained in the country, did not
pose any immediate threat to Irish independence at a time when the creation
of satellite states was not yet a part of French policy.[28]

But the Italian campaign was already changing the character of the
Directory's war policy. The huge requisitions made in Italy were not ordered
by the Directory, but the percentage transmitted to Paris came first as a
welcome, then as an essential lifeline to liberate the executive from the para-
lysing clutches of the legislative councils and from a continuing domestic
financial crisis. By his trail of victories, Bonaparte had already raised the
campaign in southern Europe to a place of greater importance in France's
war strategy than Carnot had originally intended, and both he and Hoche
looked anxiously in that direction as the Irish plans took shape, the latter
probably now regretting his refusal of the Italian position when offered it
by Carnot the previous December.[29] Reubell alone among the Directors
had the courage to pull their recalcitrant generals into line; and there is
much truth in Sorel's claim that the Directory was sometimes governed
by its generals. Carnot was happy enough to allow his generals freedom of
action, once he felt he could trust them, and the process was preceded by a
voluminous correspondence in which flattery alternated with reminders
of the debt they owed to him as their promoter. In the spring and summer of
1796 both Hoche and Bonaparte were exposed to such treatment, and Hoche
knew it. A bitter rivalry had grown up between himself and Bonaparte,
which deepened after Austria broke the armistice in July, marched into the
Rhineland, and at one stroke transferred the main concentration of military
effort from the north-west to the eastern and south-eastern frontiers.[30]
William Wickham, Britain's minister to Switzerland, claimed that Austria's
action alone prevented an Irish invasion that summer;[31] and as troops,
finance, and the Directors' attention alike were creamed away from
Hoche's preparations, it seemed unlikely that any expedition would have
sailed at all had it not been for this intensified rivalry between France's two
top generals. Hoche had been one of the few to whom Carnot had confided his
real intentions for Ireland. By July he had almost entirely delegated the
Irish plans to Hoche, who pushed ahead with obsessive determination there-

28. Debidour, *Recueil des actes*, III, 140–4; Tone, *Life*, II, 152–5, for the meeting with Hoche, and
51, 68, 93 and 161–2 for the religious issue.
29. H. Dupré, *Lazare Carnot. Republican Patriot*, 2nd edn. (Philadelphia, 1975), 209.
30. *Mémoires sur Carnot par son Fils*, 2 vols. (Paris, 1863), II, 48–67, 124–8; Dupré, *Lazare Carnot*,
219–21; and Reinhard, *Le Grand Carnot*, II, 198–211. For Hoche see Sorel, 'Vues de Hoche', 229,
233–4.
31. Hants. C.R.O. 38M49/1/22, Wickham to Grenville, 23 Jul. 1796.

after. Ireland was to be his Italy; the glory of defeating England through it would be his alone, and like the preparations themselves, the United Irish mission too was almost totally absorbed into Hoche's scheme.

II

When Tone left Ireland in mid-1795, the original United Irish Society no longer existed, and his memoranda to the Directory never referred to any national organization other than the Defenders. The nucleus of a national leadership did exist, principally among his presbyterian friends, but in 1796 France had no clear conception of the relationship between the various strands of Irish discontent. In the North the United Irishmen had been re-organized as an oath-bound society with a theoretical organization of 36-man cells and higher delegated baronial and county committees. But the new republican organization remained little more than a collection of politically-informed individuals, and the leaders kept their approach to France a close secret.[32] In the months after Tone's departure, tentative overtures were made to the Defenders, the first step in the campaign to make the United Irishmen a truly national organization. With the war slump and the escalating costs of provisions, a wave of lawlessness had swept the country in the latter part of 1795. It was accompanied by an alarming resurgence of Defenderism, particularly in the weaving communities of Armagh, Down, Cavan, Monaghan, Dublin, Meath and Kildare, where the slump coincided with the beginnings in the decline of the domestic weaving industry.[33] Government feared some sinister political motive behind the lawlessness, and with reason, for even in those areas where Defenderism was weak there were signs of a new eagerness for revolutionary change. Leonard McNally was convinced by the evidence produced at the autumn assizes 'that the whole body of the peasantry would join the French in case of an invasion, or rise in a mass against the existing government, if any men of condition were to come forward, as their leaders . . .' Other informants confirmed his reports that a general hope in a French invasion was reacting upon genuine economic grievances.[34]

In the North the intensified conflict between the Orangemen and the Defenders, and signs of actual or rumoured Orange infiltration into neighbouring counties, multiplied Defender membership.. Many United Irish leaders still had reservations about catholic aspirations, and there is no

---

32. See I.S.P.O. 620/10/121/26 and 620/54/14 for the organizational confusion of 1795.

33. Kerrane, 'The Background to . . . 1798', 57–8; see also Fitzpatrick, 'The Economic Effects of the . . . Wars on Ireland', 98–9; and I.S.P.O. S.O.C. 1015/5, 7, 22.

34. McNally's reports, Sept. 1795 in I.S.P.O. 620/10/121/27–29; see Camden's reports on the state of the country in P.R.O. P.R.O. 30/8/326/16–21, 42–4, 72–5; and R. Musgrave, *Memoirs of the Different Rebellions in Ireland*, 3rd. edn., 2 vols. (Dublin, 1802), II, 285–9.

evidence that the religious element in the conflict had any United support. But the United leaders recognized the numerical strength which an alliance with the Defenders would bring to the independence movement. Ultimately their aims were similar; but the Defenders seemed too fragmented, too vague about their overall plans and too intensely catholic to organize a movement of national liberation. The United Irishmen had an efficient central leadership but were numerically weak, and as they watched Defender-ism radiate from the north and east of the country into the more inaccessible hinterland, they realized that their own future as a national movement could only be assured in collusion with the Defenders. The northern United men sent a delegation to Dublin to confer with Defender leaders from the surround-ing counties, and after a return meeting in Belfast, some kind of formal association between the two movements appears to have been established. By mid-1796 new members in Ulster were reputedly sworn in as Defenders and United Irishmen simultaneously, and the rapid spread of the Society in the province can be traced to the time of this agreement. However, there was never a formal and complete merger of the two organizations, and the United Irishmen continued to have serious reservations about their ability to control and direct the passions of their new allies.[35]

In August Camden outlined the new developments in a letter to Portland, the Home Secretary: 'Your Grace has been long informed of the unfortunate feud which for several years has prevailed in the county of Armagh between the Dissenters and the Roman Catholics of the inferior classes ... The United Irishmen of Belfast ... took advantage of this ill conduct of the Dissenters in Armagh to form a junction with the Societies of Defenders in the Western and Midland countries, and to revive their Committees and as-semblies which the vigor of Government had almost entirely suppressed ... Recently, Emmissaries have been among them [the Defenders] to influence them against the Dissenters of Armagh, to instill into their minds that the per-secution of the Catholics is protected by Government to excite them to join the United Irishmen, and to fill them with hopes of a French Invasion ... '[36] It is unlikely that the United Irish leaders would have exacerbated religious tensions in the manner indicated by Camden. But they did use the Orange bogey to increase membership. They attacked the landed classes in their handbills, pointing to the example set by France and playing upon traditional catholic aspirations 'to plant the true religion that was lost since the Reformation' or to bring about 'a general division of the land' among them. There are

---

35. MacNeven, *Pieces of Irish History*, 119–20; I.S.P.O. 620/22/19 and 41, undated information of Bird; also S.O.C. 1015/8 and Teeling, *Observations on the '. . . Battle of the Diamond'*, 8. For the agreement of 1795 see P.R.O. H.O. 100/62/133–49 and MacNevin, *The Lives and Trials of . . . Emminent Irishmen*, 283–92; and Tone, *Life*, I, 283–4, 289–91 and II, 167 for United Irish reserva-tions about it.

36. P.R.O. H.O. 100/64/168–72, Camden to Portland, 6 Aug. 1796.

few signs of United influence among the Defenders outside Ulster before 1796; but the spring and autumn trials of 1795 show that Jackson had been accepted as a martyr and that a French invasion was already part of the Defender programme before the alliance with the United Irishmen took place.[37]

The autumn assizes of 1795 in particular highlighted the direction in which Defenderism was moving. In the face of an apparent collapse of the gentry's nerve throughout the country, Camden sought to make an example by imposing the full rigours of the law. Many capital sentences were imposed, with only a few stage pardons, and hundreds were sentenced to transportation or enforced service in the British armed forces. Instead of producing humble submissiveness, however, the assizes revealed an utter contempt for law and religion alike among the convicted, and their resolution was unmoved even by a refusal of the last rites. In September the catholic Archbishop of Dublin, Dr. Troy, declared excommunicate any catholic who joined the Defenders; but it produced no visible improvement in the situation of the countryside. Many crimes went unpunished because of Defender intimidation of witnesses and juries, and even those convicted went to the gallows with defiant unrepentance, rehearsing their roles as future martyrs in final, dramatic speeches.[38]

Camden was reluctant to impose martial law. However, the loyalist population was speaking openly of another 1641 and clamouring for protection; and on the other side the discontented were proclaiming their faith in French help. Even if the United Irishmen were not responsible, Camden saw in Belfast a treasonable nest poised to take advantage of the turmoil. Most disconcerting of all, he did not seem to be able to convince the London government of the need for extra military help or for stringent measures to counter insurgency. He genuinely lamented the mounting religious conflict, but could see little alternative to enlisting loyalist aid as a supplement to the still suspect catholic militia. An almost exclusively protestant yeomanry force was consequently added to the battery of repressive weapons the following June. More immediately he bowed to loyalist pressure and in February introduced an Indemnity Act to protect those persons who had exceeded their legal powers in suppressing the recent troubles, and an Insurrection Act which embarrassed Whitehall by its unprecedented severity. The Act made the administration of seditious oaths a capital offence and empowered

37. For the development of Defender opinion in 1795 and signs of the United Irishmen playing upon traditional Defender beliefs see I.S.P.O. 620/10/121/29, 620/18/14, 620/22/19, 49 and 620/25/136; also P.R.O. H.O. 100/58/201–7, 100/63/205–6; and Hants. C.R.O. U840/O146/3 and O150/3.

38. On the trials see P.R.O. H.O. 100/63/177–180, 195–8, 205–6, H.O. 100/64/103 (200 sentenced to transportation); I.S.P.O. S.O.C. 1015/4; *State Trials* xxvi, 225–354; and Musgrave, *Memoirs of the Different Rebellions*, II 285. For Defender reaction to Troy's directive see I.S.P.O. 620/10/121/27.

LE GÉNÉRAL O'CONNOR.

(Œuvre de J^{me} Gérard.)

Plate 17. Arthur
O'Connor (from a print
by Gérard in the
possession of the author)

the Lord Lieutenant to proclaim martial law in any district at the request
of a magistrate. In such districts a curfew would operate, and justices would
have special powers to search houses during prohibited hours, to suppress
meetings, and to send disorderly persons, untried, into the fleet.[39]

   Most reformers had already despaired of constitutional agitation and
greeted Grattan's suggestion of petitioning the King with understandable
coolness.[40] Arthur O'Connor had decided to abandon Irish politics altogether
and was in London attempting to buy an English parliamentary seat. But he
was joined there in April by Lord Edward Fitzgerald with quite a different
proposition for resolving Ireland's ills. In Dublin Lord Edward had approach-

39. See Camden's correspondence up to June 1796 in P.R.O. H.O. 100/62–4, and in particular
P.R.O. 30/8/326/1/72–5, on the Insurrection Act.
40. Lecky, *Ireland in the Eighteenth Century*, III, 384; and P.R.O. H.O. 100/63/199–201.

ed Edward Lewins, Richard McCormick, and the Ulster United leaders, Robert Simms and George Tennent, and offered to open communications with France through his former acquaintance Charles Reinhard, then French minister in Hamburg.[41] Though not as yet a United Irishman, Lord Edward had been in the confidence of its Dublin leaders for some time. His despair at ever achieving reform through parliament had pre-dated their own, and although he had continued to sit as M.P. for Kildare, his violent criticism of government measures had isolated him even from the Irish opposition. In February 1796 he alone had offered any determined fight against the Indemnity and Insurrection Acts. When the next election came around, he resigned his seat in parliament, explaining to his constituents that a seat in such a tool of biased authority was inconsistent with his principles. Lord Edward's republican principles had remained unchanged since his return from France in 1792. But the situation in the country had altered considerably, and like his fellow reformers he had graduated from passive to active republicanism when the pursuit of the former in open discussion became impossible. The status and confidence which someone of Lord Edward's noble lineage brought to the United Irish movement was considerable, legitimizing its progress towards militant republicanism, and helping to shield it from the full rigours of official reprisal. Lord Edward was a recalcitrant member of the protestant ascendancy, related to many important figures in English and Irish political life alike, and popular even with his political opponents. This, and a blind faith that such a noble could eventually be wooed back to the fold, explains the embarrassed inactivity of the authorities, and warnings to his relatives to keep Edward in line took the place of direct action.[42]

O'Connor, who was later held responsible for leading Lord Edward astray, became instead the main object of official persecution. O'Connor and Lord Edward had indeed been political allies and personal friends since about 1793, and were closely associated with the formal organization of the United movement from late 1796 onwards. But O'Connor's political development had been more erratic than that of his noble companion. Indeed many eventually came to regard him as something of an irresponsible upstart, whose ambition dragged more than Lord Edward to their fate. O'Connor was born near Bandon, county Cork, in 1763, the youngest of nine children born to Roger Conner and Anne Longfield (sister to the future Lord Longueville). On reaching maturity he and his brother Roger adopted the name of the ancient O'Connor line of Irish high kings, and with spurious legitimacy these descendants of London merchants continued to claim descent from native Irish nobility. Lord Edward's family loved to tease Arthur as 'King of Connaught',

41. See Lewins's account of the background to the mission in A.N. AF IV 1671 plaq. 1 fos. 99–105; and I.S.P.O. 620/15/3 for O'Connor's hopes of an English seat.
42. G. Campbell, *Edward and Pamela Fitzgerald* (London, 1904), 85–7, 107.

but the myth was lived out by O'Connor even after his exile in France and today his descendants still use silver bearing the family crest, that of the ancient Irish Kings. The idiosyncrasy of the Conner and O'Connor families was a living legend, continued in England by their most famous descendant, the Chartist leader Feargus O'Connor; and in the 1790s the Irish authorities were involved in a dual battle to curb the loyalist excesses of the remaining brothers and the republicanism of the wayfaring duo. The name of the eldest brother Robert, a magistrate in Cork county, became a byword for reaction, and he sought the execution of his two brothers with a determination which shocked the authorities. Roger's later actions certainly supported rumours of insanity in the family and Arthur's megalomania was to wreak havoc within the United Irish Society. On the other hand, O'Connor's confidence, his informed loquaciousness and oratorical abilities won more support for the movement that it might otherwise have attracted.[43]

In 1790 Arthur's uncle, Lord Longueville, had secured for his nephew the parliamentary seat for King's County. Contrary to his later claims, Arthur did not oppose the administration until May 1795, when his brilliant speech in favour of the catholics pulled him from obscurity to be the darling of Irish and English reformers alike. He had already been adopted by members of the opposition Whigs and radicals on an earlier visit to London, Burdett in particular becoming infatuated by the fast-talking Irishman.[44] It was to his new-found friends in London that he went to stay when he lost his Irish seat because of the speech, and where Lord Edward found him in April 1796. There is little sign that O'Connor was a republican before this date, and although it would be wrong to accuse him of insincerity or of seeking glory in a treasonable career after having failed to win it in more orthodox channels, nevertheless personal ambition was never far removed from any of his actions and became so embroiled with his republicanism as to be indistinguishable.

Lord Edward and his wife travelled independently to Hamburg where O'Connor joined them on 5 June. At first the Directory suspected Lord Edward's motives because of his wife's family connections, notably with Madame de Genlis and her cousin Madame de Sillery, prominent French *émigrés* in Hamburg. But Reinhard, the French minister there, assured Delacroix that he could personally speak for Lord Edward's probity. O'Connor's arrival removed lingering doubts; he argued Ireland's case with much ability, despite a poor command of French, and Reinhard was clearly

43. MacDermot, 'Arthur O'Connor', 48–69. I am indebted to the late Frank MacDermot for additional information supplied in several conversations with him in Paris; also to the Marquis de la Tour du Pin, O'Connor's descendant, for his information on family traditions and anecdotes. For Robert see I.S.P.O. 620/32/2 and N.L.I. MS 15,481

44. See P.R.O. P.C. 1/23/A.38; also I.S.P.O. 620/15/3/21–26, for his correspondence with Burdett, Oct. 1796. Sir Francis Burdett (1770–1844) was a disciple of Horne Tooke and the most popular and influential of the English radicals.

impressed. But although the Directory had initially agreed to Fitzgerald's request for an audience in Paris, the interest which the *émigré* underworld in Hamburg was taking in the two Irishmen rendered such a direct passage to France injudicious. Arch-*émigrés* like Dumetz, Duchrest, General Valence, who had defected with Dumouriez, and even the notorious British agent the Baron de Batz, were all claiming Irish connections in order to discover more about the mission. Valence, who like Colleville was actually attempting a return to the republican fold, was considered particularly dangerous because of his marriage to Madame de Sillery with whom Pamela was staying. In an effort to evade the royalist underworld it was agreed that O'Connor and Lord Edward should travel to Switzerland to negotiate indirectly with the Directory through Barthélemy, its minister in Basle. In both Hamburg and Basle Lord Edward and O'Connor were confronted with the Directory's reluctance to risk an invasion before the Irish revealed their hand in a rising. Like Tone they represented the ease with which a French fleet could reach and land in Ireland, the mutinous disposition of the large Irish element in the British navy, and the overwhelming support in Ireland for a rising. But because of the rigorous disarmament under the Insurrection Act, they were more insistent than Tone on the inability of the people to rise successfully without French assistance. They were not prepared to compromise on their demand that the invasion should precede the rising, and insisted that details of the invasion be fully agreed before their return to Ireland.

The confidence and determination of the two emissaries is remarkable when one considers the very flimsy foundations for the mission. Lord Edward had admitted to Reinhard that he had no official commission for his negotiations, though he offered to return for one if France doubted his credentials. Such confidence derived from the United Irishmen's overwhelming feeling that Ireland was moving irretrievably towards a confrontation with the established authorities, and that in the disarmed state of the country the people could not hold out long against the military. The time had come, as Lewins later explained, 'to ask France for the help which she had already so generously offered to us'.[45] The statements of Lord Edward and O'Connor convey the impression that the Irish saw themselves in the role of creditors seeking payment and therefore in a position to bargain for favourable terms. Like Reinhard, Barthélemy was gradually converted by O'Connor's proficiency in discussion, and his enthusiastic despatches to Paris fortified Tone's position. More immediately, the confirmation of Tone's claims by such well-known public figures intensified the impatience of Hoche and Carnot to despatch an invasion force to Ireland.

---

45. A.N. AF IV 1671 plaq. 1 fos. 99–105, Lewins's account of the mission; further details have been taken from A.A.E. Corr. Pol. Ang. 588–9; A.N. AF III 186ᵇ doss. 859; A.H.G. B¹¹1; and *Mémoires de François Barthélemy, 1768–1819*, ed. J. de Dampierre (Paris, 1914), 155.

Initially Barthélemy's reports had been sent to the Foreign Affairs Ministry and from there to the Directory. From July, however, references to O'Connor and Lord Edward disappear from the papers of the Directory and Foreign Affairs alike. They re-appear briefly in the records of the War Ministry at the end of July, when arrangements were being made for O'Connor's entry into France, then disappear altogether from central government records. Henceforth only Hoche's private papers speak of O'Connor's continued presence on the Continent. In a secret deliberation of 20 July, the Directory had authorized Hoche's assumption of total control over all matters pertaining to the Irish expedition, including the despatch and reception of secret agents.[46] Two days later Hoche's aide-de-camp, adjutant-general Crublier, was sent to Switzerland to escort O'Connor to his headquarters at Rennes. Elaborate precautions were taken to disguise the arrangement; Crublier was ostensibly appointed to escort a French prisoner from Switzerland, and a secret rendezvous was arranged with O'Connor on the Swiss-French border.

Hoche had already confirmed the patriotism of O'Connor and Lord Edward in a casual conversation with Tone on 23 July. Tone was not told of the mission, but he spoke highly of the principles of the two men and was confident that both would join the people in a rising.[47] Hoche left Paris on 12 August for Rennes, where he was to meet O'Connor. Possibly for security reasons he stopped at Angers instead, and it was here that the meeting took place.[48] No report was ever submitted to the Directory on the Angers nego-tiations; it seems none was expected. The delegation of power to Hoche had been complete, and he alone on the French side seems to have known what was agreed with O'Connor. According to Lewins, however, O'Connor had remained three weeks with Hoche and had returned to Ireland with a promise of an immediate despatch of 15,000 French soldiers and 80,000 guns to Galway Bay. O'Connor always claimed that details of the forthcoming expedition, including its place of landing, had been arranged in a secret treaty. Although Hoche never mentioned it in subsequent reports to Clarke, O'Connor's claim is substantiated by Hoche's lengthy report of 29 August, itemizing the number of men and horses France might expect on landing, and outlining a plan for the insurgents to take Dublin.[49] It does appear that O'Connor had success-fully fulfilled his instructions to remain in France until all the details of the French landing had been arranged. Lord Edward had been in Hamburg

46. Debidour, *Recueil des actes*, III, 150, 167–8.
47. Tone, *Life*, II, 165–6.
48. A. Joly, *Lazare Hoche 1768–1968 (Catalogue de l' Exposition: Deuxième Centenaire. Hôtel de Ville Versailles. Sept.–Oct. 1968*), Nos. 52 and 153, Hoche to Hédouville, 10 and 13 Aug. 1796. I am grateful to Mlle A. Joly, former archivist at Versailles, for pointing out these letters to me.
49. See O'Connor's claims in A.A.G. Doss. Pers. 2ᵉ sér. G.D. 393; and A.N. AF III 186ᵇ doss. 859 for Hoche's report of 29 Aug. 1796. See also Lewins's account in A.N. AF IV 1671 plaq. 1 fos. 99–105; and A.A.E. Corr. Pol. Ang. 590 fos. 217–23.

since mid-July awaiting O'Connor's return, and they left for England in the
latter part of September. Before their departure a secret route of communication via Hamburg was arranged between Hoche at Rennes and the
two emissaries.[50] Tone, now a commissioned officer in the French army, was
sent to Rennes at the end of September. Hoche's control of the Irish expedition
was now total. Its fâte had been decided by two highly ambitious men,
O'Connor having possibly negotiated for himself a leading place in the new
Irish government, Hoche using Ireland as an outside pedestal to establish a
position of power at home.

III

Hoche returned to Brest in September, his interviews with Tone and O'Connor
having boosted his enthusiasm for the Irish expedition. But he was dismayed to
find that the Irish preparations had been totally subordinated to the naval
commander's preference for the West Indian project. It was not entirely the
fault of Villaret-Joyeuse, the naval commander, whom Hoche accused of
sabotaging the Irish venture. The June instructions had given precedence to
the West Indian expedition and had never been rescinded. The Directory was
trying to satisfy too many conflicting interests and seemed oblivious to the
havoc this caused to naval planning. Hoche's angry complaint about the
West Indian preparations secured their apparent abandonment in October.
But the Marine Minister's reluctant directive to Villaret scarcely carried
conviction, and Hoche was later warned that Villaret never did abandon the
project. Lack of finance, supplies, pay and, most of all, sailors further handi-
capped preparations. The prisoners of war and deserters collecting at Dunkirk
for a diversionary, *chouan*-like expedition to England under General Quantin
were causing particular problems. The officers were reluctant to embark on a
seaborne venture, and many of the regular soldiers deserted rather than be
associated with deserters. By November Quantin was pleading to be relieved
of his command. When Hoche's force was plundered to reinforce the Italian
army, his exasperation erupted in a angry protest to the Directory that if the
preparations continued along present lines, it would be preferable to abandon
the whole project and use the army elsewhere.[51]

The arrival in Paris of Lord Malmesbury to negotiate peace-terms for
England introduced a new note of decisiveness into Directorial policy. No
one believed that England was sincere in her quest for peace and most thought

50. A.N. AF III 186[b] doss. 859 and AF III 408 doss. 2244 fo. 66, correspondence between the
Directory and Reinhard, Sept.–Oct. 1796.
51. For the October correspondence of Hoche and the naval authorities see A.H.G. B[11]1; A.N.
BB[4] 99 fos. 21–7, and 102 fo. 17, AF III 186[b] doss. 859; and A.D.S.M. 1 Mi 61/148/1956. See also
Tone, *Life*, II, 227–9, for Villaret's disfavour.

it little more than a temporary sop to mounting anti-war feeling in Britain. A successful landing in Ireland, however, might force her to grant favourable terms: '. . . we must humble the pretensions of this envoy of Pitt's,' wrote Truguet to Hoche on 15 October 'by opening our discussions with the words— twenty-thousand men are in Ireland'.[52] During November a concentrated effort was made to accelerate the Irish preparations: Hoche's demands for the dismissal of Villaret and a complete overhaul of the naval command were conceded, and sailors were ordered to Brest from all the neighbouring ports.

Hoche's impatience to be rid of Villaret had reached fever pitch after he received reports that a rising had taken place in Ireland. The news had been brought into port by a vessel from Liverpool. Tone was sceptical; but without checking the validity of the report, Hoche wrote to the Directory to demand the immediate departure of the invasion force. News of the Irish rising sent a flurry of excitement through the central departments involved, and it was soon the principal talking point in the Paris cafés. The news was later proved false, but it had revealed a large stock of pro-Irish feeling which would undoubtedly have concentrated Directorial efforts behind Hoche's expedition earlier, had it not been for the increasing demands of the campaign against Austria.[53] In the light of the reports, Hoche's demands were conceded, and preparations at Brest assumed a new urgency. But Hoche was already concerned that the expedition had not arrived at the time arranged with O'Connor, and news of a rising made it important to discover the exact nature of the preparations proceeding in Ireland. On 7 November Hoche sent Bernard MacSheehy, a young Irish officer in the Brest camp, an exstudent of the Irish College and another of Madgett's 'pool', to report on the Irish situation. Tone was baffled that MacSheehy was instructed not to reveal any details of the forthcoming expedition. Instead he was to travel in a trusted American vessel which would take him to Ireland and back in a very short time (Tone estimated that two weeks would suffice for the entire venture); he was to meet such persons as Tone should name (Oliver Bond and Richard McCormick) 'and learn from them as much as he could on the actual state of the country at this moment, the temper of the people, the number and disposition of the troops, whether the French were expected or desired and, if so, in what part particularly'.[54]

Hoche's confusion about the current state of affairs in Ireland is understandable. Nothing at all had been heard from O'Shee; Clarke suspected

---

52. A.D.S.M. 1 Mi 61/148/1956, Truguet to Hoche, 15 Oct. 1796.

53. A.H.G. B[11] 1, Hoche to the Directory, 3 Nov.; see also Truguet's communications in A.N. BB[4] 102 fos. 89 and 109 and BB[4] 103 fo. 26; AF III 59, Reinhard to Delacroix, 23 Nov. 1796; and Aulard, *Recueil des actes*, III, 554–66.

54. Tone, *Life*, 230–2; A.N. AF I I I 186[b] doss. 859. See F[7] 3508[A] and F[15]* 16 on MacSheehy's Irish College connections.

that he had tricked them, taken his 10,000 francs payment, and absconded. O'Shee did return to Paris on 27 October, but there is no sign that he had actually reached Ireland; most historians assume that his instructions were implemented, but no report by O'Shee to the Directory has ever been found, and his personal dossier in the Foreign Affairs Ministry makes no reference to his activities in Ireland. Lewins never mentioned him in later reports to successive French governments, though he itemized every other French mission to Ireland between 1793 and 1796. When in 1798 the United Irish prisoners were interrogated on the 1796 discussions with France, they mentioned only one agent having been sent to Ireland that year, and that was MacSheehy.[55] In addition, Hoche had heard nothing from Lord Edward since his return to Ireland, though the Directory's urgent requests to Reinhard on 26 October to check the mail at the secret Hamburg address suggests that some communication had been expected.[56] News reaching France that Britain had discovered the Galway destination cast doubts on the advisability of pursuing the original invasion plan. Such doubts were reinforced by reports of intensive repressive measures against the United movement in Ulster, including the arrests of most of the leaders.[57]

MacSheehy arrived in Dublin on 26 November, after a journey which had taken him through the British fleet blockading Brest, from Portsmouth to London, and by coach to Holyhead. On the 27th he contacted Bond and McCormick and with some difficulty convinced them of the authenticity of his mission. They later admitted that the memory of Cockayne had made them nervous of so-called French agents and as a result the meetings between MacSheehy, MacNeven, Bond, McCormick and Lewins took place in the street rather than at their houses. Eventually they gave MacSheehy a relatively accurate account of the forces in Ireland, assured him that the United Irishmen were bound by oath to separate Ireland from England, that Lough Swilly or a bay near Galway were the best landing places, and that if the French brought up to 70,000 extra arms and could initially wage war without levying contributions, success would be guaranteed. MacSheehy was particularly anxious to learn the state of the North. An agent was therefore despatched from Dublin and returned two days later with assurances that 50,000 men were ready to join the French in Ulster; they had arms for 15,000,

55. *Report from the Committee of Secrecy . . . Commons [Ireland] 1798*, Append. no. xxxi and see Clarke's correspondence for Oct. 1796 in A.H.G. B¹¹ 1. For O'Shee's expenses see A.A.E. Doss. Pers. Arrêtés et Décrets 9 fos. 88 and 96. For his return see A.N. AF III 186ᵇ doss. 859, and for his personal file, A.A.G. Doss. Pers. 2ᵉ sér. G.B. 696 O'Shee. Two recent articles also refer to the mission: F. W. Van Brock, 'Captain MacSheehy's Mission', *Irish Sword*, x (1972), 215–28, and C. J. Woods, 'The Secret Mission to Ireland of Captain Bernard MacSheehy, an Irishman in French Service, 1796', *Journal of the Cork Historical and Archaeological Society*, lxxviii (1973), 94.
56. A.H.G. B¹¹1, Reinhard's reply to the Directors' query, 26 Oct. 1796.
57. Tone, *Life*, ii, 222–3; also A.H.G.B¹¹1, Clarke to [ ], 27 Sept. 1796.

twenty pieces of cannon and able leaders, and could secure the 8,000 horses required for the French cavalry.[58]

Judging from the reports flowing into the Castle, these claims for Ulster were not exaggerated, though they could not have been made for the rest of Ireland, which had yet to be organized. Throughout the summer the country, especially the North, had remained disturbed. The Castle received reports that United Irish delegates had been to Munster and Connacht, and Camden was gloomy at the open enthusiasm with which the Defenders and United Irishmen celebrated the French victories on the Continent. Celebration bonfires lit the skies, travellers were forcibly dismounted and 'made to shout for the French', militia regiments near Belfast were feared to be disaffected, loyal protestants wrote of their constant fear of assassination, and in August, when Camden himself toured the worst-affected areas in the North, especially Down and Antrim, he assured Pelham, his Chief Secretary, that the reports were not exaggerated.

Camden called an emergency meeting of his colleagues on 6 August in order to represent the serious state of the country to the London ministers. An official statement urged 'that considerable danger is to be apprehended from the organized system which has been established at Belfast, which aided by the general disaffection that prevails, may alone lead to outrage and insurrection ... that assisted even by the probable expectation of, and much more by the actual co-operation of France *even to a small degree*, the danger is infinitely magnified ...' The statement urged the suspension of the Habeas Corpus Act, the levying of yeomanry corps, an increase in military strength, the stationing of frigates in the North Sea and the preparation of contingency plans by the Commander-in-Chief. Camden was convinced that the disaffected had actually solicited French assistance, though he was less convinced of France's ability to send it. 'It is however *that* expectation which gives energy and vigor to their exertions, and the possibility of which leads me to consider this subject with more apprehension than I should otherwise think it deserved.'[59] Portland's lukewarm response more than justified Camden's complaints of English neglect. He frequently replied to Camden's remonstrances in the tone of a patient parent, humouring an irrational child. On this occasion he brushed aside Camden's fears of an invasion, reluctantly conceded an increase in military strength, the levying of yeomanry corps and the stationing of frigates off the north coast, but refused to contemplate a suspension of Habeas Corpus—though it was conceded some weeks later.[60]

---

58. Copies of MacSheehy's report in A.N. AF III 186ᵇ doss. 859 and A.A.E. Mem. et Doc. 53 fos. 256–60; A.H.G. B¹¹1, extracts made for the Directory on his arrival at Brest, 18 Dec. and in A.N. AF IV 1671 plaq. 1 fos. 128–9. For the Irish account of the mission see Lewins in A.A.E. Corr. Pol. Ang. 590 fos. 217–23; A.N. AF IV 1671 plaq. 1 fos. 99–105; and T.C.D. M S. 873/526.
59. Statement enclosed in Camden to Portland 6 Aug. 1796, P.R.O. H.O. 100/64/168–172.
60. P.R.O. H.O. 100/64/173–6, Portland to Camden, 20 Aug. 1796. See also their exchange of letters in H.O. 100/62/190–214 and 100/65/70–98.

As the crisis continued Camden recalled parliament early, principally to push through the necessary security measures, and a stormy session it proved. Grattan, in possibly the most violent speech he ever made, attacked the Irish government for promoting religious strife by encouraging the 'Orange Boys' on the one hand, and by raising and dashing catholic hopes as it suited them on the other, and the English government for denuding Ireland of recruits and leaving it defenceless. The tone of the session betrayed the same sense of imminent crisis felt by the loyalist population as a whole; opposition attempts to deny treason in the country were greeted with contempt and the indignant loyalists poured out examples to prove the contrary. Predictably the Suspension of Habeas Corpus Act was carried on 14 October and Grattan's motion for catholic emancipation was rejected on the 17th with the same overwhelming majorities.[61]

Despite the turmoil in the North, however, it was only in the last few months of the year that the nucleus of a United Irish military organization appeared. As in 1795, this escalation of militancy was largely a response to intensified government reaction. In September the main Ulster leaders, including Neilson, Russell, Simms, and Charles Teeling, were arrested and charged with treason. The enthusiastic recruiting of the yeomanry was accompanied by a new spate of attacks on catholic homes, and catholic distrust of the government grew apace.[62] Until October new members had been sworn into the United Irishmen simply to work for parliamentary reform and 'an equal representation of all the people of Ireland'. But after the September arrests 'they plainly saw the petitioning would be of no service as government was laying hands on some of our friends and ... we must prepare for the worst by arming ourselves as best we could'. Orders had been issued by the United executive for every man to be armed, and in October the Belfast leaders sent out orders for the county committees to organize the United men into groups of twelve, each group choosing a sergeant, every six sergeants a lieutenant, and so on until a general was appointed.[63]

The arming of the Ulster movement was unmistakable. Kegs of powder were taken from the military stores at Belfast; raids for arms and the felling of ash trees for pikes were reported from Antrim, Tyrone, Derry and Down; bands of men met at night to drill, under the guise of potato-digging parties, and landings of arms were reputed to have taken place on the north Antrim coast. A search later made at Red Bay near Cushendall did reveal traces of recent arms deposits in the caves, and when the province was disarmed early in 1797, the quantity of arms seized by the military was formidable. Many of these arms appear to have come from France, possibly as part of the agreement between O'Connor and Hoche. Tone was later assured that Hoche

61. *Parl. Reg.*, xvii, 1–126.
62. See I.S.P.O. 620/26/82 for the new flood of refugees into Mayo, also 620/25/60 for the arrests.
63. P.R.O.N.I. D.272/6, Statement of Robert McCormick, *c.*1798.

had succeeded in landing 20,000 stand of arms on the Irish coasts, and the *Olive Branch*, known to have made several voyages between the two countries, was finally captured in December with a cargo of 20,000 stand of arms and an entire field-train of artillery. Camden found disconcerting the confidence with which the United Irishmen were now speaking of French assistance; the petitions from the magistrates and gentlemen of the most disaffected areas revealed mounting panic, and on 6 November Camden finally decided to place Antrim, Down, Tyrone, Derry and Armagh under the Insurrection Act.[64]

All the state prisoners agreed in 1798 that the United Irishmen only became a military organization at the end of 1796. With the return of O'Connor and Lord Edward early in October, an attempt was launched to extend the movement and to restructure its central administration. A national executive committee was set up consisting of Lord Edward, O'Connor, Robert Simms, and Richard McCormick, and five others were added shortly afterwards: MacNeven, Thomas Addis Emmet, Joseph Orr from Derry, and two friends of Tone, Bartholomew Teeling from Antrim and Alexander Lowry from Down.[65] O'Connor then set out for Cork to address a United Irish meeting convened by his brother, Roger. He said he was 'just returned from the Continent . . . That there was not a moment to be lost in opening communication with the Executive Directories of Dublin and Belfast as an Invasion of this Country would to a certainty be attempted, . . .' and the whole country should be 'in a state of the most perfect organization'. He then travelled to Galway, probably to complete the division of the country into United Irish executive departments, and MacSheehy was assured the following month that delegates had already been sent to organize Munster and Connacht.[66] Troops were pouring into the Cork area at this time because the disturbances recently experienced in the North had erupted at the other end of the country. In the North the Defenders and United Irishmen were in total agreement; both had been ordered to keep quiet until the French arrived, a sense of expectant optimism pervaded even the lowest sectors of society, and their threatening letters took on a new, confident tone.[67]

64. P.R.O. H.O. 100/65/105–9, Camden to Portland, 7 Nov. 1796, enclosing a copy of the proclamation. See also reports of arming in P.R.O. H.O. 100/62/342, 366; B.L. Add. MSS. 33102 fos. 273, 277, 283, and 33103 fo. 226; and I.S.P.O. 620/25/197 and 620/26/111.
65. *Report from the Committee of Secrecy . . . Commons* [*Ireland*], *1798*, Append. no. xxxi; and MacNeven, *Pieces of Irish History*, 182. See Lewins's claim in A.N. AF IV 1671 plaq. 1 fos. 99–105; N.L.I. MS. 873/774, O'Connor to Madden in 1842, also MacSheehy's report to Hoche, 20 Jan. 1797, A.D.S.M. 1 Mi 62/152/2029–30.
66. P.R.O.P.C. 1/44/A.155, Thomas Conway's account of the movement in Munster, Apr. 1799; and I.S.P.O. 620/15/3/4, letter to O'Connor in Galway, 14 Nov. 1796.
67. See I.S.P.O. 620/25/199 and 620/26/115 for the troubles in Cork; S.O.C. 1015/32, threatening letter of 3 Nov. 1796; and P.R.O. H.O. 100/65/136–7, Camden on the state of the North, 28 Nov. 1796.

After his Irish tour, O'Connor called briefly on Lord Edward in Kildare, then returned to Belfast to await the invasion. There seemed to be no immediate urgency about preparations, for Lord Edward had recently received a letter from Reinhard expressing his eagerness to see him again the following spring, from which the United executive inferred that the invasion had been deferred till then.[68] From Belfast O'Connor wrote on 24 December in a complacent mood to his friend in London, Charles James Fox. He spoke of how religious divisions had been suppressed in their Society, of how the Defenders, until then 'an unthinking oppressed people acting without rational view', had now become United Irishmen and no one would 'speak out' until the time had come to 'speak' for the whole nation. Three days later he received news from Dublin that the French had sailed into Bantry Bay, neither at the expected time nor at the expected place.[69] The Irish had received no warning from the French and were totally unprepared to receive them. What had gone wrong?

IV

Despite the overhaul of the naval command in which Morard de Galles had replaced the disgraced Villaret, Hoche remained dissatisfied with the spirit of the marine. It is true that there were elements of neo-royalism in the French navy, and from their different viewpoints the Director La Revellière and the British minister in Switzerland, William Wickham, held the naval command responsible for the problems surrounding the Irish expedition.[70] But Hoche's impatience cannot have helped. Relations between the land and sea command were never harmonious during the revolutionary and Napoleonic wars and the former was unable to recognize the genuine difficulties of preparing a fleet for an extended voyage. Unavoidable delays were exacerbated by the poor state of the French navy in the 1790s; it had never recovered from the effects of the emigration and the loss of expertise from this eminently royal profession. The Revolution had introduced a crippling insubordination into the lower ranks, and when every government of the revolutionary era had given financial priority to the land forces and the continental campaign, neglect had reduced the French navy to a pitiful shadow of its former self. Truguet later described the almost hopeless task confronting him, and though he fully supported the Irish project, his attempt at humouring

68. A.A.E. Corr. Pol. Ang. 590 fo. 266, Reinhard to Delacroix, 21 Apr. 1797, with Lewins's account; see also Emmet's account of this letter in *Report from the Committee of Secrecy ... Commons* [*Ireland*], *1798*, Append. no. XXXI, 319.

69. I.S.P.O. 620/15/3/7 and 9, O'Connor to Fox, 24 Dec., and Peter Kenna to O'Connor, 27 Dec. 1796.

70. *Mémoires de la Révellière–Lépeaux*, ed. by his son, 3 vols. (Paris, 1895), II, 28–31; P.R.O. F.O. 74/19/11, Wickham to Grenville, 28 Dec. 1796.

Plate 18. General
Hoche (Bibliothèque
Nationale)

the naval officers and his fears about a long voyage north in mid-winter were
born of experience, and he thought Hoche over-reacted to Villaret's tem-
porizing. Hoche's own irascibility, his tendency to read conspiracy into
reluctance, and his practice of going over the Minister's head to the Directory,
only aggravated matters without remedying defects. Moreover, the
November dismissals had created havoc in the naval staff and bitterness
among those who remained; the reverberations of the dispute had even
reached Malmesbury in Paris. The new commander was reluctant to accept
the command, and Hoche's insistence that the naval and military commanders
travel on board the same vessel when the fleet eventually sailed may well
have been an effort to pull the marine into line.[71]

In disgust at the continued difficulties Hoche had written on 8 December

71. See P.R.O. F.O. 27/46, Malmesbury to Grenville, 28 Nov. 1796; A.N. AF IV 1597A plaq.
1 fo. 10, and BB⁴ 102 fos. 87–121, 145–6, 153, on the appointment of Morard de Galles and the
continuing troubles in the navy. For good accounts of French naval weakness at the opening of
the war see P.R.O. W.O. 1/395 and 396 fo. 9, and in 1796, F.O. 27/47, report transmitted by
Dutheil in May 1796.

to Petiet, the War Minister, of his intention of abandoning the project altogether. Petiet was bewildered and asked the Directory for advice. After news of an Irish insurrection in November, the efforts made by all departments to get the fleet away had been Olympian; among other measures, Villeneuve and Richery had been ordered to bring their fleets from Toulon and Rochefort immediately, and with the arrival of the latter on 12 December, the fleet had been increased to forty-six sail (including eighteen ships of the line). But despite the Directory's genuine commitment to the Irish expedition, the Italian campaign was now its first priority. More and more finance and attention was directed that way. Clarke, one of the central pillars of the Irish preparations, had been sent to Italy in November to prepare for the peace with Austria and at the same time to tame Bonaparte's ambitions. The accession of a pacifist Tsar to the Russian throne in December had weakened Austria's position, and it was imperative that all France's military strength should be exercised against her in this final push towards peace. This, and the debilitating effect of such a long voyage on French naval power, were already causing doubts in the Directors' minds about the feasibility of the Irish project when Hoche's despatch arrived. On 17 December, therefore, the expedition was cancelled, and Hoche ordered to take the troops to Italy.[72]

But Richery's arrival from Rochefort had dispersed Hoche's pessimism; pay for the troops was still unobtainable, but apart from a handful their spirit was excellent. Taking what supplies and finance could be found quickly, and relying on the Irish for the rest, Hoche's expedition, with Tone on board, had finally sailed from Brest on 16 December, with 14,450 troops, 41,644 stand of arms, a supply of Irish national *cocardes*, and 5,000 uniforms taken from the royalists at Quiberon, which, by an ironic turn of fate, were about to be used against the country which had supplied them. Hoche had left General Hédouville behind with orders to prepare immediately a reinforcement of 14–15,000 men, a squadron of cavalry and as much artillery as could be found, and to despatch the English *chouan* expedition, now commanded by the American captain Tate and composed of the prisoners Hoche was to have taken to Ireland. Hoche's successful departure and the encouraging news brought back by MacSheehy on the 18th revived the Directory's enthusiasm, and every effort was made to meet Hédouville's requirements.[73]

But in his rush to get away and to avoid the British blockade, Hoche, against the better advice of the naval command, had insisted on taking a more precarious route via the treacherous Point de Raz. The *Séduisant* foundered with the loss of all but 50 of the 1,500 on board. It was an ill omen for the rest of the

72. Debidour, *Recueil des actes*, IV, 403; A.N. BB⁴ 102 fo. 117, order of 17 Nov. 1796; A.H.G. B¹¹1, correspondence of 12–17 Dec. 1796.
73. A.H.G. B¹¹1, correspondence of Hoche, Petiet and Hédouville, 10–19 Dec. 1796.

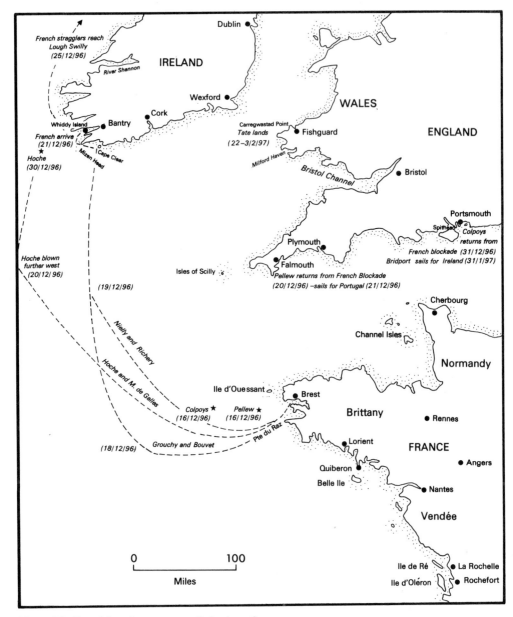

Map 4. The French invasion attempt on Ireland, 1796

expedition. During the night the remainder of the fleet was dispersed by a thick fog, and the frigate carrying both Morard de Galles and Hoche was separated from the fleet. It was an irreparable blow, since Hoche had not revealed the landing place in Ireland to the other officers. Bouvet and Grouchy, respectively the new naval and military commanders, opened their instructions in the hope of discovering their destination. But the instructions only informed them of the course they were to follow if separated from the rest of the fleet. They were to sail to Mizen Head, and cruise there for five days until a frigate arrived with further instructions. If no frigate appeared, they were to sail to the mouth of the River Shannon, wait a further three days, and then return to France. But in following these instructions, Bouvet mistook Cape Clear for Mizen Head wasted a valuable thirty-six hours, and failed to re-join the frigate carrying Hoche and Morard de Galles.[74]

On 21 December the French arrived at Bantry Bay during a raging snow-storm. Ireland must have appeared a bleak end to the voyage, and Moreau de Jonnès, though unreliable in most other respects, probably spoke for everybody on board the expedition when he described his initial impressions of the country they had come to liberate: 'Nothing in the world could have looked more sorry or desolate than the country which appeared before our eyes. It seemed uninhabited and we could see neither church towers, nor villages, nor any trace whatsoever of cultivation or of population.'[75] The troops had sailed from Brest in high spirits, firmly convinced of a warm welcome in Ireland; they sang patriotic songs about the French releasing the Irish from bondage and seemed certain of victory. But all accounts agree with Jonnès on their sense of despair at sighting the land they had come to liberate and at receiving 'no sign of recognition and fraternity from the Irish people'. Sixteen ships had entered the Bay and nineteen remained outside. During the next few days the ships outside were scattered, and a pitiful remnant under Bédout made their way to the second rendezvous at the mouth of the Shannon. The ships in the Bay were separated by a storm which had arisen on the second night, and provisions were growing scarce. After a vain attempt by Grouchy to persuade Bouvet to land, the naval commander cut his cables on 26 December, and returned to Brest. Grouchy was left with only 6,450 men and had no choice but to follow suit. The expedition had been a total failure, and there was still no sign of the frigate with Hoche on board.[76] Hoche and Morard de Galles had been blown far off course and did not sight the south-west coast of Ireland until 30 December. But the continuing winds prevented an approach to the land, and on the 31st, short of provisions and badly damaged by the storm, Hoche's little flotilla set sail for France, having already learnt of Bouvet's departure from Bantry.

74. In addition to sources already cited, details of the expedition have been taken from the following: N.L.I. MSS. 704–6 (French Invasion); E. Guillon, *La France et l'Irlande sous le Directoire* (Paris, 1888); Desbrière, *Projets et Tentatives*, I, 135–223, E. H. Stuart Jones, *An Invasion that Failed* (Oxford, 1950), and the accounts of the participating officers in A.H.G. B¹¹1, particularly those of Grouchy, Dumas and the commander of the frigate *La Surveillante*.
75. A. M. de Jonnès, *Aventures de Guerre* (Paris, 1893), 225.
76. A.H.G. B¹¹1, Grouchy's letters to the Directory from Bantry; see also I.S.P.O. 620/28/23, the information of a captured French sailor, 3 Jan. 1797.

There can be little doubt that the ill-will of the naval commanders was partially to blame for the indecision in Bantry. But given the crippled state of their fleet, and the diminishing provisions, their anxiety to return to port is understandable, and there was little justification for the witch-hunt mounted against them when the post-mortem for the failure got under way. The separation of Hoche's ship had been an irreparable blow. His determination had secured the eventual departure of the expedition and lack of confidence in the underlings who assumed command permeated the remaining force. As Sorel claimed, 'sans Hoche l'expédition n'était comme une aventure'.[77]

But Hoche's own actions were baffling. His distrust of his naval colleagues, his intensive secrecy, his obvious penchant for independent control and reluctance to delegate power even to his military colleagues, rendered failure inevitable in the event of his own loss. Bouvet replied to his detractors that Hoche had never confided in the admirals; he had issued orders which simply outlined procedure in case of separation, but said nothing about the landing. Grouchy, who had no reason to blacken Hoche's name, claimed no knowledge of the landing place. Hoche later accused him of slander and insisted that they had discussed Munster before they left. Bouvet's second packet, opened off Mizen Head, did contain a map of Bantry Bay, but no one else seems to have been so informed; Grouchy wanted to sail north and most of the stragglers, convinced that Galway or Lough Swilly was the fleet's destination, sailed in that direction.[78] In the interests of secrecy Hoche was authorized not to reveal the fleet's destination till at sea, so he was perfectly within his rights in his concealment.[79] Moreover the intensive secrecy had completely baffled Britain. Malmesbury had been specifically instructed to discover the aim of preparations in the western ports. At first the secrecy defied his attempts; then Hoche's plans to mislead, including the printing of proclamations in Portuguese, convinced him and many others that Portugal or the West Indies was the object of the preparations, and the British fleet under Pellew had sailed for Portugal on news of Hoche's departure.[80] Hoche's intensified secrecy had consequently played a major part in weakening British vigilance, but given the sudden change in all previous instructions, his failure

77. Sorel, 'Les Vues de Hoche', 243.
78. N.L.I. MS. 705 fo. 36, Bouvet's account. See A.N. BB⁴ 102 fos. 25–6, 40–1, 55, for the instructions issued to the naval command, in which their destination is left blank. For the dispute between Hoche and Grouchy see A.H.G. B¹¹1, A.N. AF III 186ᵇ doss. 860, and A.D.S.M. 1 Mi 62/152/2059; and see I.S.P.O. 620/28/35 and 620/34/1 and P.R.O. H.O. 100/65/171–3, for reports of pilots who had boarded French ships on the west coast.
79. A.H.G. B¹¹1, arrêté du Directoire, 25 Oct. 1796; see also Truguet to Hoche, 1 Nov. 1796 in A.D.S.M. 1 Mi 61/149/1971.
80. See the confusion in Malmesbury's and Wickham's correspondence of Nov.–Dec. 1796, P.R.O. F.O. 27/45 and 74/19–20 respectively; Guillon, *La France et l'Irlande*, 239, for an account of the false instructions; A.H.G. B¹¹1, for Hoche's proclamations to the Portuguese nation; and P.R.O. H.O. 28/22/96 for Pellew's movements.

to take precautions to ensure against confusion was careless, to say the least.

Nor does he appear to have taken any measures to inform the United Irish leaders of this sudden alteration, and they remained convinced that the attempt would be made in the north or north-west. A government informant later claimed that the *Olive Branch* had carried instructions to the Ulster leaders—a plausible claim, since the captain threw his papers overboard in the chase prior to its capture.[81] But there is no firm indication that Hoche had attempted to inform his Irish allies. The French preparations were completed in a rush. Hoche was convinced that his most important task was to get help speedily to Ireland; a shortage of provisions and his distrust of the navy would have dictated as short a crossing as possible. Duckett's claims for the republicanism of Munster would have been strengthened by a more recent account brought to France by the United man Barry St. Leger, who had assured Hoche of the pro-French feeling of that part of the country and, more importantly, of the absence of any British ships off its coast.[82] Most of all, the decision reflects the growing complacency of Hoche and the Directory that Irish support for a rising and a French invasion was overwhelming. Despite the claims of all the Irish agents, including Duckett, that the Irish were incapable of rising without French help, and that any invasion force must land in the North where the United Irishmen were strongest, it was their claims for the strength of Irish republicanism throughout the country which provided the final argument in favour of the shorter route. The failure of the fleet to go north, by removing the possibility of simultaneous internal rebellion, was the most important single cause of the expedition's failure. Had the fleet been greeted by a display of support from the native population, the large reserves of goodwill among the French soldiers would have compelled a landing, and those two days of indecision before the storm made a landing impossible would not have been lost.

IV

Even after Bouvet's return, the total extent of the failure was not immediately apparent in France. While there was still a chance that Hoche had landed in Ireland, efforts to send reinforcements under Hédouville and Villeneuve continued with new vigour. 'If the nucleus of a republican army exists in Ireland,' wrote Truguet, 'everything must be done to send it prompt reinforcements.'[83] Troops which had already returned from the abortive Irish attempt were kept on board pending another departure. The men under Tate

81. P.R.O. H.O. 100/65/147–9, 223, Pelham to C. Grenville, 10 and 29 Dec. 1796.
82. Tone, *Life*, II, 232–3 for St. Leger's account; A.H.G. B[11] I, Duckett's memoranda of Nov. 1796; Guillon, *La France et l'Irlande*, 302–3.
83. A.N. BB[4] 114 fo. 6, Truguet to Villeneuve, 7 Jan. 1797; also A.H.G. B[11]I, Barras's reply (undated) to Truguet's of 1 Jan.

had already been cooped up in cramped conditions for several weeks and provisions for all were running low.[84] But despite the continued hope, the search for a scapegoat for the first failure had embittered relations between the Directory and the councils, and hopes that a partial landing might be effected were dashed by Hoche's return on 12 January 1797.

Hoche was an altered person; the fatigue of the voyage and the bitter disappointment had exacerbated his already deteriorating health. Sick and angry, his temper shorter than normal, he travelled to Paris immediately after landing, lashing out at everyone he felt responsible for the failure. Bouvet was arrested and stripped of his rank, Grouchy was accused of lying to cover his own shortcomings, and the press became the forum of the ensuing conflict between Hoche and his second-in-command. Other officers fought their own battles, and the disagreement between Josnet and Chérin resulted in a spectacular duel on the heights of Montmartre.[85] The councils had complained throughout of the expense of the venture, and were not in an understanding mood when the full extent of the losses became apparent. Thirty thousand guns had been lost and shipping losses put the French navy out of action for the next year.[86] France was to become increasingly dependent on the Dutch and Spanish fleets, which would also be virtually destroyed by Britain in course of 1797.

But the embarrassment caused by the Bantry Bay failure had not yet exhausted itself. On the morning of 13 February two frigates, *La Vengeance* and *La Résistance*, a corvette and a lugger, stole out of Brest past the British blockade. On board were the more expendable remnants of Hoche's, Quantin's and Humbert's original forces. There were prisoners of war from the Lille depot, who had been gathered for Quantin's project, kept in the ships' holds off the northern coast for many weeks before the expedition was abandoned in November, returned to winter in the depot without adequate winter clothing, and eventually force-marched to Brest and re-embarked on the two frigates. There was a portion of the troublesome regiment from the Ile d'Oléron which the Directory had hoped to dispose of by incorporation into Hoche's force, a demi-brigade of grenadiers that Hoche had left behind for bad conduct, a motley assortment taken by Hoche from the prisons around Brest, and a few who had returned from Bantry Bay. The whole was commanded by the 70-year-old American merchant captain, William Tate,

84. A.H.G. B[11]1, Grouchy to Giroust, 4 Jan. 1797; see B[11]1 and A.N. BB[4] 103, Nov.–Dec. 1796, the correspondence on Tate and the terrible conditions attending the preparations on the northern coast.

85. See A.N. BB[4] 102 fo. 137, for Bouvet's disgrace; A.D.S.M. 1 Mi 62 and A.H.G. B[11]1, notably Hoche's statement for the press, 18 Jan. 1797.

86. *Mémoires de Barras*, II, 303–4, 306; A.H.G. B[11]1, reports of Sept.–Oct. on the complaints of the councils. For the losses see A.H.G. B[11]1, Chérin to Petiet, 13 Jan. 1797 and P.R.O. F.O. 27/52, information transmitted by Dutheil, 16 Jan. and 18 Feb. 1797.

who seems to have been chosen because he had already written at length on a similar project for Bermuda. He was a spirited man and just happened to be in the right place when Hoche was losing his patience with Humbert and Quantin alike for their squeamishness, as Quantin put it, 'at such a dishonourable command'. All in all, however, Tate was little more than a sophisticated pirate.[87]

How this patchwork expedition came to leave long after the Bantry Bay failure had been well and truly established is something of a mystery. The Directory had temporarily deferred Hédouville's Irish preparations on 10 February and ordered the transfer of most of the troops to the interior. The order was probably issued on Hoche's recommendation, since he had already instructed Hédouville to dismantle the expedition shortly after his return from the Irish coast. But almost simultaneously Truguet had ordered him to despatch Tate's force to England. There seems to have been little reason for the order besides the desire to be rid of such an embarrassing force, whose re-incorporation into the various regiments or prisons would have raised many questions about the emergency measures adopted for the unsuccessful Irish expedition. Truguet, Petiet and possibly Barras and Carnot also knew of Tate's departure, and although there is no record of any official orders from the Directory, there was a good deal of scuttling in ministerial corners when the secret was out.[88]

Tate's original instructions had been to sail to the west coast of England, attack and burn Bristol, land 1,000 or so of his ragamuffins in the area, and then sail to Dublin Bay to prevent any ships leaving. But in February 1797 the former part of the instructions alone were applied. Castagnier, the naval leader of the expedition, landed the men at Carregwastad Point in Pembrokeshire on the night of 22–23 February, after winds had prevented him sailing up the Bristol Channel. The object of the expedition was made self-evident by the immediate departure of the ships and the landing of only four days' supplies.[89] The officers made some attempt to control their men and Tate ordered one shot for indiscipline as a warning to the others. But the men were half-starved and they ransacked the area in search of food and clothing. Most of the damage claims submitted to Whitehall were for lost foodstuffs

---

87. See A.N. AF III 186[b] doss. 858 for Tate's communications with Delacroix and Clarke, Jul.–Aug. 1796; doss. 860 for Hoche's exasperation with Quantin, 9 Nov. and the latter's complaint, 6 Dec. 1796; BB[4] 103 fo. 33 for Hoche's instructions to Tate, 25 Nov.; A.H.G. MR. 501 and B[11]1, particularly the December correspondence, for the composition of Tate's force.

88. See A.H.G. B[11]1, Petiet's report of 14 Jan. 1797 for Barras's and Carnot's involvement with continued preparations in January; though Barras later denied all knowledge of it, *Mémoires*, II, 345–6; A.D.S.M. 1 Mi 62/152/2037, Hédouville to Hoche, 30 Jan. 1797, and 2038, the instructions issued to Tate.

89. A.N. BB[4] 112 fos. 123–4, Castagnier's report of 27 Feb. 1797; see also the account given by the captured officers in England, P.R.O. P.C. 1/37/A.114.

and the livestock that Tate's men were reputed to have devoured half-raw. Tate surrendered his uncontrollable force before nightfall on the 23rd, and after the initial British panic at what was thought to be the advanced guard of a major French expedition, Whitehall was baffled by this strange landing. Most agreed with Lord Liverpool's assessment 'that they are a Set of Ragamuffins, some of them possibly Forcats, of which the French Government wanted to get rid; and they vomited them therefore on our Coast', and by 3 March England had the first 700 re-embarked on transports off Milford Haven, ready for relanding on the French coasts.[90]

In France news of the landing had caused a public outcry and the councils, which had been kept in ignorance of the preparations, demanded a full enquiry into this apparent violation of the constitutional process by the executive. 'I would like to know,' asked one deputy, '... if the executive Directory has the right to remove condemned men from the punishment which they have legally incurred and to commute it to a milder sentence ... Moreover, is this not a deeply immoral action which violates the rights of peoples ... and if our enemies are capable of such atrocities, must we imitate them or set the example?'[91] The Tate episode and the discontent at the Bantry Bay failure exacerbated the deteriorating relations between the legislature and the executive, and the repercussions persisted throughout the following year. In March, the security forces in the north and west were put on alert because of a rumour that England was to re-land the Tate men.[92] The Minister of Justice was horrified at the thought of such convicts escaping into society, and instead of reducing their sentences, as those who took part in the Tate expedition had been promised, the embarrassed authorities intensified them, when those re-landed by England were eventually re-taken. A number had followed normal military or civilian careers for many years before their re-capture; few were the blackguards of tradition, and their fate was rather sad. In 1805 came the official declaration that they were all to serve the remainder of their sentences and several years later they were still pleading for some remission for their years of service in the armed forces.[93]

No one was happy with the events of the winter of 1796–97. At no time could an offensive depending primarily upon naval tactics have been popular in France. Conditioned to fighting upon land, the soldiers had been reluctant to embark in December 1796, and when another Irish expedition was mooted

---

90. P.R.O. H.O. 28/22/185, draft letter to the Admiralty, 28 Feb. 1797; N.L.I. MS. 5932 fo. 15, Liverpool to Blaquière, 1 May 1797. For a full account of the landing see E. H. Stuart Jones, *The Last Invasion of Britain* (Cardiff, 1950); P.R.O. II.O. 42/40, Bodl. Curzon Coll. b.16 fos. 239–53; and *The Times* 23 Feb.–3 Mar.
91. A.N. AF III 437 doss. 2527 fo. 43. See also A.N. BB³ 123 fo. 37, BB³ 124 fo. 37, BB³ 162 fo. 142 and BB⁴ 112 fo. 120, for the adverse reaction to the Tate affair in France.
92. A.N. F⁷ 7238 doss. B³ 7105.
93. A.N. BB²² 8–11 doss. 2741, Affaire des condamnés employés à la descente en Irlande.

in the early months of 1798, several divisions positively refused to repeat the experience of 1796.[94] Carnot's position became increasingly uncomfortable within the Directory, and when Letourneur withdrew the following April, his isolation was complete. The French navy had been irreparably weakened and if the United Irishmen expected a sequel to Bantry Bay in 1797, they were to be disappointed. Moreover Ireland had not stirred when the French lay off her coast, and it was difficult to avoid the conclusion that the Irish agents had secured French assistance under false pretences. The Irish argued that a rising would have occurred had the fleet sailed north, or if the French had actually landed; but the harm was already done, and henceforth Irish assurances would be greeted with scepticism.[95] Never again would France mount preparations to help Ireland on a scale equal to that of 1796, and Hoche had already transferred his attentions to the Rhine in an all-out race to secure peace with Austria before Bonaparte could do so through his Italian campaign. Lord Auckland, a former Chief Secretary for Ireland, felt that ultimately England would be the beneficiary of France's Irish experience; '... besides a dreadful waste of lives, they have purely ruined the remainder of their naval force, and have also learned by a dearly bought experience that the Irish are not so ready to be revolutionized as had been supposed'.[96]

But in Ireland the authorities had little reason to feel complacent. The incident had revealed England's complete inability, if not unwillingness, to defend Ireland. Throughout the summer and autumn Whitehall had received repeated reports confirming fears that Ireland was probably the object of the French naval preparations. But the London government's confidence in the superiority of the British fleet blinded it to the threat. In the event the confusion caused by Hoche's departure scarcely justified such complacency. Only a portion of information on the French preparations had been sent to Dublin Castle, and in the face of the United Irishmen's mounting expectation of invasion, Camden had to make a special plea for copies of the bulletins from the Continent. But requests for extra defence measures were dismissed by Portland, with assurances, even as late as December, that Ireland was not the object of French preparations. It is difficult to justify such light-hearted rejection of Camden's fears in the light of information transmitted by the Foreign Office, but it typifies the manner in which Whitehall had become convinced that Ireland could look after her own internal defence while English naval power protected her externally. Portland attributed

94. P.R.O. H.O. 69/21/55, letter from Paris, Feb. 1798.
95. See e.g. A.H.G. B[11]1, Journal de la frégate *La Surveillante*; A.N. GG[1] 67 fos. 273–80, Reinhard to Delacroix, 13 Jul. 1797, enclosing MacNeven's memoir. See also *Castlereagh Correspondence*, I, 295.
96. Hants. C.R.O. 38M49/1/1, Auckland to Wickham, 12 Jan. 1797.

Camden's scaremongering to the failure of the Irish gentry to carry out their duties of maintaining peace in the country, and he felt that Camden would be better occupied instilling some spirit into his magistracy and gentry, than crying for help to London in times of crisis.[97]

However the naval protection of which Portland boasted left much to be desired. After the last war with France Whitehall had agreed to patrol the Irish coasts in the event of another conflict. This agreement had never been implemented, and apart from Kingsmill's cruise off the south coast and the reluctant despatch of one gunboat to the North, after repeated pleas from Camden that this was the main area threatened, no full naval protection was ever accorded. Even the blockade of Brest was only partial in the years before 1800, and the British fleet persistently proved incapable of preventing French fleets from escaping. The departure of the French on 16 December had been disguised by fog; the same wind which carried them to Ireland prevented Bridport's fleet sailing from Spithead and Colpoy's and Pellew's squadrons joining off Brest. Bridport only learnt of the sailing on the 24th and immediately despatched a frigate to warn the Portugal station, so convinced was he that Portugal was its destination. The Admiralty did not learn that Ireland was France's object until the 31st, and only three days later did Bridport finally sail in that direction.[98] Little wonder that the faith of the Irish loyalists in the vaunted protection of the British navy was shattered, and a sense of abandonment and reproach pervaded the popular songs commemorating Ireland's lucky escape:

> Now fair and strong the south-east blew,
>   And high the billows rose;
> The French fleet bounded oe'r the main,
>   Freighted with Erin's Foes.
>
> O! where was Hood, and where was Howe,
>   And where Cornwallis then;
> Where Colpoys, Bridport, or Pellew,
>   And all their gallant men?
>
> N'er skill nor courage aught avail,
>   Against high Heaven's decrees,
> The storm arose and closed all ports,
>   A mist o'erspread the seas.

97. P.R.O. H.O. 100/65/87–8, 97–8, P.R.O. 30/8/326/94–5, 104–25 and I.S.P.O. 620/26/144, correspondence between Dublin and London at the end of 1796.

98. *Private Papers of George, Second Earl Spencer*, ed. J. S. Corbett, 2 vols. (London, 1913–1924), I, 368–71; D. M. Steer, 'The Blockade of Brest by the Royal Navy 1793–1805' (Liverpool Univ. M.A. thesis 1971), 69–74. See also I.S.P.O. 620/18^A, narrative of the proceedings of the squadrons under the respective commands of Vice Admiral Colpoys and Admiral Lord Bridport, 12 Jan. 1797.

For not to feeble, mortal man,
  Did God his vengeance trust;
He raised his own tremendous arm,
  All powerful as all just.[99]

Moreover, recent military surveys had shown that no more than 6,000 men could have been diverted to the Irish coasts in the event of invasion; it would have required five days to muster them at the point of attack, when Grouchy still had over 6,000 men lying off Bantry. Since the beginning of the war the regular establishment of Ireland had been repeatedly plundered to supply Britain's war needs elsewhere, and of an effective muster of 33,131 military in December 1796, 18,000 were Irish militia, only 800 were regular infantry (3 battalions), and the rest were fencibles. Nor had the command anything to offer in the way of tactical foresight, and an enemy attack on more than one point would have thrown the military into total confusion. In December all available forces were marched towards Bantry, leaving Ulster undefended behind them, though it was known to be the most disaffected part of the country. The ability of the yeomanry and the loyalty of the militia were as yet untried, and in all sections there was an acute shortage of arms and artillery.[100] When the French arrived at Bantry Bay the whole force in and around the Cork and Bandon area amounted to no more than 4,000 regulars and half a battalion of yeomanry, and even that could not have been transferred to Bantry Bay without jeopardizing internal peace in the wake of the departing tropps. The scene in Cork in the last days of December, as troops poured in to face the French, was one of total chaos, and it is difficult to disagree with General Dalrymple's gloomy conclusion that Ireland could not have been saved if the French had landed.[101]

When the crisis had passed there was a general outcry in England and Ireland alike at the failure of the London government to take the necessary defence precautions. At the Admiralty Spencer was ordered to prepare a detailed report on the fleet's movements, in anticipation of the parliamentary attack after the Christmas recess. But the fury of that attack was such that Spencer threatened resignation, and the Admiralty's reputation was already considerably weakened when the crisis of the 1797 mutinies struck. In both Irish and English parliaments a full parliamentary enquiry was demanded into the conduct of government for its carelessness in having 'trusted the

99. T. C. Croker, *Popular Songs illustrative of the French Invasions of Ireland* (London, 1845–7), 46–9.
100. For the state of the Irish defence forces at the end of 1796 see P. C. Stoddart, 'Counter-insurgency and defence in Ireland, 1790–1805' (Oxford Univ. D. Phil. thesis 1972), 91–124; W. D. Griffin, 'The forces of the Crown in Ireland 1798', in *Crisis in the Great Republic: Essays presented to Ross J. S. Hoffman*, ed. G. L. Vincitorio (New York, 1969), 155–80; P.R.O. H.O. 100/62/171–183, 100/64/129–35, 100/65/225 and I.S.P.O. 620/26/115 and 620/50/56.
101. N.L.I. MS. 809, Dalrymple to Pelham, 1 Feb. 1797; it was a conclusion fully endorsed by private letters issuing from the Castle, see e.g. P.R.O.N.I. T.3229/1/11–12, Clare to Auckland, Jan. 1797. See also B.L. Add. MS. 33113 fos. 71–9 and I.S.P.O. 620/26/155 for the chaos at Cork.

safety of Ireland to the chance of winds and waves' [102] In Ireland disillusionment with the boasted naval defence prompted the authorities to examine
and remedy the internal military situation 'like Mariners after a storm ...
examining our vessel, stopping all leaks ... '[103] The immediate aftermath
witnessed a series of defence investigations and proposals for improvement;
they were unanimous on the need for an increase in regular military strength,
and for the creation of a moveable force unhampered by internal policing
duties and able to march speedily against an enemy. All depended on
England's willingness to release additional regular units for Irish service
and foundered on her failure to do so.

But probably the most important effect of Britain's negligence was on the
loyalist population. Whitehall had made great play of the loyalty of the
Irish populace during the attempt. But as the loyalists realized only too well,
the proof of silence was no proof at all; the United Irishmen had been ordered
to refrain from action till the French landed and the inactivity of the country
could be used with equal plausibility to prove the strength of disaffection
as the reverse. The government's Irish supporters were bitter at Britain's
neglect and John Beresford spoke for the loyalists in general when he expressed
his disillusionment to Lord Auckland:

> ... the ease with which the French got into Bantry, the length of time
> they lay ... off our coasts, and the retreat they have made into their
> own ports, without, I may say, molestation, even in the very distressed
> and disabled state they were in, has truly alarmed every thinking man in
> the nation: we see that we must in a like situation depend upon
> ourselves ... No landing was made—Providence prevented it; ... we
> remain as we were, no new strength acquired; grounds given to our
> enemies to know their own strength ... and here we expect them
> again ...[104]

This feeling that the loyalists must in future look to themselves for their own
protection introduced a note of new desperation into Irish repression and
determined the brutality with which the North was disarmed some months
later.

The loyalists' fears were fully justified by the reaction of the United Irishmen
and Defenders to the attempt. Initially, news of a French arrival at such an
unexpected part of the coast was greeted with total incredulity and dismissed

---

102. *Parl. Hist.*, xxxiii, 114, and 5–127 for the full debate; *Parl. Reg.* (Ireland), xvii, 159–66;
see *Spencer Papers*, i, 377–8, P.R.O. H.O. 100/69/115 and Hants. C.R.O. U840/C102/2 and
O156ᴬ/7, for complaints of London's negligence, Jan. 1797. See *Dublin Evening Post*, 12 Jan. 1797;
Northern Star, vi, nos. 523–4; and *Manchester Gazette*, 28 Jan. 1797 for good examples of hostile
press reaction.
103. B.L. Add. MS. 33113 fos. 76–9, Camden to the Duke of York, 4 Jan. 1797.
104. *Auckland Correspondence*, iii, 375–7.

as a false rumour spread by government to promote partial risings. When the truth was known, however, the result was not the expected despair at the lost opportunity, but a huge accession in confidence and in membership. The main difficulty facing the leaders in 1797 was to restrain the enthusiasm of their increased following and to prevent a premature explosion. By early spring the numbers of United Irishmen had tripled and the Society's name was again in common usage, though it had rarely been heard of since Jackson's trial in 1795. Since no French attempt had been made on the North, the United Irishmen were confident that they would return; followers were told not to be disheartened at the quiet of the South during the recent attempt; such quiescence was to deceive government and the country would have risen if the French had landed.[105] The first few months of 1797 saw an impressive display of activity by the United Irishmen in preparation for another landing, and attempts were made to extend the military organization into the rest of the country.

But if 1797 was to be the year in which the United Irish movement was to achieve its greatest successes at home, the results of the Bantry Bay attempt were not entirely beneficial for the Society. The proximity of invasion had aroused new apprehensions among some United leaders about the French alliance and about their own ability to control popular passions. Such increasing reservations were to introduce a note of distrust into future negotiations between the United Irishmen and the French, which would make cooperation between them increasingly difficult. The successful outcome of the 1796 negotiations had accordingly both infused the nascent movement with a new confidence and implanted the seeds of its future destruction.

105. I.S.P.O. 620/34/54, notebook of John Maxwell, 1797; 620/18/14, 620/36/227 and N.L.I. MS. 54A/101, information from McNally, Higgins and to Gen. Dundas, Dec. 1796–Mar. 1797.

CHAPTER FIVE

1797: Year of lost Opportunity

The Bantry Bay attempt was such a boost to popular disaffection in Ireland that over the next six months the United Irishmen might have produced their revolution with a minimum of foreign aid. Unattuned to popular restiveness, however, the Dublin leaders preached delay until the French arrived, giving United dependence on French aid an ill-advised, and, at the time, an unnecessary prominence in the movement for Ireland's liberation. France had re-imposed its standing policy on intervention abroad after Hoche's failure, and expected the Irish to show themselves capable of winning their own independence before she would risk another force. But ineffective communication between United Irish agents abroad and the leaders at home left French intentions unclear; United Irish strength and French goodwill alike receded as each waited for the other to act first. In Ireland the absence of any immediate sequel to Hoche's attempt caused many to query French motives, making the French alliance a divisive influence within the United organization, splitting the leadership and alienating a militant minority who continued to support it unquestioningly. This inactivity of the leaders shattered the fragile cohesion produced in the Society by the general expectation of another invasion attempt, and their loss of control was manifested in mounting criticism of central policy and a tendency to independent action by the Society's lower levels. 'Every delay in sending the promised auxiliary force increased the fears and suspicions of the United Irishmen,' Dr. Madden was later told, 'their best leaders were hopeless of success without foreign aid, and were at the same time alarmed at the prospect of foreign influence in their Councils. Hence our fresh sources of dismay and disunion, which soon afforded plausible excuses for treachery to the base and for desertion to the timid.'[1] Thus the year which had opened so auspiciously was let pass in indecision and internal bickering, while the authorities regained the confidence they had lost at the time of Bantry Bay and began a systematic programme to crush disaffection.

1. N.L.I. MS. 873/397, W. C. Taylor to R. R. Madden [1842].

I

The stimulus which the French attempt had given to disaffection in the country unnerved the loyalists. In the North, United Irish membership doubled between January and April 1797, and the loyalists became convinced that the contest with the republicans would be fought soon in Ulster. The disaffected made no secret of their expectation of another French landing, and on Tate's foray into Wales, which some considered the advanced guard of another Irish expedition, many in Ulster packed their bags ready to flee to the mainland. What hope had they of their lives when the French soldiers at Bantry had admitted their intention of seeking compensation in confiscated loyalist property and the United Irishmen were 'organized to cut our throats'?[2]

The rising confidence of the Ulster United men was undeniable. The province was flooded with handbills warning the people not to purchase banknotes or quit-rents, since neither would be recognized after the revolution. The *Northern Star* was circulated free of charge in many areas and as one M.P. complained was even scattered from galleries in the Dublin playhouses.[3] O'Connor's outspoken attack on government in his letter *To The Free Electors of the County of Antrim* of 20 January amounted to a declaration of war between the United men and the authorities. But no plan of action lay behind this war of words, and the Ulster leaders counselled patience when the ebullience of the lower levels of the movement erupted in unofficial arms raids and demands for a rising. They had no need to take arms, they were told, for the military depots would supply them at the given time: ' ... let no provocation move you to strike a blow that might ruin the dawning liberty of Ireland. The plan of your enemies is to draw you forth into untimely conflict ... Be patient ...'.[4] Far from mobilizing for action, attention was devoted to benefit-type functions such as funding the defence and upkeep of prisoners and their dependents. Indeed, such was the absence of secrecy in the proceedings of the Ulster committees that informers like Nicholas Magin, a catholic farmer from Saintfield, Edward Newell, a miniature painter from Downpatrick, or William Bird, an English merchant, could filch printed documents with impunity and provide the very accurate description of the

---

2. *Parl. Reg.* xvii, 193; Bodl. Edgeworth MSS. Mrs. Edgeworth to a friend in Kent, 20 Feb. 1797; Musgrave, *Memoirs of the Different Rebellions*, ii, 244; and for loyalist fears in general see B.L. Add. MS. 33103 fo. 351, P.R.O. P.R.O. 30/8/326/144–57, and *Report of Debates in the House of Commons of Ireland* [*1796–1800*] (Dublin, 1797–1800), 147–51, 181–2; see also T.C.D. MS. 3979 fo. 1118 for French expectations of receiving land in Ireland.

3. *Parl. Reg.* xvii, 197–8. For escalating United membership see *Report from the Committee of Secrecy ... Commons* [*Ireland*], *1798*, Append. no. xiv, I.S.P.O. 620/34/54 and Kent C.R.O. U840/O152/1.

4. *Northern Star*, vi, no. 537. O'Connor's letter appeared in the 23–27 Mar. issue, and was widely circulated in handbill form, see S.O.C. 1018/5, and MacNeven, *Pieces of Irish History*, 183.

movement which appeared in the secret reports of the Irish parliament the following May.[5]

Mounting pressure from the loyalists and his own cabinet forced Camden into taking some decisive action against the Ulster movement. Military reinforcements had been pumped into the province since January, and it was there that the army first assumed the counter-insurgency role which would dominate its activities in Ireland for the rest of the war. On 2 January General Lake had been given a *carte blanche* to arrest suspicious persons, adding to the toll already taken of the Ulster leadership by the September arrests. But O'Connor's libellous letter had singled him out for particular attention, and a warrant on a charge of high treason was issued against him at the beginning of February. O'Connor had already left Belfast for Dublin, but his house was ransacked, his papers taken, and O'Connor himself arrested in Dublin on 2 February. On the 3rd the military attacked the *Northern Star* office and carried off the offending print-blocks. Robert and William Simms, two of the paper's proprietors, and among the most active of the Belfast United leaders, were taken the same day and despatched to Dublin.[6] By June 1797 103 of the main United leaders in Ulster were in detention.

There can be little doubt that O'Connor had actively courted arrest, partially to establish beyond dispute his own democratic lineage (the letter had been a reply to an accusation that he had long been a supporter of government); but most of all it was a propaganda blast to France and to the United men alike to disperse any doubts generated by the Bantry Bay failure. O'Connor quite rightly assumed that no substantial charge could be brought against him for such a publication, and brazenly challenged his accusers at the Castle to declare the charge on which he was held. He was clearly taken aback when told it was one of high treason. An obsolete act of Henry VIII had been resurrected and applied to O'Connor's offence. Dublin was determined to prosecute, despite Whitehall's reprimand for its revival of an archaic piece of legislation to upgrade a simple offence of libel. Camden admitted that the reasons for his action were 'purely political' and appealed for a different standard to be adopted for Ireland in its current dangerous situation, for O'Connor 'would make things very hot for the government' when he discovered the slender grounds for his imprisonment. However, Whitehall was

---

5. For Magin (or Mageean) see C. Dickson, *Revolt in the North, Antrim and Down in 1798* (Dublin, 1960), 164, P.R.O. H.O. 100/77/144–6, 180–1, and I.S.P.O. 620/4/29/31. But Magin's fullest reports are in P.R.O.N.I. D.714 (Cleland MSS.). For Newell see *The Apostacy of Newell containing the Life and Confession of that celebrated Informer* (London, 1798); and Fitzpatrick, *Secret Service under Pitt*, 12. For Bird, I.S.P.O. 620/34/54 and Kent C.R.O. U840/O193/2.
6. P.R.O. P.R.O. 30/18/326/144–50, Camden to Pitt, 10 Feb. 1797; and I.S.P.O. 620/28/14, Pelham to Lake, 2 Jun. 1797. For the arrests see *Drennan Letters*, 140–2; *Northern Star*, especially VI, nos. 524, 532, 537 and 546–9; and N.L.I. MS. 873/248. For O'Connor see I.S.P.O. 620/28/14 and 200, and B.L. Add. MS. 33103 fos.126–7.

adamant; Dublin Castle had lost yet another battle with the parent government to establish the principle that the crisis in Ireland demanded extra-legal remedies, and O'Connor was released on bail at the end of July. The English parliamentary opposition had quickly taken up O'Connor's case and after the recent bitter debates at Westminster on the state of Ireland, Pitt's government had little desire to reactivate the attack at a time when its image was reviving.[7] But if O'Connor had already proved himself something of a political firecracker, to be handled with caution, it was generally recognized that the rebellious situation in Ulster had gone too far, and the province was proclaimed on 13 March.

On 3 March General Lake had been privately instructed by Pelham to start disarming the province. The proclamation was simply a rubber stamp for a campaign which had already begun, and the United Irishmen were taken completely by surprise. Within the first ten days of martial law 5,462 guns were captured, a sizeable slice of the United men's inadequate arsenal. A tender was stationed at Belfast to accommodate the large numbers of prisoners from Antrim and Down alone, and as the searches radiated out from Belfast to Carrickfergus on the 13th, Loughbrickland on the 14th, Rathfriland on the 23rd and into Armagh the following week, news flooded into Belfast of military excesses. The civil authorities in Ulster were only too happy to abdicate their responsibilities to the military and Lake was in no mood to check his men's excesses at a time when he was more worried that disaffection in their ranks might lead many to act in the opposite direction.[8] United Irish enlistment among the militia was notorious, and the military camp at Blaris outside Belfast was particularly infected. A purge in April weeded out seventy sworn United men from the Monaghan militia alone, and over the next two months similar cells were found in the Wexford, Dublin, Armagh and Kerry militias serving in the province. In a macabre showpiece, *pour encourager les autres*, four members of the Monaghan militia were taken in public procession from Belfast to the camp on 14 May and there executed beside their coffins while the other regiments looked on. Like so many episodes in the disarming of Ulster 'the Battle of Blorris Moor' simply provided a fillip to United Irish propaganda, and within weeks the heroism of the victims was being proclaimed in ballad-form in the Belfast streets and in hand-bills distributed to the military.[9]

---

7. *Parl. Hist.*, XXXIII, 127–71. Kent C.R.O. U840/O193/1, Camden's correspondence with Sir John Scott, Jul.–Aug. 1797, and I.S.P.O. 620/31/15 for the decision of the law officers.
8. On the early stages of the disarming, see B.L. Add. MS. 33103 fos. 224–7 and 236–7; N.L.I. MS. 56/36 and 56; and *Northern Star*, VI, nos. 538–46.
9. Zimmermann, *Songs of Irish Rebellion*, 129–32, and *Drennan Letters*, 257; see also B.L. Add. MS. 33104 fos. 14, 71 and 85, for Lake and Pelham's correspondence, 14–20 May 1797; *H.M.C. Charlemont MSS.*, II, 301; and Teeling, *History of the Irish Rebellion*, 232–3. The United Irishmen had been steadily infiltrating the camp since at least Jul. 1796, see P.R.O.N.I. D.272/73/147.

United Irish influence in the militia was never as formidable as the Society claimed or as Lake feared, and Drennan pointed out that the fickle ardour of the militia could with equal facility be employed on either side. It was no great surprise when on 19 May the Monaghan militia destroyed the *Northern Star* presses with such ferocity that it was never again revived, though it had survived two previous attacks.[10] Nevertheless, this and other incidents of militia disaffection convinced Lake that regulars and yeomanry alone could be relied upon in Ulster. The most infected militia units were removed from the province and replaced by fencibles from England and the Channel Isles. But the scare had also tipped the balance in favour of an Orange takeover of the yeomanry. At first government had been reluctant to accept advice from the North that Orange recruitment would ensure loyalty in the security forces. But although blatant sectarian attacks during the disarming process were still condemned from Dublin, in the circumstances of the spring and summer 1797 a blind eye was turned to increasing Orange involvement on the side of the authorities.[11]

From May the campaign in Ulster took on a new vigour. A second proclamation on 17 May placed the whole province under stricter martial law, absolved officers from the requirement to act with the civil authorities, and made house-burning in disaffected areas standard procedure. A further intensification was foreshadowed after 25 June, the final date by which the disaffected could expect a pardon if they came forward, took an oath of allegiance, and gave recognizances for future good behaviour. The United Irish leaders had devoted much of their finances to securing expert legal counsel at the spring assizes, and many known United men were acquitted.[12] By the time of the autumn assizes, however, United Irish funds were exhausted, the most able Ulster leaders were prisoners or fugitives, and the success of Lake's campaign against the disaffected had made juries less timorous. With forty to fifty capital charges upheld, Camden had good reason to be pleased at the success of the disarming of Ulster.[13]

But the purge was only a limited success, and whilst it may have weakened and altered the character of the Ulster movement, it played a similar role in its extension outside the province to that of the 'Armagh outrages' in 1795. Many fled to other counties, 'poisoning the minds of the people' in areas where they settled. Northerners were reported to be actively organizing disaffection in counties as far-flung as Meath, Cork and Tipperary. No care

10. McAnally, *The Irish Militia*, 111–13; Stoddart, 'Counter-insurgency and defence', 212–29; and *Drennan Letters*, 256–7.
11. Lecky, *Ireland in the Eighteenth Century*, IV, 46–60; Senior, *Orangeism*, 64–71; see also I.S.P.O. 620/30/212, Warburton to Cooke, 27 May 1797.
12. *Northern Star*, VI, nos. 546–9.
13. *H.M.C. Charlemont MSS.*, II, 306; Kent C.R.O. U840/C31/1, Camden to Portland, 6 Oct. 1797; *Diary and Correspondence of ... Lord Colchester*, I, 109–10.

had been taken to purge suspect militia regiments before they were sent out of Ulster, and many incidents were reported of militia men introducing hitherto untouched areas to the United system.[14] But it was the publicity given to the Society by the repressive campaign in Ulster which played such an important part in spreading it further afield. In Cork, General Dalrymple was told that 'the people were greatly enraged by the accounts given of the treatment of their fellow subjects in the North and elsewhere; ... and made use of expressions ... against Individuals who they charge with barbarity and cruelty—and this ... produced most inflammatory effects'. In Wexford people were heard denouncing 'the partiality of government to the Orange men [in the North] and the cruelty exercised against the Defenders by the military' and Waterford alone remained unaffected as the United movement spread through the south-eastern counties in the course of the summer.[15]

But what Madden has called the 'judicial murder' of William Orr, in October 1797, created more sympathy for the United Irishmen than all the other repressive acts together. Orr, a young presbyterian farmer of Antrim, was capitally convicted for administering the United Irishmen's oath to two Fifeshire fencibles in April 1796. He had been arrested in September 1796 and detained for a year in Carrickfergus gaol before being tried in September 1797. At a time when juries in the North were not afraid to convict, the Carrickfergus jury was reluctant to pronounce judgement in the face of conflicting evidence and recommended Orr to mercy. After the trial the two fencibles were completely discredited and the Castle was flooded with petitions from prominent Ulster loyalists and reformers alike on the impolicy of proceeding with the execution. Lake, however, was convinced that a respite would undo the success of the summer, and the execution was duly carried out on 14 October. The publicity surrounding the affair had been immense, and Orr's dying declaration was printed and widely circulated after his death. Orr was the first real martyr of the United movement and 'Remember Orr' became the battle cry of United Irishmen everywhere.[16] His trial and execution had become a public symbol of repression, and even prominent loyalists warned government that excessive military pressure would be counter-productive if those guilty of abuse on the side of the authorities were not also punished. Instead, people coming forward to take the oath of loyalty were arrested anyway, and the uncontrolled, 'wanton brutality' of the yeomanry subjected those who had surrendered arms to the same reprisals as those

14. See such accounts, Apr.–Jul. 1797 in I.S.P.O. 620/30/257, 620/31/72 and 205; S.O.C. 1016/31; B.L. Add. MS. 33103 fos. 359 and 369, 33104 fo. 250. See also Kerrane, 'The Background to ... 1798', 90–1.

15. I.S.P.O.S.O.C. 1016/8, 51, letters to Pelham, 17 Apr. and 15 Oct. 1797; C.R.O. U840/C31/1, Camden to Portland, 6 Oct. 1797.

16. Dickson, *Revolt in the North*, 177–82 and Append. xxiii; Lecky, *Ireland in the Eighteenth Century*, iv, 103–16; *H.M.C. Charlemont MSS.*, ii, 306–7.

who had not. The blatant bias of the courts in favour of the military drove many to seek protection in the United Irish oath, for they were persecuted whether they had taken it or not. The poorer catholic sections of Ulster society suffered most in Lake's campaign, and they flocked in great numbers to become United men, making the Defender alliance a reality and totally altering the balance of the lower committees. Orr's trial was a warning of the alternative, and the United song commemorating the young Antrim farmer could well boast: 'Thy blood to our Union more energy gave.'[17]

But this influx of new members had created its own problems; and if the disarming of Ulster had not significantly weakened the movement, it had precipitated an internal crisis which would ultimately prove more destructive. With the French confidently expected in April, the enthusiasm of the lower committees was easily contained; they were even encouraged to surrender their arms to avoid reprisals and assured that the French would come with more. In February the executive held an emergency meeting in Dublin to discuss re-opening communications with France. A secret committee of Lord Edward, Thomas Addis Emmet and Richard McCormick was authorized to choose and instruct a suitable agent, and the choice fell on Edward Lewins, then a member of the executive. Lord Edward secured him a passport through Colonel Despard in London. A member of the Irish landed class, Despard had spent most of his military career in the West Indies and the Spanish Main, and rose to become military superintendent of British Honduras. He nursed a smouldering resentment against the War Office, which had recalled him on half pay in 1790, and in 1797 was a member of the London Corresponding Society and a correspondent of Duckett's, from whom the passport may have been obtained.[18]

After a careful briefing by O'Connor, Lewins left for Hamburg, arriving on 29 or 30 March. His imminent arrival had been announced by Lady Fitzgerald in a letter to her sister, Mme Mathiesson, and he was introduced to Reinhard on the 31st. Lewins explained that the United Irishmen had not acted when the French fleet lay off the Irish coast because the time and place of arrival were unexpected. Even so, Hoche might have had the help of 40,000 Irishmen had he actually landed. Although the organization had not yet been extended outside Ulster and Leinster, events in Ulster had almost trebled its adherents, and the French could now expect help from at least 100,000. Against them government could bring 18,000 regular soldiers, 25,000 yeomanry—dismissed by Lewins as mere auxiliaries—and 20,000 militia, a third of whom were sympathizers. Considerable care had been

17. Zimmermann, *Songs of Irish Rebellion*, 71; see I.S.P.O. 620/31/171 and 175 for complaints from Tyrone and Antrim, 29–30 June 1797; see Mary Anne McCracken's account of the atrocities, 26 Jul., in T.C.D. MS. 873/130.
18. I.S.P.O. 620/18/14, Higgins's information of 27 June 1797; M. Elliott, 'The "Despard Conspiracy" Reconsidered', *Past and Present*, 75 (May 1977), 47.

Plate 19. Charles Frédéric
Reinhard (Bibliothèque
Nationale)

taken to brief Lewins, and he was able to give Reinhard accurate coastal
information, details on the positions and strength of the defence forces in
Ireland and on the numerical strength of the United Irishmen. He had also
been instructed to apply to the Spanish minister in Hamburg for a loan of
£400,000. But the principal object of the mission was to renew communications with Hoche, and to repeat O'Connor's request for 20,000–25,000
French troops, 80,000 stand of arms, artillery and officers, all to be landed in
the north of Ireland. Lewins's statements confirmed accounts already reaching
France of the rising temperature in Ireland, and Reinhard was convinced of
his veracity.

But there was something about Lewins's manner which made Reinhard
uneasy. In his conversations with Mr. De Nava, the Spanish ambassador,
Lewins had spoken of Ireland's ability to liberate herself and her determination to be enchained by no foreign power. When Reinhard queried these
comments, Lewins replied that France's silence was creating a bad impression
in Ireland; she should issue a declaration outlining the help Ireland might
expect to attain independence, and the guarantees she could offer for its
maintenance. Lewins's mission had been fully authenticated by Lord Edward

himself, who spoke with Jagerhorn, an emissary sent to London to check upon Lewins. But Lord Edward had told Jagerhorn that France must send help before 20 June as the Irish could not hold back the rising after that.[19] Lewins on the other hand had emphasized United Irish control over their followers and their determination to defer the rising till the French landed. Reinhard suspected that Lewins was involved in some disagreement within the United Irish leadership, for he had read in the English papers documents published by the secret committee of the Irish House of Commons, in which the Ulster provincial committee of the United Irishmen was said to have dismissed its executive. Lewins was a pedant of the first order, lacking the enthusiasm of previous Irish agents with whom Reinhard had spoken, and the coolness between the two men was as much a product of clashing personalities as anything else.[20] The decision to send Lewins to France had been taken unanimously by the United Irish executive in February. But his caution reflected his colleagues' nascent suspicion of French intentions, and when Lord Edward travelled to London such doubts had already produced a crippling conflict within the executive on the issues of an Irish rebellion and French help.

The crisis in Ulster had forced the leaders to tighten security, principally by cutting the flow of information to the lower committees.[21] When the ranks were being swollen by men who had experienced military repression at first hand, who recognized their increasing strength, but were urged to hold back until the French came, it was difficult to keep their impatience in check when April passed, no French force arrived and no information percolated through about the French negotiations. Lack of communication between the upper and lower levels of the Society was exacerbated by a crisis in the Ulster leadership, the arrests having removed the more experienced and respected figures and filled the vacuum with younger militants. We 'hardly knew who to look upon as leaders', Samuel Turner later told Lord Downshire, '. . . we looked upon ourselves all as generals . . .'.[22] A new Ulster executive proved unsatisfactory and was reshuffled (this was the account read by Reinhard), only to be shattered shortly after by the flight abroad of most of its members.

Throughout April Ulster made secret preparations for the reception of

---

19. On Jagerhorn's mission see A.A.E. Corr. Pol. Ang. 590 fos. 224–5 and 261, 591 fos. 431–6; A.H.G. B¹¹ 1 (correspondence for April) ; and P.R.O. H.O. 100/70/113.

20. See McNally on Lewins in I.S.P.O. 620/10/121/56. For Lewins's account of his mission, see A.N. AF IV 1671 plaq. 1 fos. 99–105; for Reinhard's correspondence with Paris see A.A.E. Corr. Pol. Ang. 590/217–27, 261, 266, 310–18, 333 and Corr. Pol. Ham. 111 fos. 148–50.

21. P.R.O. H.O. 100/70/93–4, Camden to Pelham, 8 Aug. 1797.

22. Kent C.R.O. U840/O196/2. For the increasing division between the upper and lower committees see I.S.P.O. 620/10/121/58, McNally's information of 22 May 1797; B.L. Add. MS. 33105 fos. 262–3, Watty Cox's Information Dec. 1797; and *Report from the Committee of Secrecy . . . Commons [Ireland],1798*, Append. no. xiv.

the French; colonels and lieutenant colonels were appointed for their respective areas and returns of men, arms and ammunition were made at meetings of the county military committees. By May the followers were becoming restless, with Down, the United stronghold, forcing the pace. They demanded more information on the use of their funds (one of the Belfast treasurers had lately absconded to America with £1,000), the appointment of a precise date for the rising, and in particular an account of executive dealings with France. A national meeting was called in Dublin to take returns of arms and men from the lower committees, and county meetings were convened in preparation. At the Down meeting held on 11 May at Ballynahinch, it was resolved unanimously: 'That our Delegation do demand in explicit Terms the Nature of the Engagement with France; we think that men who have risked their life and property in support of Business should be entrusted with such information and that they be instructed to bring forward the Business with or without such assistance.' Further meetings held at Rathfriland and Dromara expressed similar sentiments and the feeling in Down was clearly overwhelmingly in favour of an immediate rising.[23]

The Dublin discussions took place in the first week of June and Ulster was represented by Bartholomew Teeling, Samuel Turner, Alexander Lowry, Joseph Orr and John Tennent, son of a presbyterian minister in Belfast. The main catholic delegates, Thomas Braughall, John Keogh and Richard McCormick, did not attend, and seem to have objected violently to any idea of a rising. Some of the Ulster delegates urged an immediate rising on the committee, but according to Turner 'The Dublin part of the Executive Committee did not like this plan, and after much altercation and dispute refused to act in concert with the Northerns which the latter resented very highly and accused the others of cowardice . . .'. The 'Northerns' returned to Ulster determined 'to begin the business by themselves'. But the Ulster leaders had not been unanimous at the Dublin discussions and when they convened again at Randalstown, the Antrim colonels refused to act without French aid. Shortly afterwards the main militants, Turner, Orr, Lowry, Tennent, Teeling, James Coigley, a catholic priest from Armagh, and Arthur MacMahon, a presbyterian minister from county Down, fled on hearing that warrants were out for their arrest.[24] They had a fruitful stay in England, building upon contacts already established, and by the end of the year all were reunited in France.

---

23. P.R.O.N.I. D.714/2/1, Magin's report of 15 May 1797; B.L. Add. MSS. 33104 fo. 125 and 33105 fos. 14–15, statements by W. Torney and Dr. Macarra; I.S.P.O. 620/10/121/55–63, McNally's May reports, and 620/34/54, John Maxwell's notebook, 1797.

24. *Report from the Committee of Secrecy . . . Commons [Ireland], 1798,* Appends. nos. xiv and xv; *Castlereagh Correspondence,* i, 283; P.R.O.N.I. D.714/2/3, Magin's information of 17 June 1797. See Turner's account of the June proceedings in P.R.O. H.O. 100/70/335–52.

II

The flight to England was a predictable move when the Ulster societies had been encouraged by reports of increasing support from the mainland. In particular the sight of Britain's navy immobilized by the Nore and Spithead mutinies and the fear that France might permit such an opportunity to pass had contributed to the mounting impatience of the United men throughout April and May.[25] The lower committees had good reason to think the mutinies the product of republican influence, for the punitive despatch of Defenders and United men into the fleet from areas under the Insurrection Act had become a fact of daily life, and the extension of the United movement to England and Scotland was a particular facet of the post-Bantry-Bay re-organization.

England was doing badly in the war, and when a more stable government had finally been established in France with the Directory, Pitt had seemed embarrassingly eager for peace. But France's rejection of England's peace overtures in March 1796, and the humiliating expulsion of the English negotiator Malmesbury from Paris in December, at the height of an invasion scare in Britain, were symptoms of England's declining diplomatic position. The English people were convinced that the 1796 French invasion preparations had been aimed at England rather than Ireland. Despite the shabby showing of Tate's men in Wales, their landing had an unnerving effect on the coastal communities of the south and west, and the Home Office was flooded with petitions to remove French *émigrés* and prisoners of war from such vulnerable areas.[26] An air of contagious gloom hung over English politics in the first half of 1797. England had been deserted by her continental allies Prussia and Austria, and by April, with rumblings in her own armed forces, she faced France alone. At home there was a serious financial crisis and the country was in the throes of an economic recession. Whitehall tried to derive political capital from the naval victory at Cape St. Vincent on 14 February, but with demand increasing for the dismissal of the ministers and a full enquiry into the poor showing of the navy in December, it would have required more to restore public confidence. National morale could not have been lower when news of the mutiny at Spithead reached the country in the closing days of April.

Petitions for reform in the conditions of naval service were frequently received at the Admiralty and normally ignored. But the petitions from the North Sea Fleet in December 1796, and the Channel Fleet the following February, revealed a novel combination between different ships and ports.[27]

25. I.S.P.O. 620/10/121/62-5, McNally's information, May–June 1797; Tone, *Life*, II, 428–9.
26. See P.R.O. H.O. 42/40, H.O. 28/22/194 and Adm. 1/3974 for such requests; also B.L. Add. MS. 33197 fo. 79 for Spencer's comments.
27. *Spencer Papers*, II, 105–12; see also M. Lewis, *A Social History of the Navy, 1763–1815* (London, 1960), 59; and B.L. Add. MS. 35197 fo. 81 for the petition from the *Royal George* at Spithead, 28 Feb. 1797.

On 13 April Admiral Bridport ordered the ships at Portsmouth to sea against a French force expected to sail from Brest. The men refused to sail until their petition had been answered. On the 26th the Plymouth squadron joined the mutiny. It seemed that the trouble might blow over when the sailors' demands for extra pay and the removal of unpopular officers were conceded. But the mutiny was renewed on 7 May when the Admiralty delayed implementing its promises. Mutiny quickly spread to other parts of the navy, erupting in the Nore fleet on 7 May and reaching Admiral Duncan's ships at Yarmouth in the last days of May. When Duncan was ordered out to blockade the Dutch fleet at Texel, all but two of his ships deserted and joined the mutineers at the Nore. The crews of the East India Company's ships on the Thames likewise refused to sail until wages were increased. Mutiny became contagious and signs of discontent appeared in the contiguous land forces. When ships from Spithead finally joined Admiral Jarvis's fleet off Spain in July, the red flag of mutiny was hoisted within days of their arrival. July also witnessed mutiny on the British ships off the Cape of Good Hope, and by October it had spread to those in the Indian Ocean.[28]

Initially the Nore mutiny was no more than a token of support for that of Spithead. When news arrived of the Spithead men's return to duty the Nore mutineers might have done likewise had government accorded them similar concessions, instead of adopting the high-handed policy of demanding unconditional surrender. George III was angered at the spectacle of his Lords of the Admiralty travelling to Sheerness to confer with mutineer delegates, and he refused to grant their demands. Supplies to the Nore fleet were cut in an effort to force submission. The mutineers replied by blocking the Thames, and lost the goodwill of the country which had played such an important role in the Spithead success. By mid-June impending starvation had destroyed the solidarity of the Nore men. Several ships had already broken away and surrendered to the port authorities, and in a bid to escape, Richard Parker, the Nore leader, gave the signal for sailing. Not a ship moved, the mutiny was over, and Parker surrendered on 4 June. Throughout the next month courts martial sat at Sheerness. Parker and thirty-five others were condemned to death, and Parker's ship the *Sandwich* was scuttled.[29]

The English, Irish and French authorities looked on in amazement at this spectacle of England's prized navy incapacitated by mutiny. France was elated at Britain's embarrassment. La Reveillière was reporting on British press reaction to the mutinies at a full meeting of the Directory. The use of

---

28. P.R.O. Adm. 1/53, court martial on board H.M.S. *Victorious*, 5 Jun. 1798; Bodl. Burges MSS. J. W. Dacres to Burges, 16–19 Aug. 1797; and P.R.O.N.I. D. 1748, for the Cape mutiny.
29. Details of the mutinies are taken from: P.R.O. Adm. 1/5339–41; *Spencer Papers*, II, 110–73; *The Trial of Richard Parker* (London, 1797); C. Gill, *The Naval Mutinies of 1797* (Manchester, 1913); B. Dobrée and G. Mainwaring, *The Floating Republic*, 3rd edn. (London, 1937); D. Bonner-Smith, 'The Naval Mutinies of 1797', *The Mariners' Mirror*, XXI, (1935), 428–49, and XXII, (1936), 63–86; and J. Dugan, *The Great Mutiny* (London, 1966).

the term 'a floating republic' by one newspaper to describe the current state of England's vaunted navy caused him to collapse in fits of laughter; 'toutes ses bosses s'agitèrent de jubilation,' as he exclaimed 'Une république flottante! Mon Dieu, que c'est joli.'[30] But there was no corresponding effort to capitalize on this new development. The mutinies fed the Directors' complacency about the strength of Irish sedition in the fleet and, much to Tone's dismay, they did not share his sense of urgency that advantage should be taken of the situation to send another force to Ireland.[31]

The British authorities found it inconceivable that the sailors would combine against their country at such a time of crisis. Pitt was convinced that the mutinies were 'not of native growth' and blamed French and Irish agents instead. Two magistrates sent to investigate the reputed sedition among the sailors found no evidence to substantiate the accusations. But many remained convinced that 'a spirit, in itself so repugnant to the habits and dispositions of British sailors, must have had its origin in those principles of foreign growth, which the Societies of the conspirators have industriously introduced ...', and two acts were hurried through parliament making it treason to seduce His Majesty's forces from their loyalty.[32]

The overriding cause of the mutinies was the appalling conditions of naval service, but emergency recruiting procedures had also introduced a new kind of sailor into the navy of the 1790s. Prior to the war with France, most seamen had been 'born' into the service, recruited from traditional seafaring areas and easily reconciled to the rigours of naval life. But in 1797 over 100,000 of the 120,000 to 135,000 strong naval force had been recruited in the preceding three years, primarily products of the Quota Acts of 1795 and 1796 which had extended naval enlistment to the inland counties. A fine imposed on local authorities who failed to meet the required quota some-times caused them to resort to exceptional forms of recruiting. Nowadays, the argument that many quota-men were convicts or riff-raff is played down. But the system did send a different kind of recruit into the navy, usually younger, better educated, less inured to the traditional rigours of naval life, and unprepared to accept unreasonable manifestations of authority.[33]

The trials which followed the collapse of the mutinies revealed a widespread knowledge of Painite thinking among the leaders, and a conception of

30. *Mémoires de Barthélemy*, 209.

31. Tone, *Life*, II, 228–9, 248–50.

32. P.R.O. H.O.42/41. For suspicions of treasonable infiltration see *Reports from the Committees of the House of Commons*, x, 794; B.L. Add. MS. 35197 fo. 124, Spencer to Bridport, 25 Apr. 1797; and *Spencer Papers*, II, 111–15, 156–7.

33. Lewis, *A Social History of the Navy*, 59–66; see also P.R.O. Adm. 1/3991, on the Quota Men, and Clive Emsley's introduction to *North Riding Naval Recruits, the Quota Acts and the Quota Men 1795–1797*, ed. A. M. Hill and M. Y. Ashcroft (Yorkshire, 1977), 7–13. I am grateful to Clive Emsley for drawing my attention to this document.

America and France as symbols of liberty.[34] A lurking sympathy with France was widespread in the fleet, and much to France's embarrassment hundreds of English sailors flocked there to offer their services when Amiens re-opened communications. A national break-down of those arriving at Calais between 24 April and 12 June 1802 sheds some light on the potentially volatile elements which indiscriminate recruiting introduced into the British navy. A sample of 247 included 57 French, 26 English, 26 Irish, 26 Spanish, 20 Swedish and 16 Americans. Many foreigners were of course caught up in normal home recruiting procedures, but men were also pressed in foreign ports. France constantly complained of English recruiting procedures in the Dutch and Hanseatic ports, and one United Irish sailor, later charged with sedition by the British authorities, told of how he and several others had been press-ganged on the Spanish coast. France was more wary of foreigners in her armed forces, and they were excluded by law. Foreign deserters were especially frowned upon, even those who had acted out of republican sympathies.[35]

But it was the Irish element in the navy which attracted most attention in the aftermath of the mutinies; and London, Paris and Dublin alike were convinced that these were the product of infiltration by Irish republicans. The 1799 secret report on treasonable societies claimed: 'The mutiny ... furnishes the most alarming proof of the efficacy of those plans of secrecy and concert, ... for converting what might otherwise produce only a hasty and inconsiderate breach of subordination and discipline, into the most settled and systematic treason and rebellion ... The persons principally engaged in it ... were many of them United Irishmen.'[36] The leaders of the mutiny went to great pains to refute such accusations. At Portsmouth one crew threatened to throw Admiral Gardner overboard for calling them 'skulking fellows, knowing the French were ready for the sea and they afraid of meeting them', and in reply to an article in the pro-ministrial *Sun* newspaper, the delegates issued a statement '... to convince our Country at large, that there is not in anywise the least spark of republican spirit' behind the mutinies.[37] If treason played no part in the outbreak of mutiny, however, it did have a subsidiary role in its extension and continuation. A policy of systematic infiltration of the navy was only adopted by the United Irishmen after the 1797 outbreaks

---

34. Gill, *The Naval Mutinies*, 222–3; P.R.O. Adm. 1/3974, 5336–42. Similar sympathies appeared in the 1798 mutinies, see e.g. H.O. 28/24/435–40.

35. See Marine correspondence in A.N. F⁷ 3050 doss. 2 fos. 1–29, and F⁷ 7303 doss. B⁴ 3715; and see P.R.O. H.O. 28/32/81–93, A.A.E. Corr. Pol. Ham. 111 fo. 333 and 112 fos. 200–14, for English naval recruiting in continental ports; 1700 Frenchmen who had served in the British navy were discharged in 1802, see P.R.O. H.O. 28/28/165.

36. *Reports from the Committees of the House of Commons*, x, 794.

37. B.L. Add. MS. 35197 fo. 115; see also H.O. 28/24/125, 'Parker's Dying Appeal to the Seamen'; *Dublin Evening Post*, 25 Apr. 1797.

and most of the documents supplied by the 1799 report in support of its claims are significantly taken from later cases.

The disproportionate number of Irish in Britain's armed forces, particularly the navy, was common knowledge in the 1790s. Irish agents in France can be forgiven for exaggerating their numbers when home politicians made similar claims to remind England of her neglected duties towards her neighbouring dependency.[38] In November 1796 Pelham calculated that Ireland had contributed 15,000 recruits to the navy since the opening of the war. The following spring, however, when Whitehall's fears of the real motives behind the mutinies demanded a more thorough enquiry into Irish influence, Pelham had to admit the gross inaccuracy of such figures.[39] The common practice by Irish magistrates of disposing of local troublemakers by permitting them to enlist in the navy, and the large number of Irish recruited in England, make accurate assessment impossible. But a survey of the crews which mutinied in sympathy with the Irish rebellion the following year reveals an Irish component of 50 per cent or more on board the mutinous ships.[40]

However, it was the kind of Irishmen in the fleet rather than the number which caused particular concern. In an address prepared for circulation to the Irish in the navy, the United Irish committee in Paris later claimed that 'in the heat of the action, a cluster of determined Irishmen could create as much confusion on board as the actual capture of the ships, and thereby secure their own liberation . . .'[41] The Insurrection Act of 1796 had officially sanctioned the despatch of suspects, untried, into the navy; but unofficially the practice had been common since the opening of the war. Whitehall made a determined effort to prevent it after the mutinies; but in a situation of near rebellion in Ireland, the absence of adequate prison facilities made it impossible to eradicate the evil.[42] The proportion of Defenders or United Irishmen sent to the navy in these years must consequently have been considerable, and a recent analysis of the Australian convict papers shows that the majority of those transported for their part in the mutinies were indeed Irish.[43] It would be a gross assumption to say that all the Irish sailors were republicans; but most had been nurtured on the tradition of the secret society

---

38. See e.g. *The Speeches of the Rt. Hon. Henry Grattan*, 4 vols. (London, 1822), III, 46, and Lecky, *Ireland in the Eighteenth Century*, III, 515–17; see also Kent C.R.O. U840/O143/6.

39. B.L. Add. MS. 33113 fos. 66–70, Pelham to the Duke of York, 14 Nov. 1796; and I.S.P.O. 620/31/138, 204 and 291 for the 1797 enquiries. Dobrée and Mainwaring, *The Floating Republic*, 106, calculate $\frac{1}{8}$–$\frac{1}{2}$ of the navy in 1797 to have been Irish.

40. *Reports from the Committees of the House of Commons*, x, 818–20, Lewis, *A Social History of the Navy*, 129; see also I.S.P.O. 620/36/44, 620/37/1 and 155 for United Irish plans against the navy.

41. A.N. BB⁴ 103 fo. 181.

42. See P.R.O. H.O. 100/75/341; I.S.P.O. 620/31/37, 72, 154, 167 and 291, 620/33/80; C.S.O. 1847/1/153 and B.L. Add. MS. 33103 fo. 361 for the failure of attempts to stop the practice.

43. G. Rudé, *Protest and Punishment* (Oxford, 1978), 183–4.

and opposition to the law. They were not the stuff from which loyal seamen were made. The volatile nature of such a body of men cannot be stressed too much, and it would be a misunderstanding of the nature of popular disturbance to deny the existence of treason in the navy simply because few sailors were educated enough to be committed republicans. The conviction that treason had been an active ingredient in the mutinies was voiced by too many people in authority to be easily dismissed as a desire to conceal the atrocious conditions on board the ships. Even the two magistrates who failed to find any signs of 'Jacobinism' behind the outbreak of the mutinies had noted that attempts were being made from the shore to keep them alive, and warned that traitors might exploit the discontent among the sailors.[44] There is no irrefutable evidence of a campaign by France and the English and Irish republicans to infiltrate the armed forces in the period before the outbreak of the 1797 mutinies; but the cumulative impression of the fragmentary information available is that such an attempt was made.

The French governments of these years were under no illusion about the comparative strengths of the French and British navies, and the former had become little more than a fleet of transports for troops.[45] Realizing that she could not hope to defeat England at sea, France had displayed an active interest in weakening her naval power by other means than pitched battles and needed little encouragement to recognize the asset provided by the large Irish element in the British navy. In Switzerland, Lord Edward and O'Connor were asked about the possibility of organizing an insurrection among the Irish sailors, and Berthonneau's instructions are a significant indication of how the United Irishmen had revived French interest in the Irish sailors. He was to have arranged arson attacks on the British dockyards, established Irish agents in the ports, and invited the Irish sailors to help in the liberation of their homeland by taking their ships to Irish ports.[46] Duckett and Madgett had assured France that the collapse of England's naval power would automatically follow the liberation of Ireland, not only by terminating the supply of provisions and soldiers, but by provoking a mutiny among the Irish sailors.[47] It is not surprising therefore that, from 1796 onwards, there is a marked correlation between preparations to invade Ireland and increased efforts by France to incite mutiny in the British navy. Every French fleet which sailed for Ireland carried a supply of handbills to announce the liberation of their homeland to the Irish sailors, and many felt that the mutinies

44. P.R.O. H.O. 42/41, their report of 16 June 1797.
45. See e.g. A.N. BB⁴ 102 fo. 25, Instructions secrètes [1796] and **BB⁴** 103 fos. 182–3.
46. A.H.G. B¹¹ 1, Instructions secrètes [Berthonneau]. P.R.O. F.O. 27/54, C. W. Flint to J. King, 13 Jul. 1799, and *Mémoires de Barthélemy*, 155 for the Swiss negotiations.
47. See A.A.E. Corr. Pol. Ang. 588 fos. 480–1, for Madgett's claims [1795], 589 fos. 155–6 and 592 fos. 129–30, for Duckett, Feb. 1796 and Dec. 1797.

were a delayed implementation of plans which were to have been effected before the fleet sailed against Hoche the previous December.[48]

The first signs of United Irish efforts to infiltrate the navy do in fact coincide with their preparations to receive the French at the end of 1796. In September Christopher Carey, a Dublin Defender turned United Irishman, was reported to be travelling through south-west England with a French agent (possibly Berthonneau); he had spoken with some of the sailors in the ports and introduced the United Irish system into Portsmouth. Carey had been one of William Duckett's principal contacts in his 1793-95 mission, and they remained in touch throughout the 1790s.[49] Duckett's position in any discussion of subversive influences in the navy is crucial, but extremely difficult to track down. In his pioneering re-appraisal of the Anglo-Irish intelligence system, W.J. Fitzpatrick dismissed the claims of Tone, Madden and many contemporary United Irishmen in France that Duckett was at best a thorough scoundrel, at worst an English spy. But Fitzpatrick erred in the opposite direction by giving Duckett almost total credit for causing the 1797 mutinies. The mistake is understandable, for British officials later became so intrigued by Duckett's interests in the British navy that concentration on this aspect of his activities, to the exclusion of all others, is a characteristic of surviving sources. Fitzpatrick's description of Duckett as 'an amateur rebel envoy' is thoroughly misleading. Rather he was another of the intelligence professionals referred to in chapter two, with the important difference that he was not for sale to the highest bidder; his sense of mission to liberate Ireland and to regenerate its people fostered a degree of private enterprise in his activities which makes it difficult to assess the level of official French sponsorship behind them. After his early mission in 1793 Duckett remained intermittently in the pay of his original employer, the Minister of Marine. He became part of the marine crusade to liberate the seas from English domination, of which Léonard Bourdon, ex-Montagnard and French agent in Hamburg from December 1797 to May 1798, became the principal instrument. It was through Bourdon that Duckett was able to exert particular influence on this programme, and from Bourdon's correspondence with Paris we learn something more of Duckett's activities in England and Ireland.[50]

Bourdon transmitted to Paris Duckett's recommendations for an intelligence

48. See A.N. AF II 186ᵇ doss. 859, BB⁴ 103 fos. 180-3 and BB⁴ 123 fo. 235 for French addresses to the Irish sailors.

49. I.S.P.O. 620/18/3, Boyle's information, Apr.–Jun. 1797; P.R.O. H.O. 100/65/140, 9 Dec. 1796. See also A.N. AF III 57 doss. 225 pᶜᵉ 1–3, for Duckett's claims to Léonard Bourdon.

50. Fitzpatrick, *Secret Service under Pitt*, 105–15; Tone *Life*, II, 32–3, 141, 151–2, 171, 206, 208, 219–20. For British interest in his naval connections see *Castlereagh Correspondence*, I, 308, 417; P.R.O. F.O. 33/14–16; and N.L.I. pos. 210, Life of William Duckett, 70. See also Duckett's correspondence in A.N. AF III 186ᵇ doss. 858–9, AF III 58 and BB⁴ 122 fos. 284–99, and the Ministers' statements in AF III 206 doss. 943 fos. 29–30.

J. J. LÉONARD BOURDON.

Ancien instit.^ur Dep.^te du Loiret à la Convention,
Président des Jacobins,
Administ.^ur de l'Hôpital de Toulon,
membre du comité de salut public.
Né à Orléans en ?....+ vers 1819.

Vignères Ed.^r 4, Rue du Carrousel, Paris.

Plate 20. Léonard Bourdon
(Bibliothèque Nationale)

network in the British Isles, with Carey and Despard as linchpins in Ireland and England respectively. Despard in particular had figured prominently in Duckett's French correspondence, and they had probably met during his early mission when he had become an active member of the London Corresponding Society. He also began associations at this time with such future L.C.S. militants as John Ashley, a London shoemaker and one-time secretary of the L.C.S., and the Scot Dr. Robert Watson, then a member of its executive committee.[51] Watson's connection is particularly intriguing. Most historians assume that it was Richard Watson who was active in the ports at the time of the mutinies. It was in fact Robert Watson, Duckett's acquaintance, who travelled to Portsmouth. Henry Hastings, a young Irishman in London, a member of the L.C.S. and reputedly of the United Irishmen also, later told the authorities that Watson had gone to Portsmouth the previous spring on official L.C.S. orders; but as the mutinies intensified the Society lost its nerve, recalled him, and made him the scape-

51. See P.R.O. P.C. 1/23/A.38; F.O. 33/16/50; A.A.E. Corr. Pol. Ang. 592 fos. 84–5; and A.N. AF III 57 doss. 225 p^ces 1–3 for Duckett's relationship with the British democrats.

goat for its withering confidence. Watson was furious and told Hastings that 'a Revolution would certainly soon take place here, and that it would be better for those who acted than for those who behaved supinely'. Towards the end of the year Watson sent Hastings to Bourdon in Hamburg with information on the societies in England and Scotland. He claimed that 50,000 were ready to rise in Scotland and 200,000 in England, and with the Irish they awaited a French landing before rising. Hastings remained in Hamburg until late April 1798, consulting frequently with Bourdon and Duckett, and associating with a growing number of United Irish militants in the city. Watson fled shortly after Hastings' revelations, travelling via Sweden, Denmark, Hamburg and Berlin; he finally reached Paris on 10 September 1798, where for the next two years he acted as a self-appointed English republican agent to France, working in association with the Irish.[52] The activities of Duckett, Carey and Watson prior to the mutinies may not have been connected, but their association thereafter is indisputable, and in July 1797 Duckett's official mission to travel to England and contact the mutinous sailors was only prevented by news of the mutiny's collapse.[53]

The mutinies had revived United Irish confidence, shaken by the initial stages of Lake's disarming. United followers were encouraged by assurances that Bridport's fleet would mutiny when the French sailed for England. Belfast intensified its demands for an immediate rising, suggesting that if the mutineers at Sheerness could bring the ships to Cork, they could start the rising without French aid. If the United Irishmen had played no noticeable part in the outbreak of mutiny, they made a determined effort to keep it alive once it had started. Members were urged to enlist in the navy, a directive which appears to have met with considerable success, and in July some 1,200 United Irishmen were reported to have enlisted since the outbreak of the mutinies. Carey brought funds to the mutineers raised at fairs in Ireland and from the subscriptions of the lower United committees; the United committee in Portsmouth seems to have been active as an intermediary between Dublin and the mutinous ships, and there are frequent reports of delegates and supplies of handbills having been sent to it from Ireland. Francis Higgins, Thomas Boyle and Leonard McNally, who supplied most of the information on United Irish reactions to the mutinies, were particularly

52. On Watson see Thompson, *Making of the English Working Class*, 185–90; Dugan, *The Great Mutiny*, 271; J. G. Alger, *Englishmen in the French Revolution* (London, 1889), 529; and *Dictionary of National Biography*, ix, 30–1. See however P.R.O. P.C. 1/41/A.138, L.C.S. General Committee Meeting, 25 May 1797; and P.C. 1/43/A.152; and A.N. AF I I I 57 doss. 225 p[ces] 1–2 on Hastings. Watson's memoranda, Sept. 1798–Oct. 1800 are in A.A.E. Corr. Pol. Ang. 592 fo. 220, 593 fos. 18, 532–7 and A.N. GG[1] 72 fos. 114–15; and Desbrière, *Projets et Tentatives*, ii, 280.
53. For Duckett in Hamburg see A.A.E. Corr. Pol. Ham. 111 fos. 311–12; A.A.E. Corr. Pol.Ang. 592 fos. 80, 84–5 and 129–30.

effective agents, and there is no reason to doubt the picture of the zealous attempts to sustain the mutinies which emerges from their reports.[54]

It is difficult to see what effect such efforts had on board the mutinous ships, but treason does appear to have played a real, if subordinate role in perpetuating the mutinies. Unlike the more serious mutiny at the Nore, that at Spithead is generally thought to have lacked any political content. But even here several of the ringleaders were subsequently discovered to have been United Irishmen. Valentine Joyce of the *Royal George* was the first to raise the red flag on the ship, and both he and Robert Lee had administered the United Irish oath to many of their colleagues. Two others, who were later executed, proved to have been recent Irish recruits.[55] H.M.S. *Defiance*, the most troublesome ship at Spithead, had an unusually large component of Irish sailors. Although there is no evidence that they were United Irishmen or Defenders, they proved sympathetic enough to seize the ship the following year on hearing of the Irish rebellion and French landing, and to administer an oath to their shipmates 'to be true to the Free and United Irishmen, who are now fighting our cause against tyrants and oppressors . . . and . . . to carry the ship into Brest the next time the ship looks out to sea'. Twenty-five Irishmen from the *Defiance* were court-martialled and nineteen executed—the largest number from any single vessel to be executed in the era of the mutinies. The Irish on the *Royal William*, *Glory*, *Caesar* and *St. George*, all of which had been involved in the 1797 mutinies, were found to be United sympathizers in 1798.[56] It is possible that the United Irishmen had singled out the mutinous ships for future infiltration. But the events of 1798 were to show that even without such manipulation, England could not have relied upon the Irish sailors at a time when Ireland was making a bid for independence.

The vacillation of the Nore mutineers after the collapse of the Spithead mutiny and the King's refusal to grant terms, left a vacuum in their leadership into which some Irish conspirators stepped. Richard Parker was subsequently executed as the nominal leader of the Nore men. But the man who had first suggested raising the red flag on the *Inflexible* was John Blake from county Clare, and the Irish on board were the driving force behind the mutiny. The *Inflexible* was one of the last two ships to remain in a state of mutiny. At an early stage Blake had suggested taking the fleet into a friendly port. Dublin Castle received reliable information that the United Irish executive had in

54. See their information of Jun.–Jul. 1797, and that of J. Collier, in I.S.P.O. 620/3/32/27, 620/10/121/65, 620/18/3 and 14, and 620/31/236.
55. P.R.O. H.O. 100/70/7, Cooke to Grenville, 4 Jul. 1797 on Lee. See Dugan, *The Great Mutiny*, 296–7; Fitzpatrick, *Secret Service Under Pitt*, 113.
56. See P.R.O. H.O. 100/79/338 and H.O. 28/25/42 for the *Defiance*. *Reports from the Committees of the House of Commons*, x, 818–20; see also I.S.P.O. 620/36/44 for the *Royal William* and 620/37/1 and 155 for further reports of United Irish influence in the navy, 1798.

fact issued instructions to the United men in the navy to take their ships to France.[57] Several groups of mutineers did make a dash for France, but Blake and seventeen companions, half of whom were Irish, were the only ones to reach their destination. At 5.00 a.m. on 16 June, the fugitives arrived at Calais and offered their services to the French Republic. Little is known of Blake's background, but his memoranda to the Directory betray a level of education unusual for an ordinary seaman. This disposition to view France as 'la terre de la liberté' was shared by a number of the mutineers, and Duckett claimed that many more would have followed Blake's example had they not feared the possibility of being returned to England as prisoners of war.[58] All of this does not prove United infiltration; but it does show that Franco-Irish hopes in the collusion of the Irish sailors after Ireland's liberation were not entirely groundless. Many of the Irish trouble-makers during the mutinies were subsequently dispersed through other ships, a common naval practice at the time. When Ireland rose the following year, these same men organized a number of supportive mutinies, and intermittent United participation in other mutinies over the next few years suggests a continuous policy of United infiltration long after the Nore and Spithead mutinies had collapsed.[59]

Further light can be thrown on the events of April to June 1797 by looking at them in the context of the developing alliance between Irish, English and French republicanism. That year saw the beginnings of the United English-men; with them unfolds a picture of incredible complexity, that of militant English republicanism, a violent and, in the late eighteenth century, an essentially foreign tradition which was to gain its first martyrs with Despard and his companions in 1803 and was to raise its head spasmodically over the next half-century. Cultural and commercial connections between Ulster, Scotland and the north of England made United influence, especially among the weaving communities, an inevitable by-product of the florescence of the Ulster movement in 1797. Contact had been maintained between Scottish and Irish democrats since the days of the Scottish Convention in 1792 and United Irish missionizing in early 1797 produced rapid results.[60] Several agents were sent to Scotland by the Ulster executive in the spring of 1797, and committee meetings were told that the Scottish had adopted the United constitution. Societies of United Scotsmen or North Britons do begin to appear about this time, closely modelled on the United Irishmen and swearing a typical United oath 'to form a brotherhood of affection among Britons of

57. I.S.P.O. 620/18/14, information from Francis Higgins, 8 Jun. 1797.

58. A.N. BB⁴ 122 fo. 186, Duckett to the Minister of Marine, 9 Nov. 1798. The correspondence between Blake and the French government is in A.N. F⁷ 7264 doss. B³ 9686, F⁷ 7303 doss. B⁴ 3715, AF III 58 plaq. 2 fo. 20 and A.A.E. Corr. Pol. Ang. 590 fo. 388.

59. For details see P.R.O. H.O. 28/24–5 and H.O. 79/6; and see under note 56.

60. See Goodwin, *The Friends of Liberty*, 282–304, for an account of this gathering of the Irish, English and Scottish reformers.

every description', and a more general oath against betraying the movement.[61] By May Scottish sympathizers were trying to seduce the Scottish fencibles leaving for Ireland, and one agent from county Down told of having attended a national meeting of the Scots on 10 May at which 2,878 members were returned. By the time of the Edinburgh meeting on 10 September returns had risen to 9,653.[62]

The United Scotsmen played some part in extending the United movement into adjacent areas in the north of England, but once again it was the Ulster leaders and the more militant Leinster men who attached the flagging English democrats to the system. As in Scotland, contacts between the United Irishmen and radical reform groups in England had been maintained since the early 1790s. But by 1797, the new, activist United Irish Society was losing patience with its former English friends. William Putnam McCabe, the talented son of one of the original Belfast leaders, probably spoke for his colleagues and for many democrats in England when he dismissed the famous L.C.S. publicist, John Thelwall, as 'a damned cautious fellow', and the Ulster leaders found a ready audience on the mainland for a new political initiative.[63]

Manchester was to become England's Belfast, and again it was the Ulster militants who were largely responsible for spreading the United organization through Lancashire. James Dixon, a Belfast man living in Manchester, was actively swearing in United men as early as November 1796; in January 1797 he was appointed delegate to Belfast to discover information on the French negotiations and to bring back copies of the United oath and test, and there was a steady stream of Ulster agents to the north of England thereafter. By May 1797 Whitehall was receiving reports of 900 having taken the United Irish oath in Manchester, and when the Rev. James Coigley arrived after the clash with the Leinster leaders in June, he was introduced into working-class reform circles with an ease which suggests that the United system had already taken a firm hold.[64] He brought an official address from the Ulster United

---

61. T. Johnston, *A History of the Working Classes in Scotland* (Glasgow, 1922), 231–2. The same oath was administered by George Mealmaker, tried for treason in Jan. 1798, see *State Trials*, XXVI, 1137. See also H. W. Meikle, *Scotland and the French Revolution* (Glasgow, 1912), 185–7.

62. P.R.O. H.O. 42/40, Dunbar to Pelham, 15 May 1797. For the extension to Scotland see I.S.P.O. 620/27/1, 620/34/54; P.R.O. H.O. 100/70/329 and B.L. Add. MS. 33119* fos. 80–111. See also *State Trials*, XXVI, 1179–90.

63. I.S.P.O. 620/27/1, J. Bird's information [1797]. For such disillusionment amongst the English societies, see N. Cox, 'Aspects of English Radicalism: the Suppression and Re-Emergence of the Constitutional Democratic Tradition, 1795–1809' (Cambridge Univ. Ph.D. thesis 1971), 121–9 and see P.R.O. P.C. 1/44/A.161 for Scottish missionizing in England.

64. P.R.O. P.C. 1/41/A.136, the information of Robert Gray in 1798; see also H.O. 100/70/335–52, for Turner's information, Dec. 1797 and I.S.P.O. 620/30/158, Greville to Pelham, 23 May 1797; see also A. V. Mitchell, 'Radicalism and Repression in the North of England, 1791–7', (Manchester Univ. M.A. thesis 1958), 87–8.

leaders, telling of his own imminent departure for France and assuring the Manchester brethren that help from France would arrive shortly. In addition he seems to have firmly tied the Manchester movement to that in Ulster, which thereafter sent new signs and oaths to Manchester every month. Coigley had fled from Ireland with the other leaders repulsed at the June meeting. Turner, using the alias of Hare, was almost certainly with him at Manchester, and they travelled on to London to join the Rev. William Magaulay and the Rev. Arthur MacMahon.[65] There is certainly more than a hint that the Ulster leaders, defeated in their attempt to precipitate rebellion at home and unable passively to await the French as repression gained momentum, sought to fortify their position by pressure from outside. Although most of those taking the United oath in Manchester came from its Irish communities, a number of local radicals were also involved, notably Isaac Perrins, who kept the inn at Ancoats Lane where Coigley's discussions took place, and William Cheetham, a local employer. Cheetham in particular played a leading role in organizing the followers into divisions, distributing written signs and oaths, and handling the movement's finances. After his arrest in 1798, he and James Dixon alone of the Manchester prisoners were considered sufficiently dangerous to be detained until the expiry of the Habeas Corpus Suspension Act in 1801.[66] It was Cheetham who organized a subscription to purchase arms for the United Irishmen, raising £100 and a smaller sum of £10 to assist Coigley's journey to France. The remainder of Coigley's expenses was paid by the London Corresponding Society.

The London Corresponding Society had been declining steadily since 1795. The defence of its members arrested in 1796 and the disastrous venture of its *Moral and Political Magazine* had decimated its finances and embittered relations between the remaining leaders. Militants like John and Benjamin Binns, Joseph Stuckey, John Bone, Thomas Evans (later a member of the extremist Spencean sect), Robert Watson, Alexander Galloway, Richard Hodgson and Dr. Thomas Crossfield had been campaigning for the return to an active reform campaign when Coigley arrived in London with the offer of a new future for the militants in alliance with the expanding United movement. Coigley had already met Benjamin Binns the previous year and was convinced that he was a good republican. Both the Binns brothers were to play an important part in taking the militant wing of the London Corresponding Society into the United movement. They had come to London in April 1794 from Dublin, where they had been tailors' apprentices and where John had already been an active reformer; they joined the London Correspond-

65. I.S.P.O. 620/1/4/2, Nugent's information, 7 Aug. 1797 and 620/36/59, Wickham to Cooke, 24 Mar. 1798. See also Gray's information in P.R.O. T.S. 11/689/2187.
66. See P.R.O. H.O. 42/40, H.O. 42/41, T.S. 11/689/2187, P.C. 1/44/A.161, and P.C. 1/3514 for Cheetham and the United movement in Manchester.

ing Society, in which they quickly acquired a name as extreme democrats.[67] Despite the later tendency of some former L.C.S. members, notably Francis Place, to underplay the republican elements in the Society, in 1797 there was a very definite move towards more extreme politics within its leadership. By late 1798 Ashley and Watson had taken refuge in France, where they assured the Directory of the Society's genuine republicanism, despite its ostensible reformism.[68] Inevitable polemic aside, these memoranda point to a dramatic change taking place within the London Corresponding Society in the spring and summer of 1797, and there can be little doubt that, by the time of Coigley's departure for France that summer, a substantial number of its leaders were committed republicans. Certainly by June they had opted to throw in their lot with the United Irishmen, and Coigley later claimed that they had held negotiations with some 'United Scotch', sent to London for consultations about the nascent alliance. They financed his journey to France and asked him to present an address to the Directory, in which they pledged their support for a French invasion of Britain and the establishment of republics in both islands.[69]

The name United Englishmen was already in use in Lancashire before Coigley left for London. The ideas behind its development are elusive, and there is a startling contrast between the treasonable aims attributed to it by the secret parliamentary report of 1799 and the documents produced as proof. 'The Declaration, Resolutions, and Constitution of the Societies of United Englishmen', reproduced in Appendix No. 14 of the report, is little more than a replica of Tone's 1791 *Declaration of the Belfast United Irishmen*, with the words 'English' and 'Englishmen' substituted for 'Irish' and 'Irishmen'. It was found in a raid on a meeting in Clerkenwell in April 1798, and the United Englishmen's oaths discovered on Thomas Evans, the L.C.S. secretary who had presided over the meeting, again merely reproduced those of the United Irishmen in its constitutional period. As such, these documents reflect that faith in parliament as an institution and in parliamentary reform as an end which were such marked characteristics of the first United Irish Society, and cannot be taken simply as reflections of the United Englishmen's aims. Moreover, methods of organization such as the elaborate committee structure,

---

67. For the crisis within the Society see B.L. Add. MSS. 27808 fos. 67–91, 27815 fos. 165–6 and Thompson, *Making of the English Working Class*, 64–136. For the Binnses see I.S.P.O. 620/34/50; and P.R.O. P.C. 1/43/A.152 for Benjamin's address taken by Coigley on his first journey to France.
68. For Watson, see note 52; for Ashley see A.A.E. Corr. Pol. Ang. 592 fos. 164–5 and Mem. et Doc. Ang. 53 fos. 159–62.
69. A.A.E. Corr. Pol. Ang. 592 fo. 43, their address of 4 Oct. 1797. Coigley stayed with Thomas Evans in London, see T.S. 11/689/2187. For Binns's account of his talks with Coigley see N.L.I. MS. 873/450; and I.S.P.O. 620/1/4/2 and 620/32/88 for Nugent's information on the London visit.

Map 5. London in the 1790s. 1. Somers (Sommers) Town—Pancras just off map to the north 2. Battle Bridge 3. Tottenham Court Road 4. St. Giles 5. Drury Lane 6. Little Wild Street 7. Red Lion Square 8. Lincoln's Inn Fields 9. Chancery Lane 10. Holborn 11. Fetter Lane 12. The Temple 13. Fleet St. 14. Newgate 15. St. Martins-le-Grand 16. Cheapside 17. Hatton Garden 18. Clerkenwell 19. Compton Street 20. Aldersgate 21. Golden Lane 22. Finsbury 23. Fore St. 24. The Bank 25. Spitalfields 26. Whitechapel 27. The Tower and Tower Hill 28. Mile End 29. Shadwell 30. Wapping 31. Rotherhithe 32. Newington 33. Southwark 34. Lambeth 35. Tothill Fields 36. Houses of Parliament 37. The Treasury 38. St. James's Park 39. Strand 40. Piccadilly 41. Berkeley Square (1795 map, British Library)

the protocol to be observed at meetings, which were outlined in these replicas of early United Irish documents, were quite clearly applicable to an open, constitutional body and not to the republican and underground United English movement. In the early months of 1798, the United Englishmen were only just being organized in London, and it looks as though these United Irish documents were working models rather than the final drafts for the new organization. However, the oath, modelled closely on that of the United Irishmen, 'to form a brotherhood of Affection among Englishmen of every religious persuasion . . .'; which was found at the meeting, re-appears repeatedly in association with the United Englishmen. The Clerkenwell meeting does not conform to Francis Place's picture of the United Englishmen as a small group of fanatics, but suggests rather a co-ordinated effort to establish the movement firmly in London. By this date it was already organized in Lancashire, and it was from there that the more recognizable United English oaths were issuing: 'I swear . . . to obey . . . the Committee of United Englishmen and Irishmen then sitting in England and Ireland and Scotland, and to assist with arms, as far as it is in my power, to establish a republican Government in this country, and others, and to assist the French on their landing to free this country. So help me God.'[70]

One of the main functions of the organization was to infiltrate the armed forces. But although leaders spoke of schemes to get arms and of plans to help the French when they arrived, there is little evidence of any attempt at military preparations for an English rising, even at the height of the 1798 invasion scare.[71] Nor can the promotion of a revolution in England be clearly detected as a fundamental part of their programme. Talk of an English revolution remained vague; no coherent plan was ever worked out, and to think that 'Despard's Conspiracy' of 1803 was somehow a reflection of such a plan is to misunderstand the United movement as a whole and Despard's role in particular.

The enigma of the United movement on the mainland can only fully be understood as part of the United Irish programme. Despite the use of the term 'United Englishman' and to a lesser extent 'United Briton', the number of English participants remained small. To be 'United' was for most adherents to be a United Irishman, helping a movement in Ireland, rather than attempting to promote a revolution in England, and even the Binns brothers took the United Irish oath. The United Irishmen's campaign was not a republican struggle in the narrow nationalist sense of their twentieth-century successors. Even its lower ranks saw the English people as friends, and in 1797 reports

70. For U.E. oaths see *Reports from the Committees of the House of Commons*, x, 813–17; P.R.O. P.C. 1/42/A.144; and H.O. 42/44, 47 and 55.
71. Powell's information about talk of the London U.E. arming in Mar. 1798 is unreliable, see P.R.O. H.O. 42/44, also P.C. 1/41/A.136, and see H.O. 42/45 for attempts to seduce the military.

from the leaders of successful missionizing in England and Scotland proved as potent a boost to morale as promises of French help.[72] The mainland movement was seen principally as a fortification of that in Ireland; an additional weight in representing their strength to France; a diversion to retain troops in England when the Irish rebelled.[73]

Like the Spenceans later, the Society of United Englishmen was an amalgam of different groupings, all seeking some change in the existing system and gravitating towards a new movement after the war and the attendant repressive legislation had destroyed the national structure of the London Corresponding Society and the Society for Constitutional Information. Thus United men could be found meeting in former Corresponding Society haunts in Manchester and London at the end of 1797 and early 1798. But it would be wrong to see the United Englishmen as a coherent, formalized movement. Rather it was an umbrella-like network seeking a loose connection between existing groups. It did pose the kind of threat outlined in the secret parliamentary report, not because there was a real threat of revolution—in membership the United Englishmen were numerically insignificant—but because the intensive United Irish recruiting on the mainland had resurrected the militants from the spluttering embers of their reform groups, attached them to a powerful ally in Ireland and, through it, to France. Such participation in a wider revolutionary movement gave the United Englishmen a sense of purpose, unity and confidence which was noticeably absent from the struggling reform groups between 1795 and 1797.

III

With the collapse of the mutinies, and the failure of the Irish leaders to effect the rising confidently expected by the Ulster committees, the drive of the Ulster movement rapidly evaporated; '. . . there appears to be a general . . . depression of the public spirit . . .', wrote Mary Anne McCracken to her brother in Kilmainham prison in June. 'Belfast has greatly lost the confidence of the Country from being prudent and cautious on a matter of great importance which some violent and impatient men have been induced to consider a desertion of their cause . . .'[74] Moderate opinion favouring restraint until the arrival of the French prevailed. Dwindling information to the lower committees dried up altogether after June, when the executive suspended its meetings in the interests of security. The restiveness of the rank and file increased dramatically throughout the summer, disenchantment with their

72. See e.g. I.S.P.O. 620/18/14, Higgins's information 18 Jan. 1797; and 620/34/54, John Maxwell's notebooks, 1797.
73. P.R.O. P.C. 1/41/A.136, Gray's information on Coigley; and Powell's information in H.O. 42/44.
74. T.C.D. MS. 873/122.

leaders set in, and the carrot of French help was seen as a poor substitute for direct action. The lower ranks complained bitterly of the leaders' failure to transmit news and clearly recognized much of the information for what it was, a mere palliative to quieten their impatience. A typical example of this process was cited in Boyle's information for 1 July: '... they hold out still that Parker is not in Custody with a view of still keeping up the minds of their people which I believe is the last resource the heads of them have as the people are of late much disheartened seeing that the days on which they built their hopes passed over without anything done or properly attempted for their good.'[75]

Paucity of information on French intentions was in fact the executive's main problem. Nothing had been heard from Lewins because of his enforced delay, first in London until a passport could be acquired, and then in Hamburg. A letter which Tone had sent via Reynolds in America finally reached Ireland in May. He assured his compatriots that the French were preparing to return to Ireland and asked them to send an agent to France to help with arrangements. Any news from France, however slender, was a godsend to the Dublin leaders at this time. The communication temporarily checked Ulster's impatience for insurrection, and in June the executive sent William James MacNeven to France with new instructions dictated by the emergency which had arisen since Lewins's departure. The increase in United membership allowed them to reduce the required number of troops from Lewins's 25,000 to 5,000–10,000, but the huge increase in the quantity of arms required reflected the disarming of Ulster.[76]

The disagreement within the leadership had focused solely on the timing of the rising, and for the rest of the summer there was an uneasy agreement on the need to await a French arrival. But although there seems to have been unanimous support for the missions of Lewins and MacNeven, the militants sought to reinforce them by urging some of their own associates also to travel to France. At the request of Lord Edward and O'Connor, Turner and Bartholomew Teeling had left for Hamburg at about the same time as MacNeven. This lack of a unified policy on the French negotiations was symptomatic of the excessive individualism which was ultimately to shatter the United leadership, and the conflicting missions to France only served to discredit some of the more able negotiators. In the early summer of 1797, however, with the Ulster leaders conscious that the most favourable moment for a rising was slipping away, such impatience was understandable. When Teeling and two companions, Alexander Lowry and John Tennent, arrived

---

75. I.S.P.O. 620/18/3, Boyle's information, 1 Jul. 1797; also 620/10/121/55–68 and 620/18/14 for McNally's, Boyle's and Higgins's reports May-June 1797, and those of Magin Jul.-Sept., in P.R.O.N.I. D.714/2/4.
76. See MacNeven, *Pieces of Irish History*, 189–90, and A.N. AF IV 1671 plaq. 2 fos. 166–73, for MacNeven's requests; also Tone, *Life*, II, 346–7.

Plate 21. William James
MacNeven (Madden, *United
Irishmen*)

in Hamburg on 13 July, they told Reinhard that the principal motive for
their mission was 'the necessity of dispelling the disquiet of the mass of United
Irishmen who had been told neither of Thompson's [Lewins] nor Williams's
[MacNeven] journey and were starting to complain that indifference towards
France would result.' The Ulster committees had consequently been told of
their own mission 'to revive their hope' and Teeling returned immediately
with assurances from Reinhard that a Dutch fleet off Texel was preparing
for Ireland with Tone on board.[77]

Turner arrived in Hamburg on 10 June, MacNeven eleven days later. But
while all the agents sought French help as quickly as possible, there was a
subtle difference in emphasis in the militants' statements which was more
in tune with current French thinking. Lewins's reservations about French

77. A.A.E. Corr. Pol. Ham. 111 fos. 319–23, 353–4 and Corr. Pol. Ang. 591 fo. 230, for Reinhard's
correspondence on the missions. See also the report to the county Down meeting, 10 July 1797,
in *Report from the Committee of Secrecy Commons . . . [Ireland], 1798*. Append. no. XIV, 138.

aid were exaggerated in MacNeven who had witnessed the June disagreement. He had been sent to petition France for a force 'deemed just sufficient to liberate their country, but incompetent to subdue it', and like Lewins he demanded an invasion, to be led by Hoche, and firm assurances by France disavowing any intention of taking over the country. He made it clear that the Dublin leaders were not releasing information on the negotiations to their followers, and when Reinhard suggested that he return to Ireland with assurances to calm their fears, MacNeven answered that it was not the policy of the Leinster leaders to keep the lower ranks informed and insisted instead on continuing his journey to Paris. In contrast Turner and his companions had emphasized their trust in France's genuine intention of sending aid; their mission sought only such assurances as would revive the people's confidence and Reinhard was delighted at their declared intention of returning immediately to Ireland to deliver these assurances. Moreover, unlike the Ulster agents, MacNeven had insisted on postponing an Irish rising until the French were in the country, which was totally inconsistent with French policy after Bantry Bay. Reinhard argued that 'as French interests required the Irish to rebel without waiting for help ..., taking instead the December attempt as decisive proof of France's past and future intentions, ... for one side to say, help and we shall rise, and the other rise and we shall help, is a vicious circle from which the Irish must be the first to emerge'. MacNeven's caution had rankled with Reinhard. The bitterness of the negotiations intensified MacNeven's already mounting doubts about French invasion and injected a new caution into the Dublin movement when he returned home later that year.[78]

There is no evidence that Reinhard's preference for the younger militant United Irishmen had any appreciable effect on French policy, and both Delacroix and Reinhard himself were removed from office before the end of July. Any ill-effects for the Society were entirely domestic, another example of how United Irish attitudes towards France were frequently dictated by the lesser French officials. For the moment the growing numbers of United men in Paris worked harmoniously enough together. It was only later that the impatience which had impelled the militants to travel to Paris in the first place introduced similar quarrels to those which had already split the home society. Lewins's caution in particular was seen by Turner as part and parcel of the catholic leaders' betrayal of the Ulstermen, which he considered to have been behind the June altercation. He claimed to have discovered 'that the object of the Papists was the ruin and destruction of the country and the establishment of a tyranny far worse than what was complained of by the reformers', and an element of religious distrust played an influential

78. A.A.E. Corr. Pol. Ham. 111 fos. 311–12, 319–29 and 359, for Reinhard's correspondence with Delacroix, July 1797; also MacNeven, *Pieces of Irish History*, 190.

part in alienating him from the movement entirely. By October he had already embarked on another career as a double agent and was feeding London with accurate information on the French negotiations.[79]

Reinhard's outline of French policy towards Ireland was an accurate reflection of current French thinking. Public feeling in France was against another Irish invasion attempt in the first half of 1797, the focus of attention having shifted decisively to the Italian campaign, in hopes of an imminent peace with Austria. But the ultimate destination of the five divisions created for Hédouville's expedition remained undecided for many months after the expedition itself had been cancelled. Until the summer Truguet's plans still included some kind of venture to Ireland, and the Directory's commitment to securing Irish independence was unchanged.[80] But the divergence between intention and action was widened by a host of other commitments. The Directory was unwilling to risk any troops in overseas ventures when a constitutional struggle was pending inside France and delicate peace negotiations were in progress with Austria and England at Berne and Lille respectively. Since the beginning of 1797 Hoche's energies had been concentrated on the Rhine, where the Directory had intensified military strength, as much to contain Bonaparte's ambitions as to force Austria out of the war. With Austria pressurized by Bonaparte from the south and Hoche from the west, the rivalry of the two generals soon transformed the campaign into a contest, a race for Vienna and the popular acclaim which would accrue to the peacemaker. The beneficial effects of the successful push by Hoche and Moreau across the Rhine on 17 April, however, were nullified by Bonaparte's premature acceptance of unfavourable terms in the peace preliminaries of Leoben, signed with Austria on the 18th. The Directory was furious; Carnot's increasing pacifism determined his reaction, and he alone welcomed Bonaparte's move. Not only had Bonaparte bartered part of the Venetian Republic for a boost to his public standing, but he had failed to hold out for the left bank of the Rhine, by then one of the Directory's most cherished goals in the war.[81] The terms could not be disavowed because of popular euphoria at the prospect of peace, but the Directory determined to keep the army on the alert, ready to move against Austria if the ensuing peace conference at Berne could not secure more favourable terms. In the opening months of 1797, therefore, the Directors had little time to think of Ireland.

79. See Kent C.R.O. U840/O196/3 and P.R.O. H.O. 100/70/335–52 for his information.
80. See A.N. AF III 450 doss. 2478 fo. 21 for the cancellation order. But see the correspondence between the Directory and Petiet, A.H.G. B¹¹ 1; between Hoche and Dupont (Clarke's successor), A.D.S.M. 1 Mi 62/157/2091–7; also *Mémoires de Barras*, II, 359, 409, 419; and Aulard, *Paris . . . sous le Directoire*, III, 758, IV, 11–37, 73–5 and 80–1 on public opinion.
81. See *Mémoires de la Révellière-Lépeaux*, III, 31–3, Sciout, *Le Directoire*, II, 337–49 and R. Guyot, 'Le Directoire et Bonaparte', *Revue des Études Napoléoniennes*, I (1912), 321–34, for Leoben; see also *Mémoires de Barras*, II, 303–4, 378–91, 421–3 and A.H.G. B¹ 173 for the progress of the war.

Hoche, however, smarting from Bonaparte's latest coup, had turned his attention once more to Ireland. He and Lewins had finally met on 29 May, in Hesse-Cassel (Germany), and Hoche's adjutant Simon was despatched to Paris to sound the Directory on its Irish policy. Simon arrived in Paris on 5 June, the eve of the inception of a new Director to replace Letourneur, who had drawn the lot in the compulsory annual retirement of one Director. The new Director was Barthélemy, the former ambassador to Switzerland with whom Lord Edward and O'Connor had negotiated, who was now a confirmed royalist. With his appointment, and the loss of his supporter Letourneur, Carnot became increasingly isolated within the Directory, and a triumvirate of Reubell, Barras and La Revellière assumed more and more responsibility for decision-making.

Simon sensed an atmosphere of impending crisis; ministers proved elusive, and gave conflicting statements on Ireland when they could be found. Everyone supported another Irish expedition in principle, but no one was willing to risk French troops and 'les si, les mais ...' punctuated each conversation; 'quite frankly, I think the government undecided', concluded Simon, 'it would very much like to do something but it dare not. It has little confidence in its own resources and is afraid of the possible outcome at a time when it is negotiating peace with England.' Carnot's fortunes were clearly in decline, and Simon could only speak with him in secret. But Carnot was scarcely encouraging and had obviously been chastened by the Bantry Bay experience. He assured Simon that the Directory had not abandoned the Irish, but that England was clearly master of the seas and France could not then spare the necessary troops and ships to combat such supremacy. He would happily permit Hoche to organize the despatch of arms and some troops from Holland, and France would remember Ireland in the peace negotiations with England. But the councils could legally recognize another state only after its independence was an established fact, and there could be no further guarantee for Irish independence until the Irish had actually won it for themselves.[82] This policy for Ireland was outlined in an official statement to Hoche on 9 June:

> ... the state of fermentation in Ireland offers us ... the most favourable opportunity of defeating England; but we cannot immediately send the projected expedition. The fate of the continent must first be decided ... but we can prepare for its success, and perhaps even attain the principal results, by sending to Ireland partial and successive help in arms and munitions ... We want the Irish to proclaim the Independence of their island and we will help in this laudable enterprise, but with no formal

82. See A.D.S.M. 1 Mi 62/157/2094 and 2097, and A.N. AF I V 1671 plaq. 1. fo. 160 for Simon's correspondence with Hoche; and for his meeting with Lewins see A.H.G. B¹¹ 1, his letter of 30 May 1797, and Tone, *Life*, II, 407.

guarantee on our part. Our conduct towards them must follow the same lines as that adopted for the people of Italy who declared themselves independent. We protected their Liberty, but we made no agreement to sustain their new political status for fear of jeopardizing the Re-establishment of Peace.[83]

When peace negotiations between England and France opened at Lille in June, the United Irishmen were anxious to secure some French commitment to discuss Ireland's independence with the British representative.[84] Their fears would scarcely have been appeased by the Directory's June statement, especially after Bonaparte's betrayal of Venice at Leoben. There is no sign, however, that the United Irish ever received information on the Directory's new policy statement, and even Tone and Lewins were only shown Simon's account of Carnot's verbal communication, a much milder statement of the Directory's views. Had the home movement known of the document, it might have alienated the moderates entirely, but it would certainly have come as a timely justification for militant strategy. After all, Lord Edward had assured Jagerhorn that the Irish could turn out but for an almost total want of arms; the arrival of French artillery and officers that summer would surely have set in motion Irish rebellion plans.[85]

The Directory was happy enough to let the Dutch temporarily assume responsibility for Ireland. The Batavian Republic had offered France the services of the Texel fleet as early as March, and had been actively preparing for a naval expedition since then. Its destination had remained undecided, and although Scotland and Ireland were mooted, there was an obvious preference for the colonies. By the end of June, however, the Directory had decided to let the Dutch implement their obvious desire to prove their independent martial worth in an invasion of Ireland. Lewins and Tone were sent to the Hague for consultations with the Batavian Committee of Foreign Affairs and to provide General Daendals and Admiral De Winter, commanders of the projected expedition, with details on Ireland's internal situation.[86] But if the Dutch were eager enough to risk their fleet in March, their relations with France had deteriorated by the summer. The Dutch resented having to pay the upkeep of the 25,000 French troops occupying their country, whilst the appointment of Hoche to command their Irish expedition and the inclusion of 6,000 French troops savoured of a French attempt to curb any independent

83. A.D.S.M. 1 Mi 62/157/2095; a copy was sent to Truguet, see A.N. BB⁴ 103 fo. 8.
84. See A.N. AF IV 1671 plaq. 1 fos. 166–73 for U.I. fears about the consequences of these negotiations with England.
85. I.S.P.O. 620/3/31/3; Jagerhorn's report is in A.A.E. Corr. Pol. Ang. 591 fos. 431–6.
86. See Hoche's correspondence with Truguet, Jun.-Jul. 1797 in A.N. AF III 463 doss. 2801 fos. 41–6; Tone, *Life*, ii, 409–17; and A.A.E. Corr. Pol. Ang. 593 fo. 422 for Lewins's account.

Dutch action.[87] But it was the rejection of Dutch plans for representation at the Lille peace negotiations which rankled most, and by August the French naval commissioner in Holland attributed the delay in despatching the Texel fleet to Dutch reluctance to risk her forces before she knew the outcome of the negotiations. Indeed it is unlikely that the Texel expedition would have sailed at all had it not been for Daendels's own driving ambition.[88]

Since the Directory had already rejected any idea of a French expedition to Ireland that year, there was something distinctly odd about Hoche's appointment to the overall command, and his projected departure, not from Texel, but with a detachment of troops from Brest. After their successes in the spring elections, the growing strength of the royalists in the executive and in the legislative councils made a contest with the republicans inevitable. Barthé-lemy's appointment to the Directory and Carnot's leanings towards the Clichyens, the moderate royalists, had driven the other Directors into active alliance against their two colleagues. Their first attack on the royalist threat was a purge of infected ministers in July. Hoche significantly was appointed to the War Ministry on 16 July. The three Directors needed the support of a good republican general in their forthcoming struggle, for Moreau and his men on the Rhine were known to be royalist sympathizers. On the 18th, with Hoche already in Paris, news arrived that detachments of his army were spilling over the city limits from which the military were constitutionally barred. The outcry from the councils and from the two non-involved Directors forestalled the planned *coup* and Hoche was pulled before the Directory by Carnot to explain how 15,117 troops came to be in the suburbs of Paris. Barras, who had enrolled Hoche's services, had not revealed the non-involve-ment of the other two Directors, and an astonished Hoche was obliged to shoulder full responsibility with no effort to exonerate him by the intriguing Barras. The pretext for moving the troops near Paris was an order of 29 June, instructing Hoche to take 6,000 troops to Brest for embarkation to Ireland. Malmesbury, surveying the Paris conflict from Lille, was convinced that the Directory never had any intention of despatching an Irish expedition. Indeed, apart from the desultory preparations at Texel, which he considered little cause for anxiety, he felt that '. . . in the present state of parties they seem to have forgotten that they have a foreign Enemy . . .'.[89] Malmesbury's reading of the situation was probably valid enough in the case of the Directors them-selves, but the Marine and War Ministers had taken steps to implement the necessary preparations for the expedition and even the Directory would un-

87. See A.N. BB⁴ 112 fo. 5; A.H.G. B¹* 177 fo. 130 and B¹¹ 1, June 1797.
88. See A.N. BB³ 108 fo. 32; P.R.O. F.O. 27/50 (communiqué of 6 Aug.); and Schama, *Patriots and Liberators*, 264–9 for deteriorating relations between the two powers.
89. See P.R.O. F.O. 27/50 for Malmesbury's August correspondence.

doubtedly have gone along with the plans, if only to save face, had not an embittered Hoche returned instead to his army on the Rhine.[90]

There can be little doubt that when he left Cologne for Paris, Hoche had every intention of pushing forward with the Dutch expedition, and he had brought Lewins to Paris for that purpose. Lewins, however, was quickly caught up in Hoche's own sense of betrayal, and he was asked to have no further communications with the ministers and Directors held responsible. Apart from introducing MacNeven to the Directory when he finally arrived in Paris in August, Lewins adhered faithfully to Hoche's instructions. The Dutch had already sworn Tone and Lewins to silence about the Texel preparations and they were warned not to inform their compatriots until the expedition was due to sail. Tone was on board ship at Texel from July until September, totally out of touch with the Parisian authorities and Hoche alike. Teeling's second-hand communication about the Dutch preparations was accordingly the only information received by the home society in the course of that summer. The fate of the discussions in France and of Hoche himself had become inseparable, and Lewins and Tone accepted his judgement with a loyalty born of the interest which Hoche, more than anyone else, had continued to show in their cause.

But if Hoche's support in 1796 had been the most important single factor behind the despatch of the Bantry Bay expedition, in 1797, if not exactly a hindrance, it was the source of confusion and misplaced confidence among the United Irishmen at home. The Directory could have done little to help Ireland in the circumstances of 1797, but the United Irishmen might have had a more realistic assessment of what they could have expected, had information not been channelled almost exclusively through Hoche. From June 1796 until September 1797 Hoche had dominated the play of Franco-Irish diplomacy and his encouragement had given the Irish a sense of false confidence. Until the abortive *coup* of July, Hoche had good reason to trust in his own ability to influence the Directory's Irish policy, and for a while after the rebuff he continued to urge an expedition on the Paris government. But the campaign of vilification mounted by the press and the councils had deeply affected Hoche, and when Schérer, the Minister of War, reminded him again of the instructions to march to Brest, Hoche had banished all idea of going to Ireland. 'I repeat, Citizen Minister, that I will go neither to Brest, nor to Rennes, nor to Avranches, the expedition will not take place . . . never again

90. A.N. AF III 205 doss. 940 fo. 69, report of 12 Aug. on the Irish expedition; and AF III 463 doss. 2800–1, for a full account of the crisis; see also Thibaudeau, *Mémoires sur la Convention et le Directoire*, II, 170–242, who exonerates Hoche from any base motives in the affair; Aulard, *Paris . . . sous le Directoire*, IV, 215–87; Sciout, *Le Directoire*, II, ch. XII. A good account can be found in the personal papers of the different Directors, see e.g. *Mémoires de Barras*, II, 379–498, *Mémoires de la Révellière-Lépeaux*, II, 42–138, *Mémoires de Barthélemy*, 179–236. See Woloch *Jacobin Legacy*, 62–79, for the background.

will I play Don Quixote on the sea for the satisfaction of those who would prefer to see me at its bottom . . . '.[91]

In September, however, when MacNeven interrupted his return journey to Hamburg to bring Hoche news from Lewins, the General's old spirit seemed to have returned. Hoche promised to do his utmost to have 10,000 men, arms and artillery ready to sail from Brest to Ireland by the end of October. Some weeks later MacNeven conveyed the promise to Lord Edward in London, who returned to Ireland determined again to force the issue of a rising.[92] This, Tone's letter of May, and Teeling's July assurance, were the only communications received by the United Irish executive in the course of 1797. None had issued directly from Paris, but Hoche's support had given them an air of authority and they became the main sanction for the moderate United leaders' policy of holding back until the promised help arrived. The Brest project had continued to be discussed intermittently through the summer, and when the constitutional crisis was finally settled on 4 September, with the suspected royalists (including Carnot) ejected from the councils and the Directory, the rejuvenated executive returned immediately to its plans for a direct attack against the British Isles.[93]

By then Tone and Hoche had abandoned all hope of the Texel fleet ever reaching Ireland. Tone had languished on board the flagship *Vryheid* for nearly two months, his frustration relieved only by the surprise arrival of Tennent and Lowry on 5 August. Unsuitable weather conditions, the intensified British blockade after the suppression of the mutinies, and the increasing conflict between the Dutch military and naval command seemed to have confined the fleet indefinitely to port. Daendals had only supported the venture to further his own political position. As time passed, and the longer voyage to Ireland lost its attraction, he juggled with projects which might produce a speedier return, considering Yarmouth and London, and eventually opting for a landing in Scotland. Tone was consoled with assurances that some frigates might then be sent to Ireland, and was despatched to Hoche's headquarters on 2 September to seek approval for the new scheme. On the 14th Tone arrived at Wetzlar in Prussia. Hoche did not approve of Daendels's alterations and wrote immediately to Paris. But Tone was now more concerned about Hoche than about the expedition. He was shocked at the altered appearance of the young general and could tell from his violent cough that he was dying of consumption. The men at the camp told how the late attacks by the royalists and journalists in Paris had 'preyed exceedingly on his spirits'

91. A.H.G. B[11] 1, Schérer to the Directory, 2 Aug. 1797 and Hoche's letter of 4 Jul. 1797.
92. A.N. AF IV 1671 plaq. 1. fos. 99–105, Lewins's account; and see A.A.E. Corr. Pol. Ham. 112 fo. 120, I.S.P.O. 620/3/31/3, and P.R.O. H.O. 100/70/335–52 for Turner's information.
93. See A.H.G. B[5] 41, for correspondence concerning the formation of the *armée d'Angleterre*, Oct.–Dec. 1797; also A.N. AF III 272 fos. 315–16, for Debelle's attempt to secure implementation of Hoche's promises.

and were 'the probable cause of his . . . illness'. By 17 September Hoche could no longer walk and had to be carried from room to room as he continued to conduct military business. Two days later he was dead.[94]

Tone and Lewins were shattered by the news, for Hoche had already initiated measures to implement the promise he had made to MacNeven. Lewins was particularly conscious of Hoche's personal commitment to Irish independence and sought immediate assurances from the Directory that his promises to the Irish would be honoured. Barras's response was a foretaste of the difficulties the Irish would experience without Hoche's mediation. Barras adhered to the Directory's June position, assuring Lewins that France's views on Ireland had not altered, and that when peace was concluded with Austria, help would again be despatched; but nothing could be expected before the following spring, and Barras refused to give a commitment that Irish independence would be included in any peace negotiations with England.[95] The truth was that France had become increasingly complacent about Ireland's ability to liberate herself and the build-up of Irish in France and Hamburg, all insisting on the strength of rebelliousness in their home country, only served to feed such complacency. By the end of the year MacNeven, Turner, Teeling, Tennent, Lowry, Coigley, MacMahon, Tandy (lately returned from America), Joseph Orr, Pat and John Byrne from Dundalk, and Thomas Burgess and Anthony McCann, both from Drogheda, had all penetrated through to France with the same message.[96] No French agent was ever sent to Ireland after MacSheehy's mission, but missions continued to England; and it was a peculiarity of France's secret diplomacy that the vision of a direct attack on England gave to every glimmer of English republicanism a greater significance than the accepted fact of Irish rebelliousness. With Mengaud and Colleville claiming the existence of an English revolutionary party, Thomas Muir arguing the case for Scotland, and the United Irish themselves mistakenly thinking that information on their successful recruiting in England and Scotland would fortify their position, it is not surprising that when peace was finally signed with Austria at Campoformio on 17 October, France should have immediately embarked on plans for an invasion of England, with only a possible diversion in Ireland. Any hope of help reaching Ireland before the end of the year had already vanished. The defeat of the Dutch fleet on 11 October at Camperdown, after its eventual

94. Tone, *Life*, II, 417–46. For the Texel preparations see A.N. BB³ 108 fos. 26–39, BB⁴ 112 fos. 6–7 and AF III 70 doss. 283. For Daendels's ambitions see P.R.O.H.O. 100/70/335–52, Schama, *Patriots and Liberators*, 281–92 and 308, and C. J. Woods, 'A Plan for a Dutch Invasion of Scotland, 1797', *The Scottish Historical Review*, LIII (Apr. 1974), 108–14.
95. For Lewins's conference with Barras, see A.N. AF IV 1671 plaq. 2 fos. 175–180; and A.A.E. Corr. Pol. Ham. 112 fo. 48, for the reaction of the U.I. leaders in Hamburg.
96. A.N. F⁷ 7293 doss. B⁴ 2671.

escape from Texel on the 5th, seemed irrelevant; for Tone and Lewins it had long ceased to be an Irish expedition.

If the Camperdown defeat attracted little attention in France, it was certainly quite the reverse in the British Isles, where it was given immense publicity by the authorities as a symbol of Britain's revived fortunes. Moreover, the reaction of the United Irishmen to the defeat highlights the increasing divergence between the domestic movement and their representatives abroad. The moderates' success in restraining their followers was totally dependent on the proximity of French help. Their position had been refortified by Teeling's and MacNeven's assurances, and from mid-summer preparations to receive the French were stepped up. By mid-October, however, with no sign of a French arrival, the old divisions re-appeared. The Ulster committee again urged a rising, but were overruled. O'Connor sent Teeling back to the Continent to re-open direct communications with Hoche, in ignorance of his death. After Camperdown the moderates' insistence that the French were still expected was less plausible. When Teeling wrote from Paris in October, with a full account of the new situation there, his letter was intercepted at the Dublin post office, and United ignorance of French intentions after Camperdown meant that a crisis in the home movement could not long be delayed.[97]

The United Irish leaders on the Continent never fully understood the doubts which were altering the home movement. Direct contact with the Directory and its ministers made them confident of France's good intentions. They never seemed to realize that the rapidly changing situation in Ireland demanded frequent communication, not a policy of waiting until there was news of significant importance to send. The loss of the *Northern Star* was a major disaster for the home movement; its policy of devoting large sections to unbiased reporting from the continental press had kept leaders and people informed of the real situation abroad. In the crucial summer of 1797 secondhand and frequently biased accounts from the London press were no substitute. The second United Irish paper, the *Press*, which appeared in Dublin at the end of September, never had the same appeal; its moralistic and polemical tone did not hold the same attractions for the general reader.

Despite his geographic removal, Tone was astute enough to recognize that the moderation of the home leaders had lost them an opportunity which might never return.[98] The Ulster leaders had built up a movement of such strength that the defence forces would have been hard put to contain it. It had not yet extended much beyond Ulster and Leinster, but the sympathy it

97. See I.S.P.O. 620/3/31, 620/18/3 and 14, for information on the home movement, Aug.–Oct. 1797. For Teeling's mission see A.A.E. Corr. Pol. Ham. 112 fo. 48 and P.R.O. H.O. 100/70/339–52.
98. Tone, *Life*, II, 428–9.

had generated would have been sufficient to tie down a sizeable military force without the complications which repression and frustration were to produce the following year. Instead the year ended on a bleak note, with the United Irish Society in decline and the chances of a successful independence movement being eroded. In France too, with the unscrupulous Barras and the ruthlessly ambitious Bonaparte in charge of preparations against England after 1797, the chances of the Irish securing the kind of assistance and treaty terms they required were progressively diminishing. Hoche was ambitious, but his genuine republicanism, cosmopolitanism and recognized commitment to Ireland would have done much to secure a fair deal for the United Irishmen. With Bonaparte's meteoric rise yet to come, the United Irishmen had still to learn just how great a loss Hoche's death had actually been.

PART THREE
1798: 'Who's to Blame?'

The French to invade us had swore,
  And vast preparations got ready;
But had they in time reached our shore,
  The game was all up with poor Paddy.

We fell to work, 'hammer and tongs',
  The *Orange* and *Green* both together;
With sabres, with guns, pikes and prongs,
  Each party the other did leather;

The Demons of Discord, their brands
  High flourished throughout the whole nation,
And madmen, with parricide hands
  Spread ruin and wide desolation.

Humbert and his *Sans culotte* crew
  Just landed in time to be taken;
Of his allies, an ill-fated few,
  Got *'what the cut left of the bacon'*.

'Who's to Blame?' [I.S.P.O. 620/48/47]

CHAPTER SIX

Rebellion

There is no simple explanation for what happened in Ireland in 1798 and many United Irishmen, even those who took part in the 1798 rebellion, were baffled at the form taken by their revolution. The fear of extermination banished the sophistication of revolutionary and counter-revolutionary ideas alike, as the protagonists appealed to their external mentors, to France and to England, to provide some way out of a situation over which they had lost control. But both powers viewed the Irish situation as an extended arena for their own internal problems and failed to intervene until Ireland's bitter civil war had exhausted itself. France's complacency about the Irish situation is understandable in view of the nature of the reports from the United Irishmen on the Continent. From the end of 1797, however, England's knowledge of United Irish activities was excellent, due to the operation of an increasingly efficient intelligence system by Pitt's wartime team. But England had neglected warnings of the deteriorating situation in Ireland and was incapable of offering anything other than a military solution when the crisis finally erupted in 1798. Her previously recognized role as mediator between the Irish government and the Irish people was forgotten, and supplanted in native tradition by that of the strong-armed supporter of biased authority.

What was most shocking about the 1798 rebellion was the gulf between the play of high politics, including those of the United Irishmen, and the realities of the situation in the country. The United Irish leaders had little confidence in the abilities of their rural countrymen. They sought French aid to 'cheque the *Chounnery* of the country ... and give the men of the Executive time to form a provisional Government ... ', as MacNeven later explained, and they over-extended and splintered their organizational web, fostering diversions outside Ireland in support of the blue-print of an independent state which their countrymen threatened to spoil.[1] The rebellion was to show that the ordinary Irishman had a blind reverence for good leadership, and had it been provided by the United Irishmen, both the '*Chounnery*' and military defeat might have been averted. Increasingly in 1798 one is

1. B.L. Add. MS. 33106 fos. 79–84, Henry Alexander to Pelham, 20 Sept. 1798.

aware of a movement, hitherto loosely united in its geographically and socially limited character, now developing on several divergent planes, with the French negotiations assuming a more important role as the domestic movement grew weaker. It is important to recognize that the United Irish movement was declining in 1798. The rebellion was not a United Irish one as it would have been a year earlier, but a protective popular uprising which a spent United Irish leadership failed to harness.

The singularity of French war aims in the early months of 1798 had actually intensified interest in the Irish situation. Plans to defeat England had assumed the proportions of a crusade, and Ireland was viewed as a crucial diversion, if not the actual means, of that defeat.[2] But in the reports of the United Irish leaders in Paris, there was no sign of the new urgency of the Irish situation, or of the imminence of revolt. Despite France's other commitments, it is unlikely that she would have ignored the pleas of someone known and respected like O'Connor, had he succeeded in reaching Paris with first-hand reports on the deteriorating Irish situation in February 1798. It is too easy to view Tone and Lewins in the same light as the other foreign exiles in Paris, as respected mascots of bygone French ideals, sustained by periodic effusions of empty internationalist sentiments. The other exiles were no longer of any use to France after 1797, when she was at peace with those powers against whom they had sought her assistance in the first place. But Ireland was still a fundamental part of France's continuing war strategy against England, and since its retention after independence would not have been necessary to French security, there was every indication that Ireland liberated in 1798 would have escaped the later fates of other satellite republics.

I

The United Irish negotiators in Paris were shattered by the loss of Hoche, and although the prospects of another French expedition to Ireland were brighter in the winter months of 1797–98 than at any time since Bantry Bay, his death had removed their established medium of discussion.[3] Barras's assurances of another Irish expedition in the spring were conveyed to Ireland and formed the basis of the home Society's preparations for the next six months.[4] But the feeling prevailed that the United Irishmen were having to start from scratch in schooling a new batch of ministers and generals in

---

2. A.N. AF IV 1687 doss. 2 p^{ce} 42, and P.R.O. F.O. 27/53/341–6, Bruix's memoirs of 9 Sept. and 20 Oct. 1798.

3. P.R.O. H.O. 100/75/7–9, Turner's information, Jan. 1798.

4. MacNeven, *Pieces of Irish History*, 191; Madden, *United Irishmen*, 1st. sers. I, 159. See also I.S.P.O. 620/10/121/93 and 620/43/9.

Irish affairs, and the ease of access gained in 1796 was never re-established. Initially Lewins had tried to fill the void left by Hoche's death by cultivating his military successor, Bonaparte, and with remarkable ingenuousness he implied as much in a long memoir detailing the history of Irish negotiations with Hoche. The rivalry between the two generals seems to have bypassed Lewins, and his praise of the dead general was scarcely calculated to ingratiate the United Irishmen with the new commander of the English invasion force.[5]

When peace was signed with Austria at Campoformio, France turned her attention once again to England, her last surviving antagonist. The *armée d'Angleterre* was established in November 1797, troops were transferred from Italy and Holland to the northern ports, and England for her part began to prepare herself for a full-scale siege. Many commentators have questioned the sincerity of France's English invasion preparations in 1798, attributing them rather to the Directory's desire to be rid of Bonaparte, its need to create an army for deployment against external and internal enemies, to placate national anglophobia, or to mount a patriotic loan. All these motives certainly played some part in the invasion preparations of November 1797 to May 1798. The Directory could not easily have evaded the problems left over from Fructidor or Campoformio. The Jacobin resurgence after the *coup* of Fructidor posed as great a threat as that of the royalists in 1797, and a liberal sprinkling of troops in the interior was considered essential to preparations for the March elections. On the eastern frontier the threat of renewed war was a constant reality; relations with Austria and Prussia remained brittle, and at Rastadt the continued negotiations with Austria to settle the future of the Rhineland increasingly emphasized the absence of any foundation for a lasting peace. With England and Russia pressurizing the two German powers to rejoin the coalition, and France's internal constitutional problems unresolved, the likelihood of an English invasion was already fading before Bonaparte transferred his interest to Egypt in the spring of 1798.[6]

In November 1797, however, the crusading zeal of the French against England was real enough, and for the moment the United Irishmen were fêted by all concerned in the preparations. The Paris cafés buzzed with excited rumours about the forthcoming expedition, and the continued celebrations for Campoformio became mingled with the invasion plans for England in a premature victory celebration. The theatres vied with each other to produce dramatized versions of the projected French landing in England; Rouget de Lisle's popular *Chant des Vengeances* proclaimed England

5. A.N. AF IV 1671 plaq. 1. fos. 99–105, Lewins's memoir [1799].
6. For the background to the abandonment of the English expedition see F. Charles-Roux, *Les Origines de l'expédition d'Egypte*, 2nd edn. (Paris, 1910); A. B. Rodger, *The War of the second coalition, 1798 to 1801. A strategic commentary* (Oxford, 1964), especially 16–42; Sciout, *Le Directoire*, III, 572–84.

the cause of all France's ills; ministers held grand banquets to promote a patriotic subscription, and Bonaparte's return to Paris contributed to the atmosphere of heady excitement.[7] Such noisy publicity and the tendency to mingle threat with reality was a characteristic of French preparations against England. The economic effects of an invasion scare on England seemed as important as the invasion itself, and the fears of the naval commanders about the intensified English blockade were often brushed aside. Until March, Barras's assurances of an expedition to the British Isles remained good, and Daendels, who still sought an outlet for his ambitions in Ireland and Scotland, remained in close contact with Tone and Lewins. He had continued to urge the inclusion of Holland's non-existent navy in another French expedition and was duly rewarded by Bruix's order of 14 December 1797 for a Dutch departure the following April.[8]

At a time when the situation in Ireland demanded immediate French assistance, however small, Tone and Lewins did not object to the delays and lengthy preparations required for a large expedition to both islands. It was a further indication of the degree of their removal from home developments. Tone had already resigned the role of negotiator to Lewins, as the official appointee, and the languid progress of discussions in the early months of 1798 amply justified the United Irish militants' growing concern about Lewins. There were signs that Tone and Lewins were becoming excessively francophile and were abdicating their independent stance. Tone applauded the French invasion of Rome and the 'fructidorization' of the satellite states, without reflecting on the possible repercussions for Ireland if the French invaded.[9]

But at a time when repression at home was swelling the numbers of Irish refugees to the Continent, Tone's power over their entry to France had been intensified. The invasion preparations of the winter and spring of 1797–98 made the evolution of a French policy towards the Irish exiles peculiarly difficult. Popular anglophobia had revived Jacobin demands for a purge of enemy subjects and a freeze on new entries.[10] But the Irish side of the invasion plans was designed to produce a sympathetic rebellion, and the presence of native leaders on board the expedition was highly desirable. Tone was accordingly assigned the task of monitoring all Irish requests for permission to enter France. His patriotism and reliability were unquestioned in Directorial

7. Aulard, *Paris ... sous le Directoire*, IV, 418–665; *Réimpression de l'Ancien Moniteur*, 29, p. 115.
8. For Daendels see A.H.G. B⁵ 41, correspondence with Desaix, Dec. 1797–Jan. 1798; MR. 1420 fo. 26, his Scottish invasion project, 25 Jan. 1798; and A.N. BB³ 146 fo. 124, letter to the Marine Minister, 30 Apr. 1798; also Tone, *Life*, II, 449–50. See also A.N. BB⁴ 114 fo. 233 for Bruix's order of 14 Dec.
9. Tone, *Life*, II, 458–60, 464–6; see also the Hon. A. S. G. Canning, *Revolted Ireland, 1798 and 1803* (London, 1886), 32, on this point.
10. See A.N. F⁷ 7293–4 and 7446 doss. B⁵ 8403.

circles; he had already established a close working alliance with Sotin, the Minister of Police, and after his appointment in October 1797, the procedure of issuing passports only to those Irishmen whose patriotism he confirmed became a formal extension of police activity. But Tone's removal from home developments rendered him ill-equipped to speak for the increasing numbers of United Irishmen fleeing to the Continent, most of whom had joined the Society after his own exile. Although he did seek advice from the United men already in France, even people like Lowry and Tennent had little knowledge of new adherents, and the absence of positive identification forced an increasing number of genuine Irish patriots to pursue a perilous existence on the French perimeter.[11]

French officials abroad tended to view foreign revolutionaries with greater sympathy than did the home government, and continued to grant passports more liberally than the post-fructidorian regime would have wished. Reinhard had been a particular culprit; both he and his successor Roberjot were cautioned for their liberality, and in December 1797 Roberjot had been officially instructed to issue no further passports to the Irish without prior permission from Paris.[12] However, whilst France was reluctant to openly justify the frequent accusation that she fostered foreign revolutionaries, current policy demanded a more liberal attitude towards the United Irish arriving via Hamburg. Tone's appointment was only one aspect of the implementation of an undercover policy for such sympathetic aliens. In addition, several agents operating quite separately from official diplomats were appointed to the Hanse towns to report on the activities of the *émigrés*, enemy agents, and friendly foreign exiles such as the Irish. Duckett proved particularly useful to the successive appointees, of whom Bourdon was the first and most successful, and possibly through the influence of Duckett, who became his private secretary, Bourdon's mission was transformed into one of mediation between France and the Irish and English revolutionaries in transit through Hamburg. Bourdon's appointment, however, was a product of the post-fructidorian Jacobin resurgence and was unpopular with many supporters of the Directory. In February 1798 he was recalled to Paris, and Sotin, the Jacobin minister responsible for his appontment, was also removed.[13] Their removal weakened the system of sympathetic surveillance at a time when

11. Tone's correspondence with the various ministers can be found in A.A.E. Corr. Pol. Ang. 592; and A.N. F7 7293 doss. B4 2671, 7348 doss. B4 9145, 7383B doss. B4 2119, 7417 doss. B5 5396 and 7440 doss. B5 7855.

12. See A.N. AF III 59 doss. 231 and 232 and A.A.E. Corr. Pol. Ham. 112 fos. 51–2, for Directorial displeasure with its Hamburg officials.

13. See A.N. AF III. 57 doss. 225; A.A.E. Corr. Pol. Ham. 112 fo. 347, and 113 fo. 37 for Bourdon's mission. See also Corr. Pol. Ham. 112 fo. 390, for his relations with Roberjot, French minister at Hamburg; and Sir James Craufurd's reports on his undercover activities in P.R.O. F.O. 33/15, F.O. 97/241, H.O. 100/77/222 and P.C. 1/42/A.143.

Tone's position was already being undermined by critics within the United movement itself.

The position of Tone and Lewins, as recognized United Irish agents in Paris, was undisputed until the autumn of 1797. Things changed rapidly, however, after Tandy's arrival from America in June. Tandy's name was well-known in France and he was warmly received. He had no appointment from any group in Ireland, but he expected to assume automatic leadership of the Irish in France by virtue of his former position, and there is no evidence that he ever sought to work in alliance with Tone. It was inevitable that ministers would come to listen to Tandy's advice as much as that of Tone or Lewins. But his opinions were suspect, and he brought an air of theatricality to the negotiations, causing Turner to liken him to a madman strutting 'about in the streets in the national uniform calling himself a Major.'[14] There is no indication that the Directory ever thought seriously of accepting Tandy's advice in preference to that of Tone or Lewins; but the French press capitalized on the propaganda provided by his residence in France, and his position was fortified by the arrival of the Scottish radical, Thomas Muir, lately escaped from Botany Bay, to which he had been exiled in 1794. He was an old friend of Tandy's and voiced the same claims to patriotic leadership, and he and Tandy attempted to establish their supremacy in a series of bombastic articles in the press. On St. Patrick's Day 1798 they organized a large dinner to which everyone who was anyone in past attempts on Ireland was invited. Kilmaine and O'Shee were there, and Tandy presided with oratorical assistance from that other revolutionary veteran, Thomas Paine. But this public pirouetting was more in character with their earlier experiences than with the cultivated secrecy of Irish negotiations in 1797–98. Tone was distressed to see Tandy and Muir 'puffing one another . . . for their private advantage' and led a deputation composed of Lewins, Joseph Orr and Lowry to caution Muir about his ill-advised publications. The two groups scarcely spoke to each other thereafter.[15]

Tandy's claims were to cause immense damage to United preparations at home. Reports of his activities in Paris were reprinted in the English and Irish press and he, rather than Tone, came to be regarded as the Irish generalis-simo who would lead the French forces in Ireland. Moreover, in the absence of frequent reports from Lewins, Tandy's letters to his son in Dublin, with their glowing accounts of his own position and of French intentions, carried considerable weight, and lulled the home movement into a false sense of security. In particular, contact was established between O'Connor and

14. P.R.O. H.O. 100/70/335–52, Turner's information, Dec, 1797.
15. Tone, *Life*, II, 460–2, 466–7. For French government attitudes to Tandy see A.N. Corr. Pol. Ang. 592 fos. 101, 103, 108 and F⁷ 7293 doss. B⁴ 2671. See also *H.M.C. Dropmore MSS.*, IV, 69, and 'Memoir of Gen. Kilmaine', *Dublin University Magazine*, XLVII (1856), 471.

Tandy, and the former's sense of frustrated militancy was fed by such confident representations.[16]

Given the increasing frustration in Ireland at Lewins's lack of communication, the gravitation of new Irish arrivals in Paris to Tandy's party was inevitable. Coigley and MacMahon were early recruits to Tandy's camp. Others like Madgett, Stone, Blackwell, a contemporary of Duckett's at the Irish College and now an officer in the French army, and several Irish-Americans who had been spurned by Tone or Lewins, also joined. In many cases their commitment to Irish independence was weak, but all bristled at the policy of exclusiveness followed by Tone and Lewins and at their reluctance to share information on the Irish negotiations. Tandy tried to call the two agents to account before a mock tribunal. Lewins refused to attend. Tone responded to the summons; but Tandy's failure to substantiate the charges caused Tone to dismiss the whole intrigue as unworthy of his attention. He might have done well to devote more time to the growing rift in the exile community, for it was causing much concern to the French officials involved in the invasion preparations. Tone's reputation was too well-established to have been tarnished by such cabals; but the Directory did seek advice from Tandy, and increasingly so when Tone and Lewins were absent from Paris in the months before the outbreak of the Irish rebellion. Tone was dismayed that the exaggerated claims of Tandy were taken up by the Paris press and reprinted in London, but he did little to contradict Tandy's claims, and the French were particularly bitter when they later discovered the groundlessness of his exaggerated statements.

Lewins's non-communication worried the militants at home. They accepted the majority preference for deferring the rising until the French arrived, but hoped nevertheless to secure both by accelerating the latter. Their frustration was understandable. Orders had been issued for supporters to keep quiet and to reserve their strength for the French landing.[17] But the militant leaders were less confident of their ability to sustain such organization without a promise of imminent action, and rightly so. A wave of petty crime occasioned by the economic crisis of 1797 and the hard winter which followed indicated that the hold of the United Irish Society outside Leinster was growing weaker. The cessation of the leadership's periodic tours of the provinces was taking its toll of the unsteady, and the frantic scramble to find military leaders in the weeks prior to the rebellion testifies to the general organizational collapse since the year before. Most disturbing was the incipient withdrawal of the

---

16. For the influence of Tandy's claims on the home movement see P.R.O. H.O. 100/70/93–4 and 281, I.S.P.O. 620/121/66–88, 149, and the *Press* for 14 Oct., 16 and 28 Dec. 1797, 11 Jan., 3 and 6 Mar. 1798.
17. See U.I. handbill of Jan. 1798 in I.S.P.O. 620/35/35; also S. Ó. Loinsigh, 'The Rebellion of 1798 in Meath', *Ríocht na Midhe*, IV (1970), 30.

North. Those northern emissaries who had played such a notable part in
diffusing the Society in 1797 were seen no more, and the recurrence of nocturnal attacks in county Down indicated a new weakness in what had been the
movement's main stronghold. The Ulster leadership had been broken by
arrests and exile; its finances were in chaos because of the expense of maintaining its prisoners, and a lottery to raise funds was so undersubscribed
that the prizes were withheld. When 1798 opened, Monaghan and Fermanagh
had withdrawn from the movement altogether.[18]

Militant anxiety took the initial form of attempting to bypass Lewins
and to secure an alternative source of information from France. Bartholomew
Teeling was the first to arrive with specific instructions to this effect, and
he corresponded with O'Connor until the latter's departure for England
shortly after Christmas 1797. Although Teeling's memorials laid greater
emphasis on the need for immediate French assistance, especially in the form
of arms supplies, he worked harmoniously with Tone and Lewins and appears
to have made some attempt to calm home fears about the latter's performance.
But some of Teeling's correspondence was intercepted and the continuing
dissatisfaction with Lewins's appointment helped produce another confrontation between the moderate and militant sectors of the United leadership
just before Christmas.

United expectation of a French invasion had reached another peak at the
end of 1797. Every issue of the *Press* in October and November and the
circulars from the Dublin leaders had strengthened the expectation. 'We
really did expect the French', one United Irishmen later told a Dublin
court. 'It was such a common phrase in every one's mouth, that we all thought
it.'[19] For the moment the leaders' assurances succeeded in forestalling a
premature outbreak, but the spread of official repression outside Ulster
rendered continued inaction undesirable. Moreover there were signs that
some of the Dublin leaders would have preferred to postpone the rising
indefinitely. After his release from prison at the end of July 1797, O'Connor's
impatience with the moderates rendered another clash within the leadership inevitable. In September he paid flying visits to militant supporters
in Cork and Belfast and was reported to have convened similar meetings
in Dublin. With their support assured, he and Lord Edward attempted
to force militant policy on the executive in a crucial meeting just before
Christmas. They claimed to have received instructions from France urging
them to assist a French invasion of England by rising and drawing off the

---

18. *Report from the Committee of Secrecy* . . . *Commons [Ireland]*, *1798*, Append. no. xiv; Kent C.R.O.
U840/C31/1 and P.R.O. H.O. 100/75/162–8, Camden to Portland, 6 Oct. 1797 and 6 Mar. 1798;
P.C. 1/44/A.155, information on the Cork organization; see also P.R.O.N.I. D.607/F/49, 99,
correspondence with Downshire, Feb.–Mar. 1798; and Powell, 'The Background to the Wexford
Rebellion', 167.
19. *State Trials*, xxvii, 435. The *Press* nos. 10, 20–8, 30–6.

English troops from the mainland, and suggested that an immediate rising might be provoked by spreading rumours of a planned Orange attack on the chapels during the traditional Christmas Eve mass. The crowds converging on the chapels for the service would disguise the military preparations, and the leaders could concentrate on the capture of Dublin Castle.

The moderates were aghast at such a shock project, totally overruled the suggestion and ensured against independent action by persuading the Dublin bishops to defer mass till the following morning. The claims of Lord Edward and O'Connor were an embellished rendering of Tandy's assurances that the expedition would sail in the spring. But both were convinced that the movement was declining rapidly; a rising might revive hope and force France to act decisively. O'Connor's obvious desire to run the show, however, was creating havoc within the leadership. Hitherto the differences between the moderates and militants had been on the timing of the rising alone. But the clash of personalities threatened to magnify the quarrel, and Lord Edward was to prove more persuasive with his cautious colleagues when the explosive influence of O'Connor was removed. O'Connor was disgusted at the manner in which former members of the old catholic committee, like Keogh, McCormick and Chambers, and their allies MacNeven and Thomas Addis Emmet, seemed to be dictating Society policy. After the December conflict he was to act very much as his own master from a new base in London, to which he was reported to have travelled in a great rage after the December defeat.[20]

O'Connor spent his first weeks in London socializing with his friends among the English opposition Whigs and radicals. His activities were closely observed by Whitehall, excited at the prospect of discrediting its political opponents.[21] Secretly, however, with the active support of Lord Edward and the developing republican movement in London, O'Connor continued to work for an Irish rising. The decline of the London Corresponding Society had continued throughout the latter months of 1797, and as membership plummeted throughout the winter, signs of activity from its republican elements increased. However, although the London government's cross-channel intelligence on the United movement had improved with Turner's change of allegiance, its domestic network still left much to be desired. James Powell, a former L.C.S. assistant secretary, was the main source of information on current developments within the London societies.

20. For various accounts of the growing division, particularly O'Connor's role, see B.L. Add. MS. 33105 fos. 116–17, 268, 307; I.S.P.O. 620/10/121/85–8, 620/32/183–5 and 620/36/227, information received, particularly from McNally, Sept. 1797–Jan. 1798; also P.R.O. H.O. 100/70/335–52 and 100/75/5–9, Turner's account; and P.C. 1/44/A.155 and T.C.D. MS. 873/744 for O'Connor's version.
21. I.S.P.O. 620/18^A/14, King to Cooke, 21 Jan. 1798.

But he did not regularly attend the breakaway group of L.C.S. republicans, then meeting at *Furnival's Inn Cellar,* and his information was defective.[22] Ministers juggled the pieces of information on the United movement in England in an attempt to incriminate O'Connor, but never succeeded in establishing a picture of sufficient coherence or plausibility to secure a conviction. Surviving evidence remains fragmentary, but additional information in the Irish and French archives permits a more plausible re-ordering of the pieces.

The United movement had spread in areas like Scotland, Lancashire, Cheshire and London, where earlier democratic societies had been particularly resilient and where there was a sizeable Irish workforce. The clubbish mentality of the Irish immigrants facilitated its expansion, and the movement was carried along established communication channels from Ireland as a matter of course. But although supporters had been encouraged by vague references to a national committee sitting in England or to plans for revolution, there were few signs of any attempt to draw together the inchoate sections of the United movement before the beginning of 1798.[23] In London there was little co-operation between the Irish and English workforce, and the intense clannishness of the Irish inhibited any overall direction by the London democrats, or indeed the higher class of United Irish leader. But there was an attempt to expand the United movement in the early months of 1798, to draw upon potentially sympathetic cells, and to revitalize and incorporate surviving traces of old reform groups.

One of the main reasons for this acceleration of United activity in the winter months of 1797–98 was Coigley's return from Paris en route for Ireland. Coigley had left Paris after the mock trial of Tone and Lewins, spent some time in Hamburg, and eventually reached Yarmouth in a smuggling vessel just after Christmas. It is not clear how far Tandy's dispute with Tone and Lewins motivated the mission; but subsequent events show that the replacement of Lewins was sought, and Coigley's visit quickly became another weapon in the hands of the Irish militants. O'Connor later denied having met Coigley on his way through London. But a meeting almost certainly took place, and on 5 January Coigley explained the dilemma of the militants to the newly created national committee of United Britons in London. 'The result of what I can gather from what *Quigley* [Coigley] has said in the Committee', reported the informer who had attended, 'appears to be that France is watching for an opportunity to be given from hence by some popular commotion as anxiously as their friends here wait for some direct assurance of force from their coasts to warrant their showing their faces.' From such statements the Home Office concluded correctly that the

22. P.R.O. T.S. 11/689/2187, Thomas Evans's information on Powell; also Hone, 'Radicalism in London', 79–101, and Cox, 'Aspects of English Radicalism', 135–54.
23. See e.g. *State Trials*, xxvi, 1136, 1147 and 1153.

main part of Coigley's mission was concerned with Ireland, and Portland was relieved at being spared the necessity of arresting him in London and thereby revealing Powell as the source of information.[24] In London Coigley found a group of men already determined on forming an alliance between the United men in Ireland, England and Scotland, and Benjamin Binns had been appointed to carry the views of this 'congregated delegation . . . of United English, United Scotch and United Irish' to the Dublin executive.[25]

Coigley worked feverishly during his three-week stay in London, assisted by Valentine Lawless, then a member of the United Irish executive, who had been operating in London since November 1797. With Powell and Benjamin Binns they paid frequent visits to the *Courier* office, supervising the printing of United rules and addresses. Propaganda was to play a major role in the forthcoming preparations to receive the French, and Lawless was already feeding information to his friends in the English parliamentary opposition to fuel their current attack on the government's Irish policy.[26] The *Courier* had the third highest circulation of the dailies and Whitehall was sufficiently concerned about its influence in sensitive coastal areas to order an enquiry. The *Anti-Jacobin* had accused John Fenwick, its editor, an L.C.S. member and close friend of Coigley, of being a French agent. His connection with France may not have been so formalized, but there is evidence to suggest that he was approached by France in the first year of the war and he remained a republican sympathizer thereafter. The *Courier*'s reportage was intensely pro-Irish, so much so that it was the only English paper extracted by O'Connor for the *Press* and recommended by him to his brother, on the establishment of the militant *Harp of Erin* in Cork.[27] Republicanism was strong in the printing and press world and the United men would have had formidable allies had their plans reached fruition.

In the spring of 1798 an alliance between the militant wings of the United Irishmen and the London Corresponding Society was taking shape, and a committee had been formed of Despard, Edmund O'Finn from Cork, the Binnses, Joseph Stuckey, William Bailey from county Down (a member of the Corresponding Society since its formation), Thomas Crossfield, and William Hamilton from Fermanagh (the latter being one of the small though

24. P.R.O. H.O. 100/75/3, Portland to Camden, 4 Jan. and I.S.P.O. 620/18^A/14, King to Cooke, 12 Jan. 1798.

25. T.C.D. MS. 873/451, Queries and Responses of Benjamin Binns, 1843.

26. See T.C.D. MS. 873/451, and P.R.O. H.O. 100/87/334–5 for the *Courier*. For opposition attacks on the government's Irish policy, see *Parl. Hist.*, xxxiii, 1058–1357, and Lawless's information to Burdett, Bodl. MS. Eng. Lett. c.66.

27. I.S.P.O. 620/35/139, Arthur O'Connor to Roger, 13 Feb. 1798. For government anxiety about the *Courier* see *H.M.C. Dropmore MSS.*, iv, 79. On Fenwick see A. Aspinall, *Politics and the Press c.1780–1850* (London, 1949), 206, and the *Anti-Jacobin*, i (1798), 276–80; and on his connections with France see A.A.E. Corr. Pol. Ang. Supp. 30 fo. 72; and P.R.O. T.S. 11/555/1793.

active group of Irish law students in the Inns of Court, which Lawless had cultivated since his arrival in London).[28] Portland was sceptical of the strength of the new movement and dismissed it as 'principally . . . a detachment or sect of those very low and happily very indigent tools of sedition who compose the London Corresponding Society'.[29] It was a comment typical of Portland's unimaginative approach to secret organizations. The alliance in London was never intended as a movement in its own right, but another element in the campaign of the United Irish militants to force a rising in Ireland, and the *Press* was utilizing to the full such signs of republicanism on the mainland. A change of system in England was also envisaged; but this was to assume more importance in the second phase of United English development after 1799. The leadership of the new republican alliance was consequently an amalgam of those democrats in Ireland, England and on the Continent who had been agitating for greater militancy since at least 1795. Between them they attempted to supply the leadership which had been absent from the mainland United movement since its inception in 1797, and the London committee was designed to co-ordinate relations between the separate bodies of United Irish, English and Scots 'to manage all correspondence and delegation . . . to draw the Bond of Union close with all country places and with Ireland Scotland France and America' whilst leaving the component national parts free to regulate their own affairs.[30]

Coigley and O'Connor were anxious to get word to France about these latest developments. Coigley at first asked John Murphy, a young Irishman from Tandragee in Armagh, then teaching languages in London, to undertake a mission to Duckett and Bourdon in Hamburg, and if necessary to continue to Paris.[31] Murphy was to perform such a mission at a later date, but it may have been at O'Connor's suggestion that Edmund O'Finn, a friend and fellow Corkman, was chosen for this particular assigment. O'Finn left London with his younger brother Francis and his English wife on 18 January. They sailed from Yarmouth to Cuxhaven, arriving at Rotterdam on 23 January, where they were given passports to France by the French minister to the Batavian Republic, the former Minister of Foreign Affairs, Charles Delacroix.

The early stages of O'Finn's mission were hindered by the new French

28. I.S.P.O. 620/18^/14, King to Cooke, 12 Jan. 1798 and 620/36/227 McNally's information, Dec. 1797. For O'Finn see S. Ó Coindealbhain, 'The United Irishmen in Cork County', *Journal of the Cork Historical and Archaeological Society*, 2nd ser. LVII (1952), 91–2.

29. P.R.O. H.O. 100/75/110–12, Portland to Camden, 23 Feb. 1798; see also fos. 142–3 for his letter of 2 Mar.

30. Watson explains that all those meeting as United Englishmen also belonged to other societies, see his memoir of 10 Jul. 1799 in A.A.E. Mem. et Doc. Ang. 53 fos. 261–5. See B. Binns's account of the new committee in T.C.D. MS. 873/450–1; and I.S.P.O. 620/18^/14, report in King to Cooke, 12 Jan. 1798, for the quotation.

31. P.R.O. H.O. 100/87/334–5, Murphy's examination, 2 Nov. 1799.

obsession with security. He was imprisoned as an Englishman upon arrival at Rotterdam, but released and sent to Delacroix at the Hague when the nature of his mission was discovered.[32] Delacroix was suitably impressed by the apparent urgency of O'Finn's assignment, for he had brought maps and information on the relative strengths of the armed forces and revolutionary movement in the British Isles for Bonaparte's use in the forthcoming invasion. But Delacroix soon regretted his precipitate action in granting passports for Paris, and he wrote on 25 January to the Minister of Police warning of O'Finn's arrival and of the need to make adequate security checks. The letter arrived at a time when the Minister was complaining of the lack of caution with which officials issued passports to British subjects, and scarcely improved Delacroix's standing with a home government already chafing at his penchant for independent action. Delacroix's interest in Ireland had remained strong since his days at the Foreign Affairs Ministry and his activities are a classic example of how United Irish misunderstandings of French intentions could arise from such unofficial encouragement. His attempts to get arms to the north of Ireland, and his support for Daendels's schemes against Ireland and Scotland, encouraged the United Irishmen to think invasion more imminent than it actually was.[33]

Tone and his immediate associates were unable to pronounce on O'Finn's patriotism. But as O'Connor's friend, it was to Tandy that he gravitated on his arrival in Paris in February, and through him the fears, hopes and projects of the militants were communicated to the Directory. In an audience with Bonaparte, he outlined the increasing United Irish anxiety about French intentions. It had been so long since Hoche's expedition that they had almost despaired of another attempt. He explained how the leaders were attempting to hold the people back from premature rebellion by constant assurances of imminent French help, and assured Bonaparte of certain insurrection if France sent assistance, however small. He felt that 5,000 French troops would supply an adequate rallying point, provided large quantities of arms (20,000 guns and sufficient artillery) were despatched simultaneously, and he recommended Bantry, Galway, Shannon or Lough Swilly as the most suitable landing places. It was an understatement of the military needs of the United Irishmen and an exaggerated view of the Irish people's revolutionary capabilities which was typical of the militants. But like his predecessors O'Finn advised the French to issue proclamations on landing, assuring the people of their good intentions and guaranteeing

32. See A.N. AF IV 1671 plaq. 1 fos. 114–27, F⁷ 7383ᴮ doss. B⁴ 2119; P.R.O. F.O. 33/15/10 and F.O. 97/241; I.S.P.O. 620/36/22 and 620/37/1 for O'Finn's mission.
33. A.N. F⁷ 7383ᴮ doss. B⁵ 2108 and 2119, F⁷ 7293 doss. B⁴ 2671, Delacroix's and the Police Minister's correspondence concerning O'Finn. See A.H.G. B⁵ 41; A.N. BB³ 145 fo. 264, BB³ 146 fo. 124, BB⁴ 114 fo. 233 and BB⁴ 123 fos. 194–5, for Daendels' and Delacroix's continuing interest.

property and free practice of religion; and on the whole his recommendations illustrated United agreement on overall objectives, continuing failure alone exacerbating the clash of personalities and ultimately rendering the rupture irreparable.

But his representations concerning English, as well as Irish, republicanism illustrate the way in which the English dimension of the United movement had become the particular concern of the Irish militants, and English republicans like Ashley and Watson gravitated to Tandy's party on their arrival in Paris. In the weeks before O'Finn's departure from London, plans to infiltrate the Irish community there had already been partially implemented. The leaders meeting in Furnival's Inn 'spoke on organising societies in different parts where there was a likelihood of meeting with Irishmen' and they had prepared a large number of printed addresses for distribution to the Irish in St. Giles.[34] The papers were almost certainly a new set of United Irish rules and signs lately brought from the Ulster leaders by Hamilton. It is difficult to gauge the success of these early recruiting efforts, but in February O'Finn was confidently telling Bonaparte that the English industrial centres were staunchly republican, that 20,000 Irish workers had joined the English republican party in London and that their committee corresponded with that of the United Irishmen in Dublin.

Coigley finally left London on 6 January, reaching Dublin on the 9th. He was accompanied by William Bailey and Benjamin Binns as United British delegates, who were to present a fraternal address to the United Irish Society and make arrangements for future co-operation. By the 10th, Coigley had established contact with Lord Edward and the two delegates presented the address to one of his associates, Henry Jackson. The address of the United Britons to the United Irishmen spoke of the repression which was taking place in both countries and stressed the benefits of co-operation:

> ... the prejudice of Nations is done away, and the ENGLISH burn with desire, to hail the IRISH as *Free-men*, and as *Brethren*. Our numbers are immense, our influence still more considerable, and our sentiments accord with yours ... Our DELEGATE is entrusted to lay before you our whole proceedings ... Should you think our situation, our influence, and our opportunities calculated to serve the Common Cause, rely upon our Diligence, our Zeal and our Fidelity. With best wishes, for the amelioration of the condition of Man, and hopes that your Exertions and Virtues, aided by an UNITED PEOPLE, will SPEEDILY EMANCIPATE YOUR COUNTRY ...[35]

34. P.R.O. T.S. 11/122/333, especially the examination of William White; see also H.O. 100/87/351–4, for John Murphy's information.
35. *Report from the Committee of Secrecy ... Commons [Ireland], 1798*, Append. no. XIV, 148–151. See also I.S.P.O. 620/18^A 14 and 11 for correspondence on the mission; T.C.D. 873/449–51 for Binn's account; and P.R.O. P.C. 1/44/A.155, Thomas Conway's account, 1799.

Although the initial approach of Coigley and Binns had been to the militant Dublin leaders, it must never be forgotten that the English dimension of their activities was designed to push their colleagues to action and to distract Whitehall's attention from an Irish rising. The address was consequently discussed in a full meeting of the national committee of United Irishmen, and provincial delegates were issued with copies to take back to their respective committees. Shortly after the meeting, Binns left for Cork and Coigley for Belfast, and over the next three months news of English support, as the militants had foreseen, played an important role in the increasing acceptance of their policies.

News of the London delegation came as a timely stimulant to the flagging spirits of the Ulster provincial committee. Its February meeting in Antrim was told that 'we had three delegates arrived from France, and that the French were going on with the expedition and that it was in a greater state of forwardness than was expected; but what was more flattering three Delegates had been sent from the United Britons to our National Committee; and that from this very moment we were to consider England, Scotland and Ireland all as one people, acting for one common cause; there were legislators now chosen from the three Kingdoms to act as an Executive for the whole'. The speaker then circulated the address of the United Britons, explaining 'that was the reason ... which made him so violent, as he was certain we could now obtain Liberty although the French never should come here'.[36] It was to O'Connor's adherents in Cork that Binns addressed himself at the end of February, and the outcome of his visit was an escalation of militant activity similar to that already witnessed in Dublin and Ulster. A new militant newspaper, *The Harp of Erin*, was projected, and the first issue was to carry 'An Irishman's Address to his Fellow Countrymen in England', exhorting the Irish living in England to support the efforts of their countrymen. The *Harp* was refused a stamp by government, but Roger O'Connor also sought to increase pressure on the French Directory by prevailing on those French prisoners of war about to be released from Cork to petition their home government in Ireland's favour.[37]

Coigley left Ireland in the first week of February with what appear to have been instructions for O'Connor to lead a new delegation to France. En route to London, Coigley spent three days in Manchester talking with the United leaders and outlining the nature of the forthcoming mission to France. By this time a more recognizable working-class movement than that in London had emerged in Manchester, composed on the whole of small tradesmen and weavers. An analysis of the twenty-seven secretaries of the Manchester United English divisions who met Coigley in February reveals a mixture of weavers, small manufacturers, tailors, loom-keepers, clothiers,

36. *Report from the Committee of Secrecy ... Commons [Ireland], 1798*, Append. no. xiv 146–7.
37. For O'Connor and the *Harp of Erin* see I.S.P.O. 620/36/34 and 35, 620/53/43 and 47.

an umbrella maker, two in the printing trade and a member of the supple-mentary militia. Likewise, booksellers, shopkeepers, a shoemaker and an auctioneer were among those who subscribed to Coigley's travel expenses. The Ulster origins of many of those involved helps explain the degree of support which the militants found in Manchester and Lancashire in general. Robert Gray, Thomas Towell, Moses Fry, James Hughes, James Dixon, from Monaghan, Down, Antrim, Armagh and Belfast respectively, and Coigley's relative Cassidy, all held leading positions in the Manchester United move-ment, and through Coigley Liverpool was also brought into the system. Constitutions and oaths were re-printed by Cowdroy at Manchester for distribution to the surrounding neighbourhood, and it looks as though efforts were again being directed principally at the Irish workforce.[38]

Coigley told the assembled Manchester secretaries of his intended journey to France; 'it would be his last message and if ever he returned it would be to see the tree of liberty planted in Manchester'. He said he was going to Mr. O'Connor in London, 'and the main part of the business was left to him ... their purpose was to give the French assistance in their plan of invading' Ireland, Scotland and, finally, England. He advised Robert Gray, the government informant, to apply for arms to Ireland 'as his return to France with O'Connor would make a final end of the business', and after their rising, the Irish would help in the invasion of Scotland and England. Cheetham, Dixon and Gray organized a subscription to defray Coigley's expenses to London, where he arrived on 11 February. Within weeks of Coigley's departure from Manchester, constitutions and oaths were being distributed from a central depot at Dixon's house to areas around Man-chester and further afield into Derbyshire and Nottinghamshire.[39]

Coigley's itinerary during the fortnight after his arrival in London is tantalizingly vague. He and John Binns lodged in a room in Fetter Lane let out to Benjamin by Thomas Evans. Both attended the meetings of the United Britons' committee and Coigley was given an address by them for the French Directory. It was drawn up on 25 January by Crossfield, and was a typical piece of propaganda consistent with the other addresses and statements resulting from Coigley's mission.

---

38. Robert Gray's information in P.R.O. P.C. 1/41/A.136, A.139, and P.C. 1/42 A.140. On the composition of the working class 'movement' see Thomis and Holt, *Threats of Revolution in Britain*, 21 (though their claim that it was composed of factory operatives does not apply till a later date) and Thompson, *Making of the English Working Class*, especially ch. 9. For lists of the United men arrested in Manchester in 1798 see P.R.O. P.C. 1/3514 and P.C. 1/44/A.161. For examples of the Ulster complexion of the Lancashire movement see P.R.O.N.I. D.272/37, P.R.O. P.C. 1/41/A.139 (Thomas Towell's information), and various accounts in H.O. 42/45. The constitu-tions and oaths were originally printed by George Nicholson in June 1797 (P.R.O. P.C. 1/40/A.132) and were reprinted by Cowdroy in 1798 (P.C. 1/42/A.40).

39. P.R.O. P.C. 1/41/A.136; Walvin, 'English Democratic Societies', 676–82; and for seditious literature distributed to the militia of Derbyshire and Nottinghamshire, see H.O. 42/43.

Already have the English fraternized with the Irish and Scots and a Delegate from each now sits with us. The sacred flame of liberty is rekindled, the holy obligation of Brotherhood is received with Enthusiasm even in the Fleets and the Armies it makes some progress— Disaffection prevails in both and united Britain burns to break her chains.

United as we are we now only wait with Impatience to see the hero of Italy and the brave veterans of the French Nation. Myriads will hail their arrival with shouts of joy; they will soon finish the glorious campaign.[40]

Superficially the address is a high-sounding nothing; but it was another element in the campaign being waged by the militants to secure the immediate despatch even of a small French force, by illustrating the strength of republicanism in the British Isles.

Coigley also contacted Valentine Lawless and Alexander Stewart (another of the Ulster leaders who had come to London the preceding year). They later claimed that Coigley had come to borrow money, but both were fully apprised of the nature of his mission and it looks as though Coigley's talks with O'Connor may have taken place at Lawless's lodgings. Coigley's colleagues in London were anxious to expedite his journey to France because of signs that the authorities had got wind of his mission.[41] Despite predictable difficulties in finding a shipowner willing to take the agents to a continental port at the height of the invasion scare, the primary cause of their delayed departure was the fussy preparations of O'Connor for what promised to be a protracted residence abroad. By this stage a personal motive for flight had also entered into his calculations. On 9 February he had been arraigned to appear before the Court of King's Bench in Dublin to answer the charge of seditious libel, on which he had been bailed the previous summer. Lord Edward and Thomas Addis Emmet, as his bail, had secured a temporary respite of the trial; but the delay could not have been prolonged. The authorities were still out for O'Connor's blood, and his friends warned that if he returned to face the charge the Castle might eventually succeed in conjuring up a more serious one. O'Connor accordingly sought to arrange his financial affairs to secure an income abroad. By arrangement with Sir Francis Burdett and Hugh Bell, his merchant friend in London, rents from his Irish lands would be collected by his brother and his friend John Swiney, a woollen draper in Cork, sent to Burdett as ostensible proprietor, and transmitted by Bell to

<hr/>

40. On the address see P.R.O. P.C. 1/42/A.143 and Evans's examination in T.S. 11/689/2187; also *State Trials*, xxvi, 1250–1252; *Reports from the Committees of the House of Commons*, x, 795, and Binns's account in T.C.D. MS. 873/451.
41. T.C.D. MS. 873/451. For Lawless's part in particular, see I.S.P.O. 620/18^A/14.

O'Connor in France.[42] In addition he had secured £1,000 in gold coins, *louis d'or* and guineas for immediate use. Bell then negotiated a passage to the Continent, but was rebuffed because of current fears that the French were about to seize the neutral ports where the emissaries would have landed.

On the 21st John Binns set off for the Kent coast in another effort to secure a passage. His enquiries met with hostility and suspicion and he rushed back to town on the 25th to warn his friends. But they had departed for Kent the previous day. By this stage O'Connor's personal preparations jostled uncomfortably with those for the mission, which, above all, demanded speed and secrecy. His luggage consisted of a multifarious collection of boxes, cases and trunks which could not fail to attract attention to the party which by now included besides Coigley, O'Connor's servant Arthur O'Leary and John Allen, a young acquaintance of Lord Edward who had been sent to O'Connor for help after a brush with the authorities in Dublin.[43] On the 27th Binns finally caught up with them at the *King's Head* in Margate, where their reputation as French spies had preceded them. The following morning all five were arrested by two Bow Street Runners who had followed their movements since Coigley's arrival in London the previous month. The timing of the arrests was a credit to Whitehall's utilization of the slender means of surveillance at its disposal, and in particular to the unobtrusive detective work of the Bow Street Office under its Chief Magistrate, Richard Ford. Intelligence on the domestic conspiracy had been scarce before January 1798, but by patiently observing the movements of those known to be involved, the government had acquired enough information to make arrests and to create further internal informers.[44]

In fact the authorities never discovered the precise nature of O'Connor's mission, because O'Leary, with remarkable presence of mind, had disposed of O'Connor's documents in the privy of the *King's Head*, while the officers waited unsuspectingly in the adjacent room.[45] But we do know that Coigley had carried important documents to London. In Manchester he had shown them to Gray who was impressed by their official nature, by the expensive parchment and the green, black and red seals. But they were no longer in Coigley's possession when he was arrested in Margate, otherwise they would have been taken with Crossfield's address. The discovery of that document alone among Coigley's possessions suggests that he had already

42. The *Press*, 13 Feb. and *Dublin Evening Post*. 13 Feb.; also I.S.P.O. 620/42/18, for Erskine's advice to O'Connor, and 620/35/139 for O'Connor's preparations. See also *State Trials*, xxvi, 1349–50.

43. For Allen see Hayes, *Biographical Dictionary*, 3; also I.S.P.O. 620/36/56, and P.R.O. T.S. 11/122/33.

44. *State Trials*, xxvi, 1191–1432; Binns, *Recollections*, 78–92, and his account in T.C.D. MS. 873/451; also the examination of various witnesses in P.R.O. T.S. 11/689/2187.

45. *The Life, Times and Contemporaries of Lord Cloncurry*, ed. W. J. Fitzpatrick (Dublin, 1855), 603.

abdicated the Irish side of his mission to O'Connor, but retained his interest in the English organization which he had played such an important part in promoting since his flight from Ireland in 1797. Certainly Lord Edward was relieved that no documents had been found on O'Connor. But it is certain that those disposed of by O'Leary had contained United Irish validation of O'Connor's appointment as its new representative in Paris.[46]

The arrests were particularly useful in the London government's campaign against the parliamentary opposition, which was again using the deteriorating situation in Ireland to wage a major attack on government security policy. Such attacks forced ministers to condone publicly the policies of the Irish government, which it was privately condemning in a flow of cautionary letters to Dublin. Public justification of repressive policies in Ireland accordingly became as powerful a motive for prosecuting the Margate five as that of discrediting the opposition or discovering more information on the United movement.[47] The prospect of securing all three seemed relatively certain in view of the evidence against the prisoners, and Whitehall was justifiably excited by its catch. The Irish situation at once graduated from the position of a neglected topic into one commanding almost total attention, as every scrap of incriminating information was sought to secure the prisoners' conviction. The opposition press accused government of fabricating a conspiracy from rumours of shady groups meeting 'in night Cellars and Pot houses' and denied the suggestion that O'Connor was guilty. The ministerial press responded by creating a sense of impending drama and arousing a novel degree of public curiosity. Public expectation of startling revelations was further increased by the use of ostentatious security measures each time the prisoners were moved or brought up for examination, and rumours spread of daggers having been found in O'Connor's cell and of his attempts to bribe the gaoler. It was no secret that government was particularly anxious to secure the conviction of O'Connor, regardless of the others. The opposition sought with equal determination to establish his innocence, and over a hundred witnesses packed into the courthouse at Maidstone when the trial finally opened on 21 May.

The government had taken the precaution of removing some Irish regiments stationed in the vicinity of the town, which was exceptionally crowded for the occasion. Many opposition politicians had arrived to testify for O'Connor. 'Lord Moira travelled incognito that he might be better known', wrote one observer, and he was soon revelling in the attentions bestowed

46. A.H.G. Doss. Pers. 2ᵉ sér. G.D. 393, O'Connor; see also I.S.P.O. 620/10/121/94 and 620/3/32/26 for the relief that nothing incriminating was found on O'Connor.

47. For opposition attacks on government see *Parl. Hist.* XXXIII, 5–201, 613–39, 644–734, 735–70, 1058–1357; Lecky, *Ireland in the Eighteenth Century*, IV, 189–92 and 219–21, and P.R.O. P.R.O. 30/8/325/3–9.

upon him by a crowd of two to three hundred curious spectators. The whole affair acquired the aspect of a circus. O'Connor wrote 'anonymous' threatening letters to the government; the Judge was noticeably intimidated by the figures of Fox, Sheridan and Grey on the side of the defence and by Erskine, O'Connor's eminent counsel; and with their opposing aims of ensuring O'Connor's conviction or liberation, the government and its critics transformed the trial into a tug-of-war over his fate, the cases for and against the others becoming mere side-shows.[48] There was sufficient secret evidence to convict all five, but the channels of information, notably that of Samuel Turner, were too valuable to reveal in open court. Whitehall never contemplated bringing Turner, Gray or Powell to testify against the accused, and the trials were delayed for nearly three months as a desperate search was mounted to secure 'proveable, direct and manifest proof' against them. It was a point on which the Irish and English administrations fundamentally disagreed, and as Camden tried to placate the ultra-loyalist faction in the Dublin administration, so the exchange with London became increasingly acrimonious.[49]

In the absence of such 'proveable' evidence the case revolved around Crossfield's address, the one piece of tangible evidence of treasonable intent behind the journey to the coast, and on the basis of this Coigley was convicted of high treason. On the morning of 7 June he was taken in an open hurdle to Pennington Heath where, after a short oration to the onlookers, he was executed. But in the weeks intervening between the trial and execution he had written a series of letters to a friend, who later published them, in which the biblical theme of the sacrificial victim laying down his life for his friends was invoked. Certainly O'Connor had behaved disgracefully at the trial, repeatedly attempting to shift all the guilt onto Coigley, and drawing from the Judge a warning about the consequences of such behaviour for 'the other prisoner'. It was not without reason that Coigley came to be regarded as the sacrificial lamb of the occasion, and O'Connor's reputation never quite recovered.[50] No one was satisfied with the results of the trials,

48. For the trials and the excitement surrounding them see J. Fenwick, *Observations on the Trial of James Coigley* (London, 1798), and Binns, *Recollections*, 116; *The Life of William Wilberforce*, II, 279–80; and various official correspondence in I.S.P.O. 620/10/121/101, 620/18ᴬ/1 and 4, 620/36, 37 and 42, P.R.O. H.O. 42/43 and H.O. 100/75 and 76, and P.C. 1/41/A.139. For the build-up in the press see *The Times* 12, 13, 19 and 23 Apr., 1–2 May, and the *Sun* of 2 Mar., 7 and 19 Apr. 1798; the *Morning Chronicle* for 19 Apr. lists the witnesses called by defence and prosecution.

49. For the dilemma over the use of secret evidence see P.R.O. T.S. 11/689/2187, notes on the trial; H.O. 100/75/138–40, 150, 264 and 283, P.R.O.N.I. D.607/F/8, for Camden and Portland's correspondence; I.S.P.O. 620/18ᴬ/11, Wickham to Cooke, 6 Mar. 1798.

50. *State Trials*, XXVI 1325; Fenwick, *Observations*, 102–5; Fitzpatrick, *Secret Service under Pitt*, 21–3; S. Simms, *Rev. James O'Coigley, United Irishman* (Belfast, 1937), 31–3; *The Life of the Rev. James Coigley . . . written by himself during his confinement in Maidstone Gaol*, ed. V. Derry (London, 1798). See also the report on his conviction in P.R.O. P.C. 1/42/A.143.

least of all the government. Determined that O'Connor should not escape so lightly, it ordered his re-arrest and despatch to Ireland to face the charges against him there.[51] Allen, Binns and O'Leary were acquitted, and the evidence against Coigley had been so partial and conflicting that doubts remained in the minds of even the staunchest government supporters about the justice of the verdict. 'The fact was this', wrote Pollock, the Irish government's observer at the trials, 'Quigley it was plain must be hanged—no one cared about him—he was given up ... and the event of the trial was a shabby compromise for the execution of Quigley.'[52] Neither government nor opposition had emerged from the trials in a good light. If the former had failed to reveal the full extent of the conspiracy, the latter had fuelled the doubts about their patriotism by a flagrant disregard for the due process of the law; and the Earl of Thanet, Robert Ferguson and two others were later tried for having caused a riot in the court at Maidstone in an effort to rescue O'Connor.[53]

The arrests, however, had visibly shaken the nascent English republican movement and frightened participants were soon feeding government with sufficient information to entirely crush it over the next three months. In particular they forced a redefinition of its position upon the London Corresponding Society. Some historians have insisted that the Society as a body was never officially involved with the republican movement. E.P. Thompson tries to explain the apparent contradiction of its senior officers' involvement in both by pointing to a division within the Society, with the militants attempting to push it into the republican alliance. By the beginning of 1798 the latter had indeed taken over the direction of the L.C.S. and Thomas Evans (its secretary), Thomas Crossfield (its president), and other prominent figures like Alexander Galloway, John Baxter, Paul Lemaitre and the Binnses were already prominent in the mainland United movement. Francis Place insisted that the majority of L.C.S. members shunned republicanism.[54] But in the first months of 1798 it was becoming increasingly evident that the L.C.S. as an open reform society had no future; in the face of determined government repression and increasing popular loyalism, the choice lay between dissolution or continuation as part of the underground republican movement. On 30 January, in a strongly-worded statement criticizing government policy in Ireland and supporting the struggle

51. P.R.O. H.O. 100/76/252–3, Wickham to Castlereagh, 24 May 1798.
52. I.S.P.O. 620/37/175, Pollock to [Cooke], 26 May 1798.
53. *State Trials*, xxviii, 821–986.
54. See B.L. Add. MS. 27808 fos. 89–91; *Autobiography of Francis Place*, ed. Mary Thale (Cambridge, 1972), 176–80; G. Wallas, *The Life of Francis Place, 1771–1854* (London, 1898), 27–8; Thompson, *Making of the English Working Class*, 187–91; and H. Collins, 'The London Corresponding Society', in *Democracy and the Labour Movement*, ed. J. Saville (London, 1954), 131–2. I am grateful to Ann Hone for information on this point.

of the Irish nation, the Society had already indicated the direction which many of its members would have liked to take:

> Brave and suffering Nation, The London Corresponding Society, animated by the desire of promoting universal liberty, and alive to the general interests of humanity, have beheld with inexpressible regret the enormous cruelties which have with impunity been practised in every corner of your devoted country ... If to wish for that happy UNION of mankind, when their *religious* opinions shall be no obstacle to the performance of their *moral duties*, be criminal, we also are guilty; and if to UNITE in the *cause of reform* upon the *broadest basis be treason*, WE with YOU are *traitors*.

In the climate of January to February 1798 such an address could scarcely have emanated from a society still anxious to emphasize its constitutionalism. It was published in the *Press* for 24 February and subsequently used as evidence in the secret parliamentary report of 1799 to illustrate the increasing sedition of the Corresponding Society.[55]

The arrests in London robbed the societies of any ability to act positively, and Watson alone had the presence of mind to flee the country. Government informants claimed that the movement had spread through Pancras, Clerkenwell, Spitalfields, Battle Bridge, Somers Town, Lincolns Inn and St. Giles, but there is little evidence that any had been organized on a regular basis. Grandiose schemes were proposed for dividing the metropolis into block divisions, but more attention was devoted to matters of immediate importance like the forthcoming treason trials and the advisability of continuing with any plans at all in view of the new wave of repression. Most agreed that the movement should continue, principally it seems because of firm and timely intervention by Despard. But a suggestion that the prosecution witnesses at the forthcoming trials should be assassinated evoked a strange aversion to bloodshed among these would-be revolutionaries, and even a scaled-down proposal to detain the chief witnesses temporarily was brushed aside. The disorganization and amateurishness of London's republicans was particularly apparent in their failure to abandon their regular haunts and meeting-places after the February arrests. It was at Evans's house, which United leaders had continued to frequent, that government informants secured most information and where Benjamin Binns was taken on 18 April, two days after his return from Ireland.[56]

Amidst the mounting repression, meetings of the United Englishmen, and the London Corresponding Society were called for 18 and 19 April in Compton Street, Clerkenwell and in Drury Lane respectively. The former

55. *Reports from the Committees of the House of Commons*, x, 795; *Press*, 24 Feb. 1798.
56. Secret information taken by R. Ford [March], in P.R.O. H.O. 42/44 and T.S. 11/122/333.

Plate 22. The London Corresponding Society, alarm'd (on receipt of news about the Maidstone arrests, 1798) (by Gillray, British Museum)

was presided over by Thomas Evans, then secretary of the London Corresponding Society. Place claimed that the Clerkenwell meeting was called simply to set up a United English division, and the captured documents do suggest an organization in very early stages. Many L.C.S. men were invited to attend, and it looks as though the militants hoped for some kind of merger. The rump of the Corresponding Society was being forced by the unholy alliance of the authorities and its own militants into taking a firm decision on its future. With the country being swept by invasion fever, its reticent attitude towards France had aroused press accusations of disloyalty, and the April meeting was called to decide on their action if the invasion took place. The meeting by all accounts was an acrimonious one; no agreement could be reached and it is unlikely that the Society would have long survived one anyway.[57] In the event a government swoop on both meetings and a general warrant to arrest all who called at Evans's house the same day decided the issue, and both bodies were suppressed, though the United Englishmen were subsequently revived by those same L.C.S. men who had tried to push the Society into the republican alliance in 1798. The official purge continued for the next two months. Galloway surrendered himself, and Spence and Despard were arrested on 20 and 22 April respectively. In Manchester all the leading United men were arrested, including Cheetham, Dixon and Cowdroy, and further arrests were made in Leicester, Birmingham and Scotland.[58]

The April arrests were attended by the same kind of drama as those at Margate, and the crescendo of loyalist feeling occasioned by the current invasion scare was intensified by the same promise held out of startling revelations. The Manchester men had been brought to London in heavy chains, and flanked by a party of cavalry. The United English prisoners were taken at midnight and trundled off in six separate carriages. Government press detailed in spine-chilling terms the conspiratorial atmosphere which had greeted the officers at Compton Street: the dimly-lit lane leading to the *George*, the dingy appearance of the room where the 'Crop Society' had been discovered, the pikes, daggers and treasonable papers found there proving conclusively the existence of some dastardly plot, and above all 'the connection between the L.C.S. and the London Society of U.E.'[59] In parliament too

57. *Autobiography of Francis Place*, 178–81; B.L. Add. MS. 27808 fos. 91–2; [R. Hodgson], *Proceedings of the General Committee of the London Corresponding Society on the 5th, 12th and 19th of April, 1798, relative to the Resistance of a French Invasion stated in a letter to a friend, intended to have been inserted in the Morning Chronicle* (London, 1798).

58. For an account of the arrests and lists of those taken, see *The Times*, 19 and 21 Apr.; P.R.O. P.C. 1/44/A.161, P.C. 1/3514 and H.O. 79/10.

59. The papers found were reproduced in *Report from the Committees of the House of Commons*, x, 796; see press reports in *The Times*, 18–21 Apr., *Sun*, 20–21 Apr., *Morning Chronicle*, 20–21 Apr.; and for the Manchester arrests in particular, *The Times*, 14–18 Apr.

the arrests had provided ministers with a welcome source of propaganda. The King's speech at the opening of the session cited 'the daily apprehension of suspected persons' as proof that stronger legislation was required to curb treason; the Suspension of Habeas Corpus Act was accordingly introduced and rushed through both Houses with the minimum of opposition. Attacks on government policy by the opposition in the face of such revelations were depicted as tantamount to treason, and Tierney's accusation that the government magnified the threat posed by 'a few lurking traitors' was convincingly dismissed by the Attorney General: 'United Irishmen could make United Britons; and if as a Society they did not correspond with societies here, as individuals they propagated their mischief.' That the conspiracy was one of individuals, of Irish rather than domestic growth, only served to further justify government policy for the protection of the majority.[60]

II

At a time when the situation in Ireland was rapidly deteriorating, the mission of Coigley and Binns introduced a new sense of urgency into United Irish preparations. King's County was proclaimed in January, and as the horrors of free-quarters and torture, already witnessed in Ulster, moved south, a wave of anxious expectation spread in those areas as yet unproclaimed. By February, McNally was reporting an increase in the pace of United organization, and hurried meetings were convened in the organized counties to despatch representatives to Dublin for consultations.[61] The old question of rising before a French invasion was revived, and could no longer be brushed aside, given that the Society was facing total extinction. For the moment Lord Edward seems to have succeeded in convincing his colleagues that they could no longer expect the French to send a large invasion force and that if only 5,000 men or less were sent, the United Irishmen would be well advised to attempt a rising, before their strength was completely eroded by the escalating military campaign against them.[62] By March, Lord Edward and his supporters were sitting on the executive with former opponents like McCormick. The membership of Lord Edward, as the Society's commander-in-chief, was indicative of the new urgency in United Irish affairs, for by its constitution civil and military appointments could not be held concurrently. For the moment Lord Edward had resigned his military command to John Cummins of Kildare and was totally engrossed with the national preparations for the projected rising. Provincial committees were

60. *Parl. Hist.*, xxxiii, 1423–58 and xxxiv, 66–120.
61. See McNally's information in Camden to Portland, 26 Feb. 1798, P.R.O. H.O. 100/75/128–34.
62. Madden, *United Irishmen*, 1st ser., I, 174–7; and *State Trials*, xxvii, 480 and 487.

circulated, told to appoint adjutant-generals, and warned to reveal their names to the executive directory alone. Estimates were taken of the numbers who might take the field, and specific demands made for financial contributions from local committees. On the whole, United Irish activities of February to March 1798 portray a sense of enthusiastic urgency absent since the first flush of expansion in the early months of 1797.[63]

But if the returns of current membership showed an encouraging 279,894 ready to turn out in a rising, disagreement among the leaders continued to postpone the outbreak. William Farrell's account of Carlow in 1798 paints what must have been a typical picture at local level of the ebb and flow of preparations and the excitement as delegates departed for, and returned from, an endless round of meetings in Dublin. In February, the new Carlow delegate, Peter Ivers, returned from the provincial meeting in Dublin excited at the latest turn in United Irish policy. He 'urged everyone to increased exertions in the cause, . . . it certainly had come to a wonderful pitch, both with regard to numbers and the enthusiastic spirit that animated the people . . .' As the next meeting approached, societies were asked to send to Dublin all remaining funds and any voluntary subscriptions which they could raise. Shortly before he left for Dublin on 19 February, Ivers spoke in glowing terms of the strength of the movement and was confident that 'they would be able to gain their liberty without foreign aid'. The county members expected him to return from Dublin with some kind of 'joyful intelligence' of imminent action. But for several days after his return he contacted no one and only called a meeting with noticeable reluctance. To the delegates he appeared crestfallen. When questioned about the expected rising 'he said it had been debated by some of the ablest men in Ireland both for and against it'. Parties were so evenly balanced that it was impossible to reach any definite decision, 'but, on the whole, it was considered best to make some additional preparations'. Farrell was dismayed and felt that the leaders 'had lost an opportunity that they never again would have, for fortune is a very coy mistress and if not seized boldly when she presents herself, is very apt to take fret and leave us there'. As in 1797, the leaders seemed again to be fobbing the people off with those same directives to prepare cautiously for some mythical rising. Ivers's recommendations for continuing preparations smacked more of an attempt to hide his own embarrassment than of an official command, and Farrell dismissed such delay as senseless in view of the unquestionable enthusiasm for action in the countryside. The Carlow men were sunk in gloom after this, and as news of arrests and military repression flowed in

63. P.R.O. H.O. 100/75/195–209, Camden to Portland, 11 Mar. 1798; and I.S.P.O. 620/18/3, information from [Boyle], 10 Mar. 1798; also *Report from the Committee of Secrecy . . . Commons [Ireland], 1798*, 151–4 and 169–70.

from neighbouring counties they became 'cool in attending their duties'.[64]

Whitehall's obsession with O'Connor assumes an air of unreality in the face of the deteriorating Irish situation in the early months of 1798. In particular Camden was conscious of his inability to control the fanaticism of his own colleagues and appealed for help to London to calm 'their eager loyalty.'[65] The over-reaction of the loyalists was a perennial problem. But in the crisis atmosphere preceding the outbreak of rebellion in May 1798, there was a general conviction that the catholics were organizing to dispossess the protestant population. By the end of 1797 it was rumoured that the catholics were making out titles to estates in which they believed the French would reinstate them; and although Tone had wanted to restrict property confiscations to the church and to principal opponents, loyalist and rebel alike believed that the debt for French help would be paid from confiscated loyalist property. Everywhere the confidence of the Irish gentry had collapsed, and the timidity of the magistrates left the army as the only effective means of keeping the peace. Even in quiet areas, wrote Abercromby, the Commander-in-Chief, to Pitt, ' . . . there exists among the Gentlemen the greatest despondency, they believe or effect to believe that there is a plot in every family, and a conspiracy in every parish and they would abandon the country unless the troops were dispersed over every part of it for their protection'. The consequent ineffectiveness of such a dispersed army for defence purposes worried the Dublin and London governments alike, and loyalist fears were intensified by the obvious reluctance to respond to their pleas for a military presence in their area.[66]

It was the violence of loyalist reaction which most concerned Abercromby. He blamed the Dublin 'cabinet', that 'wretched set of politicians', for failing to restrain their supporters, and remained on bad terms with the Irish ministers for the duration of his command. He was horrified at the indiscriminate persecution of innocent and guilty alike by the militia and the yeomanry, at the policy of burning houses, and at the way in which summary sentences were inflicted on victims with no supervision by the magistrates, even in areas where the civil law was still in operation. He accordingly issued instructions to the yeomanry never to violate the law and always to ensure that

64. *Carlow in '98 The Autobiography of William Farrell of Carlow*, ed. R. J. McHugh (Dublin, 1949), 60–4. For other criticisms of the leaders' stalling tactics see Byrne, *Memoirs*, I, 21–2, and Teeling, *History of the Irish Rebellion*, 70. On the movement's finance see *State Trials*, XXVII, 489.

65. P.R.O. H.O. 100/75/162–168 and P.R.O. 30/8/326/302–5, Camden's letters to Portland and Pitt, May–June 1798. See also *Auckland Correspondence*, III, 401–5, 412–17.

66. P.R.O. P.R.O. 30/8/326/76–7 and N.L.I. MS. 54ᴬ/122/31, Abercromby's correspondence, Jan.–Mar. 1798. See also P.R.O.N.I. D.272/15 for the scattered positions of the troops. For loyalist fears see I.S.P.O. 620/30/257, 620/18/14; Cornewall Lewis, *On Local Disturbances*, 14–20; Wakefield, *An Account of Ireland*, II, 359–62; *Parl. Hist.*, XXXIII, 1066.

they were accompanied by a magistrate. Gentry demands for military aid would always be granted in an emergency, but they should ensure against unnecessary dispersal and return the troops to barracks when the particular disturbance had been subdued. Lake, of whom Abercromby was particularly critical as 'too frisky' in his methods, mocked his superior for insisting on complete co-operation with the civil authorities. Abercromby tended to view the Irish situation in a purely military light and considered the restoration of military discipline to be as important as the suppression of disturbances.[67]

This 'unco-operative' attitude of the Commander-in-Chief and opposition taunts in the English and Irish parliaments were creating a feeling of barely suppressed fury amongst government supporters. It eventually erupted on publication of Abercromby's celebrated general orders on 26 February 1798. They were prefaced by a warning that 'the very disgraceful frequency of courts-martial, and the many complaints of irregularities in the conduct of the troops of this kingdom ... [had] ... proved the army to be in a state of licentiousness which must render it formidable to everyone but the enemy'. To correct this state of affairs officers must ensure 'the strictest and most unremitting attention to the discipline, good order, and conduct of their men' and troops must not assume policing duties without the presence of a magistrate. Abercromby's phraseology was stronger than that used in his earlier communications. It was injudicious in the current state of Irish politics, and the howl of protest from the loyalists was as predictable as the use made of it by the United Irishmen. But the reaction in London was, to say the least, hypocritical, for Abercromby had simply reiterated feelings expressed frequently in previous correspondence. Nor was the reaction dictated by fears of the possible effects for Irish security, but characteristically by the anticipated repercussions in British political circles. Pitt was horrified at the boost afforded to opposition attacks on government policy in Ireland, and although everyone acknowledged Abercromby to be an officer of exceptional calibre, no attempt was made to investigate his charges. Like Fitzwilliam before him, Abercromby felt that he was the victim of a political cabal in Dublin, and resigned his command, despite Camden's appeals to him to reconsider his decision. Camden was fully alive to the dangers of giving in to the loyalist reaction, and it was with gloomy misgivings that he was forced to appoint Lake as temporary Commander-in-Chief, until a replacement was found. Lake's 'frisky' methods and the military licence so abhorred by Abercromby, accordingly became general military policy until Cornwallis

---

67. N.L.I. MS. 54A/122–31, Abercomby's correspondence; and MS. 56/143–4, Lake's letters of Feb.–Mar. 1798. See also P.R.O.N.I. D.272/33, instructions for the yeomanry.

assumed both military and political leadership of the country in June.[68]

It is difficult not to sympathize with Camden's position. Deprived of a general he could trust, dismissed as an alarmist by London and denied the military reinforcements required to appease and curb the violence of his Irish supporters, Camden's actions against the United Irishmen had become as much a sop to critics as part of a consistent programme to prevent revolution. O'Connor's arrest at Margate was used as an excuse to close the *Press*, of which he was proprietor and which had long been an irritant to the loyalists. Camden also promised imminent action against United leaders. But he was robbed of the means of acting decisively by the refusal of key witnesses like McNally and Higgins to testify in court. Lesser informers might not have secured convictions, and two of the most useful, Bird and Newell, were already poised to desert government service and return to full United allegiance.[69] Camden knew that the loyalists would call for immediate trials and convictions if arrests were made and government would be made to look foolish if leaders were merely detained under the Suspension of Habeas Corpus Act; hence his relentless insistence that Whitehall should detain Turner and force him to testify when he again returned to England at the time of the Margate arrests. The retention of information channels seemed less important in Ireland when it was clear that the conspiracy they had been directed to watch was about to reach fruition, and government only lacked reliable witnesses to crush it decisively.[70] Consequently, when Thomas Reynolds of Kildare, a member of the Leinster provincial, came forward and offered to testify against his comrades in court, the promised action against the United leaders followed immediately.

The months preceding the outbreak of the rebellion in May had witnessed a remarkable indecisiveness on the part of the government and the United Irish leaders alike. Both were being pushed to take action against their better judgement by their more desperate colleagues. But their inability to decide on tactics was no way to control the extremism, which, feeding on an atmosphere of genuine fear, burst forth in a campaign of mutual destruction that summer. United Irish preparations for the rising had continued in a

68. Lecky, *Ireland in the Eighteenth Century*, IV, 203–4; P.R.O.N.I. D.607/F/108 and 131B. Robert Ross to Downshire, Mar. 1798; P.R.O. P.R.O. 30/8/325/5–6, 30/8/326/268, 270 and 274–80, Pitt and Camden's correspondence, 13–26 Mar.; *H.M.C. Dropmore MSS.*, IV, 120, 130, 143–144; *The Times*, 27 Feb. 1798; *Anti-Jacobin*, I, 292–6; *Auckland Correspondence* III, 394–7, 400–2; and James Lord Dunfermline, *Lt. Gen. Sir Ralph Abercromby K.B. 1793–1801. A Memoir by his Son* (Edinburgh, 1861), 72–109.

69. Kent C.R.O. U840/O197/2–3, Letters of Bird and Newell to Camden, 3 and 21 Feb. 1798; and *The Apostacy of Newell*.

70 The increasing tension can be seen in Camden's March correspondence, see P.R.O. H.O. 100/75/144–294; see also Kent C.R.O. U840/C31/4.

desultory manner since the last Leinster meeting. Munster and Connacht remained only partially attached to the United movement and continued in a disturbed state when leaders elsewhere sought to preserve the quiet counselled by Dublin. In February the Leinster provincial had resolved 'that if the other P[rovinces] be in an equal State of Preparation with Leinster as soon as we can procure the Information of their State ... we should immediately proceed to Act ... '.[71] Lord Edward and his supporters accordingly made plans to collect the strength of the country and on that basis to propose an immediate rising at the next meeting of the Leinster provincial on 12 March. But assurances had again been received (almost certainly from Tandy) of an April invasion, and in the weeks before the meeting the moderates continued to oppose a premature rising, arguing that government provoked one simply to crush it before the French arrived.[72]

Everyone expected the meeting held on 12 March at Oliver Bond's house in Bridge Street, Dublin, to pronounce in favour of an immediate rising; but with Emmet's supporters arriving as determined as ever against such action, it is more likely that the indecision would have continued. In the event the outcome was dictated by the Castle's new decisiveness after Reynolds's revelations, and all those attending were arrested. The meeting had scarcely begun, and Reynolds was angry at the impatience of Major Swan and his constables which permitted latecomers, including Lord Edward, to escape. Nor were any papers of immediate importance taken, those found smouldering in the fire-grate relating only to previous meetings. A glance at the list of those taken, however, shows that not only had the superstructure of the most organized province been shattered, but apart from McCormick, Lord Edward and Teeling, all the executive had also been taken.[73] McCormick had already withdrawn from the movement and fled. Only Lord Edward remained at liberty in Dublin, and letters found from O'Connor and Coigley at his house were sufficient to convict him if caught.[74]

Those leaders still at liberty acted immediately to assure their adherents that the arrests had not harmed the movement, and county committees were ordered to fill up the vacancies.[75] But with the best leaders in prison

71. *State Trials*, xxvii 430; see also I.S.P.O. 620/43/9 and 620/15/2/9 for attempts by the U.I. leaders to maintain quiet among their followers.

72. For references to such assurances from France see P.R.O. H.O. 28/24/73, P.C. 1/44/A.155 and H.O. 100/76/69–70; I.S.P.O. 620/3/32/12, 620/18/3, 620/18^/11, and S.O.C. 1017/10.

73. For the arrests see P.R.O. H.O. 100/75/213, 217–8, H.O. 100/76/11–14; *State Trials*, xxvii, 427.

74. I.S.P.O. 620/36/9^ and 620/51/121 for Lord Edward's escape, and P.R.O. P.C. 1/44/A.155, copies of the letters found at Leinster House on 12 March.

75. Printed addresses were circulated to this effect; see I.S.P.O. 620/36/78; see also 620/10/121/96 and 620/18, for information from McNally and Higgins during March. For activities in Ulster see *Report from the Committee of Secrecy ... Commons [Ireland] 1798*, 154–5; I.S.P.O. 620/36/41; and P.R.O.N.I. D.272/1. For information on the new Dublin executive see I.S.P.O. 620/51/39.

and surviving national leadership 'on the run', the picture presented over the next two months is one of confused direction and declining faith on the part of the United membership in Ireland and France alike. The meeting of the Ulster provincial called for 25 March was obliged to flee from several towns in Down and Armagh before eluding the vigilance of the military. A delegate had come from Leinster to assure them that the vacant places on the executive had already been filled. The new, smaller executive seems now to have been composed of Lord Edward, Neilson, William Lawless (a young Dublin surgeon), and John and Henry Sheares; and militant policy for an immediate rising prevailed by virtue of the removal of its opponents. The delegate to Ulster had been instructed to secure returns of the numbers expected to join a rising, and he assured the assembled leaders of a French landing in April. But his accounts of Leinster's strength were too insistent to convince, and Magin probably reflected majority opinion in proclaiming them to be greatly exaggerated. A national committee of representatives from the executives and provincials was to meet in Dublin the following week, and the Armagh meeting was asked to choose a representative.

Superficially preparations for the rising proceeded smoothly. Military committees had been formed in the counties, adjutant-generals appointed, and reports on supplies of arms sent to Dublin. But the organization's finances were in disarray and the lottery to pay for the defence and upkeep of prisoners had collapsed, when Bond, who held the tickets, was arrested. The consequent paucity of United counsel at the spring assizes was noted by McNally. In Dublin there were signs that the executive had never been properly reconstructed after the March arrests, and one delegate to the national meeting reported that its composition had been altered a dozen times since then. Camden remained convinced that they intended to proceed with the rising with or without French aid, but it is more likely that the leaders were no longer so certain of their strength. Every piece of information from France was snapped up, and assurances were sought that they might not after all be forced to act alone.[76]

In Carlow, Farrell painted the same picture of perambulating committees fleeing from intensified military vigilance, and of the declining control of the leaders as the people's terror of military reprisals intensified.[77] On 30 March the whole country was proclaimed, the yeomanry placed on permanent duty, and Abercromby forced to mount a national system of martial law and the free quartering of troops among the people before he left the kingdom. The need for some decisive lead from Dublin became urgent as subordinate committees saw their strength eroded by the disarming, the arrests and the

76. On the state of the U.I. leadership see *Report from the Committee of Secrecy ... Commons [Ireland] 1798*, Append. no. xiv, 158–9; I.S.P.O. 620/3/32/6, on the re-organization; P.R.O. P.C. 1/44/ A.155 and H.O. 100/76/130–9, Camden's correspondence of April.
77. *Carlowin'98*, ed. McHugh, 68–70.

terror of the people. The Wexford leader Miles Byrne was to criticize the executive for not ordering the rising at this moment before military repression was permitted to develop in such a tragically brutal manner that it rapidly became uncontrollable. Everywhere Orange emblems were flaunted as symbols of loyalty, making loyalty a protestant preserve and by implication damning all catholics as rebels. Catholic fears that Orange attacks on catholics had government support were at last fully vindicated, and those who joined the rebellion did so in the belief that attack was their only remaining defence.[78] This magnification of long-standing fears lies at the heart of the Irish rebellion of 1798; they were actively fomented by interested parties on both sides, and were intensified by war-induced economic distress.

After the United Irishmen had let the chances of a controlled rising slip away, the surviving leaders themselves had become almost irrelevant to the developing crisis. But in their heyday they had created a general belief that the French were on their way to redress the people's wrongs, and magistrates all over the country reported their blind faith in a French landing, and a stubborn refusal to surrender arms in consequence. Even in areas where the United Irishmen were weak, there was a general abstention from rent and tithe payment because of the confident expectation of a rising and a French landing. The cockiness of the peasantry unnerved the loyalists, and fears were particularly acute in areas like Munster where the protestants were thin on the ground. They saw plots everywhere, and their inclination to flee the country altogether was contained only by assurances of military protection. An air of impending crisis hung over the country, and not surprisingly fears of 'a night like St. Bartholomew's day' (in 1572 when protestants were massacred in France) sent many loyalists fleeing to England when rebellion finally erupted.[79]

The role of the United Irishmen in encouraging such ideas of revenge and a restoration of property, and in particular in creating the spectre of an Orange massacre, is indisputable, despite the genuine disclaimers by Thomas Addis Emmet and MacNeven, and their own horror of social revolution. Even the Dublin leaders were not altogether exempt from references to future transfers of land to reward the victors, which in the terms of eighteenth-century thinking raised hopes that would only have been satisfied by a massive alteration in the system of landownership.[80] Such

78. Wakefield, *An Account of Ireland*, II, 366–71; Croker, *Researches in the South of Ireland*, 347–85; *An Enquiry into the Causes of Popular Discontents in Ireland, by an Irish Country Gentleman* 2nd edn. (London, 1805), 29–30.
79. G. F. Handcock, 'Reminiscences of a Fugitive Loyalist in 1798', *E.H.R.* I, (1886), 536–44; see also P.R.O.N.I. D.607/F/150, 219–24; I.S.P.O. S.O.C. 1017/12; and L. Cox, 'Westmeath in the 1798 Period', *Irish Sword*, IX (1969–70), 9, for further examples of loyalist panic.
80. See MacNeven, *Pieces of Irish History*, 197, 204–5, 211 for U.I. denials of such accusations. See however Kent C.R.O. U840/O146/3; I.S.P.O. 620/10/121/103; P.R.O. H.O. 100/78/21–2; Byrne, *Memoirs*, I, 8–9; and *State Trials* XXXVII, 484 for evidence to the contrary.

hopes rapidly alienated rural protestantism from the movement. In Meath, where the United Irish had initially been supported by the protestant community alone, no protestant was known to have taken part in the 1798 rebellion. In Ulster a remarkable polarization of parties was reported to have taken place during April and May, with protestants, even former United Irishmen, flocking in a body to the Orange standard as the only recognizable organization for the exclusive preservation of protestant lives and property.[81]

The United Irishmen had played upon catholic fears of Orangeism to increase their membership. But they were only partially responsible for the great Orange fear of the spring and summer of 1798. On a society pre-disposed to credit rumours of officially-sponsored Orange genocide was launched a militaristic purge which caused even Camden to lament the opening it had provided for Orange vengeance. The great Orange fear of 1798 was no 'bogey-man of catholic fancy', as Thomas Pakenham claims. The catholics had good reason to fear Orange reprisals in the months before the rebellion. From every county under martial law came reports of yeomanry and militia sporting their Orange affiliations as they ransacked homes for arms or tortured suspected conspirators. On the surface it looked as if the security of Ireland had been handed over to the Orangemen as its sole custodians, not because every yeoman or militiaman was an Orangeman, but because those who were not were inhibited from speaking up for the victims through fear of like treatment. In Carlow, Farrell described what must have been a typical scene throughout the country after the March proclamation; '... the town was full of army, a great number of whom displayed their Orange ribbons and their fifes and drums in every direction, playing "Croppies lie down" and every other tune that would insult or wrong the people most and though there were numbers of them that wished well to the cause, the people were engaged in, still they dare not budge, as they ... were certain of being brought to the triangles if they uttered a word in their favour'.[82]

At the spring assizes of that year the Orangemen had apparently taken over the entire process of prosecution. McNally attended the trials in many counties and warned the Castle of its foolishness in appearing to uphold such biased justice. Catholic witnesses were scorned, prisoners' defences treated with contempt and capital sentences imposed on the flimsiest of

81. See *H.M.C. Charlemont MSS.*, ii, 323, for the astonishing polarization in Ulster; for Meath see Kerrane, 'The Background to ... 1798', 120. For the intense fanaticism such fears created on both sides see P.R.O. H.O. 100/77/132 and 200-1; P.R.O. 30/8/325/204; Croker, *Researches in the South of Ireland*, 348-85.
82. *Carlow in '98*, ed. McHugh, 68 and 74. On the fear that the Orangemen and the authorities were in collusion, see P.R.O. H.O. 100/77/132 and I.S.P.O. S.O.C. 1016/51, and T. Pakenham, *The Year of Liberty*, 3rd edn. (London, 1972), 192-3. But H.O. 100/75/331-4 and *H.M.C. Dropmore MSS.*, iv, 226, show that many more in government held ambivalent views on the subject.

evidence. 'Some gentlemen of fortune wore orange ribbands, and some barristers sported orange rings with emblems. Such ensigns of enmity, I assure you, are not conducive to conciliation'.[83] The numbers of sworn rebels or Orangemen in 1798 cannot have been great. But it was becoming increasingly difficult and positively dangerous to hold the middle ground, and in troubled counties catholics and protestants came to realize that their only protection lay with the extremists in the Orange or the rebel camps. In such a situation, proof of the existence of Orange lodges or United Irish societies was not required to justify fears that every protestant house harboured an Orangeman or that every countryman was a rebel, and the rebellion which first erupted in Leinster was not so much a sectarian war as a crusade against Orangeism.[84]

Although the United Irish leaders had despatched special emissaries into the counties in February to revive activity, the advancing military quickly eroded anything resembling regulated preparation for a rising. News of floggings, pitchcappings and torture radiated from areas occupied by the military. The billows of smoke from burning houses in the distance were sufficient to scatter committees, to send terrified supporters into hiding, and eventually to force the uncommitted into the rebel forces as their only means of protection; for it was the uncommitted, the people who had no arms to deliver, or information to give, who suffered most.

Prisons and tenders overflowed with captured supporters; and faced with the prospect of a massive loss of arms through forfeiture or capture, their initiative paralysed by fear of torture and death, surviving United Irishmen looked helplessly to Dublin for a lead. By April, plans to defer action till the French arrived had been rendered obsolete by events; an immediate rising or annihilation were now the only remaining alternatives: 'we cannot wait for distant expectations;' insisted John Sheares, '*we must* MAKE A HOME EXERTION'.[85] The Leinster societies hoped that the April provincial meeting would call for a rising, but delegates returned with the same old story of indecisiveness. Michael Heydon, who had replaced Ivers, told a thinly attended baronial meeting in Carlow that 'there was a great difficulty in getting the members of the Provincial to attend at all; that they were few in number and that every man in the room had a case of loaded pistols before him on the table ... that the rulers in Dublin were not ready to commence operations for a little longer, but ordered every captain to have his men in a state of readiness'. Everybody at the Carlow meeting had jeopardized their personal safety to attend and were visibly dismayed.[86]

83. Quoted in Lecky, *Ireland in the Eighteenth Century*, IV, 239–41.
84. P. O'Tuathail, 'Wicklow Traditions of 1798', *Béaloideas*, V (1935), 154–88.
85. *State Trials*, XXVII, 299, John Sheares, speaking on 10 May 1798.
86. *Carlow in '98*, ed. McHugh, 73; see also *Report from the Committee of Secrecy ... Commons* [*Ireland*], *1798*, 157–9; *State Trials*, XXVII, 303.

The truth was that even with the removal of moderate opposition, the Dublin leaders felt unable to organize the rising without French assistance. Lord Edward had assumed beatified stature in the minds of lesser United men after his dramatic escape in March. An announcement that he was to lead the rebel forces would almost certainly have provided a much-needed rallying point for the dying embers of the organized United movement. But despite his romantic qualities, Lord Edward lacked the ability to take an overall lead at the decisive moment, and proved incapable of knitting together the persistent individualism of the remaining national leaders.[87] Still expecting the French to arrive before the end of May, they passed their time disputing the best means of taking the capital when the invasion occurred. Lord Edward and Neilson argued for a convergence of United forces from the Leinster counties; others supported the suggestion of Lawless and John and Henry Sheares for an internal movement organized with the help of their friends in the militia. Lord Edward's plan prevailed, and Lawless and the Sheares brothers were removed from the executive. The Ulster delegates in the city were clearly disgusted at the stupidity of the continuing disagreement; they were unable to report anything to their provincial other than vague plans for the capture of Dublin at some undecided date, and nothing at all on the pressing topic of a national rising. The Dublin leaders seemed rather to be totally engrossed in plans for the national assembly which would rule the new Irish republic. The irrelevance of such political niceties at a time when the country was being bulldozed into a bloody conflict, with or without the Dublin leaders, was a symptom of the latter's remoteness from their followers.[88]

The picture of events in Dublin is confused after the removal of Lawless and the Sheares brothers in early May. The executive was now composed of Lord Edward, Neilson and the informer Francis Magan. The appointment of the latter, and the confused reports reaching the Castle in the few days before Lord Edward was eventually arrested on the 19th, are representative of the total disorganization of the Dublin leadership just before the rebellion broke out. It is commonly supposed that 23 May was the date set for the rising by the executive. But Lord Edward had remained undecided right up to the time of his arrest, and there is no sign of any firm decision having been made before then. At a meeting on the 17th, in Lord Edward's hiding place in Thomas Street, letters were read from the lower committees in Dublin county censuring the city leaders for their inactivity. Some thought they should instantly attack the Houses of Parliament; others argued for an attack on the Castle the following Tuesday, the 22nd. Lord Edward preferred to as-

87. See B.L. Add. MS. 33105 fo. 262; I.S.P.O. 620/10/121/149; Kent C.R.O. U840/C562/17; A. Olson, *The Radical Duke. Career and correspondence of Charles Lennox, third Duke of Richmond* (London, 1961), 103, for opinions on Lord Edward's leadership potential.
88. *Report from the Committee of Secrecy ... Commons [Ireland] 1798*, 158–9, 323.

Plate 23. The Arrest of Lord Edward Fitzgerald (by Cruikshank for Maxwell, *Irish Rebellion*)

certain the strength of the surrounding countryside beforehand, and another meeting was called for the 22nd.[89] By now the two Sheares were acting independently of any committee and pressing ahead with their plans for an attack in Dublin, with the counties rising when the outcome was known. It is probable that this plan has been accepted as that officially agreed by the Dublin leaders and given rise to the orthodoxy about the timing of the outbreak.[90] The executive had agreed that the rising should take place soon, but still hoped that a French landing would coincide with it. Neilson sent directives into the countryside announcing the date for the general rising as sometime between 11 and 20 June. William Bailey transmitted information to France via Holland, specifying the 12th as the agreed date, in the probable hope that the United men might still have news of a French fleet off their coast before taking the plunge.[91]

89. See I.S.P.O. 620/10/121/102, 620/18/14 and 620/51/39 for the information of McNally, Higgins and Sproule, May–Jun. 1798; also W. J. Fitzpatrick, "*The Sham Squire*" (London, 1866), 122–38, 149–50.
90. *State Trials*, XXVII, 292–329; MacNeven, *Pieces of Irish History*, 219, 233.
91. I.S.P.O. 620/18A/11, Wickham to Cooke, 21 May; P.R.O. H.O. 100/77/124, Cooke to Portland, 10 Jun. 1798.

The arrest of Lord Edward on 19 May, and of the Sheares brothers the following day, finally induced the remnants of the United leadership to throw caution to the winds. When news of the arrests was known, a flurry of activity was noticed among United adherents in Dublin. The plan adopted seems to have been essentially that suggested by Lord Edward, whereby the capital would be taken with the help of contingents from the adjacent counties, and the rest of the country would then rise on a pre-arranged signal. But the communication network of the organization had been totally disrupted by the arrests of the preceding months. It proved almost impossible to get proper instructions to local leaders, many of whom were already fugitives, and Meath, Kildare and Wexford almost certainly rose prematurely.[92] In those areas of Kildare, Meath and Dublin county immediately bordering Dublin city, the insurgents began to assemble on the 24th in groups of 500 to 800. In Carlow, news of the Dublin turn-out arrived on the 25th. Despite references to military preparations in the counties made at Leinster provincial meetings of the preceding months, the tragic outcome of the rising in Carlow reflects the real disorganization in the country. Some of the leaders refused to turn out at all, and it was a pitiful group of poorly-armed and poorly-led insurgents that finally marched into the centre of Carlow town on the afternoon of the 26th. They expected that popular support would permit them to take the town without firing a shot. But the people had been silenced by several days of public flogging and military torture. The rebels proceeded along the streets vainly calling on the people to rise, and were eventually caught in a bottle-neck where the main street issued onto the square. There they were cut down by the well-prepared military, and houses suspected of harbouring the escaping rebels were indiscriminately burnt.[93]

Carlow county had been the first to rise and the United men who had been in hiding in neighbouring Wexford desperately sought to find and join the main body of Carlow rebels. The massacre of prisoners by militia, retreating from Carnew on the Carlow-Wexford border, sent hordes of terrified Wexford people into the rebel forces, and sympathetic landlords and priests were beseeched to head the leaderless bands. The rough and ready Wexford rebel army gathered strength en route and was estimated at 20,000 by the time

92. *Report from the Committee of Secrecy . . . Commons [Ireland] 1798*, 160; A.A.E. Mem. et Doc. Ang. 1ᴮ fos. 188–90, Memoir of Montmorency-Morres, 19 Nov. 1798, who had a military command in Dublin City, claiming that Wexford, Meath and Kildare rose prematurely. See also S.Ó Coindealbhain, 'The United Irishmen in Cork County', LVI (1951), 27 on the plan for Cork to rise on 23 June; P.R.O. H.O. 42/44, examination of an Ulster United man, 1 Aug. 1798; I.S.P.O. 620/18/14, Higgins's information of 20 May on the Dublin preparations.
93. *Carlow in '98*, ed. Mc Hugh, 89–92. For an account of the early stages of the rebellion, see also Byrne, *Memoirs*, 1, 26–8; P.R.O.N.I. D.607/F/185; P.R.O. H.O. 100/76/258; Teeling, *History of the Irish Rebellion of 1798*; idem, *Sequel to the History of the Irish Rebellion*.

it reached Wexford town. Initially numbers and zeal gave the rebel forces an apparent strength. But the improvised nature of their campaign and the absence of any real military expertise soon began to show. Early victories like the capture of Enniscorthy and Arklow were not followed up; captured towns, left ungarrisoned in their rear, were easily re-taken by the military, and brutal reprisals were taken against suspected collaborators among the townspeople. The retreating military destroyed their stores and ammunition, and pitchforks and pikes remained the principal weapons of the rebels throughout the campaign. Miles Byrne soon came to lament their want of proper military leaders. It proved impossible to drill new adherents, and in the absence of recognized and respected leaders local loyalties made fragmentation of the main force a recurring problem. An early confrontation with the numerically inferior military in the county would almost certainly have resulted in rebel victory. But it proved impossible to bring the crown forces to battle; they simply retreated and conserved strength until reinforcements could arrive. The march of vast numbers of disorganized rebels over the countryside inevitably provided opportunities for individual acts of revenge. In Wexford the commanders barely succeeded in dissuading their men from wasting valuable time to return and burn Carnew in retaliation for military atrocities on the eve of the rebellion, and a cry of 'Orange, Orange' would send rebel splinter groups to dispose of offending protestants.[94]

Initially the authorities were relieved when the rebellion finally erupted. At last the conspiracy had become visible and might be defeated before the French arrived. With the invasion scare in England reaching new proportions because of uncertainty at Bonaparte's plans, it was unlikely that Dublin could call on reinforcements from the mainland if Ireland was threatened. Camden's pleas for military aid were meeting with even greater resistance than normal. The shortage of manpower in England was so acute that Pitt hurriedly attempted to legalize the unconstitutional procedure of drafting militia into the regular army. Moreover, Abercromby, a stern advocate of forcing the Irish gentry to look after their own defence, was now in England advising the government on Irish military matters and reinforcing its reluctance to grant Camden's wishes. But Pitt could not ignore the escalating attacks by the parliamentary opposition, which were being fuelled by stories of atrocities emanating from Ireland, and was privately warning Camden to curtail the excessive ardour of his friends in suppressing the rebellion.[95]

94. O'Tuathail, 'Wicklow Traditions of 1798', 159.
95. P.R.O. H.O. 100/77/9–10, 98–103, 136; P.R.O. 30/8/325/9 and 30/8/326/314, for Camden's correspondence with London, June 1798. See also *Auckland Correspondence*, IV, 4–7, 11, 14–17; *Castlereagh Correspondence*, I, 219–20; and *H.M.C. Dropmore MSS.*, IV, 231–6, for the general murmuring in Dublin against Whitehall's neglect.

Plate 24. The Irish Rebel Camp on Vinegar Hill (by Cruikshank for Maxwell, *Irish Rebellion*)

Loyalist fears had in fact been intensified when they found the rebellion less easy to crush than they had expected. The fervour of the rebels, and the capture of such a major coastal town as Wexford, had astonished government supporters and quickly destroyed their initial contempt for the rebel forces. In London too the rebellion was being taken more seriously, and at the end of May the Duke of York had relented sufficiently to send several regiments of cavalry to Ireland. It was a feeble gesture in the opinion of the Irish loyalists and generals alike, for cavalry was proving useless against the charge of ranked pikemen and in the small field-structure of the Irish terrain. On 5 June a deputation of Irish ministers waited on Camden and insisted that he write immediately to London for infantry reinforcements. Camden needed little persuasion. In his public pronouncements he still tried to maintain the pretext that the rebels would be speedily defeated. But his gloomy letters to London told a different story. The North had remained ominously quiet, but reliable information showed that the province still expected a French landing, and was quiet from caution rather than from any change of principle.

But it was the battle of New Ross on 5 June which finally convinced Dublin and London alike that English rule in Ireland was in danger, even if the French never arrived. The courage and the ferocity with which the rebel forces had repeatedly attacked the well-armed and disciplined troops betrayed a new, almost suicidal element in the rebel campaign. The first weeks of the rebellion had shown that a rebel could expect little quarter even if he surrendered. The rebels had consequently little to lose by startling acts of bravery; '. . . they were resolved to conquer or to die,' wrote one of the military commanders at New Ross, 'and so in fact they acted . . .'.[96] Rebel losses at New Ross were massive; over 2,000 were killed. But the eventual military victory was not particularly glorious and was such a near thing that it was scarcely seen as a victory by the authorities. 'Drawn battles with a rabble pikemen . . . appear to me as absolute defeats to us,' wrote Robert Johnson of the Downshire militia, 'the wealthiest of our Counties . . . ravaged and the rebels in possession of Wexford . . . All this after two years accurate notice of the plans and intentions of the rebels . . .'.[97]

On 8 June, Whitehall finally responded to Camden's pleas with a promise of 8,000 additional military, mostly infantry. A characteristic proviso was added to the effect that they were on temporary loan only, and must be returned as soon as the emergency had passed.[98] But the news provided a timely boost to Dublin's flagging morale, for Ulster had finally erupted the previous day. Camden's fears about an Ulster rising were somewhat unrealistic. The rigorous disarming, the massive arrests and the rejection by the Dublin leaders in 1797 had broken the spirit of the Ulster movement. The problem of choosing between suppression or rebellion which faced the United organization in the midland and eastern counties in 1798 had already been posed the preceding year in Ulster. The Ulster men had confidently opted for the latter course, but were not supported by their fellow United men in Leinster. By the end of 1797 the former fire of the Ulster movement had consequently spluttered to a cautious policy of waiting on events. When Robert Hunter and Henry Joy McCracken, the Ulster delegates in Dublin during May, wrote home telling of executive discussions on the possible necessity of rising without the French, their leaders were torn by an indecision which would have been unknown to the temper of the Ulster movement in 1797. The Ulster executive made no preparations at all and was replaced when Dublin eventually did decide on a rising.

By this stage the upper and lower sections of the Society's supporters were already much depleted and the list of leaders in the early summer of 1798 shows a preponderance of the middling social order, of woollen drapers, printers and small shopkeepers.[99] With few well-known leaders remaining, and

---

96. P.R.O. H.O. 100/77/82–3, account enclosed in Camden to Portland, 8 June 1798. See also H.O. 100/77/39–53, 66–74; and P.R.O.N.I. D.607/F/202–31, for the gradual erosion of confidence.

97. P.R.O.N.I. D.607/F/202.

98. P.R.O. H.O. 100/77/98–103, Portland to Camden, 9 June 1798. See, however, P. Mackesy, *Statesmen at War: the strategy of overthrow, 1798–1799* (London, 1974), 18–19, on the drastic shortage of soldiers in England in 1798.

99. P.R.O.N.I. D.272/1, 35[a–b], 'Black Book' of the rebellion, and lists of suspects.

little rank and file to talk about, the North was ill-prepared for action when the South finally rebelled. A meeting of the Ulster provincial called at Armagh for 29 May hurriedly made some preparations. A new executive was elected and the colonels for Down and Antrim were called to meet the follow-ing day to decide on some plan of action. Dublin was no longer in any position to set the pace, and a handful of Ulster leaders was struggling to push the reluctant Ulster movement to act without such a lead. The stoppage of two Belfast mail coaches was to have been Dublin's signal for Ulster to rise. But the Dublin attempt had collapsed before the second coach could be interrupt-ed. Hunter and Robert Simms refused to move until the full signal had been received and, when pushed to do so, the latter resigned his position as adjutant-general of the key county of Antrim, 'whereupon', as Hunter later explained, 'McCracken, Munro, Thompson, Orr, Dickey, and the other violent young men who had not the confidential communication, attempted to bring out the People'.[100] Hunter was not entirely fair on the men who eventually led the revolt in Ulster and was justifying his own inaction in reply to an attack by Arthur O'Connor. McCracken had seen the disastrous effects of the leaders' hesitation in Dublin; troops were pouring into Belfast to crush the last spark of their movement; he and his friends were being pushed by others to assume a lead, and reluctantly did so when they saw so many others shrinking from the duties attached to their appointments.

When the Down and Antrim commanders met on the 30th, the former were eager for action, but the latter refused to take a decision until a new adjutant-general had been appointed to the county, and called for another meeting on 5 June. In the interval Down began making preparations. Two government agents had been particularly forward in urging a rising, Nicholas Magin of the provincial committee and John Hughes of the Ulster executive, and their information facilitated the positioning of crown forces on the eve of the out-break. The new executive was to meet at Ballymena in Antrim on the 8th when a commander for the province would be appointed. What happened to provoke the outbreak on the 7th is not quite clear. But it looks as if McCracken's return from Dublin, with enthusiastic reports of initial rebel success, may have altered the situation in the North. Whatever the immediate cause of the Down men's decision to rise on the 7th, it had been taken so suddenly that even Magin had barely enough time to warn General Nugent in Belfast.[101]

But McCracken had underestimated the depth of opposition to any precipitate action, and when he proposed that the local divisions in Antrim county should capture their own towns and then converge on Antrim town,

---

100. See Hunter's account in I.S.P.O. 620/7/74/5, and T.C.D. MS. 7253/2, for the general feeling that they had reneged on their duty.
101. See P.R.O. H.O. 100/77/180–1, Castlereagh to [Wickham], 22 Jun. 1798.

many of the Antrim leaders positively refused to act. Only half the estimated United strength took part in the march on Antrim on the 7th, and three colonels were missing. The rising in Down was to have taken place simultaneously with that in Antrim, but their adjutant-general, the presbyterian minister William Steel Dickson, had been arrested at the last minute. He was replaced by Henry Munro, a Lisburn linen dealer, and with a skirmish at Saintfield, and plans for a major rendezvous at Ballynahinch, the rising in Down finally commenced on the 9th. As in Antrim, there was an overwhelming sense of relief amongst adherents that the time for action had finally arrived. They fought with an enthusiasm and total faith in their leaders which would have rendered them a formidable force, despite depleted numbers, had the projected leadership of trained French officers materialized. On the 11th, the Down insurgents took Ballynahinch with the full support of its inhabitants, and the following day an army of 5,000 rebels prepared to face the troops sent against them. But Nugent's soldiers had already completely suppressed the Antrim rising, and military strength was concentrated against the Down rebels with similar results. No quarter was given to the rebels in either county. At Antrim the yeomanry and Monaghan militia had vied with each other to see who could dispose of most rebels, and their bodies were left hanging on nearby trees as a warning to others. Most of the carnage at Ballynahinch occurred after victory had already been gained by the military. The fleeing rebels were pursued by mounted troops and cut down in the neighbouring woods, and reprisals continued for many days after the defeat.[102]

None of the other Ulster counties had risen. Derry had dithered on receipt of news about the risings in Antrim and Down, but held back because of lack of leaders and signs of failure elsewhere.[103] In the South, Munster had expected no action till June, and then only after a French landing. The province's organization had been disrupted by the eleventh-hour arrest of its adjutant-general, John Sheares, and the skirmishes which occurred in Cork, between Clonakilty and Bandon, were the result of rumours trickling in from the Leinster counties rather than a product of pre-arranged plans. Indeed, given Cork's feeble response to the rebellion, it is difficult to accept glowing militant accounts of the strength of the movement there. Rather, the later confession of Thomas Conway, one of the Cork leaders, that the movement had never really spread beyond the towns, would appear to be a more accurate description of United Irish influence in Munster generally.[104]

102. For full details of the Ulster rising and the events preceding it, see *Report from the Committee of Secrecy ... Commons [Ireland] 1798*, 160–1; P.R.O.N.I. D.272/1–6, 25, 29–36, 72, D.607/F, D.714/2, 78; P.R.O. H.O. 100/77, especially fos. 44–6 and 135–7; also Dickson, *Revolt in the North*.

103. *H.M.C. Charlemont MSS.*, II, 333.

104. P.R.O. P.C. 1/44/A.155; see also I.S.P.O. 620/18/14, Higgins's information, 1 May and S.Ó Coindealbhain, 'The United Irishmen in Cork County', LVI, 27–9, 95.

By the middle of June Camden felt confident that the rising had been contained. But a powerful force of rebels still held out in the Wicklow Hills under Joseph Holt and Michael Dwyer, and the loyalists, anxious at their repeated forays into neighbouring areas, did not share Camden's optimism. A system of bloody repression had been maintained as though the rebellion were still in progress, and even Under-Secretary Cooke felt that the time had come for some clemency from the victors.[105] In view of the danger to Ireland's security, Camden had repeatedly advised London to appoint a Lord Lieutenant qualified in addition to assume the military command of the country. When Lord Cornwallis arrived at the end of June to assume both positions, he was horrified at 'the ferocity of the troops' which he had been sent to command, and determined to adopt a new policy of leniency towards the 'deluded wretches' still in arms. They would be permitted to return home safely upon taking an oath of allegiance, and Cornwallis pledged himself to 'suppress the folly which has been too prevalent in this Quarter, of substituting the word *Catholicism* instead of Jacobinism, as the foundation of the present Rebellion'.

But Cornwallis was soon to find that his reading of the Irish situation had been much too facile. The terrors and bitterness bequeathed to Irish society by the events of the past year were to prove less easy to remove then he had imagined. By 18 July he was writing in exasperation to London about the indiscipline of the militia and their ferocity towards the people. More shocking still was the overwhelming feeling against clemency in the Irish parliament and among the Irish gentry generally. 'The words Papist and Priest are forever in their Mouths, and by their unaccountable policy, they would drive four fifths of the Community into irreconcilable Rebellion.' In reply to the howl of protest at his conciliatory policy, Cornwallis adopted the simple expedient of ceasing communication altogether with parliament and several members of his own government. Initially the large numbers coming forward to take advantage of the pardon seemed to justify such leniency. But terror, exhaustion and disillusionment at the apparent betrayal by many of their own leaders, and in particular by their French allies, were more often the reasons for surrender than any alteration in principle, and Cornwallis himself soon realized that 'inactivity' did not necessarily mean that the people were 'friendly or peacable'.[106]

The position of the Irish government was acutely difficult after the suppression of the rebellion. At a time when magistrates were agitating for the removal

105. P.R.O. H.O. 100/77/157–63, Camden to Portland, 16 Jun. 1798; P.R.O.N.I. D.272/40, Cooke to Nugent, 12 Aug. 1798.
106. P.R.O. H.O. 100/77/200–1, 214–18, Cornwallis to Portland, 28 Jun. and 8 Jul. 1798; for reaction to Cornwallis's conciliatory policy, see P.R.O.N.I. D.607/F/334ᴮ–40, P.R.O. 30/8/325/204, and *H.M.C. Dropmore MSS.*, IV, 280, 315, 324–5, 330–1, 343–4.

of prisoners because of the continuing inspiration they provided to the disaffected, government had insufficient information to convict even principal leaders. Lord Edward had died in prison on 4 June from a wound received at the time of his arrest and, apart from the Ulster leaders executed at the scene of rebellion, the immunity of the remainder was assured by the continuing refusal of Magin and Hughes to testify. Government moved heaven and earth to get John Cormick, a Dublin feather merchant arrested after his flight to Guernsey, to testify against Neilson. He made substantial revelations about the Dublin leadership, but refused to give evidence in court, and eventually escaped on 23 July. The evidence of Reynolds and an army captain, John Armstrong, was sufficient to convict Byrne, Bond, McCann and the Sheares brothers, and they were brought to trial immediately to appease loyalist demands for retribution. Thereafter, Cornwallis's administration was attacked by friend and foe alike for either failing to prosecute the remaining prisoners or for unjust detention. Cornwallis tried to appease all sections of Irish society: justice would accompany leniency, and a Bill of Attainder against those who did not surrender would balance an Act of General Pardon. Turner's information was sufficient to justify the inclusion of most names specifically mentioned in the proposed attainder. But London still refused to reveal its source, and the Irish government scoured the countryside in search of any snippet of evidence to publicly prove each man's treason. Even the parliamentary secret committee, which government hoped might fully justify the measures taken to contain the conspiracy in Ireland, was tied by its inability to produce secret information. Whitehall responded to Dublin's renewed pleas for permission to reveal some of Turner's information by promising that a group of ministers under Grenville's supervision would draw up a selection of Turner's communications for revelation; but on no account was their source to be disclosed.[107] Such 'anonymous' information was unlikely to satisfy the relentless critics of Cornwallis's policies.

On 26 July, however, an almost miraculous way out of this predicament was proposed by the United Irish state prisoners in Dublin. They offered a full confession in return for certain concessions, notably the reprieve of Byrne and Bond who were waiting to follow John and Henry Sheares to the gallows, and their own voluntary exile. A thrill of excited panic ran through the Castle. The executions were to take place within a few days and an immediate decision was essential. Cornwallis wrote excitedly to London, explaining his predicament, and outlining his argument in favour of acceptance. 'I did and still do consider the Establishment of the traitorous Conspiracy

107. For the exchange of letters on this problem of revealing sources, see P.R.O. H.O. 100/77; I.S.P.O. 620/18ᴬ/11, Wickham to Cooke, 9 Aug. 1798; and *Castlereagh Correspondence*, 1, 310–12. On the problems posed by the detention of such an unusually large number of prisoners see I.S.P.O. 1017/31, 35; P.R.O.N.I. D.272/39, 40; and P.R.O. H.O. 100/78/52–3.

by the Strong Testimony of all the principal Actors in it, to be a matter of much more consequence than the Lives of Twenty such men as Oliver Bond.' Whitehall shared Cornwallis's excitement. O'Connor's confession in particular would turn the ignominy of Maidstone into a victory so much greater because of the overwhelming support he had continued to receive from the parliamentary opposition. Cornwallis called together the chief members of his government; Castlereagh alone shared his eagerness to accept the offer. But he received unexpected support from Fitzgibbon, now first Earl of Clare, and an arch-loyalist, who had been out of Dublin at the time of the Castle meeting. Many loyalists were baffled at the motivation of a government which sought to crush conspiracy by 'killing 25,000 followers and pardoning 80 leaders'.[108] But an offer which would silence government critics in both islands, justify the repressive policies of past and future governments, reveal French intrigues to the world and discredit a host of United Irish leaders who might otherwise remain untouched, was not to be sniffed at, and Clare spoke for both governments in his jubilant anticipation of 'the reversal to all the Foxs, Sheridans etc.' which would result from such revelations.[109]

The state prisoners had not been unanimously agreed on this offer of a confession, and the O'Connors in particular withheld agreement until shocked into it by Byrne's execution on 26 July. Many remained unhappy about the statement produced in what came to be known as the 'Kilmainham Treaty'; it savoured too much of a moderate attempt to distance themselves from the recent bloodshed, by emphasizing their reasonable aims, and Arthur O'Connor lost little time in refuting those parts with which he was dissatisfied. The statement, detailing the progress of the United Irish movement since 1791, and in particular its negotiations with France, appeared in the first week in August. In addition, O'Connor, MacNeven and Emmet, who had conducted the discussions with government, were examined before the secret committee of the Irish House of Lords. An edited version of their replies, clarifying the points made in their statement, was attached as an appendix to the secret committee's report, also published in August.[110] Throughout the interrogation, ministers had appeared to know all the answers to their questions in advance, but were eager that the words should come from the prisoners themselves, thereby removing the need to reveal secret sources.

---

108. P.R.O.N.I. D.607/F/351, R. Johnson to Downshire, 18 [Aug.]; and P.R.O. H.O. 100/77/301–3, Cornwallis announcing the offer to Portland, 26 Jul. 1798.

109. For Clare's reaction, see Kent C.R.O. U840/O183/12; P.R.O. P.R.O. 30/8/327/86; *Auckland Correspondence*, IV, 37–40; and *Castlereagh Correspondence*, I, 310–12.

110. For O'Connor's account of the transaction see Teeling, *Sequel to the History of the Irish Rebellion*, 352–76; for Russell's see N.L.I. MS. 873/655; for MacNeven's see his *Pieces of Irish History*, 142–73. Emmet claimed that O'Connor was responsible for the later retractions, see I.S.P.O. 620/2/15/17 and B.L. Add. MS. 33106 fos. 79–84. See also Madden, *United Irishmen*, 2nd sers, I, 154–60, 164–5; and II, 100–6.

Plate 25. Evidence to Character; being a Portrait of a Traitor by his Friends and by Himself (Maidstone Trials, 1798) (by Gillray, *Anti-Jacobin Review*, vol. 1 (1978))

Government excitement at the revelations was not misplaced. The publications were an official masterpiece, and for months the government press revelled in the victory over would-be critics. The statements of various leading opposition politicians at the Maidstone Trials were reproduced in a *pas de deux* with extracts from the Kilmainham confession and in particular from O'Connor's interrogation; 'the Jacobin apologists can no longer deny a conspiracy' concluded the *Sun* triumphantly on 29 August, and ministers felt confident that they would be spared opposition taunts in the passage of future security legislation. But the potion of political capital was not yet exhausted, and the opposition was further discredited by poorly disguised insinuations that they were themselves implicated in the late conspiracy. 'They have opposed the *Treason and Sedition Bills*, and every measure brought forward, in these perilous times, for the safety and protection of the Country,' commented the *Sun* on 8 September, 'and they are now proved to have countenanced and supported men who have confessed themselves Traitors . . . with what face, then, and under what pretence will they again call upon the

People of this Country for their confidence and support?'[111] Fox was never allowed to forget his earlier association with 'traitors', and it became a particular theme of Gillray's caricatures. There was never any direct proof that the opposition had consciously supported treason. But they may have been guilty of misprision of treason by withholding information, and Wilberforce for one was convinced that cowardice alone deterred some from playing a more active role.[112]

Pitt's government would have liked to establish a more definite connection, and a remarkable dispute occurred between Whitehall and Dublin over the use of certain information implicating Grattan. John Hughes told of how he had accompanied Neilson and Sweetman to Grattan's house on 28 April of that year; Neilson had held lengthy discussions with Grattan about the United Irishmen, of which, according to Hughes, he was a sworn member. Dublin Castle was sufficiently sceptical to withhold Hughes's information from the secret committee. Grattan publicly denied Hughes's claims; but although they remained unsubstantiated, London used the flimsy excuse of Neilson's visit to have Grattan's name removed from the list of Privy Councillors.[113] There is no reason to doubt the fact of Neilson's visit. Men that we know to have been leading republicans would have been simply reformers to their social peers among the oppositon M.P.s. O'Connor, Fox, Burdett, Erskine and Lord Wycombe in particular corresponded quite openly in 1797 about the United Irish Society and its aims (though it is important to add that in such correspondence these 'aims' never went beyond radical reform), and in a demonstration of opposition support, O'Connor and Lord Edward were elected to the Whig Club in London on the former's release from prison in 1797.[114] A knowledge of the United Irishmen's more extreme aims is less easy

111. *Sun*, 8 Sept. 1798, also 28–9 Aug. and 4, 12, 13 Sept. 1798; *The Times*, 27–30 Aug. and 26 Sept. 1798; *Anti-Jacobin*, 1, 284–96, 378. The *Courier* tried to play down the affair; see issues for 4 and 27 Aug.

112. M. D. George, *Catalogue of Political and Personal Satires preserved in the Department of Prints and Drawings in the British Museum*, 11 vols. (London, 1870–1954), XI, 8826, 9160, 9167, 9171, 9217, 9245; XII, 9890; idem, *English political caricature: a study of opinion and propaganda*, 2 vols. (Oxford, 1959), II, 38–42, 69–1, 92–3. *Evidence to Character; or, the Innocent Imposture: Being a Portrait of a Traitor by his Friends and by Himself* (London, 1798). This pamphlet was reviewed in the *Anti-Jacobin*, II, 292–300. T. Moore, *The Life and Death of Lord Edward Fitzgerald*, 2 vols. (London, 1831), I, 278, claimed that Fox and Sheridan were told of Lord Edward's and O'Connor's involvement with France.

113. *Memoirs of the Life and Times of the Rt. Hon. Henry Grattan*, ed. his son, 5 vols. (London, 1839–42), IV, 408–27; P.R.O. T.S. 11/122/333, examination of William White, 1798; H.O. 100/78/268–71, Castlereagh to Wickham, 5 Sept. 1798; Madden, *United Irishmen*, 1st ser., I, 310–19. See also Grattan's refutation of the charges, *Courier*, 9 Nov. 1798, and James Hope's assertion that he did in fact take the U.I. oath in T.C.D. MS. 7253/3.

114. See I.S.P.O. 620/18/14, for Higgins's information of 1 and 24 Sept. 1797, and 620/15/3/21–6 for Burdett's correspondence with O'Connor, 1796–7.

to prove. But Lord Edward had certainly intimated their nature to Fox in March, though the United Irish leaders later absolved Fox and his colleagues of any deeper involvement. 'M. Fox ... does not know the details of the discussions with the Republic', Lewins later told Reinhard, 'but he asked Lord Edward if it concerned Irish independence. L.F. answered yes. Good God, replied M. Fox, do nothing without being certain.'[115] A widespread belief in the tacit support of the parliamentary opposition fortified the United campaign in Ireland, in England, and above all in France. But the role of the opposition in a United programme was one of government-forming when success had been achieved rather than active participation in its attainment, and given the long association between the opposition and many United leaders, the latter's belief in such co-operation was reasonable. The prospect of a French invasion, and of how they would act in the event of its success, had been frequently discussed informally by individuals of the two groups. McNally, a more reliable witness than Hughes, told of a dinner held at Grattan's on 12 November 1797 at which some leading United Irishmen were guests; '... they were unanimous that an Invasion would be attempted, and if a landing should take place, the old plan was to be adopted, namely a Convention, to treat for the country with the French in exclusion of Parliament.'[116] Even on the eve of the rebellion the United Irish leaders were more concerned about planning the future government of the country, and the provinces were requested to submit lists of those who might sit in an interim national assembly.

The United Irish leaders were misfits among the revolutionaries of the 1790s. The American system of democracy rather than the French remained their ideal model. To most, revolution and bloodshed were distasteful; a French invasion would be the means of minimizing both, and an interim national government formed by the leaders would in turn control the activities of the invasion force. There would be little confiscation of property, for Emmet and MacNeven believed that even former opponents would quickly recognize the new government when they realized how little change was contemplated. As MacNeven later explained to a French agent, the aim of the United Irishmen was 'to secure through the alliance with France, a government which would be representative without being hereditary; they would like such a government to have a strong and concentrated central power much like that of America. It would require few alterations in existing structure to attain such a government in Ireland.' Even the question of Ireland's future relationship with England was to be resolved in a manner which

---

115. A.N. Corr. Pol. Ang. 590 fos. 217–23. See also MacNeven, *Pieces of Irish History*, 188–9, for United Irish denial of opposition involvement.
116. I.S.P.O. 620/33/6, McNally to Pollock, 15 Nov. 1797; see also his information of 8 Dec., 620/36/227.

France would not have much cared for, and MacNeven did not dismiss the possibility of a federal connection if Ireland had a free parliament.[117]

The reaction of the main United Irish leaders to the events of 1798 raises many questions about the nature of their republicanism, and certainly about their commitment to an armed struggle. Rebellion was never their preferred means of attaining independence, and it is unlikely that one would have taken place at all in 1798 had they been at liberty to prevent it. People like Thomas Addis Emmet, MacNeven, McCormick and Keogh may already have been digging their heels in over the issues of revolution and invasion, and their delaying tactics may well have been the preliminary to total withdrawal. Certainly there were fears that Keogh might betray Lord Edward after his March escape, and there is some evidence that his associations with the Sheares brothers may have been one of the reasons for their removal from the executive.[118] There is a remarkable element of self-exculpation in both the Kilmainham statement and the account of this period published by Emmet and MacNeven some years later. The intention of causing bloodshed is disavowed and the search for French assistance justified as a means of minimizing it. The French were to have been paid as mercenaries for their services, and there was never any question of continuing French influence in their councils.[119] One may well ask if the 1798 confession was seen as a possible way out of the republican phase of their reform activities, and if it was government's refusal to accept such an easy re-integration into constitutional reformism, rather than their own desire, which dictated their continuing republicanism. Certainly the events of 1798 marked a turning point in the history of the United Irish movement in Ireland, banishing the woolly thinking and disagreement of pre-rebellion days, and making it potentially a much more effective revolutionary organ. But the response of the authorities and the Irish people had also changed after the bitter experience of 1798, and the dramatically altered situation which faced the French when they eventually did arrive was to show that the only real chance of United Irish success had already passed.

117. A.A.E. Corr. Pol. Ang. 601 fos. 43–6, 'Mémoire sur l'Irlande'; see also *Report from the Committee of Secrecy . . . Commons [Ireland] 1798*, 159, 163.
118. I.S.P.O. 620/37/45, anon. information to Cooke, 9 May 1798, also Sproule's information (undated) in 620/51/39.
119. MacNeven, *Pieces of Irish History*, 218–19.

CHAPTER SEVEN

Invasion

The failure of the French to arrive had baffled the Irish rebels and was the most important single reason for the indecision of the leaders, the consequent erosion of United strength, and the confused campaign which followed. But there is no sign that the Directory was aware of a commitment to send help to Ireland at any specific time in 1798. The intention was there, but the specified dates which emerge from the Irish sources seem to have been entirely the creation of the United Irish militants in Paris. With most of its army and fleet in Egypt, the Directory was genuinely incapable of sending substantial help to Ireland after April. The decision to confront England in Egypt rather than on home territory was seen in retrospect as disastrous. But the planned invasion of England seemed inadvisable, given the recent build-up of British naval force in home waters; an expedition against Hanover was impolitic in view of the coveted Prussian alliance; and, quite apart from a desire to distance Bonaparte and his army from France, an attack on English interests in the east seemed the best alternative to one on England herself. The army was becoming restive in the Channel ports, and Reubell's fear of an unemployed army eventually overcame his objection to Bonaparte's proposal for an expedition to Egypt.[1] From the outset the plans for England had lacked the decisiveness required to surprise. As with Hoche's 1796 forces, the *armée d'Angleterre* became a reserve of strength to be plundered when more immediate needs arose. Regiments were diverted to police the spring elections, and others were sent to Switzerland and to the Rhine, where there was a build-up of 120,000 men by late spring. The unitary project against England had already disintegrated before Bonaparte left for Egypt.[2]

The Irish part of the original invasion plans was left to smoulder in the Dutch cauldron. But no definite date was set for departure, and it seems certain that for the moment such ostensible preparations were retained to

---

1. *Correspondance de Napoléon 1ᵉʳ*, 32 vols. (Paris, 1858–69), III, 2419; see also Charles-Roux, *Les Origines de l'expédition d'Égypte*, 296–335. For naval criticism of the decision to sail for Egypt rather than Ireland see A.N. AF. IV. 1687 doss. 2 pᶜᵉˢ 41–2, 46.
2. A.H.G. B⁵ 42, Ministry of War orders for Mar.–Apr. 1798.

keep Ireland simmering and England guessing. The Directory had little idea of the havoc caused within the United Irish movement by this policy of raising expectations with no immediate intention of fulfilling them. France's insistence that the Dutch should continue to prepare for an expedition, of which they knew neither the destination nor the departure date with any real certainty, only served to further exacerbate relations with the sister republic, and France might have been well advised to have abandoned such preparations altogether. It is difficult to find any statement of Directory policy towards Ireland after Barras's communications to Lewins. The Irish business had become so much a part of the English invasion plans that their fates rose and fell together. The Irish expedition was inevitably a secondary project, and from his exile in Switzerland Carnot predicted the eventual scaling down of the English operation and the despatch of a smaller force to Ireland under a less important general than Bonaparte.[3]

France's bumbling attitude to the coastal preparations was in startling contrast to the escalating expectation in Ireland. The protracted preparations on the French coasts, without any sign of sailing, seemed to verify official propaganda that France only wished to send a force large enough to dominate Ireland.[4] The personal interest taken by General Kilmaine in Ireland exaggerated the hopes of the Irish exiles, at a time when there were no immediate official plans to justify his assurances. Kilmaine had been born in Ireland and had come to France as a student in 1765. He had a distinguished military career, from his campaign in the American War of Independence until his most recent participation in the Italian campaign. His appointment as interim commander of the remnants of the *armée d'Angleterre*, on Bonaparte's departure for Egypt, was a tonic to the United Irish exiles, but produced no visible alteration in the apparent stagnation of the invasion plans. By July, disillusioned United men writing home from France reinforced the growing doubts about French intentions.[5]

The main reason for the absence of any sense of urgency in the Irish preparations was lack of French awareness of the deteriorating Irish situation. The antics of Tandy and Muir had debased the value of the information they had to offer. The isolation of Tone and Lewins from home developments was becoming increasingly apparent. Tone's comments on the arrests in England and Ireland were those of a mere observer. He scarcely recognized the names of those arrested at Oliver Bond's house, and could not even guess at the reason

---

3. For Carnot's assessment see P.R.O. F.O. 27/53; for the continuing Dutch preparations see A.N. BB³ 145 fo. 264.

4. See e.g. A.N. BB⁴ 122 fos. 296–7, information transmitted by Duckett, 16 Oct. 1798; and F⁷ 7422 doss. B⁵ 5933, Tone to the Minister of Police, 21 Apr. 1798.

5. See P.R.O. H.O. 100/77/226–9, and I.S.P.O. 620/18ᴬ/11, for Wickham's correspondence of Jul. 1798.

for O'Connor's journey to France. Lewins was in Holland in the crucial months before the rebellion, and had failed to establish a regular communication route with Ireland.[6] News of the Irish rebellion found the Directory totally unprepared to help. France's best generals and the bulk of her navy and army were inaccessible in Egypt. The remnants of the *armée d'Angleterre* were dispersed along the Rhine, in Holland, Italy and Switzerland, and a march of thirty-five days would have been required even to transfer divisions from the northern to the western coasts, at a time when speed was imperative. But at last a sense of urgency had been introduced into the Irish preparations. The Directory realized that it was in no position to send substantial assistance; but instructions were issued for the despatch of arms and some men, and the near-panic that reigned in the departments concerned and the impatience to send immediate help, however small, was a token of what Ireland might have expected if the rising had occurred before the *armée d'Angleterre* had been dispersed.

Tone had heard the news on 17 June at Le Havre and left immediately for Paris. The United Irishmen in Paris had already lost heart, and several had contemplated leaving to settle in the provinces.[7] News of the rebellion, however, placed the United Irishmen on the Continent on general alert. The flow of letters and memoranda to the Directory recommenced and for once were not set aside but sent to the Minister of Marine, who had been placed in overall charge of the Irish preparations.[8] Tandy and his friends were so confident of imminent triumph in Ireland that they formally organized themselves into a United Irish committee in Paris, giving a publicity to their activities which would have been inconceivable before June.[9] Indeed, the reception of the Irish in Paris by their French hosts was reminiscent of the heady days of 1792. On 14 July the new United Irish committee sent a delegation to the councils to present their national emblems. Other patriot groups were also represented, but the Irish were singled out as particular examples of continued monarchical tyranny, and promises of liberation were extended suitable to the mood of the national fête. 'Unfortunate Ireland, vengeance is near, only bear up a little longer, all France will arm if necessary to help you. Soon, like us, you will be able to celebrate the foundation of your new Republic, sister to the Batavian, Helvetian, Ligurian, Cisalpine and Roman;

6. Tone, *Life*, II, 294–7; see also Tandy's memoranda in A.H.G. Doss. Pers. 2ᵉ sér. G.B. 755 Tandy. Even O'Finn says nothing of the urgency of some kind of French landing in Ireland: A.N. AF IV 1671 plaq. 1 fos. 114–26. See A.N. BB³ 146 fo. 124 and P.R.O.N.I. T.3048/G/9 for Lewins's absence in Holland.

7. Tone, *Life*, II, 503–10, and A.N. F⁷ 7435ᴮ doss. B⁵ 7317–46 and F⁷ 7293 doss. B⁴ 2671, for the situation of the Irish in France.

8. See e.g. A.N. BB⁴ 122 fos. 301–6.

9. For the committee see A.N. F⁷ 7449 doss. B⁵ 8623, AF III 274 pᶜᵉ 48, and A.A.E. Corr. Pol. Ang. 592 fo. 227.

and our own ... a mother embracing its children.' Much of the speechifying was little more than hot air; but news of the rebellion had revealed a surprising knowledge of Irish affairs and there is no reason to doubt the sincerity of French support. The Directors had always promised to help if the Irish showed a genuine willingness and ability to rebel, and proved as good as their word when the Irish finally acted. The temperature of Directorial enthusiasm for foreign causes did tend to rise and fall according to their potential for success, and in the summer of 1798 the rebellion had pushed Ireland to the forefront of official concerns.[10]

As the first refugees from the rebellion began to trickle to the Continent with heartening news of early successes, so the pace of the French preparations quickened. A hastily constructed army was put together for Ireland from the remnants of France's military forces, and rushed to the western ports. Four frigates were to be despatched immediately with 1,200 soldiers, 4,000 stand of arms and 160,000 rounds of ammunition. By 1 July the numbers of men and arms had been increased by a third and efforts were being made to secure assistance also from the sister republics.[11] Overnight, France's passive interest in Ireland had been transformed into a desperate attempt to keep the Irish rebellion alive until a larger force could be sent. In France, Ulster was still considered the United Irish stronghold; the Directory was clearly concerned to hear that only Leinster had risen and was anxious to produce a rising also in the North. A small advanced force of 280 French and Dutch soldiers and 20 officers, under the command of Major Michel, were ordered to Ulster from the Dutch ports, with 6,000 stand of arms and 480,000 cartridges on board; and two United Irish emissaries, Joseph Orr and Arthur McMahon, were to be sent in advance to assure the Ulstermen that a larger force would follow.[12]

France hoped that the Batavian Republic (Holland) would supply help to the Irish until the funds and forces required for the larger expedition could be found. But after the losses at Texel, the Batavian government was less willing to subsidize France's peripheral war aims, and plans for the advanced force were bedevilled from the outset by Batavian ill-will. Although France could sometimes find it easy enough to support the cause of foreign revolutionaries when someone else footed the bill, Bruix's Dutch correspondence breathes a zeal reminiscent of the early days of the war. The news that an Irish rebellion had at last occurred, the continued interest in Ireland by men involved with the 1796 preparations (Bruix, Kilmaine, Debelle and

10. See A.A.E. Corr. Pol. Ang. 592 fos. 190–3; *Réimpression de l'Ancien Moniteur*, 29, pp. 313–15, for the reception of the Irish delegation; see also Aulard, *Paris, ... sous le. Directoire*, iv, 741–3.
11. A.N. BB⁴ 122 fos. 6–11, 19. For the first Irish refugees see F⁷ 7453 doss. B⁵ 9079 and 9099.
12. A.N. BB⁴ 123 fos. 192–8; also Desbrière, *Projets et Tentatives*, ii, 54; for the despatch of McMahon and Orr see P.R.O. P.C. 1/43/A.152, Turner's information of 28 Dec., I.S.P.O. 620/18ᴬ/11 and 620/39/70.

Chérin in particular), and the intense anglophobia of 1798 temporarily produced a sort of frenzied idealism uncharacteristic of the second Directory. Hoche's influence continued to haunt the Irish preparations and disciples like Chérin saw them as in many ways the fulfilment of the dead general's commitment to that country.[13]

Bruix's personal enthusiasm did not stop at normal naval preparations. Within days of receiving the Irish news, he had sent Duckett on another secret mission, earmarking 28,000 *livres* (one-eighth of the entire allocation to the Irish expedition) for its costs, and ordering Joubert as French commander in Holland to remove all obstacles to Duckett's journey. Duckett was given an entirely free hand to implement his own plans in support of the rebellion, and en route through Holland he conferred with Joubert on the destination of Michel's small force. His recommendations were subsequently incorporated into Michel's instructions.[14] But the most important part of Duckett's mission was predictably directed at the Irish in England's armed forces, and Bruix was convinced that they would come out in support of the Irish rebellion. England's directives against the despatch of Irish rebels into the armed forces had proved ineffective, there was evidence of intensified United attempts to infiltrate the forces in the early months of 1798, and France was assured by newly-arrived United agents like O'Finn that such a campaign was in progress. Certainly there were signs that the allegiance of many Irish sailors and soldiers might have been lost if the rebellion had succeeded, and Duckett's mission seems to have been designed primarily to support a mutinous tendency which France had been given reason to believe existed. In this sense the mission was an integral part of Bruix's naval preparations, and in addition to Duckett's activities, thousands of addresses to the Irish sailors were distributed to British crews in neutral ports.[15]

But Duckett's mission was abruptly curtailed by his arrest in Hanover, on orders from the new British minister in Hamburg, Sir James Craufurd. Duckett's activities had attracted considerable interest in England since his involvement with Bourdon. His name had continued to crop up in association with England's revolutionaries, but there was a frustrating absence of information about him in Whitehall.[16] Duckett had orginally been detained in

13. See A.N. BB⁴ 123 fos. 209–14 and 235 for the influence of Hoche's memory; and I.S.P.O. 620/40/67, letter distributed to the men in Humbert's force, to the same effect.
14. A.N. BB⁴ 123 fos. 193–8, Bruix and Joubert's correspondence 4–18 Jul. 1798; A.N. AF III 149 doss. 701 fos. 67 and 71.
15. P.R.O. F.O. 33/16/50, Craufurd to Grenville, 7 Aug. 1798. Also H.O. 100/75/341; I.S.P.O. 620/3/32/1, 620/10/121/139, 620/36/223 and 620/37/155; P.R.O.N.I. T.3048/G/9; and A.N. AF IV plaq. 1 fos. 114–27 for intensified United plans to infiltrate the armed forces at this period. See A.N. BB³ 160 fo. 147 and 164, BB³ 162 fos. 65–6 and AF III 149 doss. 701 fo. 143 and doss. 702 fo. 64 for reports on British deserters.
16. See P.R.O. F.O. 33/15/4, 7, 10, 24, 27, 28, Craufurd's letters from Hamburg, May–July; I.S.P.O. 620/18ᴬ/11, information transmitted by Wickham, 1 Jul. 1798; and *Castlereagh Correspondence*, 1, 426 and 11, 6.

Hanover in mistake for another Irish agent. But Craufurd was more excited about the arrest of Duckett, and travelled immediately to Hanover to reap full benefit from such a stroke of unexpected luck. He realized, however, that difficulties might result from the nervous neutrality of Hanover. His fears were well-founded, for when Duckett produced his French passport and protested his position as an employee in French service, the Hanoverian Regency desperately sought means of correcting its embarrassing mistake before France's wrath was aroused. Because Duckett's arrest had taken place in that part of Hanover under the military supervision of the Duke of Brunswick, the Regency claimed that only he could decide the issue, knowing full well that it could thus simply dispose of the whole matter to Prussia, in her capacity as guarantor of north German neutrality. Duckett had already written to Brunswick, Joubert, Bruix, the French ministers in Prussia and Hamburg, and to his brother, who had then called on the Prussian ambassador in Hamburg. Indeed he was threatening to create a European crisis all by himself; clearly Hanover was not to be permitted to creep out of its predicament quite so easily. Lemaître in Hamburg and Talleyrand were furious at the rumpus Duckett was creating, especially since they had not known of the mission. Bruix proclaimed his full confidence in Duckett and relations between the two ministers cooled considerably when Foreign Affairs failed to secure his release.

Craufurd had placed England in an equally embarrassing situation by claiming full royal sanction for Duckett's extradition. Since 1795 England had studiously avoided any action which might have jeopardized Hanover's neutrality. France was angry at the persistence of Hanover's pro-English attitudes and was obviously looking for an excuse to attack England through what was, in effect, George III's second kingdom.[17] Consequently, when Craufurd's despatch of 19 July arrived in London on the 26th, the king was furious and warned Grenville that 'without the grossest breach of the neutrality I cannot support the irregular conduct of Sir James Craufurd in having seized a suspicious character in my Electorate, and directing from hence that the said person shall be delivered into his hands to be sent here'.[18] Many at Whitehall would dearly have liked to take Duckett with his documents, and Wickham was particularly disappointed; but the timing and the place of the arrest had been wrong, and ministers had to be satisfied with the termination of his mission. Craufurd withdrew to Hamburg, and consoled himself with intensive surveillance of Duckett when he eventually arrived

17. See G. S. Ford, *Hanover and Prussia, 1795–1803. A study in neutrality* (New York, 1903), especially 82–101.
18. *Later Correspondence of George III*, III, 100. For an account of the mission see A.A.E. Corr. Pol. Ham. 113 fos. 137–203; Corr. Pol. Ang. 592 fos. 209–14; and A.N. BB⁴ 122 fos. 284–99; and see Duckett's later reports from Altona in A.N. AF III 57 doss. 224 and AF III 206 doss. 943. For British reaction see P.R.O. F.O. 33/15/30–5, F.O. 33/16/50–7, H.O. 100/78/66–9, 85–6; and Hants. C.R.O. 38M49/1/54 and 66.

there early in September. The mission had been abandoned. Duckett was to continue to send information to Bruix on the Irish in Hamburg and to assist their activities against England. But he was never again to possess the same freedom of action. The incident in Hanover had shown England the extended nature of the threat posed by her errant Irish subjects, and Craufurd was soon to mount a crusade against them in Hamburg, their only point of entry to the Continent.

By the time of Duckett's arrest the enthusiastic confusion of France's initial naval preparations had resolved itself into some kind of coherent plan to rush aid to Ireland. Besides Michel's force, three other expeditions had commenced preparations under General Rey at Dunkirk, General Humbert at Rochefort and the main force with General Hardy at Brest. None of the commanders were of similar calibre to those sent with Hoche, a token of the poverty of military talent in France after the Egyptian expedition had sailed. But the despatch of local Irish leaders was the focal point of the Directory's plans, and, taking care to account for the existing divisions within the Irish leadership in Paris, the Directory distributed the continentally-based Irishmen among the three divisions. Tandy's supporters were sent to Dunkirk, Tone joined the main force at Brest, and Tone's brother Mathew and Bartholomew Teeling were among those sent to Rochefort. The Dunkirk expedition was to sail first. It was to provide a rallying point for the Irish until the others arrived, and it was thought that Tandy's reputation would encourage rebels and ditherers alike. As such the Dunkirk force became the receptacle of all Irishmen offering their services for the forthcoming attempt on Ireland. Hardy's expedition would follow immediately with an entire field-train of artillery, trained artillery officers, and the main body of French soldiers (significantly composed primarily of those four regiments specially formed to follow Hoche to Ireland at the beginning of 1797). All three were to sail to different points on the Ulster coast to divide the attention of the defence forces, and were eventually to join with the rebels in one army.[19] But plans were soon to be disrupted by the foolhardiness of Humbert, who would never have secured such an appointment had Bonaparte not taken the bulk of French military talent to Egypt. Few Frenchmen had any respect for Humbert's military talents. He lacked finesse and had only reached the rank of major-general because of a rash and almost suicidal courage in battle, which could not have gone unrecognized.[20]

19. A.N. BB⁴ 122 fos. 19 and 26, Bruix's instructions of 30 Jul. 1798; Guillon, *France et l'Irlande*, 366–70; Desbrière, *Projets et Tentatives*, II, 50, 54–69. For the Dunkirk expedition in particular see A.H.G. B¹¹ 2, Ameil's letter of 22 Sept. and his Journal, fo. 4; A.N. AF III 149 doss. 702 fo. 128 and F⁷ 7480 doss. B⁶ 412; and P.R.O. H.O. 100/87/334, John Murphy's account.

20. Guillon, *France et l'Irlande*, 266–80; see also Hoche's estimate of Humbert, 18 Jun. 1796, in A.H.G. B¹¹ 1.

Plate 26. Napper Tandy (Madden,
United Irishmen)

Chérin's hopes of sending immediate help to the Irish were quickly dashed. Little account had been taken of the time required to finance and provision the three expeditions, let alone to secure the stores for an army destined to wage a full-scale campaign upon arrival. Chérin experienced the same problems as Hoche in securing finance from the Treasury, and contractors were increasingly reluctant to advance supplies without payment. In the west it proved impossible to secure enough provisions for the gathering army's current needs because of the devastation of the Brest area by the civil war, and the extra supplies brought in by sea were delayed and harassed by the British ships blockading the northern and western ports. Schérer, the War Minister, was proving unco-operative and, worse still, seemed to be treating the Irish expeditions as latter-day Tate affairs, issuing brevets indiscriminately to anyone offering their services, snatching individuals from regiments scattered all over the interior of the country, and rarely transferring a full division. Chérin's letters to Bruix tell of mounting frustration and near despair at the end of July when he discovered that no money at all had reached the ports.[21]

Humbert, however, had managed to prepare his force without awaiting

21. See A.N. BB⁴ 123 fos. 212–18, Chérin's letters, 18–28 July.

the pleasure of central departments, principally by ignoring demands for the usual advance of wages before embarking on an overseas expedition. By various stratagems he raised enough money and supplies for the voyage, and having plundered the stores of a motley assortment of helmets, shirts and trousers for the Irish expected to join, he set sail on 5 August with 1,019 men, 6,000 stand of arms, 3 field-guns and 3,000 uniforms. But the unpaid sailors were semi-mutinous on the outward journey, and complained bitterly at Humbert's refusal to distribute the money on board.[22] Chérin was dismayed at such a display of ignorance of military and naval affairs by the Directors when they applauded Humbert's departure. He had totally disrupted the essential simultaneity of the three-pronged attack, and the unwieldy administration of naval and military matters was ill-suited to the rapid change in plans required by his precipitate action. The Directory put extra pressure on the Brest force to sail, without any corresponding effort to expedite the necessary supplies.[23] By now the object of the preparations was widely known. The antics of Tandy and his friends at Dunkirk were a public advertisement of the force's destination; the Directory's confidence in the strength of the Irish rebels had apparently rendered secrecy unnecessary, and the result was a predictable intensification of the British naval blockade, making an imminent French departure unlikely, and the isolation of Humbert's small force inevitable.[24]

Chérin's frustration was understandable. The impatient panic of June had not been succeeded by any effort to improve on the haphazard measures adopted in the interests of speed. There had been none of the consultations with the Irish or the careful scrutiny of maps which had preceded Hoche's departure. Bruix, in his rush, had simply requisitioned all the maps used in the first Irish expedition and sent them to the French coasts for the officers to make their own choice on routes and landing places. In their ignorance of the true situation in Ireland, the French considered a landing in any part of the island sufficient to rally the rebels, and beyond a general preference for the north-west, there were no detailed briefings on suitable ports. As a result the maps proved hopelessly inadequate, and every naval officer returning from the Irish attempt lamented the absence of proper hydrological maps which might have made the voyage to the Irish coast less hazardous.[25]

22. A.H.G. B¹¹ 2, reports of Gen. Muller, 27 Jul.–16 Aug. 1798; also MR 506 fos. 57–65, and P.R.O. P.C. 1/44/A.155, Mat Tone's letter of 28 Sept.; and for the mutinous situation on board see A.N. BB⁴ 123 fo. 36.

23. A.N. BB⁴ 123 fo. 228, Chérin to Bruix, 18 Aug.; BB⁴ 122 fos. 34, 85–6, 93, 99 and 100; also AF III 206 doss. 942 pᶜᵉ 51, Hardy to Bruix, 2 Aug. 1798.

24. For the lack of secrecy at Dunkirk, see A.N. F⁷ 7505 doss. B⁶ 2874; also P.R.O. F.O. 33/16/50, H.O. 100/78 (especially fos. 160–1), and H.O. 100/79/321–3 for British knowledge.

25. See A.N. BB⁴ 122 fos. 19, 22, 26 and 32; and the laments of the participating officers in AF III 206 doss. 943 fos. 9–11; A.H.G. B¹¹ 2, Ameil's report, 22 Sept.

As August passed with Rey and Hardy still confined to port, renewed trouble in Italy and the Vendée distracted the Directors' attention and destroyed the sense of urgency required to secure the departure of the expeditions. Detachments of the Brest force were diverted to police the troublesome hinterland, and the desperate shortage of generals caused Chérin's transfer to Italy at the end of August. Such was Chérin's commitment to the Irish venture, his frustration at the succession of contradictory commands over the previous twelve months, and the persistent denial of adequate means to effect them, that he took his removal from the Irish command as a personal insult. He wrote to the Directory resigning his military commission altogether, and reflecting gloomily on the fate of the Irish expedition. Hoche had failed even with the advantage of total surprise and 15,000 of France's best soldiers, he protested; how could the present attempt hope to succeed when one portion had already sailed without taking the elementary precaution of assuring prompt reinforcement from its other sections, and when every obstacle had been placed in the way of their departure?[26]

Humbert's expedition, as the first, albeit pitiful, French force to arrive in Ireland in the rebellion period, provides some idea of how the hypothetical results of a French landing, as envisaged by the French, their Irish allies and the Anglo-Irish authorities, worked out in reality. That the small force arrived at all was nothing short of a miracle and owed more to the persistent ineffectiveness of British naval defence than to the seamanship of the French. Desbrière points to the number of ships lying in France's ports, and attributes the insubstantial nature of the forces prepared for Ireland in 1798 to French lack of interest or to a desire simply to save face. Reliable British intelligence paints a similar picture of ships lying idle in Brest; but sailors to operate them were unavailable, virtually none of the crews were complete, and there was no money to refit them for active service. Bruix had even tried to attract old and retired seamen back into the service in an effort to save 'notre marine expireante'. Every expedition to leave French ports under the Directory was hopelessly overcrowded as a result of this dearth of trained seamen and seaworthy ships, and the large supplies of arms and artillery forced onto the inadequate transport for the Irish forces of 1798 reduced manoeuvrability and rendered capture inevitable if they were unfortunate enough to encounter the enemy. It was with good reason that they were instructed to avoid all conflict with British ships en route.[27] Low morale, indiscipline, and apathy infected crews and dockyard workers through-

26. See Chérin's letters of 11 and 23 Aug. 1798 in Desbrière, *Projets et Tentatives*, ii, 39–42 and A.H.G. B¹¹ 1.

27. For the overcrowding on the French ships see P.R.O. H.O. 28/24/356 and P.R.O.N.I. T.3048/1/8; and see P.R.O. F.O. 27/53 for reports of Sept. 1798 on the chronic shortage of sailors.

out the life of the Directory and the Consulate alike, and the conflict which raged between the military and naval parts of Humbert's force on its passage to Ireland was reminiscent of that which had so weakened Hoche's expedition in 1796.

Humbert's three frigates finally reached Killala Bay in Connacht on 22 August, after narrowly avoiding foundering on some rocks not marked on their maps. Even Killala was not their intended destination, a sudden change of wind having forced them to abandon plans to reach Killybegs Bay in Donegal.[28] The town of Killala was taken after a brief skirmish with the garrison. Headquarters were established at the Bishop of Killala's palace, and arms and uniforms were laid out in the palace yard for distribution to the Irish who were expected to join in large numbers. Such hopes were not disappointed. The United Irishmen's attempt at organizing the province had proved abortive; but as in other areas, rumours of extermination and Orange atrocities, feeding upon the existing catholic fears of the community of presbyterian weavers at Ballina, succeeded where the more formal attempts of the United men had failed, and people flocked into Killala from surrounding areas to join the French. Humbert had introduced a new sense of hope into an atmosphere of despair, and, as in the eastern counties, the call to action and the provision of leaders had generated an intoxicating confidence among the people. A strange air of festivity reigned in Killala. Mathew Tone was amused at the thought of his countrymen attired in the weird assortment of 'uniforms' brought by Humbert, and Bishop Stock's personal account of the town's occupation by the French captures the pathos of the excited, 'uncombed ragged' peasants, tasting the luxury of shoes and socks and fresh meat, possibly for the first time in their lives. They proudly strutted the streets in their new uniforms and, to the peril of friend and foe alike, displayed their new status by firing at the birds and small game in the neighbourhood. The people plied the French with everything they had to offer— drink, food, carts, horses—and they rushed out from houses along the roadside, clasping rosaries and scapulars, touching the officers' uniforms and proclaiming them as saviours 'come to take arms for France and the Blessed Virgin'.[29] At first the French were delighted at such an enthusiastic, if somewhat eccentric, response. Mathew Tone wrote excitedly to his sister-in-law, 'the People will join us in Myriads—they throw themselves on their

28. A.N. BB⁴ 123 fos. 36–79, journal of the frigate *Concorde*.

29. The account of the landing is taken from *A Narrative of What Passed at Killala, in the County of Mayo and Parts Adjacent, During the French Invasion of Ireland in 1798* [by Bishop J. Stock], (Dublin, 1800), hereafter *Narrative*; R. Hayes, *The Last Invasion of Ireland* (Dublin, 1937); V. Gribayédoff, *The French Invasion of Ireland in 1798* (New York, 1890); A.H.G. MR 506, J. L. Jobit, 'Journal de l'expédition d' Irlande'; and B¹¹ 2, Jean Baptiste Thomas, 'Souvenirs de ma vie militaire' (this has been edited and published by F. W. Van Brock, 'A Memoir of 1798', *Irish Sword*, x (1969–70), 192–206); also A.N. BB⁴ 123 fos. 179–88, Humbert's despatches.

knees as we pass along, and extend their Arms praying for our success. We will be masters of Connaught in a few days. Erin go Bragh.'[30]

The naval commander, Savary, who had been instructed to return to France for reinforcements, remained long enough to bring back glowing reports of the native response and the easy capture of Killala, Ballina and Castlebar. Savary's account reappeared in the Paris press and for a time Ireland vied with the Egyptian campaign for press coverage. Once again Ireland became the focus of French hopes against England. Within days of Savary's return, extraordinary orders were issued to expedite the delivery of supplies; the Brest commanders were given permission to recruit from the National Guard, to complete their forces and to ensure Savary's immediate return to Ireland with reinforcements.[31]

Humbert quickly became disillusioned with his Irish recruits. There was no time to train the six or seven hundred who had joined the French, and they proved little use in action besides creating an illusion of numbers. The Irish admitted frankly that Humbert could expect to find little in the way of rebel organization in such a remote spot; the United Irishmen had made no real headway in the area and the locals were astonished that the French should have chosen to land there at all. Although a body of United Irishmen managed to push through to Sligo in an attempt to join with the French, the geographic difficulties of communication in the province made it impossible to draw upon and combine the many pockets of goodwill. The activities of a handful of United Irishmen in Galway, on hearing of the French landing, typifies the dithering reaction of such isolated groups. William O'Laughlin of Galway and Peter Whelan, a servant from Cloone, made a desultory attempt at swearing in their colleagues and drilling them with farm implements, improvised as weapons. But with no higher leadership, French or native, and no sign of the French in the vicinity, the Galway United men could do little but wait on events, and like the chastened rebels all over the country they looked for a substantial French victory before showing their colours.[32] Recognition of such caution among the people dictated the preliminary campaign of the crown forces in the area. They simply withdrew before the advancing French and awaited reinforcements, in the knowledge that one French victory would attract the support of hordes of hesitant countrymen.

Dublin and London reacted to the French landing as if it were a major

---

30. P.R.O. P.C. 1/44/A.155, Mathew Tone's letter of 28 Sept. For further accounts of the reactions of the people see I.S.P.O. 620/52/118 and 123.

31. A.H.G. B¹¹ 2, Humbert's report of 28 Aug., and the Minister's correspondence for Sept.; *Réimpression de l'Ancien Moniteur*, 29, pp. 389–404.

32. I.S.P.O. S.O.C. 1018/12, examination of William Coffey, 28 Jan. 1798; see also A.H.G. B¹¹ 2, 'Souvenirs de ma vie militaire', fo. 55, for the difficulties in training the Irish recruits.

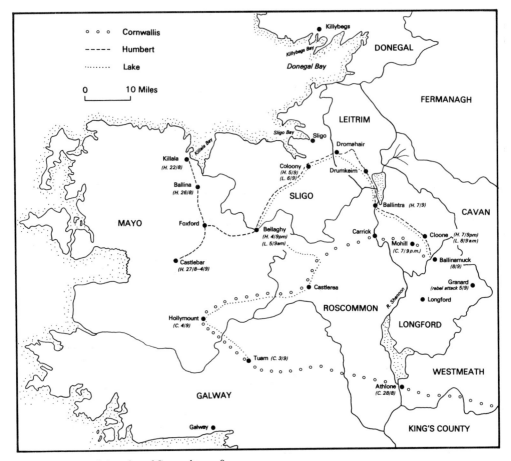

Map 6. The French invasion of Connacht, 1798

invasion, and reinforcements of thirteen English militia regiments were immediately ordered to Ireland. Cornwallis had little idea of the precise numbers landed with Humbert, which in any case he considered as an advanced guard, to be succeeded by substantial reinforcements.[33] Rebellion had smouldered in many areas throughout the summer, and the loyalists had criticized Cornwallis for thinking that it had been suppressed. News of the French landing caused rumblings in western counties hitherto unaffected by rebellion. Bands of rebels from Tipperary, Westmeath, Longford and Roscommon marched towards the Shannon to join the French, capturing towns through which Humbert was expected to pass en route for Dublin. From Kildare came reports of secret meetings to discuss the French landing; in Longford threatening notices warned 'the heretics' that the people's

33. See the correspondence of Cornwallis and Portland, Wickham and Castlereagh in P.R.O. H.O. 100/78/171–224; P.R.O.N.I. T.3048/I/2 and 8; N.L.I. MS. 54^A/146.

deliverers were approaching and that the old religion would be restored; in Tipperary the loyalists fled to the towns, in expectation of a general attack by the rebels; in the Wicklow Hills the surviving rebels received reports from Dublin that another rising would certainly take place if the French and the Wicklow men led the way and ' ... the French were in sufficient force to make head against the English army'.[34] There are certainly enough signs that a sprinkling of determined United men were still at liberty and willing to lead their countrymen in the event of a successful French invasion. Things might have been very different if Humbert had bided his time in Rochefort and news of the simultaneous arrival of Tandy, Hardy and Humbert had reached such rebel survivors.

But surviving leaders in Dublin were as divided as ever. Shortly before Humbert's landing a meeting had been convened to take stock after the rebellion. The general mood of the meeting was one of horror at the events of the preceding months and a feeling that, regardless of their position as United leaders, their own property along with that of the loyalists would fall victim to the Irish peasants in the event of a successful rising. A few stalwarts responded eagerly to news of Humbert's landing, which was falsely reported as consisting of 18,000 men; but on the whole Dublin's reaction was one of caution and a preference to defer action until the French had proved themselves in battle with the crown forces. Eventually the idea of another rising was abandoned altogether.[35] From the North, to which Humbert had originally intended marching, reports indicated that Ulster no longer posed a threat to security. The remnants of the Ulster provincial held three emergency sessions to gauge popular response to the French landing; some counties wanted another rising, but the former United strongholds of Antrim and Down had been completely subdued and refused to act.[36] The rebellion had totally altered the nature of support for the remnants of the United movement, and whilst the eastern seaboard had quite obviously been purged of its rebelliousness, Cornwallis was convinced that the rest of the country was poised for another rebellion. The massive army which he began to move towards Connacht at the end of August was designed to crush the French decisively before the anticipated rising occurred. But the 20,000 or so troops which he moved across the countryside was like taking a sledgehammer to crack a nut and was obviously intended as much to impress the natives, rebel and loyalist alike, as to crush the French.

34. Byrne, *Memoirs*, I, 234–5; see also I.S.P.O. 620/3/32/14–15; S.O.C. 1017/29, 37, 50; and the memoir of Hervey Montmorency Morres, commander of the Tipperary United Irishmen in A.A.E. Mem. et Doc. Ang. 1[B] fos. 188–90.
35. I.S.P.O. 620/18/14, Higgins's reports for 22, 28 Aug. and 1 Sept. 1798.
36. I.S.P.O. S.O.C. 1017/2, Dean Warburton (Armagh) to Castlereagh, 29 Aug. 1798, 620/40/133, information on the provincial meetings.

From the outset Humbert's rashness jeopardized the overall French objective. He was to have marched north and to have avoided all encounter with enemy forces until the larger French force arrived under Hardy. News of rebel movement in Longford and Roscommon, however, and Humbert's instinctive tendency for dramatic gestures, dictated another course of action. With no immediate sign of French reinforcements, he marched out from Killala on 26 August to meet the forces defending Castlebar. The French with 800 men and an additional 500 to 700 Irish recruits, were hopelessly outnumbered, and despite the advantage of surprise, the crown forces soon threatened to overpower their attackers. The French authorities had foreseen the danger of defeat in detail which Humbert's rashness had now made inevitable and the whole French campaign in Ireland seemed threatened with extinction before it had properly commenced.

In the middle of the battle, however, and when the crown forces were actually in the ascendant, one wing broke for no apparent reason and fled. Other divisions followed, and the officers on horseback soon outdistanced their men in the general flight. No one was more surprised than Humbert at such an unexpected victory and from Castlebar he took away a very poor opinion of the enemy generals, for such a display could only have resulted from poor leadership. Lake and Cooke attributed the defeat entirely to disaffection in the Irish militia. Such an accusation was totally unjustified. The Irish had also fled on Humbert's side, because neither they nor their compatriots in the defending forces were accustomed to battle conditions, particularly against artillery. Lake's force at Castlebar, which consisted of Irish militia, yeomanry and fencibles, was a microcosm of the crown forces as a whole, and more astute officers recognized the risk of flight by such inexperienced soldiers in similar conditions.[37] Moreover the morale of the militia was low: they were poorly fed, clothed and equipped; complaints of neglect abounded; and in Connacht they had eagerly donned the uniforms of the French killed in battle, which were of vastly superior quality to their own. They were deeply conscious of the contempt in which they were held by their own officers and in particular by the English officers and regular troops, and the ferocious zeal with which they acted against the rebels was frequently an attempt to prove their worth. As the militia had reacted with brutal reprisals in Ulster when accused of United sympathies, so those marching with Cornwallis attempted to resurrect their tarnished reputation after Castlebar by independent forays against the rebels.[38]

37. For Castlebar see A.H.G. B¹¹ 2, 'Souvenirs de ma vie militaire', fos. 58–65; I.S.P.O. 620/52/123; N.L.I. MS. 54ᴬ/146–53; and P.R.O. H.O. 100/78/238–9, for Cooke's assessment, 31 Aug. 1798. See also Gribayédoff, *The French Invasion of Ireland*, 75–99.
38. P.R.O.N.I. D.607/F/462, Maj. Gen. Mathews to Downshire, 14 Oct. 1798; also McAnally, *The Irish Militia*, 133–9.

Nevertheless, despite the groundlessness of fears concerning militia loyalty, the shock caused by the Castlebar incident was extreme. It apparently justified Cornwallis's repeated claims that English troops alone could resolve the crisis in Ireland, and reinforcements were rushed from the mainland with none of the reservations which had greeted Dublin's appeals until then. Such reservations had derived from a conviction that the Irish were perfectly capable of defending themselves and ought to be forced to do so. Castlebar had shown conclusively that their protested helplessness was real enough.

Castlebar had delivered Connacht to the French, for the news had sent garrisons fleeing from other outposts. At first, Humbert contemplated marching on Sligo and heading north according to his instructions. News of the march of Cornwallis's army and of the rebel movements in the midlands forced a change of plan, and Humbert turned abruptly to join with the Irish rebels in the first stage of a march on Dublin. Hervey Montmorency Morres, one of the Tipperary United leaders who had taken refuge in Westmeath after the rising, later provided the Directory with details of the rebel response to the French landing. He had considered Humbert's force to be an advanced guard and urged restraint on the men of the midlands until the main French force arrived. On hearing of Humbert's advance on the Shannon, however, the order was given to rise, and Morres led 3,000 poorly armed rebels north to join the French.[39] It was news of this march which caused Humbert to redirect his men southwards; a juncture with the rebels seemed the only alternative in view of the massive army sent against them.

By 7 September, after a swift forced march, the French were approaching the borders of Longford with Cornwallis's army fast closing in. They finally met at Ballinamuck on the 8th. The French put up a token fight and surrendered. The Irish were given no quarter by the victorious forces, and the Downshire, Armagh and Kerry militias were to the fore of the wholesale slaughter of Irish collaborators at Ballinamuck and in the towns retaken from the French. The bitter memory of Ballinamuck survived in the region for generations, and in the 1930s the 95-year-old Patrick Gill, whose grandmother had lived through the invasion, could still lament: 'If only the French ship that came into Killala waited for more of the other ships that were comin'' the war would have been different, but Ballinamuck was the biggest beatin'' the Irish ever got, or ever will again.'[40] Local tradition held the French largely responsible for the slaughter of their allies, for they had pushed the

39. A.A.E. Mem. et Doc. Ang. I^B fos. 188–90, and I.S.P.O. 620/3/51/29; also L. Cox, 'Westmeath in 1798', 12–13; Musgrave, *Memoirs of the Different Rebellions*, II, 165–84; and Pakenham, *The Year of Liberty*, 364–5.
40. P. Mac Gréine, 'Traditions of 1798. The Battle of Ballinamuck', *Béaloideas*, IV (1933–4), 393–5.

Irish to the front of the battle. The French maps showing the disposition of their forces on the day do not support the accusations. Rather they show the Irish flanked on all sides by the French, forcing them to remain on the battlefield after they had shown the same disposition to flee as at Castlebar. Much of the action against the Irish had occurred as they tried to join the main force, for the French had split up and approached by different routes to confuse their opponents; the Irish had separated from the French and their slaughter was thereby facilitated. Those Irish who had landed with Humbert suffered an equally summary fate; they were court-martialled and executed almost immediately, despite Humbert's pleas that Mathew Tone and Bartholomew Teeling had actively sought to limit pillage and acts of revenge and had saved the lives and property of many protestants in consequence.[41] Neither side had emerged with credit from Ballinamuck. Despite the overwhelming numbers on the side of the crown, none of those involved considered Ballinamuck an easy victory; military losses had been substantial and loyalist critics remained unappeased because of the inordinate length of time taken to defeat such a paltry force. The English officers were left with the same feeling of contempt for the abilities of the Irish military and their officers as Humbert, and lashed out at their stupidity and miscalculations and at the licentiousness of the militia which had hindered the progress of the entire army.[42]

In Dublin, Humbert and his officers were treated as guests rather than as prisoners of war; they entertained their hosts by poking fun at their Irish allies and exaggerated their bloodthirsty desire for revenge against the protestants to boost their own part in restraining it. It is true that the loyalist population in Killala breathed easier because of the restraint exercised by the French over their Irish followers. But apart from attacks on the property of Lord Lucan and that of the feared presbyterian community at Ballina, there were few reprisals even in those areas outside immediate French control. Loyalist fears were genuine enough, but they were produced by the arrogance of the victorious natives rather than by any bloodletting. Only with the news of Ballinamuck did the mutual fears of the catholics and protestants in towns under French control reach a point where a massacre on either side was possible, and both appealed to the French officers for arms

41. T.C.D. MS. 873/9–25, original letters of Bartholomew Teeling; Teeling, *Sequel to the History of the Irish Rebellion*, 314–22. For the French position at the battle see A.H.G. B¹¹ 2, 'Souvenirs de ma vie militaire', 67–75 and the attached plans. For surviving local traditions see Department of Irish Folklore, University College, Dublin, 79/634, 202/65–73, 538/263, 512–19, 624/98–101, 625/197, 310–13, 686/226, 712/61–9, 739/60–6, 995/680, 1010/48, 1158/333–5 and 1265/67–9 (just a few of the Department's extensive collection of oral traditions on the 1798 landing.)
42. N.L.I. MS. 54ᴬ/152–3; also P.R.O.N.I. D.3030/232 and *H.M.C. Dropmore MSS.*, IV, 264–5, 291 for such criticisms; and see *Castlereagh Correspondence*, II, 93, for Humbert's poor opinion of the crown forces.

with which to protect themselves when the crown forces tried to retake the towns. The only real bloodshed and destruction of property, outside the immediate area of battle during the French occupation of Connacht, occurred when the victorious military recaptured areas which had fallen to the French. An estimated 2,000 Irish caught in arms after Ballinamuck were killed, and many officers found it impossible to check the 'shameful' plunder of their men which threatened to devastate the countryside around Killala.[43]

But the most important aspect of the attempted invasion was French astonishment at the contrast between their expectations and the reality of the Irish situation. Despite Irish assurances that Connacht was not representative of the rest of Ireland, the French were visibly shocked at the character of their new allies. 'We were astonished at the extreme poverty which we saw everywhere', wrote one officer, 'never can any country have exhibited such a pitiful spectacle. The men, women and children were semi-naked, and housed by a wretched and narrow cottage, which afforded little protection against the weather ... their misery can be attributed more to extreme ignorance and idleness than to the sterility of the soil. ... Almost all these semi-savages are such fanatical catholics that they can only be pitied.'[44] The French had expected to receive support from the higher levels of Irish society and found protestant opposition incomprehensible. The impression created by the statements of the United Irishmen in Paris was of a conflict between the representatives of England and the Irish people of all denominations. Instead they found a civil war in progress and accused the Irish representatives in France of having misled them. General Charost, whom Humbert had left behind to guard Killala, told Bishop Stock 'that he was much disappointed ... to discover how extremely different the reports of the Irish Commissioners were from the truth with regard to the protestants and the people of property in Ireland'. In Dublin they continued their attacks on the United Irish in Paris, who, they claimed, had represented the country as an easy conquest. The number of Irish who joined them, however, had never exceeded 3,000 and were so unmanageable that they were an encumbrance.[45]

But such statements, issued in the aftermath of defeat, were in significant contrast to the glowing reports transmitted to Paris in the flush of initial victory. As with Bantry Bay, the French in their search for scapegoats exaggerated the more optimistic side of United Irish claims. Tandy and his friends

---

43. See *Narrative*, 28–9, 88–91, 118–73; *H.M.C. Dropmore MSS.*, IV, 329; P.R.O.N.I. D.607/F/ 433, 437 and T. 3048/1/14, for fears of massacre after the French defeat; and D. 607/F/408 for the French officers in Dublin.
44. A.H.G. MR 506, J. L. Jobit, 'Journal de l'expédition d'Irlande', fo. 7.
45. *Narrative*, 2; and P.R.O. H.O. 100/78/324–6 and P.R.O. 30/8/327/163 for remarks made by the captured French officers.

were certainly guilty of misleading the French, and tarnished the reputation of the more balanced representatives in France as a result. Tone, Lewins and their friends had never represented Ireland's liberation as the effortless task which Humbert appeared to consider it. Nor had the French made any allowances for the changed circumstances of the country after the failure of the first rebellion, the backward nature of the area in which they had chosen to land, and the predictable indiscipline of raw recruits from the local peasantry. The Irish were naturally shocked when all the rigours of French military discipline were applied to them; several were executed by the French for pilfering and other misdemeanours. The Irish had suffered terribly for joining the French forces and would not offer their services so readily a second time; 'poor Paddy never thought one was to be hanged for lying,' wrote Lord Edward's sister, Lady Sarah Napier, to the Duke of Richmond, 'and is wofully discomposed ... consequently, Paddy is all ears and eyes just now, ... steadily at harvest ... [but] if the French land in force and gain battle after battle, then it is time *after harvest* to join with their pockets full of money'.[46]

The fate of the other French expeditions to Ireland in 1798 forms little more than a postscript to this premature defeat of the overall plan. The intention behind Tandy's expedition had remained unchanged, and native leaders made up three-fifths of the 200 embarked on the fast-sailing frigate the *Anacréon*. The remaining 80 were mostly French artillery officers. It was hoped that Humbert might have gained a footing in the North and that Tandy might still arrive in time to lead the Ulster rebels. Throughout August the Irish had gathered in something of a holiday mood at Dunkirk, and the port's commissioner had lamented their lack of caution in a town known to be infested with British spies. But Tandy had ceased to be a threat to England and was proving something of a liability to his French employers. The party spirit which he had introduced into the Paris negotiations continued to complicate preparations, even at a time when victory seemed close at hand, and he refused to accept into his expedition United Irishmen who had taken the opposite side in Paris.[47] Many on board the Dunkirk expedition had been sent, without the normal security check, direct from Hamburg. Two such recruits, George Orr and John Murphy, proved particularly unco-operative and at one stage tried to desert altogether. They were eventually forced to remain after Blackwell had threatened to kill them, but attempted again to desert in Ireland, and finally succeeded when

46. Moore, *The Memoirs of Lord Edward Fitzgerald*, Append. no. vi, 463; see also P.R.O.N.I. D. 561/45 and P.R.O. H.O. 100/78/330 for French treatment of the Irish; and A.N. AF III 57 doss. 224 for Duckett's criticism of Humbert's campaign.
47. P.R.O. P.C. 1/43/A.152, copy of a letter from Turner, 28 Dec. 1798; also P.R.O.N.I. D.3030/ 336, information sent by Wickham to Castlereagh, 8 Nov. 1798.

the *Anacréon* took refuge in Bergen on the return journey. By all accounts Orr and Murphy were a disreputable pair, and they eventually sold their services to the British government. The account which they later delivered of the expedition was malicious in the extreme. But Tandy was quite incapable of leading such an expedition. Ameil, one of the French officers on board the *Anacréon*, delivered a more compassionate account than that of Orr and Murphy. He attributed Tandy's weaknesses to old age. But this was exacerbated by his many defects in character, in particular his overriding vanity and demagoguery, and there is probably an element of truth in the story Orr tells of Tandy prancing about on deck in the foppish finery of his special general's uniform, bearing more resemblance to a decadent politician than to a rebel general about to lead a nation to freedom. [48]

Since the object of the *Anacréon*'s voyage was to land as many native leaders as possible, it was detained by few of the supply shortages which had crippled preparations in the west. It reached Rutland Bay in Donegal on 17 September, having outsailed several British vessels sent in pursuit of this well-publicized expedition. Once again the enthusiastic reception by the people of Rutland village testified to the general willingness of the ordinary Irish people to turn out in 1798, if assured of proper leadership. France had not miscalculated on the magnetism of Tandy's name, and had such national leaders been provided three months earlier, the progress of the rebellion might have been quite different. Local officials, reporting to Dublin after Tandy's departure, played down the episode and claimed that the local people had been indifferent to the French landing. Tandy did not in fact stay long enough to test Donegal feeling, but Ameil is a reliable witness, and he tells quite a different story. The Donegal people informed them of Humbert's landing and subsequent defeat; they were nevertheless ready to join the French. Many on board the *Anacréon* were eager to march into the hills, where a body of Irish and French from Humbert's force were rumoured to have fled. But Tandy and Rey felt that further conflict would be hopeless, and having adhered to the strict policy of respecting property and paying for all provisions, they settled their debt with the locals and sailed again on the 18th.[49]

The decision to withdraw was probably the wisest ever made by Tandy, for the forces with which he was to have joined were still struggling to escape from the French ports, and there was no sign of their departure when the

---

48. For Orr and Murphy see P.R.O. H.O. 100/77/222, 100/79/321–3 and 100/87/318–22, 334–5. See also R. Coughlin, *Napper Tandy* (Dublin, 1977), 125–45. A.H.G. B¹¹ 2, Ameil's report, 22 Sept. 1798.
49. A.H.G. B¹¹ 2, Ameil's report fos. 5–8. For other accounts of the Donegal landing see I.S.P.O. 620/40/7, 68ª, 71 and 73; N.L.I. MS. 872/147; P.R.O. P.C. 1/44/A.155, and *State Trials*, xxvii, 1191.

Anacréon sailed away from the Irish coast. For a while, however, the fate
of the Irish expedition had seemed in the ascendant. When news arrived
of the defeat of Bonaparte at the Battle of the Nile, the Directory seems
to have decided on an all-out effort to compensate or at least to distract
attention from failure by success in Ireland. Pressure was put on the Dutch
to expedite the despatch of Michel's expedition, detained for so long by
the British blockade and by flagging Dutch enthusiasm, and to prepare
a larger force to follow. The Spanish had at last come forward with an offer
of ships for Ireland. Kilmaine was appointed to prepare an Irish force of
4,000, and efforts were intensified to despatch Bompard's and Savary's
ships. But the attention of the Directory soon wandered to seemingly more
pressing problems, first to the revolt in Belgium, then to the growing hostility
of the other powers because of the threat posed by the French forces in Egypt.
Throughout September, Paris buzzed with rumours of the probable renewal
of the continental war. Savary was ordered to take a fast frigate to Connacht
to assure Humbert that reinforcements were preparing, but he was detained
in port by the British blockade until October.[50]

By now, few of those on board the blockaded ships held out much hope of
success, and Tone wrote to his wife in a pessimistic mood. He had been a
French officer for two years, but he was poverty-stricken; and since he had not
been paid before sailing, he was unable to send any money to the wife and three
children he was leaving behind in France.[51] Bompard's expedition sailed on 16
September; but non-payment of wages had created a similar state of near-
mutiny to that on board Savary's flotilla two months earlier, and as his ships
finally rounded the north-east coast of Ireland on 12 October, they were in a
pitiful condition, weakened by bad faith on board and continual harassment
by British vessels.[52] Bompard's force was finally defeated and captured by
Admiral Warren off Lough Swilly, and its officers, including Tone, sent off as
prisoners to Dublin.

British confidence had reached an all-time high with news of the Nile
victory, and since Ireland had apparently become the new object of French
attention, the Irish coasts and French ports were closely watched for signs
of French naval support. The Dutch frigates were captured as soon as they
sailed from port at the end of August. Savary's second expedition, which
had finally sailed on 12 October, was attacked off the west coast of Ireland,
and, in an undignified scramble, officers and sailors alike rifled the money
chests which Savary wanted to throw overboard to lighten the load.[53] News

50. A.H.G. B¹¹ 2, correspondence for late Sept.–Oct. 1798; A.N. BB⁴ 123 fos. 19–32, 97–8,
103–44 and 203–7, for Michel and Savary; and AF III 63 fos. 1–2 for the Spanish.
51. P.R.O.N.I. T.3048/K/9, Tone to Matilda, 14 Aug. 1798.
52. A.N. AF III 206 doss. 943 fos. 9–11, journal of the frigate *La Romaine*.
53. See *Castlereagh Correspondence*, I, 427, A.H.G. B¹¹ 2, Schérer's correspondence 2–10 Nov.,
A.N. BB⁴ 123 fo. 82 AF III 206 doss. 943 pᶜᶜ 20 for the capture of the Dutch frigates and Savary's
second voyage.

of all the defeats arrived simultaneously in Paris. Bruix and Kilmaine argued that the preparations for the larger expedition should continue as an encouragement to the Irish, but they were overruled and the Irish plans were dropped. Once again the Directory seemed overwhelmed by the cumulative effect of catastrophe. Defeat in Egypt, defeat in Ireland, risings in the new republics, the prospect of a revival of the European alliance against France, internal criticism at a new peak—little wonder that Hardy's appeals for French intervention to save Irish officers like Tone should have fallen on stony ground.

The Irish defeats had taken the toll of French ships captured or sunk by the British in the course of the war to 942, and the Directory's financial situation at the close of the year VIII was just as bleak. Bruix reported a deficit of 901,239 *livres* in his ministry alone, and there was an acute shortage of arms and ammunition. France had sent no more than 1,700 men and officers to the Irish coasts in 1798. But the number was the most that could have been spared and is no reflection of the hopes the Directory had placed in an Irish success. Many had believed that glory could be achieved more easily and more cheaply in Ireland than elsewhere. A sense of lost opportunity and disappointment pervaded the statements of those who had recognized the potential of the Irish situation, and one officer who had accompanied Humbert lamented the 'many mistakes and ill-conceived plans . . . made by us to support a rebellion in Ireland which offered the republic its most important diversion in the war against England'.[54]

In the crash from such heights of expectation to the recognition of total defeat, scapegoats were sought as a matter of course. Bruix, like Humbert, attributed their mistakes to the exaggerations of Tandy and his 'Club de la rue du Colombier'. Bruix accused Tandy and his supporters of being optimistic visionaries and of pursuing a policy which bore little relation to the real world and its people; and he was clearly influenced by Duckett's warning that the French should never again place their faith in upper-class United leaders, who had deceived France and the Irish people alike. When the first flush of recrimination had exhausted itself, however, a more realistic assessment recognized French impatience, insufficient preparation, and the inferiority of the expeditions, in terms of both numbers and quality, as leading factors in the failures.[55]

The indictment of the old United movement, however, was more than a French attempt to find scapegoats, and similar criticisms were made in Ireland by those who had actually taken part in the rebellion. The truth was that the high politics of the United Irish movement were no longer relevant to the crisis which had developed in Ireland in the years 1797–98,

54. A.H.G. B[11] 2, 'Souvenirs de ma vie militaire', fo. 58. For the losses see Sciout, *Le Directoire*, IV, 294–5, 312; A.H.G. B[12]* 37 fo. 27; and P.R.O. F.O. 27/54, bulletin 1 Dec. 1798.
55. *Mémoires de Barras*, III, 253 and 278; and Bruix's October correspondence in A.N. AF III 45 doss. 162 p[ces] 253–4 and P.R.O. F.O. 27/53.

and the United Irish leaders on the Continent had failed to recognize their increasing obsolescence because of their removal from home realities. The sad and lonely demise of Tone was symbolic of the new situation. The man who had played such an important part in giving the United Irish movement its French dimension seemed strangely unimportant in the Dublin of November 1798. The carriage which brought him prisoner to the city on 8 November passed through the haunts of his former celebrity without raising more than an antiquarian interest. Most of the state prisoners in the city would not have known him, and little effort was made to save him in comparison to the fuss which had been occasioned by the plights of Lord Edward, Bond or Byrne, whose contribution to Irish republicanism had been minute in comparison. His presence in France was known to only a few United Irish leaders, his role eclipsed by that of Tandy in the popular mind. In many ways his return to Ireland was a tragic piece of mistiming; his reputation was largely forgotten, the United Irish movement he had founded had run amok and was no longer recognizable; and he had remained abroad just long enough to be included in the Banishment Act, by which those listed incurred the death-penalty if they returned to Ireland. His friends among the state prisoners, notably Russell, hoped to save him; but Emmet declared the case hopeless, for Clare had told him of the confession signed by Tone in 1795, which was enough to hang him if he ever returned.[56]

The discussion was academic; his arrival on board a French invasion fleet, and wearing the uniform of a French officer, was sufficient proof of his treason, and he had already confessed his guilt. A strange fatalism had been apparent in all his statements since his departure from Brest. He made a half-hearted attempt to persuade Kilmaine to intercede with the Directory on his behalf; but most of his letters to France and to his friends in Ireland were on behalf of his family, amongst whom he divided his remaining worldly wealth of £20. Tone's counsel tried to query the validity of his trial under martial law, which was operating concurrently with the civil law process in Dublin. But Tone had already decided that he might have to take his own life, even before the guilty verdict had been announced. Agitated and apparently little comprehending the scene in the courthouse, he seemed to have already removed himself from his surroundings, and his speech justifying his actions, in terms more suited to 1791 than to 1798, seemed strangely inappropriate to post-rebellion Ireland. On 11 November, after hearing of the rejection of his request to be executed by firing squad, Tone cut his own throat and died seven days later.[57] He was almost a forgotten figure in

56. I.S.P.O. 620/15/2, T. A. Emmet to Russell [Nov. 1798]; and P.R.O.N.I. T.765B/727, for Drennan's account of Tone's entry into Dublin.
57. For Tone's last days see A.H.G. B¹¹ 2, correspondence of Tone, Kilmaine and Hardy, Nov. 1798 (some reproduced in P.R.O.N.I. T.3048/J/3–8). See also *State Trials*, xxvii, 613–26; MacDermot, *Theobald Wolfe Tone* 263–76; Tone, *Life*, ii, 526–41; *H.M.C. Dropmore MSS.*, iv, 345–6, 369–70; *Courier*, 14, 16 and 23 Nov.; *The Times*, 13, 15 and 18 Nov. 1798; and P.R.O.N.I. D.607/F/537, McNally to Downshire, [ ] Nov. 1798.

Ireland. Although his name remained sacred in France and an ability to boast his acquaintance was a seal of approved patriotism, he had taken no part in the domestic movement since 1795, and in popular tradition he was eclipsed by less important leaders active at the time of the rebellion. The sense of unreality attending the Dublin drama was symptomatic of the position of the original United Irish leaders after the rebellion. The ideas which they had injected into Irish society had produced a travesty of their projected rising.

But if the 1798 rebellion had been a distortion of the United Irish vision, it had given national proportions to the conflict between the established authorities and the proponents of a new order. No section of Irish society could remain oblivious to the possibility of French-supported rebellion after 1798, and the rebellion had left an immediate legacy of social unrest which would continue to attract French interest, and would ensure widespread support if they ever again chose to invade Ireland. Most noticeable was the pervasiveness of unrest in the winter of 1798–99, affecting all four provinces simultaneously. Many of the disturbances were manifestations of socio-economic grievances, taking the form of traditional Whiteboy activities such as cattle-houghing in the west, or the destruction of crops and threats to prevent eviction in the south. But the disturbances in Clare and Tipperary had been sparked off by rumours of another French invasion, and beneath the unrest ran a current of expectation that the French would come again and that the people in general would join them.[58]

The aims of such protestors were as unpolitical as those of previous agrarian groups, and after Ireland settled back to some form of normal life, parochial interests might easily have returned to disrupt this vague sense of national wrong, had not the arrogance of the victors perpetuated it into relatively peaceful years. Orange and yeomanry attacks on catholics continued in the years immediately after the rebellion's suppression, frequently with the tacit support of local authorities, and the identification of 'catholic' with 'rebel' after 1798 was another factor legitimizing their action. Attacks on catholics at fairs in north-east Ulster became so serious that the assistance of the Grand Masters of the Orange Lodge was enlisted to curb the passions of their members. Cornwallis tried to prevent the proclamation of the west in the winter of 1799 from providing a further outlet for loyalist reprisals. But the excessive number of executions which resulted was little comfort to the catholics.[59] A sense of alienation from the established authorities and a

58. I.S.P.O. S.O.C. 1018/2, 3 (Cork), 20 and 21 (Meath), 22 (Tipperary), 23 (Waterford), 30–1 (Wexford); see also P.R.O.N.I. D.607/F/570 and G/18, 54 and 67; *Cornwallis Correspondence*, III, 19–21, 28, 66–7; and P.R.O. H.O. 100/85/87 and 259, for the role of French invasion rumours in the Clare and Tipperary disturbances.
59. See P.R.O.N.I. D.607/G/18 and D.272/16 for the proclamation of the west, and D.272/73/35, meeting of the Orange Masters, 6 Aug. 1798. For some accounts of the Orange atrocities see P.R.O.N.I. D.607/F/454 and G/89; I.S.P.O. S.O.C. 1018/30–31; and *H.M.C. Charlemont MSS.*, II, 336–40.

consequent state of undeclared war between most of the people and the government was the most permanent result of 1798 and the reprisals which followed. Passivity or loyalty went unrewarded if one was catholic. The uncommitted had suffered most in the rebellion; the ordinary people would not remain aloof in another rising.

But the ideal of uniting the religious factions behind a movement for national reform had been buried. Many felt that the protestant and propertied leaders in the United Irishmen had pushed the people into action and then left them leaderless to face the consequences when the time to rebel had arrived. The fat Belfast shopkeepers who had founded the United movement had shouldered their muskets to defend their property in 1798. The desertion of the United cause by the propertied classes was greater in Ulster than elsewhere, but prisoners taken in all the rebel counties expressed the same feeling that they had been deserted by their natural leaders. The northern presbyterians were particularly censured for having raised the catholics to act as their instruments and then abandoned them to their fate. 'The generality of the people seem to be pretty well aware that they had been first misled, then forsaken, and lastly betrayed by the leaders of the Rebellion', wrote an anonymous correspondent to Colonel Littlehales (military under-secretary at the Castle), 'and they are now convinced that it was their own ends and not the interest of the people that those incendiaries had in view ... ' But disenchantment with former leaders did not betoken loyalty, and their desire for revenge against the Orangemen and government was intensified by every act of outrage which they believed to have been committed with the sanction of the authorities; 'they conceive on this account Government to be the real source of all their real or ideal sufferings. They now have a general mistrust in every Gentleman, and they have been ... organising in many counties ... they admit no gentlemen into their secrets, but choose leaders of their own body, who had upon former occasions given satisfactory proofs of their courage and resolution.'[60] These new leaders had been thrown up by the rebellion, and its martyrology, a tradition of biased authority and a sense of alienation from upper-class leaders not of their own religion were to lie at the heart of popular organization thereafter.

The general unrest of the immediate post-rebellion era quickly became formalized in the Threshers of Connacht, Ulster and Leinster and the more localised Shanavests and Caravats of Munster, which had started out as faction groups, but later became outlets for a multitude of popular grievances. The ultimate product was Ribbonism which, with political ideas similar to those of the United Irishmen, nationalized popular discontent behind an

---

60. I.S.P.O. S.O.C. 1019/6, anon. letter to Col. Littlehales, Mar. 1800. For this sense of betrayal see also 620/10/121/155; P.R.O.N.I. D.607/F/244; N.L.I. MS. 54ᴬ/145; and Hewitt, 'Ulster Poets 1800–1870', 127.

ultimate goal of independence, in a manner which would have been inconceivable before the 1790s. But it also enshrined the catholic takeover of the independence ideal which was to characterize later nationalism. As the protestants turned away from republicanism in the period of the rebellion, commentators had noted a general resort by the people to their priests for leadership. Before 1798 the priests were scorned and ignored by the secret societies. The changing role of the catholic church in nineteenth-century Irish society was the product of many social and educational processes, and Ribbonism retained some of the open defiance of its predecessors towards the dictates of the catholic hierarchy. But with the intense catholicism of Ribbonism, the hallowed role played by many local priests in the rebellion, and the less submissive attitude of the catholic clergy towards temporal authority, after their involvement with Daniel O'Connell's Catholic Association, the almost total identification of catholicism with nationalism was already in progress in the first decades of the nineteenth century.

The United Irish Society survived the rebellion; but, as with the people who had suffered in 1798, its reaction to failure was a resolve to act more cautiously in future. A French invasion was still the prerequisite for another rising, but no action would be taken until the French had proved themselves successful. France, however, was more sceptical of United Irish claims after the 1798 failures, and with more reason to resist requests for help after the destruction of its navy at the Nile, there was little likelihood of a French attempt on Ireland until another rising took place. The obvious weakness of the home organization, and increased dependence on France, had eroded the United Irishmen's bargaining power in Paris. The loss of Tone had left Lewins—who had never enjoyed the same respect and confidence—in sole charge of continuing the negotiations; whilst Tandy's departure had placed Muir in control of the United Irish club in the rue du Colombier, which continued to attract newly arrived United men. But this group had been discredited, and although the Directory never entirely abandoned the prospect of again invading the country, it had ceased to consider the United Irishmen as a reliable mouthpiece for Irish grievances. The year 1798 had marked the passing of an era in the relationship between the United Irishmen and France. It had opened with England abandoned by her allies and weakened by the domestic turmoil of the preceding year. France had won the war of the first coalition and was confident that England, her last remaining antagonist, could be quickly subdued. The invasion of Ireland had been a means of attaining this aim. By the end of the year, however, England had proved herself mistress of the seas, and her destruction of French shipping in the Irish Sea and in the Mediterranean had rendered the despatch of any further naval expeditions by France unlikely.

For the United Irish Society, the events of 1798 were catastrophic. None of the principal leaders remained active. Most were in prison or dead; others had withdrawn. The loss of Tone in particular was irreparable for the future of the French negotiations. His imprisoned colleagues had been discredited in French eyes by their compact with government. France was astounded by the revelations of the confession. Humbert had been told of it on his arrival in Dublin and had spoken for his countrymen in proclaiming it a dishonourable betrayal of their allies.[61] Many of the local leaders had fled to the Continent. A new generation would arise to take their places, but they would never hold the same prestigious position as their predecessors.

The rebellion closed the second phase of United Irish development. It was a short but eventful period, and in comparison the inactivity of its next phase was demoralizing. In the two years from 1796 to 1798 the United movement had been revived on a republican and military basis. It had extended itself throughout the British Isles and the Continent to pose the greatest threat to English rule in Ireland since the seventeenth century. The decline in United strength from the end of that period was partly the product of England's reaction to the threat, partly that of its own internal squabbles. Despite the divisions, however, the movement's achievements had been remarkable. It had attached parochial Irish protest to a national movement in a way that would have been inconceivable only a few years earlier. In England and Scotland it had annexed an existing democratic network and republicanized it to an extent which the militants in the London Corresponding Society could never have achieved alone. But the movement's principal achievement was on the diplomatic side in France. From a mission initiated by a man of thirty-three, who arrived in Paris in 1796 with a poor knowledge of French, no finances of any consequence and no connections with any French officials, there had developed by 1798 a relationship between the Directory and the United Irish delegation as strong, though unofficially so, as that between France and any visiting embassy. Four expeditions had sailed for Ireland, several more were projected, and incalculable quantities of arms had been sent. However, the removal of most of the men on both the Irish and French sides responsible for such achievements destroyed the foundations on which they had been built, and few of the profits were to remain to the United Irish survivors after 1798.

61. P.R.O. H.O. 100/78/355-8, Castlereagh to Wickham, 17 Sept. 1798; and F.O. 27/53, Bruix's report, 20 Oct. 1798.

PART FOUR
1799–1815: Society in Exile

'The aid of France was their great dependence. Without it they will not, they cannot act.'

(P.R.O. H.O. 100/115/15–18, Leonard McNally's information,
enclosed in Wickham to J. King, 5 Dec. 1803.)

CHAPTER EIGHT

1799–1801: Coping with Defeat

The period between the collapse of the 1798 insurrection and the rupture of
the Peace of Amiens in 1802 forms a hiatus between two phases of intense
United Irish activity. The Society was temporarily crippled by the events of
1798. But the political changes in France were to exercise a more permanent
influence on the future United Society, and when the former leaders tried
to renew negotiations after their release from prison in 1802, they found a
new political system in operation, a system which abhorred republicanism
and which was alien to their most cherished ideals. The advent
of Bonaparte was the crucial turning point in the history of United
Irish negotiations with France. The Directory was rapidly declining
towards the Brumaire *coup d'état* throughout 1799, too engrossed in the
struggle for survival to think of Ireland; and Bonaparte, after his seizure of
power, was eager to make peace with England. 'La période d'abandon' is
how Desbrière describes these years,[1] and although both the United Irishmen
and the British authorities imagined that every military preparation on the
French coast was destined for Ireland, there is no evidence that France
seriously contemplated sending another expedition to Ireland between 1798
and 1803. The United Irishmen, however, had yet to discover that the last
chance of a successful invasion of Ireland had passed in 1798, and both in
France and Ireland they attempted to resurrect the Society from the chaos
of the rebellion. In France they sought more normal forms of employment
to support themselves during an extended residence abroad, whilst simultaneously continuing to petition the French government for another expedition. In Ireland the same re-organization progressed under the aegis of new
and inexperienced leaders. Unfamiliar names suddenly emerged, their very
unfamiliarity causing confusion both among the rank and file members and
in the reports of government spies. Such leaders had little patience with the
delays incurred in protracted diplomatic discussions and were less inclined
to trust France after Bonaparte's assumption of power.

For the United Irishmen at home, the 1798 fiasco had settled the dispute

1. Desbrière, *Projets et Tentatives*, II, 229–53.

about the timing of another rising by making a French invasion the essential prerequisite. A novel unanimity now reigned within the surviving leadership, and the lessons of 1798 were implemented in a new military structure designed to defy infiltrators and defectors alike. The task of preparing for another rising would fall to a handful of top leaders; the activities of inferior committees would be suspended until the French arrived and had proved their ability to defeat the crown forces. United Irish experience in 1797 had shown the difficulty of maintaining popular momentum over a protracted period, and the new structure was not designed to weather a long delay; but renewed assurances from France seemed to justify the leaders' faith in its viability. By thus attaching the fate of their movement to a French invasion, the leaders alienated from themselves any real say in the future of their revamped organization and placed it firmly in the hands of an increasingly unsympathetic foreign power. United Irish dependence on France was total after 1798; its leaders no longer possessed any independent ability to dictate the barometer of revolutionary agitation in Ireland, which reacted instead to signs of movement in the French ports.

But the United Irishmen were never sufficiently conversant with continental politics to recognize that with the Directory in 1799 they had attached their fate to a broken reed. After its fall, support for another Irish invasion receded and with it any chance of a successful application of the new United Irish strategy. With lower committees suspended until then, the non-arrival of the French caused grass-roots support to evaporate, where before it would have been sustained by visible leadership. Popular disaffection was a permanent factor in Irish society after 1798 and provided a more fertile ground for United Irish expansion than at any time in the 1790s. Uncultivated by an increasingly remote leadership, however, the groundswell flowed instead into pervasive Defendersim, and religious antagonisms were permitted to grow apace. One cannot help but feel that increasing distrust of the motives of the Irish rural classes was dictating the new exclusiveness of the United Irishmen as much as their vaunted aim of minimizing bloodshed, and in the years 1799–1803 the United Irish leaders dissipated their efforts on the Continent and in England. A disillusioned Thomas Addis Emmet would later lament their folly in having pegged their fortunes to the whims of France. But while the United Irish structure survived, an element of their dependence on outside help would linger, as much to save the leaders from their terror of popular guerilla warfare as to save Ireland.

I

The passions which had produced the rebellion and the attendant repression remained unabated into 1799. Throughout the winter, reports of arms raids and general lawlessness reached the Castle from all four provinces. Armed bands attacked the Dublin mail-coaches under the very nose of the government and Cornwallis considered such general destructiveness more embarrassing than open rebellion. Even the more traditional agrarian protesters made no secret of their French sympathies, and juries could not be found to convict in sedition cases; 'the people do not consider assisting the French a crime', complained one Mayo magistrate, and military proclamations were laughed at by houghers and tithe-protesters, who confidently claimed that the French were expected in the spring.[2] In addition, bands of rebels remained active in the hills of Wicklow, Wexford and to a lesser extent in Connacht. Michael Dwyer's men in Wicklow proved particularly resistent to the repeated attempts to dislodge them, and each dramatic escape accentuated their heroic reputation, even in areas far removed from their immediate centre of operations. But the isolation of such bands rendered them ineffective as national organizers, and by the spring the weaker groups in the west had already disintegrated.[3] All the signs were that without a speedy return of the French the latent support for the independence movement would remain untapped.

Indeed, the destruction of centralized United control in 1798 had been so complete that the time required to rebuild it rendered the attempt all but hopeless. This time-lapse was to generate its own problems, principally by permitting the less able or lower-class rebel survivors to set themselves up as petty godfathers, with little or no control from above. Their local position was to breed an independence and an insubordination which would defy plans to re-impose central control on the eve of another rising. Michael Dourly was such a figure: a yeoman turned rebel, whose house in Kildare was to remain the organizational centre and armoury for a band of ex-rebels until 1803. From there he organized drilling sessions and forays against defectors and selected loyalists. Though Dourly was a United man and was prepared to join another rising, his activities were entirely freelance and the oath administered to his followers bore little relation to that of the official movement. Apart from the ritualistic cropping of hair—forced upon new recruits regardless of the obvious dangers of such a visible admission of rebelliousness—there were few signs that Dourly was creating anything other than a personal mafia, vaguely identified with the United Irish cause.[4]

Another such figure was William Caulfield, a flax-dresser of Ballymoney in county Antrim. But whereas Dourly and the rebels in the Wicklow Hills represented some form of United survival, in its passions if not its principles, Caulfield's activities testified to its virtual collapse in Ulster. As the dissenters withdrew from republicanism, the division between protestant and catholic

2. See I.S.P.O. 620/7/73 and P.R.O. H.O. 100/87/138–66, 188–200 and 212–16, for reports on the state of the country.
3. See P.R.O. H.O. 100/86/195–6, 248 and 273 for reports of such rebel bands.
4. I.S.P.O. 620/11/138/46–9.

became more rigid; and the word 'protestant', which had been obsolete for many years, was revived in 1799 to demonstrate a group identity in contradistinction to the catholics. In 1799 the term 'United Irishman' was rarely heard in Ulster, a resurgence of Defenderism had established a monopoly of popular disaffection, and there was a corresponding flood of protestants into Orangeism. Such developments were watched with interest by Dublin, and by the middle of the year Castlereagh considered the province sufficiently loyal to administer its own defence:

> ... the protestant dissenters in Ulster have in a gt degree withdrawn themselves from the Union, and become Orangemen. The Northern Catholics always committed in feeling agt the Presbyterians, were during the early period of the Conspiracy loyal—the religious complexion of the Rebellion in the South gradually separated the Protestants from the Treason, and precisely in the same degree, appear'd to embark the Catholics in it—defenderism was introduced, and it is principally under that organization, ... that whatever there is of Treason in the North, is at present associated. They are destitute of Leaders, and the people of substance, manufacturers as well as farmers have withdrawn from them—the Province of Ulster comprises at this moment a numerous body of determined Loyalists.[5]

Caulfield's conversion to Defenderism was representative of the process described by Castlereagh. He had been an early recruit to the United Irishmen and was instrumental in attaching many Ballymoney men to the Society. In 1798, however, 'finding that the schemes of said United Irishmen cou'd not succeed', Caulfield 'became desirous of making defenders', and took with him many of those whom he had originally sworn into the United Irishmen. The low social class of Caulfield's recruits to Defenderism was a further sign of class alienation from the gentry leaders of 1798. This pattern of class polarization was repeated throughout the province, and the incoherent nature of Defender arms raids supports Castlereagh's claim that central leadership had entirely collapsed. But if United organization was shattered, Castlereagh was not optimistic about a return to tranquillity, '... enough of it remains ... to render a formidable insurrection inevitable, should the Enemy land in force'.[6] Even in the North the overall aims of the Defenders differed little from those of the United Irishmen. Caulfield's men were organized 'for the purpose of aiding the French in case they should land in this Kingdom,

5. P.R.O. H.O. 100/87/5–7, Castlereagh to Portland, 3 Jun. 1799; see also I.S.P.O. 620/46/38, for Caulfield, and P.R.O. H.O. 100/86/247, Kent C.R.O. U840/O81*/1 and *H.M.C. Charlemont MSS.*, II, 354, for the changed situation in Ulster and the revival of Defenderism.
6. P.R.O. H.O. 100/87/5–7, Castlereagh to Portland, 3 Jun. 1799. For other examples of this continuing expectation of the French, see H.O. 100/85/87–8, 100/86 and I.S.P.O. 620/7/73.

Dethroning the King and overturning the Constitution'. But the rebellion had revived sectariansim with a vengeance and these revamped Defenders were as concerned about 'taking away the lives of the Yeomen and all other loyal Men who may oppose them ... ', as changing the political system.[7]

Given the many difficulties attending a revival of the United Irishmen, the surviving leaders took what, at the time, appeared the wisest course of re-building support on the one unifying element of French invasion. In January 1799 information reached the Castle of an attempt to revive the United Irish Society. But if the rebellion had shattered the structure of the Society, it had had equally devastating effects on official intelligence channels. McNally had lost favour with the United Irishmen even before the rebellion, and the only consistent information came from the recently enlisted Belfast lawyer James McGucken. Although the new leaders confided many details of their plans to him, McGucken was not directly involved in the re-organization, and the overall picture remained blurred.[8] Gradually, however, it became clear that the United Irish movement was re-forming under the direction of the old leaders in the Dublin prisons. The Dublin state prisoners considered their continued detention in Ireland and government editing of their 1798 statement as a breach of the Kilmainham agreement. Those who had been hostile to the compact from the outset were now repaying such apparent betrayal with a vengeance. Russell and O'Connor were the most active in the promotion of the United Irish revival, but it is clear that they had the tacit support of most of their colleagues.[9] The instructions emanating from the prisons were put into effect by a small group of lesser leaders, who had come forward in 1798 to fill the places vacated by the arrested principals. Thomas Addis Emmet's younger brother Robert, Hugh O'Hanlon, who had served in Spain's Irish Brigade, and Henry Baird, Reynold's successor as secretary to the Leinster provincial, were particularly active; George Palmer, one of Lord Edward's main confidants before his arrest, James Farrell, a printer, another who had come to the fore of the Dublin movement after the March arrests, and the two Ulster men, George Teeling, Bartholomew's brother, and William Putnam McCabe, were also involved.

The new United structure took its character from two basic assumptions: that another French invasion was imminent, and that the Irish people were generally willing to rise again. The latter in particular justified the dismantling of the movement's lower levels. The new leaders attributed the failure of the

---

7. I.S.P.O. 620/46/38, the examinations of various Ulster Defenders 15 Jan. 1799.

8. *Castlereagh Correspondence*, I, 217–20, 255, 261; see also I.S.P.O. 620/3/32/13 and 620/18ᴬ/11 pt. 2 for his early information; and Fitzpatrick, '*The Sham Squire*', 149–50 and P.R.O.N.I. D.607/G for McNally and signs that he is out of touch with the United Irish remnant.

9. Madden, *United Irishmen*, 2nd ser., I, 152–205, 216–18; *Castlereagh Correspondence*, I, 329–30; also McGucken's information in I.S.P.O. 620/7/74.

rebellion to loose organization, which had permitted easy infiltration by government agents, and to the licentiousness into which the poorly led rebels were permitted to drift. To ensure against both, the revived Society would be more exclusive; new members would be accepted only on personal recommendation and after close scrutiny. The elective and ascending structure of the former movement, with lower committees electing the superior bodies, would be abandoned. Instead a cadre of officers would be selected by a handful of generals, who in turn would be handpicked by the executive or national committee. The country would be divided into a number of baronies (156 in all). A colonel, lieutenant colonel and adjutant would be appointed to every barony, each succeeding level in the military structure choosing the ranks immediately below it until a battalion of 1,000 had been formed for each barony. For security reasons, however, the lower ranks would be filled only on the eve of the invasion. At that stage military drilling would be unnecessary; the role of the people would be one of harassing the crown forces in the countryside, rather than fighting pitched battles, which would be left to the French, and such last-minute apprisal of the localities was not therefore considered unrealistic. Precautions were taken to avoid the disruption caused by the arrest of the leaders on the eve of the '98 rebellion. At the outset, plans for the reception of the French would be conveyed to primary assemblies of sergeants and colonels. No further meetings would take place until the invasion. There would be no proliferation of committees as before. Rather one of the colonels would be chosen in each locality, and through him executive instructions would be transmitted to the other county colonels and to a selected officer from each of the inferior grades. All instructions were to be transmitted by word of mouth; nothing would be put in writing. Arms would only be distributed at the last moment, and whilst the executive worked to secure the invasion, no visible organization would exist to arouse suspicion, only a general understanding that the people should hold themselves in readiness to come forward at a moment's notice.[10]

Such was the plan on paper: a military organization, divested of all the civil frills of its predecessor, in themselves a legacy from the United Irishmen's constitutional period. The plan had a simplicity of organization and a singularity of purpose which would prevent internal bickering over means and aims. This novel sense of unity within its leadership was the greatest strength of the new movement. All agreed that any thought of another rising was unrealistic without a French invasion. The task of securing such an invasion accordingly took precedence over matters of internal organization, and Palmer and McCabe were already in London en route for Paris by the beginning of

10. Details of the new organization have been taken from I.S.P.O. 620/8/72/2, 620/47/100, and 620/7/74/1–22; P.R.O. H.O. 100/86/301–2; A.A.E. Corr. Pol. Ang. 592 fos. 386–7; and T.C.D. 869/1/437.

January 1799. Ultimately the weaknesses of the internal organization were all too obvious. Its fundamental components of spontaneous mass support and an exclusive military leadership were incompatible without the connecting element of the rural middle class, the farmers, the manufacturers, and all those natural leaders of the people who had been alienated by the rebellion. The new organization was to become even more exclusive than its founders had intended, as its leaders were progressively forced to operate outside Ireland. Since the French invasion was to have been the signal for mobilizing the organization, all attention was devoted to its attainment. But with no immediate sign of another invasion, the leaders made no effort to modify the original plan. Their complacency about the strength of popular support for another rising, without any real effort to cultivate it, betrayed a singular ignorance of the complexities of Irish society.

In the short term such weaknesses were not necessarily harmful to the overall plan. The new organization was never intended to mirror the semi-permanence of its predecessor. It was an action force designed to implement a specific plan, and its success depended on relative immediacy of application. In the first months of 1799, United expectations of another invasion and a successful rising seemed realistic enough. Popular support for a French invasion was common knowledge, and reports of movements in the French ports had put the English and Irish authorities on full invasion alert.[11] Moreover, Lewins had received new assurances from Bruix of another attempt on Ireland before the summer and had transmitted the good news to the Dublin leaders sometime in February.[12] It was the non-appearance of the French over the next few years which revealed the inherent weaknesses of the organization.

The deliberate cessation of written reports makes it difficult to assess the extent to which the new structure was applied. Not all counties were re-organized, as Hugh O'Hanlon freely admitted to the Directory in July, the intention being to confuse the authorities by leaving certain areas organized on the old footing.[13] It is more likely, however, that in those areas which had remained inactive during the rebellion, the handful of confidential leaders required by the new project could not be found. Certainly evidence suggests a concentration of effort in counties like Dublin, Wicklow, Wexford, Kildare, Meath, Westmeath, Antrim and Down, which had proved their patriotism in the past. James (Jemmy) Hope, a Templepatrick muslin weaver, was the

11. For government correspondence on the invasion scare, Mar.–May 1799, see *Cornwallis Correspondence*, III, 56–100; *Castlereagh Correspondence*, II, 265–312; P.R.O. H.O. 100/86; and I.S.P.O. 620/18^A/11 pt. 2.
12. A.N. AF III 58 doss. 228 plaq. 2, Lewins to the Directory, 27 Apr. 1799; P.R.O. H.O. 100/85/281–3, Wickham to Castlereagh, 28 Feb. 1799, tells of the receipt of such information by the Dublin leaders.
13. A.A.E. Corr. Pol. Ang. 592 fos. 386–7, O'Hanlon to the Directory, 15 Jul. 1799.

agent appointed to introduce the new plan to Antrim and Down. Robert
Henry, a United Irish prisoner in Carrickfergus Gaol, later claimed to have
seen the plan of the new military organization. Several who had been active
United men in the past helped Hope re-organize the two counties, men like
John Henderson and Robert Kirkpatrick, wheelwrights of Drumail and
Ballyclare, John Nevin and James Kerr, farmers from Ballyrhoshane and the
outskirts of Antrim, and Robert Robinson, a muslin manufacturer from
Muckamore. Henry was arrested shortly after he had seen the document, but
he was later assured that parts of Antrim had been re-organized. In April
the national committee had sent down assurances of a French invasion, and
a series of bonfires on the Antrim hills to transmit such reports does suggest
the existence of some kind of organization seeking to limit personal
communication.[14] Similar agents were also reported in other areas. John
Sheegog, an attorney from Enniskillen, was sent to the other Ulster counties;
Francis O'Flaherty, a Galway attorney, Reilly of Westmeath and Robert
Stowell of Cork were invited with the other agents to come to Dublin and
carry the plan back to their home counties. By March, Castlereagh noted 'a
general whisper running through the United Irishmen that they are to be
ready at a moment's warning', and since the names of these agents reappear
constantly over the next four years in association with the new movement, it
seems likely that the new plan was implemented in selected areas, as O'Hanlon
claimed. The Castle found these hushed preparations unnerving, and although
there was little information about the organization and its leaders, let alone
sufficient to secure a conviction, it was decided in April to arrest those known
to be involved, including Robert Emmet, O'Hanlon, Baird and Farrell.
Emmet escaped and O'Hanlon and Baird were the only leaders of any consequence to be detained; but O'Hanlon also escaped and reached France in
June. The arrests were the product of another invasion scare and many old
offenders were also taken up as a precaution.[15]

But it was the activities of the state prisoners which caused most concern.
McGucken's warning that as long as they remained in the country they would
find means of continuing the conspiracy had been fully substantiated, and
measures taken to restrict their freedom of communication were to no avail. In
the hope that the despatch of many republican prisoners away from the country
would remove a major inspiration for continuing disturbances, the Castle
became irresponsibly eager to dispose of them. Many were liberated on the
simple condition of voluntary exile; plans to secretly land some at Hamburg
were only shelved because of a continental crisis brewing over the number of

---

14. I.S.P.O. 620/47/100, statement of Robert Henry, 23 Jul. 1799; also *H.M.C. Charlemont MSS.*,
ii, 348.
15. See P.R.O. H.O. 100/86/5–12, 195–6, 242, 301–2; I.S.P.O. 620/7/74/2 and 22; and N.L.I.
MS. 56/215 for details of the arrests.

such revolutionaries operating from the neutral port. The main United men in Kilmainham were given permission to exile themselves to America; but the project foundered on the American refusal to accept such potentially troublesome elements. The Dublin prisoners were bitter at the rejection, and even the authorities were taken aback, Castlereagh remarking scornfully ' . . . the majority of our prisoners are not more dangerous than the general class of American settlers'.[16] Eventually the bulk of the rebel prisoners were accepted by Prussia to serve in her armies or in the mines; the remainder were either transported to Australia or sent to British regiments overseas.[17]

Such open-handed despatch of republican ambassadors abroad was a characteristic of Irish security policy in the 1790s, a tendency to dispose of the immediate evil regardless of the future threat. But London was taking more notice of the Irish situation because of signs that the imprisoned Irish leaders were also responsible for sustaining the Irish agitation on the mainland, and found this short-sighted policy unacceptable. Whitehall's annoyance at Dublin's continuing failure to contain its security threat was exacerbated by insufficient communication from Cornwallis, because of his personal dispute with Portland. His silence gave more weight to the flood of loyalist complaints about his excessive leniency towards the rebels. Stringent passport controls had been introduced the preceding year to prevent the spread of disaffection to the mainland, but the influx of ex-rebels into England continued. The London government was convinced that Dublin was not implementing the new measures, and in a thinly veiled criticism of Dublin's security measures, Whitehall made plans to transfer nineteen Irish state prisoners to Fort George in Scotland. The Home Office was to assume responsibility for their future detention, and they sailed from Dublin on 19 March, stopping at Belfast on the way to collect the Ulster prisoners.[18] Loyalist relief at their removal, and the success in dispersing the fountainhead of the renewed conspiracy, produced a novel sense of calm in the country, and the protest of 1799–1800 against England's plan to unite the Irish and English legislatures with an Act of Union remained entirely constitutional. With the removal of the state prisoners, the attempted purge of the new leaders, and the flight of many to escape it, the United Irish leadership was forced into almost total exile.

---

16. *Castlereagh Correspondence*, I, 414, also 394–6; *Cornwallis Correspondence*, II, 423–6, 430, III, 70–4; P.R.O. H.O. 100/85/31–3; and I.S.P.O. 620/7/74/3, for the problems caused by the state prisoners.

17. See P.R.O. H.O. 100/86/156, 210, 252–3, 295 and 339; H.O. 28/25/272–4; and I.S.P.O. 620/47/138–40 and 620/56/170–86 for the disposal of the prisoners.

18. P.R.O. H.O. 100/86/163–4, Castlereagh to Wickham, 19 Mar. 1799; and P.R.O.N.I. D.607/G/132 for the Ulster prisoners. For the dispute between Portland and Cornwallis see H.O. 100/79/73–8, 100/86/140–1; P.R.O. 30/8/327/191; and *Cornwallis Correspondence*, III, 89.

II

But if Whitehall criticized Dublin's attitude towards the disaffected in Ireland, its uncharacteristic and, in retrospect, its precipitate response to a revival on the mainland was equally unwise. In former times it would have observed the development of the suspected conspiracy and chosen its moment of action to ensure the maximum of public exposure. But in the early months of 1799 it struck when a re-organization on the mainland was in planning stage only. The untimely intervention was dictated by the latest invasion scare, and by a pressing need to justify a new batch of security measures. With what ministerial supporters thought uncommon effrontery, the opposition had returned in force to parliament at the end of 1798 and recommenced the attack on the government's security policy, as if Maidstone, O'Connor and the Kilmainham confession had never existed. They claimed that there was no longer an English conspiracy and certainly no connection between Ireland and the few 'lurking traitors' on the mainland. Their claim that the English conspiracy had been destroyed was partially correct, for the arrests of 1798, and the widely publicized sufferings of the political prisoners, had broken the spirit of the English movement. But the Irish conspiracy, already the directing force in England's political underworld by 1798, was proving remarkably resilient. Secret information suggested that it was regrouping, and government sought new legislation to curtail the flow of recruits from Ireland. In the pre-Christmas session of parliament Pitt had responded to opposition claims of government scaremongering with a promise of another secret committee report 'which would more fully display that system of treason which had been carried on, and those links by which Irish traitors were connected with traitorous societies in this country.'[19]

As the committee sat through January and February, and opposition attacks continued unabated, ministers intensified their efforts to secure proof of the Irish conspiracy on the mainland. But it was proving particularly difficult to penetrate the Irish communities. Their traditional clannishness had been intensified by a new hostility even towards the English sympathizers, whom they damned as cowards for having failed to organize some kind of diversion at the time of the Irish rebellion. A continuous stream of unconverted rebel fugitives had arrived in London throughout the winter, and raids into the city's Irish areas revealed a build-up of arms. Any official incursions into such rookeries invariably took on the aspect of a full-scale invasion and were scarcely calculated to secure the kind of inside information required for the secret report.[20] Wickham appealed to Dublin for some undercover agents to infiltrate England's Irish movement. But the acquisition of Orr and

19. *Parl. Hist.*, xxxiv, 124–5, also 111–24; 169–79; and *Life of Wilberforce*, ii, 318.
20. See P.R.O. P.C. 1/43/A.152; H.O. 100/86/13–14; I.S.P.O. 620/47/33; and A.A.E. Corr. Pol. Ang. 593 fos. 516–19 for this build-up of the Irish on the mainland, particularly in London.

Murphy, the defectors from the *Anacréon*, was scarcely a symbol of successful recruitment. They were already suspect to the leading republicans; they were reluctant to supply any information which might be used in a treason trial, and Murphy soon absconded rather than continue in such a perilous career.[21]

Orr tried to penetrate former areas of United activity such as Holborn and Lincoln's Inn Fields. In the latter he talked with two United men in the *Black Horse*, Little Wild Street, and learnt of plans to revive the movement. Of his informants, Whelan, a tailor, had been secretary to a London United division in 1798 and was arrested at Winchester on a mission to seduce the troops; John Dunn was a substantial farmer in Kildare, a leader in the 1798 rebellion who had escaped to London by forging a magistrate's signature on a passport. Dunn and Whelan told of a new plan to assist the French invasion of Ireland: major diversions would be arranged in the English industrial centres to draw off the troops from Ireland, even at the risk of almost certain defeat on the mainland; contingents of Irish rebels would be sent over to prevent a repetition of the inaction of the preceding year; but if all else failed, as much confusion as possible was to be created by starting fires in the dockyards or assassinating political leaders. These plans were originally brought over by McCabe and Palmer and were elaborated upon by instructions from the Dublin state prisoners to Valentine Lawless. Lawless was still the key figure in the United Irishmen's external activities. Orr was unable to discover the names of any other leading men in London and it was from Craufurd's sources in Hamburg that government learnt of the part played by McCabe and Palmer. They had remained in London until later that summer, when they left for Scotland and eventually for France.[22] Orr's information was accurate as far as it went; but it told government little about the extent of the organization or its leadership, concentrating rather on those figures already prominent in former attempts to organize the mainland. All the signs were, however, that the main danger lay with an incalculable number of rebel fugitives who had merged with the existing Irish communities. They were not yet regularly organized in the winter of 1799, but when the attempt was made, the leaders would find it difficult to restrain their impatient eagerness.

In March reports trickled in of mounting confidence among the United men, as expectations increased of a French invasion of Ireland; 8,000 were reported to be organized in Manchester and as many as 15,000 to 40,000 in London. But none of the reports were substantiated and tangible evidence

---

21. For Orr's and Murphy's career as government agents see P.R.O. H.O. 100/86–7 and 100/94/82–118; P.C. 1/44/A.161; and I.S.P.O. 620/49/39 and 43.

22. P.R.O. P.C. 1/43/A.152, copy of Orr's information of 28 Jan. 1799; also H.O. 100/85/281–3, Wickham to Castlereagh, 28 Feb. 1799. For Dunn in particular see I.S.P.O. 620/47/33, and for McCabe see 620/7/74/1, 8, 22 and 620/46/104.

continued to elude government. Many of the documents presented to the secret committee concerned the 1798 movement, and committee members were sceptical about claims for a continuing conspiracy. Government accordingly decided to arrest known United Irishmen in London, and a hamfisted operation it proved; for in the absence of conclusive information against more than a handful, the peace officers simply arrested all those known to have been active in 1798, detaining them long enough to make a fitting show of apparent treason and to feed the usual shock articles and promises of startling revelations to the government press.[23]

On 25 February Orr told Wickham that a messenger was expected from the Dublin leaders. The messenger, Thomas Doyle, had carried such communications before and had a semi-permanent base in London at his brother's jeweller's shop in Chancery Lane. But he had the uncanny knack of eluding government vigilance, even to the extent of basic biographic detail. Doyle's communication was to be delivered to the three principal leaders in London: Lawless, John Bonham, and, as government suspected, John Binns. The document would then be presented to a more general meeting on one of the following Sundays. Pitt was clearly excited at the prospect of securing tangible proof of treason to present to the secret committee, and tried to time the arrests to secure the maximum number of papers which would prove the association between the old traitors and the revived movement in Ireland.[24]

Pitt's optimism, however, was ill-judged, for he entirely depended on Orr to indicate the best moment for action, and Orr was scarcely at the heart of the plot. The raid of 10 March on United Irish Division No. 2 at the *Royal Oak* in Red Lion Square surprised a group of twenty discussing Doyle's letter. Doyle had escaped. Lawless, Binns and Bonham were not at the meeting, and though they were later arrested, their absence destroyed the picture which Pitt had hoped to paint. Everyone in the *Royal Oak* that night had also been taken up. They were Irish, with only one exception, and most were catholics; but they were scarcely the material from which the picture of an Irish conspiracy could be drawn. The *Oak* was no more than 'a regular house for working men', claimed its landlord, a claim upheld by subsequent examinations. There were few of the expected rebels lately arrived from Ireland; most had lived and worked in London for many years, as tailors, cooks, warehousemen, milkmen or coal dealers, and were in the habit of

23. See e.g. the *Sun* for 19 and 26 Mar., 2 and 3 Apr. 1799; and P.R.O. P.C. 1/43/A.152 and A.153; and H.O. 42/46, for reports on the U.E. in Lancashire, also the examination of William Graham, 12 Mar., and information from Sam Singleton, 28 Apr. 1799. See H.O. 100/85/277–80 and 100/86/165–6 in particular for the scepticism of the committee members.
24. Hants C.R.O. 38M49/1/38, correspondence of Pitt and Wickham, 26–7 Feb. 1799. See Wickham and Castlereagh's correspondence on the elusive Doyle in P.R.O. H.O. 100/79/102, 100/85/281–3 and I.S.P.O. 620/46/65 and 117.

calling at the *Oak* on a Sunday evening after mass in Lincoln's Inn Fields chapel.[25]

But the documents taken at the *Royal Oak* were sufficient for immediate needs. They included a list of sixty-eight proposed divisions in London, an address to the United Irishmen in Ireland and a copy of Doyle's letter, which proposed 'that the United Irish here should rise even with the certainty of being defeated, the moment the French should land in Ireland ...'.[26] A series of admission cards to the proposed United Irish societies were found on a prisoner taken up elsewhere, and fragments of a plan to seduce the seamen were extracted from the chinks in the floor-boards of another suspect's house. The document outlined the grievances of the sailors and urged the formation of United societies for their redress. The seamen would be sworn 'to do everything ... to unite English, Irish and Scotchmen in brotherhood for the purpose of having the entire grievances of the Fleet redressed and to give Liberty to all the people.'[27]

The documents certainly proved that an effort was being made to re-organize the United movement on the mainland, but they scarcely supported the claim that a dangerous plot already existed. They spoke of proposed rather than existing divisions, and the arrests of former United men over the following weeks were a stab in the dark rather than the product of con-clusive information against them. On 9 April a warrant was issued for the arrest of all those known to have attended United English meetings at the *Nag's Head* in Clerkenwell. But most of the thirteen arrested had to be released for want of evidence, and it is a significant reflection on the government's inability to trace any connection between these United English and United Irish meetings that the former was not even mentioned in the secret report. Of the twenty detained from the large number taken at the *Royal Oak*, only one remained in prison after July, despite intensive efforts to find information against the others. Even Beadle McKinley, the 24-year-old coach painter of Edgware Road, who was suspected of having been a rebel fugitive from Belfast, had to be released for lack of evidence.[28] For the next five years the government continued to make similar mistakes, because it insisted on looking for well-known leaders and regular committees on the mainland, and failed to recognize that neither was to be found in the post-rebellion United movement. Organization was consciously pared to a minimum and periodically serviced

25. P.R.O. H.O. 42/46/66 and 81, examination of those taken at the *Royal Oak*, 10 and 21 Mar. 1799. See H.O. 100/86/165, 179, P.C. 1/44/A.161 and P.C. 1/3514; *Reports from the Committees of the House of Commons*, x, 798–9; and the *Sun*, 15 Apr. for details of the arrests.

26. *Castlereagh Correspondence*, II, 238.

27. P.R.O. H.O. 42/47/144, Copy of the Secret paper found at Mr. White's Lodgings; also H.O. 100/86/198–9, 268–9, Wickham to Castlereagh, 26 Mar. and 14 Apr. 1799.

28. P.R.O. H.O. 100/86/189 and 224–6, correspondence between Wickham and Castlereagh, 30 Mar. 1799. See P.R.O. H.O. 79/10 for the *Nag's Head* arrests.

by a core of peripatetic leaders passing between Ireland, England and France. In the early months of 1799 such messengers passed through London unobserved; they included McCabe, Palmer, Doyle, George Wilkinson, an Irish printer described as 'an old offender', St. John Mason, a first cousin of Emmet, and Michael Farrell, considered as one of the foremost Dublin leaders in the 1799 re-organization.[29] Indeed the most startling example of this new ineffectiveness of the domestic intelligence network was the timing of the *Royal Oak* arrests. On the previous evening the group had met a French agent, possibly to plan some action against the royal dockyards.[30] Whitehall's knowledge of United activities in England did not measurably improve with time, and in the absence of startling discoveries or spectacular trials it came to rely increasingly on secret reports to justify the continuation or introduction of repressive legislation.

If the arrests of 1799 had little effect on the progress of the revived Irish movement, however, they had achieved government's immediate objective, and permitted the secret committee to show that the conspiracy outlined in its report had continued unabated. The report '. . . contains a history of the Societies that had been formed in the metropolis and rest of the kingdom since the French revolution', wrote Wickham to Castlereagh on 20 March, 'connecting the whole together, and showing that, under different names, shapes and pretences, they have all pursued but one and the same object, namely, the destruction of the existing Government and the establishment of a Democratical Republic, after the manner and under the protection of France. The report then goes on to explain the present state of things in a manner that must draw the attention of the public as well to a sense of the general danger as to the means of preventing it.'[31] Much of the report, as Wickham admitted, was a synthesis of existing information rather than a fulfilment of Pitt's grandiose promise to make startling new discoveries. But the recent arrests allowed the committee to claim that the aims of the conspirators and their reliance on French aid had remained unchanged, and Pitt was given his excuse for introducing his most comprehensive programme of emergency security measures since the opening of the war. Parliament was told of how the Irish state prisoners had continued to organize the United movement from prison, and their recent removal to Scotland received retrospective justification. But the claim that the English state prisoners had acted likewise, and their transfer to various provincial prisons in consequence, was unjustified, and savoured rather of an attempt to remove a source of opposition ammunition. The United Irishmen, the United Englishmen and

29. For details on McCabe, Farrell etc. see P.R.O. F.O. 33/19/65–8; H.O. 100/86; and I.S.P.O. 620/11/130/60.
30. A.H.G. MR 1420 fo. 106–7, report from a secret agent, 4 Apr. 1799.
31. *Castlereagh Correspondence*, II, 216.

the London Corresponding Society were suppressed by name with all other secret societies, and greater controls over the press were introduced to curb its recent tendency 'of calling the attention of the lower orders of the people to objects of discussion of the most mischievous tendency'.[32]

The impatience of government to tack a new Combination Act on to this extensive legislative programme has bewildered historians of England's early trade unions, since it added little to existing powers of control. It was prompted by a petition from the millwrights against combinations among their journeymen; but its use by government to proscribe all combinations can only be adequately explained by another invasion scare and government's belief that another conspiracy was organizing. From the counties ministers received reports of the development of a powerful weavers' association fanning out from Manchester and Bolton and of United divisions in the same areas. Reports from Ireland told of attempts to revive the United organization in Lancashire, of an active correspondence through Liverpool and intense activity among the Irish weavers in the Manchester area.[33] Efforts had already been made to tighten control over migrating Irish workers, and in April Pitt sent a special agent to investigate the revival in Manchester. The agent reported in May that weavers from Ulster were prominent in some kind of organization and that their combination to secure better wages was part of the revived United movement.[34] The report confirmed Pitt's fears, but it was only partially correct. Many Lancashire weavers would have been members of both trade and secret political organizations; but the wave of combining in the spring of 1799 was for genuine trade purposes, particularly to petition parliament for measures to regulate wages. This is not to say that when the time for action arrived, the United men in the combinations would not have used them to increase the commotion on the mainland. Many skilled craftsmen were of Irish nationality and would have provided the nucleus of leadership required to produce such an effect. But the new United leaders were not interested in a simple increase of numbers on the mainland, which might lead to discovery before the French arrived. Signs of any extensive swearing-in are consequently absent from the 1799 revival, and the flurry of activity in the workers' combinations provides the best proof that at this stage they had not yet been infiltrated.

Opposition to Pitt's draconian package was feeble. The tide was turning against reformers and radicals. The arrests of 1798–99 had finally secured

---

32. *Parl. Hist.*, xxxiv, 984–8; *Reports from the Committees of the House of Commons* x, 800.

33. I.S.P.O. 620/46/91, 101, 138; P.R.O. H.O. 42/47/144; and P.C. 1/44/A.161, for information on combinations and the 'United system', particularly in Lancashire, Mar.–Aug. 1799; A. Aspinall, *Early English Trade Unions* (London, 1949), i–ii, xxiii, 20–7; and Thompson, *Making of the English Working Class*, 556–7.

34. I.S.P.O. 620/18^A/11 and P.R.O. H.O. 100/85/281–3, 100/86/13–14 and 361, Portland's and Wickham's letters to Ireland, Feb.–May 1799.

to government a monopoly of popular loyalty. The invasion scare rapidly evaporated in May, when news arrived of the French fleet having sailed in the opposite direction to relieve the trapped French army in Egypt. In Ireland popular disillusionment at France's failure to invade was reflected in a novel tranquillity that summer, and the changing military situation on the Continent was a guarantee that the French invasion required to ignite the United movement would not easily materialize.[35]

III

At the close of 1798 England's conflict with France entered a decisive phase and for the first time since the opening of the war her star was in the ascendant. Bonaparte's Mediterranean venture had thrown Turkey and Russia into alliance with England; and the dream of Lord Grenville, Britain's Foreign Minister, of forming a full-scale continental coalition to crush France, had started to materialize. But despite signs that Austria was about to recommence hostilities against France, her poor performance in the first coalition had won Grenville to Pitt's preference for a continental strategy based primarily on a Prussian alliance. In November 1798 his brother, Tom Grenville, was despatched to Berlin to woo Frederick William from his neutrality. Grenville's 'Grand Design' against France took shape over the next few months. Holland was to be liberated by a land campaign, conducted by Russian, Prussian and English troops. The combined forces from Holland and an Austro-Prussian force from Switzerland would then converge on the French frontier and an Anglo-Russian naval expedition would support a royalist rising in the west of France. With a credulity which France herself would have mocked, England was led to believe that discontent in Holland, Switzerland and western France was sufficiently strong to spark off native risings in support of the invading armies. The extensive plans made on this assumption overstretched military and naval resources in a manner which shocked the experts. But it was the mutual jealousies of the allies which undermined the project from the outset, and at an early stage Tom Grenville's frustrated letters from Berlin warned of the incipient collapse of the original plan.[36]

Given the precarious nature of Britain's continental negotiations in 1799, the appearance of the secret committee report was designed as much for

35. P.R.O. H.O. 100/87/31, Castlereagh to Portland, 29 Jun. 1799; and I.S.P.O. S.O.C. 1018/20–21, for September reports on the state of the country.
36. Mackesy, *Statesmen at War; H.M.C. Dropmore MSS.*, v; J. M. Sherwig, *Guineas and Gunpowder: British foreign aid in the wars with France, 1793–1815* (Cambridge, Mass., 1969), chs. 5–6; A. B. Piechowiak, 'The Anglo–Russian Expedition to Holland in 1799', *The Slavonic and East European Review*, 41 (1962–3), 182–95.

foreign as for domestic consumption. In a section on Hamburg it touched upon the sensitive question of French support for disaffected foreigners, the focus of Russia's current campaign against France. The report spoke of the extension of the United Irish Society to the Continent and warned of French activities in Hamburg in support of the dissidents of neighbouring powers:

> Hamburgh has also been the resort of the disaffected of every other country, whose intrigues are constantly directed to the object of spreading the principles of jacobinism in Holstein and the north of Germany, and generally in all the northern parts of Europe. Many emissaries, English, Scotch, and Irish, have been dispatched from time to time from Hamburgh to Great Britain and Ireland, and to various parts of the continent, as circumstances required. There has recently been established at Hamburgh, Altona, and the neighbourhood, a society called '*The Philanthropic Society*', for the purpose of correspondence with the republicans of all countries, . . . whose avowed object is the reform of all kingdoms and states. The leading members of the society, who direct all the rest, compose a committee of about twenty persons, British, French, Dutch and Germans. . . . This committee constantly corresponds with Great Britain and Ireland, and all parts of Germany. . . . It may become a formidable engine in the hands of the French Directory, and it appears to be making considerable progress; but there is reason to hope that it has at length attracted the notice of the governments of those places.[37]

The report on Hamburg was reprinted in the continental press, much to embarrassment of the city's Senate and its French resident, Lemaître. Lemaître, in genuine ignorance, hotly denied the existence of the United Irish Society in the city and insisted that the Philanthropic Society had never been anything more than a charitable committee.[38] But in France's two-tiered diplomacy, Lemaître had never been at the centre of its dealings with foreign dissidents, and in 1799 Parandier, French Consul at Altona, was fulfilling the role previously occupied by Bourdon. As Sieyes's secretary in Prussia, Parandier had already acquired valuable experience in his undercover relations with the Polish dissidents, and in the Hanseatic towns Talleyrand had come to rely almost exclusively on him for information on royalist intrigues and patriot activities.[39] Like Bourdon, Parandier had found Duckett an indispensable assistant, and through Duckett at Altona France was indeed

37. *Reports from the Committees of the House of Commons*, x, 799–800.
38. A.A.E. Corr. Pol. Ham. 114 fos. 141–2, Lemaître to Talleyrand, 13 Apr. 1799.
39. See A.A.E. Corr. Pol. Ham. 113 fos. 325–6, 355–7, 366–7, 379–80, 395, for Parandier's and Talleyrand's correspondence; also Personnel, 1re sér. 55, Parandier. See also Craufurd's reports in P.R.O. F.O. 33/18/37, F.O. 33/19/66–7, and Hants. C.R.O. 38M49/1/54.

operating an informal programme of assistance for Irish refugees fleeing from the rebellion.[40] In addition, it is clear from Duckett's correspondence with Paris that some kind of secret Irish revolutionary committee did exist in Hamburg, and by November 1798 he was acting as its secretary. But it was never as formally organized as suggested in the 1799 report. It did not exist before Duckett helped promote it in October-November 1798, and its membership fluctuated rapidly as refugees or agents travelled on to their intended destinations. It was scattered within weeks of its formation by the crisis which arose over the activities of such foreign patriots, and it was formally suppressed the following May. Craufurd had welcomed the formation of such committees as channels of information and he lamented their disappearance in the May purge. He assured London that the city authorities did not encourage such clubs, though their existence was facilitated by the notorious ineffectiveness of the Hamburg police system.[41] The veracity of the report was beyond question, even if it exaggerated the intrigue in Hamburg and conveniently ignored the activities of the French royalists, the largest single group of foreign dissidents there, and one which England herself was supporting. But its foreign section was a cleverly-timed piece of propaganda, thrown into a delicate diplomatic situation which had arisen initially over the arrest of some United Irishmen in the city and which was fanned by England and her friends to isolate France in the forthcoming conflict.

Duckett's arrest had convinced the Directory that the Irish in north Germany must be protected if France's restrictions on passports were not to deprive her completely of Irish recruits for future attempts on the British Isles. No public statement could be made, but leading members of the Hamburg Senate were privately informed that France had placed all the Irish in the city under official protection and Lemaître was to draw up a register of all newly arrived Irish refugees, indicating in particular those in need of urgent help. The Senate members with whom Lemaître conversed assured him that no Irish refugee would be harmed; but they refused to compromise the city's neutrality by publicly guaranteeing their immunity from arrest by the English authorities. France considered the Hamburg Senate excessively pro-English, and the first test of their unwritten agreement justified her worst fears.[42] As Craufurd's embassy became increasingly one of policing the communication route between France and 'His Majesty's rebellious subjects', the feeling grew in Paris and London that Hamburg

40. A.N. AF III 57 doss. 224 p^ce 15., AF III 206 doss. 943 fos. 29–30, and BB4 122 fos. 284–98, correspondence of Duckett and Bruix, Sept.-Nov. 1799.

41. See P.R.O. F.O. 33/16/58 and 63, 33/18/36, 43 and 47, for Craufurd's correspondence, Sept. 1798–May 1799.

42. A.A.E. Corr. Pol. Ham. 113 fo. 153, the Minister of Police to Talleyrand, 3 Aug., and fos. 159–70, Lemaître's correspondence, 12–27 Aug. 1798.

might prove the flashpoint in the diplomatic contest which preceded the formal renewal of hostilities in 1799. When Craufurd received word from Denmark that fugitives from the *Anacréon* expedition, including Tandy, Blackwell and William Corbet, were about to return to Paris via Hamburg, he acted with a swiftness and sense of urgency which set the melodramatic tone of the Tandy affair from the outset, and which was to focus attention on France's undercover activities abroad in a more dramatic manner than England could ever have achieved by paper propaganda alone.

The three fugitives had taken rooms in the City's *American Arms Hotel* with Hervey Montmorency Morres, the rebel leader who had joined Humbert and then escaped to Hamburg. In reply to their request for permission to enter France, Talleyrand had waived normal restrictions for those Irish returning from the expeditions. By the time his letter arrived, however, the four men were in prison, pending a reply to Craufurd's request for their extradition to England. In the early hours of Saturday 24 November, the day after their arrival, Craufurd had roused the city *Praetor* (its chief magistrate) demanded the arrest of these British subjects, and personally accompanied the city guard to the hotel to put the order into effect. Within a matter of hours he had returned to the *Praetor's* office and requested their transfer to his house, to await extradition. But a protest from the French Consul had frightened the *Praetor*, who had been unaware of any French interest in the prisoners, and he was now less willing to accede to Craufurd's demands. The Prussian minister, Schultz, had accompanied Craufurd, and both suggested that the *Praetor* should sanction the prisoners' transfer and then plead ignorance to the French. In the middle of these exchanges Lemaître arrived with the French commissions of Tandy and his companions, much to the Prussian's embarrassment at being caught red-handed in league with the English, and he speedily absented himself on a trumped-up excuse.

The arrests had caused a sensation; even the ordinary people were taking sides on the issue. The *émigrés* and foreign patriots alike had fled the city in fear of possible reprisals, and the confidence of the business community was badly shaken because of its known associations with the *émigrés* and its fear that France might impose economic sanctions. The tacit agreement to warn the French authorities of English extradition requests had not been implemented, for Craufurd had acted with such speed that none of the relevant authorities had been informed before the arrests were made. Marragon, Lemaître's successor, recognized Hamburg's difficult position and lamented the irregularities in Tandy's commission which prevented a firm decision in France's favour. All attempts by the French authorities to see the prisoners had been refused; their only direct contact was a note written in blood by Blackwell and picked up in the street outside the prison by a Hamburg woman. It told of the appalling conditions in which the prisoners were held, and if Marragon was unable to secure their release, he at least forced the city authorities to improve their conditions of imprisonment.[43]

By December, several emergency sessions of the city's legislative bodies, and increasing pressure from England and France, had failed to resolve Hamburg's dilemma. To offend either power would entail certain sanctions, and the most sensible move in the circumstances was to dispose of the problem to Prussia, as guarantor of German neutrality. Marragon had pre-empted such a move by warning Prussia that a decision in favour of the prisoners' extradition would be considered a violation of that neutrality. France knew that England was trying to woo Prussia and Austria into another coalition and that external diplomatic factors might decide the issue in her favour. Furthermore Prussia was anxious to acquire a seaport, and Austria was querying the neutrality of the north German towns at the increasingly acrimonious negotiations at Rastadt. The merit of the individuals concerned was progressively swamped in the feverish diplomatic intrigue attending the renewed war preparations. 'The Importance of the present Discussion', Grenville warned Craufurd, 'arises from the open manner in which the Question is now brought to issue in the face of all Europe, whether the King shall suffer States professing amity towards him to alledge their Fear, whether real or pretended, of the insolent menaces of the Enemies as an Excuse for violating the Laws of neutrality ... With respect to the persons of these Traitors themselves, their Importance is very small indeed when compared with that of such a Question.'[44]

By the spring of 1799, Hamburg's embarrassment was acute. England, Russia and France had removed their diplomatic representatives to Altona, where they now jostled in uncomfortable proximity. England had moved her fleet to the mouth of the Elbe, poised to apply the threatened blockade; France was ready to impose an embargo on Hamburg's shipping in French and allied ports; Russia was rattling her sabre in the Baltic, preparing to occupy the city if the prisoners were not extradited to England and the city's revolutionary societies suppressed. Tom Grenville favoured the move of Russian troops into Hamburg, thus assembling them within striking distance of Holland; but Grenville was less enthusiastic. The Tsar's antics might just as easily push Prussia into the arms of France, as those of the coalition, since Russian menaces on the Polish frontier had already cooled

43. For a full account of the arrests, see A.A.E. Corr. Pol. Ham. 113 and 114; Corr. Consul. Ham. 12–14; A.N. BB⁴ 122 fos. 290–91; P.R.O. F.O. 33/16/66; S. Ni Chinnéide, *Napper Tandy and the European Crisis* (Galway, 1962); G. Servières, *L'Allemagne française sous Napoléon 1ᵉʳ* (Paris, 1904), 37–9, and 'A famous Franco-Irish soldier: General William Corbet', ed. F. J. Healy, *Journal of the Ivernian Society*, III (1910–11), 239–44.
44. P.R.O. F.O. 33/16/216–7, Grenville to Craufurd, [ ] Dec. 1798. and A.A.E. Corr. Pol. Ham. 113 fos. 312–13, 327–8 and 114 fos. 7, 14, 103–5, for French action.

Frederick William's ardour for the coalition and necessitated an alteration of the allied strategy against France.[45]

In April, however, Grenville was still supremely confident that Prussia would join the coalition, and he haughtily rejected a plea from the Hamburg Senate that Tandy's group should be released: 'this is a point from which the King will not depart and ... rather than suffer Hamburgh to become a station from which the Irish Rebels may with impunity carry on their treasonable Designs, His Majesty is determined to incur the Inconvenience ... of placing that Port in a state of Blockade'.[46] It was at this stage that England introduced her secret parliamentary report into the contest, with quite the opposite effect to that desired. It simply intensified the existing stalemate by terrifying Prussia into total inaction and increasing the already embarrassing frenzy of the Tsar. Hamburg had again appealed to Prussia to resolve its dilemma. But by this stage Prussia had decided that her best interests lay in making no decision at all, and had advised Hamburg to follow her example and sit out the crisis until a general peace relieved them of any necessity of opting for either side. The initial victories of the Austro-Russian forces in Italy scarcely justified Prussia's optimism about a general peace, and Hamburg's difficulties would not have permitted such prevarication. In the face of British accusations that the city was harbouring international conspirators and Paul's threatened invasion, the Senate did order an enquiry into the charges and found that the Philanthropic Society had been disbanded six months previously. But Paul remained unsatisfied, and even Craufurd had become irritated by his unsolicited interference. In May the Russian ambassador was withdrawn from Hamburg; in July an ultimatum threatened Russian occupation of the city if the prisoners were not immediately surrendered. When Prussia failed to respond to another of Hamburg's appeals for advice, and Russian ships started to seize Hamburg shipping, the Senate capitulated and, on the night of 30 September 1799, Tandy and his three companions were furtively transported to the mouth of the Elbe for conveyance to England.[47]

By this stage, the Irish fugitives were of no further use as a diplomatic counter. Hopes of Prussian participation in the coalition had been abandoned. The centre of interest had moved away from Germany, and an overland attack on Holland by the Anglo-Russian forces had been put aside in favour of an

45. Hants. C.R.O. 38M49/6/9, Secret Despatches from Col. Durell at Bremen, Feb. 1799; and P.R.O. F.O. 33/18/36, on the threatened Russian blockade. For Grenville's correspondence see *H.M.C. Dropmore MSS.* v, 33; and Mackesy, *Statesmen at War*, 77–8.

46. P.R.O. F.O. 33/18/12, Grenville to Craufurd, 5 Apr. 1799; see also *H.M.C. Dropmore MSS.*, v, 13 14.

47. A.A.E. Corr. Pol. Ang. Ham. 114 fos. 73–243, 287–8, tells of the months of speculation about Prussia's decision. See P.R.O. F.O. 33/19/67, 80, for the final crisis and extradition.

amphibious operation. France had imposed her threatened embargo on Hamburg shipping, but it was quickly relaxed when its effects proved more damaging to French interests than to those of Hamburg.[48] The quarrels and jealousies of the coalition powers had enabled France to reverse some of the earlier defeats in Italy and Switzerland, and by rethinking her strategy and restructuring her military command she had succeeded in averting the threat of an allied invasion by the end of the year. Grenville's overriding confidence in victory had caused him to sweep aside all military and naval caution, and the Walcheren expedition to liberate Holland had been a disastrous failure. The political appointment of the Duke of York to its command and the naïve acceptance of reports about Dutch discontent had doomed the expedition from the outset. The capture of the Dutch fleet was poor compensation for the collapse of the campaign, and with it Grenville's 'Grand Design' for invading France. Russian disgust at the conduct of her allies soon alienated her altogether from the coalition, and Whitehall's attempt to pull victory from defeat by deflecting attention to the destruction of Dutch naval power, did little to silence home critics.[49]

The return of Tandy and his companions at this stage was most unwelcome and the ship's captain was ordered to sail straight to Ireland without calling at any English port. A veil of silence was imposed on the proceedings which until recently had received an unmerited degree of publicity, and although the prisoners would have to stand trial in Ireland, every precaution was taken to prevent a revival of the controversy. Tandy was capitally convicted, but a decision on the sentence was deferred long enough to permit his unconditional release with Blackwell after peace was signed at Amiens, and the escape of the others was winked at.[50] A minor incident in France's support for the Irish republicans had thus been blown up out of all proportion to its intrinsic importance, because of the propaganda England had hoped to derive from it. It is not surprising that critics of government were bemused at the object of all the fuss, a republican veteran that few outside France took seriously. 'Now that all our objects [in the war] seem lost and given up,' observed Dennis Taafe, the Irish satirist, 'a fresh bone of contention has been started, that may cost these nations 50 millions more. Guess what that weighty prize is . . . ? . . . Why, . . . it is no less than the great Napper Tandy! . . . St. Michael,

48. A.A.E. Corr. Pol. Ham. 114 fos. 300–1, 339, and 115 fos 4, 6, Reinhard's correspondence, Nov. 1799–Jan. 1800.
49. P.R.O. H.O. 100/87/222–5, Portland to Cornwallis, 14 Oct. 1799; also *Parl. Hist.*, xxxiv, 1397–1409.
50. For official correspondence on the prisoners, see P.R.O. H.O. 100/87/226–338, 100/109/3, I.S.P.O. 620/10/115/1, and B.L. Add. MS. 35707 fos. 221–2. See also *State Trials*, xxvii, 1191–1279, for Tandy's trial and A.H.G. Doss. Pers.2ᵉ sér., J. B. Blackwell, for Blackwell's account. Coughlin, *Napper Tandy*, 185–208, argues that the government was out for Tandy's blood; the correspondence cited above proves quite the contrary.

the Archangel, disputed with the Devil about the Body of Moses, and cities contended for the honour of Homer's birthplace; but Napper, greater than both, is the prize of a contest that halves the globe.'[51]

After the extradition, France had gone through the motions of expelling Hamburg's representatives, publicly reprimanding the Hamburg Senate, and initiating negotiations for the exchange of the prisoners. At the close of 1799, however, France was as reluctant to revive the dispute as England. General Don, offered in exchange for Tandy, had been arrested in Holland for subversive activities similar to those which England had chosen to make the central issue of the Tandy crisis. But France made no attempt to derive any capital from the comparison.[52] The Directory had recognized the value of nurturing Irish rebelliousness. The Consulate, however, which had assumed power when exchange negotiations commenced, was already hoping to make peace with England.

IV

The plight of Tandy and his companions in Hamburg was symptomatic of the situation in which the United Irish survivors found themselves after 1798. The four men had no other asylum but France, and they were arrested because French security policy prevented the automatic issue of passports to sympathetic aliens. France was the only country which could supply a haven for the United men who wished to continue plans for Ireland's liberation. A fugitive leadership would henceforth make plans far removed from the country of their intended application. The Society had never been so remote from Irish realities and its organization needed a radical overhaul, particularly to accommodate the new needs of the Irish refugees who flocked to the Continent after 1798, seeking material as well as political assistance from France.

The arrests of the original leaders had raised a new generation of younger and relatively unknown men to head the home Society. But after the departure of Tone and Tandy, the Directory had come to place exclusive trust in Lewins, and in 1799 Lewins was an anachronism. He had left Ireland in 1797 and proved unqualified to speak for those leaders who had emerged in 1798. Since his recommendation was the requirement for French recognition, however, it was difficult enough even for established leaders to enter France, let alone the many refugees who had fled from reprisals after the rebellion. Lewins continued to conduct his mission according to the terms of his original appointment, negotiating secretly and exclusively for military aid. He scarcely recognized the existence of an Irish refugee problem and preferred

51. I.S.P.O. 620/8/75, 'Napper Tandy and the War'.
52. A.N. AF IV 1672 plaq. 1 p^{ces} 5 and 14, reports on Don and the Tandy affair, Feb.–Mar. 1800; A.A.E. Corr. Pol. Ang. 593, correspondence for the exchange, Nov. 1799–Apr. 1800

to restrict their entry into France to reduce the risk of infiltration by British spies. This intensive secrecy was no longer necessary in 1799. The British government was fully informed of United activities in Paris and had publicly revealed its knowledge in the reports of 1798–99. Moreover, in the absence of any formal organization at home, such secrecy was inadvisable, and a widespread knowledge of the French negotiations would have helped sustain hope. The establishment of an open United Irish Society in Paris testified to this redefinition of their role abroad. But Lewins was appalled by this lack of caution. Although he had continued to transmit French assurances to individuals in Ireland and England, Lewins had little contact with the new United Irish executive. The unilateral nature of his embassy in Paris rendered changes at home unimportant to its continuation. He simply abided by the terms of his original appointment and continued to petition the Directory for military assistance. At no time did he represent the exact nature of the new organization to the Directory, and for most of the new leaders he had ceased to be an effective mouthpiece.[53]

For the moment the material needs of the new arrivals were the first priority of the reformed United Irish committee in Paris. Its members were prepared to work through Lewins if he agreed on a more liberal interpretation of his mission to accommodate the new needs of the post-rebellion Society. But it was a transition which Lewins was unwilling to make. He insisted on maintaining the exclusivity of his mission and remained aloof from his fellow countrymen at a time when increasing claims from other foreign refugees made the intercession of some respected negotiator imperative. Since the arrival of the first war refugees from Mainz and Liège in 1793, France had attracted a steady flow of patriot exiles. But the numbers seeking asylum had never been large enough to require any specific policy. Only in 1799 was the Directory forced to formulate such a policy when the victories of the second coalition sent collaborators fleeing from the recaptured gains of Bonaparte's early campaigns.[54] Hitherto, foreign refugee relief on an *ad hoc* basis had been relatively generous. It had not been difficult to assist small groups such as the Irish seminary students stranded by the outbreak of war. Those who wished to remain were assisted from public funds, and by 1795 their special claims on their adoptive country were recognized; they were attached to the larger colonial relief scheme and were allocated monthly stipends of between 35 and 150 francs according to individual

---

53. See A.A.E. Corr. Pol. Ang. 592 fos. 390 and 409, for correspondence from the committee and Lewins's objections, Aug.–Sept. 1799. See P.R.O. F.O. 33/18/42, H.O. 100/86/337–8, 100/87/91 and I.S.P.O. 620/7/74/39, for examples of his correspondence with Britain in 1799, and 620/10/121/127, for his loss of credit by 1800.

54. For the Italian and Corsican refugees in particular see A.N. F15 3511, 3359, 3438–9; A.A.E. Corr. Pol. Sardaigne 279 fos. 27, 48, 222; and A-M. Rao, 'Les Réfugiés Italiens en 1799', *A.h.R.f.*, no. 240 (Apr.–Jun. 1980), 225–61.

needs. Only twenty-one students were still receiving such relief by 1796, and their continued residence in Paris facilitated checks on eligibility and the issue of the *cartes de résidence* and *civisme* required for any kind of public relief. The administration of the relief, however, remained chaotic, and the pleas of ministers and deputies alike did little to reduce arrears. Nevertheless, the seminarists' relief scheme seemed an obvious precedent for the petitioners of 1799 to have cited, particularly since it was still in operation. It is a token of the isolation of the foreign refugee groups and of the lack of co-operation between the different departments of the Directory that neither the United Irishmen nor the ministers involved in their negotiations ever seemed aware of the scheme.[55]

This belief in their automatic right to French help was typical of second-generation patriots. The unofficial promises made by generals like Hoche and Kilmaine, by emissaries like Duckett and Jackson, and by French officials like Bourdon, had a cumulative effect. By the time they had reached the middling and lower levels of the United Irish Society, such promises had been transmuted into firm assurances of France's commitment to the Irish struggle, in success and failure alike. In each stage of the transmission, vague assurances had been embellished by junior French officials and United leaders, and when the real victims of such misapplied propaganda arrived on the Continent, their plight only served to highlight the diverging levels on which the leaders and the led operated. Those who fled to France after the rebellion did so on the assumption that their material needs would be cared for until another invasion restored them to their homeland, and reports of their distress shocked those who had stayed behind.[56]

When his Irish property was confiscated under the terms of the Banishment Act, Lewins sought some payment for past services in France. But the basis for his request was quite different from that of his struggling compatriots. He had been employed on various missions by the Directory and felt entitled to some recompense. But he denounced those Irish exiles who demanded relief as a right without having earned it. His mission did not include any duty to act as some kind of welfare secretary to impecunious Irishmen abroad, and he told the United exiles this in no uncertain terms. Such diverging opinions were as much a product of social as political divisions. The expatriates of Lewins's vintage were professional men, doctors, surgeons, merchants, lawyers, and in general men of independent means, with sufficient resources to establish

---

55. For earlier schemes see A.A.E. Mem. et Doc. Affaires Diverses Politiques France 10 doss. 233, A.N. F^{15} 3508^A, F^{15}* 16, and *Réimpression de L'Ancien Moniteur*, 20, pp. 575–6. See R. C. Cobb, *The Police and the People. French Popular Protest 1789–1820* (Oxford, 1972), 23 for the isolation of foreign groups in Paris.

56. See e.g. I.S.P.O. 620/18^A/11, Wickham to Castlereagh, 18 Jul. 1798, and 620/10/121/11, McNally's information, 9 Jun. 1802.

themselves in Paris before the confiscation of their property in Ireland. Those arriving after 1798 were younger, mostly artisans or small farmers; they had little wealth at the best of times, and many were already destitute before they reached Paris.[57] The removal of any source of finance in Ireland eventually caused considerable hardship to those already established on the Continent, but it was a gradual and partial impoverishment; Lewins failed to realize that total and immediate destitution lay behind the insistent urgency of his troublesome countrymen. He had never envisaged a situation in which the United Irishmen might be reduced to begging dependence on France and a kind of snobbish pride prevented his recognition of their altered circumstances. He recoiled from the prospect of accepting French charity, and responded to the exiles' pleas by arranging voluntary enlistment into the Polish legions forming on the eastern front, where they could earn their keep and secure military training for the return to Ireland. But such a solution was unattractive to most United men because of the removal from France, the loss of freedom of action by submission to regular military discipline, and the apparent permanence of such a solution to a subsistence problem deemed purely temporary. Only a handful of the United men who had come to Paris before 1798 took up this option in the summer of 1799, and all had returned to France by the following February.[58]

Lewins's reluctance to ask for French charity was purely personal and was unjustified by current French attitudes. The disillusionment of those officers who had taken part in the 1798 expeditions was swamped by overwhelming French sympathy for Irish sufferings in the rebellion, which had been widely publicized in France, and the Minister of Police had instructed his agents to assist the struggling Irishmen in Paris. In the west and south-west of France, where those who had not entered via Hamburg would have been most likely to land, the generous reaction of the local authorities was such that it invoked a reprimand from Paris.[59] The stringent requirements for entry into France were relaxed for those returning from the Irish expeditions. The fate of the Tones and of Teeling had awakened the Directory to the dangers attending Irish participation in French expeditions; and Nion, the commissioner in London for the exchange of prisoners, was ordered to secure the exchange of those Irish captured with Hardy and Humbert before their identity was discovered. The English government had already mounted an investigation

57. See A.H.G. C¹ 14, État nominatif des officiers attachés à la Légion Irlandaise, Jul. 1804; A.A.E. Corr. Pol. Ang. 592 fo. 409, the U.I. committee to Talleyrand, 13 Sept. 1799; and 593 fos. 22–3, Lewins to Talleyrand, 28 Oct. 1799; for Lewins's claims see Corr. Pol. Ang. 592 fo. 213; Personnel, Arrêtés et Décrets 8 fo. 11; and A.N. AF III 546 doss. 3649 fo. 3.
58. A.A.E. Corr. Pol. Ang. 593 fos. 22–3, 229; also Lawless's account in A.H.G. X^h 16, and Doss. Pers. 2ᵉ sér. G.B. 1840, William Lawless.
59. See A.N. F⁷ 6192 doss. 2524, 7348 doss. B⁴ 9145 and 7459 doss. B⁵ 9641, for correspondence on the Irish exiles, 1798–1799.

into rumours that many Irish had been transferred inadvertently to Liverpool with the French prisoners of war. But Nion carried out his instructions with remarkable efficiency, and by the end of 1798, Maguire, Sullivan, O'Kean and McDonnell, who had joined the French in Ireland, had been transferred from Humbert's group; Hamilton, Carey and Thomas Corbet from Hardy's; and McCann, Donavan and Burgess from the *Anacréon* expedition had made their way back to France overland from Denmark.[60]

Automatic entry for fugitive rebels was not, however, the norm, and the difficulties in proving the patriotism of the more recent arrivals at Hamburg ensured that few would ever reach France. Lewins's intransigence denied the Parisian United Irish committee any say in the investigation of requests for passports. Yet it justifiably claimed better qualifications to pronounce on such matters than Lewins. Its members included such representatives from the earliest stages of the Franco-Irish negotiations as Madgett, Sullivan, John Delaney from the Irish College, and Arthur MacMahon's brother Patrick, who had served many years in the French armies; the first generation of United Irish exiles was represented by Joseph Orr, William Hamilton, Samuel Turner (its representative in Hamburg), Arthur MacMahon, Anthony McCann, Thomas Burgess, John Donavan, William Bailey and Edmund O'Finn; whilst the new home organization was represented by William Putnam McCabe, George Palmer, William St. John Mason, George Wilkinson and some like Blackburn from Antrim, Corr from Meath, O'Heale from Wexford and McDonnell from Mayo, who had actually held commands in the rebellion. The entire country and every stage in United Irish development was accordingly represented by the committee.[61] But habit died hard; Tone and Lewins had established a recognized and respected channel of consultation on Irish affairs, and in the crucial months of 1799, when the Directory worked out its Irish relief policy, Lewins's opinions prevailed.

Until 1799 the impossibility of predicting demand, or of testing the eligibility of refugees who rarely remained long enough in one place to acquire the necessary papers, had defied the attempts of successive regimes to formulate an effective refugee policy. But the influx of 1799 forced François de Neufchâteau, as Minister of the Interior, and Quinette, his successor, to establish firm guidelines. Given the novel dimensions of the problem, it is not surprising that they should have proved unsympathetic to United Irish claims for special treatment. 'I would not hesitate in proposing that the Directory should help those Irish who have sacrificed their fortunes in the cause of liberty', Quinette protested 'if these fugitives were the only ones claiming government benefit, but large numbers of refugee Italian patriots at Briançon are likewise soliciting immediate help. We must assume that in the present

60. See A.A.E. Corr. Pol. Ham. 113 fo. 339; also A.N. AF III 206 doss. 943 p^cc 108.
61. A.A.E. Corr. Pol. Ang. 592 fo. 409, the U.I. committee to Talleyrand, 13 Sept, 1799.

circumstances, many citizens will flee to France from countries now occupied by the enemy. Consequently we can provide for the needs of all these fugitives only by a general measure.'[62] The question of refugee relief was caught up in the administrative rationalization of the last ten months of the Directory's life, and the two Interior Ministers were its main exponents. They were horrified at the confusion into which such individual claims threw their attempts at standardization, and Quinette was particularly impatient at the conflicting claims submitted by Lewins and by the United Irish committee. Such a committee was the preferred channel for administering relief, and committees for the colonial and Italian refugees were already fulfilling the functions to which Lewins, with Talleyrand's support, had laid exclusive claim. Talleyrand agreed with Lewins that a large committee should not be allowed to participate in Franco-Irish negotiations and he alone was em-powered to vet claims and to administer relief payments.

Throughout the summer of 1799 Quinette and Talleyrand clashed over their differing interpretations of the Irish position, Talleyrand arguing that the United Irish refugees ought to be considered a special case by virtue of services rendered in the past and those which they might still perform in the war with England. The latter required continued residence in Paris, since a re-mobil-ization of the naval forces against England might occur at any moment. In contrast, Quinette wanted the Irish to be assimilated to the colonial refugees for administrative purposes and sent to reside in the provinces where relief would be cheaper. His ministry could not cater for exceptional cases, and if Talleyrand insisted on exclusiveness, he would have to assume the respons-ibility himself. Quinette took his case to the Directory in September and succeeded in transferring all the routine duties to Foreign Affairs, his own ministry acting purely as paymaster. After all, Foreign Affairs had been responsible for such foreign patriots since the opening of the war, and in 1799, with the progressive delineation of duties and constant shortage of funds, few ministers wished to be burdened with additional, and potentially expensive, responsibilities.[63]

Even after payment procedures had been settled, Lewin's adherence to an outmoded security policy prevented relief from reaching many of the now destitute exiles. For security reasons he had persuaded Talleyrand to apply a draconian list of prerequisites for relief, which included compulsory residence in France, firm proof of persecution for their principles, and total destitution. He rejected the suggestion that if the matter were brought before the legislative councils they might grant as much as 60,000 francs, vastly superior to anything

62. A.N. F¹⁵ 3511, report to the Directory, [Feb.] 1799; also AF III 615 doss. 4327 pᶜᵉ 86, Interior Minister's report, Jul. 1799.
63. A.N. F¹⁵ 3511 doss. 'Réfugiés Irlandais', and A.A.E. Corr. Pol. Ang. 592 fos. 391–414, 593 fos. 7–9 and 22–3.

which the ministers could offer. This left the secret funds of the ministries involved as the only source from which relief payments could be made. The Interior Minister was to pay 10,000 francs in monthly instalments of 80 francs to successful claimants, until the fund was exhausted, and Talleyrand would provide immediate relief until claims could be investigated. The sum was generous enough, four times as much as the average *émigré* received in England, and twice as much as that voted to the Italian refugees. But the overall grant was sufficient to relieve only a handful for a short period. Lewins had made no attempt to plead the case of the majority of Irish refugees stranded in Hamburg, even though the Paris committee saw their plight as part of their own and the Directory itself seemed disposed to help them. He had no desire to increase the numbers of United men in France, neglected to push claims for passports, and was clearly censoring the lists of claimants for relief submitted by the committee.[64]

Not surprisingly, the committee, ignorant of the genuine administrative difficulties, blamed Lewins for delays in payment, and in September submitted a formal complaint against him. From the committee room in the rue de l' École-de-Médecine they issued a long statement to Talleyrand, outlining their superior qualifications to speak for the Irish exiles, and claiming that Lewins was ignorant of recent developments in the home Society and had totally ignored the plight of their colleagues in Hamburg. By the end of October, with no relief payment having yet been made, and Lewins's energies concentrating instead on the side issue of enlistment into the Polish legions, the committee was at war with its official representative. Lewins continued to answer ministerial queries on relief matters, but his pique at the committee's interference brought an angry outburst on 28 October. 'I have had, nor wish to have, any kind of communication with them, and I can in no way be responsible for the persons composing the committee . . . ; it is not that I think them traitors—but . . . such an association can only be harmful, and even serve as an instrument for English espionage.'[65]

By the end of the year relations had deteriorated so far that the committee was convinced the money allocated to them in July had been appropriated by Lewins.[66] Nothing could have been further from the truth, and Lewins's voluminous correspondence with the Directory and Consulate indicate that he had continued to conduct his mission with unflagging industry. Given the conviction that his mission was to secure armed aid for Ireland, it is not difficult to understand how his unfamiliarity with the altered circumstances in Ireland

64. For the assistance allocated to the Irish, see A.N. AF III 615 doss. 4327 p^ce 85 and AF III 620 doss. 4379 p^ces 5–7; A.A.E. Corr. Pol. Ang. 592 fo. 391, 593 fos. 22–4, 106, 162, 398 and 594 fo. 180.

65. A.A.E. Corr. Pol. Ang. 593 fos. 22–3; also 592 fo. 409, for the committee's claims.

66. I.S.P.O. 620/10/121/127, McNally's information of 7 Sept. 1800.

could breed a sense of annoyance that a group of interlopers were detracting from the central issue by disputing over such insignificant matters as subsistence allowances.[67] But the correspondence of the committee with the home leaders was more regular and direct than that of Lewins. Complaints about his behaviour had been received throughout 1799 and 1800 and his credit in Ireland was destroyed. How far requests for his replacement succeeded is unclear, but when two representatives were sent to Paris by the Irish executive at the end of 1800, they negotiated with the French authorities independently of Lewins. By that date the Paris committee had gained a measure of respectability with the Consulate. Time had eroded the suspicions of Lewins and the French authorities alike, and in the two years before Amiens its members were regularly consulted on Irish affairs.[68] Relief payments had finally commenced in January 1800, when thirty United men were listed as eligible. Their distress had eventually convinced Lewins of the need to mount a more determined campaign for prompt and adequate relief. In March the original fund was exhausted. The Interior Minister was experiencing genuine difficulty meeting the expense from his secret funds, but he agreed to continue payments from the colonial relief fund. Arrears were paid in June, but nothing further was received until the following March, when the stipend was reduced to 40 francs per month. A final payment was made in September, but when peace preliminaries were signed with England the following month the unsatisfactory Irish relief scheme came to an abrupt end.[69]

The collapse of the Directory had left the United Irishmen strangely unmoved, and many welcomed Bonaparte's assumption of power. The arrival of Joseph Bonaparte at the Interior Ministry caused no alteration in the refugee relief policy, and the return of Talleyrand to Foreign Affairs, after Reinhard's brief term of office, contributed to the impression that little had changed. But Bonaparte was biding his time, and the exiles' political insensitivity did little to prepare them for the rejection of 1801. Tone alone of the Irish exiles had gained a sense of the direction of French political winds. In 1799 any United Irish diplomatic expertise had been swamped by the wave of new immigrants, who had been conditioned to view continental politics in terms of 'us' and 'them', the republicans against the old monarchies. Their indiscriminate memorializing of falling and fallen ministers before and after Brumaire was a token of this new clumsiness, which Lewins's gradual withdrawal was to accentuate. The threat to France posed by an English-sponsored invasion on the one hand and the continuing success of Jacobinism on the other should have

67. See his correspondence of winter 1799–1800 in A.N. AF IV 1101 doss. 1, AF IV 1671 plaq. 1 fos. 106–11 and BB³ 175 fo. 241.
68. See A.N. F⁷ 7459 doss. B⁵ 9648; for the decline in Lewins's credit see I.S.P.O. 620/10/121/10 and 127, and see below pp. 275–6.
69. A.N. F⁷ 3511; A.A.E. Corr. Pol. Ang. 592–4.

warned the United Irish exiles to have maintained a low profile in the early years of the Consulate. Instead they continued to cavort with ex-Jacobins like Humbert and Madgett, and attracted unfavourable attention at a time when all foreigners, particularly British subjects, were suspect. The French were heartily sick of the foreign refugees who congregated around the Palais-Egalité (the former Palais Royal), complaining of French neglect and providing an inlet for enemy agents.[70] A clearer conception of French thinking might have cushioned the Irish against the disillusionment which would set in after 1801.

Bonaparte's accession to power had also boosted the hopes of the Hamburg refugees, but as Bruix had predicted, unrelieved distress had depleted their numbers and enthusiasm, and by all accounts their situation was wretched by the time of the Brumaire *coup d'état*. The efforts of Duckett, and the unofficial relief scheme established at the end of 1798, had promised to preserve this source of recruits for any future Irish expedition without necessitating their admission to France. The Tandy affair, however, had intensified enemy surveillance and harassment, and had scattered them all over north Germany in such a way as to render any regular scheme impossible. It had focused such attention on French undercover activities abroad that any renewed contact with the Irish in the area was, for the moment, diplomatically unthinkable. All the powers involved in the European war sponsored the rebellious subjects of their enemies. But France under the Directory had difficulty outliving that reputation as Europe's revolutionary mentor which had been established by its predecessors, and by 1799 many officials were disturbed at the way in which this reputation disrupted normal diplomatic activities.[71] The Revolution was coming of age and rebel refugees were an anachronism. The Irish dispersed from Hamburg became a lost subject. That they remained in the area is certain; and they were to re-emerge each time hopes of another Irish invasion were revived. Otherwise no information has survived on their fate.[72]

V

In the first years of the Consulate, United Irish hopes of another French invasion were realistic enough. As calm was restored in France, and hostilities in the continental campaign declined, the French armies were liberated for

70. A. Aulard, *Paris sous le Consulat*, 4 vols. (Paris, 1903–9) I, 236, 296, 328, 393–4, 707, 722, 823, III, 30, 85, 104, 160–61, 317. For Bonaparte's dislike of republicans see A.N. AF IV* 204 no. 142 and *Correspondance de Napoléon I*er, VI, 4707; and I.S.P.O. 620/10/121/127, for Irish response to the change of regime.

71. A.A.E. Corr. Pol. Ham. 114 fo. 141, Lemaître to Talleyrand, 13 Apr. 1799.

72. B.L. Add. MS. 33112 fos. 4–11; P.R.O. F.O. 33/19/69 and 84, 33/20/41; and A.N. BB⁴ 122 fos. 256, 290–1, for the United Irishmen in Hamburg.

possible use against England. England's lack of frankness had alienated her allies. Russia in particular was smarting after her forces had been left to languish in the Channel Isles through the winter and spring of 1800. By October she had withdrawn from the coalition and had joined the northern powers in hostile alliance against England. In France, Bonaparte's success in winning back royalist allegiance had finally whittled away the remnants of England's 'Grand Design'. She had been deluded by royalist agents into thinking internal discontent greater than it was and, in the belief that Bonaparte could not long survive, had haughtily brushed aside his peace overtures in January 1800.[73] But Bonaparte went from strength to strength, and the following year was able to impose his own peace terms. By February 1801, England had been deserted by her allies and her army was locked up at home by serious food riots. Little wonder that news of naval preparations in France's western ports should have raised United expectations of another expedition against the British Isles.

France's renewed success in the war had already revived disaffection in Ireland, and Cornwallis was sufficiently apprehensive of another French invasion attempt to review the country's defences. What he discovered did not inspire confidence: 6,000 regulars had been withdrawn over the past year and the militia, recently plundered to supply the deficiencies in the regular army, was full of raw recruits. Although the worst troubles in the country were devoid of political content, the latest rumours of another French invasion had sent such a wave of excited expectation through the countryside that Cornwallis thought another rising inevitable if the French ever again succeeded in landing. Ignorance of the nature of the United Irish re-organization contributed to official unease in the summer of 1800.[74]

During the invasion scare, Dublin was offered a unique opportunity to penetrate the revived Society. In July, Turner sent information that two emissaries had been despatched to Ireland by the Paris committee. But the mission of Edward Carolan and Thomas O'Meara to Ireland tells us more about the decline of England's domestic intelligence system than the United Irish Society, for the bungling surveillance of the two emissaries produced little more than a list of those still operating in Dublin. Carolan had been an officer in the Monaghan militia and was one of the catholic delegates in 1797. O'Meara was a Tipperary man who had served in France's Irish regiments before the Revolution, and had been responsible for recruiting Irish prisoners of war into Hoche's expedition of 1796. In August 1800 the two arrived at Gravesend after crossing from Hamburg, and their journey via London was watched by the authorities from the outset. O'Meara stopped in London, possibly to

---

73. *Parl. Hist.*, xxxiv, 1196–1397, debate on the rejection; *H.M.C. Dropmore MSS.*, v, 346–7, vi, 3, 52–3, 79, 99–104, 146–7, 153–6, 227–8.
74. *Cornwallis Correspondence*, iii, 287. See also I.S.P.O. 620/18/14; P.R.O. F.O. 33/20/40; and H.O. 100/94/139 for rising United expectations.

transmit Carolan's communications to France, though the English government was never able to discover anything further on his activities. Carolan was permitted to continue his journey to Ireland. A reluctant Murphy was deputed to follow him, but he was already so distrusted by the authorities in both countries that he was watched as closely as Carolan himself, and the services of Higgins were enlisted as a precaution. Murphy bungled his assignment from the outset. He failed to book a passage from Holyhead and was forced to kick his heels in Chester while Carolan sailed unimpeded to Dublin.

From 8 September Murphy submitted accounts of Carolan's movements in and out of his Eustace Street residence, but supplied no further information. He had neither the inclination nor the opportunity to penetrate the Dublin movement. The United men there had already been apprised of his new employment and had warned the two agents to avoid him. O'Meara was arrested in London on 21 September and the Irish government was instructed also to take Carolan, to prevent his flight on news of his companion's fate. But he had already absconded. McNally admitted that he was baffled by Carolan's mission. His arrival in Ireland was common knowledge and yet McNally could find no one who had actually seen him. He thought that Carolan's main object was to tell of Lewins's activities in Paris and to secure a replacement.[75] But this was a misreading of the facts, a further indication that the Irish government was missing information because of its excessive concentration on old leaders. Divisions within the United movement were never strong enough to detract from its central policy of securing French help, otherwise the home leaders would have made a more determined effort to remove Lewins. Instead, they simply duplicated his mission by sending additional agents to supply the information which he was incapable of giving. As a result of Carolan's mission, Robert Emmet and Malachy Delaney, one of the Kildare leaders in the 1798 rebellion, were sent to Paris, not to replace Lewins, but in another attempt to enlist military assistance.[76]

Emmet and Delaney arrived in Hamburg in August and applied for passports to General Augereau in Holland. Augereau invited them into Holland and both he and the First Consul, to whom he transmitted their memoir, were impressed with what they had to say. The memoir is a remarkable document, portraying the new pragmatic approach of the post-rebellion organization to the French alliance. It is devoid of obsequiousness and exaggeration and offers France a straightforward, business-like relationship. It provides an

---

75. For an account of the mission see I.S.P.O. 620/10/118/5 and 620/10/121/128–36; McNally's information, 620/18/14; Higgins's information for September, 620/18^A/14 and 620/49/38–58; also P.R.O. F.O. 33/20/38 and H.O. 100/94/143, 159–160, 165–70, mainly letters to and from Marsden, Aug.–Oct. 1800.

76. I.S.P.O. 620/11/130/26, 620/49/38, information sent to government on the mission, and 620/51/131 for Delaney in particular.

accurate picture of the current state of Ireland's defence establishment, making no attempt to portray the country as an easy conquest, and showing how the United Irish movement had been re-organized for the sole purpose of assisting a French invasion. Military requirements had been increased to 25,000–30,000 men, and arms for a further 75,000, and there is an air of determined finality about this latest approach to France. Emmet and Delaney imply that this is the United Irishmen's last request. France had been approached on five previous occasions; the United Irishmen had remained faithfully attached to the alliance, despite the years of fruitless waiting; but patience was running out. More than anything else, the documentation of this mission reveals the complete consistency of United thinking after 1798. It shows that although the United Irishmen still depended on French help to effect their aims, it was to be contracted help, financed by the Irish and leaving no excuse for conquest through a debt unpaid. France was to be fully compensated for her assistance and would receive retrospective payment for previous invasion attempts.

At first it looked as if this new mission might have succeeded where Lewins's endless and monotonous memorializing of the past two years had singularly failed. Bonaparte was sufficiently impressed by the memoir to finance and approve the authors' journey to France. They arrived in Paris in January 1801 and were recommended to the First Consul in a glowing report from Talleyrand. In a lengthy audience with the Minister, the two agents had elaborated upon their military demands and the preparations which would be made in Ireland to receive the expedition. Peace had been concluded with Austria at Lunéville and Bonaparte's reaction to the mission suggested that another attack on the British Isles was in contemplation. The two agents were referred to Bernadotte, who as commander in the west would have been entrusted with the command of any expedition to Ireland. But the Irish were to learn that Bonaparte's statements and actions were not always a true reflection of his plans. After Lunéville he sought peace with England, and the Irish mission was valued more as a means of forcing England to negotiate than as another weapon in the war against her. Bernadotte was instructed to consult the Irish refugees in Paris; 'and you need not be worried,' added Talleyrand, 'about giving a little publicity to any arrangements which might be made. The rumour itself might produce the desired effect.'[77] A few United Irishmen, including Delaney, had been sent to Brest for 'effect'. The subterfuge was a total success and British agents in France and Hamburg told of plans to send 12,000 to 15,000 men to Ireland.[78] The real object of the Brest

77. A.A.E. Corr. Pol. Ang. 594 fo.173, Talleyrand to Bernadotte, 18 Jan. 1801; 593 fos. 288–9, Emmet and Delaney's memoir, received 5 Sept. 1800; and 594 fos. 150–1 and A.N. AF IV* 204 No. 1182, for Bonaparte's comments in particular; see also AF IV 1672 plaq. 2 fos. 191–2, for Bernadotte's discussion with the U.I. committee.
78. See P.R.O. H.O. 100/100/164–72, H.O. 42/57–8, Hammond's letters of 14 Aug. and 2 Sept. 1801; also F.O. 27/58, F.O. 33/20/44 and W.O. 1/397/117–21, 149, for further reports from France and Hamburg, Jan.–Apr. 1801

preparations, however, proved to be St. Domingo, to which an expedition sailed in May 1801.

How far the French military and naval authorities themselves were aware of the subterfuge is unclear. With a hopeless disregard for naval logistics, Bonaparte had issued a bewildering series of instructions for the western fleet, which in the first eighteen months of the Consulate had outlined the West Indies, Ireland, Louisiana, Malta, Egypt, Trinidad, and Surinam as possible destinations. Little wonder that the British authorities and the United Irishmen could read their own hopes and fears into such apparent confusion. Nor can any of the projects be dismissed as exercises in pure propaganda. The St. Domingo preparations had been used initially to divert attention from the sailing of Ganteaume's fleet to the Mediterranean, and had sailed nevertheless four months later. The First Consul had mooted an Irish expedition to the Dutch and Spanish, though the unwillingness of either to risk their navies in uncertain ventures, the difficulties which Ganteaume encountered in the Mediterranean, and the urgency of extricating the army which had been abandoned in Egypt in 1799, soon banished such thoughts.[79] Bonaparte suffered from the delusion that his navy, like his army, could train and prepare en route to its destination and that orders could be altered at will. The United Irishmen could not have been expected to understand such complicated reasoning. Their hopes had been fanned by the consultations, the rumours, and particularly by the unofficial assurances of Humbert, who had set himself up as the self-appointed champion of Ireland.[80] The disillusionment after falling from such heightened expectations contributed to the growing feeling that their total dependence on French military aid should not automatically place their country at the mercy of France's unscrupulous leader.

The signing of the Leoben peace preliminaries with England in August 1801 confirmed this disenchantment with France's new ruler. But if the Parisian-based United men were already suspicious before Leoben, the tendency of the ordinary Irishman to deify Bonaparte made such apparent betrayal all the more difficult to take. 'Some yet of the Peasantry don't credit the News,' wrote McGucken from Belfast, 'always relying on the attachment and fidelity of the Chief Consul to this Country.' By the end of the year, however, the reality of their rejection was abundantly clear; Bonaparte was execrated as a usurper and a traitor, and 'French treachery' became 'the Order of the Day.'[81] For a while the blow was softened by rumours that Bonaparte might stipulate for some measure of catholic relief in the peace terms. The United Irish in Paris

---

79. Desbrière, *Projets et Tentatives*, II, 274–8; *Correspondance de Napoléon Ier*, VI, 5219, 5285, 5328, 5329, VII, 5336, 5340, 5342, 5568; Rodger, *War of the Second Coalition*, 219–29; see also J. E. Driault, *Napoléon et l'Europe. La politique extérieure du Premier Consul, 1800–1803* (Paris, 1910), 6–7.

80. For Humbert's correspondence on Ireland, 1799–1801, see A.H.G. M R 1420 fos. 34, 39–43; A.N. AF IV 1101 doss. 1, AF IV 1600^A plaq. 1. p^ces 2 and 4; and I.S.P.O. 620/49/82.

81. I.S.P.O. 620/10/118/17, McGucken to [Cooke], 15 Sept. 1801; also B.L. Add. M S. 33107 fo. 48, for the reaction of the U.I. in Hamburg.

had certainly considered asking the First Consul to negotiate terms for the Irish. But when Robert Emmet called on Talleyrand for just such a purpose, his hopes were not high, and 'having received an evasive answer,' as he later explained to a friend, 'I left the place without making any demands, telling them at the same time, that we merited their intervention at least as much as the patriots of Naples'.[82]

The coolness of Emmet's reception was scarcely surprising. Bonaparte was planning to use the United Irishmen as a bargaining counter for the expulsion of the royalists from England. To Lord Cornwallis, in France to negotiate peace terms, he had suggested 'that we could agree to remove disaffected or dangerous persons from either country, at the request of the nation to which they might respectively belong, and declared his willingness to send away the United Irishmen.'[83] A similar offer made by the French representative in London was reproduced in the *London Chronicle*. It was not quite so explicit as that of the First Consul, but the United Irishmen recognized well enough its import. The following autumn when Robert Emmet rejoined his brother in Brussels, he confirmed Thomas in his determination to give up the struggle and settle in America, by relating some expressions made by someone in 'high auth' respecting the willingness of Government to deliver up the United Irishmen, tied neck and heels, to England.'[84] England had no great love for the *émigrés*, but if a handful of United Irishmen deported from France would have attracted little attention, the mass expulsion of the *émigrés* would have caused an international outcry, and England wisely ignored France's suggestion.

Over the next year the British authorities were lulled into thinking the United Irishmen no longer a threat by the disillusioned letters sent home by the exiled leaders.[85] However, only a handful actually left France in the peace period. By 1802 the idealism binding them to France may have disappeared, but their dependence had not, and in the confident expectation that the peace would prove little more than an interlude in the hostilities, many settled down to a life of temporary normality. Almost all left Paris for the provinces, many taking employment as teachers of English or with Irish merchant houses in Bordeaux. Some joined McCabe, George Wilkinson and George Smith, a Dublin hatter, in an abortive attempt to establish a cotton manufacture at

82. H. Landreth, *The Pursuit of Robert Emmet* (New York, 1948), 112; I.S.P.O. 620/18/14, information from Higgins, 28 Dec. 1801.
83. *Cornwallis Correspondence*, III, 403; see also P.R.O. F.O. 27/60/34, despatch from Amiens, 5 Feb. 1802.
84. Quoted in Madden, *United Irishmen*, 3rd ser., III, 25, 51.
85. I.S.P.O. 620/10/121/8–11,18, McNally's information, Apr.–Oct.1802; 620/12/143, [Delaney] to St. John, 19 Sept. 1802; also P.R.O. F.O. 97/241 and F.O. 33/22/5, information from Hamburg, Dec. 1801 and Feb. 1802.

Rouen.[86] But few prospered. Skilled workers, however, were in demand, and people like Michael Quigley, a mason from Kildare, had little difficulty finding employment in the building trade. In time, Bonaparte came to value the Irish more for their contribution to France's economy than to its war effort. Large numbers of Irish workers flocked to France during the peace period, in some ways substantiating English fears of disloyalty in the Irish workforce. An attempt was also made to persuade Prussia to release those textile workers among the rebel prisoners exiled there in 1799.[87] On the whole, however, Bonaparte preferred to disguise such contacts, and to obliterate all traces of the republican past. Patriot exiles were ostracized, Paine's works removed from the Bibliothèque nationale, and the international aristocracy, which flocked to Paris in the peace years, regaled in a manner befitting the old monarchy. Former republicans were an embarrassment to Bonaparte in his quest for respectability.[88] The United Irishmen were wise enough to keep in the background, but their resolve to renew negotiations when hostilities recommenced was fortified by the release of their original leaders from prison in the general amnesty of 1802.

The Irish state prisoners had not ceased to be a headache for the English and Irish governments, and one suspects that they were glad of the excuse of Amiens to release them on condition of permanent banishment. Glaring shortfalls in security legislation had been highlighted by their detention, and the prospect of their unconditional release when the Habeas Corpus Suspension Act expired in 1801 caused panic in Whitehall. Although the Banishment Act of 1798 had excluded most from ever returning to Ireland, a legislative oversight had failed to extend its terms to England, and government was horrified at the thought that they might choose to reside there on their release. When the Belfast prisoners did petition for their release on the Act's expiration, a hastily produced secret parliamentary report provided sufficient justification for another batch of emergency measures and the continued detention of the prisoners until peace.[89] Lesser United leaders were released after Leoben. But Whitehall was more hesitant about the arch-conspirators

86. See Hants. C.R.O. 38M49/5/31; I.S.P.O. 620/12/145 and 620/13/177/3; T.C.D. MS. 873/767, for the Rouen venture. For other Irish in France during the peace period, see I.S.P.O. 620/11–12; P.R.O. H.O. 100/114/179–184; and A.N. F⁷ 6463 doss. 9980 fo. 48.

87. A.N. F⁷ 8595 doss. 2260, the Irish in Prussia, 1807; also F⁷ 3050 doss. 2 fos. 37–66, for the influx, from England, 1802.

88. R.I.A. MS. 12.L.32, Journal of Kitty Wilmot for Apr. 1802; see B.L. Add. MS. 33108 fos. 256–8; P.R.O. F.O. 27/62/8; *H.M.C. Dropmore MSS.*, VII, xxv–xxvii; Thomas Holcroft, *Travels from Hamburg through Westphalia, Holland, and the Netherlands to Paris*, 2 vols. (London, 1804), I, 55, for correspondence from Paris, 1801–2.

89. For the various crises, see B.L. Add. MS. 33108 fos. 250–1, 35713 fos. 105–6, 35770 fos. 15–16; I.S.P.O. 620/49/90–2; and P.R.O.N.I. D.1748.

Introduction of Citizen Volpone & his Suite, at Paris — Vide The Moniteur & Cobbetts Letters

Plate 27. Introduction of Citizen Volpone (O'Connor introduces Fox to Bonaparte, 1802) (by Gillray, British Museum)

in Fort George. They were detained until June 1802, and even then refused leave to regulate their affairs in Ireland before their permanent banishment. Instead, they were shipped direct to Hamburg and deposited with that same lack of caution about their future behaviour which had characterized similar proceedings in 1799. By 1802, however, the authorities were more concerned to eradicate entirely the bad memory of the past few years.[90] O'Connor and Chambers travelled on to Antwerp and eventually to France. Russell, Dowling, Sweetman, Swiney, Cormick and Wilson accompanied Thomas Addis Emmet and his family to Amsterdam, where they were joined by Robert Emmet in August. After travelling on to Brussels, the party split up, MacNeven making his way to Switzerland, Dowling to Rotterdam, and Sweetman to Lyons. There was little sign that their political views had changed, except to accommodate a greater distrust of France, and Thomas Emmet soon abandoned his intention of sailing for America because of rumours that the war was to be renewed. 'If they should turn out to be well-founded,' he told MacNeven, 'our views would be, indeed, changed.'[91]

90. P.R.O. H.O. 28/27/296, 302, 316 and H.O. 28/28/89; also H.O. 100/104/209, 216 and 221.
91. Madden, *United Irishmen*, 3rd ser., III, 26–7, also 22–3 and 29. I.S.P.O. 620/12/142 and 146, letters of John Dunn and Robert Emmet, 29 Jul. and 7 Aug. 1802. See also M. MacDonagh, *The Viceroy's Postbag* (London, 1904), 259, for Hunter's account.

Of all the leaders it was Russell who was most determined to renew preparations for another rebellion. But he was also the most distrustful of French intentions and his own deep religiosity was particularly offended by the immorality of Bonaparte's regime. He found the prospect of French control in Ireland only fractionally less odious than that of England, and was determined to forestall any attempted takeover if the French were again invited to help in the country's liberation. In a series of letters to some Ulster friends, he lamented the 'usurpation of Bonaparte', but 'so far from conceiving the cause of Ireland lost or being wary of its pursuit', he claimed to be 'inflexibly bent on it'. For this reason he had chosen to stay in Europe 'to join anybody I can find in arms in support of their rights and that of mankind'. Russell was convinced that the Irish people were again ready to rise and he lamented having been denied permission to travel to Ireland to assess the situation. It seems certain that he would have preferred to win Irish independence without invoking French aid, and it may have been the influence of his more realistic comrades which tempered such overriding confidence in Ireland's ability to liberate herself and dictated another approach to the French.[92] At this stage, however, none of the released leaders who eventually made their way to Paris had any clear idea of how they would put their resolution into effect. That an attempted rebellion in Ireland and an associated outbreak in England should have occurred within the next eight months was the result of a strangely interlocking series of emotions and events, the products of a desire to secure French help for Ireland, whilst mitigating its harmful potential, and not a little of boredom and frustrated inactivity on the part of the exiles.

92. T.C.D. MS. 873/638–40, Russell's letters, Jun.–Jul. 1803.

CHAPTER NINE

1802–1803: Conspiracy to Rebellion: Despard and Emmet

'Emmet's Rebellion' and the 'Despard Conspiracy' are traditionally assumed to have been the work of fanatics: the one a final desperate attempt to secure Irish independence by a group of young, impatient United Irishmen who had lost faith in France; the other a plot by a broken ex-colonel, driven mad by official persecution; and both predestined to failure. A tenuous link between the two is generally recognized, though grossly underestimated because of the absence of synchronization. But as Despard's activities can only be understood in the light of later events in Ireland, so Emmet's story unfolds in London and France, for it was there, rather than in Ireland, that the rebellion was conceived and planned. The reality is far removed from the picture of tradition, and it can be shown that the United Irishmen of 1802–03 had departed less from their elders' determination to do nothing without the French than is generally assumed, that Despard and Emmet were calm, calculating leaders, and that Thomas Russell's reflection that their 'failure alone was surprising' was not simply the verdict of a devotee.[1]

I

In the years 1800–02, a state of virtual war existed between the upper and lower levels of English society, with nation-wide food rioting, intensified combination in illegal trade societies, an apparent revival of the United Englishmen, and the overall mischief-making of the United Irish Society. The authorities were convinced that these were all connected, but despite repeated efforts they failed to substantiate this conviction. In the past, suspicious actions on the part of known leaders would have triggered off the government's intelligence network and arrests would have opened new channels of information. But the United movement of this period was consciously unorganized and had few main leaders, apart from those in transit between Ireland and France. It was to have become fully operative only when the French landed in Ireland, and in the event no invasion took place.

1. T.C.D. MS. 873/642, Russell to Frank McCracken, Oct. 1803.

282

Whitehall thought it had discovered the mastermind of the movement in November 1802, when Colonel Despard was arrested in London with a group of suspected conspirators. But the arrests produced little more than tap-house tittle-tattle from a handful of labourers and soldiers who knew little of any overall movement, and a broken and isolated ex-colonel who was passionately determined not to divulge what little he did know. The Irish evidence shows, however, that to search for an organized conspiracy on the mainland would be to misunderstand the nature of United planning after 1799, which sought to keep formal organization to a minimum. The kind of commotion which occurred in England in these years was exactly what the United Irish leaders would have liked to produce when the French arrived. But they were not responsible for it, and it faded long before it could have been put to effective use.

The distress caused in England by the corn shortages of 1800–01 was extreme, and food riots were reported from all over the country. But it was the novel level of participation by the manufacturing classes and the undertones of treason which caused the government most anxiety. Government agents sent to investigate reports of subversion in the worst-affected area around Birmingham and Wolverhampton found that the disturbances were produced instead by genuine distress, and that their object was the traditional one of price-fixing.[2] The argument put forward by some historians that the rioters of these years possessed a degree of political sophistication lacking in those of earlier riot years is not entirely convincing. But it does throw additional light on the contribution of subversive movements to protest which was essentially economic in character.[3] The latest wave of combining among trades was particularly susceptible to such influences. Intensive combining occurred in almost every trade in the wake of the 1799 and 1800 Combination Acts. Government was concerned at the co-operation between such geographically separated groups as the Yorkshire croppers and the Wiltshire shearmen and papermakers, and at the strong resemblance of their organization to that of the United societies. Portland concluded in a letter to the Bolton

2. P.R.O. H.O. 42/55/223–8, A. Graham to King, 26 Dec. 1800; J. R. Dinwiddy, 'The "Black Lamp" in Yorkshire, 1801–1802', and J. L. Baxter and F. K. Donnelly, 'The Revolutionary "Underground" in the West Riding: Myth or Reality', *Past and Present*, 64 (Aug. 1974). 113–35, also their 'Sheffield and the English Revolutionary Tradition, 1791–1820', *International Review of Social History*, xx (1975), 398–423.

3. See in particular A. Booth, 'Food Riots in the North-West of England 1790–1801', *Past and Present*, 77 (Nov. 1977), 84–107; E. P. Thompson, 'The Moral Economy of the English Crowd', *Past and Present*, 50 (Feb. 1971), 128–9; and his *Making of the English Working Class*, 516. For the riots see also P.R.O. H.O. 42/51–5; J. Stevenson, 'Food Riots in England, 1792–1818', in *Popular Protest and Public Order*, ed. R. Quinault and J. Stevenson, (London, 1974), 33–74; J. Stevenson, 'Disturbances and Public Order in London, 1790–1821', (Oxford Univ. D. Phil. thesis, 1973), 78–89; R. A. E. Wells, 'Dearth and Distress in Yorkshire 1792–1802', *Borthwick Papers*, 52 (1977).

magistrate, the Rev. Thomas Bancroft (a zealous organizer of the intelligence network in the north) that ' . . . if nothing injurious to the safety of the Government is actually in contemplation, Associations so formed contain within themselves the means of being converted into a most dangerous instrument to disturb the public tranquillity.'[4] The monthly meetings held at Ryeton Moor outside Oldham, at Rivington Pike near Bolton, and similar gatherings near Sheffield and Manchester caused particular concern. But an entire squad of agents recruited to watch them, failed either to substantiate or remove government fears, and Bancroft wondered if the expense was justified by the pitiful returns in information.[5]

But Bancroft's agents had discovered some movement in which there were elements capable of treason, if properly mobilized. The Irish among the Manchester weavers and the Blackburn print-workers had been particularly forward in the organization of local trade disputes and made no secret of their expectation that something would be organized in England in support of another Irish rising. Moorhouse and Magee, two former United leaders in Stockport, were still active at the end of 1800. There were signs of continued communication between the United Irish in Ireland and Lancashire, and assurances of another Irish rising were periodically transmitted.[6] But despite some indiscriminate swearing-in using the old United oath, and incidents of old literature being dropped in sensitive areas, there was no overall attempt to organize surviving pockets of conspiracy. The two Lees, arrested in Stockport for administering such oaths, were admitted to have been 'so low in rank and attainments that they cannot be supposed to be primaries in a scheme of such extended mischief'. Although government took the precaution of tightening security at the arms depots in the region, on receipt of reports about a planned rising, Bancroft's tendency to dismiss such reports as mere bravado was more realistic.[7]

It is virtually impossible to prove or disprove the existence of some new conspiracy from the reports of the northern magistrates and their agents, and the collation of facts by Bancroft's over-zealous fellow magistrate, Colonel Ralph Fletcher, is particularly misleading. The mass meetings in the north reflected a return to active protest after the expiration of the 1795 Seditious Meetings Act and were designed to support the passage of the Weavers' Bill through parliament. But accounts of a secret movement develop-

4. Quoted in Aspinall, *Early Trade Unions*, 26, also 36–7.
5. P.R.O. H.O. 42/61/122–3, Bancroft to King, 9 Feb. 1801; see also H.O. 42/53–6, for reports on the meetings.
6. P.R.O. H.O. 42/53/297, 318–20, H.O. 42/61/122–3 and H.O. 42/62/302–3; also H.O. 100/100/107 for signs of continuing activity by the United Irishmen in Lancashire.
7. P.R.O. H.O. 42/53/355, H.O. 42/61/166–7, Bancroft's correspondence of Nov. 1800–Feb. 1801; and see H.O. 51/347–8, H.O. 42/53/428, H.O. 42/61/201–2 and H.O. 100/42/62/199–200 for the use of old handbills and oaths, Sept. 1800–Mar. 1801.

ing in Lancashire and Yorkshire describe one so remarkably like that adopted in Ireland in 1799 that one must accept the possibility of a similar attempt to re-organize old United strongholds on the mainland. Reports tell of a military organization, with the generals appointed by a London assembly, and committee-men or 'conductors' recruiting ten men each, these recruiting further members, and so on down through the grades until a brigade was formed. The old United oath had been dusted down and was being widely administered among the weavers, and if as yet there was no regular organization in the north of England, all the signs are that there was a demand for one, and a spontaneous revival of the old United movement to supply the need. Information on the involvement of former leaders such as Wardle, Magee, Moorhouse, Cheetham and Crome of Sheffield may simply reflect the official tendency to concentrate on old offenders. There is certainly an element of this in the 1801 reports. But their undoubted role in the attempt at re-organization in 1802 lends credence to the earlier reports.[8]

There is, however, little sign that the initiative for such a revival had come from the United leaders in Ireland. McCabe had passed through Manchester at the end of 1800 and again in July 1801, and given his later role in the promotion of the United movement on the mainland, it seems likely that he may have confided the United plans to some local leaders.[9] But if the United Irishmen had wished to extend their new organization into England at this stage, it is unlikely that so many members at its lower levels would have been in the secret. This would have been a negation of the strict secrecy which lay at the heart of its re-organization, and any sign of such on the mainland in 1801 was the product of freelance effort by the survivors of the old, rather than instructions from the leaders of the new, movement.

The release of the English state prisoners in March 1801 promised to provide the leadership so obviously desired by such survivors from the earlier movement, and was undoubtedly one of the factors contributing to the revival of disaffection that summer. Some members of the old committee for distributing relief to the prisoners organized a dinner at the *Green Dragon* in Fore Street, London, to celebrate their release. Notable among the organizers was the shoemaker Joseph Bacon, who had remained active in the underground movement since 1798. He was assisted by Robert Oliphant, Joseph Patten, Jasper Moore, John Nicholls and Michael Doyle, all alike ex-members of the London Corresponding Society, who were to figure prominently in the events leading up to the 'Despard Conspiracy'. Many of the released

8. P.R.O. H.O. 42/62/302–3 and 441–3, Fletcher's reports of 28 Jul. and 31 Aug. 1801; also H.O. 42/61/201–2, 222–3, 232, 461–4 for information on 'swearing-in', and Devon C.R.O. MS. 152M/C1801/O2132, Rev. Dr. Thomas Blackburne to Addington, 22 Mar. 1801.
9. For McCabe's journey see I.S.P.O. 620/49/111; T.C.D. MS. 873/767; and P.R.O. H.O. 100/94/242.

prisoners were unwilling to continue the political agitation. Their spirit had been broken by their rigorous confinement, and many emigrated to America. Despard had remained isolated from the others in prison and disappeared after his release, possibly to his family lands in Ireland. Others, particularly those involved in the United Englishmen, emerged in fighting spirit: Hodgson, Lemaitre, Galloway, Evans, Charles Pendrill, a bootmaker arrested in the 1798 purge and again in November 1800, and Wallis Eastburne, arrested in 1799 as one of the United Englishmen involved in the Clerkenwell meeting, resumed their former political activities. They were present at the celebratory dinner when Evans upbraided his friends for their inaction while the others were in prison. Powell, the informer, claimed that some decision was reached at the dinner to continue such meetings on a casual basis. This report followed an accusation of negligence by Sir Richard Ford, and may have been dressed up accordingly. But Powell's information had been essentially correct in the past and there is no reason to suspect him of outright falsehood. His reports on the renewed political activity of the released prisoners are substantiated by other sources and there are signs that a small group of London United men, which included Pendrill, did continue to meet at the *Green Dragon* 'to keep a set of persons united together that if occasion offered they might act with effect'.[10] All the surviving evidence, therefore, does suggest that the most hardened republicans had not been chastened by their imprisonment, and that they sought to revive the movement in both London and the provinces.

After the release of the prisoners in March, there was certainly a revival of that tendency in provincial disaffection to look to London for a lead, and Burdett's name figured prominently in such reported expectations. Burdett had actively campaigned to improve living conditions for the English state prisoners, and remained in contact with them after their release. His involvement may have gone no further than a continuing desire to relieve their distress. But there is much to support Ann Hone's suggestion that he may have been more deeply implicated in their political schemes, and his recommendation to the 'Friends of Liberty' to play upon the discontent of the soldiery, whilst falling short of firm proof of his collusion in conspiracy, would nevertheless have encouraged others to expect his support. The Home Office was excited at this latest prospect of implicating Burdett with treason, for other sources told of the disaffected's hopes of winning over the soldiers who had been disbanded on the signing of peace with France. But despite such reports that the disaffected were regrouping, even Powell could secure no substantial proof beyond an overwhelming feeling that 'the same spirit

10. P.R.O. P.C. 1/3528 and 3535, and H.O. 42/61/187–8, 484–5, various reports, particularly those of Powell and F.J. (almost certainly Jordan, the Fleet St. bookseller); also T.S. 11/121/332 for Pendrill.

exists and ... will soon rouse into action. Yet it certainly is inactive at present.'[11]

That it was so inactive at the end of 1801 owed much to the government's immediate purge of suspects. Amidst escalating reports of seditious meetings and swearing-in sessions in Lancashire, the authorities arrested the suspected leaders in Manchester and Bolton. But these seemed ignorant of any overall organization, and ultimately charges were only brought against a handful. In London warrants were issued against those who had attended the *Green Dragon* celebration (twenty-one in all). Nicholls, Patten, Doyle and Moore were arrested immediately; Oliphant was taken on 31 May and the remainder in the course of the summer. Ten were detained until November, under a new Suspension of Habeas Corpus Act which had been rushed through parliament in the wake of government revelations in another secret report.[12]

Although Addington's new government lacked conclusive evidence, ministers were convinced that the disaffected were re-organizing, and were genuinely concerned at the consequences of the expiration of Pitt's counter-subversive measures. To justify their continuation they were forced to resort to the old expedient of a secret parliamentary report and to disguise the lack of concrete evidence by the passage of a new measure, the Habeas Corpus Suspension Indemnity Bill, which among other things permitted magistrates to make arrests without having to reveal either the nature or the source of their information. The report of April 1801 testified more to government bewilderment at the revived disaffection than to any success in proving its existence. More than any of its predecessors, it was a transparent piece of government propaganda, devoid of that veneer of plausibility which Pitt's government had always taken pains to create. Whilst allowing for opposition exaggeration, it is difficult not to agree with their charge that when 'hard-pressed', ministers had 'hatched plots and found their best ally in the old plot bag'.[13] Throughout the war, government action had shown that it actually needed an element of treason in the country to justify emergency wartime legislation. Its reports were never fabrications, but the juxtaposition of facts and the careful placing of emphasis to produce the maximum effect was such that the exaggerated picture presented amounted to near falsification. The 1801 report was an undisguised attempt to justify emergency legislation, in this instance the renewal of martial law in Ireland, the Habeas Corpus Suspension Act and a new Indemnity Bill for England. The entire document is confused; and

---

11. P.R.O. P.C. 1/3535, Powell to Ford, 25 Dec. 1801; P.C. 1/3528, the examination of Oliphant, 2 Jun. 1801; J. A. Hone, 'Radicalism in London, 1796–1802: Convergences and Continuities', in *London in the Age of Reform*, ed. J. Stevenson (Oxford, 1977), 79–101.

12. P.R.O. H.O. 79/10, Portland to J. Shaw, 18 Apr. 1801; H.O. 42/61/232, 323–4 and 42/62/110–1, 537–8, for the Lancashire arrests.

13. *Parl. Hist.*, xxv, 1277, and 1275–1507 for the debates; *Reports from the Committees of the House of Commons*, x, 827–44, for the report.

Connacht houghers, benefit societies, workers' combinations, Spenceans, Corresponding Societies, old United Britons and new United Irishmen are lumped together indiscriminately and portrayed as operating under some mythical London executive. In the parliamentary debates which followed, the absence of plausible evidence was explained away by references to O'Connor, Coigley and the Maidstone trials as proof that a conspiracy might operate without leaving visible traces. But this revival of the Irish spectre rang false in view of the unusual state of tranquillity then prevailing in Ireland. Food shortages had quite a different effect in Ireland, where the line between subsistence and starvation was so thinly drawn that the all-consuming problem of survival tended to reduce the level of disturbances in times of dearth.

The 1801 report had been accurate in one sense, if inadvertently so. Its very confusion mirrored the confused state of English disaffection, in which central direction seemed non-existent. Evidence produced by later arrests was to show that long before the national leaders made any attempt to revive the revolutionary network, the Irish on the mainland and their English sympathisers were agitating for such a revival and 'itching with impatience' for action.[14] United leaders resident in England, or travelling through it, were convinced of the strength of popular support for revolution on the mainland and of their ability to tap it with the minimum of formal organization. Their followers could never understand how a rising could be organized independently of such a network, and by 1802 their impatience had reached such a pitch that they began to force the pace of the revived movement, causing it to veer dramatically from its post-1798 course of abandoning all open organization until the French arrived.

In London the arrival of the exiles from the 1798 rebellion intensified the immigrant community's sense of collective oppression. While nothing as formal as an Irish relief committee existed, those who had suffered in the United cause were quickly assimilated into London's close-knit Irish community, and were assisted through informal fund-raising activities. The colony's strength lay in the area from the Strand to Cheapside, Aldersgate, Finsbury and most of all in Spitalfields. It was to Spitalfields that Patrick Finney travelled in the summer of 1798, where his sufferings brought automatic assistance and quickly elevated him to a position of leadership among the United men resident there. Other prominent figures among the newly exiled were James Farrell, clerk in the mercantile house of Gordon and Murphy, Peter Finnerty, former editor of the *Press*, the Coughlin brothers, carpenters in Golden Lane near Aldersgate, and John MacNamara, who had been arrested with Finney in Dublin the previous year. From 1798

14. P.R.O. H.O. 42/61/484–5, report by 'F.J.', 8 Apr. 1801; also his report for 28 Dec. in P.C. 1/3535.

these men maintained contact with those United Irishmen in France and Ireland who were to engineer the 1803 Irish revolt, notably John Allen, William Hamilton, Thomas Russell, William Dowdall and William Putnam McCabe. Their activities in London differed only marginally from those of their predecessors, and old liaisons with the press world were maintained, particularly with the *Courier*, the *Traveller* and the *Albion*, and most of all with Fenwick. There is no proof that these press men knew of the more revolutionary motives of their associates. Outwardly these United men were simply radical reformers; but they did hope to feed information to a sympathetic press.[15] The real push for action, however, was no longer coming from the Irish student or artisan elite of Holborn or Lincoln's Inn Fields, but from the mass of working Irish in the riverside parishes and in the East End, an army of Irish disaffection mobilized by the events of 1798.

Despite their sense of bitterness at English inaction in 1798, the London Irish were nevertheless impatient to renew the connection in preparation for another attempt in Ireland. John Connell, a labourer, later told of a meeting in the summer of 1801 at the *Queen's Head* near St. Martins-le-Grand, at which cards were distributed to recruit into the new movement. John MacNamara and Charles Pendrill were there, and plans were put forward to send 'conductors' to meet the 'English Committee.' It was also proposed to send someone to Dublin 'for the purpose of encouraging the Business there.' Even this scrap of information raised considerable excitement in government circles: 'it was evidently attached to the Irish Branch of the United who were taken up at the Green Dragon,' wrote John King at the Home Office, 'of which Branch our informants could never give us any precise or distinct account'. Connell attended no further meetings until the following summer, but although other evidence suggests that no proper organization had materialized before the end of 1801, Connell's information does show that the London Irish were trying to push not only their English friends but also the Dublin leaders into adopting a more active role. By the time of Connell's return to the Cheapside meetings, some plan of action was under way and he was rebuked for his non-attendance.[16] The term 'conductor' to describe the co-ordinating agents, was also in general use in Ireland and in the English counties by 1802. But there was still no sign of imminent action, and by the closing months of 1802 the London supporters were becoming increasingly restless.

Their impatience was intensified by the knowledge that thousands of

---

15. I.S.P.O. 620/11/130/3 and 40, and *State Trials*, XXVI, 1019–34, for Finney; and see 620/12/143–5, 620/13/178/8, 620/18/14 (information of 18 May 1801), and P.R.O. H.O. 42/62/495 for the others.

16. See P.R.O. T.S. 11/121/332, and 333 for Connell's information and government reaction; also *State Trials*, XXVIII, 418.

demobilized and unemployed soldiers would soon flood the country, and
there seemed little preparation to capitalize on such potential discontent.
Powell's friend, the Fleet Street bookseller Thomas Jordan, had listened to
many Irishmen talking along such lines, and at one meeting of both Irish
and English attended by Moore and Patten, Moore had claimed that
'There never was a better opportunity than there was at this time if they
would but unite and put aside all fear, . . . If they wou'd stand forward now,
they would find plenty of friends for the generality of the people had an
opinion if they cou'd obtain peace things would be better, but they find things
very little the better: . . . and *when* the Sailors came to be paid off, and the
Soldiers disembodied, there will be no employment for them, that wou'd be
the time if any thing was to be done, but that would be of no use unless there
was some kind of correspondence.' He was sorry that the English had proved
such cowards in 1798, or their object would have been gained by then. But
he assured them that although Ireland was quiet, there was a new plan in
progress, stronger than before and certain of success.[17]

By 1802 many of the English leaders had withdrawn. Hodgson and Stuckey
had joined the latest exodus abroad, though Nicholls, Bacon and Pendrill of
the distribution committee remained active. As before, however, it was 'the
Irish Branch of the United' which took the leading role in the developments
on the mainland over the next months. Despard's reappearance in February
1802 requires some explanation; it can be found in the new impetus provided
by the release of the Irish state prisoners. The determination of those released
to Hamburg to recommence preparations for another rising was shared by
their lesser colleagues who had been allowed to remain in Ireland. William
Dowdall, one of the Fort George prisoners, recommenced his old activities
after his return to Belfast in January 1802. Despard had been in Ireland
until then, having to all intents abandoned his career in subversion, and his
Irish friends hoped that he would settle permanently in the country. Any plans
he may have had for the future, however, were abandoned after a meeting
with Dowdall, and by the end of February 1802 he was back in England
attempting to attract a better class of leader into the English movement. The
prospect of revenge for his recent victimization fed his new enthusiasm, and
he told a friend that many great men had joined who would soon be elevated
'at the Head of those who walked over him then'.[18]

There is no further information on Despard's activities during the next few
months, but there are signs that the Irish leaders hoped to revive activity on
the mainland during the summer. In March they sent a full account of
developments in Ireland to Lancashire and London. By April government

17. P.R.O. P.C. 1/3535, report by 'F.J.', 28 Dec. 1801.
18. P.R.O. T.S. 11/122/333, and H.O. 100/100/332 for Despard in Ireland; see I.S.P.O. 620/10/
120/2 and 121/2, and 620/12/143 for Dowdall.

was receiving reports that delegates were being sent from the provinces to London to form a national committee, and special efforts were made to seduce the battalions of guards recently brought to London from Chatham to protect the public buildings. The government was never able to discover the members of this national committee, though it is probable that, as in Ireland, it never reconvened after its initial formation. Certainly the only account received of a meeting of leaders in London suggests that the so-called national committee was little more than an intermediary meeting designed to brief inferior leaders, and that the top men never met in such a formalized body. The Leeds delegate who gave the information to Fletcher's agent was taken by Nicholls and Farrell to the meeting near Holborn. It was attended by delegates from the provinces, from the London United Irishmen and from the guards, each of whom submitted returns of the numbers expected to join. From the outset it became clear that the ardour of the soldiers would be difficult to control. The guards were eager to seize all the public buildings in London, including the Houses of Parliament when still in session. Other leaders shied away from the bloodshed implicit in such a plan and the proposal to capture the buildings was only accepted after considerable modification.[19]

The enthusiasm of the soldiers and of the working Irish now propelled the movement forward, as the pent-up frustration of four years was suddenly released. The activities of John Hayes, a journeyman leather-breeches maker, typified the holiday atmosphere which prevailed in London's Irish community, and the tendency to revolutionary freelancing which it produced. Hayes accosted Daniel Krantz of the Swiss Guards in the *Star* near Piccadilly, and questioned him about the Irish rebellion. Krantz feigned sympathy, and Hayes promised to swear him into the movement that evening. When Krantz arrived at Hayes's lodgings in Lancaster Court, he found him in a drunken stupor after his recruiting activities of the morning. He told Krantz that he had been at a number of taverns 'making soldiers and sailors all morning' and that so many guards had been sworn-in that the attack on the Tower planned for the following Sunday would succeed without a struggle.[20] Such lack of caution and excitement at the prospect of renewed action was typical of the London movement in 1802, and proved virtually impossible to contain. It was that same impatience and lack of caution which was to seal the fate of the journeyman carpenter John Woods, the shoemaker John Francis, and all with whom they came in contact, notably Despard. It was the swearing-in activities of Woods and Francis which first attracted government attention, when Thomas Windsor, a soldier in the first regiment of foot

19. P.R.O. H.O. 42/65, Benson's and Fletcher's reports of Mar.–Jul. 1802; also *State Trials*, XXVIII, 392–423, for the role of the guards.
20. P.R.O. T.S. 11/127/333, declaration of Daniel Krantz, Aug. 1802.

guards, reported their attempt to enlist him into a new United Irish conspiracy. Windsor was encouraged to join the movement as an informer, and the train of events which was to produce the 'Despard Conspiracy' was set in motion.[21]

In the provinces the activities of the workers' combinations had taken a turn for the worse. Reports of military drilling and of a new militancy in the West Riding of Yorkshire were sufficiently alarming to entice a sceptical Earl Fitzwilliam, its Lord Lieutenant, into the north 'to put an end to the sort of conspiracy, which, I fear, does exist, in a greater or lesser degree, I mean, the true Jacobinical sort of conspiracy'.[22] Fitzwilliam's scepticism was soon revived when he discovered the paucity of tangible evidence for such claims. The famous case of Lee and Ronkesley some months later did suggest treasonable influences in the area. They were members of a committee which used the United English oath and claimed to be arming for an expected rising.[23] But no proof has ever been put forward to show that they were responsible for the greater militancy of the Yorkshire combinations at the time, and until such proof can be found we must assume that such local pockets were survivals from a former period rather than an element in the 1802 revival. That they were any the less dangerous, however, is doubtful. United plans envisaged the application of strong central leadership to harness such disaffection when the French landed. Since the event designed to produce such coherence never materialized, the existence and strength of such groups remain clouded in obscurity. Lancashire, as usual, is a case apart, and in 1802 the United leaders still looked to it as their main area of strength outside Ireland. But its organization proved sluggish, and in July McCabe and Dowdall expressed their dissatisfaction to the Manchester leaders when they passed through the county en route for London and France.[24]

In the event Dowdall did not accompany McCabe to France. Had the situation in England caused enough anxiety to alter the nature of their plans? Certainly the supporters in London were getting out of hand and threatening to disrupt the entire plan of suspending open activity until the French arrived. By August they were arguing that 'they must begin, the soldiers would wait no longer'.[25] In the context of overall United plans any immediate action was of course out of the question. It was at this stage, in September, when the impatience of the London followers required taming, that Despard reappeared on the London scene. Given the stalling tactics adopted by him thereafter, despite the attempts of Windsor to draw him on

---

21. For Windsor's information see P.R.O. H.O. 42/66 and T.S. 11/121/332.
22. Quoted in Aspinall, *Early English Trade Unions*, 6; also Fitzwilliam's correspondence for Jun.–Sept. 1802 in P.R.O. H.O. 42/65 and 66.
23. See Elliott, 'The "Despard Conspiracy" Reconsidered', 54–5.
24. P.R.O. H.O. 42/65, Fletcher to King, 31 Jul. 1802.
25. P.R.O. T.S. 11/121/332, the examination of John Connell, 10 Dec. 1802.

the question of direct action, it seems likely that his reappearance was at the request of Dowdall. More than anyone else, Despard might have succeeded in restraining the impatient soldiers because of his popular standing and his military experience. A premature outbreak in London was the last thing Dowdall wanted, for he had just received an important letter from Phil Long, one of the Dublin leaders who had recently joined McCabe at Rouen, which almost certainly told of the exiles' belief that war was about to be renewed, of their growing distrust of Bonaparte and of their determination to pre-empt a possible conquest of their country by starting preparations for another Irish rising. This was at the end of August. Shortly afterwards Robert Emmet left France for Ireland and Dowdall, still in London when the letter arrived, also returned.[26]

The English government too was getting wind of this restiveness among the disaffected, but scarcely knew whether to credit reports of a new plot in which the obvious leaders seemed unwilling to participate. 'What is the report I hear everywhere from our friends of an attack that was to have been made on the Tower, the Bank and the Treasury on Monday the 6th Inst.?' wrote Sir Richard Ford to his secret agent John Moody on 21 September. 'I do not much credit it, and I have heard from Citizens that there was nothing in it but idle talk and boasting, but others say it really was to have happ'd, but it went off by quite an accident—pray give me your opinion—they tell me Blythe, Eastburne, Nicholls, Farrel and Despard are the leaders . . . but that the wiser part will have nothing to do with it . . .' Ford suspected correctly that 'the lower class have some separate game playing, which you and your friends are kept in ignorance of', and his correspondence with Moody shows that the government was much closer than it imagined to the truth about the renewed agitation.[27]

The authorities were baffled at Despard's reappearance on the London scene and at the places he began to frequent, and attributed his patronage of working-mens' pubs in Newington, Hatton Garden, Finsbury, Tower Hill and Lambeth to mental derangement. His actions were not so very unusual in the circumstances. The United movement possessed little in the way of liaising machinery between its fluid leadership and its potential or actual supporters, and when the impetuosity of one section threatened to reveal the whole plan at such a crucial stage, extraordinary measures had to be taken. Despard did not act as indiscreetly as suggested in the evidence of Windsor, much of which appears to have been pure fabrication. Rather he operated from only a few public houses in areas of proven sympathy, taking care to speak with only those whose principles he had verified. All the evidence

26. I.S.P.O. 620/11/138/4, the examination of Phil Long, 18 Aug. 1803; also 620/12/143, 148 and 620/13/169/5 for Dowdall's movements.
27. See P.R.O. P.C. 1/3117 for the correspondence between Moody and Ford.

Plate 28. Colonel
Despard (National
Library of Ireland)

suggests that he had come to subdue rather than to incite the followers.
Windsor's attempts to provoke him into uttering compromising statements
failed completely, and the government would have had difficulty constructing
any case against him without Windsor's embellishments. In September
Despard had successfully contained a move to organize some kind of commotion on the day of St. Bartholomew's Fair, and when asked about the
timing of the rising he had replied that nothing could be attempted until
word had arrived from France. He answered queries about the absence of
any formal organization by pointing to the need for secrecy, and when
pressed on 16 November to name a day for the rising, he disarmed his in-
quisitors by convening another meeting on the 23rd to discuss the matter.
The authorities claimed that this was the date set for the conspiracy to capture
the public buildings and to assassinate the King on his way to open the new
parliamentary session. There is no evidence to support such a claim, and even
Despard's accusers admitted that he had 'interfered in restraint of the too

great precipitation of his confederates' and had rejected 'some very extra-vagant projects which they put forward'.[28]

By this stage plans for some form of direct action in London had been agreed upon and Dowdall was full of them when he returned to Dublin in September 1802. The outbreak in London was expected to spark off a larger movement in the provinces. But the formation of an overall strategy had only just begun, and there were no immediate plans for its implementation. In October Finney had joined Dowdall in Dublin and returned almost imme-diately to Manchester and London with news of the Irish plans.[29] The inten-tion seems to have been to draw together all the strings of the loose movement which had survived since 1798, though there is nothing to suggest any plan for imminent action, and the nascent conspiracy received a rude shock when Despard and about thirty others were arrested at the *Oakley Arms* in Lambeth on the night of 16 November. Further arrests followed elsewhere in London. The casual nature of the meetings at the *Oakley Arms* and the other alehouses visited by Despard scarcely supports the official claim that some dastardly conspiracy was about to erupt. The landlord of the *Oakley Arms* testified that no-one seeking admission to the group of reputed conspirators drinking upstairs was ever refused. Few of those arrested on the night of 16 November had any idea that they were involved in anything illegal. Thomas Philips, a plasterer, was one of the few to experience any unease, and he gave a false name on the assumption that the object of the raid was to enforce a paternity claim which had been filed against him. A United constitution was found on Philips, but it was the only seditious evidence discovered that evening. Nothing was found on Despard, and his own insolent indignation at being so disturbed suggests that he felt in no danger. Only one of those arrested was in regi-mentals, though soldiers were supposed to have played a dominant role in the forthcoming attack. Even he seems to have joined the group drinking upstairs quite by accident, the barmaid having told him that it was a 'free and easy' where he might hear of work. The remainder were a motley collection of labourers, journeymen carpenters and hatters. Many were Irish, but of those arrested, sufficient evidence could be found to detain only a handful.[30]

Of these, seven, including Despard and MacNamara, were condemned and executed at Newgate on 21 February 1803. But the evidence against them

---

28. *State Trials*, xxviii, 373, 414; also P.R.O. T.S. 11/121/332–3 and P.C. 1/3552, the examinations of Connell and William Francis, and Windsor's attempts to draw Despard.

29. I.S.P.O. 620/67/33 and P.R.O. H.O. 42/70, Fletcher's information of 8 Apr. 1803; P.R.O. T.S. 11/121/332, Windsor's examination; Madden, *United Irishmen*, 3rd. ser., iii, 29–30, 90–141. See also *State Trials*, xxviii, 427.

30. P.R.O. P.C. 1/3552 and 3553, examination of those arrested at the *Oakley Arms*, and H.O. 42/70, Graham's petition.

had been so flimsy and so suspect that in the interval between the trials on 7–8 February and the executions, government moved heaven and earth to secure confessions from the condemned men. Several were very frightened and penitent for their wayward past and would almost certainly have divulged any information had they known more. They did know that some kind of action was planned and were willing participants in some form of illegal activity, but they were very subordinate conspirators. Nicholls and Pendrill were later arrested, but no proof was found against them, and they were released. Several others active in the London preparations, Finney, Farrell, Finnerty, John Donavan and Frederick Cline, had fled to Ireland on news of Despard's arrest, and were to play on active part in the preparations for 'Emmet's Rebellion'.[31]

Ministers had learnt nothing new about the English movement from Despard's trial. Indeed, their decision to make an example of him, despite the insufficient nature of the evidence, threatened to actually increase support for the movement in which he had been involved. Burdett's campaign against his treatment during his earlier imprisonment had successfully created the image of Despard as the victim of official tyranny. The government had not deliberately trumped up a case against Despard. The obvious restlessness of the Irish in the metropolis was causing much concern, and the lack of clear information only intensified the government's feeling of imminent danger. The multitudes of Irish attending Sunday hurling matches in Tothill Fields were suspected as a build-up to the attack supposedly planned for 23 November, and the Home Office felt that such a conspiracy should be forestalled immediately, even at the expense of forfeiting further information from more patient surveillance.[32] But Despard's trial and execution in the face of the Jury's recommendation to mercy, and on the evidence of disreputable informers and approvers, was popularly regarded as another episode in the saga of government persecution of an honourable man. The crowds which started to assemble outside Newgate on the eve of his execution had quite obviously come out of sympathy rather than vulgar curiosity. They witnessed the execution in respectful silence, and many were heard to mutter their disgust at 'these poor men' being 'murdered'. The authorities had found it virtually impossible to secure an executioner willing to carry out the sentences. The Worship Street magistrates were ordered to remain in their offices overnight, and extra troops were drafted into the area in anticipation of riots.

---

31. See P.R.O. H.O. 100/112/335–7, 100/113/101, 103, 135–41 and I.S.P.O. 620/11/130/3, 39–40 for accounts of Finney, etc. See P.R.O. H.O. 42/70, and P.C. 1/3117, for attempts to secure last-minute confessions from the prisoners.
32. See P.R.O. T.S. 11/906/3099; H.O. 42/70; H.O. 100/119/112; P.C. 1/3553; and the *Sun*, 20 Feb. 1802, for reactions in the country to the execution, and H.O. 42/66 for government fears before the arrests.

In the provinces too the trial and conviction had uncovered a wealth of sympathy for Despard. Lancashire and Nottingham in particular were reported to have contributed liberally to the costs of his defence. John Emblin, one of the chief prosecution witnesses, was burnt in effigy, and printed handbills of Despard's dying speech were eagerly sought throughout the country. Much of the sympathy was for the man rather than the cause; but it was examples such as this, which gave the impression that popular figures of higher social status were at the head of the 'conspiracy' and which attracted recruits, and government had inadvertently substantiated such beliefs by the conscious publicity given to the trials. The lesson of Jackson had obviously never been learnt.

The executions did little to stop the progress of United preparations. Indeed, for the United men on the Continent and in Ireland, the revelations at the trial came as a timely stimulant to flagging spirits. Ministers had simply brushed the perimeter of the conspiracy with the arrests of November 1802. A conspiracy did exist, but it was neither of the dimensions nor in such an advanced stage as suggested at the trials. An attempt was being made to revive United support in England; but the Irish leaders had a poor opinion of English mettle and the activities on the mainland were to be of a diversionary nature only.[33] That there were indigenous pockets of militancy which hoped for some national lead is undeniable. But there is little justification for reading a national conspiracy back to the agitation of 1801–02 from the limited revelations of the Despard incident. An Irish rebellion or a French landing might have acted as a cohesive for such inchoate elements. 'Emmet's Rebellion', however, produced no reaction on the English side; possibly because the rebellion itself was premature. But it seems likely that the United Irishmen had miscalculated on the revolutionary content of English protest and more particularly on the ability of England's Irish population to act with the minimum of central direction. We may never know the true dimensions of the mainland movement. It did exist, but was subordinate to the main plan of an Irish rebellion and a French landing, which in turn were to act as signals for the English diversion. In the event those signals were never given, and Emmet's attempt was too insignificant to qualify as one.

II

At the time of Despard's arrest, Ireland seemed more peaceful than at any time in the past two years. Miles Byrne and several other fugitive United

33. See A.A.E. Corr. Pol. Ang. 601 fos. 43–6, for the opinions of the Irish exiles in France; also P.R.O. H.O. 100/112/158–72, and Hants. C.R.O. 38M49/5/31 for the effects on Ireland of Despard's arrest.

leaders had been working quietly in the Dublin building trade since the
rebellion, having to all intents abandoned their rebel careers.[34] Even Defenderism seemed dead, and despite the alarmism of some magistrates, investigations
proved that disturbances in Limerick and Tipperary were purely agrarian in
character. If the 'Despard Conspiracy' was to have been part of a wider
attempt in November 1802, there was certainly no sign of it in Ireland. But
something was afoot, and there were signs of leaders regrouping from mid-
summer 1803 onwards. Rumours that Dwyer was giving up hope and planned
to disband his men were soon dispelled, and in June the Irish government
was told that he had received a letter thought to have come from France,
assuring him that the United movement was reforming and that they expected
French assistance. The following month McCabe and Dowdall travelled
to England on their way to France, and by the close of that year the authorities
were concerned about signs that many banished rebel leaders were returning.[35]
The impatience of the supporters in England played some part in promoting
the renewed activity, but behind both lay the expectation of another French
invasion on the renewal of war.

France's attitude towards British disaffection during the peace period was
ambivalent. Lewis Goldsmith, then editor of the English language *Argus*,
printed in Paris under French auspices, later claimed that Despard had
been sponsored by Colonel Beauvoisin, a French agent in London, and that
his arrest and trial was an embarrassment to the Consulate. Beauvoisin did
undertake a secret mission to London at the time, and a French agent was
reported to have travelled through the most disturbed areas of Lancashire;
and although Goldsmith's account is grossly exaggerated, France's continued
sponsorship of internal disaffection in Britain is undeniable.[36] Bonaparte
was furious at the sanctuary which England continued to give to France's
enemies, and Whitworth, her ambassador in Paris, warned the London
government of the seriousness with which he viewed the scurrilous attacks
made by them in the British press. Whitehall was in an impossible position.
The show trial of Peltier for such writings in February 1803, and the arrests of
several French conspirators in London, had failed to satisfy the First Consul's
more sweeping demands for the ejection of the royalists altogether, and had
caused a howl of protest in England at such apparent pandering to the French
dictator. As long as England continued to prevaricate on the *émigré* issue, it
was unlikely that Bonaparte would totally abandon the United Irishmen,
and although Talleyrand indignantly denied England's accusations of such

34. Byrne, *Memoirs*, 1, 241–8; and see I.S.P.O. S.O.C. 1025 and Hants. C.R.O. 38M49/5/3 and
31 for the state of the country.
35. I.S.P.O. S.O.C. 1021/1; and 620/62/60 on Dwyer.
36. L. Goldsmith, *The Secret History of the Cabinet of Bonaparte*, 5th edn. (London, 1811), 253;
Correspondance de Napoléon 1ᵉʳ, VIII, 6475; Madden, *United Irishmen*, 3rd ser., III, 28–9, 32–3.

continued support, all the evidence suggests that some kind of official French encouragement did lie behind the renewal of United activity at the close of 1802.[37]

In October 1802 Talleyrand had asked an old hand at French undercover activities abroad, Pierre Claude 'Marquis' de Poterat, to find means of supporting the disaffected Irish, without giving rise to any accusations that the Consulate was continuing the war against England by subversive means. Poterat consulted with MacNeven and over the next few months submitted a succession of memoranda on Ireland based on his consultations. MacNeven made it clear that the Irish would no longer accept the role of mischief-makers to distract English attention, and whilst he agreed that no formal negotiations could take place in time of peace, he assured Poterat that ultimately they would not be satisfied with 'des demies mesures' or any enterprise 'conduite en tatonnant'. France had failed so often to fulfil her promises in the past that British propaganda depicting France as using Ireland for her own ends was eroding popular support there, and he felt 'that it would be difficult to bring the people out again unless their suspicions could be dispelled by the implementation of the promises which had been made to them'.[38] Thomas Addis Emmet did not fully approve of such negotiations, but agreed that 'if they look to war, they will scarcely treat us with neglect', and that the talks might at least provide some insight into current French thinking.[39] This *ménage à trois* situation, with Poterat as intermediary between Talleyrand and MacNeven, is baffling. Although Poterat had considerable experience of discussions with foreign revolutionaries, he was suspected of having betrayed information to the royalists in 1796.[40] His employment with the Consulate in 1802 might have been an indirect means of warning England to pay more attention to *émigré* activities, since he might have been expected to reveal information on the talks with the Irish. Another possible explanation is that his unofficial status might have supplied the Consulate with a means of wriggling out of accusations about French sponsorship of foreign revolution, as Poterat himself had suggested. Ultimately the consultations had no immediate sequel, and MacNeven left France for Brussels in February 1803. But since negotiations with the United Irishmen

---

37. *H.M.C. Dropmore MSS.* VII, xxviii; *State Trials*, XXIX, 529–620. See A.A.E. Corr. Pol. Ang. 597 fo. 455; 600 fos. 118, 139–40, 266; Mem. et Doc. Fonds France 1774 fos. 18–19; A.N. AF IV 1672 plaq. 1 pᶜᵉ 115; and Aulard, *Paris sous le Consulat*, II, 28, 429 and III, 197, 149, for French anger at *émigré* intrigues.

38. A.A.E. Corr. Pol. Ang. 601 fos. 81–4, second memoir on Ireland, 17 Feb. 1803; see also 596 fos. 190–310, 601 fos. 42–6 and 60 for Poterat's memoranda on Ireland.

39. Madden, *United Irishmen*, 3rd ser., III, 23.

40. For Poterat's earlier mission see P.R.O. F.O. 74/18/36; A.H.G. B¹¹ 1, doss. for July 1796; Biro, *The German Policy of Revolutionary France*, I, 456–62, 515–21, 551–8, 568–83; and Palmer, *The Age of Democratic Revolution*, II, 269–73.

were officially re-opened as soon as war started again, the overtures to MacNeven cannot be entirely dismissed as a propaganda exercise.

The Irish exiles had continued to receive unofficial assurances from sympathetic generals like Humbert, MacSheehy and Harty. But rumours of another Irish expedition, under the guise of one for Louisiana, do appear to have originated from official sources. To protect the Consulate from being implicated, a staged disgrace of Humbert was to have been followed by his assumption of the command of the expedition, ostensibly as an independent venture. The naval preparations in the western ports were real enough, and although in November the expedition eventually sailed for the West Indies, the Irish government remained convinced that it had originally been intended for Ireland. Desbrière denies any suggestion that Bonaparte made offensive preparations against England during the peace, and there certainly is no sign that he ever intended seriously sending a force to Ireland.[41] But the entire episode resembles that involving Poterat too closely to be dismissed out of hand. Both Poterat and Humbert were in bad odour with the Consulate and could have been disowned if necessary. On the other hand, their demagogic characters could be relied upon to divulge information and embellish rumours and half-truths to the parties for whom they were destined, and Humbert's claims certainly encouraged the United Irish exiles to regroup in the closing months of 1802.

The exiles needed little encouragement to renew preparations. The Louisiana affair had intensified their distrust of Bonaparte, and Russell remarked cynically that as the Polish exiles had been packed off to the West Indies, Bonaparte was more likely to use the Irish as mercenaries than to send them on board an expedition to Ireland.[42] This did not, however, reduce his faith in the French generally, and just as the republican generals hoped that a successful attempt on Ireland would revive their fortunes, so the United Irishmen felt that their involvement might mitigate the worst effects of Bonapartist intervention. But if they encouraged their friends at home to expect the French when war was renewed, they also took precautions to forestall a French takeover of Ireland, and the uncomfortable alliance of need and apprehension produced those conflicting statements and actions which have made 'Emmet's Rebellion' such a riddle.

As the renewal of war became imminent, the United Irishmen re-opened communications with the Consulate. But they were reluctant to admit their dependence on French help, and many almost preferred to risk a rebellion unaided rather than suffer Bonapartist domination after a successful in-

---

41. Desbrière, *Projets et Tentatives*, III, 15, and *Diary and Correspondence of Lord Colchester*, I, 445; see B.L. Add. MS. 35770 fos. 142–3, 168–9; I.S.P.O. 620/13/177/11; H.O. 100/112/361 and 100/122/220–3, for Humbert and the rumoured Irish expedition.
42. See the enclosures in P.R.O. H.O. 100/114/113–23 and 100/122/220–3.

Plate 29. Robert Emmet (by Cruikshank for Maxwell, *Irish Rebellion*)

vasion. Although they had clung steadfastly to their decision never again
to risk a rising until the French had actually proved themselves victorious
in Ireland, their demand for only 10,000 troops in 1803 was surprisingly
low. Ignorance about the potential strength at home partially explains such
an inadequate estimate, but it was primarily the result of fears about French
intentions. They also made a number of recommendations designed to further
dilute French influence in Ireland. They proposed recruiting for the expedi-
tionary force among Spain's foreign legions, providing all the supplies in
Ireland, and paying the cost of the expedition in full, and they were quite
explicit about their conception of such assistance as a loan, rather than a gift
which might create ties of obligation. In addition, they started to make their
own plans to prevent a French take-over. Most believed that Bonaparte
would look on Ireland as a mere side-show to the main attack on England,
and that they might be able to take advantage of the withdrawal of crown
forces to capture Dublin, establish a provisional government, and thus place
themselves in a position to negotiate with the French when they eventually
arrived.[43]

Contrary to general opinion, however, the return of Robert Emmet to
Ireland in October 1802 did not announce the beginning of those preparations.
Emmet had returned partly for family reasons, partly as a messenger to convey
news from France. Since he was one of the few leaders against whom there was
no charge in Ireland, he was the natural choice as courier, and he lived a
normal, public life until the following March. Only in January 1803, when
Hamilton returned from France, was there any clear indication that the
United exiles had decided to stage another rising as soon as war was renewed.
Hamilton had been instructed to gauge the degree of support for another
rising and to secure adequate financial assistance. Emmet supplied the
small bequest recently inherited from his father; Hamilton tried to raise
some capital on his own property; Phil Long, a prominent Dublin merchant,
contributed handsomely, and there was talk of assistance from other leading
businessmen in Dublin.[44]

Hamilton's mission had taken place against a backdrop of increasing
agrarian troubles in the south-west of Ireland. Official investigations found
them completely apolitical in character.[45] But the United Irishmen mis-
interpreted their significance, and a feeling that Ireland was after all more
prepared to fight for its own liberation than they had imagined clouded their

43. Madden, *United Irishmen*, 3rd ser., III, 92, 116; Desbrière, *Projets et Tentatives*, III, 317–22.
44. *Diary and Correspondence of Lord Colchester*, I, 447–8; T.C.D. MS. 873/654, notes on Russell
and Emmet; I.S.P.O. 620/11/138/40, for an account of Hamilton's return; see also Madden,
The Life and Times of Robert Emmet (Dublin 1847), 53, 370, on their finances.
45. For the troubles in Munster see I.S.P.O. S.O.C. 1025/29; P.R.O. H.O. 100/112/13–18,
42–3; Hants. C.R.O. 38M49/1/7; and MacDonagh, *Viceroy's Postbag*, 302.

conviction that French help was still the essential prerequisite. Reports of popular support for another French invasion were as rife as they had been for the last five years, but there was little to justify the view that the people would also support another rising without the French. Nevertheless, Hamilton returned to France in February in buoyant spirits, convinced that Ireland was not as dependent on French aid as they had believed, and with sufficient financial support to mount preparations for another rising.

A flurry of excited activity followed his return. Hamilton himself travelled to Brussels to persuade MacNeven and Thomas Addis Emmet to come to France and replace those leaders about to leave for Ireland. He and McCabe then began recruiting from among the Paris exiles. Russell acted as paymaster and McCabe and Swiney, in Rouen and le Havre respectively, made the necessary preparations for the next stage of their journey home. Hamilton, Michael Quigley and Brian McDermot, a recent migrant to France, were the first to reach Dublin on 5 March. Two days later Robert Emmet called on them at their hotel in Capel Street. Emmet was particularly concerned to discover the state of opinion in Kildare, the home county of Quigley and McDermot, and they were sent there the following day on a fact-finding mission with Thomas Wylde and John Mahony, two Kildaremen working in Dublin. Mahony and Wylde then conducted similar missions into Dublin and Wexford counties. Quigley returned after a few days with assurances that their supporters in Kildare would be ready to turn out at two days notice, thereby contributing to the cumulative impression that the people would rise spontaneously.[46]

It was only in that month that the Castle started to receive reports of renewed activity among the disaffected. The leaders adhered to the framework of the 1799 plan, and no formal organization was ever re-established. Quigley had simply been instructed to contact a few acquaintances. But such narrow organizational confines meant that the vision of widespread support was created solely by the enthusiasm of the converted. Emmet told Miles Byrne that their object was to become acquainted 'with all those who had escaped in the war of '98, and who continued still to enjoy the confidence of the people'.[47] It was along such lines that plans for the rising progressed. Leaders were hand-picked, mostly from a lower social grouping than those who had taken the lead in 1798, tradesmen who would have the confidence of the ordinary people and who could be trusted to bring groups of workmen

---

46. I.S.P.O. 620/11/130/44 and 135, statements of Thomas Frayne and Michael Quigley; 620/14/194, statement of charges against the prisoners in Kilmainham; 620/64/2, 7–9, and S.O.C. 1025/22, reports from Sir F. Aylmer and Wogan Browne, Jul. 1803. See also T. A. Emmet, *Ireland Under English Rule*, 2 vols. (New York, 1903), II, 279 and 285, for Hamilton in Brussels.
47. Byrne, *Memoirs*, I, 249; I.S.P.O. 620/11/160/1, 620/64/7; S.O.C. 1025/22; and Hants. C.R.O. 38M49/5/31, for information received by the government Mar.–Apr. 1803.

together from Dublin and its environs at the prescribed time. Notable among
this class was James Hope, who since 1798 had operated as a linen weaver
in the Coombe area of Dublin. He was already highly thought of by his peers
in the Liberty, that area of Dublin adjacent to the Castle, and was crucial to
the United Irishmen's plan of capturing the seat of government. Another
was Mathew Doyle, one of the '98 leaders in the Wicklow rising, now commissioned to organize his countrymen working in Dublin City. Byrne, Doyle
and Hope were typical of those former '98 men who had drifted to the anony-
mity of the capital through fear of Orange reprisals at home. In them the
United Irishmen possessed the nucleus of a national leadership with ready
contacts in the most important counties, and Emmet estimated that nineteen
counties could be organized in this manner. The risings in the counties were
to follow that in Dublin, and provincial preparations took second place to those
in the metropolis.

By March, Emmet had left his family home in Milltown for the house of
Mrs. Palmer at Harold's Cross, and the United leaders had started to purchase
a number of buildings in the city for use as arms' depots. McCabe had suggested a plan for taking Dublin by purchasing and firing a number of houses to
confuse the military, and it was a variation of this plan which was eventually
adopted. Depots were established in Thomas Street, Patrick Street, Marshalsea Lane, Winetavern Street and Smithfield, and smaller supplies of arms were
deposited adjacent to the public buildings which were to be attacked. In
the event, insufficient funds confined the preparations to the first three depots
only. They were manned constantly by a small core of faithful adherents,
who emerged only for essential supplies, and only at night-time. Quigley and
another '98 man, the carpenter Henry Howley, took charge of the principal
depot in Thomas Street. The area was inhabited by the Kildaremen in the
city in whom Emmet placed most confidence. Not more than twelve men
entered the depot in the four months of its operation. All the wood for the
pikes was taken from Edward Kennedy's timber yard by his brother-in-law
Miles Byrne, and Byrne also secured a reliable gunsmith. From March till
July 1803 these preparations proceeded unobtrusively inside the depots and
not more than thirty to forty men were ever in possession of the secret. At the
outset, Michael Dwyer was called to Dublin for consultations. Dwyer was
willing to bring his men forward only if Dublin rose first and was successful;
but he would never again be the first to take the field. In the following months
Emmet maintained contact with Dwyer, and his men were to assist in the
capture of Dublin. But Dwyer's caution was more representative of opinion
in the country than the glowing reports brought back by Quigley and should
have warned the leaders against any premature action.

It was in April that Thomas Russell returned from France. Many considered
his return injudicious at such an early stage of the preparations. They could
ill-afford the expense of his passage, and as one of the main state prisoners after

1798 he was bound to attract attention. Emmet took a house in Butterfield Lane, from which he, Russell, Dowdall and Hamilton directed the preparations for the rising. A meeting of about thirty of the Dublin leaders was called at the house to hear Russell's report from France. It was scarcely encouraging, for Russell offered little prospect of an imminent invasion, and he seemed more concerned about gaining agreement for his own opinion that the people of the North needed no French help to rise in force, and that 'the Irish people should begin at once and free themselves'. Those assembled were surprised at Russell's statements, for it was common knowledge that opinion in the North had considerably changed since 1798. Even Emmet was bemused by Russell's enthusiasm; but they considered his claim sufficiently important to despatch Hope and Michael Berney north to investigate. They returned a fortnight later with more encouraging news than might have been expected. Like the Wicklow men, those with whom they had spoken had said they would come forward if the rebels succeeded in capturing Dublin, and word of Russell's participation had aroused particular enthusiasm.[48]

The plan of using hand-picked leaders to rouse the counties seemed sound enough; the absence of local leaders had been one of the main causes for the collapse of the 1798 rebellion. In the first months of the preparations there was good reason to believe that a core of leaders could be found in key counties bordering Dublin from among those '98 men who had 'kept their pikes for another day', as Duckett claimed, and who were eager to support any new attempt. Michael Dourly in Kildare was representative of this dormant leadership which Emmet believed to exist. Through the winter months of 1802–03 he had received word of renewed preparations; by April he was preparing seriously for another turn-out, and in July he had marched with his men to Dublin to join the rising.[49]

But surprise was considered the rebels' main weapon, and apart from Kildare and Wicklow there was little attempt to maintain contact with the other counties. The leaders had good reason to feel proud of the secrecy they had preserved in Dublin. No suspicion had been aroused by the vast quantities of wood being moved into the depots, for care had been taken to employ only recognized tradesmen in the movement of supplies. But Emmet realized that such preparations could not be concealed for long. Russell's eagerness to start without the French was purely personal, and at this stage Emmet showed no desire to act independently. He merely wished to be ready to secure Dublin for the Irish when news arrived that the French had landed. Pat Gallagher, a Dublin shopkeeper, was accordingly sent to Paris to tell Thomas Addis Emmet

48. See I.S.P.O. 620/11/130/44, statement of Thomas Frayne; P.R.O. H.O. 100/114/113 for Russell's return; and Byrne, *Memoirs*, I, 265–8 for the meeting and the mission to Ulster.
49. I.S.P.O. 620/11/138/48, James Nagle's information on Dourly, 9 Dec. 1803.

of his brother's fears. Gallagher was to report that they still intended waiting for the French before rising, but that they would be compelled to act if attacked. The French were urged to send help, and if they agreed an agent should travel to Ireland to appoint a date for the rising. Robert also told of their shortage of leaders, particularly for Connacht, and asked Thomas to send several back from France. Contact with France had virtually ceased after Russell's return, because of the drift towards war and the rupture of communication on its renewal, and some key leaders like Swiney had been arrested in the general purge of British subjects.[50] The net result was that in those tense months before the Dublin rising the Irish leaders had almost no communication with France.

Gallagher arrived in Paris on 31 May to find that the Irish had already reopened negotiations with the Consulate, and General Dalton from the War Ministry had been appointed to consult with both Emmet and Arthur O'Connor. The re-entry of the latter into United Irish diplomacy had already revived old animosities. The open hostility of the two main leaders surprised the French, who had hoped to negotiate with a unified Irish committee. But both Emmet and O'Connor claimed independent credentials for the exclusive right to lead the Irish negotiations. Their wrangles confused and angered the French authorities, contributing to the delays which so complicated the position of the rebels in Ireland, feeding mounting doubts about French sincerity, and strengthening support for Russell's insistence on going it alone. In view of the deteriorating situation in Ireland, Thomas Addis Emmet did urge the French to send a small force immediately. This departure from the belief in the need for a full-scale invasion was just another symptom of growing United Irish disenchantment with France, and on the side Emmet was sounding out the possibility of securing Dutch help, and removing their dependence on France altogether.[51] Bonaparte was too pre-occupied with Hanover in the summer of 1803 to devote any immediate attention to Ireland, but on 19 July Emmet secured an audience with the War Minister, Alexandre Berthier. At this stage the dispute with O'Connor had not yet split the Irish exiles, and all, including O'Connor, recognized the urgent need to send a messenger to Ireland. But in the confused aftermath of the declaration of war, passports were at a premium and British subjects were in a particularly unfavourable position. Negotiations for a passport to send someone to Ireland were still in progress when news arrived on 4 August of Robert Emmet's rebellion in Dublin.[52]

Since Gallagher's departure, the Dublin leaders had grown progressively more disillusioned about the state of the country. Those leaders whom they

50. See A.N. F⁷ 6338 doss. 7123.
51. Emmet, *Ireland Under English Rule*, ɪɪ, 287–8, and 266 for Gallagher.
52. Aulard, *Paris sous le Consulat*, ɪv, 285.

had presumed to exist, the professional and the trades people who had formed the backbone of the original United Irish Society in Dublin, failed to come forward. Execution, persecution, or exile had decimated the local leadership since 1798 and had made the remainder timorous; and while the Castle recognized that the number of francophiles and republicans in principle had not declined, they were equally confident that few wished to alter the system by violent means.[53] The financial support which the leaders had expected from this class was not forthcoming, and lack of funds prevented the completion of preparations in Dublin. Certainly the scenes inside the depots when they were raided after the rising betrayed all the signs of incomplete preparations. On the night of 23 July when the military reached the Marshalsea Lane depot, they found their way blocked by a solid wall of pikes, let down from the depot's hatch for transportation to the scene of action. Inside they found enough ammunition for 10,000 men and about 7,000 additional pikes behind a false wall. But there were no muskets or blunderbusses whatsoever and the rebels' frantic efforts to secure them at the last minute contributed to the confusion in which Dublin had finally risen on 23 July.[54]

Nor had there been any serious effort to co-ordinate action with sympathisers in England and Scotland. Scotland seemed steady enough, and a United Irish deputation had recently returned with assurances of Scottish support if the Irish chose to rise without the French. In England, however, despite the prevailing discontent, there was little attempt at organization, and the sympathy generated by the execution of Despard was left uncultivated. Some attempt was made to revitalize the English movement when serious preparations began in Ireland, and in April an agent sent to Manchester by the Dublin leaders told of their anxiety at 'the backwardness of the Manchester citizens.' This and further reports of Irish agents having travelled through Lancashire, Yorkshire, Nottinghamshire and Lincolnshire in June and July, indicates an effort by the United Irish leaders to revive the mainland movement. But any success was cut short by news of the premature Dublin rising.[55]

In April a disillusioned Irish agent had told Charles Bent, Fletcher's principal agent in Lancashire, of their determination 'to shake off the yoke by themselves', even if no outside help was forthcoming.[56] Throughout the Irish preparations this note of defiant independence had run concurrently with claims that they could not act without the French. But their rush to forestall a French takeover by embarking on preparations for another rebel-

53. B.L. Add. MS. 35708 fos. 127–8, Hardwicke to Wickham, 11 Mar. 1803; see also I.S.P.O. 620/11/130/44, statement of Thomas Frayne; and Hope's account in Madden, *United Irishmen*, 3rd ser., III, 100–1, for the shortage of leaders.

54. *State Trials*, XXVIII, 721–2.

55. See I.S.P.O. 620/10/121/15 and MacDonagh, *Viceroy's Postbag*, 278 for Scotland; P.R.O. H.O. 42/70 and I.S.P.O. 620/65/126, 620/66/166 and 620/67/33 for contacts with England.

56. I.S.P.O. 620/67/33, information transmitted from Fletcher, 8 Apr. 1803.

Plate 30. Emmet preparing for the Insurrection (by Cruikshank for Maxwell, *Irish Rebellion*)

lion, even before war restarted, made an independent attempt inevitable if calculations about the timing of the invasion proved incorrect. On 16 July an explosion in the Patrick Street depot had alerted the authorities. The refusal of the inmates to admit the city firemen, and the death of one of their number through lack of medical attention, confirmed suspicions that the disaffected were planning some action. There was another incident the following day, when a party delivering arms was interrupted by a watchman. After such mishaps, the leaders were threatened with discovery before they had made any significant show of strength to prove to both the Irish people and to the French that an independence movement existed of sufficient dimensions to merit their support. Given the direction of Emmet's thought, his desire to show the French that the Irish were not a force to be trifled with and his blind conviction that the country people would turn out if Dublin rose first, the decision to attempt a rising rather than risk the discovery of their preparations was predictable. It was primarily the leaders lately returned from France and out of touch with the country who thought this way, and the Dublin leaders were bitterly divided on the eve of the outbreak about the advisability of proceeding without French help.[57] The result was that no attempt was made to inform supporters until the last moment. Wylde was only sent to tell the

57. See Madden, *Robert Emmet*, 82; P.R.O. H.O. 100/113/181; I.S.P.O. 620/11/138/11–12; and *Diary and Correspondence of Lord Colchester*, i, 450, for the disagreement.

Map 7. Dublin at the time of Emmet's
Rebellion (1801, map, British Library).

1. To Island Bridge**
2. Royal Barracks**
3. Smithfield*
4. Newgate Gaol
5. Kilmainham Gaol (just off map)
6. Marshalsea Lane*
7. Thomas Street*
8. Bridge Street
9. Francis Street
10. The Coombe
11. To Harold's Cross and Rathfarnham
12. Patrick Street*
13. The Liberties
14. Winetavern Street*
15. Capel Street
16. The Castle**
17. Eustace Street
18. Dame Street
19. Parliament House (taken over in 1802
    by the Bank of Ireland)
20. Trinity College
21. Custom House*
22. To Milltown
23. Pigeon House** (just off map)

* Depots in 1803 rebellion
** Points of rebel attack

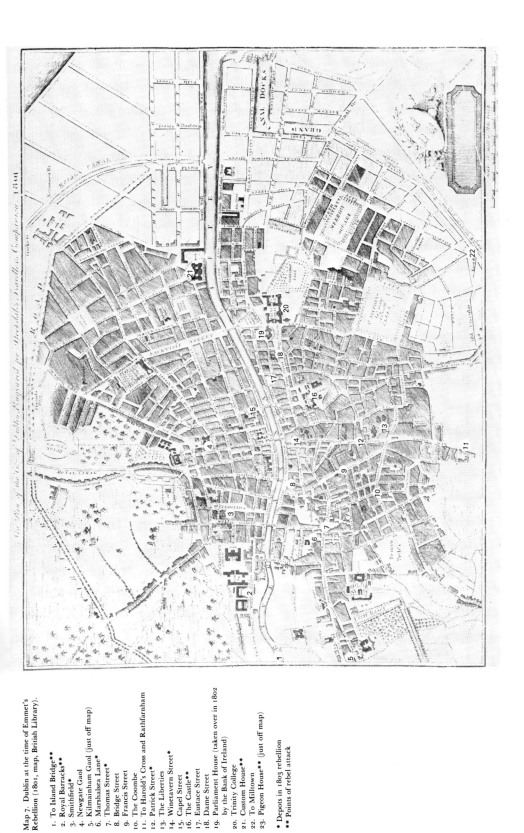

Kildare men on the 22nd; Pat McCabe, like so many others, was not told until the day of the rising itself. The predictable result was one of utter confusion. Many orders were never carried out, not through treachery, as Hope was to claim, but because 'the time came on in such a hurry that Everyone was beausey preparing themselves to go out', as Pat Farrell later explained.[58] Because of the intensive secrecy which had surrounded the preparations, few were practised in their roles, and when surprise and speed were essential to success, uncertainty and indecision invited disaster.

The plan for the attack on Dublin was of intriguing simplicity. All effort was to be concentrated on the capture of the Castle, and with the fall of the seat of government, it was felt that the country would immediately rise. Just before the attack was to take place, arms were to be transported to the smaller depots near the Castle. The Pigeon House, Island Bridge, the Royal Barracks and the Custom House would also be taken to prevent reinforcements reaching the Castle. From these depots local leaders would distribute arms to the people and to the Kildare and Wicklow men expected to march on the city. The main leaders were to set out for the Castle in carriages from the depot in Thomas Street, on receipt of assurances that the rebels in its vicinity were ready. They felt that the psychological effect of the fall of the Castle would ensure the success of the rising, and there seems little doubt that it would have dispelled the paralyzing effect which the last minute instructions seemed to have produced among the rank and file. By mid-evening the leaders had ascertained that the Castle gates were still open. Government obviously suspected nothing. But the carriages had not yet arrived. Ned Conlon, commissioned to secure them, started the train of misadventure which quickly engulfed the entire project. Earlier that evening he had hired six hackney coaches with their drivers and was leading them to Thomas Street, when they were stopped by a soldier and asked their destination. Conlon panicked and shot the soldier, and the frightened drivers rushed off, taking the coaches with them. When they did not arrive, Emmet and his co-leaders decided to make the attack on foot, but were interrupted in their preparations by a false report that troops were surrounding the depot. They decided to come out and fight in the street and the confused bustling which ensued alerted the authorities. The Castle gates were closed, troops began to fill the surrounding streets, and the original plan became obsolete. Emmet, Dowdall, the baker Nicholas Stafford, Wylde, Quigley and Mahony, the leaders who had emerged from the Thomas Street depot, recognized that further efforts were futile and simply continued on up Thomas Street to their hideout in Butterfield Lane. Most of the other leaders in the city had taken fright. The messenger sent to tell Dwyer of the plans for the 23rd had delayed drinking at Rathfarnham, and the

58. I.S.P.O. 620/11/138/11, evidence given by Patrick Farrell, 1 Sept. 1803; MacDonagh, *Viceroy's Postbag*, 303.

Plate 31: James Hope, (Madden, *United Irishmen*)   Plate 32. Thomas Russell (National Library of Ireland)

Wicklow men had never reached Dublin. The Wexford men had started to come in from the Coal Quay direction in the evening, but they turned back on hearing a false report that the rising had been postponed. From Butterfield Lane, Emmet sent countermanding orders into the countryside to postpone any movement until the French arrived, and then went into hiding in the Wicklow Hills. The piking of the Attorney General, Lord Kilwarden, and his nephew in Thomas Street, and the desultory attacks in other parts of the city, had occurred after the leaders had already abandoned the rising.[59]

Miles Byrne later claimed that the absence of Hope, who had organized the area around the Castle, had contributed to the confusion of the 23rd.[60] Hope had left on 18 July with Hamilton and Russell to prepare the North. But the enthusiasm which they reported from their earlier mission had been in response to the question: would they turn out if the French arrived? In July they found reaction to the suggestion of rising without the French decidedly

59. For Emmet's countermanding instructions see N.L.I. MS. 9706/95 and P.R.O. H.O. 123/6/12, Wickham to King 13 Oct. 1803. The account of the rebellion is taken from I.S.P.O. 620/11/128–38, 158–60, 620/12/145–56, 620/13/177 and 620/14/195; P.R.O. H.O. 100/113–15; N.L.I. MS. 5973/169–70; and Hants. C.R.O. 38M49/5. The following published sources have also been used: Madden, *United Irishmen*, 3rd ser. ; idem, *Robert Emmet;* MacDonagh, *Viceroy's Postbag; Diary and Correspondence of Lord Colchester*, I; *Castlereagh Correspondence*, IV; *State Trials*, XXIX; but the fullest and most accurate account is in Byrne, *Memoirs*, I, which was unavailable to Madden.

60. Byrne, *Memoirs*, I, 271.

lukewarm. Hope had only spoken with his social peers on the first visit, and the professional class with whom Russell and Hamilton had formerly associated remained aloof. Efforts were concentrated on the old strongholds of Antrim and Down and some of their former colleagues did attend the meetings. But Russell's refusal to reveal their plans and his bias against French aid was scarcely calculated to woo them from their cautious inaction. Russell, like Emmet, was convinced that once the rising started, the people would be roused from their torpor. He told a meeting at Castlereagh, on the outskirts of Belfast, that he was 'anxious that a beginning should be made and said that if fifty or an hundred would assemble, they would encrease rapidly; . . . Dublin and the South were compleatly ready, perfectly organised, and . . . with the assistance of the North, would be sufficient to subdue the Kingdom without the assistance of Buonaparte, whom he wished to retain only as an ally not as a master, because he had often shown the diposition of a Despot.'

To dismiss the Ulster reaction as a damp squib, the traditional approach, is to misinterpret the evidence. Those who attended the meetings were not averse to another rising; they were simply reluctant to act without the French. Other counties, like Wicklow, in which an active United Irish movement had survived, had voiced similar reservations. Certainly both Hope and Russell's nephew later denounced the historian Samuel McSkimmin for playing down the 1803 attempt in Ulster in *Fraser's Magazine* for 1836. Yet, although those who had taken part in the 1803 rising regarded McSkimmin's article as a travesty of its real nature, the article was to become the source for many later accounts, perpetuating the picture of Russell as a hopeless romantic.[61]

The facts do not entirely support such an interpretation and there were signs of continued preparations among the northern men long after they had heard of the Dublin failure. Men were reported to be drilling in those areas visited by Russell, notably Castlereagh, Ballynahinch, Knockbracken and Newry in county Down, and in those parts of Antrim adjacent to Belfast, particularly in Hope's centre of operations at Carnmoney. Some of these incidents were undoubtedly a part of the Defender revival in the area. But the training sessions and the increased talk of another rebellion were certainly products of the latest mission. Although the response was 'trifling' compared to that in 1798 and scarcely measured up to Russell's expectations, the fact that many were willing to rise again when the North was thought to have been completely subdued is a token of what might have been achieved had there been more time to train leaders, had Emmet succeeded, or had the

61. S. McSkimmin, 'Secret History of the Irish Insurrection of 1803', in *Fraser's Magazine*, 14 (Nov. 1836), 566–7 and the riposte of Hope and Capt. Russell in T.C.D. MS. 873/648–52 and MS. 7253/2. See I.S.P.O. 620/11/130/15, 620/11/158 and T.C.D. MS. 873/377, for Russell in Ulster.

French arrived. Russell's return to Dublin in a bid to rescue Emmet (captured in August) was not the action of a man who had despaired of success.[62]

The traditional view of Emmet and Russell as romantic visionaries, and of their rebellion as a project doomed from the outset, requires some re-appraisal. It was an image encouraged by Emmet, who depicted himself as the sole organizer, in an effort to spare the lives of others. It was taken up by the Irish government to refute accusations that it had been caught napping by a dangerous conspiracy. Certainly Emmet was to some extent led astray by his distrust of France and his faith in the ability and willingness of the people to rise spontaneously. But it was not only the Irish prediliction for martyr-worship which prompted later nationalists to look to Emmet as the incarnation of their ideal. He had deliberately set out to restore the dignity which Irish republicanism had lost in the 1798 rebellion and in its subservience to an external French master. He later wrote to his brother in Paris that he had wanted to give the attempt in Dublin 'the respectability of insurrection'[63]— hence the almost theatrical sense of drama with which it was surrounded, the elaborate uniforms worn by the leaders in Thomas Street, the impressive array of arms, which had included sophisticated rockets and combustible planks to hamper troop movement, the dignified manner in which the Castle was to have been taken, the strict instructions to take enemies prisoner rather than kill them, the authoritative addresses of the 'Provisional Government' which were rushed from Stockdale's printing presses for distribution on the day of the rising, the effort made to disavow any slavish dependence on the French and most of all Emmet's own explanation in his famous speech. Emmet had proved himself a powerful orator in the past, and his old college friend, the poet Thomas Moore, claimed that he rarely required notes when he spoke. But he did require them at his trial in October 1803 and had taken considerable trouble to explain the beliefs and motives behind the rebellion. He insisted that the new plan for rebellion was not brought from France, but was native-born and had been in existence when he returned to Ireland, and despite the repeated interruptions of the presiding judge, Lord Norbury, his speech had a lasting effect on supporters and detractors alike.

> I am charged with being an emissary of France, for the purpose of inciting insurrection in the country and then delivering it over to a foreign enemy. It is false! I did not wish to join this country with France ... the only question ... was:— whether France should come to

62. I.S.P.O. 620/11/138/14, Daniel Murley's account of Russell's stay in Dublin, 10 Sept. 1803; also T.C.D. MS. 869/7/118. For activities in the North see I.S.P.O. S.O.C. 1024/4–5 and 1025/2–4. Many felt the revolt in the North proved the loyalty of the province, see S.O.C. 1025/11,34 and *H.M.C. Dropmore MSS*, VII, 196. But Wickham did not agree, see MacDonagh, *Viceroy's Postbag*, 327.
63. Hants. C.R.O. 38M49/5/42, his intercepted letter to Thomas, 20 Sept. 1803, also quoted in *Diary and Correspondence of Lord Colchester*, I, 454.

Plate 33. Trial of Robert Emmet (by Cruikshank for Maxwell, *Irish Rebellion*).

this country, as an enemy? ... If the French come as a foreign enemy,
Oh, my countrymen! ... receive them with all the destruction of war—
immolate them in their boats before our native soil shall be polluted
by a foreign foe ... Deliver my country into the hands of France!—
Look at the proclamation ... Where is it stated? ... Is it in that part,
where the people of Ireland are called upon to show the world, that
they are competent to take their place among nations? ... that they
have a right to claim acknowledgment as an independent country,
by the satisfactory proof of their capability of maintaining their
independence? ... by wresting it from England, with their own
hands? ... No! Let not then any man calumniate my memory by
believing, that I could have hoped for freedom from the government
of France, ... Let no man write my epitaph ... and when I am
prevented from vindicating myself, let no man dare to calumniate me.
Let my character and my motives repose in obscurity and peace, till
other times and other men can do them justice; *Then* shall my character
be vindicated. *Then* may my epitaph be written. I HAVE DONE.[64]

64. *State Trials*, XXVIII, 1172–7, also various pamphlet editions of the speech published in London.
Dublin and Manchester 1802–1845. I am indebted to Dr. N. Vance, for permission to use his
unpublished article 'Texts and Traditions: Robert Emmet's Speech from the Dock', which gives
a full account of these different versions, their significance and influence. The trial and speech
also appear in MacDonagh, *Viceroy's Postbag*, 388–96 and Madden, *United Irishmen*, 3rd ser.,
III, 238–47; and see Thomas Moore's account in the *Irish News*, 16 May 1845. There is a
manuscript copy of the speech in T.C.D. MS. 7253/9, which contains the 'epitaph' lines, though
not the melodramatic lines about Ireland as a nation which appear in later editions.

The anti-French element of the speech caused a sensation and was widely publicized by government to discredit the United Irishmen in the eyes of France. But Emmet was not proclaiming a rupture with France; he was simply qualifying a standing invitation. He sought to show that Ireland was willing and able to win her own independence without exchanging one foreign tyranny for another, and that France would still be welcomed if she came as a friend. Neither he nor Russell had ever believed that Irish independence could be properly established without such help, and the rebellion had been organized on the assumption that an invasion would not be long delayed. After its failure, Emmet had urged the Kildare men not to lose hope, as he expected a French invasion before October, and in August he had sent Miles Byrne to Paris to accelerate its despatch.[65] McNally spoke with Emmet in prison and warned government not to be misled by some of the statements in his speech into thinking that he rejected the idea of French assistance. 'Mr. Emmet assured *my friend* [McNally himself] . . . that his brother and others in Paris had negotiated for a French Force. That if they came with a Treaty they ought to be joined and that if Ireland was once separated from England, by means of France, then Ireland, connecting with *England* by Treaty ought to establish her independence against both France and England, by beating the French out of the Island—If they remained as Conquerors. Emmet had no objections to French aid by Treaty—he only objected to France conquering Ireland for herself . . . The aid of France was their great dependence. Without it they will not, they cannot act.'[66]

Nor were Emmet's expectations that the country would rise again unrealistic, even if he miscalculated on the spontaneity of popular response. The enthusiasm of the small bands in Dublin who attacked the well-armed soldiers in the Coombe and in Francis Street, was a sample of how things might have been, particularly if the French had been on the coast. They recoiled from the attack by the troops because there was no one on the spot to tell them how to act next. John Croker, Surveyor of the Port of Dublin, witnessed such an attack by an ill-armed group of rebels and was amazed that they withstood three volleys from the soldiers before they broke and fled.[67] Emmet had not envisaged any difficulties in securing local leaders to direct popular enthusiasm when the time for action arrived. This was one of his main mistakes. The North in particular was to show that the old leaders could not be relied upon to come forward again, and the people would not move without them. McGucken, as the main survivor from the '98 leadership

---

65. Byrne, *Memoirs*, I, 285–6; also P.R.O. H.O. 100/113/199–200 and 100/114/56; I.S.P.O. 620/11/138/12; and B.L. Add. MS. 33112 fo. 14 for evidence that Emmet and Russell still expected the French.

66. P.R.O. H.O. 100/115/15–18; see also MacDonagh, *Viceroy's Postbag*, 401–2.

67. *Diary and Correspondence of Lord Colchester*, I, 434; see also I.S.P.O. 620/11/129/17, information of Sylvester Costigan, 1 Sept. 1803.

in Down, was expected to command the county's forces. But as a government agent he persuaded them to hold back and thus paralysed support from the strongest county in the North.[68] Elsewhere there were signs of movement in response to news of the Dublin attempt, and there were larger attacks on Maynooth and Naas. But everywhere the story was the same: lack of leaders to give directions to the people who were willing to turn out.[69]

The timing of the outbreak was wrong, but the original plan of a surprise attack on the nerve-centre of English rule in Ireland, with action radiating out from Dublin, was admitted by the authorities to have been a work of 'talent and judgement'.[70] They were astounded by the secrecy with which preparations had proceeded within earshot of the Castle, and two years later were still fighting off accusations that the attempt had taken them completely by surprise. If he had achieved little else, Emmet had succeeded in cooling relations between the London and Dublin governments and made both look foolish at a time when Addington's administration was under attack from a formidable array of critics. Whitehall was angry at the scrappy information received from Dublin about the rising, and was obliged to push through emergency legislation for Ireland on what critics felt to be the flimsiest of evidence that such an emergency existed. The need for such measures seemed all the more questionable in the face of the government's attempt to explain away its ignorance by depicting the whole episode as the insignificant action of a young visionary, and the numbers involved were proportionately whittled down to accommodate this claim. Such devices simply tarnished government credit, and many agreed with Windham's sardonic remark that he 'wished that ministers would tell them, when they should have made up their minds upon the subject, whether the late insurrection was really a contemptible riot; . . . or whether it spread to greater extent, and had taken deep root in the country?'[71]

In Ireland it was the surprise rather than the nature of the attack which caused the wave of loyalist hysteria. The rebellion reinforced the prejudices left over from '98; it intensified religious divisions and many again insisted that it was a popish conspiracy, despite Emmet's claim that all the leaders were protestant. Orangeism revived with a vengeance, and even moderate government officials recognized that the best hope for crushing disaffection now lay in promoting the Orange ticket against a population which had

68. Landreth, *The Pursuit of Robert Emmet*, 176, 178, 181; also MacDonagh, *Viceroy's Postbag*, 277.
69. For the rebellion outside Dublin see I.S.P.O. 620/11/129/5–7, and 620/11/130/5; MacDonagh, *Viceroy's Postbag*, 326–7.
70. P.R.O. H.O. 100/114/19, Wickham to Pole Carew, 5 Oct. 1803.
71. *Parl. Deb.*, I, 1630, also 1521–1690; *Parl. Hist.*, XXXVI, 1672–1712; B.L. Add. MS. 33112 fos. 25–35; Hants. C.R.O. 38M49/5/30; MacDonagh, *Viceroy's Postbag*, 282–366; and *Diary and Correspondence of Lord Colchester*, I, 435–7, for the accusations and the Irish government's attempted defence, also its draft report on the rebellion in P.R.O. H.O. 100/115/175–92. The official statement is in *Castlereagh Correspondence*, IV, 316–36.

once again proved itself generically disloyal. Loyalist resentment against the Act of Union was revived, and the blatant ignorance of the authorities was attributed to London's indifference. A native parliament would not have permitted such neglect.[72] This bitterness at London's reaction was shared by British officials in Dublin. The ministers in London had echoed the general attack on the Irish government, and Wickham, now Irish Chief Secretary, resented their accusations with no acceptance of responsibility for negligence on their own part. He felt that Dublin had operated an effective intelligence system in the peace period, and had London been more vigilant about United Irish activities abroad, ministers might have been better alerted to the possible results on the home front.[73]

Both governments recognized their error in having thus relaxed their surveillance of the United leaders because of peace, and in the clumsiest manner possible they tried to resurrect the old intelligence network, only to reveal the extent to which it had collapsed. It had depended on a few key people like McNally and Turner at the very heart of the United movement. Turner's withdrawal and return from Hamburg at the beginning of 1803 was a particular loss. There had been no need to employ a multitude of inferior agents when he had supplied such full and accurate information. Sir James Craufurd had also been transferred from Hamburg, and with the arrest in Paris the previous autumn of the Prince de Bouillon, who had directed British correspondence with the royalists through the Channel Isles, intelligence channels on the United men abroad had all but dried up.[74] At home, ministers scoured both islands for new agents with only limited success. They could find no one to watch the flow of Irish through Liverpool, and the information which Thomas Jordan had continued to supply since 1802 told them little more about the Irish in London than they knew already. The prospect of securing information from Robert Carty, a former United Irishman recently returned from Paris, caused sufficient excitement to draw an official from the Home Office to a secret rendezvous with Carty in Berkeley Square. Carty was able to supply much background information on the activities of the United Irishmen in France during the peace period, but he had already withdrawn from the movement and was useless for future employment.[75] Despite the intensification of vigilance after Emmet's Rebellion, lack of information prevented any decisive action against the United men on

72. *State Trials*, XXIX, 504–50; *H.M.C. Dropmore MSS.*, VII, 188; and *Castlereagh Correspondence*, IV, 298–313.

73. *Diary and Correspondence of Lord Colchester*, I, 460; also Hants. C.R.O. 38M49/5/20, Wickham to Sir Charles Yorke, 20 Aug. 1803.

74. See P.R.O. F.O. 33/21 for Craufurd's replacement; F.O. 27/64/64 for Bouillon; and see Hants. C.R.O. 38M49/5/20,36; and I.S.P.O. C.S.O. 1847/449, and 620/11/160/4, for Turner's pardon.

75. For renewed concern about the Irish on the mainland see P.R.O. H.O. 42/71–2, H.O. 79/6, H.O. 100/119, P.C. 1/3117; and I.S.P.O. 620/11/130/52, 620/12/141/27.

the mainland, and Wickham became increasingly exasperated by London's new ineffectiveness in matters of domestic intelligence. But Dublin's efforts were no better. The melodramatic despatch north of an agent posing as a French general was a token of the desperation to which failure to secure any substantial information on the disaffected had driven both governments. Wickham sought to gain more information by sending Coigley's brother to Paris. But he was a weak individual, desperately trying to curry favour with the authorities by making groundless claims about his contacts with the United men, and he never succeeded in penetrating the Paris movement. This continuing failure to secure information on the United Irish in France enabled both Swiney and Putnam McCabe to travel unmolested to Ireland the following winter.[76]

The truth was that Emmet's attempt had been an embarrassment for both governments; they had been caught unawares, and Hardwicke, the Lord Lieutenant, admitted as much to his brother, though it was publicly denied.[77] Even after the arrests, the examinations and the trials and executions had taken place, the Irish government remained ignorant of most of the preparations prior to the explosion of 16 July. The new Commander-in-Chief, General Fox, had been so ill-informed of anything untoward in Dublin that he had stayed in Connacht till the 21st. He had not received the despatch telling of the explosion, and when government suspicions began to be aroused on the 23rd, he failed to inform the military commander of Dublin. There are few signs that the authorities were taking any extra precautions because of the explosion on the 16th, and since it was this explosion which had persuaded Emmet to proceed with the rising, he might have avoided detection by delaying a little longer. Only on 21 and 22 July had the Castle received any hint of the proposed attack, and even then the reports had been so unreliable that they were rejected by Marsden, a decision which caused him to be singled out in the ensuing recriminations. It was only on the 23rd that he was sufficiently alarmed by reports of groups of men moving along the Naas to Dublin road to send for the Lord Lieutenant and the Commander-in-Chief;[78] and it was the attempt by government to call an emergency meeting of the Privy Council that day which caused the main casualties of the Dublin rising, when Lord Kilwarden and his nephew were attacked and killed on their way to the Castle in response to the summons. Given the confusion and panic on both sides, it was a miracle that only fifty deaths occurred in the city that day.

The embarrassed ignorance of the authorities and the panic of the last-

---

76. P.R.O. H.O. 100/112/331, 335 and 100/113/131, Wickham's correspondence of 23, 28 Aug. and 15 Sept. 1803. See Hants. C.R.O. 38M49/5/29 and below p. 328 for Swiney; 38M49/1/8 and Emmet, *Ireland Under English Rule*, I, 272, for McCabe.
77. MacDonagh, *Viceroy's Postbag*, 313.
78. See I.S.P.O. 620/13/163/1–3 and 179/19 for the information of Wilcocks etc.

Plate 34. The Murder of Lord Kilwarden (by Cruikshank for Maxwell, *Irish Rebellion*)

minute attempt to defend the city is sufficient to counter the preposterous suggestion that the rising had been encouraged by the authorities to facilitate suppression before the French arrived.[79] Dublin Castle's attempt to play down the seriousness of the rising was totally out of character and was designed to reduce in proportion its own negligence. Attempts to encourage the prisoners to divulge information failed miserably. Few outside the main leaders had anything to divulge; Dowdall and Allen had escaped; Russell attempted to rescue Emmet and was arrested within a stone's throw of the Castle; but both refused to give information, admitted their guilt at the trials, and removed another possible source of information by making no attempt to defend themselves. Emmet had been less concerned about his own fate than about that of the young woman with whom he had fallen in love that summer—Sarah Curran, daughter of the famous liberal barrister John Philpot Curran. The relationship had added to Emmet's anxieties on the eve of the rebellion, and after his arrest he desperately sought to protect Sarah's name. But the association of the family name with treason helped erode Philpot Curran's reforming sympathies, and Emmet was denied his services as defence counsel, though he had defended many of the United leaders in the past.

Despite his admission of guilt, Emmet's trial had been excessively pro-

79. Landreth, *The Pursuit of Robert Emmet*, 181.

longed, as the only opening left for government propaganda. Cobbett singled out the trial in his attack on government's handling of the episode, and the success with which he established the image of a callous administration, vilifying the essentially noble character of young Emmet to disguise its own inefficiency, effectively removed the benefit which the Castle had hoped to derive from the trial.[80] As with Despard, Emmet's martyrdom was created as much by official incapacity as anything else. The indecent haste with which the executions followed the trials in October was in contrast to the deliberate calculation of the Cornwallis administration in the aftermath of 1798. But Cornwallis had had an informed idea of the extent of the threat in 1798; Hardwicke in 1803 had not, and with the petulance of a frightened child his government had lashed out at an unknown enemy in the only manner it knew how.

Although the elitist form of the United movement devised in 1799 lingered on, the 1803 rebellion was the delayed epitaph for the national body which had preceded it. The authorities' complacency about its disintegration in 1803 was not entirely founded, but the rebellion had epitomized its essential weaknesses since 1795, when it had made the decision to extend the movement to all sections of Irish society. Denis Browne, M.P. for Mayo, dismissed Emmet's attempt as having been '. . . too refined . . . to make it *deep* rooted'.[81] It was a fitting comment on the United Irish Society as a whole, which had never understood the basic aspirations underlying the popular support it attracted, and in this Emmet was no different from his predecessors. In 1803 Hope had asked about his attitude to the land question and in particular to popular hopes of some dramatic change in land-ownership. Emmet had answered that any alteration in the system of land-holding would mean certain bloodshed and should be avoided at all costs. Apart from the abolition of church dues and tithes, Emmet had envisaged little change in the status quo and felt that even religious equality could not be granted immediately. His prime concern had been to organize a new system of central government and the proclamation in which he was to have announced the revolution to the people concentrated almost exclusively on this. A few references to British tyranny were considered sufficient to entice the people from their retirement.[82]

The exiles' plans in the winter of 1802–03 had revealed a fatal flaw in United Irish strategy. The re-appraisal of the situation in 1799, and the

---

80. See Hants. C.R.O. 38M49/5/35 and I.S.P.O. 620/11/132, for attempts to influence the prisoners; H.O. 100/113/167, for Emmet's failure to defend himself; I.S.P.O. S.O.C. 1025/75, for Russell's arrest; and 620/13/168/4, for the escape of Allen and Dowdall.
81. I.S.P.O. S.O.C. 1025/71, Denis Browne to [   ], 27 Jul. 1803.
82. See T.C.D. MS. 7253; also I.S.P.O. 620/12/155, the papers found at the Thomas Street depot and 620/11/134, address of the provisional government.

project which had resulted, was produced by a basic distrust of the people to effect their own liberation without a bloody civil war. The plan of giving new priority to French help was sound enough. But when the leaders distrusted both the essential components of their plan of liberation, the French invasion and the popular uprising, the United Irishmen had little future as a national movement. To have relied exclusively on the latter would have required a new approach to the Defenders, who were still active in Ulster, and in 1803 there was no sign whatsoever that such an overture was made.[83] The former alternative had increasingly assumed the appearance of a simple change of masters. The plan for 1803, which had sought to minimize the worst effects of both, was realistic enough, but it had relied on a precision of timing which past experience of French help scarcely justified. In the weeks before the rising, however, there are signs that Emmet had already started to move away from the social and political exclusiveness of the United Irish Society. Both he and Russell were shocked at the failure of their former comrades to come forward and at their trials had publicly denounced those who had taught them their principles and then abandoned them when they attempted to put them into practice.[84] In his use of Dublin tradesmen to lead the attack in the city, Emmet had taken an important step away from United Irish elitism, and what is more, had proved the effectiveness with which such inferior leaders could elude government vigilance. He had also begun to query the expansive republicanism of the United Irishmen, their tendency to look everywhere for help, to England, Scotland, France, Holland or Spain, rather than to their own people. He had recognized that the process of dependence on French help had gone too far to be reversed; it could, however, be neutralized.

The home movement disintegrated rapidly after 1803, but Emmet had succeeded in perpetuating its ideals. He had represented Ireland's right to nationhood as such a reasonable aspiration that the English government could only appear unreasonable and arbitrary by refusing it, and the contrast between the two images was taken up by English radicals long before his speech had become one of the gospels of Irish nationalism. Even such a career politician as Wickham was struck by the contrast, and the episode reacted upon a protracted illness to bring about his total withdrawal from politics. He later wrote a long letter explaining the reasons for his resignation, and though a toned-down version was actually delivered, the sentiments expressed in the original were confided to friends:

83. Hants. C.R.O. 38M49/5/31.

84. *State Trials*, xxix, 53–79; T.C.D. MS. 7253/1, Dr. Croker's reminiscences in 1864; and MS. 873/626, Mrs. McCleland's letter to Mary Anne McCracken, 1843.

... in what honours or other earthly advantages could I find
compensation for what I must suffer were I again compelled by my
official duty to prosecute *to death* men capable and acting as Emmett has
done in his last moments for making an effort to liberate their country
from grievances the existence of many of which none can deny of which
I myself have acknowledged to be unjust, oppressive and unchristian. I
well know that the manner in which I have suffered myself to be
affected ... will be attributed to a sort of morbid sensibility ... but
no one can be capable of forming a right judgement on my motives
who has not like myself been condemned by his official duty to dip
his hands in the blood of his fellow countrymen, in execution of a portion
of the laws and institutions of this country of which, in his conscience
he cannot approve.[85]

Thirty years later Wickham still spoke of Emmet and of the effect which the
events of 1803 had had on him. It was a remarkable testimony to Emmet's
achievement. The picture of him as a romantic visionary is quite wrong and
one suspects that it derives from an excessive concentration on his tragic
relationship with Sarah Curran. 'I know there are men without candour
who will pronounce on this failure without knowing one of the circumstances
that occasioned it', wrote Emmet to his brother shortly before his execution,
'they will consider only that they predicted it ... they will not recollect that
they predicted also that no system could be formed, that no secrecy nor
confidence could be restored, that no preparations could be made, that no plan
could be arranged, that no day could be fixed without being instantly known
at the Castle; ...' Emmet had proved that careful planning and able leadership could defy superior strength on the side of the authorities. Furthermore,
he had succeeded in representing the dignity and reasonableness of the pursuit
of Irish freedom to contemporaries and successors alike. It is true that he
had revealed the futility of United Irish operations abroad; but if the future
of Irish republicanism lay not with an organization like that of the United
Irishmen, it did with their ideals, especially with that of the honourable fight if
all else failed. He had succeeded in giving his march down Thomas Street 'the
respectability of insurrection'[86] and what then was dismissed as a mere scuffle
was transmitted to posterity under the epithet of 'Emmet's Rebellion'.

85. Hants. C.R.O. 38M49/1/55–7.
86. *Diary and Correspondence of Lord Colchester*, I, 454.

CHAPTER TEN

1803–1815: Last of the Wild Geese

After Emmet's Rebellion the United Irish leadership was based entirely on the Continent, and although it gained a new lease of life with the renewal of war in 1803, the kind of Franco-Irish negotiations which had predated the 1798 rebellion could not be revived. Years of exile and imprisonment had embittered the United Irishmen. Neglect, broken promises and finally betrayal at Amiens had rendered them less tolerant of the French. Bonaparte was no longer the shining hero of Italy but a manifest tyrant, and although the Consulate in 1803, like its predecessors in 1793 and 1794, had made the first overtures, the United Irishmen were not disposed to sell their services cheaply. Advance guarantees against a French takeover were considered more important than the assistance itself, and the negotiations were marred by United Irish suspicion or outright hostility. The United Irishmen were demanding too much at a time when they had less to offer France than formerly. They no longer had an organized leadership or following in Ireland, and the internal divisions so deplored by the Directory had become more acrimonious in the intervening years. In the period after Amiens the final contest took place between the two principal leaders, Thomas Addis Emmet and Arthur O'Connor, and this personal struggle was to play a greater part in the disintegration of the movement on the Continent than the growing disenchantment with France. Napoleon was to return intermittently to plans for an invasion of Ireland right up to 1812. But as a formal organization the United Irish Society had ceased to exist by 1806.

I

France was totally unprepared in 1803 to wage another war against England. A report commissioned from the Marine department told of complete maritime impotence: forty-eight ships were away in Saint Domingo, and of those remaining in home waters, two-thirds were disarmed and the others were in an appalling state of disrepair. For the moment the continental situation seemed quiet, and since England had attacked French shipping before a formal declaration of war, Bonaparte could discourage potential allies by depicting her as the aggressor.[1] In France a new wave of anglophobia had made the war popular. But the position of Bonaparte, only recently made Consul for life, was still insecure, and his enemies considered the war, particularly the plans to invade England, as the first step in his downfall.[2] In view of the delicate home situation and the state of the navy, Bonaparte hoped to win a swift land victory over England. Seven days after the declaration of war, he issued orders for the invasion of Hanover. By mid-June, with the operation completed, he launched preparations for an invasion of England.

Throughout the eighteenth century an invasion of Ireland had always figured in such projects, and in 1803 ministers in London and Dublin alike considered it a natural by-product of the renewal of war. Attention was immediately focused on Brest and Texel,[3] and Bonaparte's attempt upon 'the Potatoe Bag' became one of the stock themes of anti-French caricature.[4] In Dublin, Emmet's Rebellion was seen as the herald of imminent invasion, and the Castle became concerned about its total ignorance of United Irish activities in France since the signing of peace. In 1803 the British intelligence network abroad was as disorganized as it had been at the opening of the war ten years previously. Although some attempt was made through royalist channels to secure information on the Irish in Paris, such information was unreliable, and there was no direct source of intelligence on the Society in France after Turner's withdrawal. In September 1804 even the defective royalist channel was closed by Napoleon's purge of its agents in France,[5] and official ignorance prolonged fears of an Irish invasion long after the threat had receded.

An invasion of Ireland began to figure in Bonaparte's correspondence on 8 August.[6] However, the task of re-opening negotiations with the Irish proved more difficult than the French government had anticipated. MacNeven had made another attempt to revive French interest in January 1803, but he was ignored, and by May he had joined the thirty or so disgruntled and unemployed United men in Bordeaux.[7] In Paris other exiles were eking out a frugal existence in shabby lodgings. An organized United movement seemed a thing of the past; little wonder that the French did not know who to approach in

1. Desbrière, *Projets et Tentatives*, III, 48; A.H.G. B¹⁴ 5, War Ministry's correspondence, Mar.–May 1803.

2. P.R.O. F.O. 27/70, secret information from France, Dec. 1803.

3. See B.L. Add. MS. 35708 fos. 163–4; P.R.O. F.O. 27/69, H.O. 100/113/131–2; I.S.P.O. 620/50/40; and Hants. C.R.O. 38M49/1/45, for correspondence on possible invasion.

4. George, *Catalogue of Political and Personal Satires*, XII, 10050, also 9998 and 10009.

5. P.R.O. F.O. 27/70, Brébillon's reports until Sept. 1804. See also A. Aulard, *Paris sous le Premier Empire*, 3 vols. (Paris, 1812), I, 755–7, 763, 796, 814, 822–4, and 828 on the disruption of the royalist network.

6. *Correspondance de Napoléon Ier*, VIII, 6994; also A.N. AF IV 1671, 1597^A and 1598.

7. For MacNeven's overture see A.A.E. Corr. Pol. Ang. 601 fo. 54, and for the United Irishmen in Bordeaux see I.S.P.O. 620/66/30.

Plate 35. Thomas Addis
Emmet (Madden,
United Irishmen)

1803. After the departure of Robert Emmet, Hamilton, Russell and their colleagues at the beginning of the year, the United Irish committee in Paris had ceased to exist. Thomas Addis Emmet, its nominal president, was in retirement in Cormeil, outside Paris. Lewins, although still living in Paris, had ceased to associate with his compatriots, and there was no recognized leader to whom the French could address their enquiries. When Thomas Addis Emmet and O'Connor were approached, each denied the claims of the other, and forced the Consulate to consult both individually until the merits of one might render the services of the other superfluous.[8]

The temporary agreement of the United Irish state prisoners in Dublin at the time of the 'Kilmainham Treaty' in 1798 did not long survive their arrival in Scotland as prisoners in March 1799. Relations at Fort George, where they were imprisoned, were acrimonious; their passions were restrained by a tacit agreement not to exacerbate imprisonment by quarrelling, and the

8. Emmet, *Ireland under English Rule*, II, 265.

agreement was maintained by the simple expedient of avoiding each other. However, on the eve of his release, MacNeven had issued an ultimatum demanding satisfaction from Arthur O'Connor for some earlier insult. O'Connor had genuinely forgotten the incident.[9] He was typical of vainglorious men, who make rash statements only to forget them almost immediately, and would have been quite prepared to compose his differences with the Emmet group had he been permitted to pursue his own ambitions. Thomas Addis Emmet and MacNeven felt that the United Irish Society was no place for flippancy or ambition and considered O'Connor a threat to the entire organization. A duel between Emmet and O'Connor had only narrowly been averted on the passage to Hamburg, and although the accusations had been withdrawn, Thomas Addis Emmet warned O'Connor 'that he should not be expected to renew any intimacy'. By August 1802, MacNeven was in Amsterdam with Emmet's group. O'Connor travelled on to Calais, where he found his old friends among the opposition Whigs en route for Paris. But few, apart from Lord and Lady Oxford, would speak to him, and most of them rejected invitations to civic receptions to which he also had been invited, on the grounds that he had betrayed his cause and his comrade at Maidstone. O'Connor demanded satisfaction from Tierney, who had made the charge, then characteristically omitted to send the letter in the flurry of preparations for his Italian trip with the Oxfords. The Paris authorities, however, had been informed of the affair, and it is a token of O'Connor's resilience that he should have survived the bad publicity to become France's principal adviser on Irish affairs.[10]

In February 1803, both Thomas Addis Emmet and O'Connor arrived in Paris, Emmet having been invited by Hamilton to replace him as leader of the United Irishmen in France. There is no record of Emmet's arrival in the French archives; but to have arrived unannounced would have been uncharacteristic of O'Connor. With typical aplomb, he wrote to Talleyrand in November 1802, and to the Minister of Justice on his return from Italy the following February, outlining his previous association with France and claiming the appointment as United Irish ambassador to France since 1796, when he had concluded a treaty with Hoche. A diligent search uncovered no trace of such a treaty, but the glowing reports of Reinhard were discovered, and O'Connor's claims were accepted before anything was known of Thomas Emmet's new role in the organization.[11] Emmet's claims were consequently treated with scepticism, and from the outset the negotiations were coloured by the feud between the two leaders.

9. I.S.P.O. 620/12/143, correspondence between O'Connor and MacNeven, June 1802; Madden, *United Irishmen*, 3rd ser., III, 22–9; and T.C.D. MS. 873/578, for Madden's source.
10. For Emmet in Amsterdam see I.S.P.O. 620/12/146, and A.N. F⁷ 6330 doss. 6988 for O'Connor in Calais.
11. See A.N. BB³ 200 fo. 202 and A.A.E. Corr. Pol. Ang. 601 fos. 88 and 105 for ministerial correspondence on O'Connor, Nov. 1802–Mar. 1803.

On Monday 30 May 1803, Alexandre Dalton called on Thomas Addis Emmet at Cormeil. Dalton had served in the old Irish Brigade, sailed in Hoche's expedition of 1796, and was now attached to the War Ministry as aide-de-camp to the minister, Alexandre Berthier. Dalton, and in his absence General Harty, had been commissioned to negotiate with the United Irishmen. Ireland was to become the preserve of this ministry, with Marine taking a secondary role. Foreign Affairs, formerly so prominent in such discussions, played no part in those of 1803 to 1805, an indication of Bonaparte's view of these Irishmen as simply another factor in his military and naval plans against England. Dalton had already spoken with O'Connor. This angered Thomas Addis Emmet, who suspected him of having fallen under his rival's influence. Emmet was particularly annoyed that O'Connor had succeeded in speaking with 'the Great', the Marine and War Ministers and General Massena, commander designate of the Irish expedition, whilst he, despite repeated demands, did not secure an audience with the War Minister until 19 July. Discussions with both Dalton and the Minister centred on the notorious dispute between the two leaders. Berthier asked Emmet if O'Connor was popular in Ireland. Emmet replied in the negative, that O'Connor had no communication with the new executive and that his 1796 appointment had been nullified by the collapse of its predecessor.

By this date the dispute had become the talk of the Paris cafés and was causing concern in government circles. Emmet was cautioned for arranging a referendum among the Irish to establish his own position; but he considered the warning a ploy by O'Connor, and it was ignored. The quarrel had not yet spread to the Irish exiles as a body and most were dismayed at its effect on the negotiations. Miles Byrne had planned to visit both Emmet and O'Connor on his arrival in Paris that September, but was deterred by the rumour that they were on bad terms. Every day he listened to the United Irishmen in the London Coffee House lamenting the consequences of the quarrel. An attempt to secure a reconciliation had failed, and although O'Connor was happy enough to work jointly with Emmet, he would not recognize his appointment. On Sunday 18 September the two men met accidentally in the rue de Rivoli. Emmet was surprised at the warmth of O'Connor's enquiries about his family and replied coldly in an attempt to rid himself of his enemy. O'Connor persevered. He thought the French were playing them off against one another and suggested an exchange of information on their discussions. Emmet, suspecting that O'Connor was trying to discover which had the confidence of the government, rebuffed the overture and the attempt at reconciliation was not renewed.[12]

It proved even more difficult to re-establish contact with the remnants of

12. Emmet, *Ireland Under English Rule*, II, 263–5, 273–311 and Byrne, *Memoirs*, I, 307–8. For Dalton see A.A.G. Doss. Pers. 2ᵉ sér. G.D. 852 and G. Six, *Dictionnaire Biographique des Généraux et Amiraux de la Révolution et de l'Empire 1792–1814*, 2 vols. (**Paris**, 1931), I, 282.

the United Irish Society in Ireland. France, like England, had lost touch with the movement during the peace years. Consequently in 1803 its most immediate concern was to discover if it still existed. The United men in Paris were told to inform their compatriots that the First Consul had determined to send another expedition. Arms would be landed in advance, and they were to refrain from partial risings until the French arrived. John Swiney was appointed to convey the intelligence to Ireland. He left Paris in August and travelled via Hamburg to Cork. There he learnt of the collapse of Emmet's Rebellion, and increased government vigilance deterred travel into the countryside. Instead he despatched messengers to tell of the French plans. The mission appears to have been a success and there is some evidence of United Irish re-organization in consequence. Dublin Castle had wind of a French agent in the country, but failed to discover either his identity or his whereabouts until he was safely back in France. Swiney returned to Paris at the end of October, convinced that French plans to send a large force to Ireland were impracticable after the collapse of Emmet's Rebellion and that a smaller force should sail immediately if hopes of liberating Ireland were not to be lost forever. It was an opinion also held by Thomas Addis Emmet after he had heard of the abortive rising and which he was urging on Dalton when Swiney returned.[13]

News of Emmet's Rebellion seemed to confirm Thomas Addis Emmet's claims for the existence of a new executive in Ireland, and Berthier offered to prepare an Irish invasion force immediately.[14] The news had created a sensation in the Paris press and cafés, but if French reaction was generally favourable, it was intermingled with mounting criticism of the Irish for not postponing the rising until France's preparations against England had been completed. The report of its failure came as a blow, and Thomas Addis Emmet tried to prevent discouragement by concealing it from his fellow exiles. He was particularly anxious about the effects of Robert's speech on the French government and tried to convince Berthier that it had been misrepresented by the British press. Three days later the speech appeared in the *Argus* divested of its anti-French paragraphs. But this was essentially a piece of anti-British propaganda, and Emmet's fears were justified.[15] Robert's unilateral action raised doubts about Thomas's own attitude towards France and confirmed the growing preference for O'Connor.

Berthier was growing impatient with such bickering and insisted that

13. A.N. AF IV 1672 plaq. 2 fos. 203–8 and Emmet, *Ireland Under English Rule*, II, 263 and 312, for Emmet's account of the mission; also I.S.P.O. 620/11/130/68, 620/13/178/23 and 620/50/38, information sent to Dublin Castle, Dec. 1803–Jul. 1804.

14. *Correspondance de Napoléon 1ᵉʳ*, VIII, 6994.

15. The *Argus*, no. 189, also nos. 123–31, and Aulard, *Paris sous le Consulat*, IV, 285–7 for the effect of the news in Paris; Emmet, *Ireland Under English Rule*, II, 304, 312; and A.N. AF IV 1672 plaq. 2 fos. 203–8, Emmet to Berthier, 8 Jan. 1804.

O'Connor and Emmet should settle their differences and form a new United Irish committee. Emmet was more inclined to be reasonable at this stage, for Bonaparte had lately conceded all United Irish demands. In a long document sent to Berthier on 13 January 1804, and transmitted to Emmet and O'Connor the following day, he had agreed not to conclude peace with England until Irish independence had been recognized, to award French commissions to all those taking part in an invasion of Ireland, to take reprisals against English prisoners in France if United Irishmen captured by England were not treated as prisoners of war, and, if the expedition failed, to incorporate the Irish corps into the French army. Emmet was confident that he could introduce enough of his own supporters into the committee to neutralize O'Connor's influence, but when Dalton announced the names of the new committee he saw with dismay that his own recommendations had been laid aside and those of O'Connor substituted.[16]

The conflict between the two men was one of personality rather than policy and the demands of O'Connor differed little from those of his rival. It was rather his pretensions to power and his potential for dictatorship if he were sent to Ireland with French support that caused most friction. At every opportunity Emmet had emphasized Ireland's loss of faith in French promises, and his suspicions angered Dalton. O'Connor had no reservations about soliciting French aid, and was particularly insistent on the need for a large invasion force. He had already quarrelled with Robert Emmet over this, asserting that the United Irishmen could no longer act independently of French aid, Emmet retorting that he was about to prove the contrary by organizing an Irish rebellion.[17] Robert's fears of French domination were shared by his brother, and as French policy turned in favour of a full-scale invasion, Thomas's reservations took on the appearance of downright hostility. 'We understand from M. Emmet', wrote Berthier to Bonaparte, 'that he and his friends only want the French to win Irish independence and that they are afraid of introducing the French into the country in case they interfere in the establishment of an Irish government.' He had been warned of this by O'Connor who said that the same faction had been responsible for the latest rebellion in Ireland; 'his own party had little time for these people; they had complete trust in the French and were discreet, whilst the others he considered to be some kind of jacobins'.[18]

Despite the propaganda to the contrary, Emmet's Rebellion was considered

16. Emmet, *Ireland Under English Rule*, ii, 318–24; also *Correspondance de Napoléon Ier*, ix, no. 7475; and A.A.G. Doss. Pers. 2e sér G.D. 393 for the January communiqué.

17. P.R.O. H.O. 100/114/56, Wickham to J. King, 13 Oct. 1803.

18. A.N. AF IV 1672 plaq. 2 fo. 202, Berthier to the First Consul, [Jan.] 1804; also fos. 203–8 and 209–16 for T.A. Emmet's letters to Berthier and Bonaparte; AF IV 1195 doss. 4 fos. 9–10 for O'Connor's claims, and Emmet, *Ireland Under English Rule*, ii, 265, 295, 304–6, for Emmet's acrimonious exchanges with Dalton.

as anti-French in Paris, and together with Thomas's reservations it had
convinced the Consulate that this group was inherently antagonistic towards
France. In February 1804 O'Connor was appointed general of a new Irish
Legion, and since all the United Irishmen in France were expected to join,
overall control of United Irish affairs had been effectively placed in his
hands.[19] For Thomas Addis Emmet the appointment proved that O'Connor
was feathering his own nest, and that Bonaparte, in supporting such a power-
seeker, had no intention of establishing a democratic government in Ireland.
By March, Emmet had again retired to Cormeil. His last meeting with
Dalton had taken place on 17 February; his diary ends abruptly on 10 March,
and in October he sailed for America. Dublin Castle considered his departure
from France a significant commentary on the state of United Irish affairs.
'I consider this intelligence to be of importance', wrote Marsden, 'for he is
undoubtedly the ablest man of those sent from hence; ... ' and he watched
with mounting satisfaction as 'the more efficient ... exiles' were alienated
by O'Connor's advancement.[20] From New York Emmet wrote to Robert
Simms in Belfast explaining his reasons for abandoning the mission in Paris.
He had doubted the sincerity of France from the outset; what he saw there
convinced him that every vestige of republicanism in Ireland would be
eradicated if the French were ever permitted to land and that O'Connor
'would ... be selected under the auspices of the *Protecting Country*, to be a
greater man than Schimmelpenninck is likely to be in Holland and to revive
the ancient title of O'Connor King of Ireland ... '.[21] It had already been
rumoured in Ireland that O'Connor was encouraging the French to impose a
ready-made constitution on the country. He had certainly never made any
secret of his vision of another O'Connor kingdom, and many sympathizers
were dismayed at his rising star: 'he has a bad, very bad countinance,'
wrote Drennan's sister from Belfast, 'and will never rest till he is some how
exalted—I like him not and hope he never may come to Ireland ... He
would try to be an Irish Buonaparte, ... and drive far from him honester
men and greater sufferers, who bore the brunt of the day, and perhaps
lost it from more virtuous principles.'[22]

The moderate section of the United Irish leadership had tended to be
over-moralistic about matters of politics and power and to overlook the
fact that O'Connor had shown himself to be a diplomat of quite exceptional
talent. Nevertheless, it was O'Connor's pre-eminence which caused Thomas

19. A.N. AF IV 118 doss. 669 fo. 13, arrêté of 23 Feb. 1804.

20. P.R.O. H.O. 100/128/129–30, A. Marsden to J. King, 20 Apr. 1805; also his letter of 2 Aug.
1804 in H.O. 100/123/3. Emmet, *Ireland Under English Rule*, II, 324–7, for his last days in Paris.

21. P.R.O.N.I. T.1815/4, Emmet to Simms, 1 Jun. 1805.

22. P.R.O.N.I. T.765/1072, Mrs. McTier to Drennan, 21 Nov. 1803; see also I.S.P.O. 620/14/42;
S.O.C. 1031/35; and A.H.G. X^h 14 (MacNeven to Donzelot, 10 Aug. 1804), for similar sentiments among other United leaders.

Addis Emmet's withdrawal from France and the progressive disintegration of the remaining leadership. But at the close of 1803, the division within the United Irishmen was not yet irrevocable. It was confined to the old leaders nursing prejudices from earlier days. The only confirmed O'Connorite was Thomas Corbet, with MacNeven, William Lawless and John Swiney on the opposing side. The final schism had yet to take place in the Irish Legion.

Bonaparte's English invasion plans were launched on 24 June with orders for the construction of a flotilla of flat boats to transport 125,000 men across the Channel. On 16 August he ordered transports for 12,000 troops to prepare for Ireland at Brest. Thirty-six thousand stand of arms for the Irish expected to join the French were ordered from neighbouring ports, and the expedition was to be ready to sail by 20 January 1804. Truguet and Augereau were appointed to the naval and military commands respectively, and preparations were to be made in close consultation with O'Connor.[23] The creation of the Irish Legion by the decree of 31 August 1803 injected new life into the moribund Society: United men converged on the assembly point at Morlaix in the west of France, and many made the journey on foot to accustom themselves to the long winter marches which they expected to make after their arrival in Ireland.[24] Hope and self-respect had been restored after years of surviving on French charity, and destitution during the peace period. By supplying such a body of leaders, Bonaparte was filling the void left by the collapse of the United Irish executive in Ireland. But the Legion did not replace the old executive's ability to negotiate. As an adjunct of the French army, owing allegiance to Bonaparte, it was scarcely in any position to dictate Ireland's future government. In effect the United Irish Society both owed its temporary revival to Bonaparte and had fallen completely under his control.

The Legion was to consist of several brigades of infantry, Irish nationality was the only requirement for enlistment, and Bonaparte fulfilled his promise of awarding commissions to every recruit.[25] It was to be organized under Adjutant-General Bernard MacSheehy, taking his orders from General Donzelot as area commander at Brest and General Augereau as overall commander of the Irish expedition. The object of the Legion's creation was multiple. It was designed to supply the native leaders found wanting when Humbert landed. But an element of propaganda was present from

23. For initial preparations see Desbrière, *Projets et Tentatives*, III, 86–113; *Correspondance de Napoléon 1ᵉʳ*, VIII, 7009, 7233 and 7273; A.N. AF IV 1195 doss. 2; and A.H.G. C¹⁷* 160, III, no. 744. Details of the discussions with O'Connor can be found in A.N. GG² 23 fo. 35 and P.R.O. F.O. 27/70, secret information from France, 10 Jul. 1804.
24. Byrne, *Memoirs*, I, 318–37; A.H.G. C¹ 16, Berthier's correspondence, Jul.–Aug. 1804; and A.N. AF IV 103 doss. 578, arrêté of 31 Aug. 1803, establishing the Legion.
25. *Correspondance de Napoléon 1ᵉʳ*, IX, 7475 and A.H.G. C¹ 3, Berthier to MacSheehy, 19 Jan. 1804.

the outset. The choice of Morlaix, the point of assembly for prisoners of war about to be exchanged back to England, betrays Bonaparte's plans for publicizing the Legion's existence. One English officer in Morlaix had recognized MacNeven and Lawless, and his enquiries provided the British authorities with a fairly comprehensive report on the Legion after his return home. It is possible that Bonaparte had overlooked the danger, but he had been warned of it by Decrès, the Minister of Marine, and MacNeven's efforts to prevent the departure of MacNamara, the English officer, were deliberately thwarted. Decrès had suggested that the prisoner-of-war assembly station be moved to another town, but Bonaparte's object had already been served and it was the Legion instead which moved. In February it was transferred to Quimper and subsequently to Carhaix, which remained its home until the following August.[26]

It was, however, Bonaparte's failure to effect his invasion plans quickly, rather than prior planning, which elevated the propaganda element above all other considerations. Bonaparte was impatient in the months immediately after the Hanover campaign. He travelled to Boulogne on 2 November 1803 and was impressed by the narrowness of the Channel and the ease with which he might avenge England's 'six centuries of outrage' against France. But Decrès had examined the preparations at Brest and conclud-ed that they would not be ready before January 1804, if at all. He had never been enthusiastic about the Irish expedition and suggested that the Brest preparations would be better employed for propaganda purposes. As the preparations at Brest dragged through the early months of 1804, Bonaparte decided to adopt his Marine Minister's suggestion of diverting British attention to Brest to facilitate the sailing of the Channel fleet.[27] Until the close of 1803 Bonaparte had not doubted France's ability to successfully invade both England and Ireland. But as obstacles accumulated, the Brest fleet gradually assumed the diversionary role which it was to retain for the next two years.

The process had commenced in January 1804 with the discovery of the correspondence between Mehée de la Touche, in Paris, and Sir Francis Drake, British minister in Bavaria. Mehée, a fairly unscrupulous double agent, who had sold his services to England and France alike, was persuaded to inform Drake of Dalton's negotiations with the United Irishmen and of the formation of the Irish battalions on the western coast, and to suggest that naval preparations in the northern ports were a feint to disguise those

26. A.H.G. C¹ 5 and C¹ 7 for displacement orders, 19 Feb. and 31 Mar. 1804; C¹ 4 and A.N. BB³ 235 fo. 27, for Decrès's correspondence, Jan.–Feb. 1804; and I.S.P.O. 620/13/178/35 for MacNamara's account.
27. A.N. AF IV, 1195, doss. 4, correspondence of Truguet and Decrès, May and Nov. 1803; *Correspondance de Napoléon rᵉʳ*, VIII. 7279.

for Ireland at Brest and Texel. Truguet was ordered to distract the British blockading force by making occasional sorties from Brest. By May, when Truguet was reprimanded for not implementing such instructions, the British ships outside Brest had increased to thirty-one of the line and innumerable smaller vessels. The ploy had clearly been a great success. But Truguet had not guessed at the motives behind the instructions, and in a frustrated outburst he argued that it was impossible to comply with them. Partial sorties would simply expose the small forces to attack and jeopardize the success of the entire expedition. France would have to decide between the threat and the reality of an Irish expedition, for naval procedure would not permit the pursuit of both simultaneously.[28]

Such frustration at the torpor of the naval preparations was exacerbated by problems in the Irish Legion. Despite the overwhelming response of the United leaders, recruitment into the rank and file of the Legion was disappointing. In April 1804 it consisted of 62 officers and never increased beyond 67 officers and 24 men. Since the principal function of the Legion was to provide officers for the native Irish, this paucity of ordinary soldiers was not disastrous. But it did create a vacuum in the training programme by denying the officers the opportunity of exercising authority over subordinates. Recruitment in Hanover or Ireland, sponsored desertion of the Irish in English service, or a negotiated return of the deported Irish in Prussia, were put forward as solutions. Some Irish deserters from Jersey assured Donzelot that many more would follow their example if they knew of the Legion's existence. But there is no indication that any of these suggestions were implemented, and in October 1804 two battalions of French soldiers were attached to supply the deficiency.[29]

The officers in the Legion represented almost every county in Ireland, amply supplying the French need for local leaders. A complete list survives for July 1804: Leinster and Dublin had supplied thirty officers, Ulster and Connacht each seven and Munster eight. Of the remainder, five had been in the Irish Brigade before 1792, one was an Irishman in Spanish service, one an Irishman who had been living in England, one was a Scot and there were three Frenchmen. Most of the captains were professional men, men of private means, or ex-students; the lieutenants and sub-lieutenants, though continuing to reflect a sprinkling of professional men, tended to be farm-workers, small merchants or tradesmen. Most had taken part in earlier expeditions to Ireland, fought in either one or both rebellions, or had been involved

---

28. A.N. AF IV 1195 doss. 2 p^{ce} 35, Truguet to Decrès, 27 May 1804; *Correspondance de Napoléon Ier*, VIII, 7539 and IX, 7800. See also A.H.G. C^1 7 for the British blockade.

29. A.H.G. C^{2*} 461, État de Situation, Brest, Apr. 1804–Aug. 1805. See A.N. AF IV 1195 doss. 3 p^{ce} 14, A.H.G. C^1 3, C^1 4 and C^1 7, for suggested remedies to the recruiting problem, Jan.–Nov. 1804.

in the upper levels of the United Irish Society.[30] They had consequently asserted authority over subordinates and would not accept inferior positions in the Legion without protest.

The early stages of its organization went well. Each day MacSheehy instructed the officers in the use of arms and the art of command and seemed pleased with their progress. MacSheehy, however, was a reluctant commander; he felt the appointment would weaken his position in the French army, and he considered O'Connor's generalship a direct threat to his own authority. O'Connor wrote to MacSheehy on 4 March telling of his appointment, expressing his hope that good relations would prevail in the Legion, and announcing his imminent arrival at Carhaix. Instead of replying directly, MacSheehy sent copies of the letter and of his own reply to the Minister of War. He refused to supply O'Connor with any details about the Legion, claiming that his orders were to correspond only with the Minister, and when O'Connor arrived at Carhaix in July, he reputedly admitted his desire to undermine the new commander's authority. MacSheehy was certainly a poor commander. Even Miles Byrne thought him capricious, vindictive and totally unqualified to command a political corps like the Legion.[31] His biased and exaggerated reports painted a blacker picture of the Legion's internal troubles than existed in fact, and every misdemeanour characteristic of garrison life was represented as a plot to undermine his position or as the work of English agents. But the virtual removal of his authority, only two months after his appointment, was an irreparable blow at a time when he was experiencing considerable difficulty appeasing those officers who felt that they had not received the rank commensurate with their abilities and past services. Unable to discipline a body of men who taunted him with his reduced authority after O'Connor's appointment, MacSheehy predictably gravitated towards Thomas Addis Emmet's former supporters, now the core of an anti-O'Connorite party within the Legion.

Administrative shortsightedness rather than favouritism on the part of MacSheehy was the initial cause of the discontent. Nominations to commissions were required before permits to travel to Morlaix could be issued. It is not quite clear what criteria were adopted in the allocation of such commissions. But Emmet's belief that they were made on O'Connor's recommendation seems to have been entirely justified. Emmet himself was never consulted, and many of his supporters were assigned inferior grades. Many others who had taken part in the 1803 rebellion, or whose names were unknown to France because of years of imprisonment, also found themselves in subordinate positions, and naturally felt that their sufferings merited a more

30. A.H.G. C¹ 14, list compiled in Oct. 1804.
31. Byrne, *Memoirs*, II, 6. See A.H.G. C¹ 1, 3, 6–7 and 14, for the correspondence between O'Connor, MacSheehy, Augereau and the Minister, Jan.–Jul. 1804.

just reward. Their reaction reflected the conflicting French and Irish conceptions of the Legion's function. To France it was a training school for future leaders, and superior rank was awarded to those Irishmen of known local standing or with proven qualities of leadership.

In contrast most of the Irish considered their commissions to be rewards for their services in the United cause, and they were horrified when some who had never been United Irishmen were appointed to superior positions. Thomas Markey Johnston was an Ulsterman who had fought in the 1798 rebellion and had languished in prison until Amiens. In July 1802 he had sailed for Bordeaux, where he was living at the time of the Legion's formation. He was therefore unknown in Paris when the appointments were made. In January 1804, when a captaincy fell vacant, he demanded promotion as a right and appealed to Augereau when MacSheehy refused. His letter listed all those holding captaincies in the Legion, distinguishing between those who had suffered in the United Irish cause and those whom he considered to have no claim to such positions. Of the latter, Jeremiah Fitzhenry had come to France voluntarily during the peace and had never been a United Irishman; William O'Meara had been a soldier in the Berwick Regiment of the old Irish Brigade and had served in England's service from 1793 to 1801, when he had responded to Bonaparte's amnesty for the *émigrés*. Some had been in British service in the previous war, others had been long-standing French residents. Those who had been clamouring for promotion soon accused MacSheehy of supporting a party within the Legion, which he undoubtedly appeared to be doing, since by February many Emmet supporters, all prominent leaders in Ireland, had been given captaincies.[32] Insubordination became the order of the day, as the disgruntled officers formed themselves into an O'Connorite clique and refused to obey the authority of either their immediate superiors or of MacSheehy. By mid-July MacSheehy's authority had entirely disintegrated.

In June the dispute between the two factions reached a climax in an incident which was to be the first of several to cast doubt upon the Legion's loyalty. On Sunday 4 June MacSheehy assembled the officers to present the Legion with its flag and to administer an oath of loyalty to the new Emperor and constitution. John Swiney stepped forward and expressed some doubt about taking the oath, since he felt that it might encroach upon his duty to Ireland. MacSheehy's assurances that Napoleon was the only person who could liberate Ireland seemed to calm Swiney's fears and he took the oath with the rest of the Legion. That evening, however, Thomas Corbet, James Blackwell and Edmond St. Leger, members of the Legion's administrative

---

32. A.H.G. C¹ 15, MacSheehy to Berthier, 28 and 30 Jul. 1804, and his communications of Jan. and Jun. 1804 in C¹ 12–13. Differing accounts, exonerating the Legion, came from the Carhaix Municipal authorities in March (C¹ 12) and Thomas Markey Johnston in August (C¹ 17).

council, refused to sign a declaration that the oath had been taken unanimously. Swiney demanded an explanation from Corbet; a quarrel ensued and quickly deteriorated into a general affray between the two parties. The fracas was terminated by MacSheehy, and Corbet and Swiney were placed in confinement. The arrests did little to appease tempers and several further altercations ensued. The divisions which had been confined to the principal leaders in Paris had now spread throughout the exiled movement, former Emmet supporters adopting MacSheehy as their leader, the others looking to O'Connor.

MacSheehy recommended the removal of Corbet, Blackwell and St. Leger, for their refusal to sign the declaration. He defended Swiney, and though he recognized that he too would have to be punished, he recommended his restoration to the Legion. Berthier accepted MacSheehy's recommendations, but the arrival of O'Connor at Carhaix on 24 June altered the entire situation. 'I found the Irish Legion in the greatest confusion on my arrival,' he wrote to Augereau. 'It was split into two parties. Adjutant Commandant MacSheehy at the head of one, and the other complaining that the good of the corps had been sacrificed by a spirit of intrigue and faction.'[33] O'Connor blamed MacSheehy for the troubles and recommended his replacement by an impartial French officer. Augereau had worked closely with O'Connor in the first six months of the Legion's formation and was only too willing to support any accusations against an officer who had persistently corresponded directly with the War Minister in defiance of his own commanding position. On Augereau's advice, therefore, the Minister suspended the implementation of MacSheehy's suggestions until a full report could be submitted by O'Connor and Donzelot. News of the decision caused a further deterioration in MacSheey's authority. On the night of 29 July O'Connor's supporters held a dinner to celebrate the victory, after which some ran amok through the town in what MacSheehy described as 'a victory orgy', rousing angry members of Carhaix's municipality from their beds and displaying the total disintegration of MacSheehy's authority.[34] In several further reports, O'Connor took Corbet's part against MacSheehy and Swiney, and on 18 September the Minister accepted his recommendation that Swiney should be punished and MacSheehy removed from his command. Two days later, before the order had reached Carhaix, the final episode of the dispute was played out in a fatal duel between Corbet and Swiney.

Corbet did not wait for the decision from Paris, but sent Captain Ware on 20 September to challenge his opponent to a duel. MacNeven acted as

33. See Emmet, *Ireland Under English Rule*, II, 315, and various complaints by the Irish officers in A.H.G. C¹ 2–7, and X^h 14. Of the list of officers drawn up in Jul. 1804 (C¹ 14), 13 of the 21 captains were known adherents of Emmet, only 2 of O'Connor.

34. A.H.G. C¹ 13, O'Connor to Augereau, 24 Jun. 1804.

second to Swiney, Ware to Corbet. The passionate mutual hatred exhibited by the combatants was symptomatic of the irreparable division which now existed within the exiled movement. Corbet failed to await the signal to fire on three different occasions. Swiney received a leg wound at the second attempt, and when Corbet broke the rules a third time, he lost his temper, called Corbet 'a bloody awful shot' and proved his point by inflicting a mortal wound on his opponent at the first attempt. When the Minister's order arrived it could not be implemented. MacSheehy alone remained of the original antagonists. Swiney and MacNeven had resigned their commissions and retired to Bordeaux, the first of a stream of Emmet supporters to withdraw in the next six months. Thomas Corbet was dead; his younger brother William was inconsolable at the loss and contemplated leaving to join his family in New York. MacSheehy was sent back to Rennes, forbidden any further communication with the United Irishmen and given no other posting for over a year. His fears on taking up the appointment had been fully justified.[35]

After the removal of his opponents, O'Connor was in complete control of the Legion and of the United Irishmen on the Continent. He was closely consulted by the naval and military commanders of the invasion force, and his suggestions were generally implemented.[36] His undisputed command brought relative peace to the Legion, though the frustration and boredom of inaction played upon personal animosities and occasioned several further duels and disturbances in the course of the following year. The Swiney–Corbet dispute, however, was a turning point in United Irish fortunes on the Continent. The issue which had sparked off the dispute was Bonaparte's assumption of the title of Emperor.[37] Swiney, like the other partisans of Emmet, had never quite trusted Bonaparte, and opposed the move. The tinge of disloyalty had been attached to the Legion. In 1805–06 several further incidents increased fears that British agents were active in the Legion, and although there is no record of Napoleon's reaction, his failure to invite the Irish officers to his coronation in November, when every other battalion in the army of invasion was represented, looked like a mark of his disapproval.[38]

The inaction of 1804 had magnified the troubles in the Legion. But in

35. A.A.G. Doss. Pers. MacSheehy; T.C.D. Corbet MSS, T. Corbet to his father, 20 Sept. 1804. A full account of the disputes of the summer of 1804 can be found in A.H.G. C¹ 12–19.
36. See e.g. letters of Decrès, Donzelot etc. in A.N. AF IV 1195 doss. 2. p^{ce} 9, BB⁴ 205 fo. 150, C¹ 15 and C¹ 25.
37. T.C.D. MS. 253^{A}/312, W. P. Lyons submitting information on Corbet; A.H.G. C¹ 25–6, correspondence, Jan.–Feb. 1805, and X^{h} 14, for Aug. 1805; also A.N. F⁷ 3751, report on a duel between Powell and Swanton, Oct. 1805.
38. A.H.G. C¹ 19 and 26, Donzelot and Berthier to Augereau, 18 Sept. 1804 and 18 Feb. 1805 respectively.

September Napoleon had returned to the invasion preparations with renewed enthusiasm. At the end of 1804 a swift maritime victory over England was even more desirable than in the preceding year. France's capture on neutral territory and execution of the Bourbon Duc d'Enghien in March, and the proclamation of the Empire in May had intensified the fears of the other continental powers. Tsar Alexander I was bitter at Napoleon's refusal to let him mediate between France and England, and had been attempting to form an alliance against him. But despite the growing strength of internal war parties, Prussia and Austria were not yet ready for war and were thankful that the French Emperor's belligerent tendencies were engrossed by his English preparations. Napoleon was even less anxious for a continental war which would interrupt the English invasion plans, and preparations were pushed ahead with intensified urgency after September. Ganteaume, Truguet's successor as Minister of Marine, was told to consult with O'Connor and report on the prospects for a landing in Ireland that winter. But Ganteaume had misgivings about the venture. The English ships blockading Brest had become so confident that the French commanders were daily subjected to the humiliation of small English vessels sailing unharmed within sight of the new Brest batteries. The leaders of the Irish Legion were hopelessly divided and Ganteaume was confused by their conflicting advice. O'Connor was optimistic of success if the French landed in Ulster; others called O'Connor a charlatan, claimed that the French would find no support in Ireland, and that the project was doomed from the outset.[39]

Ganteaume's official report of the 13 September, however, did not mention such reservations. He assured the Minister that the required force would be ready by October, and O'Connor's recommendations were reproduced in full. Decrès transmitted the report to the Emperor, enclosing several maps of Ireland, and impressing on him the need for swift action if he had indeed decided on the venture.[40] Napoleon was delighted with the report and wrote enthusiastically that he had resolved to send 18,000 men from Brest and 25,000 from Texel to Ireland, whilst 125,000 would invade England from Boulogne. In Ireland the invading armies would join with the insurgents and march on Dublin. But the English invasion was still the primary concern. The Brest fleet would land 18,000 men and 500 horses in Ireland, and return to assist the passage of the *armée d'Angleterre* across the Channel. On the same day Napoleon issued instructions for smaller expeditions to Martinique, Surinam and St. Helena and mused on the total confusion which such a multiple attack would cause to the English navy, as it scoured the seas in quest of the French.[41]

39. A.N. BB⁴ 205 fos. 143–4 and 150, Ganteaume's correspondence, Sept. 1804; *Correspondance de Napoléon 1er*, ix, 7996.

40. A.N. AF IV 1195 doss. 2. pᶜᵉ 9, Decrès to Napoleon, 19 Sept. 1804.

41. *Correspondance de Napoléon 1er*, ix, 8048, 8060 and 8063; A.H.G. C¹ 20, letters from Berthier and Donzelot to Augereau, 4 and 11 Oct. 1804.

On 3 October, however, Decrès wrote anxiously that the instructions and the maps, which had been returned in the same packet, had not yet arrived. By the 8th Napoleon assumed that they had fallen into enemy hands and asked Fouché to make enquiries. At the same time he wrote to Decrès warning him that the entire plan for the winter campaign would have to be altered if the enquiries proved fruitless, since the packet had contained outlines of the expeditions to Ireland, Surinam and St. Domingo. The packet eventually reached its destination on 11 October, by open post from Boulogne, though it had been sent by courier from Paris. There was no proof that it had fallen into enemy hands, but the whole affair was extremely suspicious. The Brest embarkation was cancelled and Napoleon's attention was transferred to Villeneuve's fleet which was trying to escape from Toulon. Desbrière has concluded from this incident that Napoleon had never really been sincere about the October plan and that his mind was already focusing on the West Indian expedition which would lead directly to Trafalgar the following year. The enthusiasm of Napoleon's letters, however, and the tone of panic after the loss had been discovered do not support Desbrière's claim, and in October 1804 an Irish expedition was in total conformity with the plan of causing complete havoc in Britain's naval defence by attacking her at a dozen different points.[42]

The abandonment of the October scheme necessitated a complete change of programme. In December the Toulon and Rochefort fleets were ordered to the West Indies to attack the English colonies, secure the French islands, and return to the Ferol in Spain to join with the Spanish fleet. With the Brest fleet the combined forces would then sail into the Channel to assist the Boulogne flotilla in an invasion of England. Bad weather and the intensified blockade of Brest produced another alteration in plan in May 1805, when Villeneuve was told to return instead to Brest and remove the blockade. The new instructions never reached Villeneuve and the resulting confusion set in motion the train of events which would terminate at Trafalgar. In the 1805 plans Ireland was ignored except as a diversionary factor. In July General Marmont in Holland received instructions to make ostentatious preparations for an expedition and to foster the rumour that it was destined for Ireland. In addition, three frigates would sail from Rochefort and draw attention to themselves by attacking shipping in Irish ports. The ploy was designed to weaken the blockade of Brest and Boulogne and to facilitate the projected juncture of both fleets with Villeneuve in a last desperate attempt by Napoleon to avert a continental war.[43] In November 1804 Austria had

42. For the crisis see A.N. AF IV 1195 doss. 4 p^{ce} 19, Decrès to Napoleon, 3 Oct. 1804; *Lettres inédites de Napoléon 1er*, ed. L. Lecestre, 2 vols. (Paris, 1897), I, 46; *Correspondance de Napoléon 1er* X, 8115; Desbrière, *Projets et Tentatives*, IV, 210–13; and A.H.G. C^1 21, Berthier to Napoleon, 17 Oct. 1804.

43. *Correspondance de Napoléon 1er*, X, 8206, 8231, 8379 and 8700, 8809 and 8953; A.H.G. C^1 32, instructions to Marmont, 5 and 13 Jul. 1805; and A.N. AF IV 1196 doss. 1 p^{ce} 106, Decrès to Napoleon, 6 June 1805.

signed a pact of friendship with Russia and the renewal of the French threat in Italy finally pushed her into Russian arms. In July an alliance was formed between England and Russia, and with Austria joining on 9 August, the third coalition against France became a reality.

Napoleon offered Hanover to Prussia in an attempt to retain her neutrality, and he still hoped that the invasion of England might avert the threatened war. Villeneuve had returned to Spain at the end of July and sailed again for Brest on 14 August. If he could effect the juncture with the Brest fleet and sail into the Channel, the situation might yet be saved. 'There is still time,' wrote Napoleon to Talleyrand with unflagging optimism, 'I will be master of England.' But Austria invaded Bavaria before the plans could be implemented. Napoleon lifted his camps at Boulogne and ordered the Brest fleet to disembark.[44] The movement of the massive army towards the Rhine had commenced, and with it the continental campaign which was to end at Waterloo. Napoleon had hoped for a short campaign, after which he could return to the invasion preparations. But such hopes were dashed by the destruction of the combined Franco-Spanish fleet at Trafalgar on 21 October 1805. News of the defeat, which arrived in Paris on the 30th, left the Emperor unruffled. He had already abandoned the invasion plans, and it had been towards the Mediterranean rather than the Channel that Villeneuve was sailing when he was attacked.[45] In June 1806 the remnants of the Irish Legion were marched from Quimper to Alençon for incorporation into the Grand Army. France's dilatory attitude in implementing her promises, her patronage of the ambitious O'Connor, and finally the creation of the Empire, had convinced the more dedicated leaders that their initial doubts about Bonaparte's sincerity had been justified, and when the fate of the Legion was known, several of its most important members withdrew. The others remained because, for the moment, there was little else for them to do.[46]

II

The organization of the Irish Legion had engrossed United Irish attention since 1804, and there is no sign of any corresponding revival in Ireland. Emmet's Rebellion had eradicated any traces of the United Irish Society as a working political movement. Irish governments of the period felt that the

44. A.A.E. Mem. et Doc. Fonds France 1776 fos. 22 and 26, Napoleon to Talleyrand, 22 and 23 Aug. 1805; *Correspondance Inédite de Napoléon I*[er], ed. E. Picard and L. Tuetey, 5 vols. (Paris, 1912–1925), I, 83.
45. A.N. AF IV 1196 doss. 3 p[ces] 34, Decrès to Napoleon, 30 Oct. 1805. *Correspondance de Napoléon I*[er], XI, 9210.
46. Byrne, *Memoirs*, II, 13, 20–1; P.R.O.N.I. T.1011/1–4, for names of those who sailed to America.

country was more free from disaffection than at any time in the last decade, and the image of a newly loyal Ireland and a united offensive against the French became a favourite theme of the anti-Napoleonic propaganda which flooded England over the next two years.[47] The bigoted outbursts of some Irish M.P.s in the united parliament were scorned after 1803. Their comments on the catholic issue in particular sounded strangely archaic, and although they were always to be found voting on the side of government, ministers came to dread their intercessions and the parliamentary uproar which followed as a matter of course.[48] Cries of 'Jacobin' were outmoded in Britain after 1803, and despite the renewal of agrarian warfare in Ireland after 1806, little proof of treasonable influence was ever produced in support of such intermittent scaremongering.

Dublin Castle was sensible enough to recognize the apolitical nature of the agrarian disturbances which returned with a vengeance after 1806, and preferred to deal with them without invoking emergency powers. But in expressing this view the successive Viceroys and their Chief Secretaries were at variance with the bulk of the Irish gentry, and although no visible leadership came forward to direct this discontent, it was clear that the old United example was never very far from the minds of the agitators. The sworn bands of agrarian redressors who infested Munster throughout the period, the Threshers operating principally in Sligo, Roscommon, Longford, Mayo and Westmeath, the Caravats and Shanavests in Cork, Waterford and Kilkenny, all sought the redress of well-defined economic grievances;[49] it was their ability to terrorize an entire county and to prevent normal operation of the law rather than any sign of political motive which disturbed government. But most of the resident gentry could not believe that the military parading, the arming and oath-taking of these secret bodies was not based ultimately on ideas of political subversion, and most genuinely believed that tithes were a pretext for 'swearing of United men.'[50] Dublin Castle recognized well enough the dangers of such tumult in the event of a French invasion or a republican resurgence. Indeed there was sufficient incidental information on agitators insinuating neo-Defender or United Irish clauses

47. George, *Catalogue of Political and Personal Satires*, XII, 10009 and 10050. Reports from *The Times* on Ireland's peaceful disposition were reproduced in Paris, see Aulard, *Paris sous le Premier Empire*, I, 396.
48. See e.g. *Parl. Deb.*, IV, 834–1082; Senior, *Orangeism*, 178; N.L.I. MS. 61/435, Peel to Richmond, 3 Mar. 1813.
49. For various accounts of the aims and methods of such groups see I.S.P.O. S.O.C. 1120/41, 47 and 52, 1121/53, 1188/13 and P.R.O. H.O. 100/148/97–108; see also R. B. McDowell, *Public Opinion and Government Policy in Ireland, 1801–1846* (London, 1952), 59–65; N. Gash, *Mr. Secretary Peel*, 3rd edn. (London, 1964), 168–71; and *Parl. Deb.*, I, 1385–1900 and III, 118, 311–53.
50. P.R.O. H.O. 100/135/36–9, Marsden to King, 12 Feb. 1806; I.S.P.O. S.O.C. 1091/61, 1120/61–74, 1192/9, 1277/64; N.L.I. MS. 59/162; and *State Trials*, XXX, 83–5, 160–6 and 179, for this conflict of opinion between government and gentry.

into Thresher oaths, or playing upon the current agitation for catholic emancipation, to prevent complacency.[51]

Moreover, there were signs that, despite its overwhelming loyalty, Ulster might still provide the leadership for a revived republican movement, and that the Defender or United movements, or both, were smouldering at inferior levels. From December 1806 Dublin Castle received information about 'Regenerated Defenders' active in counties Monaghan, Down, Antrim and Armagh. Randle McAllister, a coach-driver from Antrim, was tried and capitally convicted for attempting to swear a militiaman into the Defenders. But the movement to which he had been loosely attached seemed an amalgam of surviving Defenderism and of the United Irishmen, rather than a simple revival of the former. Its secrecy was impenetrable, and in an effort to avoid the mistakes of its predecessors it had abolished all regular meetings, even at committee level; it had also forbidden any overt acts of militancy, the use of force to secure new members, or anything which might attract the attention of the authorities. Although government felt that surviving treason had not 'extended beyond the lower order of peasants and mechanics', sworn United men had automatic right of membership of these Defenders; they looked confidently to another French invasion and were sworn 'to aid and assist our friends from abroad ... and our brethren at home'.[52] Over the next few years reports of surviving pockets of disaffection were received from other counties, but every effort to infiltrate a movement which lacked both formal organization and a command structure failed miserably. No substantial information on surviving disaffection was received again until 1811, when adherents were referred to by the generic term of 'Ribbonmen'. The appellation mattered little: 'Regenerated Defenders' in north-east Ulster, 'Standard Men' in Donegal, 'a new Croppy System' in King's County, or Ribbonism— all represented that revolutionary survival from the 1790s, which had started at the top of the social ladder and moved steadily downwards to become a semi-permanent element of Irish discontent, notably in the towns.[53]

The vision of another national rising, when the people could find leaders, was a constant theme running through such disturbances. Notable reformers like the Duke of Leinster or prominent catholics like Standish O'Grady and Daniel O'Connell were all looked to at various stages as potential leaders. But the continuing expectation of a French invasion focused attention on the

51. See *State Trials*, xxx, 11, xxxi, 414; I.S.P.O. S.O.C. 1092/3, 1158/2 and 620/14/188, for examples of individuals encouraging popular expectation of French assistance.

52. I.S.P.O. S.O.C. 1120/4, Hamilton to Trail, 7 Aug. 1807; also 1120/3-8, 32 and 98, 1158/2 and P.R.O. H.O. 100/136/236-8, 423-32, for communications on the same subject, Dec. 1806-Sept. 1807.

53. M. R. Beames's unpublished article 'The Ribbon Societies: lower-class Nationalism in pre-Famine Ireland' describes this changing status of republicanism; and see I.S.P.O. S.O.C. 1120/5, 7, 32, 41 and P.R.O. H.O. 100/159 for the various names to describe the disaffected.

exiled United men. The finer points of the power struggle within the exiled leadership, or their growing despair of the French, were lost on the Irish populace, and O'Connor was hailed as the native liberator who would lead the French invasion force. 'The day is near approaching,' read a notice affixed to the door of the catholic church in Wicklow in September 1804, 'when O'Connor, the apostle of Liberty will be on our oppressed shore with an army, that will root out Tyranny from the Impoverished land of Ireland.'[54] The overwhelming defeat of the Franco-Spanish fleet at Trafalgar did little to dull such hopes, and Napoleon's continued victories on the Continent sustained the belief that another attempt would be made on Ireland when victory liberated the French armies abroad.

Reports of this continuing expectation of the French came from every part of the country in the years 1804 to 1807.[55] Some smacked of traditional protestant phobias about 'popery' or of eleventh-hour confessions by sentenced prisoners, and were dismissed by Irish governments less prone to credit scare stories than their predecessors. But many were substantiated, and the restiveness of a new generation which looked back to 1798 with pride convinced the Castle that any victory over the United movement would be dispelled by a French landing. At fairs, football matches, patterns and weekend dances, young men were heard to boast of relatives who had been out in '98. They spoke of the battles of Ballynahinch or New Ross and of how close they had come to victory that year; and within two years of his execution Robert Emmet had already taken pride of place in the martyrology developing around the memory of the fallen United men.[56] In August 1805 the funeral of Tone's father at Naas attracted huge crowds of ordinary people, and even the Dublin printer John Stockdale, who had played such a secondary role in the events of the 1790s, was surrounded by eager interpolators seeking news from France. Stockdale by this stage was a government informant, and as one of the last of the original leaders to have remained in touch with the exiled United men, he was well-placed to pronounce on any treasonable tendencies in the country. His information confirmed the feeling that the French would receive willing support from a large sector of the population, but for the moment the people were leaderless and there was no organized

54. I.S.P.O. S.O.C. 1030/100, seditious notice transmitted by Lt. Col. Caulfield, 12 Sept. 1804; see also S.O.C. 1193/1 (1808). 620/14/188/51 (1805); T.C.D. MS. 869/111 (1804); and Arthur Wellesley, Duke of Wellington, *Supplementary Despatches*, ed. by his son, 15 vols. (London, 1858–72), v, 119 for similar reports on popular attitudes towards O'Connor.

55. Rev. J. Hall, *Tour Through Ireland*, 2 vols. (London, 1813), II, 11; Wakefield, *An Account of Ireland*, II, 380; and for examples of such reports, see I.S.P.O. S.O.C. 1030/24, 1031/85; and P.R.O. H.O. 100/122/250, 316 and 324 for Leinster; S.O.C. 1032/24 for Munster; S.O.C. 1091/24 and H.O. 100/135/42–5 for Connacht; and S.O.C. 1120/55, 90 and 1091/77 for Ulster.

56. Zimmermann, *Songs of Irish Rebellion*, 175; see reports in I.S.P.O. S.O.C. 1031/16, 52–4, 1120/8 and P.R.O. H.O. 100/142/150–3, chiefly from areas most affected by the events of 1798.

treason in the country. A handful of former rebels in Dublin, notably William Henry Hamilton and Malachy Delaney, would come forward in such an event, and they talked of it among themselves. But they would do so only after the French had won a substantial victory, and the lower orders would not be called upon until then.[57]

Satisfied, therefore, that the manifest Irish sympathy for the French and the United exiles would remain dormant until either appeared at its head, government attention concentrated on preventing either from ever regaining a footing in the country. The years between the rupture of Amiens and Trafalgar witnessed Irish defence preparations on an unprecedented scale. Whitehall also believed that Ireland would be attacked first, and the main strength of the British blockading fleet lay off France's western rather than her Channel ports. But it was the continued existence of a treasonable core in the country, and the failure to make any substantial discoveries, which caused most anxiety. It was in the old areas of disaffection that government still expected to find traces of a dormant movement, and infuriatingly vague information of agents radiating out from Dublin, counselling calm until the French arrived, only reflected government failure to get at the nerve-centre of a conspiracy which it believed to exist, in however nebulous a form.[58] In 1807, Sir Arthur Wellesley, as Chief Secretary, was 'so well convinced of the existence of this organized body' and 'of its communication with France', that he suggested the compilation of a list of former traitors, and their immediate arrest on news of a French landing, as the only remedy to such continued ignorance. There is little evidence to support Wellesley's picture of an efficient and centralized system of treason during the Napoleonic Wars, and on the whole communication between Ireland and France had deteriorated to a trickle of personal correspondence from exiles like Tennent, Fitzhenry or Byrne. In the absence of substantial information on Irish treason, the bogey of a United Irish committee in Paris became the favourite means of justifying the continuation of extraordinary security measures, though the committee was never reformed after an abortive attempt at revival in 1804. But this conviction that any revival of the conspiracy in Ireland would come from the old leaders was shared by every administration of the period, and the list of rebels included in the 1798 Banishment Act was already a ready-reckoner of potential trouble-makers before Wellesley suggested it.[59]

57. I.S.P.O. S.O.C. 1031/36, W. Corbet to [   ], 28 Aug. 1805, submitting Stockdale's information.

58. Examples of official opinion on this matter and of the information on which it was based may be found in P.R.O. H.O. 100/123/57–8, 100/136/38–9, 100/142/221–3 and 296–9; W.O. 1/612/214–8 and P.R.O. 30/8/327/70.

59. For references to the Paris committee, see *Parl. Deb.*, III, 311–36, 477, IX, 1189; and P.R.O. W.O. 1/612/214–8 and 305–23, for correspondence between Wellesley and Castlereagh, Dec. 1807. On the trickle of correspondence between France and Ireland see I.S.P.O. 620/13/164 and P.R.O. H.O. 100/142/54 (from Jeremiah Fitzhenry), 1804 and H.O. 100/148/67–70 (from Miles Byrne), 1808, and P.R.O.N.I. D.1748 (from John Tennent).

Inadequate information perpetuated Dublin's fears. The intelligence network abroad, which had secured such accurate information prior to Amiens, was never re-established during the Napoleonic Wars, and the victory over disaffection on the mainland had also produced a run-down in the domestic service. From Bolton, Colonel Fletcher, now a leading Orangeman with a vested interest in tracking down Irish revolutionaries, continued to be a willing assistant, and he hounded the few old rebels who chanced to pass through Lancashire. But investigations showed that the few ex-United men living in England had been following normal and un-eventful lives for years, and could produce impeccable testimonials to prove it. Even McCabe had turned over a new leaf in Scotland, where he had been living with Whitehall's blessing. Despite the Irish community's persistent disposition for mischief in London, government informants agreed that there was no longer anything to fear from would-be Irish conspirators on the main-land. 'You know the Genius too well of our Erin-go-brah fellow Citizens;' wrote Moody, 'therefore I need not comment on their vain-boasting preten-sions. I scarcely ever met with an Irishman, but he would bring a force of five or six Thousand men of straw into the Field. The Metropolis at present is more quiet than I have known it during any period within the last Ten Years. I neither hear nor know of any organized malcontents . . . '.[60] In Lancashire too disaffection had disappeared, and in 1805 Fletcher's Lanca-shire network was dismantled.[61] The national offensive against Napoleon had decimated anti-war feeling in England, and just as Emmet's Rebellion had impelled the Irish radicals towards ostentatious constitutionalism, so in England radicals and francophiles were frightened by hairbrained schemes like that of Despard's and were anxious to distance themselves from such associations. Thomas Hardy and Lord Oxford made public denials when accused of continuing Jacobin sympathies, and such prominent old conspir-ators as Cowdroy, Bone, Lemaitre, Finnerty and Frost had eschewed their past and massed instead behind Sir Francis Burdett's constitutional agitation.[62]

The attempt to secure any inside information on the United Irish exiles met with even less success. Dublin's reluctance to permit the former leaders' return to Ireland reduced the choice of agents to the most unimportant. As disillusioned United Irishmen in France such as Alexander Lowry, Hampden

60. P.R.O. H.O. 42/78, Moody's information of 23 Feb. 1804; see H.O. 100/119/123, 195 and 202 for Jordan's and Colclough's information to the same effect; also government correspon-dence for Jun.–Aug. 1807 in H.O. 100/141/326–7 and 100/142/104–8.
61. See Senior, *Orangeism*, 154–7; P.R.O. H.O. 42/82–3; and I.S.P.O. S.O.C. 1063/1 for Fletcher. Reports from French agents sent to London in 1804 and 1807 reveal no attempt to encourage domestic subversion, see A.A.E. Corr. Pol. Ang. 602 fos. 196–209 and 604 fo. 92.
62. G. H. C. Mason, 'The Radical Bequest: Continuity in English Popular Politics, 1799–1832' (York Univ. M. Phil. thesis 1976), 80, 88–9, 107–8, 135; J. A. Hone, 'The Ways and Means of London Radicalism', 110, 121, 160–74; Thompson, *Making of the English Working Class*, 491–514; *Parl. Deb.*, IV, 744, for Oxford; Manchester City Lib. F 324/4273/S.3. (Shuttleworth's scrapbook) for Cowdroy; and P.R.O. H.O. 100/153/280–6, for Finnerty.

Evans, Jeremiah Fitzhenry and eventually the prize catch of William Putnam McCabe, followed the example of Rowan and Sampson in appealing for permission to return to Ireland, the Dublin administration became more than ever convinced that such arch-rebels should never again be let loose in Ireland's volatile society. Fox argued Evans's case personally in 1806, and Portland's administration was happy enough to let McCabe live in either England or Scotland. But McCabe's talents were recognized by friend and foe alike, and his return was particularly opposed by Dublin. 'I am against permitting any to return,' argued Wellesley, 'the rebellion is too recent and the sentiments to which it gave rise to permit this;' and if there was no republican party in Ireland, there were individual republicans who might still cause mischief.[63]

McCabe's name had appeared most frequently in reports of ex-rebels having returned to Ireland. None of these journeys appear to have had any political motivation; McCabe's disillusionment with Bonaparte had pre-dated that of most of his friends, and in an audience with Castlereagh he had offered to return to Ireland to disabuse the people of their French sympathies. But when he was finally arrested in 1814, after having entered Ireland illicitly, he was still considered a danger, and was refused permission to stay. In fact, as Chief Secretary Robert Peel admitted with embarrassment, McCabe was as entitled as Peel himself to live in Ireland. He had not been one of those specifically pardoned in 1802 on condition of permanent exile. The device of granting the pardon retrospectively was adopted by the embarrassed authorities to disguise the omission, and McCabe was escorted out of the country by the Chief Police Officer.[64] The affair had revealed the flaws in the hasty emergency legislation of the post-'98 period, which had already caused similar problems in the treatment of other ex-rebels. The only sure means of depriving Irish disaffection of potential leaders was to prevent them from ever returning to Ireland, legally or otherwise, and reports of banished rebels attempting to return in the years 1806–1811 invariably produced a flurry of preventive action in Dublin.[65]

The steady flow of disillusioned United men away from France heartened the home governments, and eventually Dublin's need for information from the

63. N.L.I. MS. 58/81, Wellesley to Trail, 11 Jul. 1808. For the return of Sampson and Rowan see P.R.O. H.O. 100/128/242–5, 274–82 and, H.O. 42/84–5; for Lowry and Evans see H.O. 100/135/225, 295–7; and for Fitzhenry, see H.O. 100/164/1–10 and I.S.P.O. Priv. Off. Corr. viii^A/1/4/307.

64. For McCabe's reputed journeys to Ireland see I.S.P.O. 620/13/177, 620/14/188/20; P.R.O. H.O. 100/122/288, 100/123/46, 100/149/259–62 and 332, 100/153/4–5 and 243–5 and H.O. 123/6/173–4. For the dispute over his right to return to Ireland see N.L.I. MS. 58/81; P.R.O. H.O. 100/153/2–5 and 100/176/1–29.

65. Until 1811 such rumours caused perennial panic in Dublin see I.S.P.O. S.O.C. 1091/5 and 1389/35, 620/14/198/5, and Priv. Off. Corr. viii^A/1/4/146; also P.R.O. H.O. 100/141/326–7, documents concerning ex-rebels living in England 1807.

Continent lost any sense of urgency. Nevertheless, as long as any United men remained alive and at liberty anywhere in the world, no Irish government could afford to relax its vigilance. With the most talented United leaders now in America, and relations between Britain and America deteriorating after 1807, many began to fear that help was as likely to come from across the Atlantic as the Channel. No government could ever believe that people like Thomas Addis Emmet or MacNeven had renounced their former principles. Emmet's campaign against Rufus King in 1807, for his refusal to let the state prisoners enter America in 1798, and recurrent rumours that he and O'Connor would eventually reconcile their differences in a new United offensive, were sufficient to sustain such fears, and their activities in America were closely watched by the British Consul in Philadelphia.[66]

One of the most spectacular efforts to secure rehabilitation had come from Arthur O'Connor. But O'Connor's return would have evoked too many embarrassing memories with his former associates among the English radicals, and when the Foxite Whigs finally gained office in 1806 in the 'Ministry of All the Talents', they sought to establish their political respectability by playing down their radical past. Caricaturists had a field-day lampooning their inconsistencies; Fox and Sheridan in particular were teased with references to their former associations with Irish rebels.[67] Such embarrassment at his past associations explains Fox's reaction to O'Connor's overture in 1806. In February, Richard O'Reilly, a banished United Irishman, arrived in London from Paris with letters from O'Connor to Hugh Bell. Whitehall had known for some time that O'Connor had continued to correspond with Bell, though intercepted letters had never shown any trace of treasonable communication.[68] On 4 February, O'Reilly called at Whitehall and told one of the clerks that he had been sent on an important mission to Pitt. After hearing of the change of ministry, he called at Fox's house that evening, and again on the 6th. All communication was by letter only, and as credentials O'Reilly showed the letters from O'Connor to Bell. He explained that he had been sent by O'Connor as spokesman for 'a strong and well-organized political party in Paris' to communicate with London and to propose a plan for over-throwing Napoleon, 'that enemy of anything like liberty'. In return for financial help from England, the new French government, with O'Connor and General Moreau at its head, would immediately re-open peace negotiations. In any event, O'Connor would never take part in any expedition against

---

66. See P.R.O. H.O. 42/80 and 100/142/111–6, 430–1, correspondence concerning the exiles in America, 1805–7; and McNally's information, Jun. 1806 in I.S.P.O. 620/14/198/8; and see Madden, *United Irishmen*, 2nd ser. II, 166–81 for their dispute with Rufus King.
67. J. Ashton, *English Caricature and Satire on Napoleon I* (London, 1888), 268, 279.
68. See P.R.O. H.O. 42/70 and 79/6, intercepted letters from O'Connor to Bell, 26 Mar. and 3 Nov. 1803.

Ireland, and if he were permitted to return, he would do all in his power to turn the Irish against Napoleon.

O'Reilly's claims seem to have had some foundation in reality. After his implication in the royalist plot of 1804, Moreau had been exiled to America; but he had remained popular with the army and was the natural focus for any discontent against Napoleon.[69] It is unlikely, however, that O'Connor had any formal contact with such a group. He was far too clever to have thus committed himself before having ensured his own safety, and it is likely that a successful outcome to such overtures would have seen him operating from the British Isles rather than France. But O'Connor was a talented statesman and the mission was not entirely an attempt at self-aggrandisement. He warned England that she should abandon any idea of ever restoring the Bourbons to the French throne, and that in Ireland a grant of catholic emancipation would be an essential pre-requisite for a return to loyalty. But although such recommendations were worthy of an astute politician and his dis-illusionment with Napoleon was genuine enough, the whole affair typified the conduct which had alienated so many United men from O'Connor. The other leaders had chosen to abandon France altogether for the same reasons, and although O'Connor could blithely compose his differences with England, Dublin was right in thinking that the principles of many of the other leaders had remained unchanged. When O'Connor's overture proved abortive, he was quite happy to remain in France, enjoying the emoluments of his military position and the confidence which France continued to place in him as United Irish spokesman.

But it is Fox's response to these overtures which startles most. Although O'Reilly admitted that he was included in the Banishment Act, Fox tried to ignore this strange emissary and does not appear to have told anybody else about the overtures. O'Reilly was 'disappointed in the mode Mr. Fox received him' and felt Pitt might have acted quite differently. He would have return-ed to France immediately if Fox had fallen in with his plans. Instead he travelled to Ireland for personal reasons, where his brother advised him to tell everything to the Irish government. Marsden was amazed that he should have placed himself in such a dangerous position, since his life was forfeit if he returned to Ireland. But O'Reilly was not to know that Fox had told no one of his overtures, and understandably felt that his reception in Dublin ought to have been more favourable. Certainly the Dublin government was glad of some free information on the Irish in France, though O'Reilly assured ministers that they no longer had any communication with Ireland. Marsden asked the Home Office to investigate O'Reilly's story; but this is the last we hear of him in English sources. In September he was back in France,

---

69. For Moreau see Aulard, *Paris sous le Premier Empire*, ii, 107–15; J. Tulard, *Napoléon* (Paris, 1977), 168–70; and P.R.O. H.O. 42/74, Rossolin to Baron d'Imbert, 8 Nov. 1803.

where he was arrested for having no travel papers, but released on O'Connor's assurance that he had been employed on a mission to Ireland. What had happened on the English side is unclear. Fox was clearly embarrassed by the whole incident, especially as peace negotiations had again been opened with France. O'Reilly's free passage back to France looks suspicious, and there is no sign that it had been granted in return for information. Had the Talents Ministry been glad to let him go in an attempt to spare its own reputation? It certainly looks that way, and the whole incident was symptomatic of the efforts made by old reformers to disguise their embarrassing past.[70]

III

The slumbering rebelliousness of Ireland in these years was quite insufficient to attract Napoleon's interest, though it would be wrong to think that he had entirely abandoned the idea of a direct attack on the British Isles after 1805. In France Trafalgar was never seen as the end of the French naval offensive against England, whatever the English might think. Villeneuve's suicide on his return journey to Paris obliterated an embarrassing reminder of the bungled campaign of 1805 ; the defeat had received scanty press coverage and was quickly swamped by news of the victories against Austria.[71] In 1805, 1807 and 1812 Napoleon returned to his English invasion plans, and each time the Irish Legion was overhauled. Indeed Napoleon's treatment of the Irish Legion after 1806 became the temperature gauge of his attitude towards Irish liberation in general. With its original function of preparing a cadre of political and military leaders removed, many recognized that new terms of reference would need to be supplied to bring it into line with other French regiments. Recruiting and promotion procedures, particularly the practice of appointing officers on political rather than military grounds, needed regulating. Over the next seven years attempts were made to implement these recommendations, but the conflict between the military and the political conception of the Irish Legion's role was never quite resolved, in the minds either of the Irish themselves or of the French officials.

The number of former United men was small and diminishing, and by 1815 only half a dozen of the officers were identifiable United Irishmen. A few more were added in 1807 and 1813 when former '98 men were found among the Prussian prisoners of war. But few United men had any desire to

---

70. See P.R.O. H.O. 100/135/61–78 for a full account of the mission; for his departure from England, with Home Office blessing, see H.O. 42/85, his letter of 13 Apr. 1806; for his return to France see H.O. 100/141/222 and A.N. F⁷ 3753, police bulletins for 24 May and 27 Jun. 1806.
71. See Aulard, *Paris sous le Premier Empire*, II, 296–348. For his periodic return to the British invasion project see A.A.E. Mem. et. Doc. Fonds France 1776 fos. 13 and 22; *Correspondance de Napoléon Iᵉʳ*, XIV nos. 11335, 11377, 11568, XVI, 13738, XVII, 13877, and for the most serious renewal of plans in 1811–12 see A.N. AF IV 1199 and 1200 and BB⁴ 309.

become just another cog in the French military machine, and there were further resignations after the move to Mainz in 1806 and to Flushing the following year.[72] Although the character of the Legion was considerably altered in the second phase of its development, by the addition of a rank and file taken primarily from prisoner of war depots, the core of its general staff was still composed of United Irishmen, and officers like Lawless, Tennent, St. Leger, Dowdall and Byrne were determined to maintain the Legion's political role. Of the sixty-eight foreign regiments serving with Napoleon, the history of the Irish Legion was unusually turbulent because of this insistence on the maintenance of its corporate, national character; and the loss of the Irish name, when it was incorporated into the *Légion du Nord* and the third *Régiment étranger* in 1807 and 1811 respectively, led to further withdrawals and demoralization among those who remained. But the fight to retain its national identity did not stop at the name: despite its multinational rank and file, the officers insisted on a purely Irish command structure, on the restoration of its corporate life by the re-unification of the various battalions scattered through northern France, Flanders, Spain and Portugal, and on the provision of a regular supply of recruits. The Irish officers were particularly bitter about recruiting procedures. The English prisoners of war deserted, the Poles remained discontented at not fighting for their own country, and discipline could rarely be imposed when most of the recruits could speak neither English nor French. The net effect was to make the Legion a byword for military indiscipline.[73]

The nationality of the command was also a constant annoyance. The Irish particularly objected to serving under the command of the Italian, Petrezzoli, who had replaced MacSheehy in 1804, and after the move to Mainz many of the new Prussian and Polish recruits were promoted over the heads of former United men. As early as 1806 Lawless had complained of this practice: '. . . it is truly desolating for an Irishman to see the reputation of his country in the hands of men who have no desire to cherish it or to see the Irish corps blamed for actions of men who have never set foot in Ireland . . .'[74] The Irish officers with the detachment sent to Spain in 1807 complained bitterly of the appointment of Jean Mahony and several other officers from the old Irish Brigade, which had actually fought for Austria and England after 1792. Fitzhenry organized a petition requesting more

72. See A.H.G. X^h 14–16, for the Irish Legion, 1804–15; and recommendations for various reforms in A.A.G. Doss. Pers. 2e sér. G.B. 1840, Lawless to Berthier, 1 Mar. 1806.

73. A.N. AF IV 1114 doss. 1 fos. 66–8, and AF IV 1117 doss. 2 fos. 210–17, reports on Irish battalions and other foreign regiments; A.H.G. X^16, particularly the correspondence of O'Reilly and Lawless, 1812–13; E. Fieffé, *Histoire des troupes étrangères au service de la France*, 2 vols. (Paris, 1854), ii, 185; Lt. Col. P. Carles, 'Le corps irlandais au service de la France sous le Consulat et l'Empire', *Revue historique des Armées*, ii (1976), 31.

74. A.A.G. Doss. Pérs. 2 sér. G.B. 1840, Lawless to Berthier, 1 Mar. 1806.

Irish appointments, but it was condemned as unmilitary practice and only served to underscore the bad reputation which the Legion seemed to be acquiring with the military authorities. Fitzhenry never recouped his reputation, and after persistent harassment he eventually threw in his lot with Wellington. The Irish were embittered by their experience in Spain. They had arrived exhausted after marching from Holland, and were left with an inept command, insufficient supplies and no reinforcements to permit the removal of the sick and wounded. Moreover, to have sent a corps recruited from rebels and British deserters to fight against British forces in Spain, seemed a singularly foolish move, and the worst fears of the Irish were fulfilled when one of their battalion was summarily executed by the British near Burgos.[75]

In 1807 the return to the War Ministry of Henri Clarke, now Duc de Feltre, with whom Tone had negotiated, opened a new era for the Irish Legion. It was increased by two more battalions to form a complete regiment, and bounties were offered to encourage recruitment.[76] The Irish had been employed primarily to defend the northern coasts, and as such formed part of the force sent against the British when they landed on Walcheren in 1809. Their role in the defence of Flushing was the first action many had seen since the Legion's formation in 1804, and the symbolic importance of such a campaign against the English aroused a sense of enthusiasm among the Irish which impressed the French, including the Emperor. It marked a turning point in the Legion's history, for not only did it rescue its reputation, so badly tarnished in previous years, but those elements which had prevented its easy incorporation into French service were removed. Almost the entire first battalion, with such United Irish veterans as Arthur MacMahon, Pat McCann, and Edward Gibbons, were taken prisoner of war. Several others, including William Dowdall, were killed in action, and with their loss the United Irish element was almost eradicated. The remainder accepted proudly the laurels awarded for the defence of Flushing, and seemed perfectly content to fight for France and to abandon their hope of ever returning to Ireland. As a regiment in French service the Irish Legion was coming of age. Recruiting and appointment procedures were gradually regularized, and the officers' grievances, particularly in relation to the appointment of non-Irish officers, were rectified. By 1810 twenty-one of the twenty-seven officers serving with the second and third battalions in Spain, and eleven of the seventeen attached to the fourth battalion in Belgium, were Irish, and plans were in progress for

75. See A.H.G. X^h 14 for 1808–9, and X^h 15, for O'Mahony and Fitzhenry; also Byrne, *Memoirs*, II, 212, 217–19.
76. A.H.G. X^h 14, correspondence, May–Aug. 1809; X^h 15, the Minister's notes on Lawless's report of 18 Feb. 1811.

further Irish appointments. Finally, in 1813, Lawless was raised to the overall command of the Legion.[77]

The Irish were able to settle to their new military career because their republicanism was evaporating. The last memoir on Ireland had been submitted to the French government by Fitzhenry in October 1806.[78] By 1810 only twelve officers of the Irish Legion were former United men, and nine of those serving in Spain. Moreover their sons were likely to prefer French regiments to the Irish Legion, and Tone's widow, Matilda, was sufficiently apprehensive about the possible ill-effects on her son's military career to make a special plea against his automatic placement in the Irish force.[79] Hopes that Napoleon might yet send a force to Ireland were temporarily revived in 1806, 1807 and again in 1815, with his return from Elba. Otherwise the idea that the Irish regiment existed primarily to assist in Ireland's liberation had entirely disappeared. Just as patterns of protest in Ireland had flowed back into channels established before the interlude of the 1790s, so the new generation of Irish exiles on the Continent had taken up where their ancestors of the old Irish Brigade had left off. But the ideals of the United Irish Society had not been laid entirely to rest by either, and whilst France remained at war with England, former membership was still viewed by the French authorities as the only real guarantee of patriotism. Until 1808 O'Connor maintained a political nucleus in Paris, and was usually consulted on the principles of new Irish arrivals in much the same way as Lewins and Tone had been in the past. The conflict between O'Connor and the Legion's officers had long ceased, and he sought their advice in cases on which he himself was unable to pronounce. But the instances were few, and there was little communication between the United men in the regiment and their former colleagues elsewhere in France. For much of the period O'Connor, Lewins, McCabe, Hampden Evans and several other former leaders still lived in the Paris region.[80] But most had reconciled themselves to the collapse of their movement. They responded eagerly to signs of any revival of French interest, but the French archives are devoid of any unsolicited communications from them after 1806.

Napoleon, however, needed little reminding of the continuing utility of the Irish in his plans against England. In practical terms France thought that the

---

77. Carles, 'Le corps irlandais au service de la France', 41–3. The fullest account of the regiment's composition is in X^h 16, list of personnel for 23 Jun. 1812. See A.H.G. X^h 15–16, C^2 103, C^{18} 25, and Byrne, *Memoirs*, II, 286, 292–5 for the Irish Legion's role in the Walcheren campaign.
78. A.H.G. M R 1420 fos. 53–7, Fitzhenry's memoir.
79. Byrne, *Memoirs*, II, 31, 35, 160. For young Tone see Tone, *Life*, II, 567–84; and A.A.G. Doss. Pers. 2e sér. W. Tone.
80. For O'Connor's position see A.N. BB^3 287 fo. 47, F^7 3753, F^7 6338 doss. 7123 and F^7 6510 doss. 1108; also Aulard, *Paris sous le Premier Empire*, II, 82. For the Irish in Paris see Byrne, *Memoirs*, II, 177–236, 263–8, 324–8 and P.R.O. H.O. 100/135/61–78.

Legion would act as a magnet for the Irish serving in the English forces, and Irish deserters received preferential treatment. In 1812 a number of desertions from the British fleet blockading Brest boosted French hopes that their reports of favourable treatment in the Legion would encourage many more defections, and Clarke was particularly optimistic about the effects on the Irish serving with Prussia and with the British forces in Spain.[81] There were a number of Irish deserters from all three sources, but the trickle did not justify Clarke's inflated hopes, and the Irish component in the Legion's rank and file remained weak throughout its existence.

The positioning of the battalions in key defence areas, or at points threatened by British attack, can also be explained by such surviving political consider- ations. The Police Ministry was aghast at the defence of Boulogne by a battalion recruited from English prisoners of war and potential English spies, and the conflicting interpretations of the Legion's role caused Clarke and Fouché to clash on several occasions.[82] Even Fieffé, the historian of the foreign regiments in French service, complains of Clarke's blatant favouritism for the Irish, and attributes the retention of the 'pompous' title of 'Irish Legion' for a multi- national corps to Clarke's desire to flatter his own national pride. But Clarke was probably more in tune with Napoleon's own thinking than many of the other ministers, and the retention of the Irish title made good sense in the propaganda war against England.[83]

It was in 1810–12 that Napoleon made his most serious effort to return to his British invasion plans; and the renewal of disturbances in the British Isles once again convinced him of the possibility of reviving an internal French party there. In England and Ireland alike a combination of economic hard- ship, trade disturbances and radical campaigning had brought slumbering disaffection again into the open. In the years 1810–11, the British economy suffered considerably from the effects of Napoleon's Continental Blockade, and a severe economic depression provided the backdrop to Luddism in England and the revival of politico-religious groupings in Ireland. The textile industry was hit particularly badly by the Blockade, and the slump led to parliamentary petitions, mammoth meetings and eventually to militant strikes, with the Irish weavers in Lancashire again forcing the pace.[84] The deteriorating relations with America, which erupted in war in 1812, caused particular suffering in Ireland because of the domestic linen industry's

---

81. A.H.G. X^h 15–16, A.N. F⁷ 8225 doss. 6318; *Correspondance de Napoléon Ier*, XVI, 13587; and Byrne, *Memoirs*, II, 279–80, correspondence on Irish deserters, 1809–14.
82. A.N. F⁷ 8225 doss. 6318 and F⁷ 3755 doss. 17.
83. A.N. AF I V 1674 plaq. 5 doss. 2, especially fos. 574–5, Clarke to Napoleon, 10 Nov. 1811; A.H.G. X^h 15, Clarke's notes on Lawless, 1812; Fieffé, *Histoire des troupes étrangères*, II, 185; and Carles, 'Le corps irlandais au service de la France', 35.
84. F. Crouzet, *L'Économie britannique et le Blocus continental* (1806–1813), 2 vols. (Paris, 1958), especially I, 266–354 and II, 563–700.

dependence on America for flax-seed and for markets. By 1814 there were
18,000 unemployed in Belfast alone, and many businesses had gone bankrupt.
With markets dwindling and drying up altogether during the 1812 war, the
already depressed textile towns in the north of England became flooded with
unemployed Irish weavers.[85]

This was the background to the national campaign for catholic emancipation in Ireland, which reached a climax in 1811. It had expanded from small
beginnings in 1804–05 to pose, by the turn of the decade, one of the greatest
threats to law and order since Emmet's Rebellion. In October 1804 a committee of leading catholics was founded in Dublin, its members ranging from
the moderate catholic aristocracy, like Fingall and Sir Thomas French,
through to ex-United men like Edward Hay and John Keogh.[86] At the outset
business was conducted in a gentlemenly fashion, and a moderately-worded
petition was presented to parliament by Grenville and Fox the following
March. The Houses were unusually full and a heated debate ensued, a token
of the passions which 'popery' could still arouse. The examples of the rebellions of 1798 and 1803, and the statements of MacNeven and the other state
prisoners about popular apathy towards catholic emancipation were freshly
aired as arguments against granting any concession to the Irish catholics,
and with Auckland's resounding warning, 'If you admit the catholics to a
participation of power, you admit the enemy into your camp', the motion
was overwhelmingly defeated.[87] The catholic leaders had not expected such
hostility or such indifference on the part of Pitt, their former champion, and in
the aftermath of the rejection they had difficulty controlling their more
militant adherents in compliance with Fox's plea for restraint during the
difficult run of the Talents' Ministry. With its fall in March 1807, after
Grenville's failure to secure the very modest reform of opening higher civil
and military appointments to the catholics, such restraint, and the catholic
Lords who had enforced it, were totally discredited.

With popular passions already inflamed by the sudden rise in prices,
unpopular distillery laws and a heated general election, government received
reports of mounting catholic disillusionment with constitutional processes and
rumours that another rising was expected. The campaign in the Spanish

85. See Fitzpatrick, 'The Economic Effects of the . . . Wars in Ireland', 99–133 B.L. Add. MS.
40280 fos. 137–8; Gill, *Rise of the Irish Linen Industry*, 220; and F. L. Wilson, 'The Irish in Great
Britain During the first half of the Nineteenth century' (Manchester Univ. M. A. thesis 1946),
8–9 for the economic effects of the Continental System on the Irish weavers. Hall, *Tour Through
Ireland*, II, 139, reflects on the great numbers emigrating from Ulster, 1812–13.
86. N.L.I. MS. 60/264, 'Notes as to Irish Catholics, 1806'; Wyse, *Historical Sketch of the Late
Catholic Association of Ireland*, I, 137–75.
87. *Parl. Deb.* IV, 97–110, 651–1040; *Diary and Correspondence of Lord Colchester*, I, 544, II, 1–3.
See Wyse, *Historical Sketch of the Late Catholic Association*, I, 140; and P.R.O. H.O. 100/135/59–60
and 79–80, for Fox's request and catholic reaction.

peninsula, with its direct confrontation between English and French forces, and the move of French troops to a viable position to mount another invasion, had been the main cause of such restiveness.[88] But the changing character of the catholic leadership was too reminiscent of the transfer which had occurred in 1792–93 to be viewed with complacency. Keogh was publicly praising the work of his old friend, Wolfe Tone, and many old United men, particularly in Belfast, were re-emerging to collect signatures for another catholic petition.[89] Temperatures in the country continued to rise throughout 1810, and at a time when government thought the country ripe for another rising, the catholic committee began preparing for elections to produce a more representative catholic body. From December, meetings were held each week in Dublin and circulars were distributed throughout the country to prepare the people for the elections. The proposed assembly was declared illegal under the 1793 Convention Act, many of the Dublin leaders were arrested, and their trials were held against a background of mounting political turmoil.[90]

The publicity surrounding the catholic elections had brought many old reformers into the limelight again, creating an image of leadership for the discontented, and producing a spontaneous revival of disaffection in old Defender and United Irish strongholds. In its early years Ribbonism was Defenderism's direct offspring in its republican, sectarian, urban and essentially lower-middle-class or artisanal character (though it was to assume a more traditionally agrarian character after the 1820s). But it lacked the leadership and the centralization which the United Irish Society had brought to political disaffection in the 1790s; and because of this basic organizational difference, no government of the period was able to infiltrate it, and there is still considerable uncertainty about its place in the history of Irish popular protest.[91]

The main period of Ribbonism's history lies outside the scope of the present study, but its origins can be found in 1811, a period closely resembling that which had fostered the union of the Defenders and the United Irishmen. It was a time of intense economic hardship and mounting sectarian conflict,

88. See P.R.O. H.O. 100/142/120–5, 100/147/280–90, 100/148/21, for reports on mounting catholic militancy, effect of events in Spain etc. during the summer of 1807.
89. For the re-emergence of old militants to head the agitation, see P.R.O. H.O. 100/158/81–3, 461–71, 100/159/1–6; I.S.P.O. S.O.C. 1382/56, 64–7 and 1383/3; and Wyse, *Historical Sketch of the Late Catholic Association*, I, 144–52.
90. I.S.P.O. Priv. Off. Corr. VIII^A 1/4/163–286 and P.R.O. H.O. 100/163/31–57, 100/164/73, 188–91 and 252–3, for details of the catholic elections and the petition crisis.
91. Beames, 'The Ribbon Societies', and idem, 'Peasant Disturbances', 27, 58–63, 83–7, 156–63; J. Lee, 'The Ribbonmen' in *Secret Societies in Ireland*, ed. T. D. Williams, 26–35; K. B. Nowlan, 'Agrarian Unrest in Ireland 1800–1845', *University Review*, II (1959), 7–16; Rudé, *Protest and Punishment*, 38, 57; T. N. Brown, 'Nationalism and the Irish Peasant, 1800–1848', *The Review of Politics*, 15 (Oct. 1953), 428.

of political reform agitation by upper-class leaders, who nevertheless raised
hopes of a less constitutional nature among the lower classes, and one when
the expectation of another French invasion ran high. Defender and United
Irish remnants had re-emerged intermittently in the preceding decade, and it
was from these that Ribbonism developed in the years 1811–13. Initial information was confused and often exaggerated at a time when news of a revival of
sectarian attacks found a ready audience among the local magistracy. But the
spring assizes of 1811 provide further evidence of surviving pockets of the United
or Defender movements in Ulster, despite the fashionable labels of 'Thresher'
or 'Carder' sometimes applied to them by the authorities. Men like James
Anderson, a Belfast watchmaker, Francis Oprey, a schoolmaster, or John
McShane, a cloth-merchant from county Down, had been United men in the
1790s and had continued in loose association thereafter. By 1811 they called
themselves Ribbonmen, though their goals of a national rising and a French
invasion remained unchanged. But unlike either the United Irishmen or the
'Regenerated Defenders', these Ribbonmen were belligerently catholic, and
all the signs are that Defenderism and Ribbonism thrived in Ulster, not because
the Ulster catholics were more politically-minded than their co-religionists
elsewhere, but in direct response to Orange harassment. The first Ribbon oaths
to be found that year in Donegal and Down were clearly the result of Orange
attacks, and signs of similar, though unconnected, disaffection were reported
from Mayo, Kildare, Meath, and King's and Queen's Counties.[92]

By 1812, disappointment at the failure of the catholic emancipation campaign had alienated many catholics from constitutional agitation: 'they
would soon make Government wish the[y] had granted them their Emancipation,' one English agent was told in Belfast, 'as Ireland had not her rights
the[y] was determined to have them or loose all that was dear to them and
all the Catholics in Ireland was of the same way of thinking'.[93] The national
campaign by the catholic leaders in 1811 had succeeded in making catholic
emancipation a panacea for widely divergent catholic groups in Ireland
and England alike, and the despair at the official reaction to the campaign,
after the high expectations generated by the Prince Regent's accession to
power, created a ready climate for the resurgence of disaffection. Many
looked to the catholic delegates for leadership, and in an effort to dissociate
the catholic cause from any imputations of treason, its main leaders, Fingall,
O'Connell, O'Gorman, Grattan and others went to the Castle in January 1812
with information of a conspiracy organizing in Dublin. Their informant
claimed that it was the 'old system' of United men, consisting of brewers,
bakers, butchers, grocers, shoemakers and the like, but looking to higher

92. I.S.P.O. S.O.C. 1383, for Ulster; and for disaffection elsewhere in the country see S.O.C.
1382/1, 19, 49, Meath, King's and Queen's Counties, 1390/1–2, Kildare and 1404/20–21, Mayo.
93. P.R.O. H.O. 40/1/1/91–2, Bent's information, headed 17 Apr. 1812.

leaders like the catholic delegates, or former United Irishmen; and one of the 'conspirators' claimed to have been told that it was 'a new business . . . similar to the plan of Robert Emmet in 1803 . . . that an Embassador . . . had arrived from France stating that the French would soon invade England or Ireland'.[94] Since they were unable to discover further information on this group, ministers dismissed it as of little consequence. But a French agent had recently been in Dublin and it can be reasonably assumed that government had chanced upon some kind of treasonable grouping remarkably like the Ribbon movement which developed thereafter. The agent was Luke Lawless of the Irish Legion, who had been commissioned by Napoleon to ascertain the degree of support which France might expect if she invaded Ireland.

It was in 1810 that Napoleon decided on a final, desperate effort against England. He was incensed to find that secret intrigues for peace by Fouché and his brother Louis, without full consultation beforehand, had made him the object of an insolent rejection by England. Louis's behaviour as King of Holland had at first disappointed, then infuriated Napoleon, and the threat of formal annexation to France had been hovering over Holland for some time. The threat which such a move would pose for England had long been considered good reason for retaining the semblance of Dutch autonomy.[95] The enforced abdication of Louis in July 1810, however, and the formal annexation of his kingdom and the Hanse towns announced the abandonment of any hopes of concluding peace with England except by defeat. A massive programme of naval construction was ordered, and a full offensive against England planned for 1812. The naval levy for 1813 was called up, the Senate applied to for an additional 40,000 sailors; once again a flood of orders set in train a series of frantic naval preparations all around the French and Dutch coasts, and Napoleon's determination hardened as England intensified her campaign in Spain. 'I want to look at all the projects relating to Ireland again,' he wrote to Clarke. 'Since England is denuding herself of troops to send to Spain, nothing would be easier than to land 25,000 men in Ireland towards the end of October.'[96]

As part of the new offensive he investigated the organization of the Irish battalions serving in Spain and at Landau, and was angry at the preponderance of English prisoners of war in their ranks. He instructed Clarke to return all English nationals to the prisoner of war depots and to submit a list of the remaining Irish. The enquiry uncovered a bitter national quarrel between

94. P.R.O. H.O. 100/166/17–56, information enclosed in Richmond to Ryder, 7 Jan. 1812.

95. See A.N. AF IV 1674 for the missions of François Fagan and Pierre-César Labouchère to London. See also Sorel, *L'Europe et la Révolution Française*, VII, 436–52; and Schama, *Patriots and Liberators*, 606.

96. *Correspondance de Napoléon I*[er], XXII, 17846, also XXI, 16916, 17434; and A.N. AF IV 597 doss. 4723 p[ce] 11, decree of 14 Nov. 1811; and BB[4] 309, for the naval preparations.

the Irish and English and an unusually high rate of desertion among the latter. The second Irish battalion alone had lost almost all its recruits through English desertion. At Landau 932 soldiers and inferior officers were found to be English, and after their withdrawal the regiment became Irish in reality as well as name. The purge had a remarkable effect on Irish morale, and many of the practices which had blackened the regiment's reputation disappeared.[97] But it was a token of the decline of Irish republicanism abroad that Napoleon's new interest in the Legion did not awaken any hopes of another Irish invasion, even among the officers. The conception of the Irish regiment as a cadre of political leaders for Ireland had entirely disappeared, and although Napoleon still considered its services essential to his invasion plans of 1810–12, he chose to treat the politicians and the military men separately, and to look to old hands like O'Connor and Lewins for information on Ireland.

The surviving United Irishmen in Paris were surprised at this revival of interest, and were clearly unqualified to supply the required information. There had been no formal communication between the exiles and Ireland for many years, and their replies to Clarke's queries revealed a total ignorance of the current state of Irish opinion. O'Connor frankly admitted this, but warned of the effects French neglect must have had upon popular opinion. 'I cannot deceive Your Majesty about the state of public opinion in Ireland today—the abandonment of the United Irishmen by the Directory made a great impression upon their minds. Hopes were revived when you came to power and there is no doubt that, had your expedition of 1804 sailed, you would have been wholeheartedly supported. But the years you have let pass by without giving them hope have alienated them.' This sudden interest had also revived suspicion of Napoleon's intentions and the exiled Irish responded less enthusiastically than might have been expected. The form of government which the French might establish was discussed with greater vigour than the fact of invasion itself, and it was eventually to the newer exiles that Napoleon had to turn to re-establish contact with Ireland.[98]

Napoleon accepted O'Connor's advice on the need to re-establish communication with the disaffected in Ireland, and on 8 September he ordered Clarke to send a secret agent there. Within three days Clarke had despatched William Lawless's nephew Luke, a former ensign in the British navy, who had joined the Irish Legion in 1810. Lawless was to discover the dispositions of the Irish people and the identity of the leaders of any party still seeking independence from England; to re-establish communication routes between Ireland and France by sending agents from this national party,

97. *Correspondance de Napoléon Ier*, xxi, 16818 and 16943; A.N. AF IV 1118 doss. 1–2 and A.H.G. X^h 15 for the enquiry and resulting action. See Markey's statement of 14 Aug. and the correspondence of the Irish officers, Jul.–Sept. 1810 in A.H.G. X^h 15.
98. Copies of O'Connor's letters of Sept. 1811 are in N.L.I. MS. 10,961; see A.N. AF IV 1674 plaq. 5 doss. 1–2 for the consultations, also Somers's report, 20 Aug. 1811, P.R.O. F.O. 27/82 and *Correspondance de Napoléon Ier*, xxi, 17331, xxii, 17875, 17909, 18034, 18123.

or from the catholic emancipationists if no such party existed; and finally he was to discover the state and distribution of the defence forces. The excitement at the inauguration of the Regency in England was public knowledge, and the Irish exiles warned Clarke that if the Prince granted catholic emancipation, which they thought he would, the catholics would be conciliated and would defend the country against all invaders. Speed was therefore essential if Napoleon did intend invading, and the preparations made for Lawless's despatch betray a sense of urgency absent from French documents on Ireland since 1798. All passport restrictions were lifted, and on 11 September the Police Commissioner at Boulogne secured a passage for Lawless across the Channel. By the 14th he was in London and arrived in Dublin ten days later.[99]

The problems facing Lawless were immense. The United Irishmen had long ceased to have any communication network in the country, and Lawless knew nothing of the little coterie of former United men in Dublin. Nor had Clarke secured the names of any other sympathisers from O'Connor or Lewins, probably because they knew of none. Lawless, therefore, did not even start with the advantage Oswald had had nearly two decades earlier, and spent the first weeks of his mission with his brother in Dublin, wondering who to approach. His brother's position as catholic deputy for Fermanagh made an approach to the catholic committee an obvious way out of his predicament. He accordingly related the object of his mission to James Ryan, the Dublin merchant who had been prominent in the 1805–06 discussions with Fox, to Dr. Dromgoole, one of the Dublin deputies and an outspoken exponent of catholic emancipation, and finally to Hamilton Rowan, who had continued in reform politics after his pardon and who was then in Dublin attracting unfavourable government attention by his association with the more extreme catholic leaders. Ryan had been a moderate 'on the make' in 1805, more Foxite than nationalist; but his demagogic leanings made him receptive to Lawless's overtures. The year 1811 had been a harrowing one for the catholic leaders. They had been snubbed by the Prince and by the pro-emancipationists of the parliamentary opposition in February; July saw the suppression of their committee and the trials of those accused of organizing it; many were becoming more militant in response to the repressive tactics of the authorities, and Lawless spoke with other catholics in Dublin who claimed to support the idea of a French invasion.[100]

The advice he received was moderate in the circumstances. He was assured that there was no organized conspiracy in the country and Ryan warned

99. A.A.G. Doss. Pers. 2ᵉ sér. Luke Lawless; A.N. F⁷ 4291, F⁷ 8255 and F⁷ 8646, for details on preparations for the mission, and P.R.O. F.O. 27/82, Somers's report, 20 Aug. 1811.

100. See Wyse, *Historical Sketch of the Late Catholic Association*, I, 165–85, P.R.O. H.O. 100/164–5, for developments within the catholic committee, and H.O. 100/135/80, 100/163/248, 100/164/250–1, 376–88 and N.L.I. MS. 60/264 for Ryan and Dromgoole. Rowan's pardon had been forced upon a reluctant Irish administration in 1803, see Hants. C.R.O. 38M49/5/30.

that he would gain little support from the catholic aristocrats. But the catholics in general cared little for catholic emancipation and although the catholic middle classes had been content to use constitutional means to secure reform, they had been shocked at the King's hatred for the catholics and the Irish. With hope in the Prince of Wales also receding, he felt that they might be found more sympathetic to any scheme which would restore the Irish parliament, especially when Ireland's natural affinity for France had been strengthened by the religious tolerance of Napoleon's regime. Ryan agreed to travel around the country to sound public opinion. What he discovered confirmed his belief that there was no organized conspiracy. But he found the southern and south-western counties in a state of near rebellion; the people were armed and he felt they would form a huge insurrectional force if the French ever invaded. Rowan also assured Lawless that despite the government's campaign to separate the presbyterians from the catholics, their love of independence remained strong and they would join again with the catholics if another rising occurred. The decline of the linen industry, the closure of the American and continental markets, and the competition from English cotton had intensified the northern presbyterians' distrust of England, and he had been assured by the county Down people that they would welcome another opportunity to overturn English rule in Ireland.

Lawless concluded from such communications that another invasion would be welcomed; but French attempts had been so ineffectual in the past and their promises of help so 'illusory' that they would encounter considerable Irish distrust at the outset. Moreover, despite widespread discontent, the rebellions of 1798 and 1803 had created 'a terror of conspiracy and rebellion' and the people would be slow to rise again without the arrival of a French force large enough to inspire confidence. A force of at least 40,000 would be required, and at the outset the French would have to publicize their intentions of granting the Irish independence and freedom to practice their religion, to hold property and to form their own government. Lawless's enquiries about the disposal of the crown forces confirmed Rowan's claim that the French would be best advised to land in the North. There were only 12,000 regular troops in the country, most of whom were in the south and south-west; otherwise the defence forces consisted of 30,000–35,000 yeomanry and 30,000 militia. But the French could no longer count on the disaffection of the latter, for the government's efforts to remove the militia from popular influence had been entirely successful.[101] Lawless left Dublin on on 18 October and was

101. Lawless's original report on his mission, written in English, is in A.A.E. Corr. Pol. Ang. Supp. 15 fos. 460–512; a translated version, sent by Clarke to Napoleon, is in A.N. AF IV 1674 plaq. 5 doss. 2 fos. 545–62, but the names of all those with whom he had spoken in Ireland are omitted. It was this latter version which F. W. Ryan used in his 'A Projected Invasion of Ireland in 1811', *Irish Sword*, 1 (1949–53), 136–41. Lawless's account of Ireland's defence forces is relatively accurate, see e.g. P.R.O. H.O. 100/149 and 169 for the militia and yeomanry in particular, also Gash, *Mr. Secretary Peel*, 134–5, 186–9.

back in France by 11 November. The collapse of United Irish communication with Ireland had brought about a corresponding deceleration in government surveillance, and Lawless had been and gone before Dublin Castle learnt of his mission.[102] By now England also had lost interest in United Irish activities on the Continent, and contrary to French hopes, there is no evidence that the existence of an Irish regiment in France was causing any real concern to the British authorities.

Lawless's mission provides the only real insight into the problem of revolutionary leadership in Ireland after 1803. The willingness of Rowan and of Lawless's brother to take part in another rebellion seemed to justify Dublin's fears of the potential mischief of former leaders in the event of another invasion. There is no reference to those whom the government most feared, people like the former Ulster United leaders, the Simms and Tennent brothers. But Rowan's connection with reform politics continued long after this latest brush with treason, and it is unlikely that his fellow reformers would have remained in the side-wings if another invasion and rebellion had occurred. The incident reveals the knife-edge course between constitutionalism and treason followed by many reformers, and given the precedent in the 1790s, it is difficult not to sympathize with government fears. But the mission also confirmed government findings that no organized conspiracy existed. Local discontent had increased dramatically since 1803, but its fragmentation deterred efficient organization. Lawless's difficulty in tracing a centre at which he could make his enquiries was symptomatic of the dilemma of any real revolutionary, and like Hamilton and Palmer before him, he accepted that no movement could be organized until the French arrived. Instead, Lawless advised the French to appoint one leader in each county. Upon receipt of information about a French invasion, he would inform a number of subordinate officers, who in turn would rouse the people when the landing had actually taken place. No more eloquent testimony could be found to the total collapse of any organized United Irish or Defender movement, or to the total ineffectiveness of endemic rebelliousness without overwhelming outside aid, so overwhelming that the invader would be placed in a position to dictate his own terms.

Napoleon was angry at Lawless's delay in Ireland. He had been ready to send an Irish expedition before O'Connor had cautioned delay until the state of the country could be investigated. 'I am waiting impatiently for news from Ireland,' he wrote to Clarke on 3 November, 'and I receive none; you must send new agents. All is ready, and if I could be assured of support, I would send the expedition at the end of February or the beginning of March. You must therefore send agents and fill up the Irish regiments.'[103] Clarke tried to calm the Emperor by pointing to the false hopes France had given

102. P.R.O. H.O. 100/165/209–12, Wellesley-Pole to Beckett, 22 Nov. 1811.
103. *Correspondance de Napoléon 1ᵉʳ*, XXII, 18237.

the Irish in the past, and the total absence of any encouragement since 1803. The revolutionary movement had collapsed in consequence, and Lawless would find it extremely difficult to re-establish contact. He agreed that more agents should be sent, but who could perform such missions? All the Irish with whom he had spoken had ceased communication with Ireland, and they could not return without risking execution. Many of them seemed to have little desire to return anyway and had become totally estranged from their homeland. It was with some relief, therefore, that Clarke reported Lawless's return on 23 November and forwarded his translated report to the Emperor. Napoleon was pleased with it, and Lawless was promoted to a captaincy in the Legion. No further agents were sent; Napoleon had, after all, been told exactly what he wanted to hear, and the naval preparations continued into 1812.[104] Ireland remained disturbed throughout that year, and as the contest between France and England quickened on the Continent, Irish expectation of French help increased apace. The Lord Lieutenant ordered ostentatious celebrations for the victory at Leipzig, in what had once been the most disaffected part of Dublin; but many in Ireland stubbornly refused to credit reports of French defeats and clung doggedly to their belief that victory would soon liberate Napoleon's forces for Ireland.[105]

It is unlikely that an invasion would have brought the people out again in open rebellion. Potential leaders were still to be found in the old, mainly urban, strongholds of the United Irishmen, but the growing strength of Orangeism and the yeomanry in the same areas might well have sufficiently contained disaffection before emissaries could have been sent to remoter parts. Lawless's scheme was designed to cater for such a situation, but there is no proof that it was ever implemented.

There was no invasion scare in Ireland in the years 1812–13. Dublin Castle did not feel that there was any danger of rebellion at the end of the war and played down reports of surviving disaffection. But if the defensive role of the military had almost disappeared, its policing duties had increased, and Peel felt that the wartime establishment could not safely be reduced after peace. Most government commentators were shocked at the level of lawlessness in Ireland in the first decades of the nineteenth century, and although reform was used to wean the peasantry from the influence of the secret societies, Peel felt the establishment of some permanent mode of policing the country a necessary prerequisite for the restoration of order. A more permanent measure would have the additional advantage of dispensing

104. See A.N. AF IV 1674 plaq. 2–5 for Clarke's correspondence with the Emperor, Nov. 1811, and BB⁴ 309 and AF IV 1200, for the continuing naval preparations.
105. Wakefield, *An Account of Ireland*, ii, 380; I.S.P.O. S.O.C. 1537/7 and 1560/11, information of 8 Dec. 1813 and 23 Feb. 1814, and P.R.O. H.O. 100/174/53–4, Whitworth to Sidmouth, 6 Nov. 1813.

with those interminable parliamentary wrangles each time the many temporary emergency measures came up for renewal. Working on the principle that people would be deterred from violence if their own parishes were made liable for the costs of restoring peace, and that the establishment of a paid and moveable magistracy would destroy the existing paralysis in the face of localized terrorism, Peel succeeded in passing his Peace Preservation Bill in July 1814. Consequently, when the final act of the struggle against France was being played out on the Continent, popular agitation was fading, and Peel's new system appeared to have restored internal peace to Ireland.[106]

The threat from the Continent had also receded after Napoleon's disastrous Russian campaign, and his invasion preparations were swamped by English victories in the ports of Holland and north Germany. During Napoleon's first period of exile, the Irish officers seemed to accept the Bourbon restoration with surprising alacrity. Mahony in particular was overjoyed at the prospect of this return to the traditions of the old Irish Brigade, and even pleaded for the restoration of the flag and the uniform of Dillon's regiment. There was no trace of Irish republicanism in the letter of homage sent to the French King on 1 January 1815, signed by all the surviving United leaders, and proclaiming the glories of their compatriots who had fought for Louis's ancestors, rather than those of their own political past. However, with Mahony flaunting his Bourbon lineage, and all the old malpractices creeping again into the organization of the Legion, the Irish began to see excessive English influence behind the monarchy's policies and welcomed Napoleon's return. They refused to follow Mahony and the King over the frontier, explaining that they fought for France, not for a person. In Paris too the Irish re-adopted the tricolour and were ostracized when Louis returned a second time. The regiment was disbanded on 28 September 1815, and many of its officers, including Lawless, left for the United States. With their departure, and the taint of disloyalty attending those who remained, the last ember of the exiled United organization faded.[107]

Thomas Addis Emmet's premonitions about the future of the United Irishmen on the Continent had proved correct. He had foreseen their depression of status if they tried to mix Irish with French politics, for the dictates of the latter would always triumph. Independence of thought could only be guaranteed by removal from France altogether. 'I do not blame the resolution you have taken, of waiting a little longer for the victory you are promised,' he had written to MacNeven before he sailed for America, 'but I am much mistaken if you will not be disappointed.' Taking military service

106. Gash, *Mr. Secretary Peel*, 169–79; *Diary and Correspondence of Lord Colchester*, II, 515–20; and see Peel's correspondence in P.R.O. H.O. 100/176/547 and 100/178/79–82.

107. A.H.G. X^h 16; Byrne, *Memoirs*, II, 166–72; A.A.G. Doss. Pers. Luke Lawless, Lawless to Clarke, 16 Nov. 1815; also Doss. Pers. 2e sér. John Allen and GB 2774, Corbet.

with France was all very well if they did not lose sight of the object which
had first determined them to do so. 'When you went down [to Morlaix]
you intended to be *Irishmen*, and as such to fight under the French banners
in your own country, and for its freedom. Have you all determined now to
become subjects of the French empire, and to follow a military life? ... *there
will be peace* ... What then will become of your band, your regimentals,
and your rights of French citizenship, etc.? ...'[108] Emmet did not consider
the reverse side of his argument against foreign influence. For most of its
existence the United Irish Society had been entirely dependent on outside
aid to implement its aims. However unsavoury they found such dependence,
once they turned their backs on France they proclaimed their own demise.
But United Irish distrust of France was so intense by the time war re-opened
in 1803 that nothing short of immediate invasion would have proved her
sincerity. In the absence of this, the United Irish movement rapidly disintegrated with the exodus of its principal leaders from France between
1804 and 1806. What remained in both Ireland and France was a memory and
an ideal, and a collection of individuals still anxious to implement it, but
progressively diverted into more muted channels of expression as opportunities
for its successful application became more remote. The memory of the
United Irish Society has lived on to inspire later republicans and nationalists; but as a sophisticated reform movement it had been the product of an
era of confident liberalism in the late eighteenth century, and had passed with
it.

108. Madden, *United Irishmen*, 3rd ser., III, 79–81.

CONCLUSION

The Making of the Myth

Emmet's verdict on the United Irishmen's French alliance scarcely did justice to its role in the development of the Society over the previous decade. The United Irishmen had proved more powerful outside Ireland than they ever could have been at home and their influence did not fade after they had apparently sunk their ambitions in French military service. Until the death in Paris of Miles Byrne in 1862 and Edward Byrne in 1869, the residence in France of many former United men had attracted the periodic pilgrimages of Irish nationalists and republicans, reminding them of the mission left unfinished, of 'the account they keep open'. The contributions of surviving United men to debates in the Irish press, and the frequent resurrection of the United Irish bogey by the authorities, kept their memory alive for much of the nineteenth century. Honourable exile in what Irish nationalists recognized as the traditional 'asylum of the banished Irish insurgents'[1] had endowed the former United leaders with a nobility and an authority which would have almost certainly been submerged in Daniel O'Connell's crusade for catholic emancipation and repeal of the Union, had they been permitted to return. As late as 1812 Thomas Addis Emmet, reflecting on his experiences in 1803 to 1804, could still denounce the French alliance as having been 'fatal to the Union', and Bonaparte as 'the worst enemy Ireland ever had'.[2] But the fact remains that without French assistance Irish republicanism would have been still-born in the climate of repression which developed in Ireland and England after 1793. Second-generation republicans in the Young Ireland movement recognized France's contribution to the development of Irish republicanism and hoped again to secure assistance from that quarter.[3] But

---

1. See Byrne, *Memoirs*, II, 324–34, 356–62, 399–401; Sir Charles Gavan, Duffy, *Young Ireland*, 2nd edn. (Dublin, 1884), 64, 70, 103–4; Kee, *The Green Flag*, 301, P.R.O.N.I. D.1748/14 and 18, for the continuing inspiration provided by the exiled United men.
2. Madden, *United Irishmen*, 2nd. ser., II, 38.
3. D. W. Leonard, 'John Mitchel, Charles Gavan Duffy and the legacy of Young Ireland' (Sheffield Univ. D.Phil. thesis 1975), 192–4; J. Mitchel, *Ireland, France and Prussia. A selection from the Speechès and Writings of John Mitchel* (Dublin, 1918), 36–7; J. Savage, *'98 and '48. The Modern Revolutionary History and Literature of Ireland* (New York, 1884), 51–8; Kiernan, *Irish Exiles in Australia*, 83–5, and Duffy, *Young Ireland*, 60–4, 117–19.

the strength which French support had given to the movement was soon forgotten in the nationalist myth created from the late nineteenth century onwards. The weakest elements in United Irish history were now seen as its major strength; attention was concentrated on the idea of the just struggle by the few noble spirits against the powerful tyrant, their martyrdom hailed as some kind of national catharsis, their failure a form of triumph in itself.

Although remnants of Dwyer's men were still active in Wicklow and Kilkenny in 1814, any organized United Irish Society had already faded by the time of Emmet's Rebellion. Nevertheless, contemporaries recognized that it had changed the climate of popular discontent, which a group of determined leaders might again harness to rebellion.[4] The vague lamentings of popular balladry still reflected the old sense of oppression, but its tone had been altered by the events of the recent past. In many cases fallen United men and acts of oppression from the '98 era had replaced those of the seventeenth century, and for the first time the sense of national wrong was being identified with England.[5] The Ribbon movement, which had absorbed the remnants of Defenderism and the United Irishmen alike, perpetuated the United ideal of the armed struggle right through the constitutional agitation of the O'Connellite years into the second half of the nineteenth century. But Irish society, however much it might grieve lost heroes or vow revenge, had proved itself consistently incapable of united action except when driven to desperation or directed by outside or upper-class leaders, and the Ribbonmen epitomized this national failing.[6] The persistence of the Napoleonic myth in particular filled the leadership vacuum for many years, for there was no active republican movement in Ireland between the collapse of Emmet's Rebellion and the rise of the Young Irelanders in the 1840s. O'Connell's brilliant mobilization of the populace was for peaceful purposes only, and when he evoked precedents for his demands of catholic emancipation and political reform, he preferred to took to the Volunteers and to 1782 rather than to the United Irishmen.[7] The United leaders had recognized only too well the lulling effect of reform on popular passions, and the grant of catholic emancipation in 1829, followed by a more sympathetic rule of Ireland, drained Irish nationalism of its martial ardour for many decades.

4. Hall, *Tour Through Ireland*, ii, 46–50; and P.R.O. H.O. 100/176/115, for Dwyer's men.
5. D. J. Casey, 'Wildgoose Lodge: The Evidence and the Lore', *Journal of the Co. Louth Archaeological and Historical Society*, xviii, no. 2 (1974), 153–60; Croker, *Researches in the South of Ireland*, 328–9; Zimmermann, *Songs of Irish Rebellion*, 39; and G. Broeker., *Rural Disorder and Police Reform in Ireland, 1812–36* (London, 1970), 108.
6. Beames, 'Peasant Disturbances', 111–14; and idem, 'The Ribbon Societies'; Zimmermann, *Songs of Irish Rebellion*, 32–3; O. D. Edwards and I. R. H. MacDiarmid, *Celtic Nationalism* (London, 1968), 84–7.
7. Kee, *The Green Flag*, 188–9, 232, 265; Col. P. Roche Fermoy (Robert Johnson), *A Commentary on the Memoirs of T. W. Tone* (Paris, 1828), 163.

In times of adversity, however, the example of the United Irishmen was always resurrected, and they entered the twentieth century as the recognized prophets of physical force republicanism; their own fears and reservations, which had motivated the approach to France in the first place, were conveniently forgotten. It was O'Connell, the self-proclaimed prophet of moral rather than physical force, who helped create the image of the United Irishmen as violent republicans. This was all very well if moral force succeeded, and the United Irishmen themselves would have preferred it to armed conflict. But when repeal was floundering in the British parliament, many became increasingly impatient at O'Connell's denunciation of the right to take up arms as a last resort. The methods of the United Irishmen may not have inspired emulation in the first decades of the nineteenth century, when memories of the horrors of '98 proved a more powerful deterrent to active republicanism. But the United Irishmen had been accepted in popular thinking as noble heroes and O'Connell's vituperative attack on them in the 1830s and 1840s seemed a shabby attempt to monopolize popular adulation. 'As to 1798,' he stated in an address of May 1841, 'we leave the weak and wicked men who considered sanguinary violence as part of their resources for ameliorating our institutions, and the equally wicked and villanously designing wretches who fomented the rebellion, and made it explode in order that in the defeat of the rebellious attempt, they might be able to extinguish the liberties of Ireland. We leave both these classes of miscreants to the contempt and indignation of mankind . . . ' It was a singularly ill-timed piece of invective, for MacNeven, with whom O'Connell had been at loggerheads for some years, had just died in New York, widely regarded as one of America's leading citizens and an honoured Irish patriot.

In fact, few United Irishmen had been doctrinaire republicans; as American exiles they were enthusiastic supporters of O'Connell's catholic emancipation and repeal campaigns, and the Emmet and MacNeven families were prominent organizers of the New York repeal committee at the time of O'Connell's attack. The attack had angered the surviving United men, and many wrote of their feelings to Dr. Madden, then researching his fiercely partisan history of the United Irishmen which would appear in 1842–6, at the height of the controversy over the use of moral or physical force.[8] The vision of the United Irishmen as the first champions of Irish nationalism in arms had been established; they were brought back into the splendour of national adulation after

8. T.C.D. MS. 873/584; also *Freeman's Journal*, 22 May 1841; and on the conflict between the former United men and O'Connell see Madden, *United Irishmen*, revised edn., 4 vols. (London, 1857–60), III, 177–9, 212–52; T.C.D. MS. 873/186–7, 742, MS. 7253/3, 7255/8; and Byrne, *Memoirs*, II, 317. See also T. F. O'Sullivan, *The Young Irelanders* (Tralee, 1944), 555–6, 577; J. F. Lalor, *Collected Writings*, ed. N. Marlowe (Dublin, 1918), 53–4; and C. L. Falkiner, *Essays Relating to Ireland* (London, 1903), 118–19.

decades of neglect, and Ingram's famous poem, 'The Memory of the Dead',
which appeared in the *Nation* for 1 April 1843, set the scene for the United
Irishman's splendid if distorted second coming in nationalist mythology:

Who fears to speak of Ninety-Eight?
   Who blushes at the name?
When cowards mock the patriots' fate,
   Who hangs his head for shame?
He's all a knave, or half a slave,
   Who slights his country thus;
But a true man, like you, man,
   Will fill your glass with us.

We drink the memory of the brave,
   The faithful and the few—
Some lie far off beyond the wave,
   Some sleep in Ireland, too;
All—all are gone—but still lives on
   The fame of those who died;
All true men, like you, men,
   Remember them with pride.

Some on the shores of distant lands
   Their weary hearts have laid,
And by the stranger's heedless hands
   Their lonely graves were made.
But, though their clay be far away
   Beyond the Atlantic foam—
In true men, like you, men,
   Their spirit's still at home.

The dust of some is Irish earth;
   Among their own they rest;
And the same land that gave them birth
   Has caught them to her breast;
And we will pray that from their clay
   Full many a race may start
Of true men, like you, men,
   To act as brave a part.

They rose in dark and evil days
   To right their native land;
They kindled here a living blaze
   That nothing shall withstand.
Alas! that Might can vanquish Right—
   They fell, and pass'd away;
But true men, like you, men,
   Are plenty here to-day.

Then here's their memory—may it be
   For us a guiding light,
To cheer our strife for liberty,
   And teach us to unite.

> Through good and ill, be Ireland's still,
>   Though sad as theirs your fate;
> And true men, be you, men,
>   Like those of Ninety-Eight.[9]

Most immediately the debate over United Irish methods accelerated the break of Young Ireland with O'Connell and was to influence the thinking behind the attempted rising of 1848, as it would again in 1867 and 1916.

This idea of total United Irish commitment to armed insurrection was not the only travesty of reality in the developing myth. Later republicans, particularly those like James Fintan Lalor or James Connolly, who saw the land war as a fundamental part of the republican struggle, and popular sovereignty as one of its main goals, built the image of the United Irishmen as social reformers, particularly from Tone's phrase about bringing 'the men of no property' into the struggle. The absence of any major social programme and their instinctive fear of the people was, in fact, one of the principal contradictions in United Irish thinking. James Hope alone expressed any realistic ideas on the land question. But he was a secondary leader who escaped the romantic fate of the others and he is significantly ignored in this aspect of republican mythology.[10]

Nor was the question of separation from England as clear-cut in the United Irish programme as their successors implied. Patrick Pearse was to reiterate Tone's famous passage about breaking the connection with England, 'the never failing source of all our evils', and he felt that his own destiny was 'to complete the work of Tone'.[11] But too many latter-day republicans failed to see the ambiguities of the United Irish definition of 'breaking the connection', and even Robert Emmet was prepared to form some new tie on a more equitable basis. The United Irishmen had always sought co-operation with the English people; there was no national hatred of England as such; their dispute had been with the English government alone. Yet their own conception of themselves as part of a wider European movement was later transformed into an intensely chauvinistic nationalist cult. The catholic takeover of their ideals by the twentieth century was perhaps inevitable. Internationalism and liberalism were products of the unusual confidence of the late eighteenth century and they were already fading before the United Irishmen became militant republicans. Even in that more tolerant climate they had difficulty implementing their ideal of national unity and, the repression of the 1790s had resurrected and fortified sectarian divisions.

---

9. Zimmermann, *Songs of Irish Rebellion*, 226–7.
10. T.C.D. MS. 7256, The Death-bed Book of James Hope, 1846; P. H. Pearse, *The Separatist Idea* (Dublin, 1916), 18–20, idem, *The Sovereign People* (Dublin, 1916); F. S. L. Lyons, *Ireland Since the Famine*, 3rd edn. (London, 1975), 54, 111–12.
11. P. H. Pearse, *How Does She Stand?* 2nd edn. (Dublin, 1915), 6.

Protestant nationalism had flourished because of its insulation from any involvement with the populace as a whole. It had been the peculiar creation of the Volunteer era, and despite the prominence of protestants such as Thomas Davis, William Smith O'Brien, or William Butler Yeats in the history of modern Irish nationalism, recollections that the first Irish nationalists had been protestants were fleeting.[12]

But it was the myth of the noble failure, the sanctity of the hopeless struggle, which paradoxically was to exercise most influence on nationalist imagination, and in the 1848 and 1916 risings republican nationalists used the myth in justification of rebellions pre-ordained to fail. Michael Davitt, speaking about Emmet in the centenary year of his rebellion, claimed that 'There was more in that failure ... for the cause of national liberty than many a success has won in other causes. There is a triumph of failure as well as a penalty ... a triumph for principles, for truth, for a great idea, when won by sacrifices which most rational considerations overlook ... '[13] This triumph of failure, taken from the United Irish myth, became the stock theme of republican thinking and has been cleverly incorporated into the title of Ruth Dudley Edwards's book on Patrick Pearse, its principal exponent.[14] In fairness, it was a myth initiated by the United Irishmen themselves when things started to go disastrously wrong. As consummate propagandists, they took over the older tradition of the dying oration and made it their tool to mould the thinking of posterity. It was Emmet's achievement in this sphere which made him 'Ireland's most popular hero'. The celebrations for the '98 centenary were impressive, but they were outshone by those in 1903. The famous last lines of Emmet's speech 'Let no man write my epitaph ... [until] my country takes her place among the nations of the earth ... ' became such a part of popular culture that they re-appeared time and time again in songs, books and everyday speech, though it is almost certain that he never actually spoke them.[15] 'No failure', Pearse told the New York Emmet commemoration meeting in March 1914, ' ... was ever more complete, more pathetic than Emmet's. And yet he has left us a prouder

12. *The Northern Patriot*, 25 Jan. and 22 Feb. 1896; E. MacNeill, *Shall Ireland be Divided?* (Dublin, 1915); Cullen, 'The Cultural Basis of Modern Irish Nationalism'; Jack White, *Minority Report: the Protestant community in the Irish Republic* (Dublin, 1975), 3–4. See also the review of F. Hacket's *The story of the Irish Nation* (Dublin, 1924), in *The Irish Statesman*, 13 Jan. 1925, 631–2. Of course the catholic 'takeover' corresponded with the protestant rejection of '98 and the United Irishmen as part of their own heritage, see I. Budge and C. O'Leary, *Belfast: Approach to Crisis* (London, 1973), 42–3, 90; and M. Farrell, *Northern Ireland, the Orange state* (London, 1976), 148, 190.
13. N.L.I. I R 92 E.43, Robert Emmet in Poetry, 1, newspaper cutting, 15 Mar. 1902.
14. R. D. Edwards, *Patrick Pearse, the triumph of failure* (London, 1977).
15. N.L.I. IR 92 E.43, 1, cutting from the *Evening Herald*, 21 Sept. 1803; see also *The Northern Patriot*, 25 Jan. and 24 Apr. 1896, and Lyons, *Ireland Since the Famine*, 247–8, 260–1, for the unifying effect of the 1898 celebration on the Irish Parliamentary Party, and Vance, 'Texts and Traditions', for the debate about Emmet's speech.

memory than the memory of Brian victorious at Clontarf . . . It is the memory of a sacrifice Christ-like in its perfection . . . he uttered the most memorable words ever uttered by an Irishman: words which . . . forbid us ever to waver or grow weary until our country takes her place among the nations of the earth . . . Be assured that such a death always means redemption . . . His attempt was not a failure, but a triumph for that deathless thing we call Irish Nationality.'[16] Emmet gained pride of place in the litany of glorious failures, later to include Pearse himself, and entered the twentieth century as part of the established contortion of nationalist reasoning which felt that a 'succession of failures' would somehow bring ultimate victory.[17]

United Irish speechifying was aimed at posterity to disguise their failure in Ireland. But their most important work had been performed outside Ireland and it is here that their real strength can be found. A French invasion was not sought in desperation, but as the most natural way of securing independence efficiently and with the minimum of bloodshed. In France they negotiated as equal partners, holding out for an invasion force large enough to prevent such bloodshed, in the face of an established French policy of withholding support until the supplicants had first proved their ability to liberate themselves. In 1796 they had secured the despatch of nearly 16,000 French troops to Ireland under one of the French Republic's leading generals. Hoche's own ambition had played a major part in this success, but the United Irishmen were also in a stronger negotiating position than many of the other foreign exiles seeking French aid. Behind them they could boast a country in which the French armies would be greeted as friends, and for a time France came to view them as her most important weapon against the British enemy.

The fact of a major war with France had created the conditions which made republicanism an inevitable response to intensified reaction in Ireland. Thereafter, the French alliance helped ensure the survival of the new movement, providing a major accession of strength in the eyes of its followers, permitting its leaders a freedom of organization and planning outside Ireland, which in the repressive climate of the 1790s would have been difficult within Ireland before 1798 and impossible after it, insulating it from the more unsavoury incidents of that year, and sustaining a cause already fading in Ireland by providing an asylum for its leaders and a source of hope for a 'second coming'. Disenchantment with the French alliance had set in rapidly after the fall of the Directory. But it was not the product of first-hand experience of French occupation, to which the Belgian, Rhenish, Dutch or Italian patriots had already fallen prey. It was rather due to the United Irishmen's re-

16. Pearse, *How Does She Stand?* 9–10.
17. See e.g. *Slór na bfiann* (Dublin, 1919), 11, and *Robert Emmet, A Commemorative Booklet* (Dublin, 1921), both issued by the Wolfe Tone Memorial Committee; also A. Newman, *What Emmet Means in 1915. A Tract for the Times* (Dublin, 1915), 4–5, published by the Irish Volunteers.

cognition of their total dependence on France, which their own fears of
social turmoil had created at the outset, but which they had never before
admitted until the '98 rebellion had destroyed their strength in Ireland
and forced their leadership into almost total exile in France. Even then
that alliance was a source of strength, keeping the movement alive in exile
long after it had ceased to exist in reality at home. It is important also to
recognize that, apart from the disappointment at the conclusion of peace
in 1802, the disenchantment of the exiles with the French was never felt by
the Irish populace as a whole. Ireland was never given any cause to doubt
the purity of either French or United Irish motives, since neither her patriot
leaders nor her French ally returned to experiment in government-forming;
and the romantic vision of both, quickly destroyed in so many other countries
which had welcomed the republican armies only to find that they came as
conquerors, was left unsullied to dominate the myth, as it had done the
history, of the United Irishmen.

   In times less turbulent than those in which it had arisen, early Irish republicanism, a movement which had spent most of its life exiled in France,
was nevertheless to provide both the inspiration and the justification for later
republicans. Tone was not entirely representative of United Irish thinking,
but his writings were so compelling, his ideas so in tune with later republican
thinking, that Tone's *Life* became the first 'gospel of the New Testament
of Irish Nationality'. With the other subtle distortions of United Irish thinking,
it became part of the necessary myth of later republicanism, legitimizing
the armed struggle, however hopeless, dignifying the principle of separation,
and national sovereignty, and through the heroic tales of their noble failure,
reminding future republicans of 'the task left unfinished'.[18] Despite their
social elitism and internal bickering, there was nothing inevitable about
United Irish failure and modern historians who dismiss them as hopeless
romantics are unaware of the extent to which they have been duped
by the republican nationalist myth. Their sociability and love of public
debate and esteem made the United Irish leaders clumsy and uncomfortable
conspirators, and the crippling divisions of later years were the product of
frustration at the prolongation of such an existence. With success or failure so
dependent on France after 1795, the real fate of the United Irish movement
was sealed at Bantry Bay. But Tone and Hoche in Ireland in 1796 would
have proved an irresistable combination; it is no idle speculation to think
that Britain's role in the Revolutionary War would have been quite different
if she had been forced out by a successful campaign in Ireland that year;
and in view of the coincidence of events in December 1796, who can deny
that only a remarkable series of accidents prevented United Irish success in
the heyday of their diplomatic activities abroad?

18. P. H. Pearse, *Political Writings and Speeches*, 2nd edn. (Dublin, 1966), 168; and idem, *The
Separatist Idea*, especially 19–20.

BIBLIOGRAPHY

Primary Sources: Manuscript

ENGLAND

London   . . . .

BRITISH LIBRARY, ADDITIONAL MANUSCRIPTS

27808–9, 27813–8 and 35143	Place papers
31237	Misc. papers of Lord Bexley
33101–22	Pelham papers
34455–6	Auckland papers
35197	Bridport papers
35707–14 and 35770–2	Hardwicke papers
37845	Windham papers
40280–1	Peel papers

GENERAL POST OFFICE

Post. 42/65–72	Postmaster General's reports, 1793–6

PUBLIC RECORD OFFICE

Admiralty: Adm. 1/3974	Intelligence
3991	Letters relating to Ireland
5336–45	Courts Martial
5486	Petitions
6033	Intelligence
Adm. 2/1119	Mutiny, HMS *Cambridge*
Adm. 12/82	Register for 1799
Chatham Papers: P.R.O. 30/8/325–7	Letters relating to Ireland, 1794–8
30/8/331	Letters of Lord Westmorland, 1790–5

Colchester Papers P.R.O. 30/9/9/12	State prisoners, 1799–1801
Colonial Office, Ireland:	
C.O. 902/2	Pensions and expenses, 1792–1808
902/7–8	Ribbonism, 1798–1841
902/20	Extracts from speeches by prominent Nationalists
9061–8	Irish Office records, 1796–1814
Cornwallis Papers:	
P.R.O. 30/11/264	Amiens, 1801–2
30/11/270	Letters from important people, 1781–1807
Foreign Office: F.O. 5/79	Intercepted French papers, 1811–13
27/40–92	France, 1792–1813
33/9–30	Hamburg, 1794–1805
37/51–3	Holland, 1794
74/3–5, 17–22	Switzerland, 1793–8
95/8	Switzerland, miscellaneous, 1781–1810
95/605	Bouillon papers
97/240–2	Hamburg, supplementary, 1781–1810
Home Office:	
H.O. 28/22–33,63	Admiralty correspondence, 1797–1805
40/1/1–4 and 40/2/1–2	Disturbances, 1812
42/21–140	Letters and papers of George III, 1792–1814
69/27–9	Bouillon papers
79/1,6,10	Ireland, private and secret entry books
95/605	Bouillon papers
100/34–179	Ireland, principally private, secret and confidential correspondence, 1792–1814
101/2	King's letters, Ireland, 1791–1803
119/1	Law Officers, private, secret and confidential correspondence, 1792–9
122/3 and 123/6, 19	Ireland, entry books, 1793–1805
Privy Council:	
P.C. 1/19/A.27	Corresponding Societies—letters of Stone, 1792

1/22/A.36^{a–c}	Examinations of those accused of revolutionary designs, 1794
1/22/A.37	Treason. Corresponding Societies. Trials, Oct.–Dec. 1794
1/23/A.38	London Corresponding Society, 1794–6
1/28/A.62	Corresponding Societies, 1795
1/34/A.90	Treason, 1796
1/37/A.114	Miscellaneous, 1797, including prosecution of officers landed with Tate
1/38/A.123 and 1/40/A.129–33	Corresponding Societies, 1797
1/41'/A.136–9 and 1/42/A.140–4	Corresponding Societies. Treason, 1798
1/43/A.147	Mutiny at the Nore. Ireland, 1798
1/43/A.150	Treason and Corresponding Societies, 1798
1/43/A.152–3	Corresponding Societies. U.I. Societies in London, 1799
1/44/A.155	Corresponding Societies. Ireland, 1799
1/44/A.158–9 and A.161	Corresponding Societies. Irish prisoners. United Englishmen, 1799
1/3117	Treason. Corresponding Societies, 1797–1806
1/3514, 3526, 3528, 3535–6 and 3552–3	Treason (Despard). Corresponding Societies, 1800–2
1/3564, 3581–3	Secret information. Irish insurrection, 1803
1/3586^a, 3596–9, 3602–6, 3611, 3624, 3627–8	Suspected persons. Ireland, 1804

Treasury Solicitor:

T.S. 11/121/332 and 11/122/333	Trial of Despard, 1803
11/541/1755	Prosecution of J. Binns and J. Gale Jones, 1796
11/555/1793	Trial of W. Stone, 1795
11/689/2187	Maidstone Trials, 1798
11/906/3099	Trial of T. Smith for attack on Emblin, 1803

| 11/1067/4835 | Trial of Rev. W. Jackson, 1795 |
| 24/1/1–3 | Sedition, misc. cases, 1792–5 |

War Office, Ireland:

| W.O. 1/395–8, 612, 778 | Intelligence, 1789–1808 |
| 30/63, 65, 73 | Defence, 1796–1804 |

Maidstone

KENT COUNTY RECORD OFFICE

| MS U.840 | Pratt papers |

Oxford

BODLEIAN LIBRARY

Bland Burges Deposit (uncatalogued at time of use)
MS. Eng. Hist. b.196, c.295–6 and MS. Eng. Letters, c.64, c.66 (Burdett–Coutts papers)
Curzon Collection, b.2–41
MS. Eng. Letters 234–8 and MS. French c.37, d.32 (Napier MSS.)
MS. Percy, b.1–3, c.1–9, e.1–9

Winchester

HAMPSHIRE COUNTY RECORD OFFICE

| MS. 38M49 | Wickham papers |
| MS. 31M70 | Tierney papers |

FRANCE

Paris

ARCHIVES DES AFFAIRES ÉTRANGÈRES QUAI D'ORSAY

Correspondance Politique:	Angleterre 582–606, 1792–1815
	Supplément 15, 19, 21, 29, 30–31, 1788–1815
	Hambourg 107–17, 1792–1804
	Supplément 14–15, 1793–1802
	Hollande 595, 1797
	Sardaigne 279, 1800
	Suisse 458, 1796
Correspondance Consulaire:	Altona 12, 1799–1800

	Hambourg 10–15, 1794–1804
	Londres 10, 1793–1815
Mémoires et Documents:	Affaires Diverses Politiques France 8–10, Irish in France
	Angleterre 1ᵇ, 2, 9, 18, 19, 32, 48, 53, 56
	France 590, 596, 601 (Fonds Bourbons) 1770–6 (letters and orders of Napoleon)
	France et Divers Etats 651–4
Personnel, première série:	1 Aherne
	8 Berthonneau
	19 Coquebert de Montbret
	25 Duckett
	39 Jackson
	47 Madgett
	55 O'Shee, Oswald and Parandier
	65 Sullivan
Personnel, Arrêtés et Décrets:	8–10, 1794–1808
Personnel, Consulats:	50–51, 1790–1813

ARCHIVES ADMINISTRATIVES DE LA GUERRE, CHÂTEAU DE VINCENNES

Dossiers Personnels, première série:	Markey, Thomas
deuxième série:	O'Reilly, Terence
	GB 1430 Ameil, Baron Auguste
	MF 6 Augereau, Pierre François
	Blackwell, James Bartholomew
	GB 2774 Corbet, William
	GD 852 Dalton, Alexandre
	Lawless, Luke
	GB Lawless, William
	MacMahon, Arthur
	MacSheehy, Bernard
	GD 393 O'Connor, Arthur
	GD 1518 O'Meara, William
	GB 696 O'Shee, Richard
	Swanton, Jacques
	GB 755 Tandy, James Napper
	Tennent, John
	Tone, William T. W.
	Ware, Hugh

(Of the above, those without reference numbers are classified alphabetically.)

ARCHIVES HISTORIQUES DE LA GUERRE, CHÂTEAU DE VINCENNES

B¹ 172–7: Armées du Nord et de la Sambre et Meuse
B¹* 177: Armée de la Sambre et Meuse
B⁵ 41–4: Armée d'Angleterre
B⁵* 114–6: Armée d'Angleterre, régistres
B¹¹ 1: Première Expédition d'Irlande, 1796–7
B¹¹ 2: Deuxième Expédition d'Irlande, 1798
B¹²* 37: Rapports du Ministre au Directoire, 1799
B¹⁴ 5–6: Correspondance des Côtes de l'Océan, 1803–5
C¹ 1–35: Armée des Côtes de l'Océan, 1803–5
C² 101–3: Armées du Nord et de Brabant, 1809
C²* 285: Bureau du Mouvement, 1811–12
C²* 365: Défense des Côtes, 1809
C²* 461: Expédition d'Angleterre, 1803–5
C¹⁷* 96, 158–60, 194: Napoléon Bonaparte, ordres, correspondance, 1800–6
C¹⁸ 24–5: Police militaire, 1809
MR (Mémoires historiques) 499–506: Armée de L'Ouest
1420: Projets de descente
1444: Angleterre
Xʰ 14–17: Bataillons et Régiments Étrangères, 1804–15

ARCHIVES NATIONALES

Pouvoir exécutif:	AF II	5, 20, 29, 42, 49, 61, 63–4, 66, 174, 294–5 (Committee of Public Safety)
	AF III	16, 45, 51ᴬ, 57–9, 64, 70, 81, 147, 149, 186ᵃ⁻ᵇ, 203ᵇ, 205–6, 268–9, 271–4, 280, 337, 362, 369–70, 373, 377, 400, 408, 431–2, 450, 452, 463, 505, 529, 546, 553, 579, 615, 620, 632, 635 (Directory)
	AF III*	20, Secret deliberations
	AF IV	103, 113, 115, 118, 204, 308, 314, 328, 345–6, 417, 494, 597, 609, 861, 1046, 1092, 1101, 1114, 1117–18, 1195–6, 1198–9, 1200, 1219, 1325, 1505–6, 1597ᴬ⁻ᴮ, 1598, 1600ᴬ, 1601, 1671–4, 1680–1ᴬ, 1687 (Consulate, Empire, Hundred Days)
	AF IV*	204–5, Registers, 1800–5

Justice:	BB²² 8–11	Prisoners sent on Tate's expedition
Marine:	BB¹	3–32, Minister's reports, 1792–1806
	BB²	2, 5, 11, 17, 18, 23, 31, 39, 45, 55, 78, 87, 94, 98, 101, 106, 547 (Marine correspondence, out-letters)
	BB³	15–16, 36, 39, 44, 58, 61, 64, 66, 87, 102–8, 124–5, 143, 145–6, 160–3, 174–5, 187, 200, 203, 214–5, 220, 235, 249, 269, 287, 310, 330, 340, 367, 386, 402, 417, 429 (Marine correspondence, in-letters)
	BB⁴	99, 102–3, 112, 114, 119–23, 130, 180, 191, 205, 309–12 (Campaigns, 1796–1805)
	FF²	137, prisoners of war, Hardy's expedition, 1798
	GG¹	31, 36, 67–72 (Memoirs and projects)
	GG²	22–3 (Truguet papers)
Comptabilité générale:	F⁴	1401 (Matilda Tone)
Police générale:	F⁷	3050, 3643–6, reports from the coasts, 1802–10; 3712, 3746–66, Police bulletins, 1804–10; 4225, 4230, 4269, 4291 (Lawless's mission, 1811), 4298, 4304, 4307, 4331, 4374, 4390ᴬ, 4774, archives, intercepted and captured papers; 6192, 6213, 6245, 6281, 6330, 6337–8, 6351, 6355, 6430, 6446, 6448, 6460, 6462–3, 6509–10, 6574–7, 6595, First Empire, political affairs; 7107, 7111, 7114, 7131–40, 7144, 7151, 7155ᴬ, 7164–71, 7175–7, 7185–8, 7192, 7194–7, 7202, 7206, 7208, 7212, 7215–25, 7233–8, 7240–2, 7249, 7251, 7262–5, 7293, 7300–3, 7310, 7321–3, 7328, 7348, 7365, 7379, 7383ᴮ, 7390, 7401, 7411, 7417 7422, 7435ᴮ, 7437–40, 7446,

| | | 7449–59, 7480–8, Directory, misc. affairs, mostly passports; 8115, 8141, 8198, 8217, 8225, 8255, 8273, 8280, 8282, 8318, 8331, 8552, 8555, 8595, 8646, First Empire, misc. affairs. |
| Hospices et Secours: | F^{15} | 102–3, 3359^{A-B}, 3438–9, 3508, 3510–1 and F^{15}* 16, refugees |

BIBLIOTHÈQUE NATIONALE

| Nouvelles acquisitions françaises: | 20097–9 Travels of Coquebert de Montbret in Ireland |

Rouen

ARCHIVES DÉPARTEMENTALES DE LA SEINE ET MARITIME

| 1 Mi 54–71 | Papiers Hoche |

Bignon

CHÂTEAU DE BIGNON, DÉPARTEMENT DU LOIRET

Private papers of Arthur O'Connor

IRELAND

Belfast

LINENHALL LIBRARY

Joy MSS. 8–13

PUBLIC RECORD OFFICE OF NORTHERN IRELAND

D. 272: McCance collection
D. 561: John Galt's diary
D. 572: MacCartney Papers
D. 607 and 671: Downshire MSS.
D. 638: De Ross MSS.
D. 714: Cleland MSS.
D. 729: Drennan–Duffin Papers
D. 1748: Tennent Letters (partially catalogued)
D. 3030: Castlereagh Papers

T. 765: Drennan Letters
T. 1075: Despard Family, genealogical notes
T. 1101/1–4: Immigrants to New York, 1802–18
T. 1722: Paterson MSS.
T. 1815: Emigrant letters to R. Simms
T. 3048: McPeake Papers
T. 3229: Sneyd Papers

Dublin:

IRISH STATE PAPER OFFICE, DUBLIN CASTLE

C.S.O. Official Papers (M.A.) IA.76.3, IA.77.4, IA.80.6 and 9, misc. papers, Chief Secretary's Office

C.S.O. 1847, misc. letters to the Irish Office, 1801–3

C.S.O. 1–2, official letters received at the Irish Office, 1801–9

Private Official Correspondence, 1789–93, vol. VIII^A/1/3–4 and 10

General Private Correspondence, 1804–14, vol. VIII^A/1/13

Westmorland Correspondence, vols. 1–4

Rebellion Papers, 620/1–67

State of the Country Papers 1015–32, 1062, 1080, 1091, 1120–1, 1158, 1188, 1191–3, 1207, 1227–30, 1275–80, 1381–90, 1401–9, 1531–44, 1560–5

NATIONAL LIBRARY OF IRELAND

Manuscripts:	
54A–55	Melville Papers
56	Lake Correspondence
58–75^A	Richmond Correspondence
611–4, 630, 635	Fitzgerald Correspondence
704–7	French Invasion
809	French Invasion, Defence
1576	Account of the 1798 Rebellion
1577	David Powell's Campaigne, 1794
2123	Leinster MSS.
3212	Misc. Letters of T. W. Tone
3151	La Touche MSS.
4156–7	Musgrave MSS.
4239, 4813	Tighe MSS.
4472	Account of the 1798 Rebellion by Mrs. Newton
5181	1898 Centenary Celebrations
5932	Blaquiere MSS.

5973	Crown Circuit, Judge Finucane
8822	Blackwell MSS.
9706	Luke Cullen Papers
10961	Copies of letters from A. O'Connor to Napoleon, 1811
13665	Letters of W. Duckett
13799–800	Misc. papers of Dr. R. Hayes
13842	Rosse Papers
15473	O'Connell Papers
15481–3	Letters and Notes of W. J. Fitzpatrick
IR 92E43	Robert Emmet in Poetry (Scrapbook)
Microfilm: pos. 210	MS. Life of William Duckett
pos. 597	Hamilton MSS.
pos. 2609	Le Fanu Papers
pos. 5308	Pollock MSS.

ROYAL IRISH ACADEMY

MS. 23.K.53	Burrowes MSS.
MS. 24.K.48	Memoirs of A. H. Rowan
MS. 12.L.32	Journal of Kitty Wilmot, 1801–3
MS. 12.P.13	Journal of D. O'Connell

TRINITY COLLEGE

MSS. 868–9	Sirr Papers
MS. 872	Courts Martial 1798
MS. 873	Madden Papers
MSS. 2041–51, 3805–9	Tone MSS.
MS. 3979	Connolly Papers
MS. 4833	Sheares Letters
MSS. 7253–6	Hope MSS.
Uncatalogued	Corbet Papers

Primary Sources: Printed

NEWSPAPERS AND PERIODICALS

Annual Register
Anti-Jacobin
Courier
Dublin Evening Post

Dublin Magazine
Faulkner's Dublin Journal
Freeman's Journal
Irish News
Irish Statesman
Manchester Gazette
Manchester Mercury
Moniteur (*Réimpression de l'Ancien Moniteur*, 31 vols. (Paris, 1858–63))
Northern Patriot
Northern Star
Press
Sun
The Times
Union Star

COLLECTIONS OF OFFICIAL DOCUMENTS, PARLIAMENTARY
PROCEEDINGS ETC.

Archives parlementaires. Recueil complet des débats législatifs et politiques des Chambres françaises, 1ʳᵉ série: 1787–1799, 91 vols. (Paris, 1879–1976)

Buchez, P. J. B. and Roux-Lavergne, P. C., *Histoire parlementaire de la Révolution française, ou Journal des Assemblées nationales depuis 1789 jusqu'en 1815*, 40 vols. (Paris, 1834–8)

The Debate in the Irish House of Peers on a Motion made by the Earl of Moira, 19 Feb. 1798 (Dublin, 1798)

Journals of the House of Lords, Ireland, 1634–1800, 8 vols. (Dublin, 1779–1800)

The Parliamentary History of England from the earliest period to the year 1803, 36 vols. (London, 1806–20), continued as *Cobbett's Parliamentary Debates* and *The Parliamentary Debates*, 41 vols. (London, 1812–20)

The Parliamentary Register: or, History of the Proceedings and Debates of the House of Commons of Ireland, 15 vols. (Dublin, 1784–95)

Reports from the Committee of Secrecy of the House of Commons respecting Seditious Practices (London, 1794)

Report from the Committee of Secrecy of the House of Commons of Ireland (Dublin, 1798)—also reproducing the 1793 and 1797 secret reports

Reports from the Committee of Secrecy of the House of Lords in Ireland (Dublin, 1798)

Report from the Committee of Secrecy of the House of Commons relative to the proceedings of different persons and societies in Great Britain and Ireland engaged in a treasonable conspiracy (London, 1799)

Report from the Committee of Secrecy of the House of Lords relative to a treasonable conspiracy (London, 1799)

Reports from the Committee of Secrecy of the House of Commons on the State of Ireland (London, 1799)

(Of the above, the Irish reports are available in pamphlet form. The English reports appear in pamphlet form, in the *Commons Journals, British Parliamentary Papers, Parliamentary History* and the Abbot Collection in the British Library. However, all the English reports are collected together in *Reports from the Committees of the House of Commons, printed by order of the House 1715–1801,* 16 vols. (London, 1803–6), which I cite for purposes of clarity.)

Report of Debates in the House of Commons of Ireland, [*1796–1800*] (Dublin, 1797–1800)

A Complete Collection of State Trials, ed. T. B. and T. J. Howell, 33 vols. (London, 1809–28)

CONTEMPORARY WORKS AND PAMPHLETS

An Account of the Late Insurrection in Ireland (London, 1798)

The Journal and Correspondence of William, Lord Auckland, ed. the Bishop of Bath and Wells, 4 vols. (London, 1861–2)

Aulard, A. *La Société des Jacobins,* 6 vols. (Paris, 1889–97)

——*Recueil des actes du comité de salut public,* 33 vols. (Paris, 1889–1951)

——*Paris pendant la réaction thermidorienne et sous le Directoire,* 5 vols. (Paris, 1898–1902)

——*Paris sous le Consulat,* 4 vols. (Paris, 1903–9)

——*Paris sous le Premier Empire,* 3 vols. (Paris, 1912)

Bannantine, J. *Memoirs of Edward Marcus Despard* (London, 1799)

Mémoires de Barras, ed. G. Duruy, 4 vols. (Paris, 1896)

Barruel, A. *Mémoires pour servir à l'histoire du Jacobinisme,* 4 vols. (London, 1797)

Mémoires de François Barthélemy, 1768–1819, ed. J. de Dampierre (Paris, 1914)

Beauties of the Press (London, 1800)

Recollections of the Life of John Binns (Philadelphia, 1854)

The Correspondence of the Rt. Hon. John Beresford, ed. the Rt. Hon. W. Beresford, 2 vols. (London, 1854)

Brooke, C. *Reliques of Irish Poetry* (Dublin, 1789)

Memoirs of Miles Byrne, ed. his widow, 2nd. edn. 2 vols. (Dublin, 1906)

Correspondance générale de Carnot, ed. E. Charavay, 4 vols. (Paris, 1892–1907)

Mémoires sur Carnot par son fils, 2 vols. (Paris, 1861–64)

Memoirs and Correspondence of Viscount Castlereagh, ed. 3rd. marquess of Londonderry, 12 vols. (London, 1848–54), I–IV.

Charlemont MSS. The Manuscripts and Correspondence of James, First Earl of Charlemont, H.M.C. 12th Report, Appendix pt. 10; 13th Report. Appendix pt. 8, 2 vols (London, 1891–94)

Clifford, Hon. R. *Application of Barruel's Memoirs of Jacobinism to the Secret Societies of Ireland and Great Britain*, (London, 1798)

The Life of the Rev. James Coigley, . . . written by himself during his confinement in Maidstone Gaol, ed. V. Derry (London, 1798)

Personal Recollections of the life and times, with extracts from the correspondence, of Valentine Lord Cloncurry, (Dublin, 1849)

Diary and Correspondence of Charles Abbot, Lord Colchester, ed. his son Charles, Lord Colchester, 3 vols. (London, 1861)

'A Famous Franco-Irish Soldier: General William Corbet', ed. F. J. Healey. *Journal of the Ivernian Society*, III (1910–11), 239–44

Correspondence of Charles 1st. Marquis Cornwallis, ed. Charles Ross, 3 vols. (London, 1849)

Crawford, W. H. and Trainor, B. (eds.), *Aspects of Irish Social History, 1750–1800* (Belfast, 1969)

The Speeches of the Rt. Hon. John Philpot Curran, ed. T. Davis, 2nd edn. (Dublin, 1853)

Curry, J. *An Historical and Critical Review of the Civil Wars in Ireland* (Dublin, 1750)

——*Historical Memoirs of the Irish Rebellion in the year 1641* (London, 1758)

Discours de Danton, ed. André Fribourg (Paris, 1910)

Debidour, A. *Recueil des actes du Directoire exécutif*, 4 vols. (Paris, 1910–17)

de Jonnès, A. M. *Aventures de guerre au temps de la République et du Consulat* (Paris, 1893)

The Whole Proceedings of the Trials of Col. Despard and the other State Prisoners, 7–9 Feb. 1803 (London, 1803)

The Drennan Letters, 1776–1819, ed. D. A. Chart (Belfast, 1931)

Dropmore MSS. The Manuscripts of J. B. Fortescue Esq., preserved at Dropmore. H.M.C. 13th Report. Appendix. pt. 3, and 14th Report. Appendix pt. 5, 10 vols. (London, 1892–94)

Emmet, T. A. *Ireland Under English Rule*, 2 vols. (New York, 1903)

An Enquiry into the Causes of Popular Discontents in Ireland, by an Irish Country Gentleman, 2nd edn. (London, 1805)

Evidence to Character; or, The Innocent Imposture: Being A Portrait of a Traitor By His Friends and By Himself, 2nd edn. (London, 1798)

Fenwick, J. *Observations on the Trial of James Coigley* (London, 1798)

The Later Correspondence of George III, ed. A. Aspinall, 5 vols. (Cambridge, 1962–70)

Goldsmith, L. *The Secret History of the Cabinet of Bonaparte*, 5th edn. (London, 1811)

The Despatches of Earl Gower, ed. O. Browning (Cambridge, 1885)

Trial of Francis Graham for Attempting to suborn Joseph Corbally, Taylor, to swear that A. H. Rowan and J. Napper Tandy Esqs. were at the Head of the Defenders (Dublin, 1794)

Memoirs of the Life and Times of the Rt. Hon. Henry Grattan, ed. his son, 5 vols. (London, 1839–42)

The Speeches of the Rt. Hon. Henry Grattan, 4 vols. (London, 1822)

Hall, Rev. James. *Tour through Ireland*, 2 vols. (London, 1813)

Hodgson, R. *Proceedings of the General Committee of the London Corresponding Society on the 5th, 12th and 19th of April, 1798, relative to the Resistance of a French Invasion stated in a letter to a friend, intended to have been inserted in the Morning Chronicle* (London, 1798)

Holcroft, T. *Travels from Hamburg through Westphalia, Holland, and the Netherlands, to Paris*, 2 vols (London, 1804)

Memoirs of Joseph Holt, ed. T. Crofton Croker, 2 vols. (London, 1838)

Hunt, H. *The Green Bag Plot* (London, 1819)

Trial of Rev. William Jackson (Dublin, 1795)

Joy, H. and Bruce, W. *Belfast Politics or, Collection of the Debates, Resolutions and Other Proceedings of that Town in the Years 1792 and 1793* (Belfast, 1794)

'Memoir of General Kilmaine', *Dublin University Magazine*, XLVII (Apr. 1856), 464–74

Mémoires de la Révellière-Lépeaux, ed. his son, 3 vols. (Paris, 1895)

Lawless, J. *The Belfast Politics, enlarged; being a compendium of the political history of Ireland for the last forty years* (Belfast, 1818)

MacDonagh, M. *The Viceroy's Postbag* (London, 1904)

McHugh, R. J. (ed.) *Carlow in '98. The Autobiography of William Farrell of Carlow* (Dublin, 1949)

MacNeven, W. J. *Pieces of Irish History* (New York, 1807)

MacNevin, T. *The Lives and Trials of A. H. Rowan, the Rev. William Jackson, the Defenders, William Orr, Peter Finnerty and other Emminent Irishmen* (Dublin, 1846)

The Correspondence of William Augustus Miles on the French Revolution, 1789–1817, ed. Rev. Charles Popham Miles, 2 vols. (London, 1890)

Molyneux, W. *The Case of Ireland's being bound by Acts of the Parliament in England, stated* (Dublin, 1698)

Correspondance de Napoléon 1ᵉʳ, 32 vols. (Paris, 1858–69)

Lettres inédites de Napoléon 1ᵉʳ, ed. L. de Brotonne (Paris, 1898)

Lettres inédites de Napoléon 1ᵉʳ, ed. L. Lecestre, 2 vols. (Paris, 1897)

Correspondance inédite de Napoléon 1ᵉʳ, ed. E. Picard and L. Tuetey, 5 vols. (Paris, 1912–25)

A Narrative of what passed at Killala, in the County of Mayo and parts adjacent, during the French invasion in the summer of 1798. By an Eye-Witness [Bishop J. Stock], (Dublin, 1800)

The Apostacy of Newell, containing the Life and Confession of that Celebrated Informer (London, 1798)

North Riding Naval Recruits. The Quota Acts and the Quota Men 1795–1797, ed. A. M. Hill and M. Y. Ashcroft, Yorkshire C.R.O. Pubs. no. 18 (Scarborough, 1978)

The Trial of Richard Parker (London, 1797)

Payson, S. *Proofs of the real existence, and dangerous tendency, of Illuminism* (Charlestown, 1802)

Autobiography of Francis Place, ed. Mary Thale (Cambridge, 1972)

Reid, W. H. *The Rise and Dissolution of the Infidel Societies in this metropolis* (London, 1800)

'Reminiscences of a Fugitive Loyalist in 1798', communicated by G. F. Handcock, *E.H.R.*, 1 (1886), 536–44

Report on the Proceedings in Cases of High Treason ... Dublin, Dec. 1795 (Dublin, 1796)

Autobiography of Archibald Hamilton Rowan, ed. W. H. Drummond, I.U.P. reprint of 1840 edn. (Shannon, 1972)

Russell, T. *Letter to the People of Ireland on the Present Situation of the Country* (Belfast, 1796)

Memoirs of William Sampson, (New York, 1807)

The Life and Correspondence of the Rt. Hon. Henry Addington, First Visc. Sidmouth, ed. the Hon. G. Pellew, 3 vols. (London, 1847)

Private Papers of George, Second Earl Spencer, ed. J. S. Corbett, Navy Records Society, 2 vols. (London, 1913–24)

Sweetman, J. *A Refutation of the Charges Attempted to be made against the Secretary of the Sub-Committee of the Catholics of Ireland, Particularly that of Abetting Defenders* (Dublin, 1793)

Mémoires du Prince de Talleyrand, ed. P. Léon, 2nd edn. (Paris, 1953)

Taylor, J. *Records of My Life*, 2 vols. (London, 1832)

Teeling, C. H. *History of the Irish Rebellion of 1798*, and *Sequel to the History of the Irish Rebellion*, I.U.P. reprint of 1876 edn. (Shannon, 1972)

——— *Observations on the "History and Consequences of the Battle of the Diamond"*, (Dublin, 1838)

Temple, Sir J. *The Irish Rebellion: or, an history of the beginning and first progresses of the general rebellion raised within the kingdom of Ireland upon the* . . . *23 Oct. 1641* (London, 1646)

Thibaudeau, A. C. *Mémoires sur la Convention et le Directoire*, 2 vols. (Paris, 1824)

Life of Theobald Wolfe Tone, ed. his son William T. W. Tone, 2 vols. (Washington, 1826)

The Usurpations of England. The Chief Sources of the Miseries of Ireland (Dublin, 1780)

Wakefield, E. *An Account of Ireland Statistical and Political*, 2 vols. (London, 1812)

Wellington, Arthur Wellesley, Duke of. *Supplementary Despatches*, ed. his son, 15 vols. (London, 1858–72), v, Ireland

The Journals of the Rev. John Wesley, 4 vols. (London, 1827), II

The Correspondence of William Wickham, ed. his grandson W. Wickham, 2 vols. (London, 1870)

The Life of William Wilberforce, ed. his sons R.I. and S. Wilberforce, 5 vols. (London, 1838)

The Windham Papers: the life and correspondence of the Rt. Hon. William Windham, 2 vols. (London, 1913)

Young, A. *A Tour in Ireland*, ed. Constantia Maxwell (Cambridge, 1925)

Secondary Sources: Published Works

Adams, E. D. *The Influence of Grenville on Pitt's Foreign Policy, 1787–1798* (Washington, 1904)

Aldridge, A. O. *Man of Reason, the life of Thomas Paine* (London, 1960)

Alger, J. G. *Englishmen in the French Revolution* (London, 1889)

——— 'The British Colony in Paris 1792–1793', *E.H.R.*, XIII (1898), 672–94

——— *Napoleon's British Visitors and Captives, 1801–1815* (Westminster, 1904)

Ashton, J. *English Caricature and Satire on Napoleon I* (London, 1888)

Aspinall, A. *Politics and the Press c. 1780–1850* (London, 1949)

——— *The early English trade Unions* (London, 1949)

Atkinson, A. *Ireland Exhibited to England in a political and moral Survey of her Population*, 2 vols. (London, 1823)

Aubin, T. 'La rôle politique de Carnot, depuis les élections de germinal an V jusqu'au coup d'État du 18 fructidor', *A.h.R.f.* no. 49 (1932), 37–51

Baxter, J. L. and Donnelly, F. K. 'The Revolutionary "Underground" in the West Riding: Myth or Reality', *Past and Present*, 64 (Aug. 1974), 113–35

—— 'Sheffield and the English Revolutionary Tradition, 1791–1820', *International Review of Social History*, xx (1975), 398–423

Beames, M. R. 'Peasant Movements: Ireland 1785–1795.' *Journal of Peasant Studies*, 2 (1975), 502–6

—— 'Rural Conflict in Pre-Famine Ireland', *Past and Present*, 81 (1978), 75–91

Beckett, J. C. *Protestant Dissent in Ireland 1687–1780* (London, 1948)

—— *The Anglo-Irish Tradition* (London, 1976)

Benda, K. 'Les Jacobins Hongrois,' *A.h.R.f.*, no. 155 (1959), 38–60

Benn, G. *A History of the Town of Belfast from the earliest times to the close of the eighteenth century*, 2 vols. (London, 1877–80)

Berman, D. 'David Hume on the 1641 Rebellion in Ireland', *Studies*, lxv (1976), 101–12

Berthaut, Col. H. *Les Ingénieurs géographes militaires, 1624–1831*, 2 vols. (Paris, 1902)

Bigger, F. J. 'The Northern Star,' *U.J.A.*, 2nd. ser. 1 (1895), 33–5

—— 'The National Volunteers of Ireland, 1782', *U.J.A.*, 3rd. ser. xv (1909), 141–8

Biro, S. S. *The German Policy of Revolutionary France*, 2 vols. (Mass. 1957)

Birley, R. *The English Jacobins* (Oxford, 1924)

D. Bonner-Smith, 'The Naval Mutinies of 1797', *The Mariners' Mirror*, xxi (1935), 428–49 and xxii (1936), 63–86

Booth, A. 'Food Riots in the North-West of England 1790–1801', *Past and Present*, 77 (1977), 84–107

Bouloiseau, M. *La République jacobine* (Paris, 1972)

Bourke, F. S. 'The Rebellion of 1803. An Essay in Bibliography', *The Bibliographical Society of Ireland*, v (1933)

Broeker, G. *Rural Disorder and Police Reform in Ireland, 1812–36* (London, 1970)

Brown, T. N. 'Nationalism and the Irish Peasant, 1800–1848', *The Review of Politics*, 15 (Oct. 1953), 403–45

Budge, I. and O'Leary, C. *Belfast: Approach to Crisis* (London, 1973)

Butler, W. F. 'Irish Land Tenures: Celtic and Foreign', *Studies*, xiii (1924), 291–305, 524–40

Cambridge History of British Foreign Policy, 3 vols. (Cambridge, 1922–3)

Campbell, G. *Edward and Pamela Fitzgerald* (London, 1904)

Canning, Hon. A.S.G. *Revolted Ireland, 1798 and 1803* (London, 1886)

Canny, N. 'Hugh O'Neill and the changing face of Gaelic Ulster', *Studia Hibernica*, x (1970), 7–35

——'Early Modern Ireland: An Appraisal Appraised', *Irish Economic and Social History*, IV (1977), 62

Carles, Lt. Col. P. 'Le corps irlandais au service de la France sous le Consulat et l'Empire', *Revue historique des Armées*, 2 (1976), 25–54

Caron, P. *Manuel pratique pour l'étude de la Révolution française* (Paris, 1912)

Casey, D. J. 'Wildgoose Lodge: The Evidence and the Lore', *Journal of the County Louth Archaeological and Historical Society*, XVIII, no. 2 (1974), 153–60

Charles-Roux, F. *Les Origines de l'expédition d'Egypte*, 2nd edn. (Paris, 1910)

Christianson, G. E. 'Secret Societies and Agrarian Violence in Ireland, 1790–1840', *Agricultural History*, 46 (1972), 369–84

Church, C. H. 'In Search of the Directory', in *French Government and Society 1500–1850. Essays in Memory of Alfred Cobban*, ed. J. F. Bosher (London, 1973), 261–94

Cobb, R. C. *The Police and the People. French Popular Protest 1789–1820* (Oxford, 1972)

Cobban, A. 'British Secret Service in France 1784–92', *E.H.R.*, LXIX (1954), 226–61

——'The Beginning of the Channel Isles Correspondence', *E.H.R.*, LXXVII (1962), 38–52

Collins, H. 'The London Corresponding Society', in *Democracy and the Labour Movement. Essays in honour of Dona Torr*, ed. J. Saville (London, 1954), 103–34

Cone, C. B. *The English Jacobins: reformers in late Eighteenth-century England* (New York, 1968)

Coquelle, P. *Napoléon et l'Angleterre 1803–1815* (Paris, 1904)

Corkery, D. *The Hidden Ireland*, 2nd edn. (Dublin, 1925)

Cornewall Lewis, G. *On Local Disturbances in Ireland* (London, 1836)

Coughlin R. *Napper Tandy* (Dublin, 1977)

Cox, L. 'Westmeath in the 1798 Period', *Irish Sword*, IX (1969–70), 1–15

Crawford, W. *Domestic Industry in Ireland. The experience of the linen Industry* (Dublin, 1972)

——'Landlord–Tenant Relations in Ulster 1609–1820', *Irish Economic and Social History*, II (1975), 5–21

Croker, T. C. *Researches in the South of Ireland* (London, 1824)

——*On Local Disturbances in Ireland* (London, 1836)

——*Popular Songs illustrative of the French Invasion of Ireland* (London, 1845–7)

Crotty, R. D. *Irish agricultural production: its volume and structure* (Cork, 1966)

Crouzet, F. *L'Économie britannique et le Blocus continental (1806–1813)*, 2 vols. (Paris, 1958)

Cullen, L. M. 'The Hidden Ireland: Re-assessment of a Concept', *Studia Hibernica* 9 (1969), 17–47

——*An Economic History of Ireland since 1660* (London, 1972)

——'The Cultural Basis of Modern Irish Nationalism,' in *The roots of nationalism: studies in northern Europe*, ed. R. Mitchison (Edinburgh, 1980), 91–106.

Desbrière, E. *Projets et tentatives de débarquement aux îles britanniques*, 4 vols. (Paris, 1900–2)

——*Le Blocus de Brest* (Paris, 1902)

D'Hauterive, E. *La Police secrète du Premier Empire*, 5 vols (Paris, 1908–1964)

Dechamps, J. *Les Îles Britanniques et la Révolution française, 1789–1803* (Brussels, 1949)

Dickson, C. *Revolt in the North. Antrim and Down in 1798* (Dublin, 1960)

Dinwiddy, J. R. 'The "Black Lamp" in Yorkshire, 1801–1802', *Past and Present*, 64 (1974), 113–35

——'Luddism and politics in the northern counties', *Social History*, 4 (1979), 33–63

Dobrée, B. and Manwaring, G. E. *The Floating Republic*, 3rd edn. (London, 1937)

Donnelly, J. S. Jr. 'The Whiteboy Movement, 1761–5', *I.H.S.*, xxi (1978), 20–54

——'Propagating the Cause of the United Irishmen', *Studies*, lxix (1980), 5–23

Driault, J. E. *Napoléon et l'Europe. La politique extérieure du Premier Consul 1800–1803* (Paris, 1910)

Dowling, P. J. *The Hedge Schools of Ireland* (Dublin, 1935)

Duffy, Sir C. G. *Young Ireland*, 2nd edn. (Dublin, 1884)

Dugan, J. *The Great Mutiny* (London, 1966)

Dunfermline, James, Lord. Lt. Gen. *Sir Ralph Abercromby K.B. 1793–1801. A Memoir by his son* (Edinburgh, 1861)

Dupré, H. *Lazare Carnot. Republican Patriot*, 2nd edn. (Philadelphia, 1975)

Durand, Y. *Les Républiques aux temps des monarchies* (Paris, 1973)

Edwards, O. D. and MacDiarmid, I.R.H. *Celtic Nationalism* (London, 1968)

Edwards, R. D. *An Atlas of Irish History* (London, 1973)

———*Patrick Pearse, the triumph of failure* (London, 1977)

Elliott, M. 'The "Despard Conspiracy" Reconsidered', *Past and Present*, 75 (1977), 46–61

———'The Origins and Transformation of Early Irish Republicanism', *International Review of Social History*, XXIII (1978), 405–28

———'Irish Republicanism in England: the first phase, 1797–9,' in *Penal Era and Golden Age. Essays in Irish History, 1690–1800* ed. T. Bartlett and D. W. Hayton (Belfast, 1979), 204–21

Robert Emmet. A Commemorative Booklet, ed. Wolfe Tone Memorial Committee (Dublin, 1921)

Emmet, T. A. *Memoir of Thomas Addis Emmet and Robert Emmet*, 2 vols. (New York, 1915)

Emsley, C. 'The Home Office and its sources of information and investigation 1791–1801', *E.H.R.* XCIV (1979), 532–61

———*British Society and the French Wars 1793–1815* (London, 1979)

———'An Aspect of Pitt's "Terror": prosecutions for sedition during the 1790s', *Social History*, 6 (1981), 155–84

Falkiner, C. L. *Essays Relating to Ireland, Biographical, Historical and Topographical* (London, 1909)

Farrell, M. *Northern Ireland, the Orange state* (London, 1976)

Ferguson, T. G. F. 'The County Armagh Volunteers of 1778–1793', *U.J.A.* 3rd. ser., IV (1941), 101–27; V (1942), 36–61; VI (1943), 69–105

Fermoy, Col. P. Roche. *A Commentary on the Memoirs of T. W. Tone* (Paris, 1828)

Fitzgerald, B. *Emily, Duchess of Leinster, 1731–1814* (London, 1949)

———*Lady Louisa Connolly, 1743–1821* (London, 1950)

Fieffé, E. *Histoire des troupes étrangères au service de la France*, 2 vols. (Paris, 1854)

Fitzpatrick, W. J. *The Life, Times, and Contemporaries of Lord Cloncurry* (London, 1855)

———'*The Sham Squire*'; and the Informers of 1798 (London, 1866)

———*Secret Service under Pitt* (Dublin, 1892)

Ford, G. S. *Hanover and Prussia, 1795–1803. A Study in neutrality* (New York, 1903)

Gash, N. *Mr. Secretary Peel*, 3rd edn. (London, 1964)

George, M. D. *Catalogue of Political and Personal Satires preserved in the Department of Prints and Drawings in the British Museum*, 11 vols. (London, 1870–1954)

———*English Political caricature: a study of opinion and propaganda*, 2 vols. (Oxford, 1959)

Gibbon, P. 'The Origins of the Orange Order and the United Irishmen', *Economy and Society*, 1 (1972), 135–63

—— *The origins of Ulster Unionism: the formation of popular Protestant politics and ideology in nineteenth-century Ireland* (Manchester 1975)

Gieysztor, A. *et al. Histoire de Pologne* (Warsaw, 1972)

Gill, C. *The Naval Mutinies of 1797* (Manchester, 1913)

—— *The Rise of the Irish Linen Industry* (Oxford, 1925)

Godechot, J. *France and the Atlantic Revolution of the Eighteenth Century, 1770–1799* (New York, 1965)

Goodwin, A. 'The French Executive Directory—a re-evaluation', *History*, XXII (1937), 201–18.

—— *The Friends of Liberty. The English democratic movement in the age of the French revolution* (London, 1979)

Gooch, G. P. *Germany and the French Revolution*, 2nd edn. (London, 1927)

Green, E. R. R. 'The Cotton Hand-Loom Weavers in the North-East of Ireland', *U.J.A.*, 3rd. ser., VII (1944), 30–41

Gribayédoff, V. *The French Invasion of Ireland in 1798* (New York, 1890)

Griffin, W. D. 'The forces of the Crown in Ireland 1798', in *Crisis in the Great Republic: Essays presented to Ross J. S. Hoffman*, ed. G. L. Vincitorio (New York, 1969)

Guillon, E. *La France et l'Irlande sous le Directoire* (Paris, 1888)

Guyot, R. *Le Directoire et la Paix de l'Europe* (Paris, 1911)

—— 'Le Directoire et Bonaparte', *Revue des Études Napoléoniennes*, 1 (1912), 321–34

Hampson, N. *La Marine de l'an II. Mobilisation de la flotte de l'océan, 1793–1794* (Paris, 1959)

Handley, J. E. *The Irish in Scotland, 1798–1845* (Cork, 1943)

Hardiman, J. *Irish Ministrelsy or Bardic Remains of Ireland*, 2 vols. (London, 1831)

Hayes, R. F. *Ireland and Irishmen in the French Revolution* (London, 1932)

—— *The Last Invasion of Ireland* (Dublin, 1937)

—— *Biographical Dictionary of Irishmen in France* (Dublin, 1949)

Hayes, R. J. ed. *Manuscript Sources for the History of Irish Civilisation*, 11 vols. (Boston, Mass. 1965)

Hyde, D. *A Literary History of Ireland*, 7th edn. (London, 1920)

Homan, G. D. *Jean-François Reubell. French Revolutionary, patriot, and Director, 1747–1807* (The Hague, 1971)

J. A. Hone *For the Cause of Truth: Radicalism in London, 1796–1821* (Oxford, 1982)

Irish Rebellions: No. 11. The United Irishmen (London, 1866)

Jackson, J. A. *The Irish in Britain* (London, 1963)

Jacob, R. *The Rise of the United Irishmen, 1791–4* (London, 1937)

Johnson, J. H. 'The Two "Irelands" at the Beginning of the Nineteenth Century', *Irish Geographical Studies*, ed. N. Stephens and R. E. Glasscock (Belfast, 1970), 224–41

Johnston T. *The History of the Working Classes in Scotland* (Glasgow, 1922)

Joly, A. *Lazare Hoche 1768–1968 (Catalogue de l'Éxposition: Deuxième Centenaire. Hôtel de Ville Versailles. Sept.–Oct. 1968.)*

Kee, R. *The Green Flag: A History of Irish Nationalism* (London, 1972)

Kennedy, W. B. 'The Irish Jacobins', *Studia Hibernica*, xiv,(1976), 109–121

Kiernan, T. J. *The Irish Exiles in Australia* (Dublin, 1954)

Kuscinski, A. *Dictionnaire des Conventionnels* (Paris, 1917)

Landreth, H. *The Pursuit of Robert Emmet* (New York 1948)

Lalor, J. Fintan, *Collected Writings*, ed. N. Marlowe (Dublin, 1918)

Latimer, W. T. *A History of the Irish Presbyterians* (Belfast, 1893)

Lecky, W. E. H. *A History of Ireland in the Eighteenth Century*, 5 vols. (London, 1892)

Levy-Schneider, L. *Le Conventionnel Jeanbon Saint-André: 1749–1813*, 2 vols. (Paris, 1901)

Lewis, M. *A Social History of the Navy, 1763–1815* (London, 1960)

Lucas, C. 'The Directory and the Rule of Law', *F.H.S.*, x (1978), 231–60

Lyons, F. S. L. *Ireland since the famine*, 2nd edn. (London, 1973)

Lyons, M. *France Under the Directory* (Cambridge, 1975)

McAnally, Sir H. *The Irish Militia, 1793–1816. A social and military study* (London, 1949)

Maccoby, S. *English Radicalism, 1786–1832* (London, 1955)

MacDermot, F. 'The Jackson Episode in 1794', *Studies* (1938)

—— 'Arthur O'Connor', *I.H.S.*, xv (1966), 48–69

—— *Theobald Wolfe Tone*, 3rd edn. (Tralee, 1969)

McDowell, R. B. *Irish Public Opinion, 1750–1800* (London, 1944)

—— *Public Opinion and Government Policy in Ireland* (London, 1952)

—— 'The Personnel of the Dublin Society of United Irishmen, 1791–4', *I.H.S.*, ii (1940–1), 12–53

—— 'The Fitzwilliam Episode', *I.H.S.*, XVI (1966), 115–30

—— *Ireland in the Age of Imperialism and Revolution* (Oxford, 1979)

MacGréine, P. 'Traditions of 1798. The Battle of Ballinamuck', *Béaloideas, The Journal of the Folklore of Ireland Society*, IV (1933–4), 393–5

MacNeill, E. *Shall Ireland be Divided?* (Dublin, 1915)

McEvoy, Rev. B. 'The United Irishmen in Co. Tyrone', *Seanchas Ardmhacha*, III (1959), 283–305; IV (1960–1), 1–32; V (1969), 37–65

—— 'Father James Quigley', *Seanchas Ardmhacha*, V (1970), 247–59

Mackesy, P. *Statesmen at war: the strategy of overthrow, 1798–1799* (London, 1974)

McSkimmin, S. 'Secret History of the Irish Insurrection of 1803', *Fraser's Magazine*, 14 (1836), 566–7

—— *Annals of Ulster* (Belfast, 1849)

Madden, R. R. *The United Irishmen, their Lives and Times*, 3 ser. 7 vols. (London, 1842–45), and revised edn., 4 vols. (London, 1857–60)

—— *The Life and Times of Robert Emmet* (New York, 1856)

—— *The History of Irish Periodical Literature from the End of the 17th to the Middle of the 18th Century*, 2 vols. (London, 1867)

—— *Literary Remains of the United Irishmen of 1798* (London, 1887)

Marion, M. *Histoire financière de la France depuis 1715*, 6 vols. (Paris, 1914–31)

Martin, M. 'Les Journaux militaires de Carnot,' *A.h.R.f.* no. 229 (1977), 404–28

Masson, F. *Le Département des Affaires Étrangères pendant la Révolution, 1787–1804* (Paris, 1877)

Maxwell, M. Perceval. *The Scottish Migration to Ulster in the Reign of James I* (London, 1973)

—— 'The Ulster Rising of 1641, and the depositions', *I.H.S.*, XXI (1978), 144–67

Maxwell, W. H. *History of the Irish Rebellion in 1798* (London, 1894)

Méautis, A. *Le Club Helvétique de Paris, 1790–1791, et la diffusion des idées révolutionnaires en Suisse* (Neuchâtel, 1969)

Meikle, H. W. *Scotland and the French Revolution* (Glasgow, 1912)

Miller, D. W. *Queen's Rebels: Ulster Loyalism in Historical Perspective* (Dublin, 1978)

—— 'Presbyterianism and "Modernization" in Ulster,' *Past and Present*, 80 (Aug. 1978), 66–90

Mitchel, J. *Ireland, France and Prussia. A Selection from the Speeches and Writings of John Mitchel* (Dublin, 1918)

Moody, T. W. 'The Political ideas of the United Irishmen', *Ireland Today*, III (1936), 15–25

——'The Treatment of the Native population under the scheme for the Plantation of Ulster', *I.H.S.*, I (1938–9), 51–63

Moody, T. W., Martin, F. X. and Byrne, F. J. eds. *A New History of Ireland*, III, *Early Modern Ireland, 1534–1691* (Oxford, 1976)

Moody, T. W. ed. *Nationality and the Pursuit of National Independence, Historical Studies*, ed. T. W. Moody, XI (Belfast, 1978)

Moore, T. *The Life and Death of Lord Edward Fitzgerald*, 2 vols. (London, 1831)

——*The Memoirs of Lord Edward Fitzgerald*, 2nd edn. (London, 1897)

Murphy, D. *A Place Apart* (Harmondsworth, 1979)

Musgrave, R. *Memoirs of the Different Rebellions in Ireland*, 3rd edn., 2 vols. (Dublin, 1802)

Newman, A. *What Emmet Means in 1915. A Tract for the Times* (Dublin, 1915)

Ni Chinnéide, S. *Napper Tandy and the European Crisis*, O'Donnel Lecture (Galway, 1962)

Nicholls, K. *Gaelic and Gaelicized Ireland in the Middle Ages* (Dublin, 1972)

Nowlan, K. B. 'Agrarian Unrest in Ireland, 1800–1845', *University Review*, II (1959), 7–16

Nabonne, B. *La Diplomatie du Directoire et de Bonaparte d'après les papiers inédits de Reubell* (Paris, 1951)

Ó Coindealbháin, S. 'The United Irishmen in Cork county', *Cork Historical and Archaeological Journal*, 2nd. ser., LV (1950), 50–61, 73–90; LVI (1951), 18–28, 95–103; LVII (1952), 87–98; LVIII (1953), 91–6

O'Daly, J. *Reliques of Irish Jacobite Poetry*, 2nd ed. (Dublin, 1949)

O'Driscoll, J. *Views of Ireland, Moral, Political and Religious*, 2 vols. (London, 1823)

Ó'Loinsigh, S. 'The Rebellion of 1798 in Meath', *Riocht na Midhe*, III–V (1966–70)

Olson, A. *The Radical Duke. Career and correspondence of Charles Lennox, third Duke of Richmond* (London, 1961)

Oman, Sir C. *The Unfortunate Col. Despard and Other Studies* (London, 1922)

O'Reilly, A. *Reminiscences of an emigrant Milesian* (London, 1853)

O'Tuathail, P. 'Wicklow Traditions of 1798', *Béaloideas, The Journal of the Folklore of Ireland Society*, V (1935), 154–88

Pakenham, T. *The Year of Liberty*, 3rd end. (London, 1972)

Palmer, R. R. *The Age of Democratic Revolution*, 2 vols. (London, 1959 and 1964)

Parssinen, T. M. 'Association, Convention, Anti-Parliament in British Radical Politics, 1771–1848', *E.H.R.*, 88 (1973), 504–33

Patterson, T. G. F. 'The County Armagh Volunteers of 1778–1793', *U.J.A.*, 3rd ser., IV–VI (1941–3)

Pearse, P. H. *Political Writings and Speeches*, 2nd edn. (Dublin, 1966)

——*From a Hermitage*, 2nd edn. (Dublin, 1915)

——*How Does she Stand?* 2nd edn. (Dublin, 1915)

——*The Separatist Idea* (Dublin, 1916)

——*The Sovereign People* (Dublin, 1916)

Piechowiak, A. B. 'The Anglo-Russian Expedition to Holland in 1799', *Slavonic and East European Review*, 41 (1962–3), 182–95

Plowden, F. *The History of Ireland from its Union with Great Britain in Jan. 1801 to Oct. 1810*, 3 vols. (Dublin, 1811)

Powell, T. J. 'An Economic factor in the Wexford Rebellion of 1798', *Studia Hibernica*, 16 (1976), 140–57

Quinault, R. and Stevenson, J., eds. *Popular Protest and Public Order* (London, 1974)

Rafroidi, P. *L'Irlande et le romantisme* (Paris, 1972)

Rao, A-M. 'Les Réfugiés Italiens en 1799', *A.h.R.f.* no. 240 (1980), 225–61

Reinhard, M. *Le Grand Carnot. L'Organisateur de la Victoire*, 2 vols. (Paris, 1950)

Robbins, C. *The Eighteenth-Century Commonwealthman* (Cambridge, Mass, 1959)

——ed. *Two English Republican Tracts* (Cambridge, Mass. 1969)

Robinson, P. 'British Settlement in County Tyrone 1610–1666', *Irish Economic and Social History*, V (1978), 5–26

Rodger, A. B. *The War of the second coalition, 1798–1801. A strategic commentary* (Oxford, 1964)

Rogers, P. *The Irish Volunteers and Catholic Emancipation, 1778–1793* (London, 1934)

Ross, S. T. 'The Military Strategy of the Directory: The Campaigns of 1799', *F.H.S.*, V (1967), 170–87

Rousselin, A. *Vie de Hoche*, 2 vols. (Paris, 1792)

Rudé, G. 'Early Irish Rebels in Australia', *Historical Studies*, 16 (1974–5) 17–35

——*Protest and Punishment* (Oxford, 1978)

Ryan, D. *The Fenian Chief* (Dublin, 1967)

Ryan, F. W. 'A Projected Invasion of Ireland in 1811', *Irish Sword*, I (1949–53), 136–41

Sagnac, P. *Le Rhin Français pendant la Révolution et l'Empire* (Paris, 1917)

Savage, J. *'98 and '48. The Modern Revolutionary History and Literature of Ireland* (New York, 1884)

Schama, S. *Patriots and Liberators. Revolution in the Netherlands 1780–1813* (London, 1977)

Schlereth, T. J. *The Cosmopolitan Ideal in Enlightenment Thought* (Notre Dame, 1977)

Sciout L. *Le Directoire*, 4 vols. (Paris, 1895)

Senior, H. *Orangeism in Ireland and Britain 1795–1836* (London, 1966)

Servières, G. *L'Allemagne française sous Napoléon Ier* (Paris, 1904)

——'Un Episode de l'Expédition d'Irlande. L'Extradition et la Mise en Liberté de Napper Tandy 1798–1802', *Revue Historique*, XCIII (1907), 46–73

Sherwig, J. *Guineas and Gunpowder: British foreign aid in the wars with France, 1793–1815* (Cambridge, Mass. 1969)

Sigerson, G. *History of the Land Tenures and Land Classes of Ireland* (London, 1871)

Simms, J. G. *The Williamite Confiscation in Ireland, 1690–1703* (London, 1956)

——*Jacobite Ireland* (London, 1969)

Simms, S. *Rev. James O'Coigley, United Irishman* (Belfast, 1937)

Six, G. *Dictionnaire Biographique des Généraux et Amiraux de la Révolution et de l'Empire 1792–1814*, 2 vols. (Paris, 1931)

Slór na bfiann (Dublin, 1919)

Smith, A. W. 'Irish Rebels and English Radicals 1798–1820', *Past and Present*, 7 (1955), 78–85

Smith, E. A. *Whig Principles and Party Politics* (Manchester, 1975)

Smyth, P. '"Our Cloud-Cap't Grenadiers": the Volunteers as a military force', *Irish Sword*, XIII (1978–9), 185–207

Sorel, A. *L'Europe et la Révolution Française*, 8 vols. (Paris, 1885)

——'Les Vues de Hoche', *Revue de Paris*, IV (1895) 225–53, 533–66

—— *Bonaparte et Hoche en 1797* (Paris, 1896)

Stevenson, J. ed. *London in the Age of Reform* (Oxford, 1977)

Stewart, A. T. Q. '"A stable and unseen power": Dr. William Drennan and the origins of the United Irishmen', in *Essays presented to Michael Roberts*, ed. J. Bossy *et al.* (Belfast, 1976), 80–92

——*The Narrow Ground: aspects of Ulster 1609–1969* (London, 1977)

Stewart, J. Hall. 'The French Revolution and the Dublin Stage, 1790–94', *Royal Society of Antiquaries of Ireland: Journal*, XCI (1959), 183–92

Stuart Jones, E. H. *An Invasion that Failed* (Oxford, 1950)

—— *The Last Invasion of Britain* (Cardiff, 1950)

Thomis, M. I. and Holt, P. *Threats of Revolution in Britain 1789–1848* (London, 1977)

Thompson, E. P. *The Making of the English Working Class*, 2nd edn. (Harmondsworth, 1968)

—— 'The Moral Economy of the English Crowd', *Past and Present*, 50 (1971), 76-136

Tohall, P. 'The Diamond Fight of 1795 and the Resultant Expulsions', *Seanchas Ardmhacha*, 3 (1958), 17–50

Tulard, J. *Napoléon ou le Mythe du Sauveur* (Paris, 1977)

Van Brock, F. W. 'A Memoir of 1798', *Irish Sword*, IX (1969–70), 192–206

—— 'Captain MacSheehy's Mission', *Irish Sword*, X (1972), 215–28

Wall, M. 'The rise of a catholic middle class in eighteenth-century Ireland', *I.H.S.*, XI (1958–9), 91–115

—— *The Penal Laws, 1691–1760* (Dublin, 1961)

—— 'The United Irish Movement', *Historical Studies*, ed. J. L. McCracken, v (London, 1965), 122–40

Wallas, G. *The Life of Francis Place, 1771–1854* (London, 1898)

Wedd, A. F. *The Fate of the Fenwicks. Letters to Mary Hays* (1798–1828), (London, 1927)

Wells, R. A. E. 'Death and Distress in Yorkshire, 1793–1802', *Borthwick Papers*, 52 (1977)

White, J. *Minority Report: the Protestant community in the Irish Republic* (Dublin, 1975)

Williams, G. A. *Artisans and Sans Culottes: Popular Movements in France and Britain during the French Revolution* (London, 1968)

Williams, R. C. 'European Political Emigrations: A Lost Subject', *Comparative Studies in Society and History*, 12 (1970), 140–8

Williams, T. D. ed. *Secret Societies in Ireland* (Dublin, 1973)

Williamson, A. *Thomas Paine, His Life, Work and Times* (London, 1973)

Woloch, I. *Jacobin Legacy: the democratic movement under the Directory* (Princeton, 1970)

Woods, C. J. 'The Secret Mission to Ireland of Captain Bernard MacSheehy, an Irishman in French Service, 1796', *Journal of the Cork Historical and Archaeological Society*, LXXVIII (1973), 93–108

—— 'A Plan for a Dutch Invasion of Scotland, 1797', *Scottish Historical Review*, LIII (1974), 108–14

Woodward, L. 'Les projets de descente en Irlande et les réfugiés irlandais et anglais en France sous la Convention', *A.h.R.f.*, VIII (1931), 1–30

Woronoff, D. *La République bourgeoise: de Thermidor à Brumaire 1794–99* (Paris, 1972)

Wyse, T. *Historical Sketch of the Late Catholic Association of Ireland*, 2 vols. (London, 1829)

Zimmermann, G. D. *Songs of Irish Rebellion. Political Street Ballads and Rebel Songs 1780–1900* (Dublin, 1967)

Secondary Sources: Unpublished Theses and Papers

Baxter, J. L. 'Origins of the Social War: a history of the economic, political and cultural struggles of working people in South Yorkshire 1750–1850' (Shffield Univ. Ph.D. thesis 1976)

Beames, M. R. 'Peasant Disturbances, Popular Conspiracies and their Control, Ireland, 1798–1852' (Manchester Univ. Ph.D. thesis, 1975)

Beresford, M. de la Poer. 'Ireland in French Strategy, 1691–1789' (Univ. of Dub. M. Litt. thesis 1975)

Booth, A. 'Reform, repression and revolution: radicalism and loyalism in the North-West of England, 1789–1803' (Lancaster Univ. Ph.D. thesis 1979)

Bracken, J. R. 'British Relations with France from the Establishment of the Directory to the coup d'état of Fructidor' (Oxford. Univ. B. Litt. thesis, 1939)

Cassirer, R. 'The Irish Influence on the Liberal Movement in England 1798–1832, with special reference to the period 1815–32' (London Univ. Ph.D. thesis 1940)

Church, C. 'The Organization and Personnel of French Central Government under the Directory 1795–99' (London Univ. Ph.D. thesis 1963)

Connolly, S. J. 'Catholicism and Social Discipline in Pre-Famine Ireland' 2 vols. (New Univ. of Ulster D. Phil. thesis 1977)

Cox, N. 'Aspects of English Radicalism: The Suppression and Re-Emergence of the Constitutional Democratic Tradition, 1795–1809' (Cambridge Univ. Ph.D. thesis 1971)

Duffy, M. 'British War Policy: The Austrian Alliance, 1793–1801' (Oxford Univ. D.Phil. thesis 1971)

Elliott, M. 'The United Irishmen and France, 1792–1806' (Oxford Univ. D.Phil. thesis, 1975)

Fearn, E. 'Reform Movements in Derby and Derbyshire 1790–1832' (Manchester Univ. M.A. thesis, 1964)

Fitzpatrick, A. J. 'The Economic Effects of the French Revolutionary and Napoleonic Wars on Ireland' (Manchester Univ. Ph.D. thesis 1973)

Hewitt, J. 'Ulster Poets 1800–1870' (Queen's Univ. of Belfast M.A. thesis 1951)

Hogan, P. M. 'Civil Unrest in the Province of Connacht 1793–1798: The Role of the Landed Gentry in Maintaining Order' (Univ. Col. Galway M.Ed. thesis, 1976)

Hone, J. A. 'The Ways and Means of London Radicalism, 1796–1821' (Oxford Univ. D.Phil. thesis 1975)

Kennedy, W. B. 'French Projects for the Invasion of Ireland 1796–8' (Univ. of Georgia Ph.D. thesis 1966)

Kerrane, J. G. O. 'The Background to the 1798 Rebellion in County Meath' (Nat. Univ. of Ire. M.A. thesis, 1971)

Leonard, D. W. 'John Mitchel, Charles Gavan Duffy and the Legacy of Young Ireland' (Sheffield Univ. Ph.D. thesis 1975)

McLaughlin, J. P. 'The Annexation Policy of the French Revolution, 1789–1793' (London Univ. Ph.D. thesis 1951)

Mason, G. C. H. 'The Radical Bequest: Continuity in English Popular Politics, 1799–1832' (York Univ. M.Phil. thesis 1976)

Mitchell, A. V. 'Radicalism and Repression in the North of England, 1791–1797' (Manchester Univ. M.A. thesis 1958)

Morton, R. G. 'The 1798 Rising in Ulster,' (Univ. of Dublin B.Litt. thesis 1951)

Powell, T. J. 'The Background to the Rebellion in Co. Wexford, 1790–98' (Nat. Univ. of Ire. M.A. thesis 1970)

Ross, S. T. 'The War of the Second Coalition' (Princeton Univ. Ph.D. thesis 1963)

Schwarz, L. D. 'Conditions of Life and Work in London, *c.* 1770–1820, with Special Reference to East London' (Oxford Univ. D.Phil thesis 1976)

Seaman, W. A. L. 'British Democratic Societies in the Period of the French Revolution 1789–99' (London Univ. Ph.D. thesis, 1954)

Smyth, D. H. 'The Volunteer Movement in Ulster: Background and Development 1745–85' (Queen's Univ. of Belfast Ph.D. thesis 1974)

Steer, D. M. 'The Blockade of Brest by the Royal Navy 1793–1805' (Liverpool Univ. M.A. thesis 1971)

Stevenson, J. 'Disturbances and public order in London, 1790–1821' (Oxford Univ. D.Phil. thesis 1973)

Stewart, A. T. Q. 'The Transformation of Presbyterian radicalism in the North of Ireland, 1792–1825' (Queen's Univ. of Belfast M.A. thesis 1956)

Stoddart, P. C. 'Counter-insurgency and defence in Ireland, 1790–1805' (Oxford Univ. D.Phil. thesis 1972)

Taylor, J. R. 'William Windham and the Counter-Revolution in the North and West of France 1793–1801' (Manchester Univ. M.A. thesis 1967)

Vance, N. 'Texts and Traditions: Robert Emmet's Speech from the Dock', forthcoming in *Studies*.

—— 'Celts, Carthaginians and Constitutions: Anglo-Irish Literary Relations 1780–1820' forthcoming in *I.H.S.*

Walvin, J. 'English Democratic Societies and Popular Radicalism 1791–1800' (York Univ. D.Phil. thesis 1969)

Wilson, F. L. 'The Irish in Great Britain During the First Half of the Nineteenth Century' (Manchester Univ. M.A. thesis 1946)

INDEX

Informers, spies and *agents provocateurs*, 64–7, 73, 79, 125, 140, 142–3, 173–4, 182, 184–6, 193, 199, 205, 211, 232, 247, 252–3, 275, 286, 290, 293, 307, 316–17, 332, 343, 345.

Ingram, Richard, 'The Memory of the Dead', 368–9.

Ireland, attitudes to English rule in, 3–4, 7, 9, 10–12, 14, 17, 29–30, 32, 37, 68–9, 71, 74, 165, 212–13, 321–2, 360, 366, 369; French missions to, 17, 63, 87–91, 104–6, 160, 274–5, 328, 357–62; impact of French affairs on, xiii, 3–5, 11, 16, 30–1, 42, 51–74, 106, 274, 277, 343, 360; land settlement in, xvii, 3, 6–8, 14, 17, 27, 37, 39, 45, 72, 87, 96, 191, 196; military forces in, 44, 97, 105–8, 121–2, 126–30, 191–2, 203–7, 225–30, 274, 344, 360, 362–3; popular unrest in, xiv, xvi, 3–4, 6–7, 15–17, 39–40, 44–6, 71, 74, 95, 97, 106, 108, 124–5, 171, 226–7, 237–8, 244–5, 302, 341–4, 352–7, 360–2, 366; religious divisions in, xvi-xvii, 3–4, 18–22, 35–9, 81, 93, 95–7, 107, 153, 196–8, 207, 224, 226–7, 230–1, 244–7, 316, 341, 356, 369–70; social and economic conditions in, 15, 70–1, 95, 171, 353–4.

Intelligence, British and Irish governments, xix, 59, 140, 165, 184–5, 193, 208, 210, 247; domestic, 64, 66, 73, 173–4, 182, 252–7, 274–5, 282–4, 286, 289, 291, 293, 296, 303, 317–19, 344–5; foreign, 57, 66, 92, 153, 173, 218, 223, 253, 260, 266, 274–6, 317, 324, 345, 346–7; *see also* informers, spies and *agents provocateurs*.

Intelligence, French, 59, 61–2, 90, 91, 102, 140, 259–60.

Irish Brigades in foreign service, 7n, 247, 274, 333, 335, 350, 352, 363.

Irish Legion, 330–40, 349–53, 357–8, 361–4.

Jackson, Henry, 25, 70, 178.

Jackson, Rev. William, 60, 62–8, 71, 73, 78, 85, 96, 123, 267, 297.

Jacobins, French, 34, 82, 86, 167–9, 272–3.

Jacobites, Irish, 4, 9, 17, 29, 51, 81, 85.

Jagerhorn, J. W., 132, 156.

Jeanbon Saint-André, André, 63, 68.

Jones, William Todd, 26.

Jordan, Thomas, 290, 317.

Joubert, General Barthélemy Catherine, 218–19.

Joyce, Valentine (mutineer), 43.

Keogh, John, 36, 43, 73, 79, 88, 133, 173, 213, 354–5.

Kildare, 95, 109, 201, 226, 245, 249, 305, 310, 315, 356.

Killala, French landing at, 224–32.

Kilmaine, General Charles Edward, 170, 215, 217, 234–5, 267.

'Kilmainham Treaty', 208, 213, 240, 247, 252, 325.

Kilwarden, Arthur Wolfe, 1st baron, 311, 318, *319*.

Lake, General Gerard, 127–30, 142, 192, 228.

Lancashire, 147, 149, 174, 180, 284–5, 287, 290, 292, 298, 307, 346.

La Reveillière-Lépaux, Louis Marie, 77, *89*, 109, 135–6, 155.

Lawless, Luke, secret mission to Ireland, 357–62.

Lawless, William, 195, 331–2, 350–2, 358.

Lawless, Valentine, 2nd lord Cloncurry, 25, 175–6, 181, 253–4.

Lebrun (-Tondu), Pierre Marie Henry, 53, 57, 60–2.

Leinster, William Robert Fitzgerald, 2nd duke of, 25, 85, 342.

Lemaitre, Paul Thomas, 185, 286, 345.

Lemaître, 219, 259–60.

Leoben, peace preliminaries of, 154, 156, 277, 279.

Letourneur, Charles Louis François Honoré, 84, 119, 155.

Lewins, Edward, 26, 36, 60, 61, 64, 70, 71, 73, 99, 101–2, 105; negotiations with France, 130–2, 152–3, 155–6, 158–61, 166–72, 174, 212, 215–16, 232, 239, 249, 265–72, 275–6, 325, 352, 358–9.

Liverpool, 104, 180, 317.

Locke, John, 10, 27–8, 32–3, 71.

London, 148, French agents in, 57–9, 92, 132, 256, 298; Irish in 57, 178, 252–5, 288–9, 295–6, 317, 345; United Irish in, 146–51, 159, 173–8, 181, 248, 253–6, 288–94.

London Corresponding Society, xix, 52, 130, 141–2, 146, 150, 173–6, 185–8, 240, 257, 285.

Long, Phil, 293, 302.

Lowry, Alexander, 108, 133, 151–2, 159, 160, 169–70, 345.